DR WILLIAM PRICE

DEAN POWELL

D1439967

AMBERLEY

*This book is dedicated with the utmost gratitude to three doctors,
whose lives were inextricably linked by their studies and years of
service at London Hospital, Whitechapel, and the profound effect
they had on the life of the author who underwent treatment there.
To Dr Michael Jones for being the guiding light in leading the
author's first difficult steps. To Mr Brian Roper, a surgeon, friend and
saviour whose dedication and genius can never be truly repaid for
guiding the author to a full and accomplished life. Finally, to old Dr
Price himself, for inspiring the author as a child while growing up in
the shadow of East Caerlan in the beautiful little town of Llantrisant.*

First published 2012

This edition first published 2014

Amberley Publishing
The Hill, Stroud
Gloucestershire, GL5 4EP

www.amberley-books.com

British Library Cataloguing in Publication Data.
A catalogue record for this book is available from the British Library.

ISBN 978 1 4456 4356 4 (paperback)
ISBN 978 1 4456 2052 7 (ebook)

Typeset in 10pt on 12pt Sabon.
Typesetting and Origination by Amberley Publishing.
Printed in the UK.

CONTENTS

PRICE FAMILY TREE 1640-1800

Thomas Price
Innkeeper of Caerphilly
d 1685

Nicholas Price
Yeoman
Buried 16/2/1733

Nicholas Price
of Pontypandy
Tanner, Ironmaster of Pentyrch
1681 - 9/12/1757
m **Elizabeth Williams**, Coedybrain

William Price
of Ivy House, Tongwynlais
Ironmaster of Pentyrch
1713 - 23/12/1777

Nicholas Price
of Pontypandy
Ironmaster of Pentyrch
1709 - 4/2/1764

Nicholas Price
of Pontypandy
Tanner
1741 - 20/6/1793

Nicholas Price
of Pontypandy
1778 - 18/1/1805

Charles Price
Tanner, Lessee, Iron Blast Furnace
of Porsett Farm & Redbrook
1725 - 24/5/1786

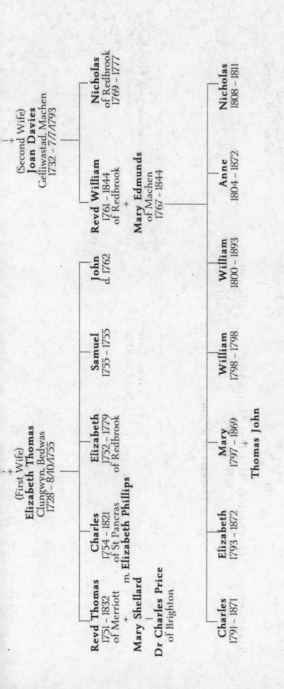

(First Wife)
Elizabeth Thomas
Clungwyn, Bedwas
1728 – 8/10/1755

(Second Wife)
Joan Davies
Gelliwastad, Machen
1732 – 7/7/1793

Revd Thomas
1751 – 1832
of Merriott
+
Mary Shellard

Charles
1754 – 1821
of St Pancras
m. **Elizabeth Phillips**
|
Dr Charles Price
of Brighton

Elizabeth
1752 – 1779
of Redbrook

Samuel
1755 – 1755

John
d. 1762

Revd William
1761 – 1844
of Redbrook
+
Mary Edmunds
of Machen
1767 – 1844

Nicholas
of Redbrook
1769 – 1777

Charles
1791 – 1871

Elizabeth
1793 – 1872

Mary
1797 – 1869
+
Thomas John

William
1798 – 1798

William
1800 – 1893

Anne
1804 – 1872

Nicholas
1808 – 1811

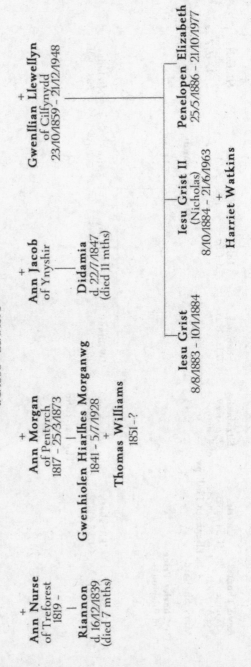

DR WILLIAM PRICE
4/3/1800 – 23/1/1893

+

Ann Nurse
of Treforest
1819 –

Ann Morgan
of Pentyrch
1817 – 25/3/1873

Ann Jacob
of Ynyshir

Gwenllian Llewellyn
of Cilfynydd
23/10/1859 – 21/12/1948

|

Riannon
d. 16/12/1839
(died 7 mths)

Gwenhiolen Hiarlhes Morganwg
1841 – 5/7/1928
+
Thomas Williams
1851 – ?

Didamia
d. 22/7/1847
(died 11 mths)

Iesu Grist
8/8/1883 – 10/1/1884

Iesu Grist II
(Nicholas)
8/10/1884 – 21/6/1963
+
Harriet Watkins

Penelopen Elizabeth
25/5/1886 – 21/10/1977

INTRODUCTION

Dr William Price was one of the most flamboyant, controversial and complex characters in Welsh history, as bright and colourful as his flaming funeral pyre, which shone across a dark, industrial Victorian age. A sparkling, dynamic, eloquent man who blazed progress and controversy by outraging a conventional society, his incredible legacy cannot be underestimated. The decision to cremate his god-like child, whom he prophesied as the future leader of a Druidic Britain, the subsequent court case and ultimately the passing of the Cremation Act, had a profound effect on the entire country. However, there was much more to Dr Price than his radical attitudes to the disposal of the dead.

Despite the unimaginable hardship of his poverty-stricken childhood, having been fathered by a 'lunatic' vicar, William became a brilliant scholar and exemplary surgeon. His frequent indiscretions, which portrayed him as being far from the epitome of the Victorian gentleman, defying in the most exhibitive fashion the conventions of his time, were forgiven due to his prowess as a healer of the sick. A pioneer of social healthcare and the embryonic National Health Service, Price was admired by the workers of the two major industries for which he was surgeon of works for more than forty years. His impressive generosity and his willingness to place his professional services gratuitously at the disposal of the poor endeared him to the many who benefited from his skill. Price's medical reputation survives untarnished. Blunt and forthright to patients who would consult him when other more orthodox methods failed, he fully supported alternative medicines, healthy living, fresh air, refused to treat smokers and advocated vegetarianism. An outspoken free-thinker and revolutionary who inflamed passions, bewildered and infuriated many, Dr Price commanded respect as a true crusader of reform; a revolutionary with an insatiable appetite for living.

Dr Price's life spanned every decade of the nineteenth century, when Britain became a victorious nation, at the height of her power and prestige. Her people witnessed some of its greatest advancements in science, engineering, exploration, industry, medicine and learning. Britain was transformed by the Industrial Revolution, during which the urban population trebled due to mass migration from rural counties to the larger cities. It was an era of political unrest, social tensions and calls for reform. At one time every other state in Europe experienced at least one forcible overthrow of government or even execution of its monarchy. Britain may have avoided such extremes, but nonetheless was a melting pot of a whole range of political upheavals.

Price was witness to them locally and nationally. Using his social standing and reputation as a surgeon, he exploited his talents as a showman and orator to further political and social causes, and his ringing speeches contain truth to us today but were heresy in his time. He saw the industrial age for what it was, recognised the squalor behind the magnificent Victorian façade, and the mischief wrought by unimaginative and greedy industrialists, to say nothing of the half-educated medical practitioners and questionable morals of the local clergy. On the one hand he was a man who understood of the needs of the working classes, whose lives were surrounded by filth and disease, and fought with all of his might to better their conditions. Yet he was also a favourite of the Glamorganshire gentry, displaying an almost aristocratic air of grace and charm, which attracted the attentions of his peers and that of their blushing wives and daughters in equal measure. However, it was as a Chartist leader, in the long months leading up to the Newport Rising, that he shocked his socialite companions. Price took the cause to his heart, and with fiery activity in his eyes; he was obviously a man bold enough to challenge the social and political system. His attempts to establish the first co-operative society in Wales are one of his many legacies.

Evidently, during his long lifetime Dr Price was no stranger to the courts, both as a defendant and petitioner. Possessing an extensive knowledge of the law, and draped in a shawl of royal tartan, he would conduct his own defence, lacing his speeches with a kind of mystic poetry. He satirically brought along to court as his learned counsel his infant daughter, who he rather incredulously named Hiarlhes Morganwg or the Countess of Glamorgan. To add to this status as both a showman and healer, the costumes he wore in public drew the greatest attention to the rather petite Welshman. Dressed in a succession of highly colourful outfits, claiming their origins were found in Welsh legend, of which he was the chosen successor, the most conspicuous item worn was a fox skin headdress, with the tail and legs about his shoulders, hanging as low as his grey hair and beard.

Dr Price questioned the justice of the social system, poured scorn on orthodox religion, despised the law and its administrators, and decried the morality of a puritanical society. Courting controversy was as natural as the air that he breathed and he displayed behaviour which shocked. He lived in a nonconformist, deacon-dominated Wales and succeeded in infuriating an entire population, fathering children out of wedlock and condemning the pulpit for the 'fire and brimstone' it spewed on the believing masses. He also saw the harm a mishandled religion could do in an uneducated working class population. He claimed that only nature was worth worshipping and man had created God in *his* own image. It was his distaste for church and chapel, coupled with his fascination for eastern religions, that endeared him to the Neo-Druidic cult sweeping across the country and enjoying a particular stronghold in the town of his adoption, Pontypridd. As the self-confessed 'master scholar', his total obsession for the pagan religion enveloped his life, following what he considered to be an epiphany while exiled in France, and he devoted his energies to attempting to bring back some form of a new Druidic society, lost with the advent of Christianity in Britain. He longed for the golden age of a Wales ruled by the Druids, of which he prophesied his first-born son would be Messiah. On moonlit evenings, while grim chapels preached their doctrine to a congregation groaning in a sense of original sin, and while the pits and the ironworks clanged in the new industrial era, Price was high above at the Druid's stones, at one with nature.

With the defeat of the French Empire and its allies in the Napoleonic Wars, the British Empire became the absolute power of the world, on which the sun literally never set. A quarter of the world's population and one fifth of the total land area came under its supreme reign. During this era of invention and discovery, there were great advances in technology, particularly biology, physics and electricity. In medicine, a better understanding of the human anatomy and disease prevention caused the rapidly accelerating population growth in Western Europe, which welcomed the railways, the first advancement in land transportation for centuries. The last remaining undiscovered lands of the Earth, including vast areas of interior Africa and Asia, saw the onslaught of the western man. Military conflicts were plentiful, and with them came the need for iron and coal to sustain a naval fleet that dominated the seas.

While Britain was ruling the waves and one fifth of the world's land area, one country more than any other provided the power to energise such dominance. That country was Wales. In the early nineteenth century some areas of Wales had already become industrialised, as ironworks were being established in the new town of Merthyr Tydfil, soon to be the largest in the Principality. Within fifty years the coal mining industry spread to the Cynon and Rhondda Valleys, bringing with it a huge industrial and social impact. The mass migration and infiltration of English-speaking landlords, colliery and ironwork owners, saw a new middle and upper class in what was once a largely rural country. What it also did was further diminish the authority of the Welsh language, which, although losing its pre-eminence, was still widely spoken. This was coupled with a direct attack on the Welsh psyche, and fears of a national crisis were widespread as the people lost confidence in themselves, their heritage and culture.

There were those who fought the trend, focusing their energies on reinventing an illustrious Welsh nationhood with distinction and honour.

Dr Price was one of those few. Fearless in support of the Welsh language and its culture, believing the ancestry of his people to be based firmly in the times of the Druids, he masterminded a major project to house a museum of Druidism and culture, a century before today's Museum of Welsh Life attracted visitors by their thousands. Dr Price should be applauded for the genuine desire he had to promote Welsh history, culture and language, the effects of which are being enjoyed by today's people, and much respect and gratitude should be shown to the early pioneers, who fought hard for their beliefs and their nationalism.

Dr William Price was admired and revered, yet some would argue he lived too long. While his younger life was filled with adventure, achievement and a vibrant, volatile outlook on the world, he later became immersed in a fabricated mysterious world of Druidism. His obsessions with litigation and desire to re-establish lost family estates and glory clouded his middle age, and scurrilous newspaper reports of his behaviour in court cases or pagan rituals left a mark on his image. With the passage of time he became portrayed as a tragicomic figure, prone to a mental instability not unlike that of his late father. Although many of his public speeches and writings were often lucid, they were equally as prone to total preposterousness and he was viewed with a condescending pity. Coupled with his close friendships with gentlemen of equally outlandish ideologies, there is little doubt why Price was observed with as much fear as respect.

Dr William Price infuriated and frightened, was ridiculed and condemned, but also held in high esteem and revered. Above all he blazed progress, and was one of the most brilliant and far-seeing men the Welsh nation has ever produced. With the passing of time and the growth of the many stories associated with this man, it has become almost impossible to separate fact from fiction, as the myth of the doctor grows stronger in the annals of Welsh history. There is no doubt that, more than a century after his death, he is still viewed with fascination for the beliefs which saw him both admired and persecuted throughout his ninety-two years. Evidently not the archetypal Victorian gentleman, his behaviour may have bewildered those around him. However, what cannot be denied is the mark he made, not only as the prime-mover to legalise cremation, but also in the wonderfully unique role he played in the tumultuous nineteenth-century Wales.

Dr William Price was a fascinating, romantic legend and around his name have been woven fantastic tales that will live to bewilder and delight generations to come.

Dean Powell
Golygfa Trisant
September 2012

1
1800–1813

Family dynasty, heritage, property and wealth were great obsessions of Dr William Price during his long, adventurous life. Childhood stories of ancestral glory were a cornerstone in the upbringing of the Price siblings and left an indelible mark on the psyche of the man himself. Living among the communities where his wealthy forefathers had resided for generations also contributed to his desire to re-establish the family honour and integrity. The Prices had been a well-established family in the vicinity of Caerphilly for centuries. Their home was the parish of Eglwysilan, of which Caerphilly was the major town, and even until Dr Price's own time they all remained close to their ancestral roots as inhabitants of that same – albeit growing – parish, which latterly included the 'new towns' of Treforest and Pontypridd.

Caerphilly was one of the major market towns of the County of Glamorgan, a town dominated by a sprawling Norman fortress that covered 30 acres of land, making it the largest in Wales, and second only to Windsor. By the time of Dr Price's birth at the opening of the nineteenth century, markets were held every Thursday in the town's Twyn Square, and as many as seven fairs took place every year. A separate cheese market was also held each Tuesday, making Caerphilly an economically prosperous town for the many local farmers, bakers, blacksmiths and dairies. Prior to the expansion of the coal industry, with the sinking of deep mines in its vicinity and the resultant flourishing railway system, Caerphilly was predominantly a rural market town that administered to its surrounding villages. It was in these villages, such as Machen, Bedwas and Rudry, that the Price family had already made their mark.

As one of the oldest families in the district, many of the Prices claimed they could trace their ancestry as far back as the famous Despenser family, the powerful Welsh Marcher Lords of Glamorgan, whose connection with Caerphilly and Llantrisant Castles – two areas where Dr Price resided – existed in the Middle Ages. Sufficiently important to be remembered with large family crypts and memorial tablets in local parish churches, the Prices were entrepreneurs. Some would have considered themselves gentry, but this did not preclude them from investing money in iron-making and other enterprises. Many of the earliest recorded members of the Price family show they were concerned with the tanning industry and no doubt their leather found an outlet through the local markets and fairs of Caerphilly and also Cardiff, as some members became burgesses of the future Welsh capital. Quite a few of the Price family entered the church as members of the clergy, and medicine was another profession favoured by a number of them.[1]

St Martin's Church in Caerphilly is the final resting place of many Price family members, although most of these 'flat stone' graves would have been within the original chapel of St Martin's, which has since been demolished. This was the church where the family worshipped for several generations before turning their allegiance to St Barrwg's Church in Bedwas, presumably when one of them married the daughter of the local vicar.

Although the Price family is extensive and complex, with two distinct parts – that of the Prices of Pontypandy and the Prices of Watford – they have, fortunately, been well documented. It can be somewhat confusing research, particularly due to the sheer quantity of matching first names over several generations, with a multiplicity of the use of the name 'Nicholas' causing the most difficulties. However, it gives us an insight into the vast expanse of the family, their influence in the parish of Eglwysilan and the wealth they had begun to amass.

More importantly, it gives an indication of how Dr Price's own obsession with his family pedigree resulted in several court cases, particularly for claims of estates which may have once been in the Price family possession. Other elements of the Price genealogy resonate throughout Dr Price's own life and the locations where he worked as a surgeon, while also allowing him usage of that ancestry to gain entry to the gentrified circles of Glamorgan. It was ironic that he resided for a large part of his life in a property in Newbridge that once belonged to the Prices. There is also the fact that he enjoyed a close association with both the Crawshay and Guest ironwork dynasties. It was another line of Price's own family that included a Thomas Price of Watford, who helped establish the mighty Dowlais Iron Works in 1759. One begins to wonder whether he used his family pedigree to his own benefit, because coupled with Thomas Price's fame at Dowlais would be his great-grandfather Nicholas Price's standing at Pentyrch Ironworks. Did those connections allow him entry to the leading ironmasters of his day and secure him a place in the hierarchical classes of Glamorgan, as well as becoming a surgeon of their works? In latter years Dr Price made claim to several hereditary titles, particularly those connected to the heroes of the Battle of Bosworth, in which his grandmother's ancestor, Rhys ap Thomas, had played such a prominent role in the victory of Henry Tudor. In fact, he went so far as to use a similar name himself in court cases, while his attire allegedly resembled that of his ancestral warriors and those who resided in the ancient bardic courts of Glamorgan. Together, so many elements of his family history remained in his consciousness and resurrected themselves periodically throughout his life.

One of the first members to have been traced is a Thomas Price (d. 1685) who lived in Energlyn, a sparse hamlet of Caerphilly neighbouring the equally modest community of Van, where he owned a large section of land in the vicinity. A lease from the Earl of Pembroke, dated 1 October 1681, mentions him as the leaseholder of the whole of Caerphilly, with an annual payment of 50s. Described as an innkeeper, possibly of the 'Boar's Head Inn', which was situated in Market Street close to the busy market place at Twyn, a seemingly convenient location to ensure excellent trade with buyers and sellers alike. However, it is also likely that while living in the nearby Court House (Dadleudy), he was the landlord of 'The Black Lion', as the figure of a black lion appears prominently on the coat of arms of the Price family, which can still be seen on the large tablet to them in St Barrwg's Church in Bedwas.

Thomas Price's Last Will & Testament bequeathed his soul 'into ye hands of Almighty God my maker hoping through ye death and passion of Jesus Christ my saviour and only redeemer to receive free pardon of my sinnes', and left the profits of the market place and a house in Bristol to his wife Christian, along with the lease of Court House and the inn and lands at Caerphilly. After her death, this was transferred to their son John. In the inventory of this property, Thomas was named as 'gent' and clearly he was a fairly rich man compared to the other inhabitants of Caerphilly. Incidentally, the rights of Caerphilly market continued in the hands of the Prices up to the 1790s, when they were acquired by the Goodrich family of Energlyn.

The Goodrichs were a principal landowning family whose name is evident throughout Caerphilly, although it originally derives from Lincolnshire. John Goodrich sailed for the American colonies in 1625 to become a cotton planter in Virginia, but his descendants fled back to Britain after the American War of Independence and bought the Energlyn estate in 1792.

Thomas Price left his other son Nicholas, the lease of 'ye house and lands wherein I now live during his own life … after ye demise of my wife Christian Price and ye brewing furnace yet therein'. Thomas left his daughter Mary £10, providing she outlived her mother. To his daughter Margaret he left 5s and to his daughter-in-law Jane, a shilling. By the time of his death he also had a grandson, Thomas, to whom he left a red bullock. The inventory left in his will includes three calves, four beasts of two years old, two little mares, one colt, six small pigs, three stacks of wheat, four stacks of oats, hay, four 'chattel' leases (as in moveable private property such as livestock, which may have included his property in Bristol), two saddles, household belongings and 'implements of husbandry', all boards and benches. There is also the mention of malt, valued at £3 and essential to an innkeeper who brewed his own ale. His entire estate culminated in a value of £62 2s, making him a fairly rich man for the period.

Thomas Price's son, John, became a glover, illustrating the long association the family had with the leather industry. John Price resided in Llandaff and it was stated that in 1692 he went to Cardiff and bought four skins, but as he was not a burgess of the town they were seized. A year later he attempted this a second time by securing seven skins, and again they were seized. In 1699 the same John Price was fined 40s for his action, and a further 40s in 1700 for the same offence. Finally in 1714 a further three sheep skins were seized from him in the town.

The second of Thomas Price's sons, Nicholas, was a yeoman (buried 16 February 1733) and 'gent'. It was his son, another Nicholas Price (1681–1747), also a 'gent', who was probably the most successful of the Price family, establishing a fortune in industry, lands, buildings and commercial interests. An innkeeper of the Boar's Head and a tanner, he made his wealth as the proprietor of the Pentyrch Ironworks. Nicholas was the owner of Pontypandy House, presumably named after the 'pandy' or 'mill' situated across the River Rhymney in the neighbouring parish of Bedwas. Pontypandy means the 'bridge of the furling mill'.

This enterprising entrepreneur and patriarch of an increasingly gentrified family even changed the spelling of his surname from 'Price' to 'Pryce' for a generation, and may have adopted the family coat of arms to add further prestige to their importance. However, his greatest asset was the Pentyrch Forge, established in the parish of Gwaelod y Garth.

The first blast furnaces discovered in Britain were established in Kent and Sussex in 1496, with two furnaces opening at Tongwynlais and Pentyrch in the 1560s, making them among the very first in Wales. A whole combination of natural factors led the early iron pioneers to consider Pentyrch as the ideal setting for a furnace. Lesser Garth contained masses of iron ore as well as the limestone necessary to remove impurities in the blasting process; the hills all around were densely wooded to ensure a supply of charcoal and later coke for fuel; the river and its tributaries provided an abundance of water to provide the motive power, and the Garth itself had not just the coal seams that would become increasingly important as the technology of iron manufacturing advanced, but also an abundance of sandstone with which to build the furnaces and forges. Carboniferous limestone, which runs from Rudry to Llanharry, stretches through this narrow area of lesser Garth, where there is a narrow iron ore of a type called haematite. Iron ore, or 'Welsh mine' was the basis of the thriving iron industry in South Wales. Those early iron-makers discovered the most effective of furnaces were those in frost pockets, as the cold air was denser and contained more oxygen, which is another reason why Cwm Llwystro or 'Hoarfrost Valley' in Pentyrch was chosen as the location of their ironworks.

With all of the ingredients in place, Pentyrch appeared the ideal location for this industry and it is believed that a member of the Mathew family of Radyr, the local landowners, pioneered this scheme. As magistrates and governors, they were in close contact with Parliament and could respond to government policies that might impact on their own area, while they may also have been shrewd enough to see the opportunities available to enrich them. Antiquarian Iolo Morganwg, who was such a major influence on Dr Price, gave an early account of the Pentyrch Ironworks in the last quarter of the eighteenth century: 'In the time of Queen Elizabeth, Sir William Mathews of Radyr ... had two iron furnaces at work in the Vale of Taff, called the higher and lower furnaces. Till very lately they remained almost entire and were built on the same place and principle as our present iron furnaces, only not so large.'

It was the second 'new furnace' at Pentyrch, founded in 1740, that was leased by Lord Talbot five years later for £5 10s a year for ninety-nine years to Nicholas Price of Pontypandy, along with his sons Nicholas and William. For more than thirty years, their regime lasted in Pentyrch. Farms, collieries and iron ore mines were run in association with the Pentyrch Works, charcoal burners cutting cording and coking timber.[2]

Nicholas Price also owned Ivy House at Tongwynlais, which is situated on the other side of the River Taff from the 'New Forge', and his will, dated at Llandaff on 17 February 1758, gives mention to a large estate at Cwm Eldag in the Parish of Eglwysilan and close to the parish church of Llanfabon. A wealthy landowner of many cottages and extensive acreage of land, he also owned a house at Ynys Llyn, a ferry and a ferry boat on the River Taff alongside the road from Cardiff to the area known as Newbridge (later Pontypridd).

He was married to Elizabeth Williams (1690–1781), heiress of the Coed y Brain farm in Eglwysilan, who died aged ninety-one, indicative of a family that enjoyed a longevity of life in generations to come. A memorial tablet once affixed in St Martin's Chapel in Caerphilly commemorated Elizabeth and bore the Latin inscription '*Immortalis est Genus, quod Mulier amat*' ('Immortal is the Family Whom a Woman Loves').

Pentyrch Ironworks was at the very heart of the family fortune. It is interesting to note that the name Pentyrch is the Welsh plural of 'boar's head', which may explain an even closer connection between the Price family and this area than previously considered, given the name of their Caerphilly tavern. It is likely the Prices built or rebuilt a house in the vicinity of the furnace, known as Tŷ Maen, on the original farm, called Ynys Tŷ Maen. It was here that the family resided for at least another generation.

Many tales survive of the Price wealth and power. As both landowners and industrialists, they grew in stature, employing a strong workforce, but not always winning favour with others. Alongside the infamous Lewis family of the Van, scurrilous tales were told of their interest in cock fighting. There is also the tale of John Williams of Bedwas who, on 19 July 1766, robbed ironmaster Nicholas Price of 3lb of bacon valued at 10*d*. Williams was found guilty at the quarter sessions and sentenced to be whipped. It is likely to have been him that wrote the following song about the ironmaster:

> *Roedd Prys o Bontypandy yn wr haeddai'I grogi,*
> *Yn hudo'r marched wrth y cant*
> *A thaflu'r plant I foddi.*

> (Price of Pontypandy, was a man who deserved hanging,
> He seduced girls by the hundred,
> And threw the children to drown.)

Whether this is a fair assessment of the man, given the author's predicament, is debatable. However, such promiscuity could well be likely and such scant regard for legal wedlock set something of a precedent for his famous descendant! Having said that, it wouldn't be the only occasion where the questionable morals of a Price came to light. Another of the Price descendants, the Revd James Price of Bassaleg, a distant cousin of Dr Price, was known to have fathered an illegitimate son with an Amy Davies of that parish.

Nicholas and Elizabeth had six sons and two daughters, the aforementioned ironmaster brothers of Nicholas and William (1713–77), James (1720–1811), Charles (1725–86) and a daughter, Anne (born 1716). Three other children, named Nicholas, Charles (1722–3) and Blanche (d. 1718) all died in infancy.

The ironmaster's will, proved at Llandaff on 2 February 1758, bequests

> to his wife, half of the household goods and plate at my house at Pentyrch, Glamorgan. To his son James the messuage and tenement in Rudy now occupied by him which I purchased from John Thomas, late of the parish of Bedwas. To his lawful sons Nicholas and William, the right to raise what iron mines they think proper now growing or under sad tenement and to pay my son James a shilling a dozen bushels.

The eldest son Nicholas Price (1709–64) inherited Pontypandy House (also known as Mansion House) on the death of his father. Typically, like so many other gentry families, they endeavoured to increase their wealth by marrying others of equal, or better financial positions. Nicholas was no exception as he was married, in December 1737, to Elizabeth Greenfield (d. 1753) of Cardiff and together they had seven children. She was a beneficiary of her uncle, a mariner of Cardiff who left the substantial sum of £4,525.

What is interesting is that one of their children, Mary, married John Wood of Staffordshire, a member of the prominent pottery family of Burslem. Their grandson, Nicholas Price Wood, married Mary Baddeley, the heiress of the Wedgewood porcelain dynasty.

A rather poignant entry in the diary of William Thomas of Michaelstone-super-Ely relates to Nicholas and Elizabeth Price's daughter Elizabeth, who died of tuberculosis and whose memorial can be seen in St John's Church, Cardiff. The entry from 11 July 1766 read,

> Was buried at Caerphilly Chapple Miss Price, daughter of Mr Nicholas Price Junior of Pontypandy, deceased about 21 of age of lingering consumption. She was to be married with William Richards Esq., of the Corner House, Cardiff – all things provided wedding suits bought and she grew worse on ye day she bought her wedding suit and continued so till her death. Doctor's tried, and then Hot Wells in Bristol but all in vain.

Tragically her beloved, William Richards, who was six years younger than his intended bride, died on 6 February 1780, aged thirty-four years, of 'melancholy'.

It is likely that Elizabeth's sister, Maria, also suffered the same fate of tuberculosis. William Thomas also wrote, in his diary on 1 December 1771, 'This day come from Bristol in Priest's boat to be buried, the corpse of the daughter of Mr Nicholas Price and wife of Mr William Lewis of the New House in Llanishen from a long lingering disease.'

Porset Farm, with its corn mill and extensive lands, was originally owned by Charles Ward, a tanner, but later leased to ironmaster Nicholas Price's second son, James (1720–1811) in 1766. James eventually moved to the large Bedwas Fawr before residing in Portishead near Bristol, where he died as the Quarantine Master for the harbour. It was his marriage to Florence Heytt in 1751, the daughter of the Revd Edward Hyett, Rector of Bedwas, which probably led the family to changing their religious allegiance from Caerphilly to Bedwas. James and Florence had one son, later to become the Revd James Price of Cardiff, Rudry and Bassaleg (1757–1836) who married a Mary Rowland of Bedwas (d. 1849), whose middle son, James Hyett Price, was a midshipman and was killed in 1801, aged just fifteen, after falling from the masthead of a ship. Another son, also named James, died on a passage to Australia.

It was William Price (1713–1777), the third son of the dynasty leader Nicholas Price, who continued to run the Pentyrch Ironworks. By this time it worked closely with the Melingriffith Tinworks, opened in 1748 on the site of an ancient corn mill, two miles south of the River

Taff at Whitchurch. Pentyrch forged the iron bars and they were sent to Melingriffith to be rolled into tinplate. The operation had a first-class communication network of two canals, two weirs, many tram roads and bridges, and ultimately the Pentyrch and Melingriffith Railway.

Although unmarried, William Price lived at Ivy House in Tongwynlais and had three illegitimate children by Jane Hopkin ap Evan, including William (1765–1821), Jane (1772–6) and Elizabeth. William ran the Pentyrch forge until his death in December 1777 'of about 60 years old of gout of the stomach'. His will, proved in London on 8 May 1778, stated that

> William Price of the Forge in the parish of Pentyrch and County of Glamorgan, Ironmaster ... desires unto my natural or reputed son, William by Jane Hopkin ab Evans, all my singular my real and personal estate, whatsoever and wheresoever the same is situate and being to hold to him my natural son William Price his heirs, executors, administrators and assigns for ever subject to the payment of all my debts, legacies and funeral expenses and to the payment of the annuity herein after given.[3]

His executors leased the Pentyrch works to William Lewis & Co. of Tongwynlais, who ran the business through the manager, Thomas Vaughan, until 1801, when he sold it to Harford and Partridge & Co., owners of the Melingriffith Works. They were formally united in 1805 under the ownership of a group of Quaker ironmasters from Bristol, who then sold it to MP and industrialist Richard Blakemore (1755–1855), who once came to loggerheads with the future Dr Price. The Ironworks remained in existence until end of the boom years of 1872 to 1874, when iron trade dramatically fell as the company faced the rivalry of steel and the import of Spanish ores. By 1888 the works were completely closed, and the site was razed to the ground.

Nicholas Price's only surviving daughter, Ann (born 1716), died of tuberculosis shortly after marrying Richard Priest, a merchant of Cardiff.

Finally we come to Nicholas Price's fourth son, Charles Price (1725–86), grandfather of Dr Price, who originally leased part of the hamlet of Van, with a meadow attached called Hopyard. Charles, also named as a 'tanner', also lived at Porset Farm and appears to have later resided at Redbrook, a house situated between the villages of Bedwas and Machen. According to local tales, the brook, which marked the parish boundary, was coloured red with rust from the former drift mine situated at Clungwyn (Glyn Gwyn). The house formed part of an estate that belonged to William Thomas, the father of Charles's first wife, Elizabeth Thomas (d. 1755) of Clungwyn, an estate that Dr Price later tried to lay claim to at the High Court. Following Elizabeth's death at the age of just twenty-seven, Charles subsequently married Joan Davies (1732–93) of Gelliwastad

Farm, Machen in 1760. Despite his second marriage, the father of his first wife left all his personal estate of Clyngwyn to Charles. His will was dated 7 December 1767, which was proved at Llandaff the next day, meaning that William Thomas was on his deathbed while signing his fortune to his former son-in-law.

According to a document written by Dr Price in later years, it was said that Joan Davies (his grandmother) was a member of the affluent Matthew family, who had held posts as stewards in fourteenth-century Glamorgan for absent English lords. She was of the same stock as Lewis of Van, whose lengthy pedigree and aptitude for the acquisition of property had made them incredibly wealthy.

Sir David Mathew (1428–84) was the son of a supporter of Owain Glyndwr. From Sir David and his wife, Wenllian Herbert, descended the lines of Mathew family of Llandaff and Radyr. The influence of their family developed under the protection of Sir Rhys ap Thomas. A controversial character, Rhys was born in 1449 and on his father's deathbed inherited the wealth of the Dinefwr estates. Although his family were Lancastrians, he served the House of York and vowed to Richard III words to the effect that Henry Tudor would land in Wales only over his body: 'Whoever ill-affected to the state, shall dare to land in those partes of Wales, where I have anie employment under your majestie, must resolve with himself to make his entrance an irruption over my bellie'.

The story is told that after Henry Tudor's return to Britain at Dale, Pembrokeshire in 1485, Rhys eased his conscience by hiding under Mullock Bridge, Dale as Henry marched over, thus absolving himself of his oath to Richard.

The fact that Rhys made a major contribution to Henry's victory at Bosworth in 1485 is undisputed. At Welshpool, Rhys had a large army of levied Welshmen with him to support the young Tudor. The Battle of Bosworth, on 22 August 1485, was a turning point in British history and Richard III's death was supposedly at the hands of Rhys. Rhys was knighted on the battlefield and made Governor of Wales as Henry bestowed upon him the Order of the Knight of the Garter.[4] The history of Rhys is of importance when examining Dr Price, for he made claim of his connection to the heroes of Bosworth, and one can imagine that such childhood bedtime tales greatly influenced him into delusions of grandeur and supremacy in later years.

Many other considerable figures in the political life of Glamorgan came from the Mathew family, of whom some effigies can be found at Llandaff Cathedral. The line produced a notable figure in Vice Admiral of the Red and one-time Commander in Chief of the Mediterranean Fleet, Thomas Mathews (1670–1751). Thomas was the uncle of Joan Davies of Gelliwastad, and therefore a great-great-uncle to Dr Price.

He was a distinguished member of the Mathew family whose home for generations was Llandaff Court, subsequently the Palace of the Bishops of Llandaff. Twice during his long naval career, Admiral Mathews settled down at Llandaff as a local magistrate, landowner, and sportsman. By a miscarriage of justice, following a bungled affair at sea and a conclusion of order, Mathews was arraigned at a court martial in 1747 and after a trial was sentenced to be dismissed from the Service. Examination of Naval records tends to show that a rear-admiral, malevolently disposed, was more to blame. The Mathews' connection with Llandaff was revived when a later ancestor, Henry Mathews QC, a famous Home Secretary, resumed the title of Viscount Llandaff.[5]

Charles Price worked the coal outcrops at Rhydygwern in Machen, and also engaged in some iron ore mining in Rudry, close to where his brother James was also involved in mining activities at Wernddu, near Rudry Common, leased from the Earl of Plymouth. Together the brothers' enterprise in the iron ore and coal pits stretched across land predominantly occupied by the village of Rudry. Iron ore from this area was also being used at the Pentyrch Ironworks. Diarist William Thomas wrote, in June 1786, 'Lately buried at Bedwas, Charles Price Esq of Redbrook in ditto Justice of the Peace for Glamorgan and Monmouthshire. He was the son of Mr Nicholas Price, deceased of the Boar's Head that built the New Furnace in 1740 and who was also a Tanner.'

Charles and Joan, the grandparents of Dr William Price, resided permanently in Redbrook, where they raised seven children, several of whom died in infancy. The eldest son, Revd Thomas Price (1751–1832), married Mary Shellard of Warrington, Somerset and brought up four children in the town of Merriott in the same county. This was a successful arm of the family, as three of the sons established themselves in a profession. William was a clergyman, Charles a physician to King William IV, and John was a captain of the Royal Navy.

However, it was Charles and Joan's sixth child, William, to whom we now turn. One of the properties owned by the original Price ironmaster, Nicholas Price, was a dwelling house with its outhouses and 30 acres of land known as 'Tir y Coedka', situated in the vicinity of Rudry village. Purchased from Thomas Morgan Esq. in 1744 and correctly named '*Tŷ'n-y-coed-cae*' ('the house in the wooded field'), it was here that the ill-fated and sadly disturbed William raised a family. The village of Rudry had only around 200 inhabitants by the time William Price (1761–1841) settled there in 1798 with his wife, Mary Edmunds (1767–1844) of Machen. They paid £1 4*s* 9*d* tax on the land that their family owned and occupied.

William was born on 26 February 1761 at Redbrook, and followed his elder brother by a decade, Thomas, in accepting the calling and becoming a member of the cloth. He received his formal early education at Cowbridge

Grammar School, before attending Jesus College, Oxford where the records of elections of Scholars and Fellows and the taking of their Oaths and Admissions confirm he was elected a Scholar of the College on 11 February 1780.

The college was established in 1571 with a set number of scholars and fellows prescribed in statutes, and although the numbers of each were increased over many years, the rule remained the same in that when a place became vacant, a new incumbent was elected by the principal and fellows. Scholars were part of the legal foundation of the college and enjoyed certain privileges and an income of £10 per annum from the Foundation Funds. Fellows had more privileges and a better income from the same source. Ordinarily all were expected to reside in the college, although leaves of absence could be granted by the principal. Marriage, however, required the resignation of either the scholarship or fellowship as was usual in Oxford colleges at this time.

Like other colleges in the university during the seventeenth and eighteenth centuries, Jesus College recruited from the ages of sixteen to twenty, sometimes with groups of brothers, cousins and neighbours coming to Oxford together to be educated, some by their private tutors. The majority were aged between sixteen and twenty-two and were drawn overwhelmingly from Wales, with which the college had had strong connections since its foundation. Undergraduates were economically and socially stratified, the richest and therefore most privileged were entered as noblemen commoners or fellow-noblemen commoners.

The next two classes down were commoners and battelers, and the poorest were servitors. Admission fees were differentiated accordingly, although all graduates paid the same college fee to receive a degree. Scholarships and exhibitions were awarded to any class, depending on academic promise.

The institution for which rules were laid down in the 1622 statutes resembled a tightly organised seminary or boarding school, with compulsory philosophy lectures for graduates and scholars and strict rules about recreation, attendance at chapel, behaviour and keeping within the boundaries. The principal, fellows and resident male servants, including a butler, cook and porter all had to remain celibate, and women only entered the college as 'bed makers or laundresses'. Some of the fellows also taught, taking turns to hold lectures in philosophy, logic, catechetical studies and rhetoric, and had the responsibility for the junior or senior class.

By the time William entered the college, the number of richer undergraduates, never large at Jesus, had declined as other more grandiose colleges attracted large numbers of noblemen commoners and fellow-commoners. Among the last was the future Jacobite MP Sir Watkin Williams Wynn, and Thomas James Bulkeley, 7th Viscount Bulkeley. From humbler backgrounds came Edward Lhuyd (1660–1709), a naturalist, Celtic scholar and keeper of the scientifically orientated Ashmolean Museum in Oxford. Another Welshman who studied there was Goronwy Owen (1723–69) who chose exile as a clergyman in North America.

In the case of William, his election was to a scholarship made vacant by the resignation of the Revd Anthony Jones MA. The election, after due examination of William, took place on 19 January 1780. He was admitted on 11 February, having taken the oaths required by the laws of the realm and the statutes – all written and signed in his own hand.

However, William voluntarily resigned his scholarship on 5 January 1781, and a John George took that scholarship at the end of the month. William proceeded to the degree of Bachelor of Arts on 18 June 1783. He was re-elected on 12 August 1783 to a scholarship, this time made vacant by the promotion of Dr John Walters to a fellowship.

William was then elected on 10 March 1785 to the fellowship made vacant by the voluntary resignation of the Revd William Morgan BD. He was admitted as a 'probationary' fellow on 6 April 1785, having taken the oaths required. His admission as an 'actual' fellow took place on 6 April 1786, after which he took his Master of Arts in April 1786.

As a scholar William Price was well aware of the requirement of the college statutes that fellows had to be unmarried and, after a period as a fellow, made the decision to resign his collegiate bachelor life and marry. This was not uncommon and many fellows, already ordained clergymen, left to occupy country livings (sometimes provided by the college itself).

Revd William Price vacated the fellowship on his marriage to Mary Edmunds, the vacancy this created being filled on 13 May 1790. Although an ordained priest of the Church of England, Price never held a living, excusing himself that he considered it was 'too serious an undertaking'. Although in later years Dr Price claimed his father was 'a Druid at heart', which might indeed have been an impediment to his preaching the Gospel, it was a far graver reason that prevented the fulfilment of his priesthood. By the age of thirty he seems to have been regarded as 'lunatic'.

Psychologists fascinated by the doctor's bizarre behaviour would benefit enormously from a closer inspection of his parentage. It was on 24 February 1790 that Revd Price married Mary Edmunds of Machen, a maidservant, and consequently relinquished his fellowship, but he probably officiated at services in local churches in the Rudry and Bedwas areas. His wife was considered well below him in class status, since he was regarded as a pillar of society given his ecclesiastical position, whereas she was just an illiterate domestic servant who could never even sign her own name. It was, according to Dr Price's own pedigree of the family, 'a most improvident connection in the way of marriage with a woman such below him in station in life, who was in fact only a domestic servant and an unintelligent, illiterate person, and who, though she might have been able to read, was certainly not able to write'.

Incidentally, the union was coincidental with some strange behaviour in the young vicar. A newspaper report by journalist Owen Morgan (Morien) of Pontypridd, something of a unreliable source given his dislike of a 'rival Archdruid' in Dr William Price, and written following the doctor's death, said of his father,

> He was very eccentric, but not insane according to the usual meaning of the term. A woman of the neighbourhood had once offended him. He saw her going with a basket on her arm in the direction of Caerphilly. Knowing she would return over a footbridge across the Rumney River, he procured a saw and sawed the bridge nearly through. He then waited for the return of his enemy. When he saw her approaching the bridge he called out 'Take care, you will fall in the river!'. The poor woman, knowing he was not quite right in his head, took no heed of this warning and on reaching the middle of the bridge it gave way under her, and she and the basket fell into the flood. The woman was rescued with no other injury than a wetting.[6]

When discussing his union with Mary Edmunds, the report continued, 'This man fell desperately in love with his mother's maid, and they married at Machen Church. Old people, who heard it from their parents, state that when returning home from the church after the wedding, the bridegroom was dancing about the road, and with great glee was shouting, "I have had her – Look! Look!" at the same time pointing her out to the people.'

The vicar's arrival at Rudry must have been a great disappointment to the vicar of the parish, who had hoped for an aide from Oxford. It was a parish that had already suffered its fair share of scandal, particularly with the appointment of Revd Thomas Rimbron of Peterston-super-Ely, who became curate of Bedwas and Rudry in 1769 by Hon. Shute Barrington, Bishop of Llandaff. It was there that he married the widow of his predecessor, Revd Watkin Jones. Up to 1775 his ministry was described as 'an uncommonly conscientious priest' who was of 'strong and independent intellect'. But one Sunday in May 1775 Revd Rimbron was accused by one of his parishioners, Robert Thomas, of having 'begotten a bastard on the body of his servant maid – who happened to be Thomas's daughter. Rimbron was forced to admit his fault. His ministry in the parish was over and he abruptly left, returning ultimately to Bristol. Sadly, the child, born in July 1775, was laid to rest in Bedwas churchyard the following month.'[7]

Evidence of Revd Price's insanity appeared more clearly directly after the marriage. For two or three years it was not, apparently, very severe, but was nevertheless evidently the reason he did not follow his career. He became dishevelled in his appearance and engrossed in walks in the woods to collect pieces of bark from the trees in order to burn them piece by piece while muttering uncouth words beside the hearth at Ty-yn-y-coed-cae. Armed with a saw, he became a nuisance to his neighbours as he trespassed on their land to cut wood. He also collected stones to spit on and clean, which he believed added greatly to their value and put them away carefully around the cottage. He kept grass snakes, secreting them in his clothing until he hid them in the stones of the grey tombs of his ancestors in the local churchyards. Much to the displeasure of the parishioners, he often carried them in his pockets for days on end.

The vicar had a love of water, bathing in local ponds up to his neck, sometimes fully clothed or only wearing his hat. Occasionally he bathed naked, but even after he had stripped, he would still drop his clothes in the pond and wear them soaking wet. After his death a post mortem took place so his surgeon son could bizarrely attempt to prove he was *non compos mentis* by showing the vessels of his brain were unduly large. The necropsy examination suggested that the clergyman's desire to immerse himself in water was in order to 'relieve the throbbing'.

In 1814, an attempt was made to prove him insane, and the testimony of two of his former servants, Edmund William and Elizabeth Samuel, was used in court. Edmund William testified the Revd Price 'carried his own excrement in his pockets, burned it on the fire, and rubbed it on his head and on the walls of his room saying it was paint' and that he had threatened his servant 'with a knife'. Elizabeth Samuel explained that Revd Price was in the habit of 'running in the field in his shirt or naked'.

On his death, the bulk of his property was divided between his brother, Revd Thomas Price, and his eldest son, Charles Price – at least that was the claim by the young Dr Price. During the trial between Fothergill and Price in Bristol in 1848, it was said that

> more than twenty witnesses were called who had known the unfortunate Revd Price from the time he had been seized with this malady until his death at the age of 76, and they deposed that they never knew him otherwise than a confirmed lunatic, at times a dangerous maniac, at others more tranquil and under control, but at all periods utterly hopelessly insane, at one time flying through the fields and woods, stark naked, shouting, hollering, bellowing, and again in ragged and torn clothes, carrying bundles of sticks which he would burn, muttering all disjointed sentences. Totally disgusting in his habits and person, frequently dangerous to himself and to others, he presented all the features of the most confirmed debasement of intellect.[8]

Other individuals were called to show that he had lucid intervals. There were testimonies from numerous witnesses who swore that although Price was insane, and committed all manner of extraordinary and extravagance actions, yet on different occasions, when they met him, he was what one called 'civil', another 'easy', another 'sensible' and yet another 'good'. The majority of the witnesses, however, only spoke of more casual intervals of a few minutes at the most, and of hearing only a sentence or two spoken by Rev Price. The only witness who spoke to a conversation of any length was a Wesleyan preacher who deposed that in the late 1820s he had a conversation with the reverend in a wood, who told him that at Cowbridge School he went to hear John Wesley preach, and that Wesley said he would rather read a chapter in the Bible than the whole *Book of Homilies* (a collection of sermons used in the Church of England) and that predestination, the doctrine that all events were willed by God, was not the doctrine of Wesley but of Calvin, and that God had foreordained a certain number to be eternally elected and a certain number not to be.

A great number of witnesses were welcomed and examined through an interpreter, saying that they could not speak '*Saesneg*' (English), though it almost invariably turned out, much to the amusement of the court, that on being pressed they gave their answers in very good English.[8]

On one occasion Revd Price allegedly fired off a gun at a young woman who he claimed had been taking sticks from his hedge. He frightened a pregnant woman called Mrs Davis so much it allegedly caused her to go into labour and result in the premature birth of her child. On another occasion he attacked a man by flinging at him a sharp spear that fortunately missed by inches and embedded itself in the ground. His wife could usually calm him, but often his behaviour would terrify the children so much one of them would be 'frightened into fits'. Or was it a case that there was a genetic mental disorder running throughout the children from their 'lunatic' father that caused the seizures? There was even the need to call his friends, Owen, Davis and Williams, to restrain him physically, although he never resisted them and would suddenly become incredibly docile on their arrival at Tŷ'n-y-coed-cae.

Arguably, the vicar suffered from paraphrenia, a condition that was often associated in later life with his famous son. Distinctly separate from paranoia and from schizophrenia, this psychotic illness usually occurs in mid-life and although there is no intellectual deterioration, there is a preoccupation with delusions and the sufferer experiences distress, irrational behaviour and may accuse others of persecution. Although the condition wasn't identified until 1863 by Karl Ludwig Kahlbaum, many of the symptoms are easily recognisable in Dr Price during his twilight years, as they are in his father.

Revd Price's behaviour was somewhat schizophrenic in nature. There was a late onset, after a promising academic career in the church, although the personality breakdown was incredibly severe. There's the dress disorder, the running around naked, the violence, the symbolic stones and snakes, which all direct towards a deeper mental problem. Some claimed that the vicar's helpless fits were due to an accident whilst otter hunting. It was recorded that he fell from his horse in 1787 and afterwards the manifestations of his illness presented themselves. Since this was not a hereditary disease, one cannot assume Dr Price suffered a similar mental disorder inherited from his father. However, living in such an incredibly strange environment must have had a profound effect upon him and the other children in the family. Environmentally and genetically, the young William Price could not have been born into a more troubled household.

Revd Price and Mary had seven children, the eldest being Charles (1791–1871), baptised in Bedwas on 16 March 1791, who died a bachelor at his home of Caeridwen in Radyr, aged seventy-seven. Charles was almost ruinously involved in lawsuits, usually at the instigation of his litigious brother Dr Price, before enjoying a modest life as the cashier to Francis Crawshay, the ironmaster, and settling in a property called Primrose Bank in Newbridge with his spinster sister Ann.

The second child, Elizabeth Price (1793–1872) was baptised on 23 March 1793 and died at Pentwyn, Rudry, aged eighty. The third child was Mary (1791–1869), who married a Thomas John and settled in the parish of Eglwysilan. A fourth child was Ann (1804–78), baptised on 27 January 1804, who settled in Primrose Bank, Newbridge where she died in 1878.

Two sons died while still young, the first being William (baptised 29 August 1795), aged three years, in 1798. Nicholas (baptised 10 January 1808) died in 1811 also at the age of three; the cause of his death was claimed to have been a reaction to vaccination.

The Parish Registers for Rudry of the late eighteenth century show that infant mortality was particularly high. In 1771, of the eight burials recorded, five were of children. There were also epidemics, as recorded on 27 November 1785: 'Barbara, Betty and Margaret, daughters of William Edward, all buried in one coffin.' Childbirth was also a hazard as recorded in the parish register of 8 January 1856: 'Amy Lloyd and her infant child Henry buried in the same coffin.' She was just twenty-seven years of age.

In St Barrwg's Church, Bedwas, a white marble tablet on black base crowned with a representation of the Welsh Dragon reads,

In memory of Nicholas, son of Charles Price Esq of
Redbrook in this Parish. Obit May 24th 1777 Etat. 8
Of Charles Price aforesaid. Obit May 24th 1786 Etat. 60
Of Joan Price, his widow. Obit July 3rd 1873 Etat.61
Of William grandson of the above and son of the Revd
William Price M.A. of Oxford. Obit 1798 Etat. 3 months
Of Nicholas his son. Obit April 28th 1811 Etat. 3

Of the Revd William Price aforesaid formerly of
Tynycoedcae in the Parish of Rudry. Obit January 19th 1841 Etat. 80
Of Mary Price his widow. Obit January 5th 1844 Etat. 77
Of Mary their daughter. Obit July 1869 Etat. 72
And of Charles Price Esq of Caeridwen in the Parish
Of Radyr (Glamorgan) eldest son of the above named William
And Mary Price Obit March 28th 1871 Etat. 80
Also Elizabeth Price died on the 25th October 1872 at
Pentwyn Rydri in the County of Glamorgan at twenty
Minutes past nine a.m. in her eightieth year of age. Her
Body was buried at Bedwas Church in the County of
Monmouth the 29th Oct. 1872.

In the churchyard, under the eastern chancel window is a large tombstone enclosed with iron railings bearing all the particulars above, names and one additional inscription:

Also in memory of Ann Price of Park in the Parish of
Llanishen in the County of Glamorgan, the youngest
Daughter of the Rev William Price of Rydri, Glam, who
Died Feb. 8th 1878 aged 74 years.

This brings us to the second youngest child, William, who was born in Tŷ'n-y-coed-cae on 4 March 1800 and baptised in St James's Church, Rudry on April 14. His upbringing was far from comfortable as his father's promising career was ruined, but there were clearly significant periods when the reverend was lucid. In fact he contributed to his son's education, and probably that of the surviving siblings, by teaching them Latin and Greek. Sadly, one cannot ignore the fact that the level of his sickness left the family in a state of poverty, and although the Prices' standing in the community meant that relatives assisted them financially on occasions, they were still dependent on charity, particularly various financial offerings from the Corporation of the Sons of the Clergy. The young William, growing up in the cottage of Tŷ'n-y-coedcae until the age of thirteen when the family left the premises for another cottage in the vicinity, was well acquainted with poverty and possibly periods of total destitution.

He also grew up in a household where the dominant figure was a father who, as time passed, increasingly inhabited a twilight world of his own, roaming the woods and fields, muttering all the time strange and disjointed sentences.[6]

His father's penchant for nakedness and open spaces was a trait inherited by the young William during his adolescence. He was surrounded by the most beautiful rolling hills in the vicinity of Rudry, with family haunts including the local woodlands of the Ruperra estate and the ruined walls of Castell y Van, a home to the Lewis family and patron of the bards whose Druidic influence was present throughout William's life. A little further afield there were the mysterious mounds and tumuli on Mynydd Machen. Here for the developing mind and fertile imagination of William, encouraged in his lucid moments by a father who seems to have been a passionate Welshman, were the ingredients of a heady brew.[6] Also on the tithe map of Rudry is an area named Maen Llwyd (grey rock), after which a local hostelry was named, making it clear that there were certain rock formations in the vicinity of the Cefn Mabley estate, also giving its name to a local farm, where the pagan forefathers were claimed to have worshipped.

The Rudry of William's youth was not necessarily a picturesque scene of tranquil natural beauty with clear streams and lush green valleys, because there was an embryonic industrial community in the area, particularly the workings of iron ore, in which his own grandfather and great-uncle had played such a pivotal role. Rudry had enjoyed a history of industrialisation with brickworks, iron mines, forges, tinplate works, corn mills and further back still, lead and silver mining dating from Roman times.[9]

Iron mining was a long-lasting industrial concern. During the seventeenth century, the first recorded references to iron industry in Rudry parish were made. In the Parish Registers of Machen after 1684 can be found mention of the Machen Forge, which by the following century was closely associated with the Coslett family. The forge, supplied by ore mined at Rudry, had a long history. Several decades later the furnace, store-house, coal works and woods were leased by Thomas Morgan MP of Ruperra to Messrs John Mayberry & Co., ironmasters, for a term of forty-two years. This was a piece of empire building by the company, for in 1746 John Mayberry, in partnership with Charles Price (Dr Price's grandfather), who held the lease from the Morgan family of the Rudry Iron Mine, his brother James Price of Bedwas, and Henry Morgan of Bristol, opened a mine at Wernddu. In 1775 Mayberry concluded a separate lease, with Charles Morgan, of the Rudry Iron Mine for thirty years, but in the event neither this nor the 1764 lease of the forges ran its term and in 1788 the latter was leased to Harford & Partridge & Co. of Bristol. The works were abandoned in 1826.[10]

It was several years before Christopher Pope, the wealthy West India merchant of Bristol, and his son-in-law Phillip Woodruff, indentured with the Earl of Plymouth for 'all and singular the mines, beds, seams of Iron ore, coal, culm, limestone and thereafter be' on some 170 acres of land in Rudry, for a period of fifty years at £133 per annum; this resulted in the opening of the Rudry Ironworks at Tŷ'n-y-Coedcae, where the Price family home was located.

The cost of erecting and equipping the works was estimated at £30,000. A short length of tram-line, which crossed the river by means of Tŷ'n-y-coedcae bridge and ascended the slopes of Crig y Rhacam, connected the works with the newly constructed Rumney tram road to Bassaleg and Newport. In 1833, 1,068 tons of iron was sent to Newport, but the venture failed a year later.[11]

William was well acquainted with these pockets of industry and knew how the workforce survived the many hazards and dangers which confronted them on a daily basis. After all, William's later preoccupation with the plight of the worker, his living and working conditions, manifested itself at a very early age. So too his interest in Welsh history, which he may have studied, with access to the volumes of work produced by antiquarian Iolo Morganwg.

During his boyhood, William witnessed rapidly changing times. The area where Tŷ'n-y-coedcae was situated was later renamed Waterloo, in honour of the victorious battle. Admiral Horatio Nelson actually visited Wales in 1802, when he journeyed to Cyfarthfa Ironworks in recognition of their contribution to the war effort. The Crawshay family welcomed him in more splendour than a reigning monarch. In years to come, Price and the Crawshays had a close connection.

At the beginning of the nineteenth century only two major roads existed in Rudry to accommodate the scattering of cottages and farmhouses. One followed the River Rhymney and dates to Roman times, while the other, a ridgeway road, ran from Caerphilly past St James' Church, overlooking the village. Otherwise, communication was by paths and track roads. Evidence relating to St James' Church dates back to 1254, taking the form of a wayside shrine used by pilgrims en route to worship shrines abroad, giving the site the nickname of 'The Pilgrim Church'. Given its proximity to the ancient ridgeway road to Newport, it is quite possible this was the main form of communication for pilgrims visiting Newport, then Bristol, before travelling by sea. One of the most popular pilgrimages was that to the Apostle at Santiago de Compostela in northern Spain, one of the three greatest places of pilgrimage in the medieval ages.

The Price family decided that, given William's intellectual aspirations, clear promise and his bright and scholarly attitude to life, some form of formal education was needed. Sadly it coincided with the rapid deterioration of his father's sickness, and with little opportunity to learn from his mentor any further, he was sent to a local day school. Early initiatives to provide schooling in Rudry were taken by the church. Until the eighteenth century, there is no record of any provision of education in the parish, but it is likely the curates of St James' Church provided some rudimentary education to the younger members of the congregation. Between 1755 and 1780 a total of forty-four marriages took place in St

James' and of the eighty-eight people involved, only twenty-one could actually sign their own names.

A system of circulating schools had been created in 1730 by Revd Griffith Jones of Llanddowror and his brother-in-law Sir John Phillips. The system sent schoolmasters into the country parishes when requested by the clergy, where they remained for three or four months to help children and adults to read. Usually the language was Welsh and the book used most commonly was the Bible. Rudry and Bedwas were visited in this way as early as 1739, but it wasn't until 1764 that the first was held in Rudry alone. Not until 1809 was a school established in Bedwas, which occupied fourteen 'poor girls' and a Sunday school of fifty children held by the curate. The children of Rudry would have to wait until as late as 1835 for an established school.

Parishes generally issued certificates commending the work of the teacher. One sent to Watkin Jones, Rector of Bedwas on 13 August 1753 read,

> ... hath taught a Welch School at Bedwas for the Space of three Months, during which Time he hath been diligent and faithful in the Discharge of his Duty, as appears by the Proficiency of his Scholars, who have been to say the Church Catechism before me last Sunday in the Church of Bedwas, where they answered to the Satisfaction of the Parishioners and of their Minister, who are desirous of signifying our Gratitude to the worth Promoters and Supports of this most useful Charity, praying for their Welfare and Success, and the Continuance of so laudable an undertaking.

An important development in education was provided by Ann Aldworth whose Will, dated 19 August 1729, left property to establish a trust for providing schools in the parishes of Bedwas and Egwysilan for 'teaching poor girls in reading, writing, sewing, needlework and any other useful sciences as the trustees should appoint'. In 1759 trustees, with Thomas Price of Watford as chairman, took a lease of lands at Pwll y Pant for the purpose of building a convenient school and the earliest Aldworth school established in 1763.[10]

Young William reached the age of ten and was still unable to speak a word of English when he attended Mr Gatward's school in the village of Machen. A charity school was established in the village in 1807 and by 1812 a Lancastrian school was also opened in the parish, probably for those children whose parents could afford to pay for their education, for in 1816 there was no school in the parish for the 'lower orders'.

Although no evidence exists today of Gatward's fledgling operation, it is likely the school was situated in Pandy Lane. William walked two miles each day to get there, where he was given instruction on the Lancastrian principle, a system by which the younger children were instructed by the older ones at the cost of 4s a quarter.

Revd Price and Mary, who only spoke Welsh in the family home, sought assistance from relatives for financial support to send William to the school, where he displayed unusual brilliance for one so young. Having said that, the support of family members was limited, for gradually the Price fortune itself was rapidly dwindling. As an example, by 1803, the wealth attained by Nicholas Price, the ironmaster, had almost vanished over three generations. His grandson, Nicholas, and great-grandson, Nicholas, had little financial stability, with several references to bank loans and mortgages. Nicholas and his wife, Catherine Price, had loans of several thousand pounds by using Pontypandy and Cwm Eldeg as collateral in the deal. When Nicholas died in 1793, he left Catherine, and son Nicholas, the burden of responsibility of the estate and the debts which needed to be repaid. By this time the Upper Boat properties, probably including the ferry and ferry-boat, were sold to E. Turberville. They also sold further property near the River Taff to W. Key, including several dwelling houses near the old ferry at Upper Boat. One of the properties included Porthyglo, occupied by Brocket Grover Esq. in the early 1800s and later the home of Dr William Price himself. By 1803 Catherine Price was determined to sell the estates and pay off the mortgage. It must have been a difficult decision for her to make and for her twenty-five-year-old son Nicholas to accept, for Pontypandy had been the family home for generations. Further tragedy was to come, for in 1805 young Nicholas died. By January 1806 the sale of the estate was underway and on 31 March John Wood, the potter of Burslem, Staffordshire paid Catherine £3,100 for Pontypandy. Catherine sold the Ynys Llyn (or Ynis y Lline) in Upper Boat to John Key Esq. on 24 May 1806. Only a year earlier and the Pentyrch Iron Works, once playing such a prominent role in the Price fortune, was adopted by the Quaker firm of Bristol Banks, Harford and Partridge, and linked with the Melin Griffith Works. Clearly the serious depression of trade following the Napoleonic Wars caused a huge decline in the once profitable enterprise.

Financial support for William's schooling may have been sought from his uncle, Thomas of Merriot, allowing the boy an opportunity to spend several years at the Gatward School. Despite a disadvantaged background, the young William Price passed all of the examination honours before him and the level of his intellect was recognised as being far superior to that of his fellow classmates.

His three years of schooling cost £2 8s and at the age of thirteen, claiming he had absorbed all his master could teach him, he left, despite Mr Gatward's offer of £20 a year salary to stay as an assistant.

Instead, for the next six months, the boy idled away his time, tramping the hills and walking ten or twelve miles a day while reciting Welsh poetry aloud. Influenced by the behaviour of his father, he began undressing and exposing his naked body to the sun and wind, resulting in him being admonished and threatened by the God-fearing villagers, but the next day did the same thing. His disgraceful conduct and profitless behaviour caused grievance with his family, who urged him to find a living. William hoped to follow a career in medicine, despite his mother's protestations to join the clergy, while his father, who perhaps had something of a surprising insight into the boy's future inclinations, felt he would make a good solicitor. He was sent to a solicitor's office but William, always the independent boy, decided he would become a doctor.

He remembered,

> I used to walk two miles to ... Mr Gatward's school. Before I had been there two years I had passed through all the cipher-books, every one of them, and had learned to speak and write in English. That was no easy task in those days. My father would not talk a word of English with me ... when I was about thirteen and a half years of age, a Lancaster teacher offered to appoint me as his assistant at a salary of £20 per year, but I would not accept it. I had learned all that he could teach me, and I wanted to pick up something else ... I went home for about six months and my father and mother continually urged me to do something for my living. 'What will you do William?' asked my mother one day. 'A doctor', said I.[12]

He persuaded his family that he could use this classical knowledge best by being articled to an apothecary or surgeon. It could well be argued that the illness being experienced by his own father was enough for William to wish to study medicine in the hope of finding a cure. Within a year the Prices suffered yet another tragedy with the death, at the age of just three years, of William's younger brother, Nicholas. Were any of these occurrences a factor in convincing William to become a man of medicine?

As already explained, many of the Price family members had entered either the clergy or medicine. One of the most successful of the family was Charles Price (1777–1853) the son of the Revd Thomas Price and Mary of Merriott, and a cousin to William. Charles, twenty-three years William's senior, was an extraordinary individual who attended Oxford University and matriculated at the age of sixteen in 1793. He passed his Bachelor of Arts in 1797, followed by a Master of Arts in 1801, a Bachelor of Medicine in 1802 and a Doctor of Medicine in 1804. He was a fellow of Oxford University until 1821, physician to Middlesex Hospital from 1807 to 1815, and in 1832 Charles became Physician Extraordinary to King William IV. There was no better role model within the family than his own cousin, and without further doubt a career in medicine was soon decided upon for William Price.

1814–1822

William Price became an apprentice to a well-established physician in the town of Caerphilly only a matter of days before reaching his fourteenth birthday. Despite the cruel disadvantages that plagued his childhood, including the periods of absolute poverty, the deterioration of his father's mental illness and the loss of a brother, this bright, scholarly and talented young man overcame the odds. All he needed was the guidance of someone whose own superior intellect in the world of medicine and inspirational tutelage would provide him with the introduction to a career in which he could excel and make a difference. This was a career that would possibly allow him to improve lives, or even cure the types of sickness that had robbed him of a father and two siblings. It was also possibly a career that William could embrace for the better of the working man, whom he saw toil and become sick or injured in the embryonic industrialisation of his home county.

There were few physicians in Wales that could surpass the expert teachings of someone as young and experienced as Dr Evan Edwards (1790–1848) who held a practice in Caerphilly. Only ten years older than William, Evan enjoyed a unique family heritage in South Wales. His grandfather was architect William Edwards (1719–89) who died just a year before Evan was born. The youngest son of a farmer at Tŷ Canol Farm in Eglwysilan, William Edwards became an expert at repairing and building dry walls for neighbouring farmers and learned his craft by erecting several houses, forges and mills in the nearby parish. His greatest legacy was the creation of the famous single-arch bridge at Pontypridd. In later years he also built bridges at Aberavon, Llandovery, Morriston, Usk and Glastonbury. William lived for many years at Bryntail Farm above Glyntaff, a residency that would later be occupied by Dr William Price and his own family. After being converted by revivalist Howell Harries in 1739, he became a lay preacher. An ordained Welsh Independent Minister, William gave his salary to the poor.

The single-arch bridge remains probably his most famous legacy of all, giving the area once referred to as Pont-y-ty-prydd its 'new' name – for a century at least – of Newbridge. When local farmers despaired at being unable to cross the River Taff, except when the water level was low enough to use a ford, they commissioned William Edwards to build a bridge for £500. His first bridge was a three-arch structure, built in 1746 and sited slightly downstream from the present bridge. After two and a half years, while William watched anxiously, tree trunks and other debris battered the bridge during a severe flood and it collapsed and washed away. He had pledged to maintain the bridge for seven years, and therefore had to reconstruct it. He conceived the idea of a one-arch bridge, the perfect segment of circle, 35 feet high with a 140-foot chord or span, and a diameter of 175 feet. Wheelwright Thomas Williams built a substantial centring to support the arch while it was under construction. Stone for the bridge was quarried locally, but when the bridge was nearing completion in 1751, it collapsed.

Following his two failed attempts, Edwards was in debt and discouraged, but a subscription of £700 promoted by Lord Talbot and Lord Windsor enabled him to finish the project. Until then he was not totally aware of the laws of equilibrium or balance, and the pressure caused by the 32-foot-long by 20-foot-high abutments, or haunches, of the bridge was so great that, after several years, the crown of the arch was forced upwards and the central section collapsed. Undaunted, he lightened the weight of the haunches by making three cylindrical openings of 3 feet, 6 feet and 9 feet in diameter in each. The danger that the light curve of the bridge would spring upwards again was avoided. The bridge was started in 1755 and completed in 1756, and was for many years one of the longest single-span bridges in the world. A century later a second bridge was built alongside William Edward's masterpiece, and none other than Dr Price himself contributed towards its creation. William Edward's resting place is St Ilan Church, Eglwysilan, where Dr Price witnessed the baptism of two daughters.

Of William Edwards' six children, David, who built bridges in Newport, Bedwas and Llandeilo, was the most accomplished, and he passed on his expertise as a builder to his son William, who superintended many of the locks and bridges of the Kennet and Avon navigation canal from London to Bristol, and tendered for rebuilding Caerleon Bridge in Monmouthshire.

William Edwards' grandson William had at least two brothers, both of whom broke new ground by entering the medical profession. Evan, the elder of them, settled down for life as a family doctor in Caerphilly. His residence was a house on the Twyn, later, if not in his own time, known as *Tŷ'r Meddyg* (Doctor's House). He had an expensive practice in and around the town.[1]

Deservedly proud of his achievements, one entry for his accomplishments is recorded, 'A man of the name of Morgan, many years sexton at Rudry Church in this county, has lately undergone an operation for cancer. The whole of his lower lip was removed, down to the chin, and the muscles and skin from the chin were brought up and which have beautifully formed a new lip. This operation was performed by Mr E. Edwards, surgeon of Caerphilly. The patient is doing well. The same gentleman performed a similar operation upon a female, residing near Caerphilly in which he was equally successful.'[2] Evan was also said to have undertaken an unprecedented operation on a worker who suffered a spinal injury and was able to see him walk once more. In a letter to the senior surgeon of the Royal Berkshire Hospital, George May Edwards explained that a twenty-three-year-old collier suffered an accident when the roof of the mine collapsed, and fractured several vertebrae and drove in the arch so deeply that he was paralysed. Edwards visited him twelve weeks following the accident and operated, removing some of the damaged bone elevating the pressure on the spine, relieving the injury on the spinal chord and allowing the man to walk again.

Evan's younger brother, Daniel, also studied to become a surgeon and passed his Licentiate of the Society of Apothecaries in 1820. Daniel was a room-mate to William Price during his period of medical study in London.

After a life of work among his patients, Dr Evan Edwards passed away on 21 August 1848 at the comparatively early age of just fifty-eight. He married Caroline (born 1791), in Whitchurch Parish Church in 1818, and they had three sons and two daughters. The eldest, Caroline, died in infancy and was buried at St Martin's Church in Caerphilly. The youngest daughter, also named Caroline, was born 19 November 1831 and married Samuel Batchelor (1829–1903), the son of Benjamin Batchelor, a Newport timber merchant and younger brother of the well-known Cardiff shipbuilder and Liberal politician John Batchelor (1820–83), whose statue graces Cardiff. Sadly Caroline died childless, aged forty-eight, in April 1858. Of the three sons, the eldest was Evan (1819–79), who doesn't seem to have followed any particular profession. The other two sons however, William Thomas and Daniel Thomas, both followed in their father and uncle's footsteps as physicians.

William Thomas made his mark on the Welsh medical scene during the Victorian era. Dr Price attended his birth in 1821, the year in which he completed his studies in London, and one can wonder if Dr Edwards named his son after his promising apprentice – or more likely his famous grandfather! William trained in London but returned to Wales, becoming physician to the Glamorganshire & Monmouthshire Infirmary in 1862, retaining his connection with this hospital and its successor until his retirement. His standing as the leading medical man in South Wales ensured his election to the presidency of the British Medical Association in 1885, during the year of its annual meeting in Cardiff. He was the leading advocate for the establishment of a Medical School in Cardiff and a generous donor of funds for the cause. He served for many years as Vice President of the University College of South Wales and Monmouthshire, and as Vice President of the Cardiff Liberal Association.

The young William Price could not have wished for a better mentor than Dr Evan Edwards. His sheer medical expertise alone made him the ideal candidate to guide the young marvel on his first tentative steps to a career as a surgeon. It allowed William the opportunity to travel throughout the district with Dr Edwards to treat patients and become fully exposed to the ravages of poverty, diseases and also agricultural and industrial accidents.

It was also rather fitting that William resided in the Edwards family home at Twyn, the same area where his ancestor Thomas Price had owned The Boar's Head more than a century earlier. Unfortunately not all of William's family members shared his belief that medical research and a position as a surgeon was within his reach. Several tried to dissuade him, none more so than his uncle, Revd Thomas Price. It is surprising that he of all people tried to persuade William along a career path other than medicine, given the success being enjoyed by his own son, Charles. On the other hand, Thomas saw first-hand the abject poverty that faced his brother's family on a daily basis, and when William was offered a wage as a teacher in the Gatward School, Thomas felt he should remain at home and be of further benefit to his immediate family.

Dr Price remembered in 1888,

> I had been with Evan Edwards about six months when an old uncle of mine, named Thomas Price, an elder brother of my father, came to Caerphilly with the intention of sending me back to school, but I would not go. My uncle was furious at this 'Why, you are but a little more than 14 years old, and Daniel Lancaster offered you £20 a year to commence with, and a yearly advance of £5 a year to commence with, and a yearly advance of £5 a year afterwards until you are 21 years of age! More money than many a curate receives after spending hundreds of pounds on his education. You must go William, and I will get Dr Edwards to liberate you. Why you will be a man at once.' But I would not listen to him. Not I ... my uncle used to be very kind to me, and used to give me half a crown every time he met me, but on this occasion he was so mad with my refusing Daniel Lancaster's office that he did not give me anything, and he left me with his little finger in his eye. 'I will never give you anything,' he said, 'nor will I do anything for you!' But I did not care. I did not want his money, and told him so, too.[3]

Regardless of the acute opposition, William remained determined in his endeavours, but was forced to apply for charitable support to pay towards the five-year apprenticeship, which amounted to £35 and signed a legally binding contract on 21 February 1814. It also states that if he successfully completed his apprenticeship he could apply for £20 towards setting up his own medical practice. The contract read,

> This Indenture witneseth that William Price in his fifteenth year, son of the Reverend William Price of Ruddry in the County of Glamorgan doth put himself Apprentice to Evan Edwards of Caerphilly in the County of Glamorgan, Surgeon, to learn his art and with him after the manner of an Apprentice to serve from the date hereof unto the full end and term of five years from thence next ensuing, and fully to be compleat and ended,

during which term the said apprentice his master faithfully shall or will service his secrets keep, his lawful commands every where gladly do; he shall do no damage to his said Master nor see it to be done of others, but to his power shall let or forthwith give notice to his said Master of the same; the goods of his said Master he shall not waste, nor the same without Licence of him to any give or led; Hurt to his said Master he shall not do, cause or procure to be done, he shall neither buy or sell without his Master Licence; Taverns, Inns or Alehouses he shall not haunt. At Cards, Dice, Tables or any other unlawful Game he shall not play, nor from the Service of his said Master Day or Night shall avail himself, but in all Things as an honest and faithful Apprentice shall and will demean and behave himself towards his said Master and his during all the said Term; And the said Evan Edwards in consideration of the sum of thirty five pounds of lawful money of Great Britain being Charity Money of the Governor of the Corporation of the Sons of the Clerk, the said Apprentice in the Art of a Surgeon which he now uses shall teach and instruct, or cause to be taught and instructed in the best Way and Manner that he can. And for the Performance of all and every the Covenants and Agreements aforesaid, either of the said Parties bindeth himself firmly to these Resents. In witness whereof of the Parties abovesaid to these Indenture interchangeably have set their Hands and Seal, the 21st Day of February in the fifty fourth year of the Reign of Our Sovereign Lord George The Third by the Grace of God of the United Kingdom of Great Britain and Ireland, King Defender of the Faith And in the Year of our Lord 1814.

The contract was signed by William Price and Evan Edwards with Joseph Jones as a witness.

One organisation that financially supported him was the Corporation of the Sons of the Clergy, founded in 1655 by a group of merchants in the City of London and clergymen. During Cromwell's Commonwealth, persecution of the clergy who had remained loyal to the Crown was widespread, and many had been deprived of their livings and were destitute. The charity's foundation dates from a recognition by a body of sons of clergymen that action was required to meet a pressing need among clergy families for charitable help. It was awarded a Royal Charter when Charles II came to the throne and so the 'Charity for Releefe of the poore Widdowes and Children of Clergymen' enjoyed the royal seal of approval, with Sir Christopher Wren as the first vice president.

Given William's father's profession and on recognising him as 'lunatic', the corporation were able to award the young man a certain amount for his tuition. On 18 February 1815, they saw fit to pay Dr Evan Edwards the apprenticeship fee of £35, less 6s, this being the expense of the indenture.

The document read,

The Corporation of the Sons of the Clergy have been pleased to order an apprentice fee of £35 to be allowed for binding William Price to you for five years. You, therewith, receive the Indentures as prepared accordingly; the Part having the Receipt endorsed must be executed by you in the Presence of a witness of Credit, and the Receipt also signed by you in the Presence of the same Witness, and returned to me to remain in the Office of the Corporation. After which the Money will be paid to your Order, by your Bill duly stamped drawn on me, payable at Ten Days hence and not otherwise. I am, Sir, Your very humble servant, The Registrar, Corporation House, Bloomsbury Place, London. This being Charity Money, it is not liable to the Duty on Apprentice; but the Expense of the Indenture being 6s, the Bill must be for £34.14.0.

William was still in a state of poverty in May 1815 and at the age of fifteen, he wrote a charming letter to his friend, a school keeper called Evans at Ebbw Vale, telling him the situation was extreme and 'so much in his shallow pocket as will pay the postage of a letter!' The letter, which in itself detects the fiery and forthright character we come to know in Dr Price, read,

My Dear Evans, the person to whom you entrusted your letter brought it safely to me. If you really imagine me capable of forgetting him who calls me his friend, it follows that you think very hardly – indeed, a great deal too hardly of me. You may rest assured that so long as continues your merit – that merit which first occasioned our friendship, so long shall continue our union in that sacred bond, but if my merit claims it no more, let your regard for me instantly expire. I heartily wish you the best success in school keeping at Ebbw Vale, and I earnestly hope the two years you spent in London, may turn out greatly to your benefit, if you ever come to Caerphilly, your expectations will not be disappointed, for you shall receive all the welcome, which It shall be in my power to afford you. True, my power is limited – my poverty is extreme, but when you call on my here, you will no doubt be content with what your friend is compelled to be contented. If I happen to come to your residence, I shall, of course, expect you to keep and make good your words.

The liberty of which you seem to be possessed, raises too high your expectations of having a long letter from me, who had but little liberty, for, you must know, my time is not my own, but another's. I am apprenticed for five years to Dr Evan Edwards, a surgeon, at this place. My daily occupation is to look into a pharmacopoeia, to mix medicines and to study the Latin dictionary. My leisure moments must be devoted mostly to an English dictionary, and English Grammar, the remaining portion of my leisure is allotted to trifle and now to reply to an old friends letter – I like my situation very much, and, as I try with all my might to learn my business, and to please my master, it is to be hoped that success will ultimately crown my endeavours.

It is true, Mr Gatward, your old master and friend, resides now in Reading, in which town, as my brother informs me, is the principal school on the Lancastrian plan.

Your writing, though not to your liking, is easily excused by me; but the stile of your letter would not be quite so personable, if you composed it at leisure and not, as you say, in a hurry. Your good sense will not suffer you to be offended at this freedom and those admonitions of friend, who, as he assumes that sacred name, will not, on any consideration, flatter you – let us be carefully about our writing – and very carefully about the style, the matter and the manner of our composition.

You have full and free leave to write to me whenever you please, on condition, however that you do not send your letters by post, lest it happens your now penniless friend should not have as much in his shallow pocket, as will pay the postage of a letter.

During his five years with Dr Edwards, William's eyes were opened to all manner of disease and sickness that riddled much of Wales during the early nineteenth century. In the pre-industrial areas surrounding parts of Caerphilly, housing and diet were both incredibly poor. Cottages were often squalid, where inhabitants lived in close proximity to animals, which meant contact with flies, dung and clay floors covered in straw which trapped filth and urine. People did not routinely wash themselves and infestations of lice and skin conditions were common. Things were little better in towns like Caerphilly, where the poor lived in small alleys and courtyards, overlooked by the richer members of the community. Visitors from some rural areas who came to larger towns risked infection, as they encountered diseases for which they were not immune. With the onslaught of industrialisation, more towns welcomed migrant workers from all parts of Wales and beyond. As the need to accommodate the growing population saw the rapid building of houses with few rooms and living spaces, large numbers lived together in disgusting conditions.

The invention of the steam engine meant factories, ironworks and collieries erupted in all manner of areas. In South Wales, the ironworks of the region steadily grew prior to the first penetration of rich coal seams and so too did the risk of smallpox, cholera and typhus. Cholera was usually caused through contaminated water and would cause diarrhoea, vomiting and severe cramps which could kill in hours. Typhoid and typhus often hit the poor the worst and swept through workhouses with alarming ferocity. Death rates were high, diseases were endemic and the overcrowding combined with poor sanitation left the poor vulnerable.

Medical practices at the start of the nineteenth century were a peculiar combination of chance and quackery. They were often barbaric, employing methods that had been used for centuries and yielded few results and often killed the patient with an affliction different to the original ailment. Leeching, blood letting, purgation and cold water dousing were just some of the treatments being used by physicians, surgeons and apothecaries. When new methods were being introduced, many of them feared losing their reputation if they didn't work, and continued with long-held beliefs and superstitions rather than embracing new practices. Medicines were overwhelmingly botanical, with preparations of mercury, arsenic, iron and phosphorous very popular. Some physicians recommended a 'change of air', alongside laxatives or leeches. Even the power of prayer was regularly used.

Some of these medical men practised with university degrees, various forms of medical licences, sometimes a combination of these, and sometimes with none at all.[4]

Early nineteenth-century medical training was diverse. Some were apprenticed to apothecaries and only capped bottles and rolled pills, yet others held degrees from medical colleges. Others, who were often condemned by William Price himself, were just 'poison peddlers' who practised freely without any legal sanctions. He later declared that doctors should pay the expenses of people they allowed to fall ill. 'We are suffering under the curse of mistakes of our profession,' he said.

> We have been educating the public into the false belief that poisonous drugs can give health. This belief has become such a deep rooted superstition that those of us who know better and who would like to adopt more rational methods, can only do so at the risk of losing our practice and reputation. The average doctor is at his best but a devoted bigot to this damnable teaching which we call the medical art, and which alone in this age of science, has made no perceptible progress since the days of the earliest teachers, some call it recognised science, but I call it recognised ignorance![3]

In Great Britain there were three divisions of medical groups, the Royal College of Surgeons, Royal College of Physicians and the Society of Apothecaries, all of whom had differing duties, legal privileges and ranking in the medical community. The physicians were university-educated and considered the most knowledgeable about medicine, but could not act as surgeons or dispense medication like an apothecary. Instead they could examine, diagnose and prescribe various medicines. The apothecaries were responsible for the sale, compounding and supply of medicines. In 1815, while William was in his first year of apprenticeship, the Apothecaries Act was passed, allowing them to provide medical advice and prescribe medication themselves. They were apprenticed for a minimum of five years with an age requirement of twenty-one.

It was the third order that attracted William Price. On the advice of his mentor, Dr Edwards, he had aspirations of becoming a surgeon. Their role was to perform operations, set broken bones and treat victims of accidents and disorders. Considered a skilled craftsman, surgeons 'demanded speed, dexterity, and physical strength as well as expertise'. William Price felt he had all the abilities, talents and knowledge required for such a position. Surgeons were apprenticed, as William had been, and by the time he joined Dr Edwards, there were around 8,000 members of the Royal College of Surgeons.

Usually, during Price's time, surgeons were the sons of other apothecaries or surgeons, clergymen and lawyers. Generally they were the sons of men who could afford their education, unlike William Price. It must have seemed to William that his chances of becoming a Licentiate of the Society of Apothecaries, let alone a Member of the Royal College of Surgeons, were remote.

In 1820 the five-year apprenticeship with Dr Edwards was over and Price had to produce further certificates of attendance in medical practice at a hospital or dispensary and sit examinations in Latin, pharmaceutical chemistry, *materia medica* (or pharmacy) and the theory and practice of medicine. Undeterred by poverty, he travelled to London, and it was arranged he should share the lodgings with Daniel Edwards, Evan's brother, who lived in Great Trinity Lane, which was dominated by a large Lutheran church and only a short walk from Mansion House and St Paul's Cathedral. William probably earned his keep by helping Daniel with his studies in Latin, as he had yet to succeed in becoming a Licentiate of the Society of Apothecaries by the time of Price's arrival in 1820, but qualified later in the year. Daniel had already passed examinations in anatomy and surgery that were required for membership in the Royal College of Surgeons, but the Hall of Apothecaries still eluded him.

In 1888 Dr Price remembered,

It was in 1820 I first went to London. I stayed there with Daniel Edwards. He was an excellent fellow, a very humane man, but he was not 'flush' any more than myself. We had to help each other as much as possible. He had passed the Royal College of Surgeons, but had not passed through the hall, for he had no knowledge of Latin. We studied hard together. However, I passed through the hall before he was half through his Latin. In fact, I passed the college and the hall in 12 months after I went to London – a thing never done by anyone before me.[3]

The Corporation of the Sons of the Clergy came to his aid again with the further provision of £20, but this was scarcely enough for his needs. Price was a brilliant student. He entered the London Hospital, Whitechapel on 30 October 1820 for twelve months under the instruction of Sir William Blizard, and registered at St Bartholomew's under the instruction of John Abernethy.

London was the largest city in the world, with one million inhabitants when William Price made his entry to the Voluntary Hospital at Whitechapel. This was the London of the mid-Regency period, known for its elegance and achievements in the fine arts and architecture under the patronage of the Prince Regent (later George IV). It also encompassed a time of major political, social and even economic change, but the Regency period was known for its great refinement, cultural success and the shaping and altering of the social structure of Britain as a whole. The Prince Regent ordered the building of the exotic Brighton Pavilion and ornate Carlton House as well as many other public works, although his exuberance outstripped his purse. However, despite the lavish parties, beauty and fashion of the time, there was the thievery, gambling, prostitution and squalor beneath the glamour that the Regency society provided. It was this aspect of London life that William Price encountered as he entered the nation's capital in the year in which Piccadilly Circus was constructed and only a few months before the death of the 'mad' King George III.

Today, Whitechapel has all manner of connotations, maybe as the home of Joseph Merrick, the Elephant Man, in the latter decades of the nineteenth century, or the vicinity of the East End that suffered a succession of gruesome murders at the hands of the infamous Jack the Ripper. The Whitechapel of 1820 was a filthy, degenerate, disease-ridden district of immigrants, paupers and thieves. It 'had become, as the result of the expansion of London's docks and England's sea-borne trade, the most commercially important district in the whole of the metropolis and a hotbed of vice and villages. Whitechapel High Street was not particularly horrendous, although the small dark streets branching from it contained the greatest suffering and danger. The iron hand of the Industrial Revolution too, had tightened its grip on it. Heavy industry and the mass production of cheap clothing were increasing; the density of its population had mounted as the birth rate rose, cheap labour poured in from Ireland',[5] and further waves of immigrants escaping political or religious persecution – usually poor and often sick – arrived from the Continent. Refugees were fleeing from wars in Europe and Jewish and Irish immigrants settled in Whitechapel and Bethnal Green.

In Whitechapel there was no town planning. Tenements had sprung up everywhere to house workers, but many of the inhabitants still had no fixed abode and almost every street had its quota of common lodging houses of varying degrees of iniquity and filth. Four out of five families lived in a single room; this served as their sleeping accommodation, kitchen and washhouse, and frequently their workroom, too. The graveyards among the houses were fast becoming as crowded as the tenements and there was still no sanitary authority; open sewers ran down the streets. Wages were low and Corn Laws kept up the price of bread. Abject poverty was rife, people lived on the verge of starvation.

Poverty, squalor and unsanitary conditions bred disease on a large scale. Deficiency disease was common; tuberculosis rife; accidents frequent. Typhoid was endemic due to contaminated water; typhus, on account of human infestation by lice. Cholera swept the Continent.[6]

While London was flourishing, with masters of wealth and power, the social contrast couldn't have been more divided in the East End. Public executions at Tyburn and tours of the madhouse, Bedlam, were considered attractions of the expanding capital. A growing social consciousness in the middle classes in philanthropic causes saw a number of voluntary hospitals founded. Such a hospital was desperately needed in the East End, where the greatest population boom was being experienced and the largest deterioration in health. The London Hospital in Whitechapel was founded on 23 September 1740 to 'relieve the sick and ailing poor', led by surgeon John Harrison. They met at the Feather's Tavern in Cheapside to resolve to open a hospital in Featherstone Street that could accommodate thirty patients at the rent of £15 per annum. Shortly the building was considered inadequate, and with further subscription, a 'London Infirmary' opened on Prescott Street in May 1741 and additional houses were acquired within the vicinity, and the 'London Hospital' was formed.

By the time William Price ventured to Whitechapel, a permanent, grand hospital building had opened on White Chapel Mount and Mount Field in 1752. Although resources were limited, patients were offered the best accommodation that could be afforded – iron bedsteads replaced wooden ones as early as 1772 and feather beds were purchased in 1820 for particular cases.[7] The purpose-built hospital on Whitechapel Road could accommodate 161 patients and treat outpatients. Even then, public subscriptions and charitable events were commonplace to support the hospital, for they had not enjoyed the sort of patronage or large donations afforded by the likes of Thomas Guy, who amassed a fortune out of South Sea stock and printing Bibles to open his hospital in the metropolis. In Whitechapel they relied on generous donors and benefactors such as local traders, merchants, even the patients themselves.

It comes as little surprise why William Price supported an embryonic social healthcare system on his return to Wales, witnessing first-hand the sicknesses that befell the poorest members of London society. In Price's time at Whitechapel, the treatment by physicians for diseases or 'distempers' consisted mainly of blood letting, cupping and prescribing 'elixirs, decoctions, pills and potions'. Malt spirit was used before anaesthetic and compound fractures usually resulted in amputation or often death. No antiseptic practises were used. Artificial limbs were fitted, of wood and iron. Children under seven were not admitted unless they had fractures or required amputations. Pregnant women were also turned away. Above all, the London Hospital patients relied on sanctuary, and there were few cures for disease as surgery was primitive until the introduction of anaesthesia. Patients with a fever or contagious diseases, or 'dying condition', were sent to the workhouse under the Poor Law Board to avoid over-crowding and the spread of sickness in the wards.

The state of the wards was by no means clean and in good order and one gets the opinion that standards were declining during Price's time there. 'No towels or soap in the women's Wards' reported one, or 'the dust in George ward will soon be a great nuisance if not taken away'. On one occasion, 'the sink in the bleeding room was stopped up', on another, 'all the sinks terribly out of order and no notice taken of it'. The decent disposal of the dead was a perennial problem.[6] One surgeon begged for a screen to be placed around the corpses in the lobbies as they had 'an indelicate and rather shocking appearance.' It was also noted that the burial grounds to the rear of the hospital were in a dreadful condition and 'offensive to the feelings of humanity'.

By the early nineteenth century, the atmosphere of the wards was appalling. One visitor reported that

> the west end of the Hospital was very offensive, so much so that I
> could not bear it. Even outside the hospital the stench was equally as
> vile as a plant had been created for the production of ammonia by the
> distillation of bones, but it was erected amidst vast assemblage of stinks;
> on a dunghill, adjacent to a vitriol manufactory, a bone house and a stall
> of human manure and to complete the filthy description, contiguous to a
> ditch full of common soil.[6]

Another record reports on the state of the patients themselves, some arriving in such a filthy condition that their own 'cloathes burnt on account of vermin'. Another read that 'patients not be allowed to go to the wards until examined as to vermin, filth etc., that those infested be stripped in the lobbies and their cloathes be either immersed or fumigated'. Such conditions were witnessed by William Price on his arrival.

One of the men who signed William Price's medical certificates was William Blizard, who was largely instrumental in founding the Royal College of Surgeons and who formed the first completed medical school in England with systematic formal education at Whitechapel in 1785. Blizard, an eminent surgeon, philanthropist and reformer, was elected to the staff at the London Hospital in 1780 and persuaded the House Committee to allow him rather grudgingly to present two courses of lectures on Anatomy and Surgery; but he had to bring his own patients, as pupils were not allowed into the wards. Until then, Blizard held lectures of medicine in his own home. There were other surgeons similar to him who also advertised their lectures and had been seen at 'The London' smuggling out dead bodies for dissection. One of those early students to

Blizard's new medical school was John Abernethy, who founded the St Bartholomew's Hospital Medical School, and was another figure who played a significant role in the education of William Price.

Blizard's own uncompromising stance was 'let your search be after truth, should you perceive truths to be important, make them the motives of action, let them serve as springs to your conduct. Many persons acknowledge truth with apathy, they assent to it, but it produced no other effect on their minds.'[8]

Someone else who influenced William was fellow Welshman Thomas Davies of Carmarthen, a pupil of the inventor of the stethoscope, Rene Theophile Laennec (1781–1826) at Necker Hospital in Paris. On his return to London in 1820, Davies was the first to lecture on auscultation and the use of the stethoscope at his house in New Broad Street, a short walk from William and Daniel's lodgings.

In his endeavours to establish a medical school, William Blizzard circulated a pamphlet entitled 'one the Expediency and Utility of teaching the several branches of Physic and Surgery at the London Hospital and for creating theatres for the Purpose'. He raised the sufficient funds to erect a building, costing £600, next to the hospital in 1783, with a lecture theatre and the facilities to teach a wide range of medical subjects that no other private medical college could offer at that time. The House Committee were hardly convinced and were half-hearted in their support of the proposal, but did allow some land to build the school. However, on no account was expenditure on the teaching of students to be mixed up with money for patient's treatment. As long as the school could stand alone without interfering with the hospital, then they would allow it to take place. Blizard issued his own appeal for funds with 'An Address to the Friends of the London Hospital and of Medical Learning'. He argued that clinical experience was essential training of a doctor but not enough – knowledge of the principles was also demanded. He felt this could only be properly taught with lectures at a hospital, so practical and theoretical teaching was integrated. To gain a complete education in medicine, which clearly was desperately needed, students had to attend a medical school and become a dresser and then a 'walking pupil' at one of the hospitals. The students were divided into surgical dressers and medical clerks. Each surgeon was allowed six dressers while physicians had unspecified amounts of medical clerks.

Although pompous and often a non-inspirational lecturer, Blizard had however succeeded in creating a medical school for the capital city and it was here that Price saw first-hand how he could make a difference to the lives of others who were sick – and for that matter, poor. In 1791 Blizard expressed his own 'concern at seeing patients he had discharged as "cured" being readmitted within weeks because of poverty, and lack of care that led to the foundation of the Samaritan Society. He led the way to assist patients with special needs for surgical appliances, or convalescence and financed much of the work.'[7] Such abhorrence had to be solved. Price felt equally as shocked at the state of the poor, and equally passionate to appease their suffering and plight when he established his own successful practice in Wales.

William attended as a surgical dresser for a year at 'The London' when body snatchers plied their grisly trade to keep up the supply of anatomical dissections. Without doubt, the Welshman was probably more than familiar with the 'Resurrectionists' who supplied corpses to his celebrated teacher of anatomy, Dr Edward Grainger. It would not be unthinkable that Price, himself suffering from lack of financial resources and in need of extra pennies, may well have been involved in the practice which saw bodies stolen from the Hospital Dead House or even the Burial Ground after dark.

When a patient died his body was carried into the lobby of the hospital and then over to the dead-house while the steward notified the next of kin, in the hope they would come and take it away, as each burial cost the charity 13s. When no reply was received, the clothing and personal effects of the deceased were sold 'to the best Bidder in the Presence of the Governors' and the proceeds put into the poor box.

Bodies were sometimes smuggled out of the hospital, the committee soon discovered, to be sold for dissection to one of the private schools of anatomy. Even the surgeons were not innocent in this matter. 'The Committee being informed that dead Bodys have been carried out of this Hospital contrary to the Rules of the Charity, they proceeded to Inquire into the truth of the said information and having examined John Cushee and John Smith, Two beadles, they acknowledged that on Friday night they did carry out the body of a Woman in a Hamper by order of Mr Grindall, and by him desired to leave it at the House of Mr Dougles, a Surgeon in Cannon Street,' and on being caught 'brought the Body back again, which was next day Burried in White Chapel Burrying Ground at the expense of this Charity. They confessed that they had carried or sent out to the Surgeons within Nine Months past Four Bodys.'[6]

Interestingly enough, less than a year before William Price entered the medical school, the minutes of June 1819 displayed a scandalous episode that was brought before the House Committee, including William Blizard. It appears that on Friday 1 June two house pupils, Mr Parrent and Mr Roberts, who were pupils of surgeon J. G. Andrews, made an application to dissect the bodies of two dead patients. Andrews forbade it but the young men 'got into the dead house without my permission of any one in the presence of no one but themselves, dragged the body to the adjoining room and opened the head thorax and abdomen and cut into the diseased part of which the man died and it was only by accident that the occurrence was discovered'.[9] Both were suspended for a month and forced to apologise to the House Committee and the surgeons.

On entering The London Hospital in 1820, William Price was presented with the institution's Charter, By-Laws and Standing Orders that set out clearly the rules and regulations that each medical pupil must adhere to. The seventeen-point list of regulations explained the two different types of pupils: House-Pupils, who resided in the Hospital in a weekly rotation, and Visiting Pupils. William Price was one of the latter. They were allocated places with an individual surgeon with rights to dress patients, attend operating theatres and keep accurate lists of accident victims. The charter states, 'A Pupil shall not be absent himself from the Hospital for more than seven days, without such absence being noted and the time completed, before a certificate is given.' The final points read, 'At the conclusion of a Pupil's attendance, provided he shall have conformed to the regulations of the Institution, he shall receive a certificate of such attendance, signed by each of the Surgeons, and Chairman of the House-Committee and countersigned by the Secretary.'

At Whitechapel, William Price became more acquainted with Edward Grainger, for whom he became a surgical dresser. Grainger was only three years senior to Price and yet had achieved great notoriety and success. Sadly, he died only a few years later in 1824 at the age of just twenty-seven. Born in Birmingham in 1797, Grainger had been educated in medicine by his father, and had become a student at the united hospitals of St Thomas's and Guy's in 1816. A dresser to surgeon Sir Astley Cooper (1768–1841), his plan to open an anatomical school was rejected by Guy's Hospital, leading him to open his own school at St Saviour's Church, and it proved so successful in rivalling the hospital schools that he built an operating theatre and anatomical school in Webb Street, Southwark in 1821. It remained popular until the Royal College of Surgeons changed their by-laws to eliminate independent schools.

As part of his medical schooling, William Price attended further lectures at St Bartholomew's Hospital, an institution that had been founded as far back as the twelfth century, making it the oldest surviving hospital in the country. Officially the medical school itself was not established there until 1843, but when John Abernethy began holding his own lectures at the start of the century, many considered this the starting point of the organisation that would follow. At 'Barts' there were several hundred surgical students, attracted by the reputation of Abernethy – and none more so than William Price. Fellow medical student George Hurst wrote,

> About the year 1820 I heard with satisfaction the celebrated Abernethy lecture, and his style, manner and simple elocution impressed me greatly. He has been represented as an eccentric, but as a public speaker he was clear, distinct and impressive. By the pupils of the hospital he was esteemed as the highest medical authority of the period, and each

student on leaving the hospital considered himself as only second, having received instruction from that great man's discourses.[10]

Short in stature, at 5 foot 6 inches high, as was Price, Abernethy was meticulous in dress, manner and mind. His dogmatic, illustrative method of teaching endeared him to his pupils. The son of a merchant from Wolverhampton, he became an apprentice to Sir Charles Blicke (1745–1815), a surgeon at St Bartholomew's in 1779. He attended the anatomical lectures of Sir William Blizard at the London Hospital and was employed to assist as a demonstrator. He also attended Percivall Pott's surgical lectures and on Pott's resignation as surgeon of St Batholomew's Blicke succeeded him, allowing Abernethy to be elected Assistant Surgeon in 1787. In this capacity he gave lectures at his home in Bartholomew Close that became so well attended that the governors of the hospital built a theatre in 1791 for him to practise and teach. In 1814 he was appointed Professor of Anatomy and Surgery at the Royal College of Surgeons, and in 1815, after twenty-eight years as assistant surgeon, he became Principal Surgeon to St Bartholomew's Hospital. His *Surgical Observations on the Constitutional Original And Treatment Of Local Diseases*, published in 1809, was one of the earliest popular works of medical science. Attractive, persuasive and charming, he attained an almost celebrity status, not necessarily due to his medical success and skill but also in part to his eccentricity, all the qualities that William Price would inherit in his own capacity as surgeon.

By the time young William met him, Abernethy was at the peak of his career, running an extensive practice and still an exceptionally popular lecturer. His lectures in anatomy, physiology, surgery, and pathology were considered unequalled. They were, in fact, so popular that they were taken down by fast writers and published in *The Lancet* in 1826 and 1827 – whereupon the publisher was sued by Abernethy. Although he was a generous man, he deliberately assumed a brusque manner with his patients, assuming it would inspire their confidence. Abernethy lectured in a small amphitheatre, known for its lack of comfort and the stench of the nearby surgical wards, adding to the sufferings of the patients and students alike.

One student observed, 'The seats were without rails, and therefore each ascending row of students received the knees of those above in their backs, whilst they thrust theirs into those of the sitters below.' Disease could be seen in the wards and methods of post mortems were carried out in public. Often the families wanted to get the body first, while the practitioners wanted to dissect it and it was not uncommon for post-mortems to be carried out while the corpse was still warm, causing the blood to gush in abundance.[10]

Abernethy's eccentricities probably influenced Price greatly, for the tales told of both master and pupil bear strong resemblance. He was also a man who, like Price, issued wonderful snippets of information to patients which are filled with plain common sense. Typical was the remark to the mother of a girl suffering from stomach complaints: 'Why, Madam, do you know there are upward of thirty yards of bowels squeezed underneath that girdle of your daughter's? Go home and cut it; let Nature have fair play, and you will have no need of my advice.'

He illustrated one lecture with the story of a major who suffered from recurrent dislocation of the jaw. One evening away from the regiment, he laughed uproariously and dislocated it again. A local doctor was summoned to reduce the dislocation then began to doubt his own diagnosis. The infuriated and speechless major became so angry that the doctor thought his diagnosis was certainly wrong and that the major was suffering from insanity. He sent for a strait-jacket and imprisoned the major. In a short while the major managed to indicate that he wished to have a pen and as this was taken as a sign of returning sanity, one was fetched whereupon he wrote, 'For God's sake, send for the surgeon of the regiment!' 'I hope,' said Abernethy, 'you will never forget how to reduce a dislocated jaw'.

Abernethy was visited by a patient who complained of suffering from a form of depression. 'You need amusement,' the good doctor declared after a brief examination. 'Go and hear the comedian Grimaldi. He will make you laugh and that will be better for you than any drugs.' The patient's reply? 'I am Grimaldi!'

While studying at the hands of such great practitioners, William Price continued to receive letters from his former master, Dr Edwards, who not only continued to show interest in his young apprentice, but apparently began taking his advice on treatment. One letter, written on 16 March 1821, read,

> I must confess that I have been long about answering your letter, you will I have no doubt given me credit when I say that I should be very sorry was my delay to make you at all uneasy – I am quite proud to find that you go on so well and be assured that your prosperity at all times will materially add to our comforts. The oil you were kind enough to send me has quite astonished me, for which I am very much obliged the Elaterium although I have tried yet not fairly please to let me know the price of the oil as I shall be in want are long. Your mother drank tea with us last evening and desired her kind love to you, the rest of the family I believe are quite well. I have no news to give you. Evan is getting a stout healthy boy and would divert you more than ever were you to see him. Give our united respects to my brother and sister in law and accept the same yourself. Tell Daniel I shall write to him ere long. My brother and yourself will be glad to hear that my father is better than he has been of late. My mother in law has been very ill for this fortnight back, they desire their kind respects to you both.

William studied the midwifery lectures at St Bart's given by Robert Gooch, obstetrician and militant teetotaller, who was vociferous in his criticism of the government for tolerating alcohol abuse. Gooch was dynamic and a 'performer' to his students, whose lectures were famous throughout the metropolis. Such skills as an orator may have had a lasting impression on the young Welshman, whose larger-than-life personality and strong beliefs made him an individual not to be forgotten – or meddled with.

He also studied under Edward Grainger at Whitechapel, when the surgeon was joined by Dr John Armstrong (1784–1829), of Durham, a lecturer in the 'Practice of Physic'. The son of a superintendent at a glass works factory, Armstrong studied medicine at the University of Edinburgh, where he graduated in 1807 and became physician to Sunderland Infirmary. On his arrival in London in 1818 he published *Practical Illustrations of Scarlet Fever, Measles, Pulmonary Consumption and Chronic Diseases, with Remarks on Sulphurous Waters*, which added to his reputation, and in the following year became physician to the London Fever Institution, which he resigned in 1824. A Licentiate of the College of Physicians in 1820, he rapidly acquired a large practice under Grainger. Fellow medics spoke highly of him; to quote one, 'He always spoke from the fulsome of a mind rich in a store of facts which he had collected from his observation of disease. His lectures were attended by many members of the profession, who were powerfully impressed with the originality and boldness of his views.'

Energetic and hugely talented, the rapidity of his success caused his career to be watched with surprise. His works on fevers became extremely popular.

However, in later years William Price went so far as to criticise Armstrong. Although his 1888 newspaper interview can hardly be accepted with confidence, Price claims he felt sufficiently confident to instruct Dr John Armstrong on *materia medica* because the course was deficient. Price claimed Armstrong was obliged to put himself under the young student's tuition for four months before he was competent to teach it! Dr Price explained,

> Dr Armstrong was appointed a lecturer on *materia medica* at the school but he was as ignorant a man as you could meet. He did not know one medicine from another, so he was obliged to put himself under my tuition for four months before he was competent to teach that school, which was attended by more than 400 pupils.
>
> Oh! I taught him a lot of things – physics, drugs, chemistry – and made him a master of his business. But mind you, this was a secret. It would not do to let the people know that this great man was under the tuition of Dr Price! But he was! After that I got a lot of persons to ground – sometimes I had as many as twenty or thirty at a time. I grounded them all. They call it coaching these days.[3]

William Price was at the very heart of the expanding and developing medical world during his time in London, learning at the hands of some of

Britain's foremost medical men. It was a period when strides were being made in medical anatomy and physiology and in pharmacology. Some of the drugs being developed during this period included morphine, quinine, atropine, digitalis, codeine and iodine. There was a notable period of identification, classification and description of various diseases including scarlet fever, diphtheria, syphilis, typhoid and typhus. In 1823, Laennec wrote a treatise that distinguished diseases such as pleurisy, emphysema, bronchitis and pneumonia. English physicians such as Brighton, Addison, Hodgkin and Parkinson supplied classic descriptions for conditions that were named after them. It was an exciting era of developments that would change the entire future of the medical profession.

A certificate dated 28 August 1821 confirms William Price attended the medical practice of the General Dispensary for six months. Signed by Henry Clutterbuck, George Burberick and William Lambert, Physicians to the Dispensary. Another certificate on the following day certifies he had attended courses in the theory and practice of physic, signed by Clutterbuck of the Royal College of Physicians, Senior Physician to the General Dispensary.

On 6 September 1821 William Price was made a Licentiate of the Society of Apothecaries, with a testimonial from Daniel Edwards at the cost of £3 10s. He had attended three lectures and demonstration courses on anatomy and physiology, on the theory and practice of medicine, on chemistry and *materia medica*, and had also spent six months as a probationary practitioner at a general dispensary.

A certificate dated 25 September 1821 certifies that Price had attended as a dressing pupil at The London Hospital. This certificate shows a picture of the London Hospital from a 1740 engraving, with the text below reading 'Inasmuch as ye have done it unto the least of one of my brethren ye have done it unto me' (Matthew 25:40).

The London Hospital charitably relieving sick and wounded manufacturers and seamen in merchant service their wives and children. These are to certify that William Price hath diligently attended the practice of surgery as a dressing pupil in this hospital for 12 months. Witness our hand this day September in the year of our Lord 1821 signed William Blizard.

On 19 October 1821, at the age of just twenty-one he was made a Member of the Royal College of Surgeons, in a certificate signed by Sir William Blizard, John Abernethy and others. The entry in the Extraordinary Court of Examiners of that date lists him as the third member out of thirteen to become a fully made Member of the College, at the sum of £22 each.

He was of a very young age to reach such a level of success, but was not the youngest to pass through the college as he maintained in later life. Despite his attainment, he continued to study, and that winter attended a further three courses on lectures in anatomy and physiology, under his old teacher, Edward Grainger. He also dissected during the same period.

At this time Price worked for a notable Scottish entrepreneur named John Forbes, possibly the same Forbes who was a merchant in Bombay. There are references made to a Forbes (1743–1821), better known as Bombay Jock, who founded the family fortune that led to the erection of Castle Newe in Aberdeenshire. It seems perfectly possible, since the Forbes referred to in Dr Price's life was a man who had been in India and ruined his constitution in a warm climate. He called on Price to care for him, and allegedly pleaded with the doctor to stay with him until he died. For the last ten months of his life, Dr William Price nursed the patient at his London home.

Dr Price, a brilliant young scholar, someone who greatly impressed all who came into contact with him, admired by his peers and loved by the women he so often charmed, became a handsome young man about town, with a sufficiently becoming presence to warrant the painting of his portrait by his friend and fellow student, Alexander Steward. In it he appeared as a young man of proud bearing and penetrating eyes, his thick black wavy hair framing a high forehead and his features softened by a kindly mouth. It is faintly inscribed on the back,

> This portrait of Mr William Price, Member of the Royal College of Surgeons in London by his friend and fellow student Alexander Steward in grateful thanks for various kindnesses given to him was presented to his three sisters Elizabeth, Mary and Ann Price July 11, 1822 as a memento which is ever to remind them of the first wish of his heart, namely, that they should always devote the greater part of their leisure to the cultivation of their minds and which they are to retain but on condition of complying with the wish and that of strictly attending to the wishes and suggestions for their improvement of their elder brother Charles Price.[11]

Dr Price felt that London had no more to offer him and considered travelling to India, as the late Forbes had advised, to begin his own practice as a surgeon. It was his well-respected cousin, Dr Charles Price, who gave him some sound advice. As much as £500 was needed to secure a position as an assistant to a leading surgeon in London. The physicians were a very select body whose circle Price had not penetrated; it was exceptional for anyone to gain election to their fellowship unless they were a graduate of Oxford or Cambridge. The snobbery in the higher ranks of the medical world left a bitter taste in the young doctor's mouth. However, his new qualifications fitted him well for general practice in Wales. His love of Wales, its culture, language, history and above all the needs of his people were the greatest influence on Price's decision making. It was time to return home.

1823–1834

The Wales that Dr William Price returned to was still being vastly transformed. Coalmining, iron, steel and tinplate industries formed the basis of the largest development in the history of Glamorgan. At the time of his return from London, it was iron that was recognised as the greatest of these industries in the area. The northern rim contained the major ironworks of Dowlais, Cyfarthfa, Penydarren and Plymouth. In neighbouring counties there was the growth of other works such as Ebbw Vale and Blaenavon in Monmouthshire and the Rhymney works. From the late eighteenth century onwards iron predominated, and with the establishment of major works came the creation of a new gentrified society led by the large dynasties of the Crawshays, Guests and Hills.

During the eighteenth century the Sussex ironmasters began developing the industry in the Forest of Dean and South Wales areas due to increasing fuel costs. It was there that they found essential materials, from timber to iron ore and limestone, with an abundance of free-running water for power. By 1750 there were seven furnaces operating in South Wales. Between 1759 and 1765 iron furnaces and forges were being erected in the area of Merthyr Tydfil, which eventually led to the transformation of Glamorgan as pioneers realised the wealth of the region's resources, with the greater demand for armaments during a period when Britain fought wars abroad. There was a widespread use of new technology that added to the growth of the industries, particularly the use of steam-power, which increased production and more efficient methods of hauling, and in the techniques of blast employed by smelting. Also the gradual use of coal to smelt pig-iron helped the industry expand.

In Dowlais a group of nine partners subscribed £4,000 each to open the 'Merthir Furnace'. One of those was an ancestor of Dr William Price. The entrepreneur of the ancestral line of the Prices of Watford, Thomas Price, bought leases of minerals under land in Bedwellty, Monmouthshire and Gelligaer. He was joined by Thomas Lewis of Llanishen, who owned Pentyrch Ironworks, and had a lease of a moiety of coal and ironstone in Dowlais. Another was Isaac Wilkinson of Denbighshire who had the patented machine for blowing furnaces and forges. Other financiers included Richard Jenkins, a merchant of Cardiff, Thomas Harris, a merchant of Bristol, and John Jones, also of Bristol. With financial support and a growing workforce, the first large-scale ironworks in Dowlais was formed on 19 September 1759 with the purpose of 'business of an iron master and iron manufacturer and for that purpose to build a certain ffurnace or ffurnaces for smelting or iron ore or mine or stone into pig iron in the parish of Merthyr Tidvil for a term of 99 years, and that with the joint stock of £4,000 which the said partners have agreed to bring in, advance and deliver in and before the first day of January AD 1760'.[1]

The Merthyr entrepreneurs were assisted by leases from local landlords at a ridiculously cheap rate, as no one realised the major industrialisation that would develop in this isolated region. In 1748 Viscount Windsor, who inherited the Welsh estates from the Earl of Pembroke, granted a ninety-nine-year lease at £26 a year. A decade later and the Plymouth Ironworks, located on the Dowlais brook, was under the direction of John Joshua Guest together with Isaac Wilkinson, and by the end of the century it was producing 5,000 tons of iron a year.

In 1765 a third works, Cyfarthfa, was started by Anthony Bacon and William Brownrigg of Cumberland, who also received favourable terms from the landlords of the area.

Penydarren was the site of a fourth ironworks, established by Francis Homfray and his sons Jeremiah, Samuel and Thomas of Shropshire in 1784.

The small group of English immigrants, supported by the capital of London and Bristol merchants, had a profound effect on the industrial growth of South Wales. The concentration of these new large enterprises, which saw the importance of wars as the stimulus of its early growth – particularly the Seven Years' War of 1756, followed by the American War of Independence in 1775 and the Napoleonic Wars – required new demands for iron, copper, lead, tinplate and coal to keep the British naval fleet afloat and ensure huge quantities of munitions. By making cannon and other armoury, ironworks – particularly Cyfarthfa – flourished.

It was through the contract for cannon that Richard Crawshay (1739–1810) of Yorkshire first became associated with the Glamorgan enterprise. The 'imperious' and often tyrannical Richard, born in Normanton, near Leeds and christened 'Richard Crayshaw' quarrelled with his father, William, a Yorkshire farmer, and left home at the age of sixteen. After travelling twenty days, he reached London without a penny. He sold his pony for £15 and worked in an iron-warehouse, where he won his master's confidence and his daughter Mary Bowne's (1745–1811) hand in marriage, eventually becoming the sole proprietor of the business. Over the next twenty years he created one of the largest iron merchant houses in the city, trading mainly in Swedish and Russian iron. He began working with Anthony Bacon, the owner of the Cyfarthfa Ironworks, and became his agent for supplying iron cannon to the Board of Ordnance. Realising the ironmaster's ongoing success he journeyed to South Wales to become a partner to Bacon, and after the latter's death in 1786 secured the lease of the works with James Cockshutt and William Steven, becoming sole proprietor in 1794. Creating a family crest that included a pile of cannonballs, the Cyfarthfa works became so critical to the success of the war effort that during his time as ironmaster he welcomed Admiral Nelson to the ironworks to announce his gratitude. Richard Crawshay was responsible for making Cyfarthfa's Ironworks 'by far the largest in this kingdom, probably, indeed, the largest in Europe; and in that case, as far as we know, the World'.[2]

There were smaller furnaces throughout Glamorgan that assisted the local economy and workforce, including Pentyrch. By the time Merthyr became the iron capital, Pentyrch was in the hands of William Lewis, one of the original partners at Dowlais, and much of the output was sold to the Melingriffith tinplate works in Whitchurch. In 1828 an ironworks was even established in Rudry, where the Price family had also enjoyed considerable success with their furnace during William's grandfather's era.

By the 1780s the Guests and the Crawshays were the most powerful industrial families in the country, and both families later befriended Dr Price.

What the iron industry – and much later the coal industry – did for Wales was create a huge shift of population, an introduction of waves of immigration and the development of large urban areas. It is estimated the population of Wales grew from 489,000 in 1750 to 530,000 in 1780 and by the time of the first census in 1801, this had reached 587,000 with the largest rises in the areas of large economic activity. Glamorgan saw rapid expansion due to the increase of birth rates and widespread migration as people were attracted to the new industrial communities.

These dense population growths came at a huge cost to public health, a facet of nineteenth-century Wales that faced Dr Price during his career as a surgeon. From district to district the high infant death rate fluctuated, but undoubtedly it was the industrial towns such as Merthyr Tydfil that illustrated the worst figures of all. At first the workforce at the ironworks was from the locality, including the parishes close to Brecon, but with the growth of the 'works' people came from further afield. Industrial districts were largely poor, with inadequate housing and overcrowding as people lived in dwellings of 'extreme wretchedness'. The quality of food was low and generally families lived in inferior homes with little furniture, food and there were regular episodes of poor health. The houses generally were mud-covered stone, bare ground and small windows, while their diet consisted mainly of bread made of wheaten flour and oatmeal. They ate few vegetables or meat, making labourers in Glamorgan experience the worst standard of living in the entire country.

If Glamorgan was a county of poor standards, then Merthyr Tydfil, the great frontier town, was its stench-ridden capital. There were no hospitals or clinics, no public sewers nor drains. Refuse was thrown on the street or along side the River Taff. With no Board of Health and the ironmasters denying responsibility, Merthyr was diabolical. The sanitary destitution was not helped by the fact that in the whole town there existed only three water pumps and one shallow draw-well. Disease was rife and Merthyr experienced some of the worst cholera epidemics during the Victorian era. Socially, the working classes were also becoming recognised for their dependency on alcohol as drunkenness grew to make Glamorgan one of the worst areas in Great Britain. Work was heavy, monotonous and dangerous and labourers spent those hard-earned wages on their only form of escapism from the harsh reality of their lives – the 'evil' drink.

Merthyr Tydfil was not the only town to grow and develop due to its industrial enterprises. Many of the ironmasters had interests in other forges, furnaces and tinplate works where gradually a further population shift occurred. Such an enterprise was founded under the Crawshay reign in the small hamlet of Treforest, perfectly located owing to its close proximity to the Glamorganshire Canal and, as with so many other areas near this main artery of transport, the area flourished.

In the mid-1760s Anthony Bacon's iron bars were carried to the coast on pack horses and mules, and in 1767 he built a road from Cardiff to Merthyr, but the cost of transporting the goods on carts was becoming hugely difficult to maintain. By the end of the century canals were being built, but not without massive costs and a whole host of difficulties to overcome. The very positioning of the ironworks and coalfields in Glamorgan necessitated a canal of fifty-two locks between Merthyr and Cardiff alone – in fact it dropped 160 feet in a mile from Quakers Yard to Abercynon. A barge could carry 24 tons and was worked by a horse, one man and a boy. The same amount by road took twelve wagons, forty-eight horses, twelve men and twelve boys.

Richard Crawshay engaged the canal engineer Thomas Dadford to survey the route for a canal to Cardiff, and, with the support of Lord Cardiff, the bill to authorise the canal was passed through Parliament without amendment on 9 June 1790. The Company of Proprietors of the Glamorganshire Canal Navigation was authorised to raise £60,000 in capital, with a further £30,000 if required.

In August 1790 Thomas Dadford, his son Thomas Dadford Jr and Thomas Sheasby started construction in Merthyr Tydfil. An extension from Merthyr to Cyfarthfa Ironworks was built, although payment for it resulted in a dispute that was resolved by arbitration. However, the plan to build branches to Dowlais and Penydarren Ironworks failed, and was replaced by two tram roads.

Construction of the Glamorganshire Canal began in 1790 and was fully opened in 1794, with the primary purpose of enabling the Merthyr iron industries to transport their goods to the docks of Cardiff and Barry. An illiterate army of predominantly Irish workers moved into

Merthyr Tydfil and literally cut their way through the valleys to shape the industrial future of South Wales. In the next three and a half years the navvies dug an astonishing twenty-five-mile channel from Merthyr to Cardiff. The Glamorganshire Canal was a vital link in a chain of events that turned the valleys from rural retreats into major industrial centres. While the Merthyr ironmasters built it to take their produce to Cardiff, other entrepreneurs were swift to see the potential and developed their enterprises near the canal and linked up with it by horse-drawn trams. Some of the most intense activity was around Treforest and the nearby agricultural community of Newbridge (later Pontypridd).

The entire project cost £103,600 and the Crawshays were the main shareholders. It clung to the western side of the valley, where it crossed the River Taff at Abercynon to follow to the eastern side for most of its route to Cardiff, leaving John Bird to comment in 1796, 'The canal is brought through mountainous scenery with wonderful ingenuity.' Branch canals to other works were also linked. The Crawshays had the view that iron offered greater profits than coal, therefore as independent collieries grew, new regions were being exploited. In 1812 there were coal pioneers in the lower Rhondda Fawr at Dinas. Walter Coffin was the first industrialist to recognise the Rhondda's mineral resources and by 1820 was shipping around 10,500 tons. His colleague, Dr Richard Griffiths, erected a canal at Treforest that linked to the Glamorganshire and shipped 6,000 tons a year. A decade later and Coffin sent over 46,000 tons to Ireland, and by 1841 he employed 414 workers.

Dr Richard Griffiths, of Gelliwastad Farm in Newbridge, became a shareholder in the Glamorganshire Canal and saw the potential of building a horse-drawn tram road from the new coal levels in the lower Rhondda Valley, including his own at Gyfeillion, to link with the watercourse in Treforest. That is why he commissioned the building of a bridge and tram road that ran the length of lower Rhondda, through Newbridge to Treforest in 1809. It crossed the River Taff to a feeder canal at Dynea that subsequently led into the Glamorganshire Canal. This was known as the 'Doctor's Bridge', but later renamed Machine Bridge, because a weighing bridge was constructed on the one end to measure the amount of coal which crossed the river.

Treforest was a revolutionary town, born out of the industrialisation of its surrounding valleys and transformed from a sleepy agricultural region into one of the largest in Glamorgan, and owes its development to the industrial ambitions of the Crawshays. Their association with the area began in 1794 when William Crawshay (1788–1867), the grandson of ironmaster Richard Crawshay, purchased a portion of land at Ynyspenllwch, where a small mill for the rolling of tinplate was in operation. With the crucial opening of the Glamorganshire Canal, the development of the tinplate works was bound to follow. The expansion and modernisation of the works made it the largest in Britain by 1836.

The Crawshays opened a new forge and nail works and also acquired a small ironworks on the adjoining land to their tinplates. This was later expanded to form the Taff Vale Ironworks, which in conjunction with the tinplate formed the 'Fforest Works'. The success of both industries and the link to the Rhondda coal trade led to the rapid growth of the village. In August 1811 a market opened and there was also a hide and wool market sited at the Castle Inn Bridge. Dominating the area was the large Crawshay property, Fforest House, built on the site of Fforest Isaf Farm that gave its name to the Fforest Works and the town of Treforest itself.

Richard Crawshay and his fortune at Cyfarthfa was helped greatly by his young nephews, Joseph and Crawshay Bailey, the sons of his sister Susanna. He was concerned by his sons, 'who would never follow my advice, and treated me rudely'. Eventually he was reconciled and William Crawshay I (1764–1834) received three eighths' share of the fortune on his father's death in 1810. Another three eighths' share went to Benjamin Hall MP, the husband of his daughter Charlotte Crawshay, and parents of Sir Benjamin Hall, Lord Llanover. The remaining quarter share went to his nephew Joseph Bailey.

On Richard's death, William came to power and successfully managed to buy both Benjamin Hall and Joseph Bailey's shares in the Cyfarthfa Ironworks, becoming sole proprietor. A master manipulator and businessman, he was recognised as someone who took advantage of weak opponents, giving him a lethal streak that was feared by those who knew him. He had little interest in the manufacture of iron, and instead took charge of the family's selling agency at Upper Thames Street in London, building a home there. William and his wife Eliza (1760–1825) had five children and it was their eldest son, William Crawshay II (1788–1867), who managed Cyfarthfa and Hirwaun ironworks, acknowledged as 'the most statesmanlike of the Crawshay iron kings', and guided the enterprise with a steady hand. His wife, Elizabeth Homfray (1785–1813) a member of the Homfray iron family, gave him five children, one of whom was Francis, who would inherit his interests in Treforest and live at Fforest House, while his youngest son, Robert Thompson Crawshay (1817–1879), by his second wife Isabel Thompson (1788–1827), who gave him nine more children, inherited Cyfarthfa.

During William Crawshay II's 'reign' as the iron king, he extended the fortune to incorporate Treforest and went on to build the extensive family mansions of Caversham Park and Cyfarthfa Castle in Merthyr Tydfil. Flamboyant, well educated and popular, he spent the majority of his working life locked in wrangles with his father. He retained a strong sense of moral duty to the workforce, refusing to cut their pay during difficult times in the trade and refusing to advocate the 'Truck System' where tokens were given to workers to purchase items from company-owned shops at inflated prices. Controversially, he was however linked to the hanging of Dic Penderyn, who was accused of leading the Merthyr Rising of 1831, although it appears he was personally distressed at the miscarriage of justice. William's life was not without its tragedy. He lost two wives and was outlived by his third wife Isabella Johnson. In total he fathered fifteen children, but appeared deeply affected by the death of his eldest son William Crawshay III (1810–1839) who was drowned while crossing the River Severn.

One of his greatest legacies was that of Cyfarthfa Castle, the family home. Designed by Richard Lugar, Cyfarthfa was built in 1824 at the cost of £30,000 and with its mock Tudor style, shields, huge Gothic doors and stained glass, its imposing grandeur gave the illusion of an ancient family home that dominated a town where the lower classes lived in filth and poverty. The castle was built on the site of Anthony Bacon's Cyfarthfa House and its creation led to countless feuds with William's father, who felt it was folly to build such an extravagant premises. Covering an acre, the castle had its own dairy, brew house and ice house with extensive cellars for wine and produce.

Less than a year before the foundation stone of Cyfarthfa Castle was laid, William Crawshay was introduced to Dr William Price. It would not be unreasonable to think that the young surgeon had all the necessary credentials to ensure such a meeting took place. Although his own immediate family's apparent poverty did not show it, the Prices were, after all, a family of ironmasters in their own right. It seems as if Crawshay was made very much aware of this when the first introductions were made. Dr Price was the great-grandson of Nicholas Pryce of Pentyrch furnace; he was distantly related to Thomas Price of the Dowlais ironworks, and his own grandfather, Charles Price, had run an ironworks at Rudry. These were the credences that Price was able to exploit to gain access to Crawshay society. At that time William Crawshay II continued to rapidly develop the enterprises at Treforest, and the need for a surgeon of works to administer medical care to the growing workforce was becoming apparent. In June 1823, just three months after receiving his final certificate in midwifery, Dr William Price was appointed the new surgeon to the Crawshays at Treforest. It was a relationship that continued for over forty years and was further cemented by a strong connection between Price and William's successor at Treforest, his eccentric son Francis, who inherited the works in 1835.

Despite his exceptional talents as a doctor, he could have secured a city position and earned a fortune, living a luxurious life rather than one among the oppressed people of the valleys. Instead Dr Price was interested in the working classes of his birthplace and remembered, 'I regard as entirely the fault of their employers who give them far less attendance and care than they bestow on cattle' – quite a statement for someone who became such a favourite of the Crawshays.

People derided his flamboyance but no one could mock his fame as a successful physician and surgeon, just as the ill-paid workers could not complain of his habit of giving them his services free of charge; usually he extracted high payment from the rich. He was also known to assist professionally, materially and spiritually outcast girls condemned by the chapels – 'but this could be expected of a man who preached such dangerous theories above love and marriage and, moreover, used to roam the hilltops naked, declaring the sun a healing power?'[3]

Dr William Price developed a reputation as a healer among not only the workforce, but the residents of the surrounding agricultural communities, whom he visited on horseback to diagnose and prescribe suitable medical treatments. It became apparent that he was an outspoken individual with firm ideals and strong opinions from a very young age, and was unafraid of voicing them openly.

On the completion of his studies at London, he returned to Rudry and worked for some time in Caerphilly. He engaged in general practice in the area, and felt sufficiently well established to build a house opposite Pentyrch works; which was never completed after a fracas with the industrialist Richard Blakemore of the Melingriffith Works.

Dr Price remembered,

> I began to build a house for myself opposite Pentyrch. Mr Blakemore, the owner of the site, had promised me a lease for 99 years, but he wanted me to do something there against my will and I refused. 'Very well' he said, 'I will not give you a lease on the place and I will not return you a shilling of the money you have spent there.'
>
> I had spent over £200 and the lodge is there now. So I put him in Chancery and got my money back. My brother, who was in Blakemore's employment as a clerk at the tin works, was very angry with me for this.
>
> I went to my brother's house at Pentyrch but he tried to throw me out. He was four or five inches taller than I, but I was stronger, so I soon put him on his back and gave him a good licking. He got notice to leave the works but as I was a great friend of Crawshay, I got a place for him at Cyfarthfa Works and he remained there for 16 years.[4]

In 1829 he rented the rather grand-sounding property of Ynys y Llewod Duon (River Isle of the Black Lions), which may well have belonged to the Pentyrch Ironworks. Dr Price provided medical care and advice to the workforce in the Pentyrch furnace, allowing him to live at the house, which was situated between Tongwynlais and Taff's Well, where he was said to have resided for several years.

From there he moved to Nantgarw, at that time the location for a fledgling pottery that had produced elaborate and fine porcelain between 1813 and 1814 under the guidance of potter William Billingsley and his colleague Thomas Pardoe.

Dr Price realised there was a need to open his own surgery to cater for the needs of the developing population. He found the ideal location with a building on the other side of the River Taff from Treforest in an area known as Glyntaff – or more correctly, Craig yr Helfa, sometimes spelt as Craigalva. Overlooking the Taff, the Griffiths canal and tram road, the Glamorganshire Canal and Treforest itself, this was a perfect location for his new surgery, where his talents were sufficient for him to be in constant demand. According to Dr Price, he lived in the property for seven years, later setting up home at Porthyglo Cottage in Upper Boat, rented from a solicitor from Cardiff and once owned by the Price family before it was sold by Catherine Price some twenty years earlier.

Porthyglo belonged to the farm estate of Ynys Llyn, and when Dr Price lived there and leased Ynys Llyn from the owner, Mr Grover, it had 65 acres of land attached to it. It appears that Dr Price preferred to live at Porthyglo cottage rather than Ynys Llyn Farm, although he took full advantage of the extensive land at his disposal. Dr Price's love of animals pervaded his entire life and over the years he built up a large quantity of cattle, horses, pigs and more controversially his unruly goats! It was at Porthyglo that he tentatively began to develop his interest in livestock and began purchasing large numbers of animals.

According to a newspaper report many years later by Morien, 'The goats inflicted great injury to every green tree on the farm and in the neighbourhood. After he had been there some time Mr Grover, the solicitor, gave him notice to leave, but Dr Price would not go. An action of ejectment was instituted, and, in the midst of intense popular excitement, his goats and cattle were turned out into the highway. Dr Price himself had retired into the farthest room in the house. He was carried out sitting on a chair, and placed on the road.'[5]

His reputation as a healer, however, went before him. His services were in great request in complicated cases, or when other practitioners pronounced a hopeless fate, and his mode of treatment was sometimes extraordinary to a degree. Public faith in his skill was unbounded and people travelled long distances to consult him, or sent for him at great expense as a last resort. With his aristocratic looks, sparkling eyes and strikingly handsome physique, as refined as a lady in all matters pertaining to his profession, he was idolised by his female patients, from whom he enjoyed remarkable attention. It was also a reputation that led many to suspect him of having some unorthodox beliefs that manifested themselves in his flamboyant dress and open denunciation of medical practices generally.

Dr Price strongly condemned the practice of inoculation and experiments on animals. He advocated vegetarianism, good food, clean living, fresh air, exercise and natural medicine. He regarded smoking as dangerous and unhealthy, allegedly refusing to treat patients who smoked. On 17

April 1940, James Powell of Swansea wrote to the *Western Mail* about a journey he took from Pontypridd to Merthyr by train with Dr Price. The surgeon asked a fellow passenger in his carriage to stop smoking his clay pipe and when he refused, the doctor snatched it from his mouth and threw it through the window of the moving carriage. When the passenger protested, Dr Price threatened to throw him through the window if he didn't sit quietly. The journey apparently ended in peace.

As a strict vegetarian, he believed 'that the eating of animal flesh has a tendency to revive in men the worst passions of the brute. I contend that human beings ought not to eat animal food, and the Cymmerian teachers forbade it. The man who eats animal food descends to the level of the brute, and will in time require the habits and passions of a beast.'[4]

He regarded vaccination as 'a method established by law for the express purpose of slaughtering infants'. It was hardly a surprising outburst remembering the death of his brother at such a young age from an alleged vaccination. What is interesting is that in many respects his anti-vaccination beliefs were disproved when identifying his name as the signatory on a Certificate of Vaccination in 1854.

Dr Price proclaimed,

> We are suffering under the curse of the past mistakes of our profession. We have been educating the public into the false belief that poisonous drugs can give health. This belief has become such a deep-rooted superstition, that those of us who know better and who would like to adopt more rational methods, can only do so at the risk of losing our practice and reputation.
>
> The average doctor is at his best but a devoted bigot to this damnable teaching which we call the medical art, and which alone in this age of science, has made no perceptible progress since the days of its earliest teachers. Some call it recognised science. I call it ignorance![4]

He never lost his contempt for medicines and pills; this along with expressing radical views on nudity, free love, and his unusual style of dress and his refusal to wear socks on hygienic grounds, explaining, 'stockings prevent the proper exhalation of the feet, which, in consequence, are kept damp; and the person who wears them is more liable to catch cold. My feet are always dry and warm.'

In his personal hygiene he was obsessive, wearing a clean white tunic everyday. After receiving any money he would wash the coins before putting them in his pocket and afterwards washed his own hands.

A keen walker, he was known to visit his patients at night, riding or walking ten or fifteen miles in the early hours, his theory being that people were at their worst at night and needed more attention than during the day.

He never wore a watch, which he said was not needed in his profession as the time to see patients was 'when they send for you'.

Unorthodox, judgemental and outspoken he may have been, but Dr Price was also making results in his treatment of patients. His mode of treatment was extraordinary and the public's total faith in his skill was unbounded and patients frequently visited his basic home of bare walls and little furniture and a consulting room, which testified to his disregard for bodily comforts.

A local reputation as a brilliant surgeon ensued, despite his somewhat heretical beliefs and eschewal of convention, be it medical, social, or religious. Whether his behaviour was merely quirky or a manifestation of mental illness remains the subject of speculation. He was clearly a maverick and a rebel, and his bizarre notions led him into frequent conflict with the law and the Church.

Sadly, with the growing passage of time and few documented accounts, many of the tales of Price's methodology to cure patients have become more than exaggerated and almost ludicrous in their assumption of being true. One such tale was that of a young girl in Llantrisant, dying of a stomach complaint. Dr Price ordered the parents to fill a clay pipe with tobacco and make her swallow the smoke. They didn't carry out the orders and she died.

When he held an autopsy he opened her stomach and found a live snail. On blowing pipe smoke fumes at the creature, it died. However, the fact the Price was totally against smoking somehow refutes these claims.

Once when he went to see a dying woman in a remote village, a man who suffered from rheumatism consulted him.

'How long have you used these crutches?' asked Dr Price.

'For two years, sir,' was the reply.

Dr Price said, 'Put the crutches away. You need the medicine of movement. If you refuse to use your limbs, they become useless. I will now take away your stick; walk again, as you first did as a child and then learn to walk like a man.' After this elementary physiotherapy, with a little embrocation, his complete function was restored.

An old Welsh woman once asked the doctor for 'something for the headache'. Dr Price asked to be allowed to look into her bonnet. The woman, surprised, handed him her head-gear, which was thickly lined with two layers of flannel, irrespective of the straw and trimmings, whereupon the doctor examined it, and said, 'No wonder you have a headache. This thatch is fourteen ounces too heavy. Reduce the weight, and the headache will go.'

Dr Price's cure for rheumatism was said to be ginger and salts as 'the ginger will penetrate where the salts will not, and the salts will work from there'. Another cure recounted was Dr Price's instructions to a patient to 'eat all the green vegetables in the garden'. Another was Dr Price's refusal to allow rhubarb to be eaten by his own family, following the observation that animals never eat it.

Another piece of common sense diagnoses and treatments was down to a patient suffering from overindulgence in food and drink. He was told that the trouble was due to 'consumption – table consumption of the most hopeless kind. No cure unless you live lower and eat less.'

Price was called to the Newbridge farm of Evan Evans and was not surprised to find him groaning in pain and clutching his stomach. The old farmer, a widower with two sons and a daughter, was renowned for his heavy drinking. Leaving the farmer in agony on his bed, Price went downstairs to meet Evan's twenty-one-year-old daughter Megan and together they walked to a nearby pond, where Price caught a frog. Returning to the farmhouse, he instructed Evan to take some medicine that made him vomit in a bucket into which the doctor placed the frog. Appearing shocked, Price convinced Evans that beer was causing the growth of frogs in his stomach and the farmer was so appalled that he never drank again. He paid Price a £2 fee, which the doctor secretly returned to the family.

Another farmer once asked him, 'What shall I do, Dr Price? I'm as stiff as an old horse.'

'Wash and be clean,' was the laconic reply. 'With the dirt of half a century upon your body, how can you expect to be anything but stiff?'

Price apparently had an interesting treatment for a dislocated shoulder. The story runs that it was his custom to walk from Llantrisant to Ystrad Mynach, where he would take the train to Rhymney. One day, whilst on his walk in his usual garb, he noticed a group of people standing outside the door of a house in great distress. He enquired as to the nature of the trouble and was told a man had just been brought in with a dislocated shoulder. He went inside, placed a stool, on which he told the man to stand while strongly gripping a meat hook that was protruding from the ceiling. The doctor kicked away the stool. The man fell, his shoulder jerked into place and the doctor continued on his journey.

One day an old Rhondda man with his son called on Price and asked for an opinion on his wife. Together they walked to Penrhiwfer, a journey of several miles. After examining the patient, Price recommended a prescription that could only be made up by a chemist in Pontypridd, but despite the skill of the pharmacist, the woman died. The relatives applied to Price for a death certificate. He gave it, believing that malnutrition was the blame and wrote 'Died through the laws of the land' on the certificate. They had to apply to another doctor for a proper certificate.

When a lady was suffering from intractable pruritus, a skin complaint for which there was no cause or cure, Price invited her into his house and placed her in a room with a chair and table and commanded her to undress. Then he gave her a kitten to hold under her armpit. In an hour he returned to find her shivering with cold, but still holding the kitten. The doctor took the animal away and demonstrated a large lump on her skin. He incised it and it released a myriad of lice. Needless to say, she was cured.

A pretty girl was pining away, and her debilitated condition caused her mother such great anxiety, that she took her to be seen by Dr Price, whose silence as to the nature of the illness surprised her.

'Well, sir,' said the mother, 'what do you think is the matter with her?

'Heart complaint,' was the reply. 'I did think so,' said the astute mother. 'She does look that uncommon pale sometimes, and her breath is short and there's always them stitches in her side. Will you please, sir, to have the kindness to give her something for it?'

'I can do nothing for her – nothing whatever,' said the doctor, who, observing the mother's anxious look, added, 'Many waters cannot quench love neither can floods drown it.'

When examining a woman suffering with a cataract he asked for some milk and a cat. He bathed the eye with milk and held the cat up to the eye who then licked off the milk. It was alleged the rough tongue of the cat also removed the cataract!

He once recommended the following treatment to a patient of his in Hopkinstown who was suffering from stomach and chest pain. The man was to fast for twenty-four hours, and on Saturday his wife was to prepare the Sunday joint so it would be ready at noon, when the doctor would call. He arrived and, taking the joint from the oven, placed it on the man's bare chest. With carving knife in hand, he threatened the man that if he moved so much as an inch to taste a morsel of the joint, he could cut his throat.

They waited expectantly, and from the man's inside crawled up a worm that was so hungry it was attracted by the aroma! Once he killed the worm, the man was cured of his symptoms.

Another tale speaks of a Miss Jacob of Brynmenin, who had been unable to walk since the day she was chased by a herd of pigs and collapsed on the steps of her home. On calling for Dr Price he advised to throw her in the cold stream and the shock of it would reawaken the use of her legs. The family, fearing she was drown, did not accept his treatment and the girl remained paralysed all of her life.

Although many of these tales are recognisable as 'tall', they show the type of impression he made on his contemporaries. It was certainly a reputation that would further benefit his career in the vicinity of Treforest.

Neighbouring Newbridge remained a quiet hamlet of scattered farmsteads, linked over the River Taff by the famous single-span arch bridge. The bridge did little to change the rural character of the district, and led to the growth of a small cluster of houses on either side of the River Taff. It was another century before the town was renamed Pontypridd. The original was probably Pont-y-ty-pridd (bridge of the earthen house), which is thought to refer to a small hut which may have stood near the eastern bank of the river.

Industrialisation of the area came in several stages. On the one hand the Glamorganshire Canal would bring renewed interest in lands in close proximity to it, where large-industries could be erected and take full advantage of the transportation available by water. Such an enterprise opened on the banks of the canal just five years prior to Price's arrival at Treforest.

Newbridge Chain & Anchor Works, or the 'Ynysangharad Works', was established by cousins Samuel Brown and Samuel Lenox in 1818 following an initial base at Millwall in East London. It was the first major industry to come to Newbridge due to the canal. The location of the site provided easy access to supplies of iron from Merthyr Tydfil and Hirwaun, and its proximity to abundant coal and water supplies was also beneficial. Initially, the Brown and Lenox 'works' concentrated on supplying chains for the shipping industry, but also provided chain-links for suspension bridges and engines, and trams and shackles for the collieries. The chain works first brought the great British engineer, Isambard Kingdom Brunel (1806–59), who designed the Clifton Suspension Bridge and the three largest ships in the world, to Newbridge. Among its many customers was the Royal Navy, whilst also providing chains for the suspension bridge at Hammersmith, the chain pier at Brighton, and Thomas Telford's bridge over the Menai Straits. The firm made chains and anchors for many liners, including the *Lusitania*, the *Mauretania*, the *Queen Elizabeth* and the *Queen Mary*, and for the warships *Rodney* and *Nelson*. When German warships were scuttled at Scapa Flow in 1918, they were found to be equipped with chains and anchors made at Brown Lenox.

When Dr Price initially met the proprietors Samuel Brown and Samuel Lenox and the manager of the Newbridge works, Philip Thomas, their exceptional factory had yet to reach its full potential, although it would not be long before the ever-increasing workforce moulded a company that lasted in the area for over 190 years. This was the workforce that, in 1823, were so enamoured of his success as a surgeon in the locality, they actually elected Dr William Price to become the Medical Advisor and Chief Surgeon of the Ynysangharad Chain Works. It was the only occasion known in British history up until that time where a workforce elected their own medical officer.

Many varied stories relate to the remarkable treatments he administered to the workers during this time. Although largely unsubstantiated, they again reveal the honest respect and admiration people had for his abilities as a surgeon. It was at the chain works that he allegedly performed a bone-graft operation on an injured worker from Hopkinstown who had suffered such a serious compound fracture that it was thought necessary to amputate his leg. The young boy refused to consider such a horrific surgery and Price was sent for. On arrival he sent a worker to the nearby slaughterhouse in Treforest for the leg bone of a calf, which he allegedly grafted onto the broken leg. Apparently it was a successful operation and although the boy was left with one leg shorter than the other, no amputation was necessary.

Dr Price made a clear statement that medical care should be a basic right to everyone, not just the wealthy. As far as he was concerned, there were too many medical men profiteering from acts of butchery and any physician worthy of the title should not just give cures, but look at the symptoms, the poor lifestyles, health, and the effects of machinery and industrialisation. During his early life Dr Price had already witnessed the rapid industrial growth of Merthyr and Treforest. While in London he had seen for himself the degenerate conditions of working class families. With the appointment of his position at the chain works came his opportunity to show a zeal and energy for helping the workforce improve their well-being. It was a facet of his character that placed him in the highest esteem with the workers and local population. Price was a kind and generous man who clearly cared very deeply about the conditions, pay, environment and health of those young men and their dependants experiencing this mass industrialisation first-hand. Unlike fellow medics, his purpose wasn't just to cure, but to tackle the causes of sickness and eradicate those causes where possible. He not only catered to their medical needs, but did all in his power to improve their lives generally. Whilst working at the chain works he established a system of social healthcare that would benefit injured or sick workers in his care. He devised a popular system of payment whereby workers paid him when they were well and he treated them for free when they were ill. Price felt that fellow physicians should only be paid when someone was healed, otherwise they could allow a patient to remain sick for a long time to ensure they profited from their sickness.

As an early proponent of co-operative healthcare, Dr William Price's philosophies were mirrored elsewhere throughout industrial South Wales. Nowhere was this better represented than in the formation of organisations such as the Tredegar Workingmen's Medical Aid Society in 1874. It was their work in particular that influenced the likes of politician Aneurin Bevan, whose Socialist zeal and determination led to the establishment of the most far-reaching piece of social legislation in British history, the National Health Service.

The system may have well resulted in Price making financial sacrifices of his own, for according to the *Cambrian News* of March 1831, 'William Price, late of the parish of Eglwysilan in the county of Glamorgan, Surgeon' was listed in the Court for Relief of Insolvent Debtors at the Guildhall, Cardiff. Financial problems beset Price from time to time throughout his life, but this first brush with the establishment did little to affect his reputation as a healer and he continued at Treforest and in its immediate vicinity for almost half a century.

The 1830s were an incredibly tumultuous period in Welsh history and Price, to some degree, played a role in them. The Rebecca Riots and the Chartist Rising in Newport were just two of the massive outbreaks of violence as the working classes raised arms for better conditions and livelihood. The first major impact of activism occurred in even closer proximity to his new home and in doing so involved his employers, the Crawshays. The Merthyr Rising of 1831 was the violent climax of many years of unrest among the workers of Merthyr Tydfil. Crawshay's workforces were aiming for reform and protesting against a lowering of wages and unemployment. By the end of May 1831 the insurrection had become far worse than anyone could have imagined, and for the very first time the red flag of revolution was flown. The rebels stormed through the town, sacked the debtors' court and destroyed books detailing the debtors themselves. Among the calls were cries of '*Caws a Bara*!' ('Bread and Cheese!'), a phrase Price himself used in his own political material, and also '*I lawr a'r Brenin*' ('Down with the King'). A contingency of the Argyll and Sutherland Highlanders was dispatched to quell the crowd, but found it was too large to disperse. On the second day of fighting, the High Sheriff of Glamorgan held a meeting with employers and magistrates at the Castle Inn, where a group of men led by Lewsyn yr Heliwr (Lewis Lewis) demanded a reduction in the price of bread and an increase in wages, which was rejected. They attacked the inn and after some of the rioters seized weapons belonging to the soldiers, the troops opened fire on the angry mob. There were many fatalities and hundreds of injuries before the Highlanders withdrew to Penydarren House, the sole refuge of authority for eight long days and nights. The rioters controlled the town with military precision, ambushing the Swansea Yeomanry and the Highlander's Baggage Train, beating off the cavalry. Peaceful residents and families began to flee as the rioters took control. They arranged a meeting on 6 June where 450 troops marched *en masse* to the spot in Dowlais with levelled weapons and effectively brought the rising to a close.

Although Dr Price was not involved in the Merthyr Rising, this revolutionary spirit was strong within him. On the one hand he was a close companion of the Crawshays, and his popularity with the Guests was also becoming well known. His frequent visits to the society balls and champagne parties (which gave him a genuine taste for the expensive beverage for the rest of his life) illustrated the paradox of Dr Price that, although he would later openly condemn the class system, he was in effect a part of the gentrified social crowd. Dr Price was as much a socialite as others of the higher class in the industrial south.

This was recognised by the close association he enjoyed with Lady Charlotte Guest, the wife of the Merthyr ironmaster and contemporary of the Crawshays. If there was one great love that both Price and Lady Charlotte shared, it was Wales, her culture, history and language. Dr Price was fiercely proud of his heritage and since childhood had immersed himself in the fascinating history and mythology of the Principality. As a Welshman he tried his utmost to defend his people and their heritage to the best of his ability. He wanted to join the likes of Lady Charlotte Guest and her contemporary, Lady Llanover, in their endeavours to showcase Welsh culture to the world and become a great patron of the arts. With the growth of the British Empire, he fought to glorify and celebrate Welsh culture when the battle for widespread recognition of Wales, her people and promise, could not be won. There were times when his frustrated mind could not withstand the terrible pressures of defeat, but he stayed at his post when few others did. That is why he is remembered with such affection and respect as a true Welshman.

These were the qualities that Lady Charlotte greatly admired in him, and a genuine mutual affection was felt by the two stalwarts and defenders of Wales and her traditions. Twelve years younger than Dr Price, her life also spanned a large part of the nineteenth century as she only outlived him by two years. She was one of the most remarkable women of her generation. Like Dr Price, she shared an interest in early Welsh literature, but whereas the young surgeon was proud of his natural-born heritage, she was in fact the daughter of an English earl and yet went on to translate and publish a major collection of medieval Welsh tales, the *Mabinogion*, between 1838 and 1849.

Born in Lincolnshire, the daughter of the 9th Earl of Lindsey, Charlotte showed a talent for study and taught herself Hebrew, Persian and Arabic. After a brief flirtation with a young politician named Benjamin Disraeli, she was married in 1833 to the industrialist and owner of the Dowlais ironworks, John Josiah Guest, an occasion that coincided with the advent of his own political career. He was forty-nine while she was twenty-one, and they moved to the area after he became elected a Member of Parliament for the Merthyr Tydfil constituency in 1832, an election that Dr Price openly supported and canvassed for. Lady Charlotte Guest wrote in her journal that the flamboyant doctor was 'one of our best friends at the last election'. The election, which took place in the same year as the Parliamentary Reform Act, sealed the power of the new middle class. In the 1832 election, only 402 men in Merthyr Tydfil actually had the vote – which equates to around one in seventy members of the male population – and these consisted chiefly of shopkeepers and publicans. Known as the 'poor man's friend' because of his stance during the Reform crisis, John Josiah Guest had come a long way from the days of his own grandfather, who rode from his native Shropshire to Wales to open the furnace at the Plymouth Works. Within two generations the Dowlais Iron Company was poised to become one of the largest ironworks in the world.

Lady Charlotte was a hugely influential woman. The Guests had the approval of the monarchy, as displayed in Queen Victoria's decision to sponsor their son Montague's christening and the offer to Josiah Guest of a Baronetcy in 1838. This extremely wealthy couple (one of her wedding presents was the Empress Josephine's earrings) wielded immense power and social standing, although she was hardly prepared for the role of a conventional wife and she delighted in being different and daring – qualities that Dr Price could appreciate and understand.

With an enthusiastic interest in her husband's philanthropic activities on behalf of the local community, Lady Charlotte, like Dr Price, is remembered in a number of different ways. A sharp businesswoman, collector, educator and translator, her copious amounts of journals were kept for almost seventy years and now the life-time companion has become a piece of social history. She worked closely with the people of Dowlais by developing educational and leisure facilities for the workforce. For Lady Charlotte, there was a genuine need to revive the culture of Wales and showcase its many talents and she acknowledged Dr Price's own vast knowledge of this subject. Lady Charlotte stated, 'he is a clever man and on Welsh subjects well informed'. Dr William Price embroiled himself in manuscripts of Wales, becoming one of the many who accepted Iolo Morganwg's often unsubstantiated portrayal of Welsh history. Whatever the source, Dr Price was becoming known as more than just a medical man, but also a great proponent of Welsh culture and heritage.

In August 1834, a year after Lady Charlotte's marriage to Guest, she first became acquainted with Dr Price. At the invitation of the second Marquis of Bute, an eisteddfod was held in Cardiff Castle and the money raised paid towards a new dispensary in the growing town. It marked the early years of the revitalised eisteddfod tradition. The tradition dates to the twelfth century, when the eisteddfod was held by Rhys ap Gruffydd of Deheubarth at his court in Cardigan in 1176, but with the decline of the bardic tradition, it eventually disappeared.

However, it wasn't until 1789 that a move was underway to re-establish the tradition and help raise Welsh culture above the tradition of the tavern eisteddfodau. This was put forward by the Gwyneddigion Society in London, established as a debating and cultural society for Welsh speakers in the capital. Like its contemporary, the Cymmrodorion Society, whose constitution outlined specific aims for the cultivation of the Welsh language and research into its antiquities, both organisations were an expression of the patriotic impulse of the eighteenth-century cultural revival. One can only wonder whether Dr Price attended any of the society meetings during his time as a young medical student in London, an event that could well have further inspired him to join the fight to improve Wales's position as prominent part of British history.

Throughout the early part of the nineteenth century, provincial societies were established in Dyfed, Gwynedd, Powys, Gwent and Glamorgan. Often patronised by the local gentry class, the ten eisteddfodau held between 1819 and 1834 began to transform Welsh culture. The first saw the introduction of Gorsedd y Beirdd, the tradition of honouring the winning poet with a bardic chair, one of the brainchildren of Iolo Morganwg. The Cardiff Eisteddfod of 1834 was the impetus for holding a further ten eisteddfodau in Abergavenny between 1835 and 1852 by the Cymreigyddion Society. Inspired by Thomas Price, who used the bardic name of Carnhuanawc, the vicar of Llanfihangel Cwmdu, it was patronised by the redoubtable Augusta Hall (1802–96), Lady Llanover. Another supporter and friend of Dr Price, Llanover was the wife of Benjamin Hall MP of Abercarn and Hensol, the grandson of Merthyr's founder ironmaster, Richard Crawshay. A promoter of the Welsh national revival, she was born in Tŷ Uchaf, Llanofer in Monmouthshire, daughter of landowner Benjamin Waddington. Married to Hall in 1823, she was a talented editor and illustrator, and was well connected and an accomplished hostess in the London parliamentary circle. However, it was her contribution as a patron of the language, literature and national institutions of Wales for which she was famous. At their home, Llanofer, she employed household staff who spoke Welsh and established a harp-manufacturing business.

Vivacious and resolute, she became established in Wales the day she met Dr Price at the Gwent and Dyfed Royal Eisteddfod at Cardiff on 20 August 1834, in which she won the prize for an essay entitled, 'The Advantages resulting from the Preservation of the Welsh language and National Costume of Wales.' Her nom de plume on this occasion was Gwenynen Gwent (the Bee of Gwent), the bardic name by which she subsequently became known. Lady Llanover made efforts to preserve and popularise a sense of Welsh identity. Dr Price was in essence present at the start of a huge moment in Welsh history, as Lady Llanover began to gain support for her dream to create the national costume, and did so in the presence of both Price and Lady Charlotte Guest.[6]

> Although the original idea of a national dress was promoted by the land owning and literary and artistic elite of Wales, and this was based on what was being worn in some areas of rural Wales, the widespread acceptance and wearing of a particular form of dress as a conscious expression of Welshness, was undoubtedly also influenced strongly by the tourist industry … which boomed with the expansion of the rail network into Wales. It seems undeniable that Lady Llanover's passions and energy contributed in a significant way to the development of the Welsh national dress from an ideal to an internationally recognised symbol. This is also due in part to the fact that she based her ideas on a form of dress which was actually being worn by Welsh women, rather than trying to invent a completely spurious outfit.[6]

Lady Llanover and Lady Charlotte Guest had much in common in their attempts to preserve, patronise and celebrate Welsh culture. They also shared the admiration of Dr Price, the dashing, charming and handsome young surgeon of Porthyglo. When Dr Price gave a speech on Welsh history and literature, Lady Charlotte was totally enamoured of him.

She recorded the matter in her journal later that day:

> I was early roused by the bells, which continued at intervals to ring during the rest of the week. Just as they were all departing to the

gaieties, Baby detained me, so I had to follow them alone in the carriage to Castle Gate, where I waited till Merthyr, who had been walking in the procession of the Bards from the Town Hall, came and took me in. I got a very good place under the tent in the front row opposite the platform. After a pause Lord Bute opened the Eisteddfod. His speech was miserable, and made me tremble lest I should be betrayed into a smile. When it was at length, to my great relief, and I should think to his, concluded, Mr Price came forward and made one of the most beautiful and eloquent speeches that was ever heard. He traced the history of the Welsh and expatiated on their attachment to their country, their usages and language. It was, indeed, most exciting. Mr Price was one of the judges of the claims of the Bards to the different prizes, given either by the Committee or by individuals. Mr Bruce Knight was another, and when Mr Price's speech was over, he proceeded, after an address of his own, to communicate in very elegant terms the decision which had been come to upon the merits of the various candidates. It was at this stage of the proceedings that I was invited up upon the platform, occupied by Lady Bute and her party, as well as the Bards and the Hudges ... The Medal was the first that was adjudged, and great interested was evinced as to its appropriation.[7]

On the basis of his speech, Dr Price was invited to become the judge of the eisteddfod's bardic competition, with the prize being awarded to Taliesin Williams, the scholar, historian and schoolmaster at Merthyr who was also the son of the infamous Iolo Morganwg. He received the medal from Lady Bute for his translation of the *Welsh Ode On The British Druids* and was then chaired, and it was felt to be a great triumph for the Bardic Chair to be assigned to a native of Merthyr Tydfil.

Clearly by this time Dr William Price was a recognisable figure in the growing society of Treforest and Newbridge. His popularity with the workforces of the two largest industries in the area was secured, as was his social connection to the Crawshays and the Guests. It was a period in his life when he could recall with great satisfaction that he was a self-made man who had overcome a distressing childhood to reach the very pinnacle of his profession, with a large population requiring his services. Dr Price was making his mark on the people of Glamorgan and his reputation as a surgeon, philanthropist and supporter of Welsh culture, with a focused social consciousness, made him a greatly respected individual. An established figure he may have been, but soon his own ideals of religion and political activism would result in a very different William Price being both admired and ridiculed in equal measure.

4

1835–1838

To understand Dr William Price, one must also consider the period of history in which he lived and the renaissance experienced throughout Wales and elsewhere of pagan religions. It is easy to condemn Dr Price for his dress and beliefs, which were considered alternative to the appropriate behaviour of the early days of the Victorian period. When one realises that many of these facets of his life are due to his deep-rooted worship and total fanaticism for Druidism, then many of the so-called 'eccentricities' can be readily explained. It is important to remember that he was just one of a growing movement of fellow believers, or disciples, of Druidism throughout the country.

It was this cult of Druidism which gave rise to such controversy during the nineteenth century, when Dr Price followed his obsession with the three volumes of Iolo Morganwg's *Myvyrian Archaeology of Wales*, Dr Stukeley's *Stonehenge*, and Bernard Montfaucon's *L'Antiquite Explique* and Barnes' *Odyssia* and *Iliad* – volumes he named in his will as being of great importance. Dr Price stood alone in many of his Druidic beliefs, not always accepting the ways of the 'regular Druids' in the vicinity of his home, and understandably a tension grew between the two factions. First and foremost, Dr Price had a missionary zeal to his energies regarding Druidism, as he did for the promotion of Welsh culture, the two subjects being so intrinsically interwoven. He wanted to make a positive contribution to the preservation of Welsh culture and Druidism by helping to recreate the national identity of his homeland. Dr Price felt Druidism was a facet of Welsh history that the Welsh could call their own, making them totally unique in the wider culture of the British.

The Druids may well have been the religious specialists of some of the Celtic tribes of north-western Europe over 2,000 years ago, but in truth that is all that can be said of them with any certainty. The legend has been shrouded for centuries, and in truth little is known of this mysterious and powerful cult. All that remains is a few accounts and biased portrayals of the Celts and their religious leaders by the Roman Empire. The propaganda issued by the early Roman warriors told of human sacrifices and white-robed, bearded men who gathered in circles. They claimed they were soothsayers, magicians, bards and prophets, and with the advent of Christianity the original Druids had gone forever.

The Druids were not necessarily always religious leaders and priests, and some were identified as judges and teachers, physicians and philosophers. In fact when Christianity swept through Europe, it may well have been that many of those Druidic priests became religious leaders of the new order. What is believed is that the Druidic religion was free of dogma and not an organised religion with a rigid belief system, something that would have appealed to the likes of the freethinking Dr Price. The Celts themselves, with their own Brythonic languages of which Welsh remains the most widespread today, were referred to in the fourth century BC as the 'Keltoi' who learned how to treat iron and make weapons, tools and roadways. Recognised as being courageous in battle, as Aristotle said they feared 'neither earthquakes or waves', the Celts had a well-ordered class structure of leaders, warriors, producers of goods, and labourers. When the Roman armies invaded, the sophisticated tribal Celtic societies that had been the predominant civilisation of northern Europe had survived attacks by the Jutes, Angles and Saxons. Those on the isles of Britain began to migrate to Ireland, Scotland, Wales and Cornwall.

> The Celts were no simple, mindless group of savage, barbarian tribes wandering Europe in a ruthless and bloody orgy as many writers over the centuries would have us believe. Celtic society was highly evolved and sophisticated and the Celts formulated and developed many fascinating concepts about themselves and about the world in which they lived. It was only at the height of the Celtic expansion that the writers of Greece and Rome began to speak of the Druids, not as priests, but as philosophers, educators, historians, doctors, astronomers and astrologers; in fact, as the native intellectual class of Celtic society.[1]

With a religion that forbade them to commit their teachings to writing, making their history difficult to follow, one of the earliest references comes from the invading Julius Caesar himself, who explained an aspect of Druidic beliefs that Dr Price reiterated in his latter years – the transmigration, or reincarnation of the soul. Caesar noted, 'A lesson which they take particular pains to inculcate is that the soul does not perish, but after death passes from one body to another; they think that this is the best incentive to bravery because it teaches them to disregard the terrors of death.'[1]

In fact Caesar, along with Diodonus Siculus, portrayed them with indifference and cruelty. From human sacrifice and climbing oaks to worshipping the moon and ritually cutting mistletoe, the early descriptions of the Celts and their Druids cannot be accepted as truth. What is apparent is that whereas the Druids were encouraged to become the new priests of Christianity, many pagan sites and festivals were also becoming incorporated into the 'new religion'.

In AD 601 Pope Gregory told his missionaries not to destroy pagan sites but convert them 'from worship of devils to the service of the true God'. Another of their early doctrines, which again coincides with Dr Price's own, was their positioning of fire at the central role of the primary religious experiences. The obsession with fire is of ancient origin. It is an aspect of the cult that enjoys a connection to Hinduism, another religion that Price and his contemporaries studied in great depth. It was their belief that Druids above all sought the cultivation of wisdom, creativity and love and were open to the inspiration of nature, which was at its very heart. It was also believed that services were held as the seasons turned, displaying a devotion of the natural world by celebrating the solstices and equinoxes four times during the year, which are dictated by the relationship between the earth and the sun.

The teachings of Druidic tradition came very much from the new enthusiasm in the subject that surfaced in Renaissance France during the sixteenth and seventeenth centuries. When classical writings were translated to English during this period, it led the way to a new infatuation with pre-Christian history. By then a number of influences converged to trigger an interest in the Druids once again and this gathered momentum. During the period of the Enlightenment, translations of classical texts describing ancient Druids became more readily available through the development of the printing press, and scholars became fascinated by the Greek and Roman accounts of pre-Christian religion.

Shortly, this indigenous religion became associated with the many mysterious monuments that scattered the land. One of those scholars was John Aubrey, who in 1649 wrote a sketch of ancient Wiltshire and claimed that the moments at Stonehenge were 'Temples of the Druids'.[2]

Aubrey had discussed his theories with Edward Lhuyd (1660–1709), the Celtic scholar of the Ashmolean Museum, Oxford, who agreed with him. His major work, *Archaeologia Britannica*, published in 1707, laid an important foundation to modern Celtic scholarship.

> Outwardly, the Celtic world was now 'at peace' with England. There had been no uprising in Cornwall since 1549. Ireland had been subdued during the Williamite Conquest of 1690–91. There had been no unrest in Wales since Tudor times and the Scottish Jacobite uprising had been suppressed in 1746. So it was by the mid 18th century that the English public were in a more receptive mood to believe in the romantic image of the Druids. Their association with the great stone circles, such as Stonehenge, seemed more acceptable.[1]

Probably the most important figure in the re-creation of Druidism was William Stukeley (1687–1765), the antiquarian of Lincolnshire who pioneered the investigation of the prehistoric monuments of Stonehenge and Avebury with his *The History of the Religion and Temples of the Druids*. He was also the first biographer of his friend, Isaac Newton. Also involved in the newly fashionable Freemasonry, he described himself as a Druid by believing that prehistoric megalithic monuments were part of the Celtic religion. Stukeley was a major figure in the early development of the modern movement known as Neo-Druidry. It was a concept that resulted in widespread interest, not just in Wales, but throughout the whole of the British Isles. In many of the larger cities, the 'Grand Lodges of the Ancient Order of Druids' were created to parade, worship and celebrate.

One of Stukeley's followers was William Blake (1757–1827), who remained greatly intrigued by the Druids and the concepts of his mentor. His close friend and fellow 'Neo-Druid' was William Owen Pughe, the Welsh lexicographer who helped Iolo Morganwg establish the Gorsedd of the Bards of Britain in London in 1792. This was the period of immense antiquarian study and imagination to recreate a new Druidic legacy. In fact, Wales was the part of Great Britain where the strongest Druidic traditions survived throughout the nineteenth century, but with the Druids represented as bards more than any other order. It was in the arena of the eisteddfod tradition that they began to flourish once more.

Theophilus Evans (1693–1767) published *Gweledigaethau y Bardd Cwsg* (Visions of the Sleeping Bard) in 1704, and in 1764 Evan Evans (1731–88), better known as Ieuan Bardd, published his *Specimens of the Poetry of the Ancient Welsh Bards*. He enthusiastically claimed that a Druidic literature had been discovered in Welsh poetry. Soon came Edward Jones's *Musical and Poetical Relics of the Welsh Bards and Druids* in 1784 and *The Bardic Museum of Primitive British Literature* in 1802. It was Welsh scholastic endeavours that had led to the foundation of the Cymmrodorion Society in London in 1751 for the publication of ancient Welsh texts, and the more radical Gwyneddigion, who sponsored an eisteddfod in Bala in 1789. Among its members at the time was the man who would have the most profound effect on the beliefs of Dr William Price. The renowned Edward Williams (1747–1826), better known by his bardic name, Iolo Morganwg, constructed a body of lore that he tried to pass off as ancient Druidism, which took scholars more than a century to expose as a fabrication.[3]

On meeting the Prince of Wales he introduced himself as 'Edward of Glamorgan' whereas on other occasions he referred to himself as a 'rattleskull genius', as in a noisy and empty man. He was indeed a cultural icon and phenomenon whose reputation as an influential antiquarian, poet, collector, and his tireless research and forgeries of historical literature, was unsurpassed in Wales. There were many elements to his character that could easily be recognised in one of his greatest protégés and disciples, Dr Price. An egotistical showman who displayed great eccentricity, mischievousness and frivolity, Iolo Morganwg's legacy cannot be overestimated.

Iolo was born on 10 March 1747 in Pen-Onn, near Llancarfan in the Vale of Glamorgan and raised in a small cottage in Flemingston, where he followed his father, Edward, into a career as a stone-cutter, tiler, plasterer, carpenter and joiner. His mother Ann was a descendant of the gentrified Mathews family of Llandaf, Radyr and Castell-y-Mynach. This was the same Mathews family whose descendant, Joan Davies of Gelliwastad, was the grandmother of Dr Price. Such a connection through family between Iolo and William seems more than appropriate, as not only their beliefs were shared but even their very bloodline and fascination in family pedigree. After all, they both had the wild streak of mischievousness and both appeared to court controversy wherever they went. For that matter, both had inflated egos, despite being particularly small men with a penchant for flamboyant and dandy costumes.

Iolo spoke both English and Welsh, although his education appears greatly limited as in school he was 'sullen and stubbornly silent' and sent home, claiming he learnt the alphabet by watching his father cut letters into gravestones. In latter years he claimed to have been taught elements of Welsh poetry by Sion Bradford, who was a student of the bardic system and collector of Welsh manuscripts. It was in this collection that Iolo said he found references to the bardic Gorsedd, which had survived in Glamorgan alone. Of Sion Bradford (a weaver descended of the family of which Bradford-on-Avon is named), Iolo asked him to 'step into the garden with him and taking out of his pocket a blue ribbon invested me with the insignia of the "Primitive Order of the Bards of the Isle of Britain"'.

During his early years in Glamorgan he displayed an interest in the surviving manuscripts of poets such as Lewis Hopkin, Rhys Morgan and Sion Bradford himself. When his mother died of consumption in August 1770, he claims to have wandered all over the country. In 1773 he joined his brothers on a visit to London and Kent in search of work, and while in the capital was introduced by fellow antiquarian Owen Jones to the Gwyneddigion Society, where he attended some of their meetings as a guest. On returning to Wales he married Margaret (Peggy) Roberts in St Mary Church, Llanfair.

As a businessman Iolo was a failure, and on one occasion was committed to the debtors' prison in Cardiff, where he was detained for a year. His wife shared a room with him and she became pregnant with their son, Taliesin, named after the early medieval Welsh bard.

Iolo's great concern was in preserving the literary and cultural heritage of Wales. When the English ironmasters began to exploit Glamorgan as the Norman lords had done centuries ago, Iolo genuinely feared that the culture of that county of his birth would be lost forever. In his attempt to preserve its celebrated past, he produced large collections of manuscripts, which he claimed would prove that the ancient Druidic bardic traditions had survived the Roman conquest, the coming of Christianity and the persecution of the bards under King Edward I. Through his elaborate forgeries he developed his imaginative, mystical philosophy, which he said was a direct continuation of the ancient Druidic tradition. His literary career spanned the years from 1770 to 1826, wherein he adapted romanticism and Arthurian legend to provide lyrical poetry and romantic history. Profoundly influenced by the work of Edward Lhuyd, he envisaged a wondrous future for Wales, and tried to invent a past upon which it could be built.

In 1789 he worked with William Owain Pughe to produce *Barddoniaeth Dafydd ab Gwilym*, a collection of poems from the fourteenth-century poet, several of which were Iolo's own early forgeries. The success of the folio saw him return to London, where he met many whose sympathies lay with the French Revolution, including Prince Talleyrand, Dr Benjamin Franklin and Thomas Paine. With the Gwyneddigion, who supported 'liberty', he also promised to visit the USA in 1792, in search of the 'Welsh Indians', descended from Madog ab Owain Gwynedd, who were said to have sailed from Abergele to Mobile Bay in 1169. In an effort to prepare himself for the journey, he followed the writings of Rousseau by reverting to nature and living in the forests, eating grass and sleeping under the stars. It actually led to him developing rheumatism and the entire expedition was abandoned.

On 21 June 1792 at Primrose Hill, London he founded the Gorsedd of the Bards of Ancient Britain, claiming it was based on ancient Druidic rites and linked to the Chair of Poetry where 'Merlin and Taliesin were Masters of Poetry under King Arthur'. The motto of his Chair, or 'Cadair', was '*Y Gwir Yn Erbyn Y Byd, Yn Enw Duw A'I Dangnef*' ('The Truth Against The World, In The Name of God and His Peace'). It was a piece of Iolo mythology that stood the test of time, as it continues to represent the very highlight of the National Eisteddfod of Wales.

He exaggerated the importance of small eisteddfodau where the bards of Glamorgan continued to meet in Dr Price's future home town of Llantrisant. A group was formed in the medieval town in 1771 to promote the Welsh language but there is no mention of the '*Brodoliaeth Beirdd Morganwg*' (the Brotherhood of the Bards of Glamorgan) taking place there.

Forever denouncing literary traditions of other Welsh counties in favour of Glamorgan being the pre-eminent vicinity of this bardic heritage, he referred to it as the 'Hen Ddosbarth' (The Old Order) which was also referred to as '*Dosbarth Morganwg*' (The Glamorgan Order). Iolo also wrote of the strict Welsh metres of writing poetry, which again he said had only been retained in Glamorgan. His aim was to assert Glamorgan as the true heart of Wales, where the purest survival of Welsh traditions existed. Iolo actually developed his own bardic alphabet, called '*Coelbren y Beirdd*', which was said to be the system of the Druids and consisted of twenty main letters and twenty others to represent elongated vowels and mutations. These were to be hewn on a four-sided wooden frame, known as '*peithynen*', and were the basis on which bards in Victorian Wales composed much of their works. The pieces of wood could be turned to read all four sides. *Coelbren y Beirdd* was a published as a book by Iolo's son in 1840 and illustrated the popularity of the alphabet with poets and Druids during the nineteenth century, until its authenticity was greatly questioned. It was also the basis of one of Dr Price's most elaborate and bewildering costumes.

However, many years later in 1893, J. Romilly Allen, the joint-editor of the *Achaeologia Cambrensis* wrote in a letter, 'I think the so-called Bardic Alphabet a gigantic fraud ... I don't believe you will find it repay you to look at these bogus alphabets and pseudo-Druidic antiquities as anything but the most bare-faced imposters.'

Iolo worked closely with Owen Jones and William Owen Pugh as editors of *The Myvyrian Archaeology of Wales*, a flawed magnum opus in a three-volume collection of medieval Welsh literature published between 1801 and 1807 to preserve 'the ancient manuscripts in the Welsh tongue'. In doing so he was not content to merely study the culture of the past, but compelled to add to it, and the scholars of his time failed to distinguish between the forgeries and the genuine. It was a collection of work that Dr Price prized in his collection, and we remain unsure as to whether the Treforest surgeon ever actually met Iolo on his visit to Newbridge, when Dr Price was twenty-six years of age. However, Price was closely connected to his son, Taliesin, following their initial introductions at the Cardiff Eisteddfod.

Following Iolo's death on 18 December 1826, his cottage in Flemingston was found to be crammed with manuscripts, and some of his collection was compiled into the *Iolo Manuscripts* by his son, Taliesin Williams. His papers were used by many scholars and translators, including Lady Charlotte Guest when producing the *Mabinogion*. Much of it was purchased by the Llanovers.

By the late 18th century, northern Glamorgan was one of the few places in Wales where the bards still followed their craft, a fact inflated by Iolo into a splendid extravaganza. He asserted that the traditions of the Welsh were older than those of any other country in Europe. The guardians of those traditions were the Druids, an order that had died out everywhere except in Glamorgan. He persuaded the Gwyneddigion to embrace his theories, they were published in 1792, the year in which Iolo organised his Gorsedd (assembly of bards) on Primrose Hill. Many gorseddau were subsequently held and in 1819 at Carmarthen Iolo succeeded in linking the gorsedd with the eisteddfod, a linkage which has lasted today.[4]

Iolo's forgeries represented a fusion of Christian and Arthurian influences and a romanticism similar to William Blake and the Scottish poet and forger James MacPherson, who also enthused about Celtic history. In Iolo's case however, his mental state was further tampered by an addiction to laudanum, to ease his physical troubles, which also stimulated the imagination and could develop a type of creative madness. He first used it during long periods of suicidal despair in London, which he loathed due to the dirt and squalor, to save him 'from the jaws of death'. In fact, ill health plagued him for most of his life. It was believed that the mason's dust affected his chest and he slept in an armchair for most of his later life.

Iolo's creativity was for a greater reason. He wanted to create for Wales, and Glamorgan in particular, a tradition and identity of which its people could be proud. The status of the Welsh language was lost with the Acts of Union under Henry VIII in 1536 and 1542, which effectively oppressed the Welsh people in the face of the imperialism of English. English was the language of authority and the emerging middle class in Wales, shattering the self-confidence of the Welsh people in themselves and their mother tongue. Gradually, however, it was gaining some respect as one of the recognised roots of many other languages, possibly the language of the Ancient Britons themselves, but this was a prestige that Iolo wanted to enhance. His ability to recreate a 'glorious past' also created a movement in its own right. Wales was changing in profound ways with the development of trade and mass migration to the industrial towns. There was a need to preserve and showcase Welsh culture to the rest of the world as it fell more and more under English dominance – a message that resonated well with his successors, including Lady Charlotte, Lady Llanover and even Dr Price. In fact, on his death, Lady Llanover purchased many of those manuscripts and had them installed at Llanover Court in Monmouthshire as a prized collection. Together Iolo and William inhabited many worlds and embraced many contradictory views, and nothing about either of them is straightforward. Iolo was part of an entire movement of imaginative myth-makers, which was paralleled by those across other parts of Europe who transcribed and even forged literature.

Modern scholarship has shown conclusively that there is no historical foundation for Iolo's account of the development of the Gorsedd and for the alleged connection between the professional strict-metre bards and the ancient Druids. Nevertheless, it is beyond question that this aspect of his work exercised a powerful influence on very many of his contemporaries, for it was Iolo who was pre-eminently responsible for transforming the old bardic assembly into a national institution, which became an important focus for many of the literary and cultural activities of Wales, where the warm romantic glow that so enchantingly suffused the essays in which he discussed the old bardic meetings, some of which probably never existed outside his own creative imagination, proved to be a factor of great importance in the remarkable development of the eisteddfod in the 19th century.[3]

The Gorsedd was the champion of Wales, her culture, language and history and for that very reason alone, Iolo became hugely respected throughout the country. His influence over others was widespread and bordered on the magnificent, and despite subsequent discoveries of forgeries among his work, we continually turn to the Gorsedd as his greatest inspiration of all. As he said, 'Preserve your language ... and above all, take care to safeguard her entire Gorsedd; that is her crown and splendour, and your own great witness as Welshmen that you are, from the beginning, the First among the Nations'.[5]

Iolo's immense popularity and influence found significant footholds in many aspects of Welsh life, and nowhere was this better represented than in the sleepy hamlet of Newbridge. It was located in a broad bowl between Llanwynno and Llanfabon, the two mountains and parishes on either side of the Taff Valley. It was here that the romantic fiction of Iolo, perpetuated by his son, created a fanaticism for Druidic lore that attracted the interests of many local figures of note, of which Dr William Price was one of the most celebrated.

The autocratic priesthood, with its human sacrifices, transmigration of souls, sacred groves and holy mistletoe, is changed almost beyond recognition in the 19th century version. The grave old priest, sage beneath the spreading oak, has become, in the latter day Druid, the embodiment of the traditional wisdom of the ages and an adherent of the ancient patriarchal religion, reverencing the sun as the symbol of the Creator, interpreting the cosmic meaning of natural objects such as moving stones, a master of the oldest measures of poetry and a diviner of secret things. Such a man could be no ordinary mortal. And the vein of superiority plainly visibly must be significant to the psychologist. The general air of esoteric obscurity is enhanced by the mystic significance given to Glamorgan as the home of Druidism, and the Welsh language as the medium of the sacred learning.[6]

Newbridge had a unique draw for this Neo-Druidic following, due to the famous Rocking Stone of Coedpenmaen Common. The Rocking Stone, or *Y Maen Chwyf* to give its Welsh translation, stands on the edge of the steep cliff to the east of the River Taff. Consisting of pennant sandstone, which is common in the locality, it weighs around 9½ tons and is supported by a natural rock platform that was probably moved there during Ice-Age glacial action. *Y Maen Chwyf* was considered by Iolo's disciples as a primitive Druidic temple or sacred altar for the Druids and even a burial ground for their ancestors.

Morien recalled, 'Whether the stone is there as a monument of some renowned, but forgotten chieftain, or as an old Druidical altar or centre of worship, we have no records for our guide. But the Eglwysilan mountain, or Bryn Arian as it was formerly called was the burying place of men who had attained eminence before the ground was desecrated by the foot of the Saxon.'[7]

Morien, one of the questionable disciples of Iolo, wrote the greatly fabricated history of Newbridge and its neighboring Rhondda. In it he claimed that

> Lewis Evans (Lewis y Saer) who died in the 1880s, well remembered an eisteddfod in 1815 being held at the New Inn Hotel, then kept by a bard named Gwilym Morganwg, whose surname was Williams. But what lends additional interest to that gathering is that the celebrated Welsh antiquary, Iolo Morganwg and Gwilym Morgan, a banner carried in front of hem, walked at the head of a procession over Taav Street and then over the great bridge and on to the Rocking Stone on the Common above. Ancient ceremonies were performed on the great stone by Iolo in the role of Y Gwyddon or Odin, the ArchDruid, not the least interesting being sheathing the State Sword of Wales, to convey the valuable lesson, as in Gethsemane, that there is more credit sheathing the sabre than in drawing it forth among the sons of men. Nowhere else in Wales is the sublime lesson now taught.[8]

A notice announced that a '*Cadair* and Eisteddfod' (Chair and Eisteddfod) would be held at Y Maen Chwyf, Pont-y-ty-prydd on the day of the full moon on 1 August 1814 to 'write verse on various subjects, and especially on the Restoration of Peace, and to grant a degree and honour in poetry to all who may deserve it'. The subject of peace remains central to the Gorsedd tradition today.

Y Maen Chwyf was the location for this colourful event where Iolo met with Gwilym Morganwg and sat on the stone, writing poetry as the crowd gathered. Gwilym was initiated as a bard at the ceremony and his poem 'Heddwch' (Peace) was declared at the 'Gorsedd of Morganwg Upon The Maen Chwyf'.

Gwilym Morganwg, born Thomas Williams in 1778 and the son of a miller from Llanddeti in Breconshire, settled in Cefncoedycymmer in 1781 and became a colliery boy in the Cyfarthfa Ironworks. In 1807 he moved to Newbridge to become landlord of the Butchers Arms with his wife, and on her death moved to the New Inn and became one of the most prominent figures in the eisteddfod movement in Newbridge from 1813 onwards. He held them regularly in the public house where the Merthyr Tydfil Cymreigyddion Society and the Pontypridd Cymreigyddion Society competed with fellow districts. Becoming another of the disciples of Iolo, he took the name of the county of his adoption for his bardic name, becoming the 'father' of Druidism in Newbridge. A poet and prose writer with an obsession for the history of the ancient Britons, he was a frequent competitor in the eisteddfodau held in Wales and London through the Cymreigyddion and Gwyneddigion. At the age of fifty-seven he was injured in an accident at Builth and never fully recovered. His son submitted his last essay to a local eisteddfod on his death and the adjudicator, Revd T. Price (Carnhuanawc), awarded the first prize posthumously.

Gwilym placed a notice in Seren Gomer stating a Gorsedd would be held on Alban Arthan (21 December) 1814 and the bards and poets were invited to attend to compete on a choice of nine subjects that included 'The Excellence of Brotherly Love', 'The Excellence of the Welsh Language', 'A View of a Wicked Heat', 'The Burial of the Sword', 'Y Maen Chwyf' and 'The Fall of the Miserly'. He invited Iolo and Taliesin to attend.

On 21 March 1815, Gwilym recited his poem 'Twyll y Melinydd' (The Miller's Deceit) at Y Maen Chwyf and kept his regular meetings of *Cymdeithas Y Maen Chwyf* at the New Inn, with one on 21 June 1825, at which the subject was 'Pont Y Tŷ Prydd, The Biggest, Single-Arch Stone Bridge, Maybe in the World'.

Gwilym Morganwg and his successor's fantasies, not unlike Iolo's, were intended to recreate local history and raise the area of Newbridge into an almost spiritual Druidic settlement. Morien is also guilty of this, as his book rambles on in an inarticulate manner as he attempts to explain local place names with a Druidic bent:

> the district was a great central one for national gatherings, when the religion of the Oak Groves was the national religion. The Druids, strange to say, called themselves Mabinogion, or Adherents of the Baby Son ... Now it is perfectly clear by the local place names that in very remote times, the drama of the Creation of the world and the Sun was on the occasions of the Gymmanvas, performed here with the Rocking Stone as the centre around which the performances took place.[9]

It was suggested several bardic meetings took place there, with one presided over by Iolo's son, who adopted the full bardic name of Taliesin ab Iolo Morganwg, in 1834. The schoolmaster and poet accepted his 'poisoned chalice' of forgeries, publishing much of his father's work to ensure his spirit, hopes and dreams remained fulfilled, never realising much of it was due to his own colourful imagination. Such a fact says much of the Neo-Druids of Newbridge.

Taliesin had been inaugurated an 'ovate in absentia' at his father's famous Gorsedd meeting in Primrose Hill in 1792, when he was only five years old, and fulfilled his father's ambition by attending the Gorsedd at Y Maen Chwyf with his father in 1815. An ardent competitor in the eisteddfod, apart from the success he attained at the 1834 Cardiff Eisteddfod presented by Dr Price, his essay on *Coelbren y Beirdd* was the winning piece at the Abergavenny Eisteddfod, patronised by the Llanovers in 1838. That day an open carriage held twelve harpists to lead the magnificent procession of bards, Ancient Order of Druids, Gorsedd, Archdruid and others.

A review of the competition by W. Rees of Llandovery in 1840 read,

> This is one of the most successful essays on a *vexata* question that it has been our good fortune ever to witness. When Iolo Morganwg and Dr Owen Pughe some year ago, published to the world certain characters, alleged to have been the Alphabet of the Primitive Britons, forasmuch as they did so merely on the authority of oral tradition, they failed in convincing the generality of their fellow-countrymen as to its genuineness. The more skeptical, indeed, proceeded so far as to palm its very invention on the forenamed persons. Nor were the feelings of doubt and suspicion likely to be diminished, when not a single candidate was found to aspire to the premium which the Cardiff Eisteddvod [sic] held out on the subject; indeed, an eminent Welsh scholar, rather illogically it must be confessed, considered this negative circumstance as conclusion against the claims of the 'Coelbren. However, after a while a similar appeal was made by the Abergavenny Eisteddvod, which was held in 1838, and the result was the treatise in question, which was pronounced by the learned judge at the time as 'one of the most extraordinary and important productions that had ever come under his notice, either as a prize composition or one of any other description'.

Y Maen Chwyf featured as a leading story in the *Cardiff & Merthyr Guardian* as early as February 1835 when it announced,

> Y Maen Chwyf (the Rocking Stone) of Coed-pen-maen in the parish of Eglwysilan, Glamorganshire, above the turnpike to Cardiff. From this spot may be seen the celebrated one-arched bridge over the Taff near Newbridge and the views of several ramifications of the neighbouring

hills and valleys. The romantic vale of Rhondda extends to the west and a little nearer we have the salmon-leap, and fall of the Taff under Craig-yr-Hesg to the north west the equally beautiful vale of Cynon meets the eye, and the rugged charm of mountains which divide that valley from the upper portion of the Vale of Tale, and from the parish of Merthyr Tydfil, the great metropolis of Britain ironworks. To the south-east the woods which fringe the Taff in its course towards Cardiff add to the varied beauty of the scene; nor is it quite uninteresting to the tourist to learn, that just at the foot of the abrupt fall of this hill, he will be accommodated at the Bridgewater Arms, a comfortable inn, situated in the midst of most enchanting scenery.

The name of the hill, Coed-Pen-Maen (viz the Wood of the Stone Summit), is doubtless derived from this stone, which in primitive ages, under the Druidic theology, was venerated as the sacred altar on which the Druidic offered in the face of the sun and in the eye of the light, their praises to the Great Creator. The ground around the stone is at present a bare sheep walk, but the higher ground to the east is still covered with wood. The superficial contents of this stone are about 100 square feet, it contains about 250 cubic feet. It is a sort of rough argillaceous sand stone, which generally accompanies the coal measures of this part of the country. A moderate application of strength will give it considerable motion. The underside slopes around to centre and it stand nearly in equilibrium beneath.

The prevalent opinion of the surrounding inhabitants respecting this ancient stone is that the Druids gained nobility in this country by pretending to work miracles from it and that they offered human sacrifices thereon, vulgar errors! The Maen Chwyf is rarely mentioned by ancient Welsh authors but the Maen Llog (Stone of Benefit) and the Maen Gorsedd (Stone of the Supreme Seat) is frequently occurs. These were the central stones, encompassed by circles of stones at various distances, that constituted the Druidic temples, when worship in the face of the Sun was solemnised, institutional instructions imparted and bardic evaluations and inaugurations solemnized. That the Maen Chwyf and Cromlech, such as Kit's Coity House, near Aylesford were used for such central means, cannot be reasonably doubted.

Several bardic congresses have recently been held at this stone. The late distinguished Bard, the profound Welsh antiquary, Iolo Morganwg (Edwards Williams of Glamorganshire) presided there in 1815 at the conclusion of the late war.

The Gorsedd held there took place on Monday, September 23 1834, the 21st, the exact time of the equinox and of our annual bardic festivals, giving fallen on a Sunday. This Gorsedd would have taken place at the period of the Grand Royal Eisteddfod held the proceeding month

at Cardiff, but that the indispensable notice of a year and a day had
not expired from the first announcement. At this Gorsedd, Taliesin ab
Iolo Morganwg, (son of-above named Iolo Morganwg) who gained the
chair-medal at that eisteddfod, as well as the beautiful medal given by
the Princess Victoria and the Duchess of Kent, presided, having opened
it with the very ancient Welsh proclamation usual on such occasions. At
the Gorsedd, the assembly adjourned to the house of Gwilym Morganwg,
this person and Taliesin Williams are the two Welsh Bards regularly
initiated into the arena of Druidism now existing, at Newbridge, where
an Eisteddfod was held in adjudicate the prize for the best Welsh ode
in honour of Rev.. William Bruce Knight, Chancellor of the Diocese of
Llandaff and Senior Judge of Cardiff Eisteddfod.[10]

When Taliesin held his eisteddfod at Y Maen Chwyf on 22 September
1834, the bards met at the New Inn before climbing the mountainside,
led by harpist Gwilym Ddu Glan Cynon (Richard Williams of Merthyr),
followed by Taliesin, who held his sword by the point, Gwilym Morganwg
and Gwilym Ilid (William Jones of Caerphilly) followed by a certain
character named Myfyr Morganwg.

As with Gwilym Morganwg, there was also a growing desire for the
Newbridge Druids to use the bardic name of Morganwg, both as a
symbol of their love for the County of Glamorgan (Morganwg being the
Welsh translation) and ultimately for their respect of Iolo himself. The
most prominent of these was Evan Davies (1801–88), a clockmaker who
took the bardic name of Myfyr Morganwg (The Scholar of Glamorgan)
and settled in Newbridge in 1844, and, according to Morien, 'he was
universally known as the Archdruid, having succeeded Taliesin ap Iolo
Morganwg to that dignity in 1847'. More of Myfyr to come, for he was
instrumental in developing Y Maen Chwyf still further during his period
in Newbridge, with a vision of creating an elaborate serpent of standing
stones leading to the mighty rocking stone itself.

The best that can be said for Neo-Druidism is that it was the dream
of men who refused to accept the recorded view of the history of their
country and who refurbished the past by inventing traditions which
mirrored their own aspirations. They sought refuge in the Wales of
their imaginations at a time when understanding their country's history,
language and literature had long been neglected.

Among a dispossessed people, the main objective was not so much
to demonstrate the intrinsic qualities of the Welsh language and its
literature, as to show that the Welsh people had an honourable place
in the British scheme of things – indeed, that they alone should be
considered the true Britons. Iolo's claims for his native and beloved

Glamorgan found fertile ground in the minds of Newbridge men, and his influence lingered in the district for long after his death in 1826.[9]

During the 1830s, signs of development of Newbridge were becoming more apparent. Although a market for the local agricultural population existed there as far back as 1805, its gradual growth was due to the development of Treforest and the Newbridge Chain works. By 1840, when the Taff Valley Railway opened, linking the expanding Welsh coalfields to Cardiff, Newbridge was developing into a significant market town to cater for this part of the South Wales valleys. No one had anticipated the enormous growth of the Rhondda coal industry, turning the lush green Rhondda into something of a vast black Klondike as those early mining pioneers penetrated indiscriminately into the valley floor for their precious 'black gold'. It was an event that had a tremendous effect on Newbridge, as the town found it was ideally placed for transporting coal to the docks at Cardiff. As the region produced most of the coal and iron on which the economy of the British Empire depended, the peak of production in 1913 saw 57 million tons of steam coal pass through the town to Barry and Cardiff per year. Pontypridd, as it then became known, had the longest railway platform in Britain in an effort to cope with its 500 trains and 11,000 passengers per day.

Although by the late 1830s the population was still below 2,000 people, the town had already become recognised as a lawless and disease-ridden place that required its own police force, consisting of a sergeant and six constables. Gwilym Morganwg's New Inn, originally a farmhouse dating from the 1730s, grew to become a popular hotel for the town and also a law court. Gelliwastad Farm, the home of Dr Richard Griffiths, was also to be found on the west of the River Taff as another landmark building in the growing boom years, which saw neighbouring properties built with stone coming from Craig yr Hesg quarry. So important was Griffiths to the development of the town that one area was named due to his entrepreneurship. Once the busiest coal-dram centre in the country, horse-drawn drams emptied on his tram road from Gyfeillion Colliery and Coffin's Dinas enterprise to the Machine Bridge in Treforest. The drams were literally 'tumbled' to allow laden drams passage to the Doctor's Canal, giving the name of 'The Tumble' to an area of Newbridge that exists to this day.

The opening of chapels in the vicinity is a clear indication of the need for religious worship by an expanding population. Carmel Chapel at Graigwen was the first of the nonconformist chapels to open in 1810, followed by Penuel Calvinistic Methodist Chapel in 1812. By 1834 a third chapel, Sardis, opened its doors to an ever-growing congregation.

Among this population growth came even more supporters of Iolo Morganwg's teachings, multiplying the Neo-Druidic community of

Newbridge. Over the coming years these men would create a circle of poets known locally as *Clic Y Bont* ('the bridge clique'). There was Dewi Haran (David Evans, 1812–85); Dewi Wyn O Essyllt (Thomas Essile Davies, 1820–91); Camelian (Cosleff Cosleff, 1834–1910); Glanffrwd (William Thomas, 1843–90); and Brynfab (Thomas Williams, 1848–1927), to mention only a few of the clique's leading members, and all were men of some substance and not without literary ability.

> They gave Pontypridd a literary identity at a time when the town was beginning to need one. Pontypridd was still only a random assembly of industrial undertakings of one sort or another. It consisted of hastily thrown up and unsanitary houses, deemed good enough by the coal owners and ironmasters for workers and their families to live in, and it was a place where local government was still embryonic and politics still at a semi-feudal stage of development. Still, the town was nevertheless the meeting place of this small group of writers who met regularly to discuss and practise their craft.[8]

Dr William Price did not always agree with the versions of Neo-Druidry being expressed by members of the *Clic* or those who attended various celebrations at Y Maen Chwyf. By the mid-1830s, already recognised for his notable authority on Welsh history, which in itself may have stemmed from the corrupted tales of Iolo, Price was embracing Druidry in an obsessive and addictive manner. By the end of the decade, the first accounts talk of him growing his black hair beyond shoulder length, accompanied by a thick beard, and gradually his colourful style of dress began to imitate those visions that were generally accepted as being Druidic. As middle age approached, Dr Price did little to endear himself to the Maen Chwyf Druids, acting as the renegade among them and courting controversy wherever he went. His determination to establish himself as the all-knowing leader of the cult also caused a rift with the fellow worshippers.

The manifestation of Druidry in his mind was further inspired when a new figure entered his life in 1834. William Crawshay I died in that year and his son, William II, to whom Dr Price was closely associated, was forced to turn his attentions solely to the Cyfarthfa Works. In doing so he presented the role of manager of the Treforest Tinplate and Ironworks to his second eldest son, Francis Crawshay. In Francis, Dr Price found his greatest ally. Both fascinated by Druidic lore, Egyptian and Greek history, along with an interest in Hindu literature and creeds, the new-found friends became soulmates in their desire to learn, examine and fulfil their lives as the ancient bards had done. Together their already vivid imaginations ran wild, one further inspiring the other in their unquenchable thirst for knowledge.

Francis was an interesting and enigmatic member of the Crawshay dynasty.

He possessed, in many respects, the leading characteristics of the family and in the addition had an eccentric vein which remained more or less marked to the end. Like all his family, he was fearless to a degree. He is said to have sailed down the Taff in a flood, when that usually demure stream was lashed into a fury. One time wishing to feel the full force of a mountain storm, he braved a furious gale on the Beacons with his brother Robert, when the stoutest of the Herculean rail men, who had staked the tent down with pegs of iron, fled in dismay.[10]

On coming to Treforest he also inherited his father's ambition to modernise the Treforest Mill. It was one of a number of projects that his grandfather, William Crawshay I, had criticised and the project was halted in 1831 when a general recession hit the industry which ultimately led to the Merthyr Rising. By 1833 the rebuilding of the mill had yet to be completed and it was suggested to William II, by his associate Robert Moser, to wait until his father's death for fear of losing his chances of inheriting the family fortunes. He took the advice and returned to Cyfarthfa as heir apparent, showing no further interest in Treforest. The modernisation was delegated to the twenty-three-year-old Francis and it was back in production by 1836. A stone plaque on the site bears the family motto of 'Perseverance', which may have reflected the problems encountered in undertaking the modernisation process.

As were all the boys in the family, he was encouraged to show an interest in the industry, but it was his elder brother William Crawshay III who was being groomed as heir to the Cyfarthfa works. His younger brother, Henry (1812–79) also showed great promise as an ironmaster, but Francis was considered rather eccentric even at an early age and was something of a worry to his father. He was very popular with the workers, however, most of whom spoke only Welsh and Francis was the only Crawshay to become truly fluent. In 1839 William III died in an accident while crossing the Severn Estuary. Francis was next in line, but his extravagant behaviour ruled him out. Eventually Cyfarthfa passed on to Robert Thompson Crawshay (1817–79), the eldest son of William's second marriage ... Francis thus lost his chance of becoming the last of the great 'Iron Kings' and was relegated to manager of the Trefforest (*sic*) outpost.[11]

Sadly, the Treforest works continually failed to make a profit under Francis, and only by pooling the accounts with the thriving Hirwaun and

Cyfarthfa could the tinplate works survive. Francis, or 'Mr Frank' to the workers, was blamed for inept management and would prefer to spend the day shooting rabbits on the Crawshay's property of Barry Island than run the Treforest enterprise. Such was his love for the coastal haven that it was known as 'Crawshay's rabbit shooting box' and one wonders whether Dr Price ever accompanied him on one of his 'expeditions'. Clearly 'Perseverance' was not shared by Francis and possibly the placing of it in Treforest was aimed at him as much as the workers themselves.

Francis blamed the losses of the company on the inadequate and unsuitable machinery at the works. Not a single steam engine was found on the site during the inventory of the works in 1842, and the machinery was run off just eight waterwheels. Francis argued that Nant y Fforest was not adequate as a power source and during the modernisation a weir was built over the River Taff with an adjoining sluice down to the mill. With the advent of the steam engine, such a project was rendered unnecessary.

Eventually Francis took control of both the Hirwaun and the Treforest works, which worked well as a single unit with Hirwaun supplying the Treforest tinplate factory. Pig iron and bar iron, the material to be tin-plated, travelled from Hirwaun via the Aberdare and Glamorgan Canals and was unloaded for Treforest near Glyntaf, at the weighing machine. The iron was then loaded onto the tinplate works' trams. The tram road followed the river downstream as far as the weir at Castle Inn Bridge, where it continued to the tin mills by way of a route alongside and above the feeder.

It was a hazardous job for the workers, with little protection from the dangers it could cause, including the crippling 'doublers' cut', which could sever the tendons on the front of the worker's ankle as they attempted to double the tin sheets. It was such injuries that Dr Price was required to treat and he, above all, knew of the many horrific injuries sustained in the tinplate works as well as the neighbouring chain works on an almost daily basis.

Francis remained in Treforest for thirty years, although his interests in the industry to which he was assigned dwindled as they became less and less profitable and more of a hindrance to himself and his overcritical father. In 1858 William threatened Francis with the closure of the Hirwaun works under his command and the latter began building a new ironworks at Treforest that was to be fired by coal from Troedyrhiw, the colliery he bought in 1856. The new ironworks was to be sited in the grounds of Forest Isaf farm, a mile from the tinplate works. The Crawshay residence, Forest House, was halfway between the two industries. With the death of Francis's father in 1867, he grew more disinterested than ever in Treforest and placed it in the hands of a manager, William Griffiths, allowing Francis to enjoy his retirement in Sevenoaks, Kent where he grew more and more eccentric, including wearing naval dress and striking large bells at his home, Bradbourne Hall.

> Francis's eccentricities excluded him from inheriting the Crawshay empire. No doubt the relatively minor poet that was bestowed upon him was intended as a steadying influence, but instead only added weight to his extravagance ... as a young man Francis was most indignant in his wish to be part of the workforce and not aloof from them. This was undoubtedly the real reason for his learning Welsh, his self confessed desire to 'curse his workers in the vernacular' being a cleverly disguised tool in his quest for acceptability...

Francis was alleged to have fathered many illegitimate children with local women and employees, some would argue in the region of twenty-eight to thirty in total. He would ensure each of them received £100 and a future job, either in the tinplate works if a boy, or in his own household if a girl. The 'free love' ideals, which he shared with Dr Price, were ignored by his long-suffering wife Laura, herself a Crawshay before marriage as she was the daughter of Richard Crawshay II, Francis's own uncle. His affinity with the workers was further strengthened during a cholera epidemic in 1849 when he refused to leave Hirwaun and stayed helping those suffering from the disease, also establishing churches and chapels locally, even though he was not a Christian. Again, this was an aspect of his character shared with Dr Price.

In his latter years Price exclaimed, 'I believe in nothing except what I know to be absolutely in existence. I use the Bible as it ought to be used. It is clear to me that Abraham was a cannibal, and it was the view of destroying that trait in the nature of his descendants, and to raise tame animals that the first pyramid in Egypt was built.'

Price hated the gloom of the chapels and despised sanctimonious preachers, who he said only led people at funerals. He felt religion had been used to enslave, claiming, 'Man is greater than God. For Man created God in his own image.' The only deity in his life was nature itself. 'Worship! Why I tell you, I worship nothing, I have not seen anybody or anything greater than myself to worship. All I do is ... chant a song of the Primitive Bard to the moon.' He once said, 'Preachers are paid to teach that the world of thieves and oppressors, of landlords and landowners, is a just world. Their theology is the doctrine that the powers that be are ordained by God.'

While at Hirwaun Francis refused to live in the large Crawshay house there, preferring a small cottage near the ironworks with a huge block of inscribed coal hanging outside. In Treforest the family resided in Castle House before moving to Forest House, where he and Laura raised nine children, after whom a number of streets in the community were named, including Laura Street, Francis Street, Tudor Street and Owen Street. Forest House, during his tenure, was the dominant family manor that overlooked their industrial concerns. It was here that Dr Price spent much of his time, not only sharing ideals and becoming embroiled in late-night debates, but also to attend many of the extravagant parties and balls, fuelled by William's favourite tipple of champagne.

Francis and William also shared a passion for building towers and follies. One of Francis's was the folly on Hirwaun Common, built in 1849, which he said would fortify his family against any worker's uprisings, a trend established by the Joseph and Crawshay Bailey ironmasters and relatives, who were so unpopular they built fortified towers for their own protection in Nantyglo. Francis's folly at Hirwaun was a single round tower with a diameter of around 18 feet, measuring 33 feet high with three floors, each containing only one room. He resided there during the summer, using it for hunting, and he later added two small brass cannon, such was his sense of humour. In Treforest he built another tower, of iron, near the summit of the Graig Mountain, overlooking the Treforest Works from the west. Known as the Glass Tower or Iron Tower, it was in place by around 1850. Local folklore even goes so far as to explain that this was used as a secret hideaway, particularly for Dr Price during his many skirmishes with the local magistrate and debtor's courts! In front of the tower lay a stone with the words, indicating Crawshay's atheism:

> Duw ni feddaf
> Haf ni ofalaf
> Gauaf ni theimlaf
> Angau ni ofnaf

It translated into:

> I have no God
> I heed no summer,
> I feel no winter
> I fear not death.

Francis was also influenced by the intensive Druidic gatherings in the area, and whereas they worshipped the standing stones of their ancestors, Francis began to create his own obelisks and stone circles on his property. 'The quiet folks of Treforest were startled by midnight processions to the graveyards, by day processions of Druids, and many a performance which had more or less conspicuous a dry humour about them.'[12]

The Crawshay quarry behind Forest House produced Pennant sandstone for such monuments. One of his first obelisks appeared in front of Castle House and bore his initials, along with those of his brother Henry, and was dated 1844. Around the base reads, 'I am a model of the only obelisk now standing at Heliopolis on of [*sic*] the scriptures erected by Osortsen – the earliest of Pharaohs.' Price and Crawshay's admiration for ancient Egypt, with its sun worship as with Druidry, was identified here. Other obelisks appeared in Treforest, one of which was erected in the newly opened church at Glyntaff in memory of his son Richard, who died in 1848 before his first birthday. The almost pagan memorial was altered before it could be erected in the graveyard in 1848 to include the words 'Suffer the little children to come unto me', thus appeasing the concern of the local clergy.

Obelisks later became fashionable as funerary monuments, and ironically the largest examples in Glyntaff Cemetery and Saron Chapel Graveyard both retain a link with Francis Crawshay. The former was erected in memory of William Morgan (d. 1901), an inhabitant of Forest House; and the latter a manager of Trefforest and Pentyrch Tinplate Works and inhabitant of Castle House, Benjamin Rees (d. 1907).

Francis Crawshay's other monuments followed the style and pattern of the Bronze Age megalith builders. He erected many standing stones in the grounds of his home, and at Forest House placed a large stone with the names and years of birth of the males of the Crawshay family beginning with William in 1650. At the time of his death in 1878 Francis estimated there were twenty or more standing stones in the grounds, and in his will directed his son Tudor to collect them into a circle, for which he would inherit the house. In essence, his last act was to order the creation of a Druidic temple as a monument to the Crawshay family.

Even during his retirement in Kent, he continued to display his appeal for practical jokes and created an air of eccentricity among the local population. During his eight years at Bradbourne Hall he placed a large bell in front of the property. Cast in Lyon in 1871 and weighing more than 2 tons, it was the largest bell in Kent after Canterbury Cathedral's Great Dunstain. At regular intervals during the day he would chime it, much to the displeasure of the neighbouring villages. One of his surviving monolithic stones in the area is listed by English Heritage and 'thought to have been fashioned and erected by order of the then owner Francis Crawshay (1811–78) of the Crawshay Family of Cyfarthfa Castle, Merthyr Tydfil: the Crawshays were among the leading late eighteenth and early nineteenth century ironmasters in South Wales, and owned iron tinplate works in the Merthyr Tydfil area. Francis Crawshay was a member of the Order of Druids of Wales'.

Dr William Price's own largely self-taught knowledge of ancient history, Druidism, the bardic tradition and his devotion to Welsh customs like the eisteddfod, made him a favourite among those figures whose devotion lay in showcasing the culture of Wales. He became an active participant in the eisteddfodau held by the Cymreigyddion Society of Newbridge or 'Cymreigyddion y Maen Chwyf' and in 1837, the year that Victoria took to the throne, he offered £10 in prizes at a local eisteddfod – £1 each for the best essay on the subjects of Love, Pride, Belief, Faith, Superstition, Prejudice, Fame, Opinion, Profit and Truth. There is no account of the success of the eisteddfod itself and the very little reported news of Newbridge during that period was overshadowed by the extreme spread of influenza, which was, according to the Cardiff & Merthyr Guardian, 'raging in this place and has been fatal in so many cases; there is not a house in the town but some of the members are afflicted and in several of them the whole are laid up and unable to render the least assistance to teach other. The measles also prevail among children, with a serious fatality.' Dr Price had more than his fair share of home visits to conduct.

A further news item in the same periodical of April 1837 also relates to Dr Price and his respected knowledge of history:

A labourer lately employed in opening of a stone quarry in Cwm Rhondda, when four feet below the surface, came unexpectedly to a portion of earth ... that shaped as if a human body had mouldered there – close to the side of this impress he found an old brass battle axe. This student weapon had a groove on each side, as if for the purpose of fastening the handle. It is in the possession of Mr Price, surgeon, Porth-y-glo. The quarry is rented by a son of Gwilym Morganwg, who has a similar weapon in his possession, which his father found many years ago in a limestone quarry...

Aside from his medical practice, the mythology surrounding Y Maen Chwyf was becoming more and more overwhelming in his mind. An obsession with what Dr Price and other Druids perceived as the Primitive Temple to the Bard was of huge importance in the preservation of Welsh culture and history. It was with this in mind he began the process of appealing for public funds to preserve the monumental relics of Y Maen Chwyf by erecting a tower, 100 feet high, around them at the cost of £1,000. His dream to create a showcase for the Welsh people and their history was clear; this would be the centre of Welsh culture that would celebrate its heritage and great bardic traditions.

A document printed on 7 March 1838 by W. Bird of Cardiff on behalf of Dr Price was entitled 'Y Maen Chwyf' and makes fascinating reading. It again refers to the Druids as the 'Aborigines of Wales', a message made by Iolo himself.

The Bill read,

My lords, ladies and gentlemen! I beg to call your attention, and all those who feel interested in the Preservation of the Ancient Institutions and Antiquities of Britain, and especially to this PRIMITIVE TEMPLE, 'Y MAEN CHWYF'. This Druidic Temple is situated on Coedpenmaen Common, on the left of the Taff near Ponty y Tŷ Perydd, on the verge of the precipice, a little north-east of Ynysangharad Works.

In the immediate vicinity of this temple, the graves of the aborigines occupy a space of about 40,000 square yards. While the population of this neighbourhood continued to follow agriculture, Y Maen Chwyf was in no danger of being injured, as the hereditary veneration which descended from father to son, through successive generations, was sufficient to shield it from rude hands. *But it is not so now.*

The legions of artificers, manufacturers and strangers that advance on this place from all directions, have no idea of reverence for this beautiful temple. Hence it is that some few years ago an attempt was made to destroy it. Mr Thomas of Ynysangharad heard of it just in time to save it from ruin.

From this brief history, then, it appears that it requires no great genius to foretell the fate that awaits this most ancient monument.

Under this impression, it was suggested to '*Cymdeithas y Maen Chwyf*', that a Tower of one hundred feet high be built by public subscription near Y Maen Chwyf; the space within the Tower to be divided into eight apartments for a Museum, and surmounted with a Camera Obscura. This Tower will command a horizon of ten miles radius. And that a spacious house, some distance from Y Maen Chwyf, be built for the Bard of the Society to reside in, to take care of the temple.

This proposition has been unanimously seconded by the Society and the whole neighbourhood, as will be seen by the subscriber's names, in the order given. The estimated cost of these erections is £1000. The revenue of the Tower will be about £100 per annum. With the greater part of this sum the Society will establish a Free School, to be kept by the Bard of the Society, for educating the children of the poor. The remainder will go to defray the expenses of the institution. In this way, Y Maen Chwyf will not only be preserved, but will continue to operate as a mighty engine of civilisation, the Nucleus of a Museum, the parent of the tower that is destined to protect it, and to dispense the blessings of education to the industrious classes of the community.

Y MAEN CHWYF will represent the seed, the tower, the tree, and the inimitable landscape of the Camera Obscura, the fruit of knowledge. A question has been asked us, will the brinker landlords – viz Lord Dynevor, B. Hall Esq, M.P., J. Bassett, Esq., Mrs Morgan, the Hon R.H. Clive, and the Marquess of Bute, permit the Bards to protect and preserve their temple! Our answer has been and is, WE HAVE NO DOUBT they will not only charter our prescriptive right to protect the Druid's temple,

but express their sense of approbation by directing their names to be added to the list of subscribers for its preservation,–
'One common cause makes millions of one breast,
Slaves of the East, or Helots of the Wqesy;
On Andes' or on Athos' peaks unfurll'd,
The self-same standard streams o'er either world.'

As some may question the applicability of the word Temple, at the present day, to designate an immense rude and poised fragment of the Rock, on an elevated plain, with no other covering than that of the sky, I beg leave most humbly to submit, that it is infinitely more deserving of that term, than the Temple of Jupiter Ammon, in Thebes. As none will dispute, I think Thomson's description of this Temple, not made with hands, I shall give it here, to illustrate this opinion – he sings

'Nature attend! Join every living soul,
Beneath the spacious Temple of the sky
In adoration join; and ardent raise
One general song!'

In this, and in similar temples, the music, the language and institutions of the Britons, made their first impressions on the infant and savage brain. In this, and in similar temples, civilisation was born, nursed and educated under the tuition of men of genius. In this, and similar temples, the uncivilised Britons first acknowledged the dominion of the superior intelligence. In this temple, the bards received their degrees of proficiency in the arts and sciences from age to age, from time immemorial to the present day. In this, and in similar temples, opinion, the Queen of the universe, was created to govern the rulers of the earth.

As Y Maen Chwyf then is THE temple, where civilisation was born, let the modern Britons of all grades of opinion second the motion of the Cymreigyddion Society of Newbridge, with the means to protect and preserve to the latest posterity, this sublime temple of antiquity, where, perhaps, the remains of the Genius of Serch Hudol and Gadlys lie buried unknown.

Let the respect and reverence we owe to the unknown benefactors of mankind inspire us with gratitude to preserve and protect Y Maen Chwyf, as a monument of their superior intelligence.

Let Y Maen Chwyf be the banner of civilisation, around which millions, yet unborn shall assemble to learn the music, the language, and institutions of the Britons. Here stands the Temple, wide as the horizon is, high as heaven is, infinite as time is, where all shades of opinion shall never blush to assembly 'in the face of day, and in the eye of light!'

'And see!
Tis come, the glorious morn! The second birth
Of heaven on earth! Awakening nature hears
The new creating word, and starts to life,
In every heightened form, from pain and death
For ever free!'[13]

A century before the first Museum of Welsh Life and Culture opened in St Fagans near Cardiff, Price had already thought of it. Subscriptions were received by Phillip Thomas, manager of Pontypridd Chain Works and close friend of Dr Price, who was elected treasurer with a special account opened by the West of England and South Wales District Bank and by the Merthyr Bank. Dr Price was the secretary. The list of patrons included Francis and Laura Crawshay, who donated a miserly £1 1s each! Other names included Dr Price's own family, including his brother and sister Charles and Ann, who lived together at Primrose Bank in Newbridge. Dr Price made the largest contribution of £10 10s. Other names included fellow Newbridge Surgeon Evan Davies, and Taliesin Williams. There is a fascinating list of traders from Newbridge itself, giving a clear indication of the growing commercial hub of the town, with various grocers, masons, butchers, watchmakers, shoemakers, smithy, bakers and the proprietors of a lengthy list of publicans in the vicinity. The total subscriptions of 157 were promised at £131 17s 11d. It was hardly an amount to be scoffed at, but ultimately insufficient for such a large-scale project.

Dr Price had already seen how successful public subscription had been in the vicinity of his own surgery when a call was made in 1836 for the Newbridge Church to be erected at Glyntaff. The *Cardiff & Merthyr Guardian* of September 1836 announced, 'The Foundation Stone of Newbridge Church will be laid by the Lord Bishop of Llandaff on Saturday. When we consider the short notice that has elapsed, scarcely six months, since the first attempt was made to procure subscriptions for this pious undertaking. And that the funds for the completion of the building are not only raised, but the endowment also in a state of great forwardness, we cannot but be thankful to the Providence that "put it into the heart" of his servants to erect this temple in his honour.' As a footnote to the article relating to the actual laying of the foundation stone are a few words that would undoubtedly have infuriated Dr Price: 'Within a hundred yards of the site of the intended building is the famous Druidical Stone, at Coed-pen-maen – reminding the spectator of the Druidical precept – *Da'r Maen Gyda'r Efengyl* – "Good Is The Stone Of The Gospel", "A proof," said the Chancellor of the Diocese, at the Cardiff Eisteddfod, "of how admirably calculated Druidism was for union with the sacred principles of Christianity"'.[13]

Sadly, his own subscription system to raise funds for Y Maen Chwyf project was not as forthcoming and it would be another twenty years before he broached the subject again and revealed more extensive plans for the area. In the meantime, he was infuriated by the failure of the project. Unfortunately, a letter that appeared in the *Cardiff & Merthyr Guardian* in September 1839 did nothing to soothe Dr Price: 'To The Editor of the Gazette & Guardian. Y Maen Chwyf. Sir, Will any of your readers be kind enough to inform me what has become of the money paid towards erecting a tower etc., in the neighbourhood of this celebrated stone? I am Sir, your obedient servant. A SUBSCRIBER, Cardiff, September 11th 1839.'[14]

The response from Dr William Price appeared in the following edition, of 21 September 1839, and ran almost the entire drop length of the front page of the same newspaper:

To the Editor of the Gazette ... As I am the man who suggested this scientific institution in a printed address to the public, and that upon myself the responsibility in conjunction with Mr Thomas of Ynysangharad, and others, to carry it into effect, I feel great pleasure in rendering a statement of what has been done towards accomplishing this project, to an enquirer and the public generally through the columns of the Guardian. We have not been as successful in this undertaking as we might have been, either for want of ability, or leisure, or influence to inspire a love of themselves in the privileged classes or, for want of that sympathy, to be called benevolence to be inspired with that sort of feeling in civilised society that commands one to respect himself that his neighbours may respect him. I must acknowledge an exception to this observation, that the only nobleman who has expressed a voluntary wish, more than once, to do whatever should be pointed out to him to promoter this undertaking is Lord Dynevor. As we owe our very existence in civilised society to the Arts and Sciences, I imagined like a child, there would be no difficulty in the whole length and breadth of Britain, a thousand ladies and gentlemen with a love of themselves and the power by whom they were created and existed, as such, to subscribe a sovereign each, to entry it at once into effect for the mutual benefit of themselves and the millions by whom that power created their civilised existence.

But to my great astonishment, I have found that they were either ignorant – some with a net income of £1,000 a year! – of the rations of their creation and civilised existence or that they were biased to think or suspect that some sinister motive or passion inspired the projector to plan the institution. This was expressed in some one anonymously, with a view to prejudice the public mind against the scheme. As this was answered at the time the charge was made, it is not necessary to any one word more here.

As the object in erecting the Tower near y Gwyal is not only to preserve this most ancient and interesting monument of the infant Arms of Peace but to teach the descendants of 'Tydon Tad Awen' 'Mawrth', 'Iau' and 'Sadyrn' who were revered and worshipped as Gods by the Romans of the Greeks &c. &c. &c. and even by of the inhabitants of the earth under different names in the present day, in the language they were originally taught by Caesar, was the great god worshipped by the Mercher who according to Caesar was the great god worshipped by the Gauls, one is tempted to exclaim what, in the sacred name of the most profound ignorance, sways and possesses you, to refuse or withhold your patronage and protection to that monument of the infant industry and wisdom of your immortal progenitors to whom you owe your very existence as a civilised people!

However little the privileged classes of the community, generally, may feel interested in the diffusion of the Arts and Sciences, among the industrious millions whose genuine life, liberty and health are blended and identified in those works, machinery, and manufacturers that create and maintain your civilised existence in the affluent the period, I think, is not for distance when the intelligence of the millions will not only see the design and utility of such institutions and are destined to encourage and explain to those Arts and Science that create them and diffuse affluence, contentment and happiness among them, but the reason why those ought to be foremost in the race of their diffusion, contend against each other with fiendish ferocity, who shall be foremost in the organised division of their mortal enemies!

However vain it may appear me, to urge on the attention of those who may yet have it in their power to propitiate the rising storm of public opinion, by cultivating a good understanding with those on whom their civilised existence depends, I shall always think it in my interest to recommend it wherever an opportunity offers, by calling upon them to second even such a limited scheme as I have proposed to equalize education and diffuse knowledge among the people; notwithstanding, I see a vote in the House of Commons in granting £70,000 for repairing the Queen's stables for a few horses and but £30,000 of people's own money to educate a whole nation of 26 million laughing me in the face! The amount of subscriptions already promised is about £250.

A lot of the subscribed received shall be published in the finance account. Those Ladies and Gentlemen who have already promised their aid, and others who may subscribe, will be pleased to pay their subscription in the Merthyr Bank Messr Wilkins and Co. The receipt of all subscriptions shall be acknowledged and published from time to time in one of the newspapers. I am Sir, yours respectfully, WILLIAM PRICE.[15]

A response from the same anonymous reader appeared in the *Guardian*,

> Y Maen Chwyf. Sir I am obliged by Mr Wm Price's account of the
> money collected for the proposed tower, at the above place, which is
> quite satisfactory. He is wrong, however, in thinking my former note
> insinuated anything – it contained nothing but a straightforward
> question which he has answered. I remain, Sir, your obedient Servant, A
> SUBSCRIBER, Cardiff, September 1839.[15]

Dr Price's hopes for Y Maen Chwyf never materialised. By September
1839 he had become embroiled in something far bigger than Y Maen
Chwyf. It may well have been that his disappointment felt at the failure of
the venture focused his mind on a new sense of political activism where
his energies could be better used. On the other hand, it may have been
his very entry into this delicate field of social reform that caused the
lack of financial support he so desperately wanted, particularly from the
powerful industrialists he mentioned in his letter and whose very rights
and privileges he was now bringing into question. It wasn't the end of his
scheme for Y Maen Chwyf, but it was certainly an almost twenty-year
postponement, which began with his entry into a chapter of his life that
would give him even further notoriety, respect and ultimately, fear.

1839

Wales during the 1830s was a country of discontent. Right across Britain, since the last decade of the eighteenth century through to the second half of the nineteenth, a whole host of rebellious outbreaks, movements and disturbances such as food and enclosure riots took place. Luddism, the Pentridge Rising, the Cato Street Conspiracy, Peterloo, Tolpuddle, and the Parliamentary Reform riots illustrated how the working classes made their presence felt by means of strikes, trade unionism and ultimately Chartism. At a time of rapid industrialisation and a rising population, there was an upsurge of popular radicalism while the ruling classes tried to suppress the changes that were being called for. At a time when so many other European countries, France in particular, was witnessing the level of unrest that could topple governments and behead monarchies, the British government did all in its power to quell radicalism by outlawing trade unions and public meetings.

Glamorgan was a county that had seen possibly the most turbulent period of change of any other region in the country, and with the sprawled industrial heartland beating louder by the day, it was this area that saw some of the large-scale strikes and outbreaks of violence that were either part of a national pattern, or focused purely on that particular area and set of circumstances. Chartism, the Rebecca Riots, Trade Unionism and the Scotch Cattle were not purely 'Glamorgan' issues, but had a foothold in the population. There were further strikes and violent outbursts in other areas due to the drop in wages, the truck system, high food prices or the sliding scale of coal in many Welsh towns including Swansea, Maesteg and Merthyr. The turmoil there was endemic.

Although the Rebecca Riots – where agricultural labourers dressed in Welsh costume, much to the horror of Lady Llanover, destroyed toll-houses in protest of the fees paid to pass along the highway – were mainly found in Carmarthenshire during the mid-1840s, there were attacks on the toll-houses at Llantrisant and Pontypridd. However, most of the larger conflicts took place in the coal and iron areas, including Aberdare and Merthyr. In these bleak and dangerous valleys, where people lived in poverty, debt, and insecurity, the volatile atmosphere could easily ignite under the slightest pressure. The Corn Laws of 1815 kept bread, the staple diet of most families, astronomically high while on occasion wage cuts – sometimes up to forty per cent at a time due to a sudden dip in the price of iron – turned a community of people to desperation for survival. The undercurrent of discontent was not helped by the dictatorial ironmasters or colliery owners, themselves usually English and thus behind an already uncomfortable barrier of being unable to speak the language used by the greater population; there was the widespread corruption of the local magistrates, who often worked in cahoots with whoever slipped the additional funds into their pockets.

It was under such circumstances that a movement of the magnitude of Chartism, possibly the first mass movement of the working classes, grew to a position of strength. Chartism pierced the very heart of parliamentary reform. It was established and controlled by working men to achieve democracy as a step towards social and economic change. It symbolised an unrest among the industrial areas of the working classes, and its demands fired the imagination of the more militant and rebellious temperament of its campaigners. Terrible social conditions led to the revolt. Since the 1790s the industrial valleys had suffered a culture of alienation, sedition and violent protests, and the workers had plenty to protest about. Throughout Britain, men, women and children worked fourteen hours a day for little reward. For a time workers looked to the Radicals in Parliament, but the much-talked about Reform Act of 1832 was a huge disappointment. In June 1836, the London Working Men's Association was formed and in 1838, the members launched a People's Charter and National Petition that called for radical changes to the way in which Britain was governed. These were embodied in the six principles of the People's Charter of 1838:

1. A vote for every man twenty years of age, of sound mind and not undergoing punishment for a crime
2. A secret ballot to protect the elector in the exercise of his vote
3. No property qualification for members of Parliament, thus enabling the constituencies to return the man of their choice, be he rich or poor
4. Payment of members, thus enabling an honest tradesman, working man, or other person to serve a constituency, when taken from his business to attend in the interests of the country
5. Equal constituencies, securing the same amount of representation for the same number of electors instead of allowing small constituencies to swamp the large ones
6. Annual Parliaments, to present the most effectual check to bribery and intimation, since though a constituency might be bought once in seven years, few purses could buy a constituency under a system of universal suffrage every year

In 1838 the call for the People's Charter was made, compiling all six points into an official document along with a large petition. Parliament refused it.

Chartism is often dismissed as only being about reform of the polling system, but it was much, much more. Workers believed that when the Charter was law their lives would be transformed and 'children would no longer labour ... men and women would only work for six hours a day ... the distinctions between rich and poor would be swept away'.

Following in the footsteps of the Birmingham Political Union, which demanded a widening of the franchise and took place following the 1832 Act, it only gave the right to vote to a marginal section of the middle class males, but not the ever-growing working classes who filled the new industrial towns such as those found in South Wales. The concept began in earnest when six members of Parliament, including William Lovett of the London Working Men's Association, formed and published the People's Charter. In 1837 it was Birmingham that established a second Association, and by the following year they combined to create the National Charter Association. This entity published its People's Charter in May 1838, and on receiving a lukewarm response from Radical Feargus O'Connor and the *Northern Star* newspaper as being too moderate, it began to create favour with others who supported universal suffrage and spoke of Chartism as a 'knife and fork, a bread and cheese question'.

To overcome the clear divisions that already appeared in the movement, the first National Convention was called in London in February 1839 where the followers of O'Connor's physical force appeared to have the upper hand.

When a petition of 1,280,000 signatures was submitted by the 'moral Chartists' to Parliament in June 1839, members voted not even to hear the petitioners. When refused by 235 votes to 46, the once largely peacekeeping Chartists began to advocate the widespread use of force as the only means of attaining their aims.

Wales became a perfect heartland for such a movement against a Parliament that clearly had a total ignorance of the needs of its people. In the valleys of South Wales, where a third of all pig iron in Britain came from, with its 122 working furnaces, along with fifty ironworks and a total coal output in the region of some 4 million tons per year, the large scale-exploitation of the working classes was obvious.

With a lack of education and a primitive and arbitrary Poor Relief System, which was actually guarded by the masters themselves, it was hardly surprising that organisations like the Friendly Societies, Odd Fellows, Ivorites and even the Ancient Order of the Druids were ensuring a strong foothold, providing a sense of security, solidarity and companionship to the workers and were usually law abiding and peaceful. Strikes were common, and masters and workers fought each other terminally, with some workers' leaders imprisoned. Many of the ironmasters, including William Crawshay and Crawshay Bailey, refused to employ the Scotch Cattle members, whose near-terrorist activities were seen in parts of every industrial valley except Merthyr Tydfil, or anyone connected to a trade union.

The Working Men's Association in Wales was established in Carmarthen in 1837 under the leadership of solicitor Hugh Williams, who enjoyed a close association with London Chartist Henry Hetherington. Through this connection, more Chartist doctrine began to spread in other parts of Wales. In January 1839, a mass meeting of more than 4,000 took place in Carmarthen, with Williams chosen as their representative at the National Convention in London. He also represented the newer groups established in Merthyr Tydfil and Swansea, followed by the woollen mill workers of Mid Wales. Chartism had already spread throughout Glamorgan and its neighbouring counties, and by 1839 there were thirty-four Working Men's Associations in the area.

Monmouthshire had become a central county of activity, where there were signs of political awareness and militancy. 'The world of constitutional politics revolved around the two great families of the Somersets, the Duke of Beaufort and the older Morgans of Tredegar, and the only occasion for popular participation was a rare electoral contest.'[1] The wealthy leaders had held sway in the political arena for decades. Since 1816 the burgesses of the first two towns made a serious, although unsuccessful bid for a change to the two Parliamentary seats. It was led by Whig industrialist John Hodder Moggridge, 'pugnacious lawyer and town-clerk of Newport',[2] Thomas Prothero, and John Frost, a tailor and draper of Newport, '… the son of a humble and strictly honest parents, John and Sara Frost, who kept the Royal Oak public house in Mill Street, Newport … At about sixteen years of age he was put apprentice to a tailor in Cardiff … on his return to Newport, in the year 1811 … henceforth he took an active part in the politics of Newport and carried on a paper war again his opponents.'[1]

John Frost (1784–1877), who married Mary, with whom he had eight children, was held in high esteem and affection in the locality of Newport due to his clear sense of justice, selflessness and strong sense of democratic principles. A man of medium height, who spent his formative years in London Radical circles and after a short period in Bristol, settled in Mill Street, Newport where he lived alongside three other prominent reformers in Samuel Etheridge of the 'Radical Printing Office', John Dickenson, the butcher, and William Edwards, a baker. Etheridge and Frost launched printed attacks on the corruption of the county families.

On becoming embroiled in a dispute with Prothero, a solicitor and town clerk, over his uncle's will in 1821, Frost accused him of being the reason why he was not included as a recipient of his inheritance. When Prothero sued him for libel for £1,000, Frost reacted by accusing him of malpractice and Prothero sued and won. In February 1823 Frost was imprisoned for six months. Frost himself recalled, 'No man was ever treated with more injustice and cruelty than Prothero treated me ... Indeed I believe it would be a sin to forget it.'

On his release Frost vented his anger once more against Prothero and his business partner, Sir Charles Morgan of Tredegar House, the famous landowner (and someone whose woodland in Rudry would one day be decimated by Dr Price's hungry goats!). In a pamphlet of 1830 Frost accused the wealthy industrialist of mistreating tenants and called for electoral reform to bring down the wealthy landlord. With the French Revolution alive in the collective memory, Radicals were calling for universal suffrage and if necessary a revolution in Britain to achieve their aims and transfer the political power to the masses. In such a volatile area of mass industry as South Wales, less than a decade since the Merthyr Rising, the landed gentry began calling for special constables and established defence associations to protect their properties, and, for that matter, themselves.

Frost fully supported the Parliamentary Reform Bill that had now become the centre of public attention. In the Monmouthshire county elections Lord Granville Somerset, the Tory, held one seat but Sir Charles Morgan withdrew in favour of the Whig candidate William Addams Williams of Llangibby Castle. In the Monmouth boroughs the conflict was bitter and intimidating, as the Newport burgesses refused to support Somerset's brother, Marquis of Worcester, another Tory, but Benjamin Hall (Lord Llanover, and supporter of Nonconformists and 'advocate of the use of the ballot in elections').[2]

There were widespread celebrations following the election campaign but only a few weeks later the verdict was overturned by the House of Commons Committee. Within the following months rioting had spread across Britain, while Frost and his colleagues established a branch of the Political Union of the Working Classes in Newport in 1831, committed to manhood suffrage and focusing their energies on reform of local politics.

By 1835 Frost was elected a town councillor for Newport and was appointed a Justice of the Peace. He became an Improvement Commissioner and Poor Law Guardian and in 1836 was elected Mayor of Newport, and 'was now able to defend more vigorously the interests of the poor'.[2] Frost began to consider the Parliamentary seat for himself, and when he suffered the desertion of friends and the rise of the Whigs, Frost was dejected. However, he realised that on the wider political field, the growth of the Working Men's Association was beginning to draw his attention. Its founding members included William Edwards and Samuel Etheridge, along with William Townsend, the son of a wine-merchant, meeting weekly at a pub in Commercial Street, Newport and within a few months had a membership of around 150 men.

> Their rules were similar in spirit and even word, to those of the parent body, the London Working Men's Association. In October 1838 a public meeting was convened at the Parrot Inn, and there Frost was asked to explain the points of the People's Charter ... At the end of November the Working Men's Association organised another public meeting, this time at Devonshire House and on this occasion Frost was appointed delegate for Newport, Pontypool and Caerleon to the forthcoming National Convention of the Industrious Classes in London.[2]

By January 1839 Newport boasted around 430 Chartists, meeting in a number of public houses including the Royal Oak under the leadership of Frost, with a host of fellow Radicals who had a 'missionary zeal' by attempting to encourage more members of the movement and giving lectures across the Monmouthshire area. Few alliances had been made in the larger ironwork towns like Merthyr Tydfil, until an association was formed in October 1838, followed by Aberdare in December. By the end of the year some 7,000 men had joined from the two industrial towns.

However, when his political alliance to Chartism became known, Home Secretary Lord Russell revoked John Frost's appointment as Justice of the Peace. Frost retaliated at a Chartist Convention in Pontypool with a letter to Lord Russell and a Chartist song that expressed clearly the thoughts of the Welsh working classes in support for the political movement:

> Uphold those bold Comrades, who suffer for you,
> Who nobly stand foremost, demanding your due,
> Away with the timid 'tis treason to fear
> To surrender or falter, when danger is near,
> For now that our leaders disdain to betray
> 'Tis base to desert them, or succour delay
> 'Tis time that the victims of labour and care
> Should for reap what is labour's fair share
> 'Tis time that these voice in the councils be heard
> The rather than pay for the law of the sword;
> All power is ours, with a will of our own
> We conquer, united-divided we groan.
> Come hail brothers, hail the shrill sound of the horn
> For ages deep wrongs have been hopelessly borne
> Despair shall no longer our spirits dismay
> Nor wither the arms when upraised for the fray;

> The conflict for freedom is gathering nigh:
> We live to secure it, or gloriously die.

Furious at being unable to reform politics through capturing power locally, he helped establish the Newport Working Men's Association by 1838 and was chosen as the Monmouthshire delegate for the National Convention.

Frost was aided in raising the popularity of the cause by Henry Vincent (1813–78), the young Chartist Leader from London and Hull who was responsible for promoting universal suffrage and welfare benefits of the Working Men's Association in South Wales and the West of England. He was suitably impressed by the growth of Chartism in the area and the interest of the middle, as well as the working classes in the meetings. In some cases the shopkeepers and publican landlords may have feared the colliers and ironworkers to such a degree that they felt compelled to join meetings due to possible recriminations on their livelihoods. However, there were those who clearly had a radical instinct. From blacksmiths and carpenters to shoemakers, watchmakers and cabinet makers, the Chartist followers were varied but focused on the same clear ideals and aspirations.

According to varying reports, by the height of its popularity in 1839, as many as 25,000 Welsh people were members of Chartist branches, equating to a fifth of the entire population. This type of movement was unprecedented and had become a matter of grave concern for the authorities. Chartist meetings were held in public houses, open-air venues and mountainsides, where one of many eloquent, inspired speakers would preach the doctrine of the cause to the newly converted. John Frost was joined by Zephaniah Williams of Blaina and William Jones of Pontypool to become full-time leaders of the Radical cause. There was a need to enrol even more recruits from the industrial towns of Glamorgan as well as attracting the 'artisans' of Monmouthshire. The hugely persuasive Vincent came to Pontnewydd in January 1839 and a thousand people turned up to listen to his lectures, as he called on their support to readdress the system, the crown, army, government and lawyers. Frost joined him on his membership drive, often to hostile crowds who would eventually become fervent supporters of the cause. In the coming weeks the calls for further lectures by Vincent and his entourage were rapidly increasing throughout every industrial valley. On his visit to Newport in February 1839 he told the massed gathering that if the National Petition was rejected by Parliament in May then the whole of Wales should send forth an army to which the crowd responded, 'We will! We will!' Vincent then called for the mayor, Thomas Phillips, who had already voiced his contempt for the Chartists, and his colleague Prothero, to be hung from the nearby lamp post.

Men from the collieries and ironworks were beginning to flock to new lodges, to follow the movement. Membership of each Chartist lodge was a penny a week, and by April 1839 Vincent visited South Wales for the third time, specifically to tour each of them. 'Vincent stated the working classes were the industrious classes and that the upper classes were the idle ones ... A rising of the people was a thing likely soon to happen ... "death to the aristocracy! Up with the people and the government they have established!"'[1] Gradually more of these young men became natural leaders of their own area, including the likes of William Harris of Abersychan, Lewis Rowland of Maesycwmmer, Thomas Giles of Gelligaer and William Owen of Llancaiach.

In Newbridge and Treforest a certain surgeon, whose popularity among the working classes was already cemented in his abilities as a healer as well as his fascinating orations at Y Maen Chwyf, became a valuable member of the cause – Dr William Price.

It is not at all surprising that Price should have been caught up in such a radical movement. Working as a young apprentice in the Rhymney Valley, as a student in London, surrounded as it was by the appalling slums and 'rookeries' of the East End, and as a young doctor and industrial medical officer, William Price had seen at first hand, and had wrestled with, the problems of poverty and exploitation. What is also notable is that Price's own outspoken, free-thinking view of the world around him made him a perfect candidate as a revolutionary leader of the cause. He was a true crusading son of rebellion.

In 1839 the leaders of Chartism in the area,

> Morgan Williams and William Lloyd Jones were around thirty years of age, and William Price, Zephaniah Williams and William Edwards were in their early to mid-forties. All were Welsh, and Welsh was the first language certainly of Price and the two Williamses. None was working class in origin ... with the exception of Jones, all had been previously active in radical politics. It was these men who would build up the Chartist movement in South Wales. Of the five it was William Edwards who played perhaps the most critical role ... Edwards effectively launched a campaign to mobilise the workers in the Chartist cause at a meting at Pontnewydd on 1 January 1839 ... Two guest speakers were also announced, Feargus O'Conner and Henry Vincent.[3]

On 22 April 1839, accompanied by 200 little boys and girls, Henry Vincent and Dr Price proceeded to Blackwood to meet with William Edwards, and on arriving at the Coach and Horses public house they began their business with a local committee. Price was called to the chair and opened the meeting in a Welsh speech full of eloquence and argument, concluding, amidst loud cheers from the crowd of 3,000 people, with a quotation from the *Rights of Man*.

'It was probably Price, impressed by the resolution of the Blackwood Chartists, who urged Morgan Williams in Merthyr to discuss common strategies with the Monmouthshire leaders. Morgan convened a meeting at Dukestown on 30 April.'[3]

Given Dr Price's close association with the Crawshays and the Guests, which allowed him access to people of influence and wealth, many Chartists – especially those in England – had considered him to be the perfect candidate to lead the entire insurrection in Wales.

In March, a newspaper report discussed his involvement in a glittering ball at the Cyfarthfa Castle Inn, Treforest, for the Crawshays. This is the great paradox of the situation, as despite his faithful support of the industrial dynastic families, he was willing to sacrifice it all in becoming a political leader who could undermine their Parliamentary support. John Edmunds and William Price were stewards for the party when dancing continued 'until the late hour'.

Later in April, Vincent and Edwards set off for a lunchtime meeting outside the Greyhound, Pontllanfraith. About 2.45 p.m. the audience lined up five abreast, and, escorted by 200 children carrying flowers and flags, moved up to Blackwood. There the Committee of the Working Men's Association had erected hustings, and crowds of perhaps 2,000 heard the chairman, Dr William Price, make the first speech in Welsh. After Vincent's address and tea, it was time for the leaders to return to Pontllanfraith for an evening meeting.

In the late spring and early summer, the scale and vigour of the Chartist movement in South Wales seriously worried the authorities. The Marquis of Bute, Lord Lieutenant of Glamorgan, now received regular reports of Radical activities at Merthyr and along the border, whilst in Monmouthshire Capel Hanbury Leigh (1776–1861) of Pontypool requested assistance.

The next few days were critical in the history of the Chartists, as further meetings took place in Pontypool, Blaina, Blaenavon and Newport, where the leading inhabitants were calling for better protection from the 'rioters'. On 24 April magistrates Thomas Phillips, William Brewer and Lewis Edwards issued a notice that declared the mass meetings were illegal and warned publicans not to allow Chartists to use their premises. On 25 April a hundred special constables were sworn in and the magistrates expected soldiers to follow shortly afterwards.

On defying the ban by the Justices of the Peace, Vincent crossed the battle lines and the masses were called to a public meeting that night. After a parade through the streets to cries of 'Britons never will be slaves', several thousand people waited for Dickenson to introduce the star attraction. Vincent mocked the mayor's proclamation and defied the magistrates to arrest him.

Alarmed by the growing Chartist movement and threats of physical force, the authorities realised it was time to retaliate. Frost's successor as mayor, Thomas Phillips established groups such as 'Association for The Protection of Life and Property' to campaign against the Chartists and train members how to fortify their homes and defend themselves.

Dr Price, who had by now been appointed leader of the Chartists of Newbridge and lower Rhondda, held meetings at Y Maen Chwyf, where he often gave stirring speeches, which lasted two hours on the night he was elected leader. His commitment to the Welsh language, which he spoke eloquently, was steadfast. Every Sunday morning in the 'Commonwealth Society Hall of the Industrious People of Great Britain', an unlicensed beer house on the Ynysybwl Road in Llanwynno, he organised so-called Welsh classes for around twenty of 'Dr Price's Scholars', only to see them broken up by the police, who suspected them of being a cover for lessons in the handling of muskets and military training.

6 May 1839 was originally the date chosen to present the People's Charter to Parliament, but the authorities were sensitive at this time. At Pontypool all the shops were closed and 1,500 constables were sworn in as more than 600 paraded the town. At Merthyr Tydfil there were similar incidents. On the same day Captain Howells of Cardiff, adjutant of the Royal Glamorgan Militia, wrote to the Marquis of Bute (1793–1848). According to the letter, which is quoted in *The Welsh Heretic*, their colleague Tomas Booker of Velindre had nothing further to report on the insurrection, but 'the person who was agitating about Nantgarw was a surgeon attending Mr Crawshay's works at Newbridge. I know him by sight. He has already been considered a strange, flighty character.'

The marquis was further informed in a letter dated 9 May 1893,

I have great satisfaction in informing your Lordship that I have every reason to believe the Chartist Demonstration will not take place as intended on Whit Monday. There has been no agitation of any unusual in this Valley since I had last the honour of addressing your Lordship. But Mr Stacey tells me that the leaders of the Chartists in this neighbourhood, viz, a surgeon of the name of Price, who resides near Newbridge, and a shopkeeper called Davies of Dinas, with two dissenting preachers, have been extremely active among the colliers of the parish of Llanvabon, and likewise at Blackwood during the past week.[4]

Never before had the intentions of the working classes been so plain. Industrialists and landowners such as Crawshay Bailey held speeches to attack the Radicals and Vincent in particular. With the arrival of the soldiers in Newport, the Home Secretary approved proceedings against Henry Vincent and three other Newport Chartists, William Edwards, John Dickenson and William Townsend. The warrants were issued for their arrest on 9 May. The soldiers of the 29th Regiment were on alert but kept out of sight and the 300 special constables were ordered to control the milling crowds. Outside the King's Head were Capel Hanbury Leigh, Reginald Blewitt, Thomas Phillips, William Brewer and Lewis Edwards, who joined other magistrates to begin the examinations. Then William Edwards himself arrived by boat from Bristol and was arrested in front of a jeering crowd in the High Street. Henry Vincent, who had been arrested in Bristol, also appeared at three o'clock, and a battle broke out among the crowd calling for his release. Chartist members from throughout the South Wales area protested, resulting in armed combat with the Special Constables. A woman led the assault on the constables while others attempted to attack the mayor while the case against the four Chartists continued inside. Bail for the four of them was impossibly high while the crowd outside continued to call for their release.

John Frost, who had returned from the National Convention, intervened in the situation and from the window of his house in Mill Street urged the people to be peaceful and to return home. Peace was maintained once more, but not before the magistrates committed the Chartists for trial at the Monmouth Assizes on 2 August, where they were found guilty of conspiracy and illegal assembly. Vincent was sentenced to a year in prison, Edwards to nine months and Dickenson and Townsend to six months each. The sentences did nothing to break the Chartist movements.

Frost had become concerned over the future, believing the Welsh Chartists would either be dispirited or even more rebellious. Throughout May and June the streets of Newport were quiet, but other political meetings continued elsewhere, including at Newbridge, where Dr Price, who had become a member of the more militant faction of the movement, met nightly to choose guest speakers and plan the route and time of their marches. 'On May 13, hearing of a recent meeting at Morlais and concerned at the outcome of that at Blackwood, Sir Josiah John Guest sent for Dr Price and warned him of the dangers of proselytizing among the colliers of Dinas and Llanfabon.'[2] Lady Charlotte Guest noted in her diary of 11 May 1839 at Dowlais, '... at Newbridge too, they [the Chartists] were reported to be very strong, and Dr Price of Porthyglo, one of our best friends at the last election, but an eccentric and enthusiastic character, was said to be their leader in the latter place ...'

On 13 May she wrote, '... Merthyr went to the furnaces and I had a long tete a tete till he came in with Dr Price of Porthyglo, who called in consequence of Merthyr's note to him. He owned being favourable to Chartism, but disclaimed all idea of physical force, which he said had almost determined him to abandon the doctrine altogether.' Her husband warned him of 'lending his countenance to any society of the kind – and he seemed grateful for the advice'.[5]

Lady Charlotte recalled how the local gentry would feel that she had enjoyed 'a long interview as mine with a chartist leader would be sufficient to frighten many of my friends, how much people and things are exaggerated'.

However, Dr Price continued to hold mass meetings at the Rocking Stone, one of which included fellow leaders William Jones and William David, who addressed several hundred 'eager listeners'.

When the petition for the Charter was rejected by the ruling class in Parliament that summer it was obvious their attempts had failed. Frost, Taylor of Birmingham, Bussey of Yorkshire and other leaders met in secret and decided the only alternative to reach their goal was by physical, or militant, force.

Coupled with Parliament's negative reaction to the petition, meetings began to call for 'ulterior measures'. Frost, Zephaniah Williams and William Jones began organising themselves in secret groups to obtain and store arms. Vincent, however, supported the peaceful nature of the movement: 'The Chartists have not the slightest intention of appealing to arms, except in self-defence,' he said in March 1839. As for the authorities themselves, they continued to grow increasingly concerned over the expanding membership. Although it was clear a movement was taking place, for once the Welsh language itself was benefiting the cause as many of the upper classes, educated men and gentry were unable to speak a word of it. Henry Vincent himself recalled that the secrecy of the movement was secured 'from the fact of the mountaineers universally making use of the Welsh [*sic*] language'.

The climax of the activity took place on 12 August when one of the largest gatherings took place at Dukestown, Tredegar, with some 2,500 people present and Dr William Price acting as chairman. On 13 November 1839, in the court case that followed the Newport Rising, a Morgan James was cross-examined by Revd Mr Cole who remembered the meeting:

> The person in the Chair at Dukestown had very long black hair. I believe his name was Price. I had the people all around call him Dr Price. They said, 'That is Dr Price in the Chair there.' Have not seen Price since. I never knew of Dr Price attending any other meeting. Dr Price was dressed in a round jacket.[6]

Five magistrates were also in attendance at the meeting in question and Samuel Homfray J. P. was invited to speak. Dr Price introduced a large number of speakers, some of whom addressed the crowd in Welsh. The advertisement for the meeting suggested the Chartists would petition the queen for removal of her ministers, but there were other objectives too. William Jones demanded the release of the Chartist prisoners in Monmouth and Frost was ordered to convey these feelings to Lord John Russell. It was clear that further action would depend on Russell's response, along with a request for mercy to the three condemned Chartists in Warwickshire.

The objectives of the Chartists were many, for there were those workers who called to take control of the hills and the towns and establish a Chartist Kingdom of its own in South Wales. The notion of regional revolt, not unlike the Merthyr Rising eight years previously, revived an idea.

During an open-air meeting in Cefn Cribwr, a member of the local gentry, mounted on his horse, demanded the speeches were given in the Queen's English, not in Welsh. As he attacked the chairman of the meeting it was Dr Price who rushed to defend him.

On 18 August 1839, from the Court House in Merthyr, Mr William Thomas wrote to the Marquis of Bute that 'Doctor Price, Nantgarw near Cardiff, is a fit subject, in the opinion of most, for a lunatic asylum'.[7] Becoming recognised as a prominent militant, Dr Price had undertaken significant missionary work on the Glamorgan to Monmouth border and, according the coal owner Walter Coffin, went on a political rally to Staffordshire and the north of England in September, when he told others he was in London. Morgan Williams of Merthyr, the most moderate of the Welsh Chartist leaders, was also in close contact with Dr Price and John Frost at this time and travelled to London at the end of October 1839.

Dr Price may well have journeyed once more to the capital city with John Frost at his side. Frost continued to require the support of the ironworkers and miners and looked at Dr William Price as the man who could command them. In fact Frost may well have introduced him to the delegates of the General Convention while in London.

At the same time the Cardiff Reform Association had asked Dr Price to help them in registering for voters. His reply in a letter speaks for itself:

The battle of the country for equal laws and fair play is to be fought in the brains of the working classes and not in the registration counts as the Whigs and the Tories would have us believe. I have nothing to do with Whigs or Tories and liken them to players at a card game. Just as card players throw away a pack of cards when it becomes old and dirty, so the Whigs and the Tories condemn people to the workhouse when they can no longer work or fight for their masters. Both parties permits living off the industries of the people and insighting nations to war against each other.

Dr John Taylor, the Scottish Chartist leader, heard Price had been chosen to lead an armed insurrection in Wales. Price had seven pieces of cannon in his possession (possibly made by Chartist members who worked at the Brown Lenox works) and Taylor also organised a supply of small arms for trained hands – with the business help of Richard Cule, a shopkeeper in Treforest, and William David. 'Most convincing were the references to the six or seven pieces believed to be in possession of Dr William Price; they were said to have been melted down immediately after the rising.'[3]

On 6 September 1839 the magistrates of Lower Miskin reported that three-quarters of the mining and manufacturing populations of Dinas and Newbridge were Chartists, and at Treforest a considerable number of weapons had been bought, sold and tested on targets. The quantity of firearms included several packages of double-barrelled pistols worth thirty shillings each, powder flasks and bullet moulds.

Again Captain Howells informed the marquis that Price and Davies were the two most dangerous people living in the area and a close eye needed to be kept on both of them. According to the Bute Papers, Dr Price was guarded by four armed men in the weeks before the rising and by the end of October Captain Howells asked him to remove the cannon in his possession.

A letter, dated 6 September 1839, from magistrates R. F. Rickards, Thomas Booker and E. M. Williams to the Marquis of Bute who was residing in Camden Hill, London, said that Chartism was spreading in Dinas and Treforest in particular:

> We the undersigned Magistrates of the County of Glamorgan acting for the Division of the Hundred of Miskin of our Petty Sessions held this day have received information to the state of the population of a part of our district ... We are informed, that the Principles of the Chartists have been very actively diffused throughout the popular past of this district, that among the mining and manufacturing population of Dinas and Newbridge and Treforest a considerably quantity of firearms have been received and sold at prices far below their cost and vallue, that in particular a small shopkeeper at Treforest of the name of Richard Cule has received several packages of pistols with powder flasks and bullet moulds and that their double-barrelled pistols, worth at least 30sh each, have been sold to labouring men at 7 to 10sh each, that Cule himself is an avid Chartist, ... that the working people are constantly practising firing at targets and that meetings are frequently held on the mountains near the Rocking Stone, called the Maen Chwyf.
>
> This being licensing day here, we have felt it was duty bound under strict enquiries as the character and conduct of each person who has applied for a Rev.ival of his Licence, and in two instances we have

withheld the licenses from the persons applying, one of whom admitted that he had fiercely been a Chartist, but that he had ceased to be so and had refused to allow Chartist meetings to be held in his house.[8]

The *Cardiff & Merthyr Guardian* of 7 September 1839 gave a report of a Chartist meeting at Y Maen Chwyf, although no mention is made of the doctor.

A meeting of this very redoubtable fraternity was held at the Rocking Stone here on the evening of Wednesday week 'to discuss the principles of the people's charter' – as his requisition to the chief constable described – but such a miserable demonstration, both physical and moral as the meeting and discussion displayed, we have not witnessed for a long time. The stone was taken by Mr Evan Morgan, collier at the suggestion of Mr Secretary Davies, weaver, Newbridge, who with Mr Arthur Davies, late of Victoria Works, did the needful a way of speech making ...[9]

Dr William Price was the leader of this band of men. He had exclaimed,

We must strike with all our might and owner and strike immediately, the time for hesitating is past and the day of reckoning is at hand ... oppression, injustice and the grinding poverty, which burdens our lives must be abolished for all time. We must have an understanding of our cause in our minds, the principle of our cause in our hearts, the power of our case in our conscience, and the strength of our cause in our right arm strength that will enable us to meet our oppressors boldly, fearlessly, upright on our feet. Remember that freedom is out birthright and for that we are prepared to give our lives. We are the descendants of valiant Welshmen and we must be worth of the traditions which they have passed on to us ... it is far better that we should die fighting for our freedom, than live as slaves of greed and opulent wealth.

At the final meeting of the Chartist National Convention of 14 September 1839, which was chaired by Frost, it was decided the Monmouthshire Chartists should march on Newport as part of a wider rising throughout Britain. The greatest pressure of violent conflict would come from South Wales. Soon after the convention, people like Dr Price and John Frost made considerable efforts to keep contacts with local leaders.

A series of secret delegate meetings took place throughout the Chartist heartland, including those at Dukestown and Blaina. Writing four decades after the event, Dr Price remembered some of those meetings. It was becoming increasingly obvious that he was playing a major role in the early planning of the Newport Rising and the atmosphere was becoming tense.

I remember that I was to lead the people from Merthyr, Brecon, the Aberdare Valleys, Pontypridd, and Dinas ... Six weeks before the Chartist riots he [Frost] sent for the delegates to meet him at Twyn-y-Star, Blaenau Gwent. I went there as a delegate from the Merthyr and Aberdare district. Frost, who was Chairman, said 'I have called you together to ask you will you rise at my bidding, for it must be done!' Well, upon that, one of the delegates, an old soldier named David Davies of Abersychan, who had served for 25 years n the army, and fought in the Battle of Waterloo, got up and said 'I will tell you, Mr Frost, the conditions upon which my lodge will rise, and there is no other condition as far as I am concerned. The Abersychan Lodge is 1,600 strong, 1,200 of them are soldiers; the remaining 400 have never handled arms, but we can turn them into fighting men. I have been sent here to tell you that we shall not sire until you give us a list of those we are to remove – to kill. I know that the English army is, and I know how to fight them and the only way to success is to attack and remove those who command them – the officers and those who administer the law. We must be led as the children of Israel were led from Egypt through the Red Sea'. This we understood to be the sea of blood. Every delegate gave a similar reply and Frost promised that he would not call them until he had given them the list asked for. The meeting lasted until two or three o'clock in the morning.[10]

Frost later claimed he was forced under threat of his life to take part in the planning of the Rising, which contradicts totally the recollections of Dr Price. Price never fully trusted him and other working men had begun to suspect Frost's own courage and purpose.

However, it may simply have been the fact that in the absence of a master plan for a serious attack, Dr Price, who was of the militant, not moral chartists (despite his reassurances otherwise to Lady Charlotte Guest) behaved wisely in disassociating himself from any part of the armed march, which would inevitably lead to disaster. In latter years he may have found it necessary to use this as an explanation for his failure to join the march, and would reconcile Lady Charlotte's opinion of him that he deplored the use of force, while his Chartist friends felt he had not attended because he deplored the lack of it!

In a letter from Captain Howells of Cardiff to the Marquis of Bute on 17 September, further mention is made of Dr Price. He explained that Chartism was scarcely spoken of in Neath and Swansea and the man who tried to address the people at Swansea races was nearly thrown in the canal. However, the Chartists at Newbridge had firearms and met at the Rocking Stone, in less numbers than formerly. 'They included about 150 of the lowest form, of women and children being in large proportion. Mr

Roche, Landlord of the Duke of Bridgewater Arms advised me that since the Assizes the alarm in the neighbourhood is much subsided and that he considers Chartism much in the decline. There are two dangerous persons living nearby. Price, a Surgeon and Wm Davies, a shopkeeper at Dinas.'[11]

Throughout October, plans were discussed for the march on Newport. Secret meetings took place, with little evidence being brought to the law courts, allowing very little insight into the thoughts and fears of the Chartists themselves. However, it was planned that sometime at the beginning of November men from the valleys were to march on Abergavenny, others from Merthyr were to hold Brecon and the rest were to capture Newport. There were also rumours of plans to take Pontypool, Monmouth and Cardiff, while other Chartists elsewhere in Britain would receive a signal and ultimately the government would fall.

At the Coach and Horses in Blackwood on 1 November 1839, the leaders met to make the final preparations for their march on Newport. William Davies of Blackwood gave the following evidence in preparation for the Chartist trials:

> It was agreed that all persons from that time were to get all their men together armed with guns, pikes and sticks ... and to meet in the most convenient place in their neighbourhood ... then proceed to be at Risca about twelve o'clock and then they were to be governed by circumstances but obey the orders of the leaders ... It was agreed ... that they were to seize the authorities wherever they could be found, to stop the Mails, so that the people in the North would know they had succeeded ...

Also on 1 November, a letter again from Captain Howells to the Marquis of Bute said all was quiet in Merthyr and 'I have written to Mr Price of Porthyglo to remove his cannon'.[12]

According to reports, on the weekend prior to the march, a delegate from the Chartist National Convention visited Frost in Blackwood and told him to delay the rising for ten days, as other areas of Britain were not ready to take up arms at the same time. Arms were already being gathered throughout the valleys and meeting places arranged for each of the separate marches to converge on Risca and then Newport.

It is generally acknowledged that Frost and other leaders did not agree on the course of action adopted and quite possibly Dr Price realised that the utter chaos that ensued could result in casualties. It seems as if Frost realised the English chartists were not as prepared to take matters in their own hands as the Welsh. On the one hand he wanted to lead the Welsh Chartists, on the other he needed to hold them back. Dr Price argued that Frost deliberately scuttled the ambitious schemes and ensured the failure on the march.

Despite his position in the Chartist movement in Wales, Dr Price did not attend the march, probably because of a personal disagreement with Frost over his methods of protest. In truth, it appeared that Price was suspicious of him all along. Years later he condemned Frost for keeping his men out in the rain on the day of the march, calling him a traitor since he believed Frost was allowing the army time to fill the Westgate pub – the centre of the upheaval – before their arrival. This is probably very unfair. Price was elderly and more prone to delusions when he made some of his most outlandish claims. Quite simply, there was no master plan and Price knew best not to get involved.

On Saturday 26 October he was visited by an Isaac Morgan and summoned to meet John Frost at his apartment and was asked by Frost to support the modified plan of a march on Newport on the following weekend. It was obvious that Price distrusted him and thought a listener was also in the room. Price would only whisper and still Frost would not reveal the full plan for the march.

When he asked for a copy of the plan, Frost allegedly told him the papers were still in Etheridge's office. 'A curious confirmation of this is that the plan for the organisation in groups of ten was actually seen in Etheridge's office when his papers were seized. Price declared that he would only rise on the conditions laid down at the secret meeting.'[13]

'I refused to agree to anything except what had been decided at the Twyn-y-star meeting,' Dr Price recalled in his newspaper interview in 1888. '"What" said he [Frost] "do you want us to kill the soldiers – kill a thousand of them in one night?"

'"Yes," I said, "a hundred thousand if it is necessary."'

'"Dear me," cried he, "I cannot do it, I cannot do it," and he cried like a child and talked of heaven and hell.'

Price cursed Frost, adding, 'You shall not put a sword in my hand and a rope around my neck at the same time. If I take a sword in my hand I will use it, and no one shall take it from me but at the cost of my life.'

Although this conversation may not be authentic, it does display a moment when Dr Price started to withdraw from the movement. Concern was spreading over how much support the rising would have while other more militant Chartists were prepared to take up arms. Price later called into question Frost's own honesty to the men and claimed he could well have been in cahoots with the authorities, which seems an incredibly unfair statement to make.

Later, it was claimed that soldiers had been informed beforehand to 'shoot the man with the long black hair'. Price, normally the crusader, broke himself off totally with the Chartists before the riot and had no intention to take any further part in the proceedings. In later interviews with Ap Idanfryn he said that 'if the Chartists had only been properly commanded they could have carried everything before them'.

It may be that Price and his colleagues felt that a simultaneous attack on four or five towns would not succeed, whereas an attack on the one town could. Frost did not sell the workers short and for many years his name was honoured and revered.

'The progress of the "rise" in the Pontypridd district was much affected by the differences of opinion between Dr Price and John Frost. The three lodge heads, Price of Pontypridd, William David of Dinas and Thomas Giles of Nelson were all present in Blackwood'[3] when the crucial plans of the rising were put to a delegate meeting at the Coach and Horses in Blackwood on the late morning of Friday 1 November before some twenty five people, representing Dowlais, Rhymney, Dukestown, Sirhowy, Ebbw Vale, Blaina, Brynmawr, Llanelli, Llanhilleth, Crumlin, Crosspenmaen, Pontypool and Newport and those in the vicinity of Blackwood. The fact that Merthyr was not represented, nor Rhondda, means that the egregious Price could have tried to mislead the Merthyr Chartists to do the same. According to the landlord he did come to the door of the pub, speak to Frost at midday and then leave. Dr Price, fearing the lack of planning and questionable leadership of John Frost would cause the biggest tragedy of all, would not lead his men.

We can only guess that Price learned that Frost intended to make changes in the plan agreed upon at the previous Dukestown meeting, and refused to have anything to do with them.

A confusing set of events involved Price's followers, for although he and William David from the locality were to lead the men for John Frost, neither took part in the rising itself. However, people in the area were stockpiling arms and possibly considering joining the march. With news of the last delegate meeting William David, who had shops and houses in Dinas, told collier Daniel Llewellyn that there was to be 'serious work at Newport, the great men would be secured, and if the people all cooperated they would get what they wanted. It is better for me to join with them that to turn a lout or coward and it will be that safest way for you all to cooperate with the Monmouthshire men.'[14]

Walter Coffin claimed many of his colliers escaped to the woods and hills to avoid joining the march, although some did travel to Llanfabon and Caerphilly and there were fears the Newbridge and Rhondda men had considered an attack on Newport. Morien later recalled that some had set out from Dinas along the road from Tonyrefail towards Cardiff, and it appears that throughout Monday 4 November Price and William David had their men scouring the lower Rhondda and Newbridge to stop the workers from fleeing. Coffin failed to penetrate this conspiracy of silence. Decades later and Morien, on speaking to survivors, said the Rhondda 'phalanx' was assembling at midnight and would 'dash upon Cardiff in the early hours of the morning'.[14] This is uncertain. Reports and evidence remain unclear, as some would suggest the Newbridge and Rhondda men would proceed to Caerphilly and meet with reinforced groups from Blackwood who had already successfully captured Newport, before marching on Cardiff.

Although Price and David made some attempt to continue the muster, the enthusiasm of the Taff Valley populace rapidly waned and many took to the hills and woods to escape imprisonment. Their predicament was satirised by a contemporary balladist:

> Mae son yn Nantgarw fod y Chartist yn d'od
> A phob un a'I elfin and gilo ta'r co'd;
> Mae Harriet o'r felin, Shon Tomos y Crydd,
> Ac hen dic o'r Turnpike an ffoi t'a Chaerdydd.
> Dafydd Shon Isaac a chydaid o fwyd
> A lefodd dair noswaith yn Nghraig y Berthlwyd.

Such a march on Cardiff was abandoned as the mayor, C. C. William, drew upon every available resource for its defence. Pensioners, special constables, staff of the Carmarthenshire Militia and a recruiting party of the 41st Regiment were all stood at arms. Field pieces were positioned to command all entrances to the town and Captain Foulger of the US ship *Warsaw* landed twelve of his guns to help man them. Scouting parties were sent out to report on the progress of the revels, and bell ringers and buglers were ready to alert the citizens should an attack be imminent.

A contingent led by John Frost assembled at Blackwood and left at 7 p.m. on 3 November, marching through the heavy downpour of rain to gather support in Newbridge, Abercarn and Risca until, by 2 a.m. on 4 November, they reached the Welsh Oak at Cefn with around 2,000 people.

Zephaniah Williams set off his march from Blaina at 9 p.m., with 4,000 men from the northern iron towns who met Frost at Cefn. There they waited for the main contingent of William Jones and his gathering from Pontypool, who had been gathering at the racecourse throughout the night. Some left for Newport, others waited for Jones to lead them and eventually they reached Malpas, but he halted and returned to Pontypool to gather more men. By 7 a.m. On 4 November, Frost and Williams gave up all hope of the Pontypool contingency and moved their forces on Newport with them. It may have been that Jones deliberately held them back so his men could play a big part in the Rising by saving the forces for a further attack on Monmouth and Abergavenny.

The government's commissioner, Tremenheere, remarked on the 'unusual phenomenon, of large masses of the working population capable of contriving and keeping secret from the magistrates and everyone in authority until he moment of execution, a well-organised plan for a combined attack at midnight upon a populous town'.[3]

Several thousand workers, armed with muskets, pikes and clubs were marching on Newport. They planned to free the political prisoners held in the Westgate Hotel and proclaim a Silurian Republic. Victory at Newport would be the signal for a nationwide uprising.

Short of the full contingency, and with many of the men soaked and exhausted by walking through the night in the rain, Frost led them from Tredegar Park to Court y Bella, where final preparations began. By this point the Newport authorities, prepared for the event to follow, had around 500 special constables awaiting their arrival. Mayor Thomas Phillips had requested the Home Secretary send troops to the town and on the previous night special constables joined thirty soldiers inside the Westgate Hotel, which is where Frost had learnt the Chartist 'martyrs' were being held. He decided on the Westgate as the concentration of the main attack. Whether he knew soldiers were guarding the hotel is unclear.

At about nine o'clock the cheering of many voices was heard ... from the directions of Stow-Hill ... in a few minutes ... the front ranks of the numerous body of men approached, armed with weapons of every description ... this body of Chartists must have amounted to five thousand men ... the leading ranks then formed in front of the Westgate ... One of the leaders then ascended the steps and said 'Deliver up your prisoners' ... a special constable in the hall replied, 'No, never!' upon which one of the rioters presented a gun ... A volley was discharged at the windows of the house, which broke almost every pain of glass...[15]

Lasting only twenty minutes, the soldiers opened fire on the crowd outside the Westgate and on the Chartists who had entered the hotel. Further panic followed while many Chartists fled, with around fifty wounded and twenty-two killed. Fearing all was lost, many fled back to the valleys, leaving the authorities to send troops into the coalfield in search of the leaders, who were arrested and evidence was collected for the Special Court at Monmouth on 10 December 1839. Frost, Williams and Jones were arrested and tried for high treason. They were sentenced to be hanged, drawn and quartered, the gruesome and excruciatingly painful penalty for treason. In the event they were not executed but transported to the penal colonies in Australia for life.

After being granted a full pardon in 1856, Frost returned to England and, until his death at Stapleton, near Bristol, on 27 July 1877, devoted his last two decades to writing and lecturing, mainly on the horrors of deportation.

Concern was growing about the other leaders who could exert such power over the men, and although Dr Price and William David had deprived the Rhondda and Newbridge Chartists of any leadership, the authorities were convinced they were still armed and determined to support the cause. However, the magistrates took days to get necessary warrants to search pubs and houses in search of the Chartists. In Newbridge important documents were destroyed before the constables arrived.

A letter dated 5 November 1839 from Captain Howells to the Marquis of Bute said he spoke in Welsh to two young men in Merthyr who were 'horrified' by the reports from Newport, and 'I was also pleased with the neighbourhood of Porthyglo and the Bridgewater Arms on my way up; all idle and many tipsy. Price had his shutters closed and blinds down, some people inside and some out.'[16]

The leader of the Nelson Chartists, Thomas Giles, had disappeared by the time his house was raided and the authorities discovered several guns and a bullet mould.

It was obvious that Price had to escape and – according to a later interview – a £100 reward for him, dead or alive, was announced. He remembered,

> I was in London a short time afterwards and there I saw a notice offering a reward of £100 to anyone who would capture Dr Price, the Chartist, dead or alive ... the authorities were afraid of another rising, and so they deemed it wise to secure me and others if they could. They knew very well that the men of Aberdare and Merthyr would do anything at my bidding. I expected that a warrant would be issued, as I at once decamped.

According to further correspondence between Captain Howells and the Marquis of Bute, Price disappeared by 25 October. On searching his home, and that of William David and a weaver called Francis, all of them had disappeared.

In a letter from J. Bruce Pryce of Duffryn to the Marquis of Bute on 11 November, he explained that a Richard Cule of Newbridge and Dr Price of Nantgarw had arms and ammunition which they sold before the riots and which probably armed the Chartists at Newbridge and Cwm Rhondda, and that William David of Dinas had gone to America, 'Price himself was accompanied on the day of the Newport Riots by four very notorious fellows, each with a double barrelled gun, upped capped and at full cock, it is wonder, as well as pity, they did not shoot each other!'

The Cambrian newspaper of the same day was equally as impolite about Dr Price:

> It is expected that the colliers in this vicinity will resume their work today. At present the Taff Vale Iron Works are standing still for want of coal, but this morning every indication is favourable to a return of the

men to their regular duties. A furious agitator in this neighbourhood, who assumes to be a Chartist Leader, and is generally reported of 'unsound mind' has great influence over the deluded people – many of whom he has seduced from their work during the late period of turbulence. His apprehension and lodgement to safe custody, whether in one of her Majesty's gaols or in a lunatic asylum, would go far towards restoring the peace of this thriving little town.[17]

The police were aware of his influence in the valleys and ensured the Welsh ports were closed in an effort to catch the doctor, but according to another letter to the marquis from Captain Howells on 19 November, Price had fled the vicinity.

On 28 November, Walter Coffin also wrote to the marquis, claiming, 'I am satisfied that the whole of the bad spirit in this district is to be attributed to Price and W. David. He has been sowing poison in the minds of all around him. I understand a warrant is out against Price by the Monmouthshire justices.' This is the only evidence found that a warrant was indeed out for Dr Price, as evidence had often suggested the doctor had told this 'tale' to a journalist almost fifty years after and it was considered another of his exaggerations.

Another letter from Walter Coffin to the marquis on 3 December 1839 confirmed it. In it he agrees the moral force Chartists differ from the others only in lack of courage, since their objectives were the same. He said that he and Mr Thomas had been making further enquiries among the collieries, who were reluctant to give any information. He goes on to explain that it was generally accepted that Price and William David gave the order for the men to rise on 4 and 5 November but none would admit receiving the orders from them. He also feared William David had indeed escaped the warrant, charged of treason.

Mr Booker and myself issued a warrant on Saturday night to apprehend Price, but being advised that the charge being only for riot and break of the peace, that the officers could not break into his house. To search for him, we thought it best to retain the warrant in the hope that holding it a more serious evidence could be obtained in the course of the examinations ... Mr Thomas and myself, are about to make, under all the circumstances, will it not be better that the Home Office should either send down authority to the magistrates to issue hand bills with a reward of £100 for the apprehension of Price and William David as soon as they deem it best to do so ... I need not suggest to your Lordship that there is some difficulty in determining on the course to follow where there is difficulty obtaining evidence, if for instance Price were committed on evidence which would only terminate in his being acquitted, then effect on the mind of his deluded followers would be much worse, than if by leaving the country but clearly no courses is intended with such bad consequences that there to whom the peace of the country is entrusted should not openly and fearlessly endeavour to bring to justice the controversy of such outrage, though they were not present at the scene of mischief.[18]

Two days later and Coffin wrote another letter:

I am sorry to say that neither Mr Thomas nor myself after the most diligent enquiry have found any evidence against Price ... though no manner of doubt that he and Wm. David have not only been the original instigators of all the Chartists in the neighbourhood but that they were actually in concert ... with the Monmouthshire Chartists as to the outrages committed at Newport. They were both in the meetings which took place in ... Blackwood in which I believe the details of collecting forces to attend Newport were settled ... .a weaver at Newbridge of the name of Francis was the Chartist Secretary, he absconded yesterday week having first burned a basket full of papers. He is exceedingly desirable to be able to convict Price and William David. I believe now that they have absconded and I am disposed to think the rumours of Price being in his own house on no good foundation – but to prevent their return, if they are so bold to do so, to be prepared with evidence against them is very important to the preservation of the public peace in this county.

Would it not be well that the Home Office to get a searching enquiry made of the proceedings of any meetings in Monmouthshire at which Price and David were present particularly at these proceeding the outbreak at Newport held in the week preceding the 4th of November. Two such meetings I know were held particularly on Friday the 1st at Blackwood and probably at Newport. They have some Queen's evidence who can speak to this fact.

I called at Mr Thomas, the Manager of the Chain works in Newbridge today belonging to the Brown Lenox & Co. to which works Price was the medical man – he also attended Mr Thomas himself and was intimate with him. He confirmed Price knew all that was to happen in Monmouthshire, but said he never communicated anything to him, also that Price about three months ago had been in Staffordshire and north on a Chartist tour, going out he was in London.

Morgan Thomas who works some coal at Graig yr Allt near Nantgarw was met by Price a short time before the 4th of Nov. and was urged by him to become a Chartist, and Thomas refusing Price said if he did not the Chartist would burn his house for him – he was ... disposed to get Price bond over for this, but Mr Booker and myself could not persuade him even to submit to be examined on oath on the event – he said his house was in a low evaluation and they he was afraid – all the workmen nearly are Chartists and if these happens to be one who has not joined them he is so afraid of the other, that none of them will give any information.

The great many of the Chartists are entirely ignorant of the political changes contemplated by the leader. They have been induced to join the party, by promising first of the removal of taxes that will make every shilling they earn nearly double in value ...

Mr Thomas and myself have determined to work for another communication from our Lordship before we do any thing on offering a reward for the apprehension of David and Price. The effect of using handbills of this nature would no doubt be good, the difficulty is should they succeed in providing an arrest ... what will be our situation if we have no evidence to convict them.[19]

Despite further enquiries, W. E. Williams of Pwllypant informed the Marquis of Bute on 17 December 1839 that in spite of their efforts the magistrates could only make out a doubtful case against Dr Price.

Price told an exciting tale of his movement after a warrant had been issued for his arrest. There are always rumours that he hid out in the Crawshay tower at Treforest, or possibly in the secret chamber found below Forest House a century later. However, given the evidence of his forthcoming Druidic vision at Paris, it appears that for the next seven or eight months he resided in France, although it would not be wrong to assume that Crawshay may well have offered him a safe haven before the crossing was made.

A clean-shaven doctor, disguised as a woman (and probably convincingly so given his petite figure) managed to escape on aboard a Liverpool-bound vessel at Cardiff. Police Inspector Stockdale was on special duty at the docks and carried a warrant for his arrest. According to Price the inspector assisted a lady on the deck, who was none other than Price himself. He went below, then reappeared as a man, but still disguised. When the ship stopped at Milford Haven he had a look around the town and enjoyed a drink in the Nelson Hotel. It was there that a stranger made conversation with him and Price began to suspect something was afoot. It was none other than the master of the port, sent to talk to him by the captain of the ship who was suspicious of Price.

Dr Price later recalled,

I dressed myself in women's clothes, and in that disguise I went on board a Liverpool laden vessel to Cardiff. I was assisted on board by Police Inspector Stockdale, who, deeming I was a lady, showed me every courtesy. He little thought when he handed me so politely on to the dock that I was Dr Price, for whom he was at that very moment on the lookout. Having got on board I at once went down below and when the vessel was at sea, I came to deck in man's attire, but yet disguised. Our ship turned into Milford Haven and remained there for some hours. During that time I went ashore, and entered Nelson's Hotel. I was no sooner there than a gentleman came in, and began to chat with me in a very familiar manner and did his best to make friends with me. But I knew his little dodge. He, I found, was the master of the port, and the captain of my vessel had communicated to him his suspicion I was Dr Price. The master of the port was very polite and offered to take me out to his yacht and to show me the beauties of the neighbourhood. His object was to detain me until the warrant arrived, but I knew it, so I thanked him for his invitation, which of course I took care to decline. When I got on board again I told the captain, a Welshman named Edwards that when next I met him on shore I would give him a taste of the whip for having dared to poach one of his passengers. Having arrived in Liverpool, I made my way by rail to London, where I saw the notice I told you of. Having stayed in the metropolis for a couple of days I went in a steamer from there to Havre, then to Paris. I wrote to Edwards promising I would pay him dearly for the little trick he tried to play with me at Milford.[20]

It would appear that the stranger, a police officer in disguise, offered to show Dr Price around the town while hoping a warrant would arrive in time. But the warrant was too long in coming and the ship had to sail out or miss the tide.

Once on safe shores he penned a little note to Constable Stockdale who unwittingly helped the disguised doctor on board the ship, to wish him well and thank him for his assistance. Dr Price had set foot on foreign soil for the first time – and a life-changing experience was on the horizon.

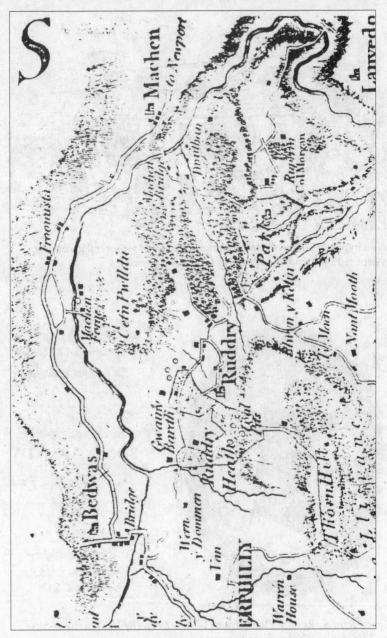

1. The area near Caerphilly where the Price family resided for generations, including Rudry, Machen, Bedwas and Van. Taken from the Yates Map of Glamorgan, 1799.

2. Pontypandy House, the home of the Price family for several generations, as depicted by Glyndwr G. Jones in *Chronicl Caerffili*.

Above left: 3. Revd William Price (1761–1841). (By kind permission of the Museum of Welsh Life, St Fagans)

Above right: 4. The sale of Pontypandy House, 24 May 1806. (By kind permission of Mary Miller)

Above: 5. The Indenture of William Price into the apprenticeship of Dr Evan Edwards, 1814. (By kind permission of the Museum of Welsh Life, St Fagans)

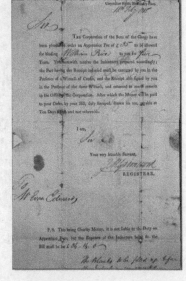

Right: 6. Certificate from the Corporation of the Sons of the Clergy who promised £35 towards Dr Price's tuition. (By kind permission of the Museum of Welsh Life, St Fagans)

Above left: 7. Sir William Blizard (1743–1835).

Above right: 8. John Abernethy (1764–1831).

9. A lecture theatre at the London Hospital, Whitechapel. (By kind permission of the Royal London Hospital Archives and Museum)

Above left: 10. A certificate proving Dr Price attended courses in General Dispensary for six months, August 1821. (By kind permission of the Museum of Welsh Life, St Fagans)

Above right: 11. A certificate, signed 1821, proving Dr Price's attendance in lectures. (By kind permission of the Museum of Welsh Life, St Fagans)

Above left: 12. A certificate proving Dr Price attended 'Practice of Surgery' as a dressing pupil, September 1821. (By kind permission of the Museum of Welsh Life, St Fagans)

Above right: 13. Royal College of Surgeons Certificate, October 1821. (By kind permission of the Museum of Welsh Life, St Fagans)

14. Dr William Price, 1822, by Alexander Steward. (By kind permission of the Museum of Welsh Life, St Fagans)

Treforest near Pontypridd.

Above: 15. Treforest, engraved by Newman, 1840. (By kind permission of Rhondda Cynon Taf Council Library Service)

Right: 16. Dr Price's certificate in midwifery, 1823. (By kind permission of the Museum of Welsh Life, St Fagans)

17. The Ynysangharad Chain Works opened by Brown and Lenox in 1818. (By kind permission of Rhondda Cynon Taf Council Library Service)

Above left: 18. Lady Charlotte Guest (1812–95).

Above right: 19. Augusta Hall, Baroness Llanover, also known by her bardic name of Gwennyn Gwent (1802–96).

20. Edward Williams (Iolo Morganwg, 1747–1826).

21. Y Maen Chwyf, Newbridge.

22. New Inn, Pontypridd, the former home of Gwilym Morganwg (Thomas Williams).

Above: 23. Newbridge *c.* 1845. (By kind permission of Rhondda Cynon Taf Council Library Service)

Left: 24. Francis Crawshay (1811–78).

25. Treforest Works, which was operated by the Crawshays and sold to a consortium in 1876. (By kind permission of Rhondda Cynon Taf Council Library Service)

26. The Crawshay Family obelisks at Treforest. (By kind permission of Rhondda Cynon Taf Council Library Service)

Y MAEN CHWYF.

My Lords, Ladies, and Gentlemen!

   I beg to call your attention, and all those who may feel interested in the Preservation of the Antient Institutions and Antiquities of Britain, and especially to this PRIMITIVE TEMPLE, "Y MAEN CHWYF." This Druidic Temple is situate on Coedpenmaen Common, on the left bank of the Taff, near Pont y Ty Perydd, on the verge of the precipice, a little north-east of Ynysyngharad Works.

In the immediate vicinity of this temple, the graves of the aborigines occupy a space of about 40,000 square yards.

While the population of this neighbourhood continued to follow agriculture, Y Maen Chwyf was in no great danger of being injured, as the hereditary veneration which descended from father to son, through successive generations, was sufficient to shield it from *rude* hands. *But it is not so now.*

The legions of artificers, manufacturers, and strangers, that advance on this place from all directions, have no idea of reverence for this beautiful temple.

Hence it is that some few years ago an attempt was made to destroy it. Mr. Thomas, of Ynysyngharad, heard of it just in time to save it from ruin.

From this brief history, then, it appears that it requires no great genius to foretel the fate that awaits this most antient monument.

Under this impression, it was suggested to "Cymdeithas y Maen Chwyf," that a Tower of one hundred feet high be built by public subscription near Y Maen Chwyf ; the space within the Tower to be divided into eight apartments for a Museum, and surmounted with a Camera Obscura. This Tower will command a horizon of ten miles radius. And that a spacious house, some distace from Y Maen Chwyf, be built for the Bard of the Society to reside in, to take care of the temple.

This proposition has been unanimously seconded by the Society and the whole neighbourhood, as will be seen by the subscribers' names, *in the order* given.

The estimated cost of these erections is £1000. The revenue of the Tower will be about £100. per annum. With the greater part of this sum the Society will establish a Free School, to be kept by the Bard of the Society, for educating the children of the poor. The remainder will go to defray the expenses of the institution In this way, Y Maen Chwyf will not only be preserved, but will continue to operate as a mighty engine of civilization, the Nucleus of a Museum, the parent of the tower that is destined to protect it, and to dispense the blessings of education to the industrious classes of the community.

Y MAEN CHWYF will represent the seed, the tower, the tree, and the inimitable landscape of the Camera Obscura, the fruit of knowledge. A question has been asked us, *will* the brinker landlords—viz., Lord Dynevor, B. Hall, Esq , M. P., J. Bassett, Esq., Mrs. Morgan, the Hon. R. H. Clive, and the Marquess of Bute, permit the Bards to protect and preserve their temple? Our answer has been and is, we have no doubt they will not only charter our prescriptive right to protect the Druid's temple, but express their sense of approbation by directing their names to be added to the list of subscribers for its preservation,—

> " One common cause makes millions of one breast,
> Slaves of the East, or Helots of the West;
> On Andes' or on Athos' peaks unfurl'd,
> The self-same standard streams o'er either world."

As some may question the applicability of the word Temple, at the present day, to designate an immense rude and *poised* fragment of Rock, on an elevated plain, with no other covering than that of the sky, I beg leave most humbly to submit, that it is infinitely more deserving of that term, than the Temple of Jupiter Ammon, in Thebes. As none will dispute, I think,

Above left: 28. John Frost (1784–77).

Above right: 29. The Memorial Stone to Philip Thomas of the Ynysangharad Chain Works, 1840.

30. Attack of the Chartists on the Westgate Hotel, Newport, 4 November 1839.

31. A vaccination certificate signed by Dr William Price, 1854.

Above left: 32. Evan Davies (Myfyr Morganwg, 1801–88).

Above right: 33. Evan James (Ieuan ap Iago, 1809–78).

34. The official opening of the Victoria Bridge, Pontypridd, 4 December 1857.

Above left: 35. Dr William Price and his daughter Gwenhiolen Hiarlhes Morganwg Price, *c.* 1850.

Above right: 36. The Round Houses, Glyntaff.

Above: 37. Dr Price's Surgery at Craig yr Helfa with the roof of one of the Round Houses visible on the far left.

Left: 38. Gwenhiolen Hiarlhes Morganwg Price (1841–1928).

39. A view of the Round Houses from Windsor Road, Treforest.

40. The former Duke of Bridgewater Arms, or Pentrebach House, where Dr Price resided with his daughter Hiarlhes.

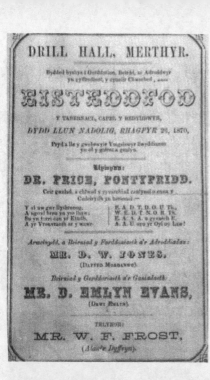

DRILL HALL, MERTHYR.

Bydded hysbys i Gerddorion, Beirdd, ac Adroddwyr yn gyffredinol, y cynnlir Cherchol, &c.

EISTEDDFOD

Y TABERNACL, CAPEL Y BEDYDDWYR,

DYDD LLUN NADOLIG, RHAGFYR 26, 1870,

Pryd a lle y gwobrwyir Ymgeiswyr Bryddiaeth yn ol y gofres a ganlyn.

Llywydd:

DR. PRICE, PONTYPRIDD.

Ceir gosod, a chlwad y cynarchiad canlynol o enou y Cadeirydd yn bersonol:—

Araethydd, a Beirniad y Farddoniaeth a'r Adroddiadau:

MR. D. W. JONES.
(DAFYD MORGANWG.)

Beirniad y Gerddoriaeth a'r Gosodiaeth

MR. D. EMLYN EVANS,
(DAWE EMLYN.)

TELYNOR:

MR. W. F. FROST,
(Alaw'r Dyffryn).

Left: 41. Merthyr Eisteddfod, 1870.

Bottom left: 42. Owen Morgan (Morien, 1836–1921).

Bottom right: 43. The notice issued by Dr Price in condemnation of the colliery owners and managers, 1871.

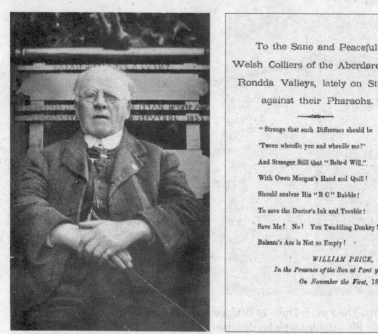

To the Sane and Peaceful Welsh Colliers of the Aberdare and Rondda Valleys, lately on Strike against their Pharaohs.

"Strange that such Difference should be
'Tween wheedle you and wheedle me!"
And Stranger Still that "Belt'd Will",
With Owen Morgan's Hand and Quill!
Should analyse His "B C" Bubble!
To save the Doctor's Ink and Trouble!
Save Me? No! You Twaddling Donkey!
Balaam's Ass is Not so Empty!

WILLIAM PRICE,
In the Presence of the Sun at Pont y Priyth,
On November the First, 1871.

GWYLLLLIS YN NAYD.

*"Yn Tayd wut Ti yn y Nevecyld! Sanctwdd vyddddo dy Enwe Di dyri dy
Dyrrenas! Byddddet dy Wyllllis Di aer ydd Ddaware meggis yn mo I yn
y Nevecyld! Dyrro inai ceddda yn Barra Byuuyldddddiol A maddddo yn
Dyled Dion eel yn madddddawmi yn Dyledxawr! Na arvwinni u Brovvidigayth
ynththnrr ynggwacred Ni rugg yd Drugg! Canrin dy yuddddot Ti uw yd
Dyrronas yg galilla a yryggogonwiaut ya ogo ogazoqdd A yu Mem! A yn
Mem! A yn Mem!"*

Arcyggraphplwyd I gann Dr. WILLIAM PRICE o yb Bont y Prityh Ymmaeryggnnwg
A yeh ehoyecrcstrwyd I yn Neuddd yll Llaennogglon yn yli Llynndann Dudd Albann
Arelbthann 1871.

Above left: 44. *Gwylllis yn Nayd*, by Dr William Price, 1871.

Above right: 45. Charles Price (1791–1871).

46. The image from Bernard de Montfaucon's collection which Dr Price used to create his own costume.

IN MEMORY OF

MR. CHARLES PRICE, LATE

Of Caeridwen Cottage, Radyr,

WHO DEPARTED ON THE MORNING OF TUESDAY, MARCH 28TH, 1871,

Aged 80 Years,

Of whom it may be truly said that " He was what he pretended to be."

47. An obituary card to Dr Price's brother, Charles, 1871.

48. Elizabeth Price (1793–1872), a sister of Dr William Price.

1840–1849

Dr William Price's political exile in France lasted eight months, as he feared that further evidence against him would be forthcoming and he would be forced to stand trial for his involvement in the Chartist uprising. Price had not abandoned the Chartist cause as has often been quoted. Instead, he merely lost faith in John Frost and was determined to continue with the aspirations of the movement by marching on Cardiff. It was this element of his involvement in the cause that could well have resulted in his trial, possible conviction and even transportation to Tasmania, a fate suffered by so many of his fellow Chartist leaders. For Price, the forced exile to Paris was quite enough.

It could be argued that by residing in this heartland of European socialism, it strengthened his Radical commitment and he certainly remained faithful to the cause on his return to Wales. Little evidence remains of his whereabouts abroad except for the surgeon's own recollections of his time there, which were shared in his latter years and are often colourful adaptations of the reality of the situation, although they should not be ignored. It appears that despite their close friendship, Francis Crawshay was not among those who were questioned over Dr Price's involvement in the political upheaval in South Wales, and in fact their shared enthusiasm for Druidism and eastern religions ensured the relationship survived and flourished despite Price's brush with authority. Only Philip Thomas, the manager of the Newbridge chain works, was visited by the local authorities to determine whether enough evidence was available to charge Price. Fortunately for the surgeon, the secrecy that pervaded the entire Chartist movement ensured he was never charged, let alone convicted of his involvement in the cause.

It would not be unreasonable to think that Francis Crawshay offered Price the use of his home and tower as a secret hideout and, given the wealth of the ironmaster, financial support was easily available to ensure his friend secured safe passage to France. It may have also been Crawshay who kept a close view of the general mood in the Newbridge area and he may well have offered Price some advice on when it was safest to return to Wales once the Chartist trials were over and the investigation by the local authorities had lost momentum.

Dr Price's time in Paris remains largely unrecorded and therefore vague at best. He claims to have sent word to a fellow surgeon with whom he was a medical student at Whitechapel, London, twenty years earlier. John Masklyn, who had married a French woman and settled in Paris to open his own practice, allegedly offered Price a room in their apartment. According to Dr Price, he actually assisted in the practice during his time in the capital and many years later Morien stated that Dr Price had mastered French 'like a true Parisian'.

Dr Price's recollection of Paris was special for another reason. He claimed to have befriended a Captain Phelps, the brother-in-law of the 'citizen king' Louis Philippe. Phelps was said to have married the king's sister and originally came from Cottrell near Cowbridge. There is no record of such a character.

Of King Louis Philippe, Dr Price later said, 'I used to see him almost every day at the palace. I often had a friendly chat with him. It was at His Majesty's particular request that I visited him and I remember that he used to laugh heartily when I told him how I had escaped the English police.'[1]

Again this was the fruit of Price's overactive imagination, along with the claim that it was Phelps who introduced the Welsh doctor to a host of his closest friends, who included the exiled philosopher, Heinrich Heine, the German writer whose poems inspired such composers as Mendelssohn, Schubert, and Schumann. Price also allegedly met the seventy-year-old Dr Christian Samuel Frederick Hahnemann, the father of homoeopathy, whose scientific mind was neither satisfied, nor convinced of the effectiveness of the existing medical practices that he felt did more harm than good to the patients. Dr Price said he was in awe of him, learning the benefits of natural herbs and plants for cure and believing the body had the capacity for self-healing.

During Price's exile he allegedly took interest in Captain Phelps's sixteen-year-old daughter, Yvonne, a beautiful and accomplished girl. The captain assumed they would marry and so Price was allowed access to society of a high standing. Unfortunately the relationship with Phelps ended when Price enjoyed taking the girl to the country, undressing her and caressing her nude body. Understandably, Price was banished from the Phelps household.

However, one event that we can be fairly sure occurred during his time in France was a visit to the Louvre Gallery in Paris, when Dr Price claimed to have experienced a hugely profound moment. It was a vision, a life-changing and prophetic juncture in his fortieth year; the effect of which would cause ripples, and indeed waves, throughout the remainder of his life. It would be another thirty years before he fully committed the intimate knowledge of the experience to paper. When he did so, it was to widespread ridicule. The publication was called *Gwyllllis yn Nayd*, a corruptible version of Welsh which roughly translates into 'The Will of My Father'. This is the name he also placed on the sight before him at the Louvre.

On a visit to the museum, Dr Price claimed to have viewed one of the ancient stones on exhibit in a widespread collection of artefacts relating to Greek history and mythology. One of those items was a large stone that had been in existence for more than 2,700 years and was decorated in hieroglyphics and primitive depictions of what Dr Price perceived to be the original Druids, who had ruled the pagan societies of his forefathers. Once again his total devotion to Druidism did not leave him, despite being far from the circles of that faith and understanding, which was pervading Welsh society on every class level.

Dr Price wrote, discussed and held lectures about *Gwyllllis yn Nayd* until his dying day. It enveloped his thoughts and actions, giving him a purpose and a sense of eminence. He would even go so far as to state the fact that he, and only he, could decipher the sacred messages of this stone, in the annual Medical Directory of the Royal College of Surgeons. Following his own list of Royal College of Surgeons credentials, there would often include a phrase relating to his ability to be the 'chosen one' of all the Druids, to whom this stone had imparted its superior knowledge.

The Medical Directory of 1886 is a perfect example of such an incredulous statement:

PRICE, William V.S.L.M, Llantrissent, M.R.C.S., Eng, A.L,S.A, 1821 (St Barthol & Lon Hospital), Decipher of 'Gwyllllis yn Nayd', Discoverer of *Gavval Lenn Berren Myurddhidin Syllt Tyurn wiallen Cyur Anuerin Gwawtrud Awennudg Priv Varrydh Nuadh y Bran Gunn Gwyklsn Lsnn ab Lannn ab Deyk ap Peyl Sarrph ynus Pruttan a ych Chyoul Brenn Privv Varrydh Dusce Cymmru a Gwyllllis yn Nayd*.[2]

It was of course a fallacy, for Dr Price described the stone as depicting one of the primitive bards addressing the moon while holding *Coelbren y Beirdd* in one hand and in the other a mundane egg, the image of immortality. As *Coelbren y Beirdd* had absolutely no historical basis and was another of Iolo Morganwg's greatest fantasies, it is clear that Price was deluded in his obsession with Neo-Druidism.

The origin of the stone he saw is difficult to ascertain, but references to cameo stones, charms or amulets depicting images described by Dr Price have been well researched. In fact, the most prominent illustration is found in the early eighteenth-century work of Bernard de Montfaucon and it is this image that Price duplicated for his book, *Gwyllllis yn Nayd*, in 1871. The figure on the stone and on subsequent cameos, which Dr Price claims to have been that of the primitive bard, is depicted wearing clothing covered with letters from neck to feet. The original large stone, which was on display at the Louvre, was not part of the permanent collection there, although it may have been on loan from one of the leading French antiquarians of the period. It appears that the stone may have been discovered with a large collection of artefacts, mostly vases and decorative crafts, during archaeological searches in Naples. However, it is only the smaller charms depicting the man in lettered costume holding a staff that can be easily attributed to Dr Price's 'vision'. Claiming he could translate the hieroglyphics, whether Greek or Hebrew in origin, is of course a fallacy. However, this was another example of Dr Price's desire to establish himself as a leader of the Neo-Druidic order of which he could claim to be the greatest scholar.

The figure on the stone has several letters running vertically on each side, with further letters along the staff and across the clothing. This is the translation that Price offered of the tablet on the right-hand side of the 'bard':

Has thou seen the strong Lord
The black rod of song of the Lords,
That sows hell
With my old ocean for the sun to generate me?
He will liberate my country
The lord in judgement!
Enslaved in my temple that gathers whomsoever you are to serve him who is
Yes, who is! 'A' that will go before 'A' I sowed my seed in
The limit of the blockhead God that has no seed in him!
'A' will go before I shall cease to shed the blood of armies.
'A' will go before the inglorious foam shall come on my lips
'A' will go before the equivalent power shall come on the wooden wands
Of the poet my soul 'A' will be my equivalent seed
The administrator of my will in the letters of books
In the custody of my tongue after I shall see myself liberated
In the might of those who will hunt out my bard's books
Who will buy the country of heaven to sow my supreme seed
They will buy the country of heaven who will sow my supreme seed.

And here is the translation of the tablet on the left of the bard:

I am a divine
And a common primitive bard
Who knows every songster
In the cave of seasons
I will liberate the place where I am confined
In the belly of the stone tower
I will tell your king
And the common people
That wonderful animal will come
From the shores of the Lord of War
To punish the lies of the bloodhounds of mankind.

I will go into his hair, his teeth and his eyes of gold in peace.
And I will visit with vengeance their lives on the bloodhounds of
mankind.[3]

Dr Price recalled,

> The Primitive Bard, you know, represents himself as the source of the
> ocean. Perhaps, you have noticed that one of the emblems of Freemasonry
> is a board with water flowing out of its centre – that, really, represents
> the Primitive Bard. It is said that it was Newton who discovered that the
> moon influenced the movement of the sea, but that was well known to
> the Druids thousands of years before he was born.[1]

The mundane egg has far more basis in pagan ritual and beliefs. It is found
in the creation myths of many cultures and civilisations and was certainly
an object worshipped by pagan cultures, with a symbolic effect even in
Christianity at Easter. Gaius Plinius Secundus (AD 23–79), better known
as Pliny the Elder, was a Roman author, naturalist and philosopher who
died following the eruption of Mount Vesuvius. He wrote extensively of
the Druids during the first century and makes references to the egg as a
treasured talisman of the order, in which they claimed the secrets of the
world are found. Secreted by a group of snakes and having the power to
win the favour of rulers and the success of lawsuits, the mundane egg was
central to Druidic lore. A translation of Pliny suggests,

> There is a sort of egg in great repute among the Gauls, of which the Greek
> writers have made no mention. A vast number of serpents are twisted
> together in summer, and coiled up in an artificial knot by their saliva and
> slime; and this is called 'the serpent's egg'. The Druids say that it is tossed
> in the air with hissings and must be caught in a cloak before it touches the
> earth. The person, who thus intercepts it, flies on horseback; for the serpents
> will pursue him until prevented by the intervening water. This egg, though
> bound in gold will swim against the stream. And the magi are cunning to
> conceal their frauds; they give out that this egg must be obtained at a certain
> age of the moon. I have seen that egg as large and as round as a common
> sized apple, in a chequered cartilaginous cover, and worn by the Druids.
> It is wonderfully extolled for gaining lawsuits, and access to kings. It is a
> badge which is worn with such ostentation, that I knew a Roman knight, a
> Vocontian, who was slain by the stupid emperor Claudius, merely because
> he wore it in his breast when a lawsuit was pending.[4]

Price was obsessed with the object, which he said was a prophecy sung by
the

Welsh prince called ap Alun, who had once ruled the entire civilised world. It spoke of the coming of a man who would understand the true secrets of the old Welsh language and liberate the Welsh people. The fact that nobody else had heard of this person or made, (anything like) the same interpretation of the inscription, was an encouragement to Price. It turned him from a long and ignominious fugitive from a political disaster into somebody granted a unique revelation of vital importance to his people, for surely he was the cultural saviour whose coming had been foretold for almost three thousand years.[5]

From this event he further claimed that one day his first-born son, called Mab Duw (Son of God), would rule the new earth under Druidic law. It was an incredible prophecy according to Price, illustrating that a new Messiah would reign the earth and the ancient Druidic system would be restored. Without question, Price felt that it would be his male offspring who would be crowned a Druidic God and restore the system to its ancient glory.

He remembered,

I should tell you that during my stay in Paris in 1839 I visited the Louvre, and there came across a precious stone, on which was inscribed the portrait of the primitive bard in the act of addressing the moon. In one hand he holds *Coelbren y Beirdd* while in the other he has a mundane egg.

Across the body I found inscribed several Greek characters and hieroglyphics and although the stone has been in existence for 2,000 years, I am the only person who has been able to decipher the inscription, and I spent twenty years of my life doing so.

The characters represent the Song of the Primitive Bard, the theme of which is Iesu Grist, and he says that his son shall walk on earth again as before. Now, although I have given a challenge and publicly offered £50 to anyone who would be able to decipher the song, no one except myself has been able to do so. I am the son of the Primitive Bard, and it is this son of mine, Iesu Grist, that the bards sings about. I therefore call it Gwyllllis yn Nayd.[1]

This turbulent, provocative, visionary man's return to Wales in July 1840 was not an easy one. The Marquis of Bute, with whom he had become acquainted at the Cardiff Eisteddfod only six years before, now maintained a watchful eye on the surgeon, and the local constabulary took extra precautions that he was not conducting political meetings in Upper Boat and Newbridge as was presumed. He continued working for Crawshay and at the Newbridge chain works, and resumed his involvement with Chartism. In June 1840 an attempt was made to assassinate Queen Victoria and meetings all over the country responded by declaring their loyalty to her and congratulating Her Majesty on her survival. Not in Newbridge. When the local gentlemen and clergy arrived at the hall in the New Inn, Price and his friends were already in occupation. The 'respectables' proposed the chair should be taken by the Revd David Williams of the new St Mary's Church, Glyntaff. Price proposed William Williams, landlord of the Prince of Wales beer house. Price won the vote and the 'respectables' adjourned to another room to vote their loyalty without interference.

A newspaper report read,

The inhabitants of this flourishing little town were almost frightened from their property on the evening of Saturday last, by rumours that the 'Fiery Cross had ta'en its road' through the neighbouring valleys, commanding the appearance of the valiant Chartists at a grand demonstration the redoubtable Dr Price purposed making in opposition to the meeting of the respectable portion of the community, who wished to congratulate her Most Gracious Majesty and her Royal Consort on their providential escape from assassination. On the arrival of some of the neighbouring clergymen and gentlemen, the room was found to be occupied by the Lenanter and his 'body guard' who mustered in considerable numbers. The Revd David Williams of Glyntaff Church, having been proposed to the chair by Mr Barber, seconded by Mr David Davies, of Cwm Rhondda. Dr Price proposed that William Williams, keeper of the 'Prince of Wales' beer house should take the chair, which was seconded by a brother chartist. A remonstrance was made to Price on the gross insult thus offered to the Clergyman. The reply of the valiant Chief was 'If I have insulted Mr Williams, he knows where to find me'. This was in good keeping with the character of the man who

In Chartist tunes did run away
And Live to fight another day.

The room was immediately left by the respectable portion of the meeting, who adjourned to another apartment and with the Revd David Williams in the chair, whose animated opening address in English, followed by the Revd William Leigh in Welsh, elicited much applause.[6]

Police constable Phil Banner gave information of meetings held by Dr Price on the road between Newbridge towards Llanwynno every Sunday, with his fourteen or fifteen 'scholars', who paraded around with walking sticks shaped like bayonets and covered in Druidic symbols. 'The house belongs to Thomas Morgan, cabinet-maker; the number who attend are usually fourteen or fifteen. They are all violent and notorious Chartists and are called "Mr Price's Scholars",' he said.

By the end of 1840 the Chartists had diminished and appeared to have little influence over workers in the area. Though in company with other Chartists Dr Price was quieter, he was by no means cowed and when in January 1841, Richard Jones, weaver of Llanrwst was charged with distributing seditious publications in Newbridge, Mr Price, surgeon, of Newbridge, a gentleman well known for his predilection for the Chartist cause, offered himself as a surety in ten pounds, with Thomas Morgan, carpenter of the same place.

Richard Jones himself was referred to in the newspaper account as 'this dirty Demosthenes', but he proudly claimed that he was 'only accountable to God for his actions'.[7]

During the general election of June 1841 significant political divisions developed in the Chartist movement, both nationally and locally. The Monmouthshire Chartists were divided over the question of what attitude to adopt towards the two political parties in Parliament – the Whigs and the Tories. The *Northern Star* newspaper recorded for several weeks the outcome of the election and the problems encountered along the way.

Some of the key players in the event included William Edwards, John Dickenson and William Townsend who had all been arrested in May 1839 with Henry Vincent in Newport. Edwards, a Newport baker, spent nine months in prison for his involvement in the uprising.

In June 1841 the Chartist nominations for a Parliamentary member for the Monmouth Borough took place and Dr William Price was invited to stand as the Chartist candidate. Brought in at the eleventh hour and sure to win the support of the Conservative interest, it was arranged that Dickenson and Edwards would propose and second the doctor's nomination for the seat, but there was treachery in the ranks of the organisation. Both men left Newport the day before the nomination, heading to Monmouth without Dr Price and leaving him to travel forty-three miles from Newbridge. In the meantime it was claimed that Edwards had reached Monmouth to hold secret meetings with John Buttery, the Whig supporter of the town. In effect, Edwards had promised to nominate Dr Price, when in fact he was hoping for election as the Whig candidate himself.

Meanwhile, not knowing of treason in the camp, Dr Price arrived in Newport at half-past five on the morning of the nomination and proceeded to Monmouth. When at Usk they found every relay of horses had been snapped up by the Whigs, they were compelled to continue on the same pair of horses to Raglan and on changing horses arrived in Monmouth by great exertion, still in ample time, but the hall was crowded to excess.

Dr Price and his supporters entered and Townsend handed Edwards a note, 'Dr Price with us, you must propose.'

To the great astonishment of Townsend, Edwards then wrote the reply, 'You must do your own work yourselves.'

Townsend remarked, 'By God there is treason in the camp, we are sold like bullocks at Smithfield.'

The election was total chaos. Townsend attempted to propose Price but was precluded from doing so by the mayor because his name did not appear on the list, as it was felt he had arrived too late to be nominated. A show of hands appeared in favour of Edwards and he was put forward for the election poll on the following day.

By this time, Edwards' reputation as a traitor to the cause had become so widespread that he didn't secure a single vote in the election. William Edwards actually went down in history as the only Parliamentary candidate in Wales, ever, to not win a single vote.

The election caused an uproar in the pages of the *Northern Star* newspaper with countless features, articles and letters condemning Edwards for his double-dealings, all of which he denied.

William Edwards wrote,

On Tuesday night, June 22nd 1841, at a meeting of the Chartists of Newport, a person proposed me as a fit and proper person to be nominated to bring the principles of the People's Charter before the public. The proposition was seconded and every man in the room held up his hands for me. Before the meeting broke up, however, a man proposed that Dr Price of Newbridge, should be invited to come forward. The secretary was directed to send a letter to Mr Buttery, of Monmouth, to inform him of what had been done, and to ask him whether he and the Monmouth Chartists approved of me or not.[8]

The letter to Mr Buttery read,

Newport, June 23rd 1841, Dear Buttery, you will see by the enclosed that our friends here have invited me to allow myself to be put in nomination at Monmouth, to give me an opportunity to bring our principles before the public; and if you cannot find a better man so to act, I will do the best I can for the cause, but of course, not go to the poll. I believe some of our friends have written to Dr Price of Newbridge and invited him to come forward. Will you be so kind as to let me know whether you approve of such a plan or not. I remain, your Chartist Leader, William Edwards.

Mr Buttery replied,

Dear Edwards, I should say by all mean bring your principles before the public at the nomination, which will be an excellent opportunity to give both the factions a good dressing; and if we can, muster a good majority by show of hands. You will in that case, when the world rageth, be the legitimate organ of our wants and wishes. Should there be any more on the carpet I will write to you immediately. If your humble servant can be of any service at the nomination, shall be very willing to render my humble service in the glorious cause that must prevail so long. John Buttery, Monmouth.

Edwards attempted to explain his actions to the *Northern Star* again:

I had nothing whatever to do with bringing Dr Price, a physical force Chartist, forward as a candidate and I told the Chartists of Newport, before I went to Monmouth, that I would not nominate the doctor or support him in any way. Yet if the Doctor had arrived in Monmouth before the court was opened, I would not have allowed myself to have been put in nomination. At nine o'clock on the morning of nomination, the secretary of the Newport society came to the Inn where I was and produced a letter from Dr Price, in which he stated that he could not make it to Monmouth, but that his friends might make what use they pleased of his name, or something to that effect. A few of the Chartist electors of Monmouth, who were with me at the time, said it was no use to nominate and second any man, except those present to explain his principle to the people. The electors asked me, then, if I would allow myself to be put in nomination to which I replied, yes, as there was no one else.

If there is any blame to be attached to any one, it is not me, but rather to Dr Price and his own party. The Mayor gave the Doctor and his friends a fair chance; and if any elector had come forward to nominate the Doctor, instead of Townsend, the lawyer, who is not an elector, all would have been right; and as there were two electors with the Doctor, I want to know why they did not come forward like men and do their duty. I knew nothing of the Doctor's intention to go to the poll; nor did I know that the Tories were going to support him. I am no Tory and I think the Chartists who have voted for Tories have acted inconsistently ... If ever a man did his duty fearlessly, I did it that day. I gained all I wanted, namely a show of hands in favour of the principles of the Charter ... I believe the time is not far distant when there will be another election; let Doctor Price's friends and the Tories return him then, but I will have nothing to do with him.[9]

The conduct of William Edwards at the election became the source of much correspondence in the *Northern Star* for the weeks ahead. One of the letters written by Jonah Williams, a tailor of Llanarthy Street, claimed that Edwards had intended all along not to support Price but to have the nomination for himself and the decision was not a last-minute one. They also claimed Edwards would continually support colliery owner Reginald Blewitt of Llantarnam Abbey, MP since 1837.

Jonah Williams wrote,

On the Monday night previous to the day of nomination at Monmouth, we had a meeting, when we had a letter from Dr Price, stating his intention to come forward to offer himself a candidate, and desiring Mr Edwards to wait until he arrived at Newport, which he declined, stating that he was going on his own business.

Soon after my arrival in Usk, Edwards and Dickenson arrived, and called to the public house where I put up ... and told me that I might come to Monmouth with him and Dickenson. We arrived at about two o'clock. We put up in the Angel ... after dinner Edwards went to see Mr Buttery ... but he was at Usk. We went out together with a view of seeing the town. I met with one of our Association Councilmen and ... told him that Edwards was not our man to be nominated, but Mr Price and that I should be very happy for the whole Council to meet, in order that I might have known the whole truth to them. The conversation took place before Mr Taylor's door, who is another council man. I went to tea to Mr Buttery ... where a great deal of the councilmen had assembled. I told them that Edwards had not come there at the request of the association, but of his own accord, that we had written to Price, desiring him to come forward as a candidate in opposite to Mr Blewitt, that Mr Price had written a reply, stating that he was not only ready and willing to serve the will of the sovereign people if such a man as he was, should be considered by a clear majority of the people worthy of being put in nomination at the next general sale of the nation to represent us. I told them that the Council met on Sunday night, at Edwards's houses, when and where Price's letter was read.

On Monday morning we sent a messenger to Mr Price, who returned that night bearing his letter, which stated that he would be at Newport on Tuesday morning and that he wished to see Edwards particularly before he proceeded to Monmouth in order to know whether the people were organised enough to return a Chartist candidate by a show of hands. This letter was read in the hearing of Edwards. We begged him to stop for Mr Price, but he would not, stating that he wanted to see Mr Buttery.

A desire to have a requisition drawn up was made known, and Edwards promised to have it ready by Monday night, on which night we had a meeting when Edwards declined having anything to do with Mr Price. We asked him if he had the requisition ready, according to his promise. He said he knew nothing at all about it and would not have anything to do with it.

I told the Council that they might fairly see Edward's disposition, and that he would not only vote for Mr Blewitt, but that he would also induce every one that he could to vote for him likewise; therefore, that we had broke all connections with him, and, whatever they would not, for them not to nominate Edwards, in the event that Mr Price should not come forth. The same night, a public meeting was called, at which Edwards and Dickinson delivered speeches. Edwards proposed himself as a candidate, and never mentioned the name of Mr Price. Here I am acknowledge that I ought to have contradicted him; but, thinking it the Chairman's duty, I refrained.

On Wednesday morning, very early, the Secretary of the Newport Association, arrived with a letter from Mr Price, stating that he was coming but that should he not arrive at Monmouth in due time – that they were at full liberty to make use of his name on every requisite occasion. This caused the Chartists of Monmouth to fear that if Mr Price should not arrive in due time, he should not have the majority by the show of hands. Edwards stated if Mr Price should come, that he would propose him, and that Dickinson would second him.

We went out together, but Edwards, Dickenson, and others went to the Mayor on some business unknown to me; I proceeded to the Hall, the place of nomination. Soon afterwards I saw Edwards there; I sat not far from the place where he stood. Before the business commenced, a note was delivered to Edwards, the contents of which I knew not; but soon afterwards I saw one of the hand bills [calling on Mr Price to come forward], delivered into the Mayor's hands, and another note delivered to Edwards, the contents of which also I knew not then. I heard a voice calling Mr Buttery out, when Edwards rose up his arm and said, 'Buttery, stop where you are, don't move.' I have seen the last note which Edwards received, which stated that Mr Price had arrived and desired him to resign and propose Mr Price, as he had proposed in the morning, which he refused to do, and wrote with a pencil the following reply, 'You must do your own work yourselves when the time comes.'[10]

Jonah Williams then went on to question why it was that Edwards turned his allegiance to the current Member of Parliament, Blewitt.

I wish to know on what account Mr Edwards felt inclined to vote again for Mr Blewitt: is it on account of Mr Blewitt's application to the Secretary of State to have Frost, Williams and Jones tried by a Special Commission? Or because Mr Blewitt came to a certain meeting, convened on last New Year's Day to intimidate the friends of Frost, Williams and Jones? Or because he left London for Newport the time petitions were to be presented to the House of Commons for the liberation of Frost, Williams and Jones, and the liberation of all political prisoners, and returned the following night to vote for Ministers? Or for having apprehended Edwards, on the Queen's highway, without having any warrant for his apprehension. I defy Mr Edwards or any other man to point out any legitimate steps Mr Blewitt has taken either in or out of the House of Commons, to advance the Chartists cause? Would I vote for such a man? No never! I would rather live and die in poverty, than I would accept a penny from either a Whig or a Tory.[10]

W. H. Cronin of Newport contradicted William Edwards's letter, claiming Edwards was not a fit and proper person to bring the principles of the Charter before the public. He said, on the contrary, that the meeting were unanimously in favour of Dr Price but in the event he declined to come forward, then Edwards would be invited. Cronin claimed that Edwards not only promised to support Dr Price, but actually to nominate him.

Two weeks later on Tuesday 10 August, a council of twenty-one assembled in Jonah Williams' house to discuss Edwards' conduct at the election. Edwards was very angry at the articles in the *Northern Star* and Cronin was first to cross-examine him, charging Edwards with 'acting in coalition with the Whigs'. He then went ahead and laid out precisely how the day unfolded. Edwards eventually replied, 'Every word … is true. I have acted wrong; and it was nothing but ambition that led me to do it! I have sustained a great loss, therefore I am willing to forgive if you will do the same.' The council replied – 'No, we will not be sold again!' Further allegations were made as to whether Edwards was seen go inside a local bank with Blewitt and at that point he left the council and refused to listen to the judgement, which summed up that, 'This council are of opinion that Edwards is guilty of the charges preferred against him this night and we, the undersigned do now warn the country to be aware of Messrs Edwards and Dickenson, let them go where they will.'[11]

Following such a disastrous entry into the political arena, Dr Price did not make a re-appearance in this field again, preferring to denounce the establishment from the centre of the law courts. Later that year, he was featured again in the pages of the *Northern Star*. In November 1841, he supported the stonemasons' strike. In a full meeting of masons and other traders at the Carpenters Arms in Cardiff on Monday 22 November, 'The Chairman handed in a letter containing five shillings from Dr Price.'[12]

Price continued to be involved in the movement for some time, but did not play any role in the next phase of the Chartist history in 1848.

One of the great legacies of his involvement in the political turmoil of the industrial communities in which he worked was his establishment of a venture to provide large amounts of food provisions to striking chain workers in Newbridge.

The first entry in the *Northern Star* of October 1840 comes in the form of a letter from carpenter Thomas Morgan of Newbridge, which reads, 'The Chartists of Newbridge, near Cardiff, and the adjoining villages, seeing that the whole of the shopkeepers are against the principles of Universal Suffrage, have come to the determination of opening a co-operative store for themselves. They would, readers who are directors of such stores would oblige them so much as to forward a copy of their rules and regulations, by post ...'[13]

A week later Thomas Morgan wrote a second letter to the periodical, thanking its readers for copies of the rules he requested, possibly from other co-operative societies that had formed in the north of England and Scotland.

The organisation was named the Pont-y-ty-Prydd Provision Company, one of the first times the Welsh place name was used in conjunction with a society in the town rather than Newbridge. Dr Price and his Chartist 'scholars' were actually creating social history by opening the first co-operative in Wales, four years prior to the Rochdale principle.

The *Northern Star* discussed the popularity of the Newbridge venture. It claimed to have been established when Chartist members were refused groceries and food from local wholesalers that refused to sell their wares to the Radicals, and Dr Price enquired with wholesalers from other districts to supply him with bulk goods which he could then sell to the workers. The company ran its business as a co-operative from the same beer house where Price's 'scholars' held their Welsh lessons on the Ynysybwl Road to Llanwynno, which was named the 'Commonwealth Society Hall of the Industrious People of Great Britain'. Another report tells of a meeting being held in the public 'Association' room above the Co-operative Store itself, giving some indication that this was a large venture, although it is difficult to ascertain its precise location in Newbridge.

The Provision Company was subject to attempts of sabotage from local traders and members of the authorities who suspected that the men met there for more subversive purposes. This was an example of a co-operative movement that was created due to the beginning of militant trade unionism and political agitation and essentially formed self-help organisations by the most political workers at the time.

Dr Price complained of a wholesaler's boycott of the Pontypridd co-operative in 1841. In a letter to the *Northern Star* he wrote,

Sir, as the Pont-y-Ty-Prydd Provision Company experiences much difficulty in claiming what they want from the wholesale dealers, for ready money, will you be so good as to make the fact known in the columns of the Star, in order that some of your Chartist correspondents may refer us to some houses who do not consider it their interest to make a political distinction between the money of Chartist companies and that of the factions. To remove all doubt on this point, I beg to transcribe a copy of one of those insidious distinctions'. The letter, from Jos Travers and Sons of London, dated 4 May 1841 read, 'We are in receipt of your favour and are much obliged for the preference of your order, but had rather decline the account altogether, as we are only in the habit of doing business with regular grocers and not companies of the description you represent. We are, Sir, your obedient servants.[14]

The store seems to have survived the crisis and existed for two years at least, for when the Newbridge chain workers struck against a reduction in wages in April 1842, he was able to supply them with a large amount of provisions. An economic crisis was developing with the iron industry particularly feeling the brunt of the depression, which led to unemployment and reduced wages. For eight long weeks the workers at Brown and Lenox went on strike, an event that was blamed on Dr Price by the local press for having such an influence over the workforce. According to *Cardiff & Merthyr Guardian*,

The works have, unfortunately been entirely idle, owing to a combination amongst the men not to work at the prices recently offered them, and from all appearances it is not probably that an arrangement will be come to soon.

The reduction proposed being very moderate, certainly not at all commensurate with the depressed state of the times, ought to have been accepted by the workmen: but unfortunately they are entirely at the command of a certain doctor in the neighbourhood, who although receiving his bread from works, makes it his study to create and keep alive dissension between master and man, to the utmost of his power, and in this instance has taken steps to provide the workers with provisions to a large amount. The poor dupes will only have heir eyes opened by a visit from the sheriff's officer; for — is just the man to exact his 'pound of flesh'.[15]

There were calls for a national Chartist strike and clearly the Radicals of Newbridge stood firm in their endeavours, particularly since they contributed handsomely to the cause, and more than 3,000 signed a second Chartists Petition.

In July 1842, a time of widespread poverty owing to the significant industrial strikes taking place in the area, a public meeting was held in the open air at Newbridge 'for the purpose of taking late consideration the property adopting the memorial to the queen, and remonstrance to the Commons'.[16] A group of Merthyr Chartists addressed the audience with the chairman, Evan Morgan. Among them were Mr David John Junior, who said he hoped the crowd understood the principles of the Charter as so many had been persecuted with transportation for defending its principles. He went on to explain the appalling picture of widespread poverty and economic downturn, while also making it clear how the Charter would make a positive impact on the lives of the working classes. He moved the following resolution, 'That it is the opinion of this meeting that class legislation is the sole cause of the present unparalleled distress, now so prevalent among the working and trading classes of this nation, and that there is no hope of amelioration until the People's Charter becomes law. Therefore, we are resolved to stand by the Charter, name and all.'[16]

Dr Price's Newbridge Chartists were a force to be reckoned with and their Pont-y-ty-prydd Provision Company, which was defunct by the end of 1842, was the first co-operative society of its type in Wales. The first co-operative that endured in Wales wasn't established until 1859 in Cwmbach near Aberdare, which was modelled on the pioneering co-operative in Rochdale, established in 1844, four years after the Newbridge venture.

Their Rochdale Society of Equitable Pioneers was a group of twenty-eight weavers and other artisans who suffered the mechanization of the industrial revolution and decided to combine their efforts to open a store selling items they couldn't afford. Following several failed attempts at cooperation elsewhere, the Rochdale Principles were established and in December 1844 opened their store to sell butter, sugar, flour, oatmeal and some candles, and within three months had established themselves as the provider of quality goods.

By the time Robert Owen (1771–1858), a Welsh cotton trader who shared similar ideals to Price – most notably as an atheist, but also as a patriot with a desire to educate the poor – established his first co-operative store in New Lanark, Scotland its principles had already been well known. The first consumer co-operative probably dates back to the 1760s, when a group of weavers began selling a sack of oatmeal at a discount in a cottage in Fenwick, East Ayrshire. Owen, however, is considered the true father of this enterprise, who had the idea of forming entire villages of cooperation where workers could grow their own food, make clothes and be self-governed.

The Cwmbach Co-operative was established by John Rees, a collier, and David Thomas, a mechanic, at the Lletty Shenkin Colliery. Inspired by the Rochdale Principle and the overwhelming poverty suffered by their community during the disastrous miners' strike of 1857, when the colliery owners closed the company provision shops, they decided to establish their own Co-operative Society near the Aberdare Canal.

Dr Price's hopes and aspirations for the Pont-y-ty-Prydd Provision Company were short-lived. There are several arguments over why the company was forced to disband. Some believe the heavy weight of boycotting from local shopkeepers was a key factor in its demise, while others would argue that Price caused the business to fail because it went bankrupt through offering too much credit to the striking workers of the Newbridge chain works. A similar story befell the Cwmbach Co-operative, which closed through over-funding the miner's lockout in the 1920s and was forced to merge with the larger Aberdare Society, which was offering a higher dividend than at Cwmbach.

At the time Chartism was continuing to gain ground in the area, a government spy infiltrated the Merthyr Chartists in September 1842, and, following the defeat of the political strike in August, sent back information about arming the workers – as Dr Price had done in 1839. This was the last piece of evidence connecting the doctor with Chartism and his attention and energies were diverted from the political cause to his cult of Druidism once again. What can be ascertained is that Dr Price was a leading figure in Chartism for almost four years, during which time he had succeeded in influencing thousands of workers in the vicinity of Newbridge to support and fight for the Charter. From his 'Commonwealth Society Hall of the Industrious People of Great Britain', with his bayonet-waving 'scholars', all of whom had pledged their oath of secrecy to the cause, Price had succeeded in striking terror in the hearts of the local gentry and constabulary. Not only was his armoury of pistols and cannon a concern, but more importantly his influence and leadership. Clearly he was a man not to be underestimated.

Dr William Price's radical views of Neo-Druidism became more extreme during middle age, and evidence suggests that periods of mental illness were apparent, not dissimilar to the symptoms described as being paraphrenic in their appearance. Convinced that the ancient prophecy of his Greek stone in the Louvre indicated he would liberate his country and revive the religion of the ancient Druids, he grew to become one of the most prominent proponents of the Neo-Druidic movement during this period of his life. His aspirations for a son to lead the new Druidic religion, which would cast out Christianity from Great Britain, was still not forthcoming, but it was not for the want of trying. Dr Price's boundless energy for the plethora of aspects which formed his rich and fascinating life was mirrored by his equally energetic sexual appetite for fair young maidens and frequent love-making wherever possible. Women were deliciously alarmed by him and his radical, even feminist views on marriage, which he claimed 'imprisoned' them and obviously the women of the parish were somewhat in awe of this figure in their midst. Many failed to resist his advances. Although his black hair was now long and he became bearded, his new evolving style of colourful dress, his manner, charm and magnetism, attracted attentions far and wide. He believed totally in free love, living with women of his own choice and feared not religion, law nor custom to live the life he chose. Known for adhering to such principles as equal democratic rights for all men, vegetarianism and the abolition of marriage, he was controversial to say the last, being labelled an 'eccentric' and 'radical'.

'Matrimony is to be mercilessly condemned as an institution which reduces the fair sex to a condition of slavery,' he said.

Marriage is of no importance, rather is it the desire to mate which Nature has endowed in us which makes people complete the union which we call marriage. I have found it unnecessary to enter into legal marriage, because I do not, as an evolved being, require any law or religious ceremony to compel me to love the woman I have chosen as my mate.

The artificial thunder of the church and the state on marriage cannot frighten me to live with an woman under compulsion. No law made by God or man can compel a man and a woman to love each other, but it can and does compel them to live with each other, which is quite another thing.[1]

He opposed legal marriage due to his interpretation of it as a property relationship, and given the state of the law at the time, this was a valid basis for his argument. Despite the growing 'Victorian Values', he was not alone in his opposition to legal monogamy and advocated the emancipation of women. Marriage was being seen by the radical thinkers of the time as the male exploitation of women, a property transaction that subordinated the female sex.

Continually denouncing the Nonconformist preachers who condemned unmarried mothers-to-be from the pulpit, Dr William Price, like his friend Francis Crawshay, was hardly innocent of causing the pregnant state of the young maidens in the first place. Condemning the deacons for frightening the congregation into submission with their fear of fire and brimstone that spread fear and hatred rather than love and compassion, Dr Price was venomous in his outbursts. In return he was often denounced by the religious leaders for spreading dark, heathen ways and the less tolerant citizens questioned his respectable position in society, for although he was a remarkable healer, his religious views were blasphemous at the least. Yet he obviously had a deep interest in religion and possibly followed in Iolo's prophecy of Druidism influencing Christianity. Although many claims have been made as to the validity of Dr Price's offspring, we can only truly depend on the recorded evidence before us.

In which case, the first child he was said to have fathered was a daughter, named Riannon. She was born of 'William Price, Surgeon of Porthyglo' and 'Ann Nurse of Treforest'. The parish church of St Ilan in Eglwysilan holds baptism records of the period that show that the child was 'base' (illegitimate) and was baptised on 16 December 1839.

It is possible the mother is the Ann Nurse who was born in the parish of Pentyrch in 1819, making her twenty-two years of age at the time of the birth, and later married to a labourer in Penderyn Ironworks named Barber. Despite Dr Price's condemnation of Christian faith, he had little say in the decision to baptise his daughter, for the timing of the event would have placed him as residing in Paris following the Chartist rising.

The few records we have of the child explain that she lived with her mother at Dynea Lock, close to the Glamorganshire Canal, and possibly Dr Price had not allowed her to be baptised at first, but given his disappearance abroad and the child's desperately sickened state, Ann decided to baptise her before she passed away. Tragically the child died of measles, aged just seven months, on 17 December 1839, which means that Dr Price was not there to see her passing. The death certificate names a John Weddes of Dynea as registering the death, placing a 'x' for his mark on the paper. Dr Price's mentor Evan Edwards was the registrar, and baby Riannon was named as 'Surgeon's Daughter'.

His return from France therefore may not have necessarily been due to the changing mood of the authorities in wanting his capture. It may quite simply have been the case that he was informed of his baby daughter's sickness or untimely death. Either way, Dr Price's return came after the demise of Riannon Price, who was buried at Eglwysilan, from where Dr Price would have enjoyed the majestic view towards Llantrisant, his future home, to the south-west, and admired the grave near the church door of architect William Edwards. It is interesting to note also that of Dr Price's surviving siblings, he was the only one to have produced heirs. Only one of the sisters was actually married.

Further sadness struck Dr Price's personal life with the death of his dear friend and employer for almost twenty years, Philip Thomas, the manager of the Newbridge chain works. Thomas, who was aged sixty-nine, had caught influenza while superintending the building of the suspension bridge at Llandovery, and had been superintendent of Bright Chain Pier. He had worked closely with Samuel Brown (of Brown & Lenox) to facilitate the manufacture of chain cables by the introduction of machinery for bending and scarfing links in preparation for making them into chains. He was the first to be interred at the new Glyntaff Church in 1840. However, for some time there was a lack of a gravestone on the site, which caused some annoyance to Francis Crawshay, his industrious colleague, and Dr Price himself. Therefore the two gentlemen took it upon themselves to remedy this deficiency and took a stone from the quarry behind Forest House. Crawshay paid for a local monumental stonemason to create a gravestone to honour the great man who had enjoyed such widespread appeal with the workforce and was known for his philanthropic causes, including Dr Price's Y Maen Chwyf. The stone read:

STRANGER HALT!
I am placed here to commemorate
the virtue and abilities of
PHILLIP THOMAS Esq.
who after managing the chain work
on my right hand side for the space of 21 years
much to the benefit of all mankind died
and was buried herein 1840 aged 69

Unfortunately Thomas's family took exception to the epitaph's ambiguity and none more so that Philip Thomas's son-in-law, Mr Irving. They were so incensed that they removed the stone by dragging it through a hole in the graveyard wall and left it lying in a nearby field. Dr William Price came upon it and with the assistance of Francis Crawshay, arranged for it to be placed in its present position near the Druidic circle at Coedpenmaen. The name Philip Thomas has been erased from the stone and it now overlooks his workplace on the Common and has become part of the history of the locality.

A third death in Dr Price's life came in the early part of 1841, with the loss of his father. Revd William Price and his wife Mary had left Rudry in the intervening years and moved to a farm cottage named Glandwr in the neighbouring hamlet of Van. It was there, at the age of eighty-one, that he passed away of 'chronic inflammation and water on the brain'. With age Dr Price's father had deteriorated still further leaving him suffering an intolerable psychological illness. The family surgeon, Evan Edwards, signed the death certificate as registrar. Revd Price was registered as a 'cleric' who was attended by an Elizabeth Thomas whom, unable to sign her own name, left the mark of a cross on his certificate. The reverend was interred in the family grave at St Barrwg's Church in Bedwas.

According to varying reports, Dr Price fathered his second child in around 1841, with Ann Morgan. She was a housemaid of nearby Pentyrch, born in 1817 to David and Alice Morgan. Dr Price remained with Ann until her death in 1872. The thirty-year relationship lasted through some of Dr Price's most traumatic years, when he faced bankruptcy, failure and the onset of depression and possibly mental health disorders. Yet Ann remained faithful to the doctor, despite his idiosyncrasies, although the same cannot be said for William himself. The second child, sadly for Price, was not the son he had hoped as proclaimed by the primitive bard vision. Another daughter, she was incredulously named Gwenhiolen Hiarlhes Morganwg (*Gwenllian Hiarlhes Morganwg* or Gwenllian, Countess of Glamorgan), although her birth was never registered. She was baptised by Price in his role of Druidic high priest at Y Maen Chwyf. Again following in the tradition of Iolo and his descendants with the use of 'Morganwg' in the title in honour of Glamorgan, Price probably felt that he was also reaffirming his own sense of Druidic supremacy in the eyes of the other Druids of Newbridge, who were not showing the respect towards him that he felt he deserved. He claimed that she received the grand title by right of her distinguished descendancy from the Prince of Wales. It was indicative of his belief that both his daughter and he were the direct descendants of the rulers of Wales, and therefore gave him the right to assume the title of leader of the Druids.

It is uncertain whether such events represented serious gestures or acts of playful and provocative misrule; 'but it seems that Price's longing for glory for his family reflected his desire to wipe out the shame he felt in his real familial past after the birth of his child he took a great interest in his descent, drawing up elaborate genealogies tracing it through many generations'.[5]

He often signed his name with a series of unintelligible hieroglyphics. It was a signature he used frequently, although not always as Dr William Price, sometimes as Arglwydd Rhys of Deheubarth. In later years he began to refer to himself and his daughter as the children of the Lord Rhys, leader of the rising against the English in 1165. On another occasion they became children of Owain Llawgoch (Owen of the Red Hand), who fought with the French against Edward III and passed into Welsh legend as a hero who would one day return to rule over Britain. Named Owain ap Thomas ap Rhodri (*c.* 1330–78), he was a Welsh soldier who served in Spain, France, Alsace and Switzerland and led the Free Company, fighting for the French against England in the Hundred Years' War. As the last politically active descendant of Llywelyn the Great in the male line, he claimed the title of Prince of Gwynedd and Wales. A number of legends grew around him, which Dr Price had heard, particularly of the cattle drover Dafydd Meurig of Bettws Bledrws, who was shown a set of stone steps leading down to a large cave under a bush where he cut his hand. The legend states that it was the resting place of Owain Lawgoch, 'who sleeps until the appointed time, when he wakes he will be king of the Britons'. The same prophecy Price had for his own first-born son. Despite his obsession with having a god-like son, for now, it was Hiarlhes who was his only known surviving offspring.

If the friendship between Francis Crawshay and William wasn't close enough by their mutual interests, then history tell us it was certainly secured by the events of 1843. Laura and Francis had nine children during a sixteen-year period from 1841 to 1857. Two of their daughters, Laura Julia and Isabel, were later married in an extravagant double-wedding at Treforest in 1862, when they were betrothed to two brothers, the sons of wealthy industrialist Roland Fothergill of Hensol Castle, whose rail works ran through Treforest.

According to unsubstantiated sources, Francis's wife suffered a difficult pregnancy with her daughter, Laura Julia in 1843. While in labour, the ironmaster's wife became increasingly distressed and when complications in the birth became more apparent, Dr Price, who had obtained his certificates in midwifery while at the London Hospital, was called to Forest House. It was there on the kitchen table he successfully delivered the child by Caesarian section.

Many claims have been made that this was the 'first' successful Caesarian birth where both the baby and mother survived the ordeal. This is not the case, but it was indeed a rare and significant event. What must be remembered is that such an operation took place prior to the general use of anaesthetic or chloroform. Until then various potions and concoctions were used to numb the senses of the patient, but many proved hopelessly inadequate. Surgery was a terrifying last resort in a final attempt to save life. Surface surgery, amputation, excising fungating cancers and cutting for bladder stones were the most common areas where surgeons would operate – and even then patients frequently died of infections, which few medicines treated properly before the advent of penicillin. For surgeons like Dr Price, operations on the abdomen, chest or skull were essentially impossible. Surgeons had to be fast and accurate and most patients were held or strapped down, others would mercifully faint from their agony and many died of their suffering because it was so intense.

Bristol was among the cities that first reported successfully using ether as an anaesthetic within the first few weeks of it being demonstrated in London, with entries in *The Lancet* during the latter part of 1846. Although some surgeons used primitive methods of subduing their patients, the ordeal of surgery was often too intense and many died of their illnesses rather than ever attempting to go under the surgeon's knife.

Caesarian has falsely been attributed to the method in which Julius Caesar himself was delivered, although in fact the Romans did require that the child of a mother, dead in childbirth, be cut from her womb as a religious requirement that she wasn't buried pregnant, and this may have evolved into a way of saving the baby. Jacob Nufer, a Swiss pig-gelder, reportedly delivered his child without the death of his wife. His wife allegedly bore five more children, including twins. The story was not recorded until 1582 and many question its accuracy. The first modern Caesarian section was performed by German gynaecologist Ferdinand Adolf Kefrer in 1881, placing it forty years after Dr Price's attempt.

For Laura Crawshay, the situation was desperate and Dr Price's meticulous surgery led to the survival of both mother and daughter. Although there is no firm evidence of this event, as presumably the Crawshays themselves made no note of such a sensitive occurrence, there appears to be truth in the tale. Morien's ambiguous history of the area makes it clear that this event did occur. Without doubt it further cemented the close bonding relationship between the surgeon and the heir to an ironmaster's fortune.

Further developments took place in Newbridge and Treforest during the early part of the decade and nowhere was this better represented than in the building of an iconic railway bridge at the growing market town. It was the great engineer Isambard Kingdom Brunel (1806–59) who made regular visits to the chain works at Newbridge, where he obtained many of the chains. His iconic photograph was taken standing before the Brown & Lenox chains. Dr Price was probably introduced to the great man himself.

Anthony Hill of Hill's Plymouth Iron Works in Merthyr asked Brunel to estimate the cost of building a railway from Merthyr to Cardiff, which was eventually put at £190,649 – and included the cost of the skew viaduct at Newbridge. This request was endorsed, although there was obvious opposition from the Glamorganshire Canal Company – the main artery for transportation to Cardiff – but following Parliamentary debate it received royal assent on 21 June 1836. Lady Charlotte Guest laid the foundation stone in 1837.

When Brunel completed the magnificent skewed stone railway viaducts over the River Rhondda in Newbridge in 1840, the stage was set for the penetration northwards by the Taff Vale Railway Company. Originally the viaduct provided a path for the railway to Merthyr and Aberdare, and later to Ynysybwl, Llanwonno, Nelson and Llancaiach, and was a single-line skew structure. The main span over the River Rhondda had a width of 110 feet and may well have attracted scepticism regarding the stability of such a wide span. Critics were proved wrong, for these viaducts have stood the test of time, and carried the weight of trains far in excess of which they were intended. When Brunel carried out a feasibility study for the proposed railway in 1836, he had assumed that its main function would be to carry iron from Merthyr. As the extraction of Rhondda coal got under way in the years following, the town found that it was ideally placed for transporting it down to the coast, especially as the railway station, unlike the road and canal, was conveniently situated on the Rhondda side of the valley.

The industrial landscape was developing at a rapid pace and coalmining soon overcame iron as the main source of employment in the South Wales valleys. This growth was assisted by the Marquis of Bute, who spent £350,000 on opening a dock at Cardiff, regarded as

one of the most remarkable ventures ever to be financed by one man. With its position at the mouth of the river which drained the richest part of the coalfield, with a dock superior to that of its rival and with a patron – the Marquess of Bute – who was determined to ensure for the town every advantage which could result from the power he enjoyed as the greatest of the landowners of the coalfield, the prospects for Cardiff were bright.[17]

Newbridge was already undergoing its transformation to coal with the opening of the Maritime Colliery in Maesycoed. The colliery was opened by John Edmunds in 1841 after he sank a shaft 800 yards deep to the north of Gelliwion Colliery, and at a depth of sixty yards he found and worked No. 3 Rhondda seam. Seven years later and the Great Western Colliery, Hopkinstown was sunk by John Culvert, attracting further migration of young workers to the locality and resulting in the building of further dwellings, chapels, shops and public houses. The Llanwynno Parish Rate Book of 1842 lists thirty-five houses and shops in Market Street, sixty-four in Taff Street, seventeen in Bridge Street, thirteen in Crossbrook Street and fifty-five in Mill Street, as well as a number of inns, blacksmiths, carpenters and a wheelwrights, one abattoir and several farms.[18]

Dr Price saw the further industrialisation and mass migration in the county of Glamorgan as a continual threat to its unique culture and heritage. Glanffrwd (William Thomas, 1843–90) in his *History of Llanwynno* wrote of his dismay over the industrial revolution,

> O! my dear Llanwynno, you too at last have sunk beneath the feet of the enemy. The sanctity of your beautiful fields have been trampled, your melodious birds driven away, the fiery stallions neighed and screams like a thousand pigs have been heard in your lovely glades! So fair, so peaceful, so pure, so silent, so dear were you before the adventurers came to burrow your breast! And not, you are like – well, like all places – where coal is to be found.[19]

Faced with a situation in which he saw the culture of his people under attack and their history denied, Dr Price reacted by reaffirming, through invention, their existence as Iolo Morganwg had done years before. While he created material of his own, not quite forging a national consciousness as Iolo had done, Dr Price immersed himself still further in the Neo-Druidism of Newbridge.

Taliesin Williams, Iolo's son, held several honorary titles in Welsh societies throughout the country, most notably the Abergavenny Cymreigyddion. He was responsible for publishing much of his father's work, including *Cyfrinach Beirdd Ynys Prydain* (1829) and *Coelbren y Beirdd* (1840), which were released with the support of the Welsh Manuscripts Society, followed by the *Iolo Manuscripts* of 1848, which were in fact printed a year following Taliesin's death. 'These contained, among a great corpus of fake medieval poetry, a collection of twenty poems which Iolo had attributed to Rhys Goch ap Rhiccert, of whom little is known ... [but he] had retained the use of the original Welsh metres and that, under the influence of the troubadours that the Normans had brought with them, a romantic school had risen in Glamorgan during the 12th century.'[8]

Even though Iolo had died almost twenty years earlier, the posthumous release of much of his work kept the vision, based on forgeries, alive – and thriving. By now Druidry had become part of the national self-image of Wales and was creating a sense of nationhood when the country felt that more and more it was under English dominance and was in fear of losing its identity. Sir Walter Scott had succeeded in Scotland with the revival of the kilt, tartan and bagpipes. In Wales the men were running the industry, and the wives were enjoying a love affair with the country of their adoption by trying to restore its national heritage and cultural identity. Lady Llanover was doing it with the Welsh costume, the triple harp and eisteddfodau, Charlotte Guest with her *Mabinogion* and eisteddfod support. The Cymmrodorion and Gwyneddigion of London had spent decades trying to recover and restore the literature, music and eisteddfod. For Taliesin Williams, the support of the Guests and the Halls were paramount as they assisted with propagating Iolo's legacy, which resulted in his publishing the reflection of his father's work and thereby influencing a whole new generation of would-be Neo-Druids.

In Newbridge people like Taliesin Williams and Dr William Price were its chief leaders. The fact that they continually referred to the area by its original Welsh name of Pont-y-ty-pridd was an indication that this was becoming a hub of Druidism in Iolo's sacred Glamorgan. It was there that a new figure appeared on the scene and overshadowed the work of his predecessors – and for that matter his few successors – in the attempts to promote Druidism as the natural religion of the Welsh people.

Evan Davies was born in January 1801 near Pencoed. He received no formal education and devoted himself to the mistrusted mastery of Iolo's Welsh bardic rules and the study of mathematics. At first he called himself a whole series of bardic names, including Ieuan ap Dafydd, Ioan Morganwg, Ieuan Morganwg and Ieuan Myfyr Uwch Celli and eventually Ieuan Myfyr, and began to preach in Congregational chapels near his home. A vociferous opponent of the temperance movement and campaigner for moderation, he challenged Revd John Jones to a public debate in Llantrisant in November 1842 and became known as a great orator, controversialist and debater in theology and moral and ethical issues.

A clockmaker by trade, he settled in Mill Street, Newbridge in 1844 where he established a clock and watchmaker's shop. He was fascinated by Druidism and came deeply under the influence of the 'fever' sweeping the town. One of those who deeply influenced him was Taliesin Williams, who first met him when he entered poetry in a local eisteddfod in the 1820s. He also went on to win an eisteddfod in Merthyr Tydfil which Taliesin adjudicated. In a Gorsedd ceremony at Y Maen Chwyf at the spring equinox of 1834, he was initiated into the circle of Druids and licensed as a bard. He returned at the summer equinox to help initiate Lady Llanover (Gwenynen Gwent).

On the death of his master, Taliesin Williams, he infuriated Dr Price by naming himself the new Archdruid of the Bards of the Isle of Britain (even though neither Iolo nor Taliesin ever used such a title) and accepted a new bardic name. 'Myfyr Morganwg', or the 'Scholar of Glamorgan' followed in the footsteps of his forefathers such as Iolo, Taliesin and Gwilym Morganwg in their desire to be considered the promoters and saviours of the Glamorgan bardic tradition. Myfyr claimed to have been invested with the '*Corwgl Gwyrdin*' (the mundane or mystic egg) which had been discovered in a Druidical burial chamber in Llandaff four centuries earlier, and, as the natural descendant of Iolo and Taliesin, he asserted to have inherited the secrets of the bard ('*Cyfrinach y Beirdd*') unlike any other. He claimed that those were the secrets of bardic teachings and traditions that had been conveyed uninterrupted from one generation to the next since the time of the Druids. Dr William Price was incensed by these assertions, since he claimed to be the Archdruid following his religious vision and Druidic message at Paris. However, it appears that Price was never actually initiated at a Gorsedd at any time, quite possibly because he refused to accept something that he considered a hereditary right. It was the beginning of a very antagonistic and acrimonious relationship between the two Neo-Druids, which would continue for the next thirty or more years.

By then Myfyr's enthusiasm and obsession with Y Maen Chwyf could only be rivalled by Dr Price himself, but whereas the surgeon's aspirations for promoting the religious site had failed, Myfyr succeeded, at least in a more modest project. For him the renovation of the site was of paramount importance, and by 1849 Myfyr's vivid imagination saw him design and create two stone circles around Y Maen Chwyf. By undergoing this transformation, which was due not only to Myfyr's imagination, but also to his time, effort and expenditure, he designed an inner circle of fourteen standing stones and an outer circle of twenty-eight standing stones. It was designed as an avenue of thirty-seven stones in the form of a serpent that led to a smaller circle to the north-west of the existing Maen Chwyf, and this smaller circle formed the head of the serpent with two eyes; below the eyes he placed three stones in the shape of the *Nod Cyfrin*, thus /I\, or Mystical Mark, which was another invention of Iolo, who propounded that 'God created the world by the melodious utterance of his holy name, and that the form of that name was /I\, being the rays of the rising sun at equinoxes and solstices conveying into focus the eye of light'.[9] The eye of the serpent bore an inscription from *Coelbren y Beirdd* with three concentric circles, while the left eye had five concentric circles alone. Myfyr was deeply influenced by the eighteenth-century antiquarian William Stukeley, which can be detected in his design for Y Maen Chwyf, with Stukeley's description in his manuscripts of the snake passing through a circle of stones.

At his completed project he performed frequent rituals and ceremonies, the largest taking place at the quarterly intervals that coincided with solstices and equinoxes, with Welsh terms that were created by Iolo – *Alban Eilir* (vernal equinox), *Alban Hefin* (summer solstice), *Alban Elfed* (autumnal equinox) and *Alban Arthan* (winter solstice). Myfyr led his members of Cymdeithas Cymreigyddion Y Maen Chwyf throughout each of the rituals, the first taking place on 21 June 1849, when Myfyr addressed those who had assisted him, giving a brief outline of the Gorsedd from the days of Gomer, the grandson of Noah, and the early poets. He declared that Gorsedd Y Maen Chwyf in the 'ancient principality of Siluria' was the oldest and most significant of them all, supreme and absolute in its authority over all the other Gorseddau of the bards in the whole of Britain.

Ceremonies at Y Maen Chwyf became more grand. In 1851 Myfyr was the first known Druid to actually expel a bard from the Gorsedd; he had committed the sin of accepting a cash prize in an eisteddfod held at Dowlais. Myfyr said he was 'excommunicated through the tail of the serpent and driven to the brook, and from the brook to the River Taff and from the River Taff to the sea, and from the sea to the state of evil, and from the state of evil to Annwn, and from Annwn to the water closet of Lucifer'.

The following year Myfyr mounted the Rocking Stone to be invested as Archdruid of the Isle of Britain, his symbol being the small crystal or Druid's egg. Myfyr won the chair at the Newbridge Eisteddfod in 1854 for the Welsh ode 'The Sacred Circles of the Bards' and held ceremonies at Y Maen Chwyf until 1878. He published several books dealing with Druidism, and was appointed to adjudicate essays in the Grand Llangollen Eisteddfod of 1858. He died in Pontypridd on 23 February 1888 and was buried with copies of his publications placed under his head. His grave, also occupied by his wife Sarah, is a few yards to the right from the entrance into Glyntaff churchyard.

Even in death, his legacy continued to infuriate Dr Price, which wasn't helped by his often savage and condescending treatment in the press by Morien, who claimed to inherit the Archdruid title from Myfyr! He explained,

Myvyr Morganwg adopted the extraordinary view that Christianity was Druidism in an Oriental disguise and his wrath was great when descanting on his theory that the Christian religion is Druidism in Jewish clothes. He wrote in Welsh several works in support of his novel approach ... from boyhood [he was] regarded as a very remarkable genius ... in *Seren Gomer*, for 1839, we find an essay by him, read at the meeting of the Cowbridge Cymmrodorion Society, in which we discover that even then the stone circles and other relics of Druidism greatly interested him and excited his curiosity.[20]

Dr Price also saw the arrival of another prominent member of the Cymreigyddion of Newbridge, a few years after that of Myfyr. It would appear their relationship was even more acrimonious than that between Price and the clockmaker. Evan James (Ieuan ap Iago, 1809–78) was born on 11 February 1809 in the parish of Eglwysilan and was one of eleven children. The family later moved to the Ancient Druid Inn at Argoed. A weaver and wool merchant by profession, he came to Newbridge in November 1847 to run a woollen mill on Mill Street. He married Elizabeth Jones of Rhymney and the couple had seven children, the eldest being James. In the 1840s The Harp at Gelligaer was the venue for an annual eisteddfod and in 1848 the president of the event was Lewis James, the elder brother of Evan, who had established himself as a successful and well-respected poet. A prize was offered at the eisteddfod for the best poem to praise Dr William Price 'for his attention and attachment to the colliers'. Evan James, who would find lasting fame with his son James as the composers of *Hen Wlad Fy Nhadau*, the Welsh national anthem, submitted an entry, but was beaten by Thomas Williams of Cilfynydd, better known as Twm Cilfynydd.[21] Dr Price's ego was truly inflated by such a celebration of his political activism after almost a decade since his initial brush with Chartism.

Evan James's poem, entitled '*Penillion o Fawl I* William Price' (Verses in Praise of William Price), was 'written for his effective skills in easing the long and excruciating pains suffered by William Jones of Gelligaer'.

The translation of the poem is:

> In Gelligaer a pale man was suffering sharp pains
> Who suffered many months until he was weak,
> Namely William Jones, collier, his condition was bad.
> Under the weight of his oppression he stooped in his pain,
> The pills were useless – he could only despair,
> As the pain he was suffering daily got worse.
>
> Renew yourself, muse, for the news to proclaim
> Of our meritorious doctor to sing his praise
> Namely William Price, Esquire, fine noble man,
> Wondrus his medicine to the sick of our land;
> By the skill of his hand he restored back to health
> And to bliss our weakly and miserable man.
>
> Of respect for his efforts for the sick everywhere
> Our esquire deserves the praise of us all.
> He understands causes and cures disease
> And how to dispense medicines, and never to fail.
> Thanks to this knowledge there was noble good
> To many who were sickly and poorly of hue.

In 1845 Dr Price chaired an event which began with a

> scene of considerable excitement and gaiety, being occasion of the anniversary of the 'Gallt Vardre Lodge' of Druids, the 'Britain's Glory Lodge' of Odd Fellows, and the 'True Ivorites Society' of Ivorites.
>
> The affair had been anticipated with feelings of the deepest interest by all classes; and in order that the workmen employed in the extensive works of Francis Crawshay, who were members of either of the above societies, might have an opportunity of attending uninterruptedly the

proceedings of the day, that gentleman, with his accustomed kindness and urbanity towards those employed by him, issued directions for the business of his great establishments to be entirely suspended in order that ALL might join in the festivities which were to take place ...

The Society of the True Ivorites proceeded from Newbridge to the Bush Inn, Treforest, where they were joined by the Odd Fellows Society, headed by their excellent brass band, and proceeded to the Castle Inn to allow the Druids to join the procession ... the whole procession was complete, and presented a most interesting and most gratifying and exhilarating spectacle.

Mr Crawshay's brass band took the lead; then came the noble Druids in their full and most imposing costumes, with banners bearing devices, the various emblems of their ancient order in the most splendid style, together with their richly finished regalia, entirely new, and procured at a considerable outlay from Bolton. The appearance of this band of brothers who cherish and keep alive remembrances of customs of ancient days was eminently calculated to produced the most intensely pleasing reflection – to remind one of old times – of the tales of Hen Gymru – of everything that to Welshmen is dear and worthy of respect ...

The procession passed the mansion of Francis Crawshay Esq., on its way to the church. Mr Crawshay, attired in the full costume of an Archdruid, was, with his truly amiable lady and family standing on the steps in front of the house ... the procession then proceeded to the church where a most admirable sermon was preached by the Revd Mr Williams ... afterwards the procession proceeded to the town of Newbridge, the bands playing most lively airs.

... the Odd Fellows and Druids proceeded along the tram road to Treforest where they arrived in their respective lodge rooms and partook of sumptuous feasts provided ... the chair was filled at the Castle Inn by Charles Price Esq., [brother of Dr Price], cashier of works at Treforest. After the usual loyal toasts were drank, the health of F. Crawshay Esq., was proposed by the worthy chairman and drank with the most enthusiastic applause. The health of the Revd Mr Williams was also drank with great cheering. The Revd gentleman responded to the toast in a neat and appropriate speech. Dr Price, the Chairman, and several others were drank and responded to in course of the evening. The utmost good feeling pervaded the assembly ... F. Crawshay Esq., presented the members of the society of which he is a member [The Druids], with a barrel of beer in which to drink his and his lady's good health. In the evening dancing commenced at both lodges, where all the beauty of Treforest and the surrounding neighbourhood seemed to enjoy themselves to a degree never to be forgotten ... On Monday night the Druids walked in procession to the Maen Chwyf ... in full costume ... accompanied with torches and variegated lamps, were sundry Druidical rites were performed.[22]

The Druid Society of Newbridge was not always held in such high esteem. In one ceremony the

> Druids cut a very sorry figure in perambulating the town on Monday last. The dresses looked sufficiently shabby and ridiculous; the wearers themselves seemed more than half ashamed of their grotesque habiliments. What a burlesque on benefit societies! If long beards are essential to the success and respectability of the society, the members will find it more consistent and economical to cultivate their own. The public will cheerfully allow them to remain in Jericho until these conditions are fulfilled. Last year a Nanny goat was actually led at the head of the procession. This ceremony was wisely omitted on the present anniversary. Perhaps poor Nanny is dead; if so, we would recommend two of three Jerusalem ponies on the future ... they would render the ceremonial somewhat attractive ... we really think it is high time – almost the noon of the nineteenth century – to lay aside all tawdry shama and mockeries of pagan antiquity; a benefit club should be a plain fact, conducted decently earnestly, faithfully. As such its annual processions and festivities will ever be regarded with pleasure and gratification by all rational and enlightened members of the community.[23]

Few would argue Dr Price's flamboyance during this period. It was an element of his character epitomised by his style of costume, every item of which was immaculately tailored to his specifications. The colourful costumes turned Dr Price into a recognisable and even iconic image, which has been continually enhanced through the passage of time. He described it as the dress of the ancient Court of Glamorgan, but in later life said it was the costume of the Ancient Bards and Druids.

With a suitable tailor found in the area, Price went about designing several grand outfits for himself that brought the greatest of attention to someone who was in fact a rather petite man, standing at only around 5 foot 6 inches tall. However, his outfits gave him a larger-than-life image to the locality, and undoubtedly assisted in his abilities to draw the attention of many young ladies. In ensembles of bright reds and green, creating a startling image as a priest of his sun god, Dr Price began to wear the conspicuous fox skin on his head, the brush stitched to the upper part of the pelt, similar to the one he claimed was worn by the primitive bard depicted on the ancient stone. The tails and legs were draped about his shoulders, symbolising his emblem as a healer.

'The fox is represented as one of the first beings in the hieroglyphics of Egypt. The primitive bard and the Druids always wore fox skins head coverings,'[24] he claimed.

The colours of his outfit were also based on Iolo Morganwg's own descriptions of Druidic costume. He claimed the ovate wore green, typifying verdant spring, and Price had trousers made of the same colour with a scarlet trim. The bard wore sky blue, typifying the summer and the Druid wore white, the colour of his tunic, typifying old age and sanctity. He also allowed his hair to grow in plaits of length, even longer than his lengthy black beard. He occasionally wore a green coat, later a red tartan shawl, which covered his bright waistcoat with its two rows of brass buttons, each embossed with a goat. These were in specially made sets, one showing a billy goat standing, another a nanny goat laying down, and a third showing a standing kid. By having these specially minted brass buttons, he began to use emblems of goats (which of course he kept at his farm in Porthyglo) and stags. He used their images on his stationery notepaper and as an emblem of his standing, possibly believing that with the transmigration of the soul, he had been a stag or a goat in a previous existence. Many an angry resident acknowledged his goats as symbolic of the sexually rampant behaviour of the surgeon himself! Price on the other hand believed in them purely as regenerated beings.

'Death! There is no death man!' he exclaimed to journalist Ap Idanfryn in 1888. With a fierce gaze in his face he said, 'That which you call death does not exist except in the imagination.' When asked why he had once said he will live to be 120, he replied, 'People do not understand me when I speak, they cannot comprehend. They are ignorant. Do you think, that I, who have existed upon this earth for ten thousand years, cannot tell what the future has in store for me? Death, indeed. I shall never see death.' On pointing to his second son, he added, 'I shall in future, exist in him. He is my offspring, and what takes place at what you call death is simply a renewal when I shall exchange this body for that of my offspring.'[24]

His spotless linen blouse, the collars and cuffs scalloped and hand-stitched in semicircular pattern, was worn outside his green trousers, made of elegant facecloth and livened with a narrow red silk braid cut in vandyke fashion around the edge. In later years he said this was a uniform worn by Welshmen when they defeated the English at the Battle of Bosworth. He claimed that Dr Coch, who carried the Red Dragon at the battle, was his ancestor. Dr Coch was an authentic person, namely Dr Ellis Price of Plas Iolyn, whose grandfather, Rhys Fawr, did in fact act as standard bearer at the Battle of Bosworth on 12 August 1485. As already stated, Dr Price claimed ancestry through his grandmother Joan Davies to that of a hero of Bosworth in Rhys ap Thomas, who had played such a prominent role in victory for Henry Tudor. The outfits were also supplemented by a sword, an emblem used often by Taliesin Williams on his Druidic ceremonies at Y Maen Chwyf.

... a beard flowing to his waist and his hair, which has evidently not been cut for many years, descends to as great a length, but is tied up with sundry long tails, *a la chi noise* [in the Chinese style]. His dress consists of a jacket and trousers of emerald green, fancifully notched and scalloped, lined and pointed with bright scarlet, and adorned with numerous small gilt buttons bearing devices. His cap is of sable, of singularly quaint form, and had attached to it three pendant tails of the same fur, one falling over each shoulder of the wearer, and the third coming down to the centre of his back.[25]

Despite his Chartist sympathies, radical views of free love and infatuation with Druidism, Dr William Price never seems to have lost favour with the Crawshays. On 9 February 1842 he received a message from the future heir of the Crawshay fortune, Robert Thompson Crawshay (1817–79), to attend a ball. Robert was the son of William Crawshay II by his second wife, Bella Thompson, and, unlike his half-brother Francis, displayed a genuine interest in his father's ironworks. He became acting manager of Cyfarthfa on the death of his brother William and when his father died in 1867 was the sole manager of Cyfarthfa, then employing around 5,000 men, women and children, receiving good wages and well looked after by the master. He was often referred to as the 'Iron King of Wales'. At the time of the ball in 1842 he had yet to marry his wife, Rose Mary Crawshay (1828–1907), someone who had interests and sympathies of the work of Dr Price. A well-known philanthropist and literary prize-giver, she was later a leading member of the fledgling Cremation Society of Great Britain, an organisation that had a great debt of gratitude to the future events of Dr Price's life.

The letter to Dr Price read, 'Dear Price. Knowing you to be a loyal Welshman I have sent you the Paper trusting that you will give me your Company at the Ball, If you will please let me know so that I may send you a ticket as I wish to send as many as I can, Yours truly, Robert Crawshay.'

Dr Price continued to socialise in the upper social circles, namely at various functions organised by the Crawshays. Robert Thompson Crawshay held another 'Princely Festivity' at Cyfarthfa Castle with his betrothed, Rose Mary Yeates of Caversham Grove, Oxfordshire in February 1847, which Dr Price attended and where he possibly met the future supporter of cremation for the first time. As always, the editor of the *Cardiff & Merthyr Guardian* heaped magnificent praise on the event, opening, 'With feelings of considerable diffidence we commence a description of one of the most brilliant, animated, and agreeable assemblies which ever enlightened the Principality; and which; probably, has never been excelled in point of general magnificence out of the Metropolis.'[26] It seems obscene that while the greater majority of the population of Merthyr Tydfil were living in a state of deprivation, in Cyfarthfa Castle which overlooked them, a ballroom measuring 140 feet long by 36 feet wide was built for this particular social gathering. The sides were hung with drapes while the ceiling was covered in evergreens and thousands of flags and banners, all lit with gas. An orchestra played throughout the evening with an embroidered plough before them covered with the family motto of 'Perseverance'. A total of 1,000 people attended, 'a most ample field of youth, beauty, elegance and fashion, calculated to dazzle and surprise ... Merthyr must not be judged by its exterior, which, like that of the pineapple, may appear to casual observers rough and rugged, yet contains underneath a social kernel of incomparable sweetness, as many a love-sick swain can by this time, we suspect, fully testify.' Such an overwhelming complement had little effect on the poorer families in the community for sure!

The long list of guests saw a whole array of Crawshay family members, Francis and Laura (who wore 'a blue brocaded Tarlatana dress, flowers and gold ornaments') included, with fellow ironmasters including Johnson of Blaenavon, Needham of Plymouth, Wayne of Gladys ironworks, and the Fothergills. There among them is the name 'Mr Price, Surgeon, Newbridge'.

Just over a month later he returned to the castle for a public dinner for William Crawshay, 'of Cyfarthfa Castle, Glamorganshire and Caversham Park, Oxfordshire, by the town and trade of Merthyr'. The magistrates, merchants, tradesmen and other inhabitants of the town entertained William Crawshay with a public dinner at the ballroom of the Bush Inn, attended by around 300 'highly respectable individuals'. The male members of the Crawshays, including Francis and Robert Thomspon, were present and again listed is 'William Price, Esq., Newbridge'. The Cyfarthfa Brass Band entertained, and a piece of music called 'Perseverance' was composed especially for the evening.[27]

In 1844 Dr Price suffered the loss of his mother, Mary, at the age of seventy-seven. In her latter years she had returned to live with her daughter at Rudry, and during her final days William cared for her medical needs. She passed away on 5 January. Her death certificate states that 'William Price of Porthyglo' was in attendance and the 'clergyman's wife' had died of 'old age'. Once again, the registrar of the death was Price's mentor, Evan Edwards, who since 1836 was Medical Advisor for the Caerphilly District at £40 per annum, followed by his appointment as Registrar of Marriages in the Cardiff Union. Dr Edwards died in 1848.

In February 1844 Dr Price's attempt to organise an eisteddfod in Pontypridd was a dismal failure, and one begins to wonder whether by this time he was losing the respect and support of the circle of Druids whom he continued to attempt to overrule. Intended to act as a showcase for his own material, nobody else entered the competition, and the only event of note seems to have been Price's own initiation of toddler Hiarlhes as a bard at Y Maen Chwyf.

In 1846 Dr Price was named as the father of a third daughter, Didamia (or Didemia) Price, who was baptised at St Ilan's Church in Eglwysilan. As with Riannon, her birth is termed by the phrase for illegitimacy, 'base', and her mother is named as Ann Jacob, daughter of Thomas and Gwenllian

Jacob. She was a spinster of Ynyshir and the third 'Ann' who bore him a child. Sadly, as with his first daughter, Didamia died at the age of eleven months on 22 July 1847. The mark of William Rees, who was present at the death, is found on the death certificate, registered by Robert Cooke, which lists her cause of death as 'debility, or general weakness and infirmity'.

With a succession of failings and personal losses during the first half of the 1840s, Dr Price began to seek a new outlet for his aggressive energies and the need to express his fury at the establishment, his hereditary rights, and the power of Druidism. This outlet was in litigation, a new public arena in which he could play a major part. Dr Price became a well-known figure in the courts of law for the next forty years. Blunt and forthright, he had nothing but contempt for the English legal system but was often found in court, enjoying every moment of the proceedings and, always the showman, shamelessly playing to the gallery. He also proved an awkward litigant, and cases were temporarily halted because he refused to swear on the Bible. On occasions he argued that he could not vouch for the accuracy of the map of Judea in it, and, when a second Bible arrived, failed to vouch for the accuracy of the name of the owner on the inside cover. There were occasions when he mocked the court system by including his infant daughter as a fellow counsel, or announced a different name for himself from the dock. Everyone looked forward to a Price court case. It became his favourite pastime and he believed it added to his stature.

Litigation is frequently associated with schizophrenia, and in it Dr Price may have found the means of expressing his paranoia. Here he had his audience to play to, an arena where he was the central character – a character away from his life as a surgeon. Generally, people accepted him in a rigid Victorian era because of his outstanding success as a healer. On one hand they were afraid or at least somewhat sceptical of his peculiarities as a self-confessed Druid, but as a surgeon, their trust in him remained unwavering. Now he wanted to challenge a new, higher social class by entering the courtroom to display his total defiance and contempt of the judicial system publicly.

One of the first recorded court cases involved Dr Price as a defendant, rather than plaintiff or accused. In June 1847 an inquest was held into the death of Solomon Lewis, a twenty-three-year-old railway labourer from Banwell in Somerset who was killed when a skip of earth fell on him while working on the top of the tunnel at Nantgarw. 'Dr Price, surgeon, was instantly sent for; he hastened to the spot but the "vital spark" was extinct as the poor fellow died within fifteen minutes after the accident occurred.'[28] The court heard that 'this unfortunate affair seemed to be entirely the result of accident and the jury have declared no blame be attached to anybody'.

In 1846 Dr Price suffered a burglary at his home, when he found that his cupboard drawers had been broken into and a large sum of £69 10s stolen from his waistcoat pocket. He employed a housekeeper, possibly

Ann Morgan, his common law wife, who had been with him some time, and a new maidservant called Jennett Lewis. Price suspected Jennett and had her arrested. When she came to be examined at Cardiff and Caerphilly the magistrates felt that the other servant was the more likely culprit!

The case was dismissed for lack of evidence. Price, smarting under his loss, refused to pay Jennett Lewis her wages. The girl then brought an action demanding her wages but Price was determined not to pay her. After the examination of her mother, he asked for an adjournment, saying, in his defence, that he was now able to bring further evidence against her and would spend £50 on the prosecution if necessary. At the close of the proceedings, Price distributed copies of the depositions in Welsh to the court.

In June 1847 it came before the Small Debts Court under Mr Wilson, who heard that the wage claim was for 7s 10d, but Dr Price again refused to pay her because he believed she had stolen the money.

> Having provided that she had earned the sum of 7s 10d, by serving him in his household affairs, he entered upon his defence which was a charge of felony against her; but after hearing several witnesses the judge decided (as had a bench of county magistrates at Cardiff and Caerphilly in June 1846) that the charge could not be sustained; and an order for payment was made upon Mr Price which he instantly discharged.[29]

However, Jennet Lewis was still dissatisfied and brought an action against Dr Price in Jul 1847 for the recovery of the damages sustained by her by the

> detention of the wearing apparel after she had quitted, or rather been driven from his service ... on the present occasion proof was given of the plaintiff's wearing apparel having been taken to, and left at, the defendant's house; of a subsequent demand by the plaintiff's mother, and refused by defendant, to deliver them up. All the articles, consisting of upper and under garments of all descriptions, were minutely detailed, not excepting a thimble and valued at £1 12s 6d for which sum and order was made.

No further information is recorded of the outcome of the case, but it was unlikely to have proceeded any further.

However, 1847 was a more memorable year for Dr Price, and for that matter the rest of the country. The Newport Rising of the Chartists in 1839 was closely followed by the Rebecca Riots of Carmarthenshire in 1843, which resulted in the growing belief that the main reason behind such a dramatic increase in social unrest in Wales was due to the lack of education of its people. It took little notice of the social changes from being an undeveloped country to a place of wealthy industries and commerce, with huge consequences to the massive migration and density of population. Believing better education and discipline was the way in which to deal with social ills and oppress the unruly population – of which forty-six per cent were under the age of nineteen – Members of Parliament suspected that the general ignorance of the Welsh people was actually the cause of the period's social problems. However, Wales was largely a peaceful country in many respects as although petty thefts and drunkenness often appeared in the local press, the major crimes such as murder, rape, violence and burglaries were all very minimal.

The concern of the MPs resulted in three commissioners visiting every part of Wales to collect evidence and statistics, a scheme which was completed in April 1847, and a report was presented on 1 July in three large blue volumes, which caused shock and disgust among the inhabitants of Wales. *Reports of the Commissioners of Enquiry Into the State of Education in Wales* was better known as the 'Treachery of the Blue Books' or '*Brad Y Llyfrau Gleision*' as it condemned the Welsh people, its language, morals and the growth of Nonconformity as a religious force. The report contained direct comment on the poor religious and moral standing of the people, accusing them of being lazy, uncouth, socially degraded, corrupt, morally depraved and ignorant, causing furore and even greater agitation. One of the results was the effect it had on the nation's psyche, making people like Dr Price, Lady Llanover and those determined to create a sense of Welsh nationhood and cultural renaissance even more determined to '*tynnu Cymru o'i hol*' – pull Wales out of this 'hole' and fight the exploitative British Empire, which considered them inferior.

The commissioners believed the Welsh language was the biggest obstacle of all as it 'isolated the people from their masters' and could also be used to plot and conceal from the authorities, as had been the case with Chartism. Such statements infuriated Dr Price, whose home parish of Eglwysilan was deemed as a place where the people were 'ignorant and immoral, though not flagrantly so', but did 'lack mental discipline'. Suddenly the Welsh believed themselves 'foolhardy', as the report explained, and the only way they could educate and improve their lives was by speaking English, introducing by the 1870s the 'Welsh Not' as a form of literally 'beating Welsh' out of the mouths of children. The reports had been constructed largely from verbatim reports of prejudiced opinions of landowners and Anglican clergy – few of whom were likely to have any positive views of the proletariat. The census of religious worship claimed the Welsh were backward on the one hand, but well advanced in worship, although it was largely through the medium of Welsh at a Nonconformist chapel and not in an Anglican church. For the next three decades the debates about Wales, its people, culture, religion, morality and role in the British Empire, were persistent. What was needed was a further injection of confidence in the insecure Welsh psyche, more than Llanover's costumes, Iolo's Neo-Druidism or the cultural renaissance of the country could do. The Welsh people had an all-embracing facet of their lives that would unite them, and in doing so project an even greater image of the country to the rest of the world. It would take until 1872 to actually secure itself, but by then Wales's universal image as the Land of Song was born from the fusion of two easily discernible features of valley life in the mid- to late nineteenth century – the strength of Nonconformity and the frantic acceleration of the coalmining industry. As musician William Matthias stated,

> The tradition of the nineteenth-century Welsh choralism was as much a sociological as a musical phenomenon, arising out of the need of the people to express religious fervour or to rise above hardship and poverty through the means of choral singing. They are to be honoured for doing so. They and their leaders were in bond to their time in taking the only means open to them with results which were often inspiring.[30]

In January 1848 Dr William Price returned to the courtroom, where an action was brought against a fellow surgeon named David Gwynne Owen of Monmouth. Heard at Merthyr County Court, Dr Price accused Dr Owen of stealing one of his books, valued at £20. It appeared from the evidence of Mr J. C. Maddever, an assistant to Dr Price, who was formerly an assistant to Dr Owen, that about ten or twelve months earlier Price and Owen entered into partnership. Dr Price at the time was surgeon to Gellygaer Colliery. Mr Maddever had been sent by Dr Owen to reside at Nelson, as his representative.

At the commencement of the partnership, a book was bought by Price and given to the care of Mr Maddever, in which was entered a list of names of the workmen on whom Price was to attend and the payments to be made by them, as well as a list of private patients, from whom Dr Owen had received £25. Dr Price, who conducted his own case, contended that since the terms of the partnership had never been complied with by the defendant, the partnership was void; besides that, the partnership did not include his private patients, but only those who were employed at the works, and that Dr Owen had no right to receive the £25 that appeared on the book. For the defendant it was submitted that this, being a partnership concern, was entirely out of the jurisdiction of the court and could only be decided in the Court Chancery.[31]

The case continued in February, by which time Dr Owen had retired. It was proved that, during the existence of the partnership, both plaintiff and defendant had private patients, to whom they individually attended, and that the proceeds arising from this practice were separate and apart from the partnership concern. It appeared also that Price had attended a private patient and that Mr Owen was a friend of the invalid and he was called to attend. Mr Owen's witnesses proved that he at first objected, stating he felt a delicacy in attending patients who had first called on Dr Price, but that if it was the wish of the invalid and his friends, he would comply.

After the dissolution, Mr Owen, on making out his bills for the private practice, discovered that the leaves of the book containing the entries had been torn out and destroyed, he alleged, by Dr Price. Dr Owen made out his bill on the patient, and received in full £25. Dr Price conceived that he – and not Dr Owen – was entitled to the sum, or at least, a portion of it. It was proved by Mr Maddever that the patient and his friends expressed a wish to have the services of Dr Owen instead of Dr Price; and that £5 10s was in his opinion a sufficient remuneration for the services of Dr Price. He went on to say that he had heard Mr Thomas (the patient's uncle) say he would not grudge a hundred pounds to Mr Owen for the restoration to health of his nephew.

On cross-examination Mr Maddever admitted the treatment by Dr Owen of the patient was preferable to that of Dr Price, and in consequence of the leaves being torn from the book, Dr Owen sustained a loss of about £150.

Mr Charles and Frank James appeared in the court and submitted that if Dr Price attended the patient for three weeks, he was entitled to a larger portion of the £25. Dr Owen's brother conducted the defence, maintaining that even if Dr Price had attended the patient for a longer period, the patient's convalescence was entirely attributable to the treatment of Dr Owen.[31] Sadly, the result of the case is not known.

The court hearing greatly annoyed Dr Price, who dismissed Maddever as his assistant, resulting in them appearing before the judge again. Price refused to pay Maddever's wages on his dismissal, and on one occasion in July 1848 Maddever made a claim of 25s per week. The contract was on this, as former occasions proved, and also the performance of the services. Dr Price said Maddever had been paid wages as his assistant and received compensation for loss of time as a witness in Merthyr Court, and was consequently paid twice for the same thing. It was stated that the allowance to Maddever as a witness was intended to recover his expenses. Dr Price was ordered to pay the full amount.

In early 1848 the coroner for the Eastern District, William Davies, had passed away, allowing a vacancy for the position. Of the five candidates Dr Price was included, but failed to gain the post.

At the end of February 1848, Dr Price was again mixing with the gentry of the vicinity when he attended the Merthyr Fancy Ball at the Castle Hotel in Merthyr Tydfil. Around ninety people attended, with nearly the whole of the gentlemen being attired in 'gay fancy costume', while the dresses of the ladies were almost as 'beautiful as the fair and sylph-like forms that floated around the room, forming a galaxy of brilliance'.[32]

Organised by Robert Thompson Crawshay, Samuel Homfray of Tredegar and Richard Fothergill, who acted on behalf of Rowland Fothergill of Hensol Castle, the room was 'well lit', with the Cyfarthfa Brass Band and a string orchestra providing the entertainment. Crawshay was dressed as a Venetian, while Dr Price was dressed as 'Robin Crusoe, in full costume – this figure attracted much attention'.

Dr Price appeared as a witness in the case involving Thomas Mostyn, the superintendent of police at Newbridge, against Richard Llewellyn-Reece, former attorney of Newbridge, to recover damages for loss sustained by Mostyn for 'libels' published about him by Reece.

It was the first case in which Dr Price's colourful costume was discussed openly in court.

A newspaper report read,

William Price, surgeon, Porthyglo, examined by Mr Hall, said in October 1846 he met Mostyn and saw he was drunk.

Prosecutor Mr Chilton asked, 'Pray Sir, are you a member of the Royal College of Surgeons?

'They say so,' Dr Price responded.

'But, really I wish to know whether you are a member of the college or not?'

'Yes I am.'

Mr Chilton enquired, 'And is this dress in which I now see you the uniform of a surgeon who is a member of college?' followed by immense laughter in the court.

'No, it is not. It is the dress of the Ancient Court at Glamorgan,' Dr Price snapped.

His dress, 'which is exceedingly peculiar', made the judge and counsel 'stare with all their eyes'.[33]

Dr Price's unconventional mode of living, his costume and what many perceived as heretical beliefs had already aroused a fury and hatred of the preachers and other pillars of respectability. Gossip, pulpit and press were used to spread stories about him. The preachers of his time invented the first Welsh atrocity with the idea of discrediting him in the eyes of the 'faithful'. Having ordered a post-mortem on the body of his father during the proceedings of one particular court case, they seized upon the incident to give vent to their hatred and spite by saying that he had the body exhumed and then cut the head off. Such stories further fuelled the anti-Dr Price feeling among the Nonconformist and Anglican clergy. Dr Price was even questioned about it in another court case in 1856. At that point he told the court in no uncertain terms, 'I should be glad to open my father's head a thousand times if I could benefit the human race by getting the wickedness and insanity out of their heads. In our profession we, medical men and men of science, do not think of our subjects as fathers and mothers, brothers or sisters, but as sticks and stones, as you regard them.'

The event came about as a result of a court case held in Bristol in 1848 to decide whether Dr Price's father had been insane in 1809 when he sold 85 acres of land in the Rudry area. Dr Price was effectively trying to reclaim land which he believed his insane father had sold, while suffering his mental deficiencies and therefore unsure of his actions, to the wealthy

Fothergill family of Hensol Castle. The reverend died in 1841, spending his last six years residing in Glandwr, near the Bedwas Bridge. A certificate declaring Revd Price a lunatic and committing him to the care of his eldest son, Charles, was dated 21 June 1839. It stated the management of the Revd Price's estate was also entrusted into the hands of Charles. The date of the certificate however is not the same as that of Dr Price's testimony in the trial as he said it was proved at the Boar's Head, Caerphlly, on 22 May 1839. Revd Price's post-mortem was undertaken by Joseph Davies of Tŷ Isaf Farm, Bedwas and Dr Evan Edwards to prove his insanity.

The Fothergills were a family of ironmasters who originally came from Kendal in Cumberland. Two brothers travelled south to establish a small ironworks in the Forest of Dean before coming to the ironworks in Tredegar and Sirhowy. One of the brothers was Richard Fothergill (1758–1821), who joined Homfray at Tredegar, later becoming High Sheriff of Monmouthshire in 1829. It was his son, Rowland Fothergill (1794–1871), who came into contact with Dr Price on more than one occasion. On becoming the chief of the Abernant works and the controlling influence in the Llwydcoed Ironworks, he made his fortune both at Llwydcoed and by erecting the Taff Vale Ironworks in Treforest, next to Crawshay's tinplate works, before retiring to the stately home of Hensol Castle. His brother, Richard (1822–1903), was an ironmaster, coal owner and politician who became the proprietor of the Aberdare Ironworks and later the Plymouth Ironworks and Penydarren. It was in Aberdare that he built his magnificent home and became a Member of Parliament for the town.

Determined to reclaim the once gentrified Price family wealth and legacy from the Fothergills, while also attempting to reassert his own nobility and standing in the community, Dr Price took the 'Trustees of the Children of the Fothergill Family' to Bristol Assizes on 28 August 1848 for a court case that caused heightened interest from the general public and the press, who stated, 'This was an issue directed to try the question whether a clergyman of Wales, the Revd W. Price, was of sound mind in the year 1809 when he executed a certain deed for the sale of some estates at Rudry, Glamorganshire.' Clearly the court case was also of interest due to 'the strange character and grotesque appearance of the defendant Dr Price ... in the costume of the Royal Court of Glamorgan'.[32]

Sergeant Kingslake, Mr Barstown and Mr Smith appeared for Dr Price, while Mr Cockburn and Mr Butt appeared for the Fothergills. The case was due to Revd Price selling a small property of 83 acres to John Hodder Moggridge in 1809. Moggridge died in 1831, a decade before the reverend. Charles Price 'asserted that his parent, at the time of the execution of the deed, was of unsound mind, that therefore the law could give no effect to it, that though his father had executed it, yet, in consequence of the unsoundness of his mind, and that he was entitled to the property'.[33]

Influenced greatly by his brother William, Charles had made an attempt in 1836 to bring into question the sale of the property which he claimed was undertaken 'fraudulently' because it was sold for less than it was worth and his father was not of sound mind when the sale took place. In 1837 a 'commission of lunacy' was taken out with the view of assisting the vicar with his interests as he had 'been a lunatic, without lucid intervals, as far back as 1798'. Given that so much time had elapsed since 1809 and since many witnesses had died, it was deemed a difficult case to solve with the absence of so much evidence.

Moggridge, of Gloucestershire, had moved to Monmouthshire in 1809, well after Revd Price's 'symptoms of aberrations of intellect became apparent'. Moggridge bought several estates, including the one in Rudry, first offered to him by a solicitor named Prothero of Newport who had conducted Revd Price's affairs. In 1805 Prothero was instructed by Revd Price to raise money from the property so he could pay off the mortgage because the lender, Samuel Rees, had been demanding payment. Moggridge became the purchaser of land for £2,000 in 1809. Of this £678 was due to the principal lender of the mortgage and £477 10s was left to Prothero's hands, to be paid either to Price or anyone who had claims on him. Moggridge was to pay the remainder, £814, with three per cent interest over time to Revd Price. The vicar was allowed to stay on the premises for some time, but after a year refused to leave and remained for several years and eventually a solicitor named Meyrick was to bring them both together to discuss the matter. When Moggridge heard that the question of the validity of the original transaction was being brought into question, he asked for the return of his money and the cancellation of the terms. By then the money had gone and the only solution was to sell the land; repayment of the £2,000 and any extra money should be given to the Revd Price, but the family objected and said they would keep the money and the estate. Moggridge then brought the ejectment notice against the family and by 1813 had possession of it until he died.

As for the remaining money owed by Moggridge to Revd Price, he had been instructed not to make any further payments because of the mental state of the vicar and should wait until Charles Price became of age to undertake his father's financial concerns. In 1820 this occurred and Charles gave release to all the claims, waiting a further sixteen years – and pressurised by William – to re-examine the situation.

No one could dispute that Revd Price was subject to periodical fits of insanity but at the same time those fits were of such a character as to be accompanied by lucid intervals, and during which time he was capable of acting rationally and that it was within one of those times the deed in question was executed.

Numerous witnesses testified that the Revd Price was insane for the last forty years of his life. The court case lasted until nine o'clock in the evening. It was admitted Revd William Price was a lunatic, was sought to be shown that he had lucid intervals, including the visits by surgeon and mortgage lender Richard Reece (who admitted they discussed his college days rather than the mortgage he was about to sign) and the solicitor Prothero, who executed several mortgages on the property during the early 1800s. However, under cross-examination Prothero admitted that on 9 February 1809, when the deeds for Moggridge were to be signed, 'the unhappy man was then suffering under his malady and could not do it'.

The only witness who spoke to a conversation of any length with Price was a Wesleyan preacher who said that twenty years ago had a conversation with Revd Price, in a wood, who said when at Cowbridge School he went to hear John Wesley preach.

On the Monday morning the court was told of his early life and promising academic career and that

In 1787 he was thrown from his horse and pitched on his head and soon after indications of insanity presented themselves. Within a brief period of his occurrence he married a person of a station much inferior to his own. Whether his mind had then received its first shock was not known, but at any rate directly after the marriage evidences of his insanity appeared. The jury would hear from the witnesses not only the painful and disastrous condition of the man but the shocking and disgusting actions which he had been led to commit under the influence of the disease.

He became disordered in his dress, and took to leaving home, and frequenting woods where he was in the habit of cutting and defacing the trees, which in fact seemed to be one of his greatest pleasures. He always went around with a saw, which nothing would induce him to part with, and thus made incurations into other people's grounds so often that he became quite a nuisance. His custom was to bark the trees, then to cut the sticks into small portions, secrete them about his person and when he went home burn these bit by bit, muttering strange uncouth words as persons in madness usually did ... he entertained that stones, after he had spat upon them, acquired a value, and he would always put such stones away carefully. Again he supposed there was a marvellous charm about snakes. He sought them and carried them about his person and would keep them in his pocket until he found an opportunity of depositing them in the family vault, among the bones of his ancestors ... He also had a great predilection for water; and one of his greatest enjoyments was to immerse himself in a pond up to his neck. Sometimes he would take off his clothes, but before he put them on again, he would dip them in the pond to make them wet. He would go in sometimes without his hat only. But if he did, he would fill it with water before he replaced it on his head. That, however, might be connected with physical causes, a surgeon made an examination of his head after his death and found the blood vessels very large; and the notion of the water on the brain might, therefore have caused relief to its throbbing, and operated to induce the desire of being in the water.[34]

Dr Edwards of Caerphilly and Dr Davies of Bedwas carried out this procedure.

He was constantly in wet clothes, sometimes he was without any dress at all ... Witness after witness would depose that they had seen this clergyman, striding with wild steps across the country in a state of absolute and complete nudity.[34]

Among the witnesses called were those who had taken care of Mr Price and had been servants in his household, and the instances of total and unmitigated madness of which they spoke were numerous. They remembered that there were occasions on which he assumed a calm and quiet form, on other occasions they would not dispute that the

maniac chained to his cell, when he had worn out in his mad struggles his physical energy, sank into that state of tranquillity and repose which human nature so imperatively demanded ... but he was not an 'innocent' but a mischievous madman, and had fired off a gun at a young woman, whom he fancied had been taking sticks from his hedge. On another occasion he nearly killed a man, by flinging at him a sharp pointed stick, which missed the mark and buried itself some inches in the earth. His wife usually exercised a great influence over him, but there were times when he would make her and the children – of whom he terrified into fits – fly from his presence. He was a man of great prowess and courage, but when the keepers, whom his wife had been advised to put over him – Owen, Dafis and Williams, found it necessary to exercise physical as well as a moral restraint upon him, he never resisted them and after they had once inflicted punishment, he was as docile as a lamp, had few paroxysms of insane fury in their presence. In one instance he so terrified a lady named Davis, who was in the family way, that premature confinement was the result. The keepers who were appointed to keep him in check used to lock him up at night, but he would sometimes contrite to jump out of the window and go about the country... he had never met so painful, so miserable, so distressing a case, one so lamentable in all its features ... Mr Price was to all intents and purposes an insane man.[34]

The jury were asked by the defending lawyer whether they genuinely believed a man in such a distressing state could in fact have had lucid enough intervals to conduct business of his sort. If he could show them that for forty years Revd Price manifested the extreme symptoms of insanity, both before and after the act of 1809, it would give Charles Price a stronger case.

Of the twenty witnesses called, all said they never knew him otherwise than as a 'confirmed' lunatic. At times a dangerous maniac, at other seasons more tranquil and more under control, but at all periods utterly and hopelessly insane. 'At one time flying through the fields and woods stark naked, shouting, hollowing and bellowing and again in ragged and torn clothes carrying bundles of sticks, filthily disgusting in his habits and person, frequently dangerous to himself and others.' The defence also added that even on the day of the signing of the deeds Revd Price had jumped through the window and flown into the woods and 'could not, therefore, execute the instrument on that day and that on the 9th [the following day] he was fastened up in a room until the lawyer arrived with the deed, was then brought down by his keeper, said to sign his name, that he did so and that immediately after, on being let loose, he started away down the river, came back with a large stone, and secreted it in his room, saying it was of immense value'.[35]

The judge summed up and the jury had no trouble to return the verdict for Charles Price and his family. However, the case was brought before the Vice Chancellor's Court on 24 February 1849 to Vice Chancellor Wigram, where the Solicitor General Burrington and Mr Headlam, for the Prices, asked that the transaction be declared void and the deeds given up to be cancelled and for certain accounts of the rents and profits to be repaid.

Mr Wood and Mr Smythe, for the trustees and executors of Moggridge's will, said the claim ought to be dismissed with costs as Charles Price on 18 March 1822 had assigned all his interest in the property to Moggridge, as the deed bound by his father had done in February 1809.

The vice chancellor gave an opinion that he could not dismiss the bill and did not see what evidence there was to suggest Moggridge had notice of Price's insanity, because it was not shown that he was in such a state that anyone in his company must necessarily perceive his insanity. The judge argued that Moggridge in fact was only one in the unfortunate position of having bought an estate of a madman.

In the supplement bill filed by Charles Price he stated as being heir-at-law, but in truth he was only an administrator of his father.

Lord Chancellor Cotton, who tried the case, was very much in Charles Price's favour, and gave him the verdict, but it was refused on appeal and Charles Price claimed to have lost £4,000.

The ongoing series of court cases of which Dr Price participated were becoming a regular feature of the newspapers and clearly much attention was aroused by the striking figure of the Druid. In March 1849 he attended another of the lavish Crawshay affairs, this time also attended by Sir John and Lady Charlotte Guest at the Castle Inn, Merthyr Tydfil, where the 'company being numerous and comprising of most of the leading families of the place, the room was in exquisite order, the lights admirable, only surpassed in brilliance by the eyes of the ladies'.[36]

Not all was well with Dr Price, particularly when he faced losing his home of Porthyglo. The first hearing of a case between William Price and Revd John Rogers took place in July 1848, when Mr Rogers demanded the possession of his house and premises. However a Mr Chilton, counsel for Rogers, announced that the record had been withdrawn. By July it reappeared in the court when Mr Chilton returned once more for Rogers, and Mr Evans QC and Nicholl Carne appeared for Dr Price. Mr Chilton said that his client took possession of Porthyglo under the will of the Revd Evan Jones, who had granted a lease to Charles Price, one of the defendants, the other defendant being Mr William Price, surgeon.

It was contended at considerable length and sought to be established by evidence that the defendants had committed a breach of covenant. Ultimately a verdict was taken for Rogers, with damages of a shilling.

At the end of May and early June 1849 the case went before the Vice Chancellor's Court under Sir J. K. Bruce, and the newspapers ran a series of articles entitled 'Doctor Price's Goats'. Revd Rogers took Dr Price to court over the state of Porthyglo. The newspaper report read,

> The value of the subject matter of the suit was stated to be very trifling, but, if properly protected as in 20 years be probably worth £20 or £30. The object of the bill was to restrain William Price, his servants, agents and workmen, by injunction from leading, driving, or admitting any goats of the defendant, or any other domestic animals noxious to young tree saplings, wood or under wood into Graig Galva, otherwise known as Craig Alfa Wood, or plantation, or into any woodland comprised in the premises which had been leased and injure any of the trees … during the term of the lease.[37]

In 1835, Revd Evan Jones of Colwinston in Glamorgan granted a lease for ninety-nine years to Thomas Thomas, of Craig Alfa, with power to dig and raise paving or tile stones but not damage trees or wood. In 1840 the premises were assigned by the lease of Charles Price, who transferred his interest to Dr Price. In July 1848, Rogers wanted Charles and William evicted from the property for destroying young trees whilst working in the nearby quarries. The subject was brought before Mr Justice Wightman and a verdict was found for Rogers. Two days after the case, Dr Price turned goats into the Craig Alva Wood and 'he had been warned not to do so, as the goats would eat off the bark and damage the young trees'.

Consequently Dr Price insisted he had every right to do so. Witnesses were called for both sides, including some who suggested the goats had bitten off the bark of the woods. Others said they were most likely to eat moss and ivy and up to fifty goats were on Craig yr Alva without doing any damage. The judge observed that Dr Price treated the goats as domestic animals. The case was eventually withdrawn.

Gertrude Jenner reminisced about Dr Price and his goats in later life, remembering a time around 1841 when she travelled to Cardiff with her father and Dr Price sent a message that he wanted to see him. Dr Price came to their hotel, The Angel, and he asked to send two of his favourite goats to graze for two or three weeks on their rough ground at Wenvoe Castle. Mr Jenner said the goats could stay for six weeks if he wanted, as long as he took responsibility for them. He then ordered a room to be made available to Dr Price and some hay and food prepared for the goats on their arrival. After waiting some hours, the group were astonished to see a whole herd of goats scampering towards them with three goat-men. Apparently Dr Price had been disappointed of pasturage and they were turned out, so he sent them all down, hoping they could all reside at Wenvoe. She said, 'My father was naturally perplexed, but always kind-hearted and good-natured, ordered the herd to be driven straight up to the upper lawns where they would have shelter under the wood and gorse and had a load of straw taken up, and hay and oats to be put down, in a sheltered corner. The three goat men then had a good dinner and given a shilling apiece, and a letter was sent to their master saying ...'[38] two goats could remain but the herd had to be recovered in a week. When no one arrived a week later a letter was sent to the doctor as the bark on the trees was all being damaged. Eventually Mr Jenner sent the goats out with Dr Price, placing a summons on him, but on reaching the court four goats named 'Jenner', 'Price,' 'Gertrude' and 'Wenvoe Castle' entered the courtroom, turning the proceedings into a kind of burlesque, causing the entire case to collapse!

Dr William Price was on the verge of turning fifty years of age. He had reached the very peak of his success as a surgeon and moved in the circles of the highest wealth and extravagance in Wales, yet had also been an exiled political activist. He was the father of one surviving daughter and lived with his mistress, who was also his housekeeper. Respected by an entire community, but often scorned by the press with a history of litigation and an obsession with Druidism, Dr William Price was an incredibly dynamic, energetic and yet complicated individual. With the dawning of a new decade midway through the nineteenth century, his life showed little evidence of slowing down. In fact, during the decade ahead he faced the legal system on the most serious charges of his life, continued to stand witness to the incredible changes of the community surrounding him and showed such dedication to his religion that he undertook his biggest project of all, one that remains an iconic landmark site in South Wales. A decade of success and failure in equal measure followed as this awkward, mischievous, proud and strong man continued to shock, stimulate and intrigue all those who came into contact with him.

1850–1859

Litigation became an obsession for Dr William Price during the second half of his life and rarely a year passed when he wasn't involved in some type of legal proceeding. Allowing him a showcase to vent his aggressions and ideals to a wider audience, his various trials and cases continued to attract widespread attention, not least of which due to his appearance and behaviour. By the opening of the new decade he had left his home of fourteen years, Porthyglo, following the court hearings with the property owner Rogers, and was now residing with Hiarlhes and her mother Ann Morgan in a property named 'Llwyn Llwydh' or Llwyn Llwyd at Craig yr Helfa, Glyntaff. According to manuscripts of the period, the site is often referred to as Craigalfa and Craigalva, depending on whether Dr Price had changed its spelling to offer a more mystic, Druidic impression!

In February 1850 Price brought an action against James Curtis, the brother-in-law of William Watson of the Castle Inn, Treforest, to recover compensation by way of damages for an assault committed near Pwll Nant y Dale in Newbridge on 15 January. Damages were laid at £5. Mr Langley appeared for the defendant while Dr Price defended himself in the court.

He explained,

On the 25th of January, at about half past nine at night I was returning homewards from various places. It was dark, but the light given by the Treforest Works enabled me to perceive two persons coming to meet me within sixty yards of me or thereabouts. They were on the right hand side of the road coming up. I recognised that they spoke English in a moment; and I fancied that they had been drinking a little. I was walking in the middle of the road as I always do, but when they came near me I turned to the side of the road. Notwithstanding that I moved very quickly, the shorter one came against me and struck me. I should have fallen from the violence of it I had not held on by the waistband and shirt of the one who assaulted me. I knew the taller person, but I did not know the shorter one. The taller one was Charles Nash, inspector of rails at Mr Crawshay's works. I knew him well.

On recovering myself from the effects of the blow, I said, 'Holio, what is the reason that you assault people on the highway at night?' The shorter one made no answer but the taller one said, 'I am very sorry for it Mr Price; we did not think it was you.' I replied, 'Whether it is me or somebody else, you have no right to assault any one on the highway.' He begged my pardon again. I said, 'What is your name that I should pardon one for assaulting me on the highway'. I did not know him and would not give me his name. The truth is that the light from the works being on my back and in their faces I was enabled to see them better than they could see me. Nash and the other man were arm in arm. I again asked for his name when he answered, 'I am an Englishman and you are a d— Welshman.' 'Well, well', I said, 'that is not sufficient for me; it is my determination to know who you are, whether you are English, French, a God, a devil or lice – I will know your name.' He said, 'No you shall not,' and threatened me.

When we had gone about sixty yards further, we came to an ash tree. I again asked for their names, when just at that point the shorter one ran at me with one hand advanced and the other a little back. I fancied he had something in his hand, a knife or some deadly weapon. The instant I saw that I drew a pistol out and held it towards him. I keep two pistols with me always when out at nights. He ran at me just as a person would who wished to attack another. I presented a pistol to his chest and swore I would fire at him. At that instant Nash stood between us or else I have no doubt, I would have fired at him ... the shorter man ran at me again ... Nash again interfered ... and a third time.[1]

In cross-examination Charles Nash reluctantly admitted he had met an intoxicated James Curtis but could not recollect an attack although he said, 'There were threats used on both side – Mr Price threatening to shoot, and the other threatening to strike.' The judge ordered 10s with full costs to Dr Price.

Dr Price was also known for causing added confusion to a court hearing, and the next court case, at the Small Debts Court, gives some indication of his behaviour. It also indicates that although he hadn't resided in his home village Rudry, he maintained close associations with the area. The 1843 tithe map lists him as the lessee of Mynyddybwlch pasture land and also as lessee of Pentwyn Farm. The farm was close to the original Ty-yn-y-Coedcae Farm and although it doesn't appear that Dr Price lived there, it was certainly occupied by his sister, Elizabeth and in fact she died in the property some years later.

The case on 12 June 1850 was held before Judge John Wilson and involved Miss Maria Price, of Crockherbtown, Pentwyn in Cardiff, who attempted to recover from the doctor the possession of a piece of land of 45 acres called Mynyddybwlch in Rudry. Price, 'who was known here and elsewhere very extensively',[2] defended himself. The extensive common land had come into the possession of Miss Price on the death of her father. She had let it to Dr Price in 1838 to graze his young cattle at £5 per annum and £1 for game, after he had convinced her to take the land from the previous tenant, a Lewis Henry, and offer the tenancy to him. At that stage the proceedings seemed clear enough to all concerned. However, when Miss Price wanted the property returned and tried to evict Dr Price, he refused and claimed he had rights to the property through his own family ancestry, whether he was in agreement with Miss Price or not.

This seemed a simple situation, but to recover the land she had to take it to court. To make the situation worse Dr Price succeeded in using ingenious delaying tactics to get the matter referred to the Court of the Queen's Bench. What added further chaos to the proceedings was the fact that Maria Price was a second cousin to the doctor.

Miss Price's servant Mary Rees explained she recalled the agreement between her mistress and Lewis Henry and the one with Dr Price, who wanted to raise his young cattle on the property because, as she explained,

> It was a convenience to him, because it was handy to a farm that he held. The farm was adjoining and it. This conversation ended in Price taking the land and giving Lewis Henry notice. Mr William Price was to give five pounds per year with a pound for the game but after the bargain was made she told him that she had heard that he was an arbitrary sort of a man and she was not willing for him to have the land. He asked for a pen and ink and paper and he wrote that he was to give it up at six months notice. He signed it and so did Miss Price. He asked Miss Price, 'Are you quite satisfied now?' she said, 'Yes'. I recollect Mr Price being out of the country (during his exile in France). I recollect a letter coming from Mr Charles Price, who managed his affairs, to Miss Price.[2]

There was a whole host of evidence suggesting that William Price had occupied the land, and by 1845 the rent book featured both his name and that of his elder brother, Charles, who was the cashier at Crawshay's tinplate works. On cross-examination, Thomas Evans, the solicitor to Miss Price, said that in June 1849 he had served a bill of £30 on Dr Price for five years' rent of Mynyddybwlch.

Dr Price sent to Maria Price's solicitor a letter which tried to change the issue completely by arguing she had usurped the legitimate claims of her half-brother James Price to some of her late father's property, and claimed James had entrusted his interests to the doctor as his relative.

The letter, dated 13 June 1849 at Porthyglo, makes interesting reading because for the first time we see written work by Dr Price where clearly his mind is somewhat less lucid than it had been before:

Dear Sir, having asked Miss Price of Crochberbtown, for those effects willed by her late father to Mr James Price and received from you the evasive answer of June the 8th, I have no alternative now but to demand the same from you, as her agent or legal advisor to whom you say she has referred me on the subject matter in dispute – I suppose I do therefore demand, on behalf of James Price, the residuary legatee of the Revd James Price (late of Cardiff) all and singular every article given and bequeathed to him, the said James Price, by his late father in his will, which can be proved he had in his possession the dwelling house at Cardiff at his deceased and at the decease of his late widow, the mother of Miss Price.

I hope Miss Price will submit or be advised by you to submit to my demand, on behalf of her half brother, in peace and good will. I will take care that every power given and every obligation entered into at Llandaff, and assigned to me by James Price, shall be duly, at the proper time and stages of his administration, requested.

When Miss Price submits to the power given in peace or otherwise then will come the time or stage of her set off or claim to be considered. To pay or to be asked to pay Miss Price £60 out of her father's estate in her possession is rather an extraordinary proposition from a lawyer and a man of business. But here it is! The desire that follows and expressed in the last paragraph is the same style of extraordinary composition or construction I presume that wonders will never cease in the confusion of ideas till the day of judgement, whence everything will move in order in all directions to the sound of music.

May that come forthwith to destroy the intervention of doctors, lawyers and priests between the wild and tame god. Looking at the animus of my first letter on this business to Miss Price, you will see that my object is justice and peace, not peace and justice. She shall not escape her father's will if I can, either shall her half brother injure her peace of mind and her interest capriciously himself or by my agoney [sic].

I have taken care of him. Let her take care of herself not to resist her father's will in respect of her half brother, James Price, who has assigned to me his authority to do what I shall consider right and just between them. If Miss Price will put the same confidence in me under your advice as her half brother has done himself I will undertake to settle their different interested to the satisfaction of both parties, without legal intervention, William Price.[3]

Apparently when a clerk working on behalf of Miss Price's solicitor returned to the farm to demand possession of it, all that welcomed him were a flock of goats! The statement caused widespread laughter throughout the courtroom.

When Price fled to France, his brother Charles managed his affairs and his name appeared on the rate book, but the rent had not been paid for five years and when a Robert Williams attempted to serve notice on the doctor, he locked him in the surgery until he agreed to serve the notice on his brother. The case excited considerable interest, particularly when the judge ruled that it was Charles Price upon whom Maria should have served notice and she had prosecuted the wrong man, letting William go free. However, this was not the end of the matter and it would once again land the doctor before a magistrate.

For the third time in 1850 Dr Price was summoned to court, this time to return once more to the Bristol Assizes in August before Mr Justice Coleridge. On this occasion Dr Price, described as 'an eccentric surgeon ... obtained some celebrity in a trial in Bristol ... he is pretty well known',[4] appeared with solicitors on his behalf, Mr Barstow and Mr Greenwood. This case related once again to his residence of Porthyglo, the house and farm of 63 acres belonging to Mr Grover that was leased for twenty-one years, which was determinable after fourteen years for either side. As Dr Price would not undertake certain repairs on the property as requested, and barricaded himself into the property, he was eventually ejected by force. Mr Grover consequently tried to retrieve £191 15s from Dr Price to carry out the repairs requested. The surgeon admitted that there was certain damage to the outside of the property but he had already paid £54 10s 10d to the court, which he felt was sufficient, but Gover added that Price hadn't actually paid rent for the past six months either, which amounted to £50 alone and that the £4 10s 10d could go towards the cost of the repairs.

On being called as a witness, Daniel Thomas, a builder and surveyor of Cardiff, described the state of the house to have been abominable. 'Some rooms had been appropriated to the use of pigeons and goats and had not been cleaned for years; while the water courses were filled up with rubbish, causing the water to overflow to the injury of the premises. The witness went through all the items which were numerous, one by one.'[4] Dr Price denied them all, claiming the property was cleaned and painted and the court fell into hysterics when he explained he had replaced the sash windows and locks. Grover's solicitor asked whether he had sold them, whereas Price answered he'd actually paid to have them removed! In return the judge criticised him for conducting the case in such a minute manner and called it a 'disgrace' and he could not expect a jury to remember all of these details or the case could last for two or three days!

Several witnesses were called who testified to have carried out necessary repairs, including fencing and roofing works, at Porthyglo. A number of other witnesses, including David Edwards, David Lewis, Thomas Morgan, David Morgan, John Davis, William John and Charles Price himself criticised Grover's exaggerated list of repairs for the building. They also said the house had been whitewashed five years earlier, although those who painted it had since 'gone to America'. Finally the jury, which also took time to deliberate, awarded costs of a staggering £140 to Grover. Dr Price was totally incensed.

In 1851 Dr Price visited the International Exhibition in Cardiff in a goat-drawn carriage, such was his love for the animal. Price had goats and sheep immortalised in a series of paintings at his home, and his proudest possession was his Glamorgan herd of cattle that he specifically disposed of in his will.

One of the largest court cases involving Dr William Price up until this point occurred in 1853, when he faced the serious indictment of perjury, the wilful act of swearing a false oath in the courtroom. The entire episode began at the Cardiff County Court on 11 March 1853 for a case entitled *Millward* v. *Millward*.

His indictment for perjury read,

> William Price, Esq., Surgeon of Llwyn Lhwidh, in the parish of Eglwysilan, Ponty Priyh, in this county, was charged on suspicion with having, on the 11th of March last, in the borough of Cardiff, committed perjury, in testimony which he gave upon oath at the trial of a certain cause, between William Millward, plaintiff, and Ann Millward and Frederick Burns, defendants at the County Court of Glamorganshire, held at Cardiff.

At the arraignment of Dr Price at nine o'clock on Saturday morning, as the case opened, Mr Price's name was called. When he didn't appear, it was stated that he had gone home on the previous night, and that the train by which he would arrive was not yet due. In the course of the day Mr Price arrived, but another court case took up most of the day until nine o'clock in the evening.

His Lordship asked, 'Is Mr Price here?'

The Under Sheriff said, 'Mr Price has gone home, my Lord; he left the Temperance Hotel under the impression that his trial would not come on until Monday morning.'

He was called again but did not answer. Mr Giffard, counsel for the prosecution, applied to his Lordship to grant a warrant for his arrest. His Lordship did not grant the application, observing that he did not see what end it would answer, unless to gratify spite, and told the counsel to speak to him on the subject on Monday.

At the reassembling of the court on Monday morning, the judge intimated to Dr Price his regret that he had left on Saturday night without having the sanction of the court because if he had remained the case might have been tried. Mr Price said he was a medical man in extensive practice and left because he was under the impression the case would not be called and he wanted to attend to his patients.

After some delay, Mr Price having challenged a large number of jurymen, the preliminaries were got through and the trial proceeded. Mr Price conducted his own defence, and was accommodated with a seat at the barrister's table. Dr Price, displaying his total contempt for the judicial system and establishment by causing chaos in the court, was called as a witness on behalf of the defendant, Ann Millward. A copy of the New Testament was put into his hands so he could be sworn, but he objected because he didn't believe in the accuracy of the map of Judea inside it. Therefore a copy of the Bible was handed to him and he objected to being sworn on that as the owner of the Bible's name was written on a blank page. Finally another copy of the New Testament was found and he couldn't find any objection to being sworn on that one.

Price was examined by a Mr Haviland and cross-examined by Mr Bird. The court heard that in 1847, Thomas Millward died and had owned a quarry and other property in Newbridge. By his will, which was prepared and witnessed by Dr Price, he left all his property to his widow, and on her death it would go to their four children, William, John, Mary and Ann. William Millward rented certain premises from his sister and for some reason she made a claim for rent and arrears of rent on the premises, the rent only being due from the brother on the day the claim was made. Instead of going to the quarry, for which the rent was payable, Ann Millward, who lived in Treforest and was supported by Dr William Price, ordered the bailiff of the County Court of Cardiff, Frederick Burns, to go to her brother William's private house so the rent for the quarry could be obtained by goods and furniture. Such an action was not allowed to be lawful and an action was then brought against Ann Millward herself along with Frederick Burns.

The question arose, in a trial on 11 March 1853, of how the bailiff himself knew which house to go to. Dr Price appeared at the trial and was asked in the witness box whether he had given instructions to Burns, but Price said he never even saw him. In court, Burns said that on 24 January he went to the Castle Inn, Treforest and was met with solicitors Edward Davies, followed by Mr Haviland and Ann Millward. As Burns began to have breakfast Dr Price entered and said, 'Leave that alone. You will have time for that bye and by.' Mr Haviland asked him if he had any warrants with him to which he produced two black forms and he was asked to make out a claim for unpaid rent. When Burns asked him who should pay this rent, Price said 'William Millward'. Burns then asked Price how much was the rent, he said it was £61 and it was due that day. Burns said they could not compel payment of debts on the day it was due to which Price replied,

'Mind your own business, do your duty' and warned Burns to be 'more civil'. Burns then wrote out the warrant to obtain the rent and showed it to Ann Millward, who consulted Dr Price to see if it was correct. Price said it was 'all right' and told him to visit William Millward's house and added that even if he tried to pay the debt, he should still obtain his goods and personal belongings because a fresh case against William Millward was also being drawn.

Burns said in court, 'The business was done from instructions you (Dr Price) gave me, and not from Mr Haviland or Miss Millward. I did not receive instructions from any other person to make the distress except the prisoner. Ann Millward did not interfere at all; she seemed afraid to interfere.'

Burns said in the second hearing in April, 'She would not have signed the authority if it had not been for Dr Price. That I swear. I persist in saying that Ann Millward gave me no instruction on the day I was there. Mr Haviland gave me no instruction at the Castle Inn. Dr Price gave me the instructions I acted. I said it was a great pity the matter could not be settled without any interference at all, as they were all respectable people. Mr Haviland did not direct. Dr Price directed.'

At the hearing Edward Davies also swore that Dr Price had given the order to obtain items to the value of £61 from William Millward, whose house was near the Duke of Bridgewater Arms.

Consequently, Dr Price was faced with the following indictment:

On the eleventh of March 1853, in the County Court, William Millward sought to recover damages against Ann Millward and Frederick Burns her bailiff, for seizing his goods by virtue of a distress for rent. It became a material question whether William Price had instructed Frederick Burns and told him where to go to make the said distress, and had met him, and had seen him at Treforest on the 24 January 1853. William Price, duly sworn, said that he had not come for the bailiff, had not told the plaintiff where to go or what to do; had not met the bailiff at Treforest and had not seen him at Treforest on the 24 January 1853. Whereas he had come, had told, had seen, had met and so did consult wilful and corrupt perjury.[4]

William Williams, Mayor of Cardiff, told the court,

Whereas information hath this day been laid before the undersigned, one of Her Majesty's Justices of the Peace, in and for the said Borough of Cardiff for that you the said William Price did, on the Eleventh day of March, instant at the Borough of Cardiff aforesaid, falsely, wickedly wilfully and corruptly, did commit wilful and corrupt Perjury in the testimony which he gave upon the trial of a certain cause between William Millward, Plaintiff, and Ann Millward and Frederich Burns, defendants, at the County Court of Glamorganshire held at Cardiff, against the form of the statute in such case made and provided. These are therefore to command you, in Her Majesty's name to be and appear on Thursday, the 17th of March at Eleven o'clock in the Forenoon at the Town Hall, in the Town of Cardiff, before such Justices of the Peace for the said Borough as may then be there, to answer to the said information, and to be further dealt with according to Law. Given under my Hand and seal, this 14th day of March in the Year of Our Lord 1853, at the Borough of Cardiff aforesaid.[5]

The case was adjourned until 4 April when Dr Price appeared before William Williams, and Gareth Phillips Esq. at the Old Town Hall in Cardiff, where 'during the four hours which the examination receipted, the court remained crowded to excess, a large amount of attorneys being present – Mr John Bird, attempted on the part of the prosecution; Price conducted his own defence'.[4]

Bird explained that the charge 'was serious to consequence to the defendant; it was very serious in the effects upon the community, striking, as it did, at the root of the due administration of justice, and destroying all confidence in the most just and best of causes'.

At the hearing Dr Price questioned Robert Francis Langley, Assistant Clerk to the County Court, remaining difficult. 'Do you know your Christian name?' he began, to which the judge interrupted, 'He was present at his christening, but probably doesn't remember it!', which caused laughter in the court.

But Dr Price claimed he merely wanted to identify him because he felt there may be a question of the name of one of the witnesses, but the judge dispelled it. Finally he said, 'But you cannot expect a man to say, "I was present at my christening, but being only about three weeks old I cannot remember it!"'

Langley was cross-examined at great length as the clerk on the 11 March court hearing and produced his documents illustrating what occurred in that court. He was followed by a series of other officers of the court who were also present at the case and gave their evidence.

At the hearing Ann Millward defended Price by claiming,

Everything that was done there was done at my direction and request. Mr Price did not instigate me to take those proceedings. He did not counsel me to take those proceedings at law. He did not advise me to take those proceedings against my brother. He always advised me not to go to law. Owing that I could not have my money from my brother I did it. Mr Price did not act at the Castle Inn on any other capacity than as a witness. He did not instruct Mr Haviland what to do. He did not instruct Burns what to do. He did not instruct the other person what to do. He had nothing to do with the bailiffs there. He did not go with the bailiffs. I did the business that was done there under the roof of that house entirely out of my own free will.

While Dr Price put further questions to Ann Millward, there was clear evidence of his occasional lapses in thought and deed, which were gradually becoming more apparent. At one point he questioned, 'If I rightly understand the book upon which I have been sworn, it appears that in the beginning was the word, and the word was God, and the word was with God. In Him was the light and this light was the light of men. And it is that light I want to get out.'

On being cross-examined Ann Millward continued on the point that Price had nothing whatsoever to do with the proceedings. She recollected, 'I did not hear Mr Price say anything about the rent. I did not hear Mr Price telling the men where to go. I was there till they went from there.'

But John Hodkinson, an officer of the court, was called by Mr Bird to contradict Ann Millward. He recalled the previous court case, where she was sworn and said that Price went to the attorney with her along with the bailiff. When she was asked, 'Who told the bailiff what to do?', she replied, 'I told Mr Price what was wanted.' He swore the notes of the court were correct and the magistrates cautioned Mr Price, who replied, 'I have nothing to say ... I'll reserve whatever I have to say.' At that point he was committed to trial.

At the close of the case on 4 April 1853, Dr Price was bound over to the sum of £200 bail to appear at the next assizes to face the indictment of perjury, of which David Edwards of Cylwach y Clyd, Llanwonno and Benjamin Evans, china merchant of Cardiff, were both bound to the sum of £100 each to ensure Price's attendance.

Dr William Price claimed that members of the court had previously extorted money from him and the grievance between them had resulted in the current case of perjury, effectively accusing him of being unlawful, dishonest and deceitful. He accused them of 'perjuring themselves' by holding the current case as a conspiracy to ruin his reputation because he had exposed their act of extortion. He called them the judge's 'satellites, Robert Langley, Frederick Burns and others in the Queen's name, under the Seal of Court, by putting an execution into my house on the 1st of December 1852 and plundering therefrom the sum of £5 11s 4d which had been paid once by me before, as the receipt proves'.

He next charged Frederick Burns with owing him 10d, whereas the judge said only an error of 6d had been made in the court costs.

Prosecutor Mr Giffard said that the accusations of Dr Price that he had paid the bailiff twice for the same cause in December 1852 was 'complained of in terms too strong as it was quite a mistake and folly to suppose anything of the kind was intended'. The judge said that if Dr Price had paid the money twice he had a right to complain, and he did not think the word extortion was too strong.

It was due to a case between William Price as the plaintiff and defendants Rebecca Thomas, Thomas Jenkins and Thomas Isaac. On 10 September 1852 an action was taken in the Small Debts Court at Cardiff, and Price said he should pay a sum to the defendants by way of costs and to the Clerk of the Court. Dr Price said on 1 December 1852 that he had a receipt from Frederick Burns, stating the receipt of £14 9s 4d. He also proved that he paid £5 11s 4d to Rebecca Thomas and others. There was a third receipt of the same day of £8 17s 6d again to Burns for the full amount of the execution in that case.

During the proceedings he went so far as to accuse Langley of a 'felony' for exacting the £5 16s 4d from him twice. He displayed County Court documents proving he had been forced to pay the amount a second time. He said it was his complaint about this 'extortion' which had resulted in the court staff conspiring to charge him with perjury.

The trial, *Regina* v. *Price* For Perjury, took place at the Glamorganshire Summer Assizes in Cardiff on 18 and 19 July 1853, before Her Majesty's Justice Baron Platt. The case began at 6.30 in the evening, once again with Dr Price making many challenges to the jurors, who were changed for 'twelve good men and true'. Mr Giffard and Mr Rees conducted the prosecution with attorney Mr Bird. Dr Price sat at the barrister's table with 'voluminous papers ... he was attired in the dress usually worn by him'.[5]

Burns again swore that Price was managing the entire business on behalf of Ann Millward, adding, 'The young lady did not sign the authority till the Doctor told her to do it, then she said, "I wish the Doctor to manage all for me." When she was handed the warrant to sign she said, "I have nothing to do with it, give it to the Doctor, I wish him to manage all the business for me."' Burns added that he took the inventory from William Millward's house. It resulted in Millward placing damages of £10 against his sister and Burns.

John Hodkinson added that under oath Price had made the statement,

It is not by my instigation, advice or counsel that the proceedings are carried on. I had no distress made on the property. I did not give instructions. I did not come for the bailiff. I have nothing to do with the bailiff. I will swear I did not give instructions to the bailiff to take the distress. I did not tell him where to go nor what to do, I did not see him in possession of anything, I do not know where he took or where he went to. I did not see him.[6]

It was at this point in the case that Dr William Price read the following address:

As my brain has been ploughed and harrowed for the last five months, and sown by the conspirators with the seeds of villainy and malice, I beg you to listen to me patiently and with all the indulgence you can afford, while I, an innocent victim of persecution, mow down their harvest of perjury! In obedience to the Throne, the Inhabitants of my Country and the Law of the Land, I yield to no man, as well as, in respect, to the seat of judgement wherein you sit, on behalf of the Queen. To enable you to understand my present position, hunted into this Dock by the bloodhounds and their huntsmen, who took away my liberty on the 4th day of April 1853, by perjuring themselves, I beg you will hear from me, patiently, the shortest possible account of the facts, circumstances and connection of events, the animus of the how, and the why, I appear now before you, to defend myself against a Charge of Perjury, that never had existence in my mind, nor in the expression of my mind, by the words of my mouth, on my oath, in *Millward* v. *Millward* on the 11th of March 1853, before the Judge of the Small Debts Court in Cardiff. I think that I shall be able to show to your satisfaction that this charge of perjury against me, was born and bred in the brain of Judge Thomas Falconer, and nourished by his sinister influence over the conspirators, John Bird, Robert Langley, Frederick Burns, John Hodkinson, and other greater and lesser lights in the background plot for the express purpose of taking away my liberty, destroying my reputation, and arresting my right course, because I have repeatedly refused to prostrate my senses in this Court and other places at his dictates and their threatening of prosecution.

I believe my name is William Price. I am a medical man, in a very extensive practice, residing near Ponty Priydh. I have been practising my profession, in the same neighbourhood, for more than 30 years. The late Thomas Millward and family, were, and are still, except William Millward, the plaintiff, herein named, among some of my oldest patients.

During the last illness of the late Thomas Millward, I made his will, by his request, and his dictation. I attended the late Mary Millward, the widow of Thomas Millward, in her late illness. At her request and by her dictation, I made her will, but, after delaying the execution of it to the last moment, she hesitated and refused to sign it, because she was afraid of Billy. This Billy is the plaintiff. I do assure you, my Lord and Gentlemen of the Jury, it is not with pleasure, but it is with pain, my present position compels me to pull up the black soul of Billy from his Mother's grave, to show you, the animus the soul of this malicious, ex-officio prosecution against me, instituted at the suit of the Queen, as a banner to enlist similar souls, to accomplish the ruin of his sister, Ann Millward, the defendant, in the inevitable ruination that awaits me, if you find me guilty of the false charge of Perjury, levelled against my innocent heart, by the conspirators John Bird, Robert Francis Langley, Frederick Burns and others, under the influence, and instigation of Thomas Falconer Esq. Nothing but the black soul of this ex-officio prosecution, in the Queen's name, against me, could induce me here publicly before your Lordship, to impeach a functionary, in the administration of Law of the Land, who encourages the black soul of the plaintiff to resist in Ann Millward, the supreme authority of the church, to administer the property of her late parents, on her oath, under a heavy penalty, and who instigates these proceedings against me, to involve Ann Millward, the administrator and destitute defendant and myself in one common ruin.

The dying words of the late Mary Millward, the mother of the plaintiff, and of the defendant, in the presence of her daughters and in my presence was, '*Mae arno hi ofn Billy o wneuthyr nghwyllyss*' (I am afraid of what Billy will do of my will). I have offended Billy, mortally, but making his late Father's will, protecting his aged Mother in her widowhood, from his insensibility and drunken hard-heartedness, and after her decease, for patronizing the unsullied character of his orphan sister, Ann Millward, the defendant, in the plaint, out of which this prosecution sprung, on the 11th of March 1853 where I appeared as a witness, for the defense, to an agreement made my me and Thomas Thomas of the Bridgewater Arms, Ponty Priydh. As peacemakers, between and at direction and request of both parties.

These proceedings in replevy, by the instigation, advice and counsel of Mr Bird could have had no other earthly object in view, but to resist, and delay, the payment of the £100, rent then due to Ann Millward, by their agreement, to starve her into compliance to her Brother's will, thereby tempting her to violate her oath, at Llandaff, as the administrator of her Father's will, where I had become one of her bail. Out of these acts of charity, grows one of the horns of my dilemma.

The other horn is the ex-officio prosecution, generated in a conspiracy in the Small Debts Courts, under the influence of Thomas Falconer, Esq., the Judge, on the self same day, of the 11th of March, 1853, for exposing the extortion committed by his Satellites, Robert Francis Langley, Frederick Burns, and others, in the Queen's name, under the Seal of the Court, by putting an execution into my house on the 1st of December 1852, and plundering therefrom the sum of £5 11s 4d, which had been paid once by me, BEFORE, as the Receipt proves. Let it be borne in mind, too, that the hearing of this complaint for extortion was the first business transacted by the Judge, on that day. Having tried in vain to excuse his Satellites from this charge of extortion, I observed that his argument was not warranted by the written evidence of extortion before him. 'What,' said the Judge, 'Do you say No to me?'

'I do,' I replied, 'say "No" to you Sir but not meaning it discourteously to the authority vested in you. The evidence of the Receipts produced is beyond doubt.'

'The Judge called up Langley to explain away the evidence of the Receipts which he mumbled in some broken sentences, I could not gather, to the satisfaction of the Judge. The effect of which was to warm his heart, to exculpate Langley by striking again at the evidence of my senses, by denying the evidence of the written documents. This induced me again to say 'No Sir!' to the Judge, 'That is impossible!'

It is contrary to the evidence of the Receipts, and the explanation of the transaction by the officer of the Court, Frederick Burns, who signed the Receipts and gave the explanation.

'What,' asked the Judge again, with a threatening countenance and malignant eye, 'Do you say "No" to me?' 'Indeed Sir,' I replied, 'I do, without meaning any offence or discourtesy to the authority vested in you. There is no man living has a greater respect for that authority than I have. I charge the officers of your Court for plundering me, in the Queen's name, under their Seal of office, of the sum of £5 11s 4d.'

Robert Francis Langley then got up and threatened me with a prosecution, if I dared to repeat the charge against him. This is the same Robert Francis Langley that has given his evidence in this Court to day against me on behalf of the Crown, and the same Frederick Burns who signed the Receipts.

Heedless of the consequences of his threatening, and the scowling countenance and malignant eyes of Thomas Falconer Esq., to back him, I repeated the same charge against that Robert Francis Langley, then assistant Clerk of the Small Debts Court (that sainted villain who swears to my meaning in this Court today) for plundering me, in the Queen's name, under the Seal of his office, of £5 11s 4d upon which, the Judge asked me what I wanted?

I replied, 'Sir, I want my money returned'.

The Judge gave me leave to mention the circumstances to him next Court. Some two hours afterwards, on the same day, the Plaint of *Millward* v. *Millward* came off in favour of the plaintiff, Billy. Just as I was leaving the Court, the Judge addressed me, saying that if the dispute on the matter in difference was left to his adjudication, he would see justice done. I replied, as it was not my business, I could say nothing. That I had always advised the party for whom I appeared as witness that day, to have nothing to do with Law and Lawyers, if she could possibly help it. And even if I did advise her to leave the matter in difference to his settlement, I knew the party had no faith in his justice.

In the course of three or four days afterwards, comes after me, the Superintendent of the Cardiff Police, from the Borough Magistrates, charging me with falsely, wickedly, wilfully and corruptly for having committed wilful and corrupt Perjury, in the plaint of *Millward* v. *Millward* on the 11th day of March, 1853, commanding me to appear on the 17th of that month, at Cardiff, before the Mayor. As commanded, I appeared on the 17th, and got the hearing of the charge postponed to the 4th of April 1853, on which day I appeared there again, to answer the charge trumped up against me, with the evidence of Ann Millward, the defendant, in my defense, and attended then as now, by my infant daughter Hiarlhes Morganwg, as my Counsel of the Defense. When the case was called in, I begged the Mayor, William Williams Esq., for the ends of justice, he would be pleased to order all persons who are to be examined, for, and against me, out of the Court, under the penalty of being objected to.

The Mayor, William Williams, in the name, and on behalf of the Queen of Great Britain, nodded his assent, and forthwith ordered all persons to leave the Court that were to be examined for, or against me, under the penalty of being objected to. I had obtained summonses, signed by the Mayor, to command the attendance of witnesses on my behalf in the Police Court that day. John Rhys, served John Bird, in the Court, in the presence, and in the sight of the Mayor of Cardiff. What do you think, my Lord, and Gentlemen of the Jury was there, and then done, in contempt of the Queen's authority, by the said John Bird, the attorney for the prosecution, in the sight and under the sanction, of the Representative of the Queen of Great Britain? Why! It is almost incredible! It is incredible, I believe, everywhere else in Great Britain, but in Cardiff, and her Lunatic Asylums!

But as faces are in Cardiff, I will dare tell you, and produce witnesses of the facts. This is what was said and done, by one of these conspirators in iniquity, John Bird, and gainsayer and undone, by the Mayor of Cardiff, in the Court on that day.

My Lord, and Gentlemen of the Jury! Observe their animus, in this preliminary stage of the prosecution! This blundering conspirator, John Bird, cocksure of his game, said in the face of the Court, that it was an unwarrantable act, and in contempt of Court, to service him, with a summons. 'He would not go out'.

He clearly proved, by his act, he felt what he spoke for once his life, for he put the Queen's authority into the fire, where it was burnt to ashes, in the sight of the Queen of Great Britain, not only with impunity, but with some favour and affection, evinced by Her Majesty's Representative, The Mayor, who appeared pleased and enamoured by Mr Bird's contempt of her authority, for he countermanded his original order, given for the ends of justice, and permitted John Bird and John Hodkinson, two of the principal conspirators, to remain in Court, in this iniquitous, and malicious ex-officio prosecution.

There was then no remedy. My Lord, and Gentlemen of the Jury! Observe the common animus of this prosecution for innocent blood, as well as the blood of the innocent, in the name of the Queen of Great Britain!!

What! Cannot her Majesty, as the mighty huntress, in her day, before the Lord, go out like the Sun, to find beasts of prey enough for her bloodhounds without hounding them to sacrifice the liberty and the life of an innocent man upon her criminal altars with the bloody hands of her Law Priesthood?

What! Does the equivalent Queen of Great Britain, the mistress of the civilised world, in her day, fear the light of the Sun, living in a drop of dew, and identified in the name of William Price? Will her Majesty, the Queen, dressed by her officers of State, in her white robes, sprinkled with Five Pounds and a Half of my innocent blood, plundered by her Cardiff officers, in her name, under the Seal of office, on the First day of December, 1852, in the Small Debts Court at Cardiff, by the conspirators, in the administration of the Law of the Land?

These are the facts, the circumstances and connection of events, on which this villainous ex officio prosecution is based, and the extreme questions I have asked, on which their solution depends. I submit them to your serious consideration, to be answered by your verdict. My blood, my liberty, and my life, are in your custody this day. Do me justice! The villainy, conspiracy, and malice of my prosecutors thirsting for my blood have sworn me guilty by perjuring themselves. Truth, justice and common sense say, 'No! No!'

There is no foundation for it. NOT GUILTY! My fate is sealed by the word of your mouth. Your will be done on earth as it is in heaven![7]

Dr Price examined Mary Edwards, a servant at the Castle Inn, Treforest; Moses Cule, a carpenter from Pentrebach who assisted in the business dealings of William Millward; Ann Millward; and Thomas Thomas, of the Duke of Bridgewater Arms. On attempting to cross-examine Mr Haviland himself, the judge forbade it.

The judge summed up the evidence very carefully, and the jury retired to consider their verdict. Following a sixteen-hour-long day in the courtroom, the jury deliberated for just twenty-five minutes and Dr Price was found not guilty, and when the trial closed at 1.15 a.m.,

The result was received with enthusiastic cheering. The hall was densely crowded, although it was then quarter past one in the morning. We can compare the scene to nothing else than the cheering with which a great public meeting would express their unqualified approbation of any circumstance that had fallen under their observation. Repeated rounds of applause greeted the defendant, which were renewed when he reached the street, and continued some time with unabated ardour.[7]

Dr Price published the entire legal encounter as *The Trial versus William Price*, which was privately printed by William Hemmons. Running at forty pages, the detailed account of the trial and the accusations made by Price to the officers of the court also contained a lithograph image of Dr Price and Hiarlhes, in which they are both dressed in the Druidic attire with matching fox skin hats. Dr Price is holding a large brass crescent moon, which in later years he had mounted on a pole. What is interesting is the fact that he is also depicted holding a burning torch, rather prophetic for the events that would transpire thirty years later.

However, the case didn't quite end there, for in the following edition of the *Cardiff & Merthyr Guardian* of 30 July 1853, letters were published questioning the position of Langley given the accusations made against him by Dr Price. The entire case had been published in the *Cambrian News* of Swansea, and Lord W. C. Spring Rice wrote to Judge Thomas Falconer to discuss an enquiry into Langley's behaviour, withholding his forthcoming 'appointment' in the court until the matter had been dealt with. Falconer ordered Langley to inform Price that he was willing to hear of any complaint made against the court regarding his overcharge of payments. On doing so, Dr Price responded to Langley, saying

Sir, take notice, that my answer to your letter, purporting to be dated at Cardiff on the 23rd, instant, is – inform the Judge Thomas Falconer, Esquire, respectfully, that having been tempted by the officers of his court, and others implicated and impeached, publicly, in the late malicious conspiracy against me for perjury, to throw five pounds and half of my blood, plundered in his court, under his supervision, upon the white robes of the Queen, I understand the duty of a British subject better than meddle in such a grave affair that must come before the Lord Chief Justice of the Queen's Bench...

The outcome was that Falconer submitted papers to the Lord Chancellor that on 10 September 1852, two actions were tried at Cardiff County Court in which William Price was the plaintiff. The fees payable on the hearing were:

William Price v. *Rebecca Thomas*	£3	3	6
William Price v. *David Thomas*	£2	5	0
	£4	8	0

In the first of these actions Price failed to introduce sufficient evidence and the case was deemed 'nonsuited' and Price was ordered to pay the defendants the cost of witnesses and the advocate's fee, which amounted to £4 16s 4d, exclusive of the sum of £2 3s 6d due for fees for which the court is accountable to the treasury. In the same month Price came to the County Court Office and paid Frederick Burns £4 16s 4d, but he ought to have also paid the fees of £2 3s 6d.

Burns, then acting for Langley, who was absent on account of illness, should have demanded the fees from Price. When Price made the payment of £4 16s 4d, he directed the issue of a new summons of *William Price v. Rebecca Thomas* and 'others'. On issuing this summons Burns permitted him to leave unpaid 12s of the fees payable for this summons, making the sum of £4 8s 6d due on the former two actions, the sum of £5 0s 6d due for fees. On 11 October the second action came for a hearing and Price attended the court, where Langley explained he could not pay in the defendants costs before the costs of the hearing. Langley handed him an account in writing showing how he was indebted to £5 0s 6d. Langley gave him credit of £4 16s 4d leaving a balance due of 4s 2d, which Price paid. When the second hearing of *Price v. Rebecca Thomas* took place, Mr Morris, who was then the County Court Clerk, permitted the hearing to take place without first demanding the payment of the hearing fees on this action and they were paid afterwards without any dispute.

On the second action against Rebecca Thomas and others, judgement was given to the defendants, whose costs for witnesses and advocate's fee amounted to £7 17s. That, accompanied by the defendant's costs of £4 16s 4d, brought the total owed by Price to £12 13s 4d and it remained unpaid, despite summonses issued to him, until 24 November. This is how Langley explained the situation to the Judge Falconer, who had 'no doubt of its accuracy. I have no knowledge of what passes at the table of the court respecting the payment of fees, but I am always ready to give my attention to any appeal that may be made to me to ascertain the propriety of any demand of fees.'

Dr Price complained the execution for the defendant's costs of *Price v. Rebecca Thomas* was irregular, saying he had once paid this sum.

There certainly was an irregularity in transferring to the fee account the sum of £4 16s 4d, paid on account of the defendants costs, for if it had so happened that this sum had not been finally recoverable, the defendants, including Rebecca Thomas, would have had good reason to complain. Mr Price, however, has no reason to complain for if the sum of £4 16s 6d had not been appropriated as explained when he paid the additional four shillings and four pence, executions might have been issued against him in three actions, namely £2 3s 6d, £2 5s 0d and £7 17s 0d amounting to £12 5s 6d. The executions actually issued against him in two of these actions were for the sum of £12 13s 4d – the defendant's costs of £4 10s 4d in the action taking place of the two sums, £2 3s 6d and £2 5s originally due for fees in the two actions. According to the rules of the County Court, which were also publicised in the newspaper report, and that Dr Price had departed from these rules by giving credit for fees, that has occasioned the present discussions; but in this Langley acted under the control of Morris, the late Clerk of the Court. There has, however been no overcharge and at all times, every desire has been expressed to aid the fullest investigation of every complaint made by Mr Price.[8]

In July 1853 Dr Price made yet another court appearance, this time as a witness in the trial of Christopher Morgan, a thirty-three-year-old collier, 'a fellow of repulsive appearance'[8] who was charged with assaulting a little girl aged four years in Llantwit Faerdref. Dr Price saw her and stated in the court she had been abused and suffered 'abominable violence'. The jury found the prisoner guilty of the charge.

Aside from his frequent and often lengthy court appearances during this period, changes were taking place in Dr Price's life and surroundings. Newbridge was developing at a rapid pace and by 1852 had become the main market town of the county, with a thousand dwellings and thirty-three public houses. In 1850 the Gaslight and Coke Company was established to light the main streets and a County Court was held at the White Hart Hotel. There was also major expansion in transport. In 1849, the Rhondda branch of the Taff Vale Railway was extended into the Rhondda Fach, with a short line from Porth to Ynyshir. This was extended to Ferndale in 1856, and finally to Maerdy. The Rhondda Fawr line was extended from Dinas to Treherbert, also in 1856. The Taff Vale Railway proved its worth immediately. At its peak, two trains a minute passed through Pontypridd. By 1850, the TVR was carrying 600,000 tons of coal per year through the town. There were two passenger trains, including Sundays. Single fares from Cardiff to Merthyr were 5s for first class, 4s for second class, and 3s for third, and were each reduced by a shilling in 1845.

In 1847 the Rhondda Valleys were described as 'this solitudinous and happy valley ... where the Sabbath stillness reigns', but by the 1850s had become a 'vision of hell' with the massive growth of the coal mining industry which had begun under the command of the Marquis of Bute, who purchased the mineral rights of Cwmsaerbren Farm in Treherbert and sunk the first Bute colliery in 1855. By the end of the century, Rhondda was the most important coal-producing area in the world. The coal industry at its peak in Wales employed one in every ten persons, and many more relied on the industry for their livelihood. Rhondda alone at one time contained fifty-three working collieries, in an area only sixteen miles long. It was the most intensely mined area in the world, and probably one of the most densely populated. From the rural population of around 951 in 1851, mass migration meant that by 1924, the population reached 169,000, approximately 20,000 people to the built-up square mile.

Such was the considerable growth of Newbridge that calls were made for a second bridge to cross the River Taff at the centre of the town, as heavily laden carriages were dangerous for the horses to pull at such a steep downward angle. In December 1853 an address was presented to solicitor Edward Colnett Spickett and the Committee of Magistrates at the Glamorgan Quarter Sessions, gathered to discuss the feasibility of erecting a bridge close to the William Edwards single-arched bridge that had become such a landmark and iconic structure throughout the district. With the express desire to 'obtain a new bridge over the River Taff', the committee, led by postmaster Charles Bassett,

> feel quite confident that upon inspection of the bridge by your worships, it will be found not only very inconvenient but absolutely dangerous for heavy carriages to be taken over it [because it was so steep] and consequently, that some means must be found to alter it without delay ... in the course of the last twenty years Pontypridd has increased ... so that a great number of wagons, carts, and other vehicles, frequent the place weekly exclusive of the regular traffic carried between the place and the canal, Merthyr and the surrounding country ... and when the river is flooded which frequently occurs in winter, all such vehicles are compelled either to brave the torrent or to attempt the bridge being in either case attended with great peril to the drivers and also to the horses and accidents have been very frequent within the last year, but hitherto no life has been lost, but some have been seriously injured and others very narrowly escaped their lives ...[9]

Bassett, a postmaster, formed a committee to raise a public subscription and meetings were held at the Tredegar Arms. To aid publicity a hot-air balloon was launched from a field adjacent to the gasworks across the river. In the following year Dr William Price himself displayed his philanthropic consciousness by holding a fund-raising tea party at the Rocking Stone in an effort to help pay for the new bridge. The structure, named the Victoria Bridge, was opened on 4 December 1857. Robert Hughes was the architect and the entire project cost £1,575. Stone was quarried from Trallwn and the bridge was built by Thomas Jenkins. It was opened by Revd George Thomas of Ystrad Mynach, who contributed £500 towards it.

In 1856 the first post office opened in Pontypridd. In the same year the town officially changed its name from Newbridge to Pontypridd, largely because the postmaster, Bassett, had grown tired of having to deal with mail intended for the many other 'New Bridges' in Britain and Ireland. It was clearly a decision supported by Dr Price and the Druids of the area as it honoured the original Welsh title of the area rather than the Anglo version, which was adopted in the 1750s.

Druidic ceremonies continued to be regularly held at Y Maen Chwyf and columns of newspapers contain the details of Myfyr Morganwg and his followers, such as David Evans (Dewi Haran), John Evans (Ieuan Wyn), William John (Mathonwy), John Emlyn Jones (Ioan Emlyn) and Jonathan Reynolds (Nathan Dyfed). Several major Welsh poets were invested as members of the society of Y Maen Chwyf, including Robert Ellis (Cynddelw), Evan James (Ieuan ab Iago), Thomas Essile Davies (Dewi Wyn O Essyllt) and Owen Wynne Jones (Glasynys). Myfyr even won the chair at the Pontypridd Eisteddfod in 1854 for the Welsh ode 'The Sacred Circles of the Bards'.

Of them all it was Evan James who achieved respect and honour throughout the Welsh people worldwide. Evan was a poet and it is believed that he wrote the words of the national anthem after his brother, Daniel, had emigrated to America. He wrote the verses to explain why he could not leave his homeland. His son, James composed the tune. The song was published in the *Gems of Welsh Melody* (1860) and soon became extremely popular.

James James (1832–1902), who adopted the bardic name of Iago ap Ieuan, worked in his father's woollen mill before opening a public house in the town – and another in Mountain Ash – in 1873. He married Cecilia Miles and the couple had five children. A harpist and musician who also earned a living playing in the inns of Pontypridd, he composed the tune of the Welsh national anthem while apparently walking along the banks of the River Rhondda in January 1856. At first it was known as '*Glan Rhondda*' ('The Banks of the Rhondda'). Some believe the words were written before James composed the melody, which was based on an old harp instrumental composition, and others believe that the melody was composed before the words. The most likely story is that father and son got together the night of James's walk and wrote the first verse, with the next two verses being completed on the following day. '*Glan Rhondda*' was performed for the first time in the vestry of Capel Tabor, in Maesteg, by a singer called Elizabeth John from Pontypridd, and it soon became popular in the locality before becoming adopted as the anthem.

Another of those who was inaugurated into the society of the Maen Chwyf was Ebenezer Thomas (Eben Fardd, 1802–63), the schoolmaster of Llanarman, Carmarthenshire, who was regarded as one of Wales's foremost poets of his day.

John Williams (Ab Ithel), was also greatly influenced by Myfyr and his teachings, and co-edited the Cambrian Archaeological Association's publications, but in doing so accepted the forgeries of Iolo and Myfyr without question. Ab Ithel was invested as a bard in absentia at the Gorsedd Rocking Stone on 21 July 1856, by which time the Gorsedd had become something of a national institution in Wales.

The same honour and distinction was not shared by an eisteddfod in which Dr Price played such a prominent role. In 1855, the editor of the *Cardiff & Merthyr Guardian* voiced his disgust at the conduct of an eisteddfod held in Merthyr Tydfil. He explained,

This event came off on Monday last. Great had been the expectations respecting it; and the announcement that two bearded Britons, namely Dr Price of Newbridge, a half-naked Aberdare man, rejoicing in the title of Myrddin and a third native in the form of a large goat, created much curiosity to witness the grotesque exhibition. The day came, and with it the Doctor and Hiarlhes Morganwg in dreams of refreshing verdure, the Aberdare man, half-naked in the garb of a veritable savage, covered with the skin of an old white horse, and making up a show very closely bordering on indecency; thirdly the goat, a fine animal, and judging from his dignified deportment, not the least respectable member of the trio, however, the popular expectation was disappointed; as instead of taking the usual course up the High Street, the procession was led through the less frequented streets of the town, towards the Tabernacle Chapel, into which, we are sorry to say, the goat and his scantily clad conductor, were permitted to enter.

We never saw a stinking goat, and a mock savage at an eisteddfod before, and we trust never to see the folly repeated. Mr David Williams, coal proprietor of Ynyscynon, Aberdare, was appointed to preside on the occasion. He was met by a deputation from the Ivorite Societies, who presented him with an address in Welsh, to which he responded in the same language. A procession was formed, and he was escorted to the place of meeting. Having opened the business in a brief address, the Chairman was greeted with a variety of bardic verses of Englynion, according to the custom on such occasions. Dr Price then delivered an oration on the mystic significance of the goat and a holly he held in his hand; but owing to some stupidity on our part, we were unable to discern his meaning.[10]

In July 1855 the goat, possibly the same goat, appeared in a court hearing of its own at the Glamorganshire Summer Assizes. Lord Chief Justice Campbell presided over several days where thirty-five prisoners were tried, none of whom on a very serious offence. Dr Price, 'an eccentric medical gentleman', was the plaintiff. Mr Morgan Thomas, the defendant, was charged with setting dogs on the goats belonging to Dr Price.[11]

A court hearing appeared in a newspaper where the attire of Dr Price was more important than the trial itself! He was described as

> a most singular spectacle ... whose beard, hair and peculiar costume have long been a theme of curiosity among all who have seen him, especially in court. Today he stood at the barristers' table, with the white skulls and huge horns of three of his Welsh mountain goats and the shaggy and long black haired skin of another lying on the table before him. His iron-gray hair fell on his shoulders, in tresses and locks, down almost to his waist; with an Asiatic beard of silver grey falling on his breast, over a turned down collar of beautifully fine and white linen. His jerkin, or jacket was of Lincoln green turned up with scarlet, the yellow buttons each bearing a different form of dog. The wrists of the jacket were scalloped, alternately green and scarlet, with yellow buttons, and the wristbands of his shirt were also scalloped. His scarlet waistcoat, was similarly scalloped. The sharp, keen, eagle eyes of the doctor, his Welsh idiom, and general appearance were the subject of close attention by all in the court, and we noticed two or three of the learned counsel engaged in sketching a likeness of this remarkable Welsh character ... his style of the olden time was more becoming in a descendant of the Cymri. But all this had nothing to do with the action.[12]

Two charges were put to neighbouring farmer Morgan Thomas; that his dogs had caused the deaths and secondly that he had dogs in his ownership knowing they could harm or kill other animals. In March 1852 Dr Price kept a herd of seven goats on the thirty-three acre farm, while Thomas occupied the nearby farmhouse that was adjacent to the mountain land. Price said Thomas and his sons had let the dogs worry and kill twenty or thirty of his goats in the first instance.

Again Dr Price proved awkward when called to swear on the Testament with a kiss. He minutely examined the pages and came to some pictures where he exclaimed, 'My Lord, I do not like these things.' Another Testament was found and finally, on being assured it was accurate, kissed it and gave his evidence. He explained how he kept goats because he preferred their cheese to that of cows, and occasionally they strayed to the neighbouring farm where Thomas and his sons would set their three sheep dogs and his mastiff on the animals, 'worrying them so savagely that they died'. He explained that despite protesting to Thomas, he still lost twenty-eight goats and several batches of kids between June 1852 and December 1854 which had a net value of £250 12s 6d. He said his 'beautiful' goats, which had names derived from Welsh history, were logged in minute detail in his manuscripts.

In cross-examination Price was accused of shooting at the dogs. Hiarlhes was called as a witness in the case,

who excited nearly as much interest as her father had done. She was about 12 years of age. A large brimmed Leghorn hat almost hid her very intellectual countenance, and her shoulders were covered by a peculiarly cut and scalloped white fur tippet. Unable to speak English, Mr Evans, the court interpreter was called. The judge said, 'Ask her if she goes to church or chapel, and knows anything of religion, or can say the Lord's Prayer.' Hiarlhes replied, 'I do not go to church nor chapel. I have been taught religion.' The judge asked if she understood the Lord's Prayer, when Dr Price declared she had been incorrectly asked that question. He said, 'She has been brought up in the Christian religion and is a first-rate Christian. She will make a splendid Christian,' causing laughter in the court. Hiarlhes said she had learned the Lord's Prayer, but couldn't say it now, although she knew that those who are wicked 'will go to the fire, they do say'. She then went on to explain the times dogs had killed or worried her father's goats, remembering being on the Craig when one of the goats was beaten by one of Thomas's sons and the animal ran to her and put its head on her lap and 'cried much'. She held it there for some time, and then, fearing it would die, she took off her apron, wrapped the goat's head in it and ran for her father. Her poor goat died that evening.[12]

Other witnesses corroborated the same evidence, although Thomas argued they had mainly died due to their age. The jury deliberated for half an hour and returned a verdict of guilty. Thomas was ordered to pay damages of £15, a far cry from the substantial sum Price had hoped for.

In March 1856 the case regarding his second cousin, Maria Price, and the item of land at Mynyddybwlch in Rudry reappeared at the Glamorganshire Assizes. Worth several thousand pounds due to its mineral resources and a railway being built in the vicinity of the land, Maria Price wanted to make claim to the property she said was left by her grandfather.

Once again the court heard how Dr Price had rented the property for £5 per year since 1838 and suddenly claimed ownership of the land, giving notice that nobody should trespass on the property. At the time a declaration of ejectment was made upon Price's siblings, Charles and

Elizabeth, but they said they had nothing to do with it and the bailiff should go to Dr Price instead.

In defence of Dr Price, Mr Evans QC addressed the jury and explained that in law this was called 'estoppel', a doctrine that may be used in certain situations to prevent a person from relying upon certain rights, or upon a set of facts (e.g. words said or actions performed) which is different from an earlier set of facts. Estoppel could arise in a situation where a creditor informs a debtor that a debt is forgiven, but then later insists upon repayment. In a case such as this, the creditor may be estoppel from relying on their legal right to repayment, as the creditor has represented that he no longer treats the debt as extant.

Evans said Maria Price had made no attempt to prove ownership of the property, only showing she had signed the agreement which they considered was enough to show their title to the land. When Dr Price took possession of the land in 1838, some circumstances showed that the agreement was soon changed and a second agreement was signed, which Maria Price claimed she had never signed or agreed to, hence the reason she wanted them evicted from the land. A claim had been established by the brothers Charles and William, who was said to have established a disclaimer.

Earlier, the will of Maria Price's father was not used in the case and Dr Price claimed he had a right to the property himself. Maria Price's grandfather, Nicholas Price, made his will in 1757, leaving the property to his eldest son, Revd James Price, who was Maria's father. However, it transpired that her grandfather had left it an entailed estate and couldn't make a will in respect to it, as the land would descend on the lawful heirs. An entail of an estate cannot be sold, devised by will, but passes to the owner's heirs upon his death. The purpose of an entail was to keep the land of a family intact in the main line of succession so the heir to an entailed estate could not sell the land, nor usually bequeath it to, for example, an illegitimate child. This was the case of Maria Price, who was not a legitimate daughter of Revd James Price and therefore the estate could not descend to her.

Dr Price revealed that a second agreement on the land took place in 1839 when, for £6 per year, he took the title of Mynyddybwlch from his brother Charles. By 1844 Maria Price had turned him off the land with the support of the police.

Dr Price argued, 'I knew the Revd James Price, the father of the plaintiff. I knew the grandfather was named James Price … I have heard from Miss Price's father, in her own presence and her own mother, that she was illegitimate. When he was betwixed of a certain bastard he used to say, "And what are you Maria, but a bastard."'[9]

On being cross-examined Dr Price was forced to relinquish, while in the court room, the two pistols he kept in his jacket. He explained how the agreement was made at the small house of his sister Ann Price, Primrose Bank, near the Duke of Bridgewater Arms (where her brother Charles also lodged) and signed in the presence of Charles and Ann, along with Maria Price and a servant called Elizabeth Thomas.

Charles had set up a claim to the property as it had originally belonged to their mutual great-grandfather, and he objected when William made the first agreement for the land because he knew Maria was illegitimate and had no rights over it herself.

He said, 'It was in the year 1838 I objected to my brother making an agreement. In 1839 my brother was out of the way in consequence of the Newport riots. I never offered to pay the rent for Mynydd y Bwlch.'[9] When the bailiff arrived Charles told him to speak to William, where he agreed to pay £5 for the premises and £1 for the game to 'keep peace between them', but he was annoyed that by renting the property William could have prejudiced his own right to the land.

Charles, Ann and William all confirmed that a second agreement was signed before them at Primrose Bank.

A witness named Amy Davies, aged seventy-nine, was called and said she knew James Price of Portishead, the father of the Revd James Price. 'The Revd James Price used to live with me sometimes. I had a son by him,' she added!

Maria Price claimed she had never signed a second agreement with William Price, but remembers signing the first agreement and the fact her tenant was forced to leave the area during the Chartist rising. She also denied being illegitimate but added her parents did not live 'an agreeable life' and Revd Price had passed a good deal of his time with Amy Davies, 'that creature'.

She added, 'I claim this property under my grandfather's will. He left it to me.'

The jury deliberated and found that Dr Price was left in possession of the land in the first agreement, but felt the second agreement produced by him was not genuine. On the third point they felt Maria Price was indeed legitimate. The documents, including the one proved a fake, were impounded by the court.

The issue of Mynyddybwlch appeared in another court case in June 1856 at the assizes. Dr Price was landed in court against someone that his Chartist colleague John Frost had openly attacked in the press, Sir Charles Morgan of Tredegar. The action was due to Dr Price's goats trespassing from the Mynyddybwlch onto the property of Sir Charles Morgan called Coed-y-Cefn, where he enjoyed 'hunting and sporting'.

The latter sued Dr Price for £49 13s 4d for the trespass. H. J. Davis of Newport appeared for Sir Charles, while Dr Price as always appeared unrepresented. Mr Davis said the goats had damaged a fence and woodland, eating the bark off trees on 7 acres of land, which amounted to around a thousand trees.

The first witness was William Rowland, aged eighty-five, who had worked as a gamekeeper for Sir Charles for thirty-three years and stated Dr Price kept so many goats he 'could never count them' and they used to trespass into the wood. He said the fence was no use because the goats jumped over it and had ruined the wood. Rowland claimed that Dr Price had fired at his dog when he was driving goats out of the wood and Price allegedly promised to use the other pistol on him.

When Price asked Rowland about the land and the amount of footpaths and highways, the gamekeeper said he was unsure.

'Come now, William, you know very well, you have poached in the wood many times,' Dr Price said.

'Yes, and so have you too,' Rowland quipped, much to the delight of the court.

Benjamin Cross, a young boy who worked for Dr Price, said there were thirty-nine goats and there was no way to prevent them from trespassing into the adjoining land.

Woodman Robert Young said the fences were in good order, but there was no way to keep out goats and Dr Price's had caused chaos on the land. In some cases the trees had been reduced to nothing but stems.

On being examined, Dr Price said he had known the land since he was a boy and the fence which belonged to him as in the best repair, just as the gamekeeper claimed Sir Charles Morgan's fence had been.

Dr Price also tried to deny that the goats were even his, but rather belong to Hiarlhes as the doctor had given them to her when she was thirteen. The jury deliberated for a quarter of an hour and Dr Price was found guilty and ordered to pay £5.

Within a few short months, Dr Price faced the wrath of the local gentry – not due to his political or religious beliefs, but once again owing to the flock of misbehaving goats he kept on his farmland at Craig yr Helfa. In July 1856 Lady Harriet Clive, known as Baroness Windsor (1797–1869), widow of the 1st Earl of Powys, claimed compensation against Price for the damage his goats had allegedly caused on her property. W. R. Grove QC explained that the baroness was not trying to obtain large sums of money, but to apply to the Court of Chancery for an injunction to stop Dr Price from allowing his animals to wander onto her land. Grove explained that on Price's smallholding of 27 acres at Eglwysilan he had six cows and a large flock of around fifty to sixty goats, and, as they were not tethered, they would trespass for grass to eat.

In 1853 the timber that grew at Craig yr Helfa was cut and 4,000 trees were planted, which were all attacked by the goats, reducing the value of the land. Baroness Windsor complained that unless there was an injunction then her property would soon be worthless. Her woodman William Morgan said, 'I have no doubt that the damage was caused by goats. The fences on Mr Price's land (Graigalfa) were sufficient to exclude cattle and sheep and ordinary farming stock. Goats could come over ... only 381 trees now remain out of 4,000 which were planted.'

Margaret Lawrence, the granddaughter of Edwards Lewis, a tenant of the neighbouring farm Graig Fach, said she remembered Dr Price moving to Craig Alfa (Craig yr Helfa) in around 1852. She added that he kept a flock of sixty goats, which often trespassed on Baroness Windsor's land 'sometimes eight times on the same day'. The previous case of Morgan Thomas was also discussed (he was the son-in-law of Edward Lewis) as he had kept goats himself in the area, but they were tethered and the only goats that were not were owned by Dr Price.

On 8 December 1855, Dr William Price put a notice on the beech tree on his land to Edward Lewis & Co. of Craigfach or Bryntela, which was witnessed by his servant Daniel Richards, the first of two servants who adopted the pseudonym of Mochyn Du (Black Pig). It read,

> I hereby give you notice, collectively and individually, not to trespass on my lands called Craigalfa, in the said parish and county, by building a fence or otherwise encroaching on my said land, with and by your party fence, where there has never been a fence hitherto to divide my land called Craigalfa from Bryntela or Craigfach land, as you, Edward Lewis, did trespass on the 7th of this month on my land in a certain beech tree on the Craigalfa woodland, as there has been no artificially fence there in the memory of man to divide the said property from one another.

Dr Price had a defence solicitor for this trial, Mr Giffard, who said Price's fences were able to support the land and keep the goats at bay, but where the fences belonged to the neighbouring farmer, Edward Lewis, they were trespassing there. He claimed that in turn Lewis drove the goats himself to Baroness Windsor's land so she could 'fight the battle' with Dr Price!

On being examined, Dr Price said he leased the property and owned goats, cows, pigs, a horse and chickens at Craigalfa. He said there was a 7-foot-high wall dividing his land and the Graig plantation, which had been in a good condition except when 'damaged by Edward Lewis and his relatives'. He said the fence between his property and that of Lewis was an old wall with some inadequate fencing on top. In December 1855 Morgan Thomas, who was infuriated with Price's goats, had allegedly broken down part of the wall. When the wall was repaired, Price had two gates placed there to prevent animals from being destroyed when driven out of the Windsor's land after they were driven in there by Lewis's relatives. Dr

Price said he had seen Lewis's people 'hundreds of times, driving goats from their land, generally into the (Windsor) plantation'.

Dr Price continued with the allegation that the trees were in fact destroyed by an Evan Williams, who was using it to build a new fence between the Windsor's land and the land owned by Sir Benjamin Hall at Craigalfa. At that point Dr Price was ordered to give up his pistols and his daughter, Hiarlhes, was examined and she supported what her father had said. Bedwas magistrate Joseph Davies attested to the fact he had also examined Price's fences and found them in an excellent state of repair whereas Lewis's were dilapidated. The jury returned and came back in favour of Baroness Windsor, ordering Dr Price to pay damages of £7 10s.

Few newspaper reports survive including references to Dr Price for the next year or so, with the exception of a short entry in the *Cambrian*, which tells of an excursion train coming to Swansea on 8 October with 700 men from Francis Crawshay's tinplate works marching with the Cyfarthfa Drum and Fife Band. Among the group was Dr Price 'attired in his usual costume of green, with fox skin cap, and presenting such a singular appearance to those who did not know what it mean, that one was ready to inquire whether the previous night's storm some "ancient mariner" had been cast ashore'.[13]

Dr Price appeared in what the newspapers called 'The Great Will Case' of *Thomas* v. *Thomas*. A special jury was called at the Glamorganshire Assizes with Sir Fredrick Thesiger, Mr Giffard and Mr Lloyd as counsel for the defence, while Messrs Coke and Jones, Mr Grove QC and Mr Davison were counsel for the defendants. Messrs James of Merthyr were agents of Messrs Wadeson and Mallison of London.

The plaintiff was Janet Thomas and the defendant was William Thomas. The action was to try whether a written paper, dated 12 July 1854, was the Last Will and Testament of Thomas Thomas; or whether another paper, dated 8 February, was in fact the true paper. Janet Thomas said the 12 July document was the genuine Will, whereas William Thomas said it was the latter.

Thomas Thomas, a landlord of a large amount of property in the parish of Llanfabon, had died aged fifty-three in 1854 in their farm of Werngaiach. On Tuesday 11 July he became very ill and Dr Price attended to him once again. He had been a patient of Dr Price for around seven years.

Dr Price was sent to Merthyr to fetch retired solicitor Mr Overton to assist with completing his will.

Thomas, unable to speak English, and Overton, unable to speak Welsh, relied on Dr Price as the interpreter. The will gave all of Thomas's property to his wife for her life, with remainder to his three brothers and three nephews in equal share. This had been signed at two o'clock in the morning with two servants as witnesses. Thomas was dead within five hours. The defendant, William Thomas was a brother.

On being asked to enter the dock, Dr Price was ordered to hand in his two pistols. He corroborated the evidence and said he had assisted with completing the will on behalf of Thomas, who signed it only a matter of a few hours before death. However, the question was whether the document was actually completed prior to the signing, or whether Dr Price had completed it for Thomas after his dying breath.

After several hours of witnesses being called to the dock, the jury decided that the will was not valid, but the original of several months earlier, which did not leave a fortune to his wife, only £300, was the correct will of Thomas Thomas.

Dr Price and his fellow members of the Druid's circle had long since hoped for a national stage for their religion and culture. It was a wish that was felt throughout the entire Principality. Wales was still in the shadow of the 'Treachery of the Blue Books' and so the need to create a new national image to defend their reputation and show they were a nation of praise, rather than ridicule, was needed more than ever. Discussions were rife and the dream was finally realised on 21 September 1858, when the National Gorsedd of British Bards under the Royal Chair of Powys was held at the great Eisteddfod of Llangollen. An advertisement read:

Under the protection of God and his peace,
will be held,
on Alban Elved [21 September], A.D. 1858,
at
LLANGOLLEN,
in the Province of Powys,
The National Gorsedd of Bards
accompanied by a
GRAND EISTEDDFOD

Ab Ithel (John Williams, 1811–62), rector of Llanymawddwy, a fanatic of Iolo's Druidic ideas (and inaugurated at the Circle of Y Maen Chwyf), decided to try to establish a national eisteddfod and Gorsedd at Llangollen. Regarded as one of the leading scholars of his day, his enthusiasm and Welsh nationalist fervour knew no bounds, and, along with fellow antiquarian and cleric Harry Longueville Jones, he founded the Cambrian Archaeological Association, whose journal was *Archaeologica Cambrensis*, which he edited until a quarrel with the editorial policy and Jones in 1853. He also published an edition and translation of the *Gododdin* in 1852, established the *Cambrian Journal*, which he edited from 1854 until his death, and was prominent in the Welsh Manuscript

Society, editing four of its publications. The 1858 eisteddfod, which he organised together with Richard Williams Morgan ('Mor Meirion', *c.* 1815–89) and Joseph Hughes ('Carn Ingli', 1803–63), caused much derision and embarrassment, largely because many of his own family won the prizes. Thousands flocked to it and the Gorsedd provided a remarkable spectacle. A large pavilion was erected on land adjacent to the Ponsonby Arms and was built in great haste, proving to be full of holes – made by the local geese! A huge storm roared for two long days beforehand, causing added concern and troubles.

Despite the initial setbacks it was a turning point for the eisteddfod and Gorsedd movements, as this was the first step towards a National Eisteddfod with the Gorsedd as an integral part of its activities. Two years later, at Aberdare's Market Hall, Ab Ithel's aspirations were fulfilled and the first National Eisteddfod and Gorsedd were held. The Llangollen Eisteddfod was a tempestuous event, where Thomas Stephens of Merthyr entered his essay exploring the myth of Madog's discovery of America. John Williams and his friends had been expecting an essay which would reinforce the myth but because it had been discredited, they were not at all willing to award the prize and matters became turbulent in the extreme.

Thousands flocked from all parts of the country. Canal transport was arranged for those coming from Cefn Mawr, Acrefair, Froncysyllte and Chirk, and excursion trains came from South and North Wales, Liverpool, Manchester and Birmingham. Many came on foot, and reached the town to find it was crammed with people and beds cost as much as a guinea a night.

The eisteddfod saw the first public appearance of a young poet who would be the idol of the nation, John Ceiriog Hughes. He travelled from Manchester to collect his prize for a love poem, 'Myfanwy Fychan of Dinas Brân', which created a wholesome, moral, well-mannered and pure image of the Welsh woman who had been pilloried in the Blue Books.

Myfyr Morganwg, now proclaimed Archdruid of the Isle of Britain, had sanctioned the Gorsedd at an eisteddfod on Kings Hill near St Brides Major in the summer of 1857. At Llangollen, his arrival was considered bizarre and eccentric. Myfyr paraded with the egg around his neck and was characterised in *Y Pynch Cymraeg* in March 1859 as a hen sitting on a nest with the egg, from which a whole weird collection of creatures appear. The Gorsedd of Bards was given the greatest prominence, with members in their respective orders wearing white, blue or green and marching along the streets of Llangollen from the Gorsedd stones to the eisteddfod ground in an exceedingly colourful and pompous procession. A report read,

Many of those who attended objected vehemently the teachings of Myfyr and Ab Ithel on bardism and complained that the mystic mark was accorded far too much prominence on the eisteddfod platform. As a consequence, a special meeting chaired by Revd Richard Parry [Gwalchmai] of some sixty major poets and literateurs of the day was convened on the first evening of the festival ... Myfyr Morganwg was also summoned to this meeting during which he was rigorously questioned on the subject of the bardic mysteries. During his taxing interrogation it became apparent that some of the doctrines promulgated by Myfyr were not entirely in harmony with Christianity. Several ministers publicly opposed his view, but Myfyr refused to continue with the debate ...[14]

Among those who took part in the procession held at ten o'clock on the first morning was Dr William Price.

> They seemed to be forming a procession, headed by two of the most grotesque persons I have ever seen – Dr Price, Pontypridd and his daughter. The young lady rode a cream coloured charger, and on her head she wore a cap of fox skin, the brush at the top, and the head falling down her back. The doctor wore the same, with very peculiar green trousers, scalloped at the bottom, scarlet waistcoat, and a green, round jacket.[15]

The scene was incredulous, with thousands flocking to the event where the foremost members of the Welsh literati appeared dressed in their colourful and wondrous costumes.

Another significant part of the eisteddfod was the performance of Evan and James James's composition, '*Glan Rhondda*'. At Llangollen, Thomas Llewelyn of Aberdare won a competition for an unpublished collection of Welsh airs that included the work. The adjudicator of the competition, Owain Alaw, asked for permission to include '*Glan Rhondda*' in his publication, *Gems of Welsh Melody* (1860). This volume, which gave the composition its more famous title, '*Hen Wlad Fy Nhadau*', was sold in large quantities. It was given large prominence in the National Eisteddfod, Bangor in 1874 and was sung by one of the leading singers of the day, Robert Rees (Eos Morlais), resulting in it later being adopted as the national anthem of Wales.

Such a magnificent showcase as the Great Eisteddfod of Llangollen further inspired Dr William Price in his endeavours to continually uphold the traditions and culture of Wales and its Druidic ancestry. Once again, the hopes and aspirations he envisaged twenty years early at Y Maen Chwyf re-emerged and he became obsessed with creating his museum to Druidism and Wales and a school for poor children.

Despite the passing of Josiah Guest and steady departure of Lady Charlotte from the area, Dr Price continued to enjoy a close relationship with Lady Llanover and her husband, Sir Benjamin. The grandson of Richard Crawshay of Cyfarthfa, Benjamin Hall, 2nd Baron Llanover (1802–67) was a civil engineer and politician and elected MP for Monmouth in 1832. Making a name for himself in the bitter attacks on the Welsh church for its exploitation of church revenues, in 1837 he returned as MP for Marylebone and served under Lord Aberdeen and Lord Palmerton as President of the Board of Health from 1854 to 1855 and was sworn on the Privy Council in 1854. In 1855 he introduced an Act of Parliament which led to establishing the Metropolitan Board of Works, and he became the First Commissioner of Works, responsible for environmental and sanitary improvements in London. He also oversaw the later stages of rebuilding the Houses of Parliament which included installing the 13.8-ton hour bell, Big Ben, in the clock tower. As a tall and imposing man, many feel the nickname was attributed to him. He remained the First Commissioner of Works until the Whigs won the election of 1858, the year in which he was elevated to the peerage as Baron Llanover of Llanover and Abercarn in the County of Monmouth. It was in this year that Price's own visions for the land leased from Hall and Lady Llanover began to flourish.

The influential couple shared a dream to build a house that would become a centre for Welsh culture. It was a place where bards, musicians, historians and academics could come to study, exchange views, and enjoy the society of like-minded people. In fact, they were almost obsessive in their aspirations, not so far from those of Dr Price himself. They held ten eisteddfodau at Abergavenny between 1834 and 1853, each one more magnificent than its predecessor. The prizes were large, and competitors came from all corners of the globe, including Karl Meyer and Albert Schultz from Germany.

On 5 March 1853 Hall leased to Dr Price the building ground, which was 'part of Pentrebach lands with a dwelling house therein situate in the parish of Eglwysilan in the County of Glamorgan for twenty one years from the 24th June 1849, renewable as within at a rent of £20 per annum'. Sir Benjamin specially reserved the mineral rights and 'for any purpose to work and use tram roads, railroads and waterways'. Dr Price was allowed to erect 'one good substantial dwelling house' in addition to the one already on the land. On 9 May 1858 Dr Price mortgaged the leasehold premises to John Snow and Miss Maria Snow for the sum of £400 plus the interest. On 7 May 1859 the leasehold premises were reassigned by William Price, who on 11 May 1859 secured a mortgage from Miss I. E. Garden of £800 plus interest. In 1859 the property contained two dwelling houses, one of which was used as a tavern called Gelhy Fedhig and was occupied by John Williams, the other being in the possession of Dr Price.

Dr William Price's project to open his cultural centre began in earnest in 1858, when excavation commenced on the woodland and quarry and building work began between his surgery at Craigalfa and Y Maen Chwyf. Remembering the towers built by Francis Crawshay decades earlier, Price's designs were more elaborate and consisted of two three-storey round towers in whitewashed rubble, with high-pitched octagonal slate roofs and wooden casements in narrow lancet openings with triangular pointed beards. By the start of 1859, the towers were prominently overlooking Pontypridd and Dr Price is likely to have lived in one of them for a period of time with Hiarlhes and Ann Morgan.

Complete with a symbol of the letter 'T' on the top of the dome, being the Cymmerian pre-Christian cross, the two 'Round Houses' as they became known were the gatehouses to his planned museum to Wales and her heritage close to Y Maen Chwyf. The Round Houses were fortress-like towers that served as flanking turrets to an imposing gateway leading to the palace beyond. The main building was planned at eight storeys high, housing his museum of Welsh folklore and culture, a centre for Druidism, and a school for the orphaned poor. His intention to make a positive contribution to the preservation of Welsh culture by founding the centre of learning cannot be doubted. It was carried out with the same energetic zeal portrayed in his fund-raising abilities in 1839, and also showed his determination and desperation to fulfil a lifelong dream of his own.

What is interesting to note is that eight years previously, Francis Crawshay had also built a Round House at Rhydyfelin. The project, started in 1850, saw eight houses built in 'slices' of a circle. There are two rumours about why they were built. Some believe the circular design was to stop housewives gossiping on the doorsteps. Others believe Francis had a bet with his brother Henry over who could build so many houses on the smallest piece of land.

At first it appears that Lady Llanover was very enthusiastic about Dr Price's scheme, understandable given their mutual admiration and enthusiasm to support a new image and identity of Wales. This would provide the perfect showcase to the rest of the world of all that was great and true about Wales and her people. Sadly the close involvement with the Llanover dynasty showed signs of deterioration as early as 1859, when issues arose over the mineral rights of the land and the terms of the lease. One can only imagine why the situation reached such an extremity. On the one hand, did Dr Price's notoriety for his various behaviours in the courts of law trouble the gentrified Llanover and her husband? There is also the question of whether Hall himself had a dislike of Dr Price for his constant philandering in the neighbourhood, and did he feel in any way threatened by the charm and quirkiness of his character that clearly attracted the opposite sex? Had he in fact attracted Lady Llanover's attentions?

There was also the question of Price's own financial stability. The constant court hearings had clearly affected his bankroll and one can only imagine the huge expense of attending such cases. After all, the properties and land under his name were all leased, and was it simply the case that he became bankrupt and could no longer continue with the work, or pay the rent on the land itself? There was also the question of his own mental stability by this period in his life. As his sixtieth year approached, his total immersion in the frantic mythology of the Druids often caused him to lose the grasp on reality he once had. In the next few years his writings supported a clear indication that some form of mental illness, possibly of a breakdown, became more and more apparent. His gross deterioration became obvious in the letters and publications that he created during the next decade or so, complete with hieroglyphics and desperate attempts to create a new family lineage connecting him to the last true Princes of Wales. Such delusions were further evidence that something was going very, very wrong indeed. Was he beginning to show early signs of this behaviour to the Llanovers, who were becoming increasingly concerned in his ability to carry out the project on their land? Some even claim he had no right or permission whatsoever to even begin the project, which seems to be possible given the fact that the lease allowed him to build one substantial dwelling house, but there is no mention of two large gatehouses also? In truth there is little evidence to support any of these possibilities.

What is available is the evidence that the Craig Alfa estates were to be sold at auction in 1862 at the Angel Hotel, Cardiff and contained several veins of coal in addition to 100 acres of a vein called, rather ironically, Gwenhiolen. The case that ensued had a dramatic effect on his mental stability and was undoubtedly the catalyst for his own decline. Before his aspiration to build the palace above the Round Houses could commence, the entire project failed a second time. What followed was a series of events that would lead to some of the darkest and loneliest days in the long life of Dr William Price.

1860–1869

Work on Dr Price's major scheme continued throughout 1859 and into the new decade. Sadly his hopes and aspirations for the project were short lived. Varying reports claim that Dr Price had no right to build his 'palace' on the land belonging to the Llanovers, and no sooner had the work commenced on excavating the site behind the towers than Lady Llanover instituted the action to eject him with heavy costs. When he refused to pay, a warrant was issued for his arrest and he escaped once more to Paris. Whether or not this is true is debatable. Some claim his disappearance lasted six long years, ensuring that by the time of his return the warrant and the debt would no longer be valid. He admitted in one court hearing to have been exiled for three years, but none of these appear true. There is also the possibility that although he did initially reach France, as several letters were sent from Boulogne, he may well have used Francis Crawshay's property, either at Forest House, his Treforest tower or even property at Hirwaun or Barry Island as a refuge.

What we can be sure of is that the entire enterprise failed in the most dramatic of fashions. It was announced that an auction by J. G. Trenery of Bryn Tail and Craig Alfa in Eglwysilan would take place at the Angel Hotel, Cardiff on Saturday 16 August 1859 at three o'clock. The estate was described as containing several veins of coal and 100 acres of the vein called, rather ironically, Gwenhiolen. One can only imagine that the name of this vein may have been an inspiration into naming Hiarlhes herself twenty years previously! The veins beneath Craig Alfa were assumed to be of exceptional quality, not unlike those in the upper Aberdare and Rhondda seams, and could yield an average of more than 42,000 tons of coal per acre. It was sold to Charles Davies of Claremont House, Abergavenny.

The land had a complicated history, and the conditions of the sale referred to the legal and equitable proceedings that were pending between the Halls and William Price and the mortgagees. The mortgagees had been in receipt of rent reserved by the lease, while the Halls had been nonsuited in proceedings at law. The Halls had intended to make a railway across part of Price's land to work the new colliery at Craig y Helfa called Bryntail but Dr Price refused to give it up, which resulted in them claiming damages against him in December 1859. Damages had been awarded by the arbitrators, but their validity was in question. The Halls then notified their intention to appeal to the Court of Error. On 14 December 1860 they filed a bill in Chancery against William Price and the persons in whom the mortgage security of 8 November 1857 was vested, in order to compel William Price to provide land for the construction of the railway.[1]

Sir Benjamin Hall specifically reserved the mineral rights and 'for any purpose to work and use tram roads, railroads and waterways'. On 9 May 1858 Dr Price mortgaged the leasehold premises to John Snow and Miss Maria Snow for £400 plus interest. On 7 May 1859 the leasehold premises were reassigned by them to William Price who then, on 11 May 1859, secured a mortgage from Miss I. E. Garden of £800 plus interest. In November 1860 the mortgage for £800 was transferred from Miss Garden to John G. Trenery. By the 1861 census Dr Price was listed as residing at Craig Alfa, and Hiarlhes was with her mother Ann at nearby Bryntail Farm, the former home of Pontypridd bridge architect and engineer William Edwards.

As Dr Price recalled,

> I owned the Craig Alfa and Bryn Tail Farms, situated behind the Glyn Taff Church, Pontypridd and a Company called Messrs Davis and Harris leased one hundred and twenty acres of this land from me to work a vein of coal three or four feet thick. It was set forth in the lease that they were to pay me £500 a year reserved rent, and that in case of a disagreement, the dispute should be submitted to arbitration.
>
> I received £500, and when a dispute did arise I found that my attorney, a man from Bristol had 'sold' me, so I conducted the case myself in Bristol for six weeks and subsequently for three weeks in London. The arbitrator, however, decided against me and ordered me to pay £2,000 for refusing permission to the company to construct a tramway over the ground. I then fled to France; but when the case afterward came before the Queen's Bench, I forwarded an affidavit, setting forth that the company had no right to claim anything save and except that which I had given them in the original memorandum, which included the words, 'These are all the parts of the agreement that I allow you, and nothing else and not otherwise.' My attorney denied the existence of this agreement, but I provided it in my affidavit that I saw it in his office, and that I had found that his clerk, a clever fellow, had taken it away. The result was that the finding of the arbitrator was quashed, and the company was ruined. I then returned home.[2]

Dr Price had caused delays in the court. One report of October 1860 suggests that the hearings in the White Lion, Bristol were continually delayed by him. One report claims 'six out of ten days' had in fact been wasted altogether.

A separate case, linked to the arbitration, was heard at Bristol in September 1860 before General Worrall and Mr Poole in which

Mr Price, a large landowner in Wales, charged Mr William Harrison with perjury in an arbitration between Messrs David and Harris, lessees for the Bryntail Colliery of which the complainant was the owner. Mr Stone appeared for the defendant, but the complainant conducted his own case. When called upon to state the ground upon which the complaint was made the complainant said that there had been an arbitration going on at the White Lion Hotel for some time past, relative to a colliery called Bryntail Colliery, in which William Mills Esq., barrister-at-law, was appointed arbitrator by the Court of Queen's Bench. On the 6th instant the defendant was examined and deposed to what he (the complainant) considered to be false, wilful and corrupt perjury. He therefore, applied for and obtained a summons from the Magistrates against him as he was a most material witness in the case with reference to two points, the first of which was whether there had not been a lease granted by him [the complainant] to Messrs. Charles Davies [the younger] and William Harris, at £500 per annum, for a certain vein at Gwenhiolen; but of that vein they had never worked one pound of ore, but in digging towards one part they came to what their considered another vein of coal. He made repeated objections to their digging in that direction, but they persisted in doing so, and went to a distance of 800 yards. They ultimately charged him a sum of £5,000 as damages for not making a railway to connect their works with a canal, and an arbitration was determined upon, in which the decision mainly depended upon the statement of Harrison. The complainant went on further to enter into the matter of the arbitration, but Mr Bruce said the Magistrates did not want to know the particulars of that any more than to enable them to comprehend the nature of the present charge. 'It would not,' he said, 'be an ingredient in the case inquiring how the colliery was worked; but what he [the complainant] would have to show would be, that the arbitration had been held in pursuance of a rule of court, and that some person made a false statement before the arbitrator.'

Mr Mills, the arbitrator, who was present, stated that the arbitration was not yet concluded. Mr Brice said that if that were the case no charge of perjury could be brought, for the witness might be able, perhaps, to explain away or qualify his former statement, even supposing for the sake of the argument; that he had committed the grossest perjury.

Mr Poole said to the complainant, 'When you supplied for the summons, the evidence at the arbitration had not been completed as it was a fortnight ago.'[3]

Mr Mills said, as in a judicial capacity from the Court of the Queen's Bench, and sitting in the case *de die in diem*, Mr Price had done everything he could to cause delay from the start and he hoped the magistrates would not allow him to create any more delay.

Mr Brice, in answer to a question from the complainant, asking the magistrates to adjourn the case, said that they had no jurisdiction at present, but that if Dr Price, when the arbitration was concluded, could make out a *prima facie* case to the magistrates, they would grant him another summons. The case was dismissed.[3]

Bryntail Colliery worked for only a few years in the 1860s, sending its coal down to the Glamorganshire Canal by a tram road incline.

A further incident occurred in October 1860, again at Bristol, when Dr Price, 'the eccentric gentleman' concerned in the arbitration cause at the White Lion, and who made an application to the Bench on the same subject several days earlier, appeared to ask for a warrant for the arrest of Mr Wm Harry Harrison, on a charge of perjury. On a former occasion he had applied for a summons to be granted, but he had been advised that the best course for him to take would be to apply for a warrant, and he now asked for one.

Mr Coates said before a warrant could be granted the magistrate must know all the circumstances. Dr Price said the alleged perjury was committed in Bristol, on 6 September, by William Harry Harrison, before William Mills Esq., an arbitrator, sitting at the White Lion. Mr Harrison swore then, a certain heading, forty-seven yards long in the colliery, had passed through a vein of coal, from 2 feet 8 inches to 2 feet 10 inches thick, into a pit, which he described as a trial pit. He also said that in that heading two stalls could be turned, and that seventy or eighty yards of coal could be worked out. That was false.

Mr Coates said that before the magistrates could grant a warrant Dr Price must show that the statement was made, and then he must prove by documentary evidence, or the testimony of two witnesses, that it was false, and that Mr Harrison, at the time he uttered it, knew it to be false. Dr Price said he could do that. He had a witness present. Mr Williams said the statement must also have been material to the issue. Dr Price said it was material. They were in a vein of coal which they had not leased, and the object was to identify it as the same vein. That was the materiality.

Mr Williams said Dr Price should bring to the magistrate a copy of the evidence. Dr Price said he trusted to his memory and had no copy. Mr Castle said memories sometimes differ on points. Mr Williams said the magistrates, before they could issue a warrant to drag a gentleman up from Wales, would require to be satisfied, from the examinations, as to what was sworn. Dr Price had better get a copy of the arbitration notes of the evidence.

Dr Price said he could not do that. Mr Coates repeated that Dr Price must show, by documentary or *viva voce* evidence, that the person complained of had sworn what he knew to be false. Dr Price said he would get *viva voce* evidence, and after some further conversation, he left the office.[4] No further evidence exists of the case, which again is likely to have failed.

There is indication of Dr Price's mental deterioration during the early part of the 1860s. One of the first letters written in the decade was addressed to Hiarlhes from the Great Western Hotel, Paddington, London and dated January 1861. During the decade he made regular visits to the city, sometimes for very long periods of time, and presumably this one coincided with the court case being heard by the Queen's Bench relating to the Gwenhiolen vein of coal. In it he talks of the authorities and suggests, '*Y mae y diawl yn gynnyl iawn yma, ond yr wyf yn meddwl yr af trwyddo.*' ('The devil here is very subtle, but I think I will get through.')

According to Dr Price's recollections, Lady Llanover insisted on evicting him from the land, with heavy costs, particularly to the unpaid builders who supplied the material for the Round Houses and the proposed project of the large mansion house. Dr Price refused to pay and a warrant was issued. According to his later interviews, Llwyn Llwyd was surrounded by police and Hiarlhes suggested he should hide in an old chest. Price scrambled inside and she locked him in so the police could find no sign of him. Later that day the trunk was allegedly carried out of the house by two friends claiming it contained clothing. Whether the local constabulary were really that naive is hard to imagine!

His specially printed headed notepaper now included a symbol of a stag surrounded by the Druidic lettering that became synonymous with much of his life from this moment onwards. There are the beginnings of a withdrawal from reality into a new world of his own fantastical creation. The surviving letters from Price during this time are fascinating, and yet are remarkably disturbing in their content. Throughout 1860 and into 1861 Dr Price had been totally engrossed in battle with the Halls, the failure of the Craig yr Helfa scheme and the court hearings relating to the colliery and railway connection. One can only assume that these were a factor in the reason why Dr Price did not attend the first National Eisteddfod of Wales, held in Aberdare in August 1861, as he was probably in France. Having made such a dramatic appearance at the Llangollen forerunner three years previously, it would not be unreasonable to have expected him to attend the Aberdare event. No evidence exists of his visit to the National Eisteddfod and probably, the organisers themselves breathed a sigh of relief at his lack of attendance, possibly concerned by the impact such a controversial figure would have on the proceedings. The event took place at Aberdare Market Hall and was underwritten by David Williams (Alaw Goch), the coal owner and eisteddfod enthusiast of Miskin Manor. Originally intended for another site, a storm destroyed the pavilion erected to welcome the thousands of visitors, and Alaw Goch stopped work at his collieries and instructed the miners to adapt the Market Hall to save the event from collapse.

By the end of 1861 Dr Price had fled to France, and in the first of his letters from Boulogne claims he and his daughter are the children of Lord

Ris (Rhys ap Gruffydd, 1132–97), Lord of Deheubarth, and leader of the 1164–5 uprising. In it he asserts that the security of his claim to his 'father's' estate and title was the reason why there was an action against him. The remarkable contents include the following.

To the Messrs Jackson, Neale and Co. and the Pretender Mortgages, or Mortgagees, under whose direction, you say, you will Act, as Auctioneers, and to the Solicitor or Solicitors, or such Pretender Mortgages or Mortgagees, Agent or Agents, or Representatives, respectively and collectively, of such pretending mortgages, or Mortgagees, and to the Public Capitalists, without exception, individually, and in company; and to all other persons, to whom it may concern, and will concern, to know, who may meddle to sell, or offer for sale, or medals to buy the Inalienable Estate and Title of Inheritance or us, The undersigned YH Hy, *, X, C, Cayroris, Arglwydd Deheudir Cymru and Genhilen Hiarlhes Morganwg; or to presume to sell, or to offer for sale, or to buy, any part or parcel thereof, identified and in our possession, known by the names of Bryntail and Craig Alfa, and Llys Ywein as described, by you, in your Public Notice, inserted, and published, in the *Bristol Mercury* of 22nd December 1861m, which, you say, you will sell, by Public Auction at the Cardiff Arms Hotel, in Cardiff on Saturday the 4th of January next, 1862.

We, YH, Hy *, X, O, Cayroris, Arglwydd Deheudir Cymru and Gwenhiolen, Iarlhes Morganwg, Being Two of the identified Children of our Father the Lord Ris of Cayroris, In His Will, in the New Greek Testament, and in His ORIGINAL Will, in His Iliad, and Odyssey, and in the Fifty Laws of His Mint House in His own language, in what is called the Greek Letter, from which there is no translation into any language, do hereby give you Public Notice that you shall not sell, nor offer for sale, the Estate we inherit from our Father, the Lord Ris of Cayroris, nor any Part of it, known by the Names of Bryntail, and Craig Alfa, and Lhys Ywein, as you propose to do, with impunity by the instruction or direction of our inalienable Estate, the Title of Inheritance from our Father and our Father's Father, through all past generations of the civilised world, by the Original Title of the Goat that carries the World on Her Left Horn!!!

This is the Reason why these Pretending Attorney Mortgages, or Attorneys Mortgagees are in such haste, to get out of their own Blue Bags before this secret shall be known, from the Court, to their Golden Geese. Their Capitalists, who are obliged to hire their Brains to carry their Purses in their title Deeds; or there they must remain to eat their own Parchments, till they get out to be condemned! They know perfectly well, they have no mortgage on our estate as ordinary individuals, under the Laws of change and commerce, and the Lease of one hundred Acres of the Bryntail Gwenhiolen vein of coals will convince everybody in His

Senses. This Lease of one Hundred acres of the Bryntail Gwenhiolen Vein of Coals (The Right and Title of Gwenhiolen, Hiarlhes Morganwg) represents These Pretended Mortgages, or Mortgagees, as Owners, Mortgages and Mortgagees of their own estate at the same time!!!

How is it possible, that say one, in His senses, To be a Mortgages, and a Mortgages of his Own Estate to Himself, and Lease a part of it to a Third Party, under such deeds under seal at the same time? There is no other construction to be put, upon this Lease, with the Authority, of their intended Escape Goat, but a swindling deed of partnership planned and executed, under the Director of the Will of the pretended owners, mortgagers and mortgagees and their lessees!!! That is the Nationals!!!

There is no other sane solution of the intention and motive element of design and construction in this lease of one hundred acres of the Bryntail Gwenhiolen Vein of Coal!!! Our inalienable estate, before the discovery, and publication in London, of our Right of Inheritance to all the Private Estate, and the Title of the Goat, of our Father the Lord Ris of Cayroris, who had woven his Immortal Title to his private estate and distinction of his race in all the written and printed law of the civilised world, with his Egg, on the top of the thumb on his right hand, that has stamped the coinage of all nations on the face of the earth, from his Mint of Cayroris or Caerphilli, unclaimed, till October 24th 1861, when the Staff of his authority, His Cross, and his New Greek Testament, were demanded by Me, His Son, from the Custody of His Steward, the Last Lord Mayor of London, in this accompanying copy of the sixth letter, addressed to him, on this subject, Dated November 4th 1861. Our Father, the Lord Ris of Cayroris, is no other Lord, nor man than Ywein Lawgoch, the author of the Iliad and Odyssey, and fifty laws to rule his Mint of Cayroris, as well as the Mints of all Nations, and a Codicil to His original Will in Four Parts at the end of Barnes edition of His Will printed at Cambridge by Professor Barnes.

There is a copy of the original law of the Mint of Cayroris, in the second volume of Montfaucon's *L'Antiquite Expliquee*, in the Plat OXL, admirable explained and illustrated, with a likeness of the Lord Ris, and his Eldest Son V on their knees, in the Presence of the Lady of the Lady or Lhyn Evan, and the other members of his Family, before he communicated the Secret of coining his own Genius into Gold, with the Blood of his eldest son, on his own cross!!! Capitalists are Hereby informed that this crossed ceased to be, and died out of Force to hold Real Estate, to bar the entailed estates under the original title of the Goat of our Father, the Lord Ris of Cayroris, and Great Britain. There is no title to hold land now, and has not been since the nine of November 1861, but the Title of the Goat of Our Father and Lord Ris of Cayroris, and Great Britain. Marriage settlements are avoidable now, in the Court of Law and Equity. A divorce court to separate husband and wife, now, is an useless court to the public! The woman, as well as the man, is freed now, and liberated henceforth, to enjoy themselves in this respect, as they will in the light of the sun and moon!!!

Again we, the undersigned, forbid you to sell, or offer for sale, by auction, our inalienable estate, as you propose to do; and, again, we warn and forbid those who may attend your proposed estate, to bid for it, or buy it, or any part of it or parcel thereof, as described, by you, in your public notice, in the *Bristol Mercury* of 22nd instant. There is another little book, in Latin, called The Breviaries, to which Lawyers refer, when they are nonplussed, which capitalists may consult with advantage at this period of revolution in the title to real estate!!!

The word 'Breviaries' is the proverb in the Cymmmerian Language, in the mouth of infants, 'Rodh a Brefar y ol'!!! dated, at Bryntail, in the Parish of Eglwysilan in the county of Glamorgan, on the 28th day of December 1861 and signed by us, YH, Hy * X,O. Cayroris, Arglwydd Deheudir Cymry Gwenhiolen, Hiarlhes Morganwg.[5]

Such an incredulous letter illustrates that at this moment Dr Price had began to suffer some type of severe breakdown. The style shows a marked deterioration, particularly in his description of himself as the son of the Lord Ris of Cayroris, accompanied by the indecipherable hieroglyphics. It also calls into question whether his decision to name Hiarlhes as Gwenhiolen the Countess of Glamorgan showed a sense of delusion twenty years previously, particularly as in this letter she is named as one of the 'identified children' of the Lord.

There is a strong case here for beginning to consider the fact that Dr William Price was beginning to show a late onset of a mental illness not totally dissimilar to that suffered by his late father. In diagnosing mental illnesses, psychiatrists use different criteria to ascertain the type of illness suffered by the patient. Karl Kleist divided paranoid schizophrenia into several categories: 'confabulating, hallucinating, somatic delusional, autistic, those with ideas or delusions of infidelity, passivity feelings, fantastic delusions, and mixed forms'. He goes on to record the average age of the onset of schizophrenia or paraphrenia as thirty-seven years, slightly later in life than Revd William Price, and arguably sooner that his son, but there is clearly indication of this prognosis affecting them both. Kleist said the diagnosis was characterised by 'an outgoing, aggressive, assertive manner, recognition of personal superiority; extreme self assuredness and condescension to others; egocentricity; pedantry, and failure to see the observer's point of view, loquaciousness in argument, forcefulness, grandiosity'.

On the one hand Revd Price had become 'lunatic' by his thirtieth year with symptoms of gross schizophrenia. Dr Price never broke down to the degree of his father.

The eccentricities and oddities, the zeal and aggression of his youth became more florid with age, but he retained sufficient integration to be a formidable opponent even in old age. He is remembered for his eccentricities, his dress, his mystical Druidism and ceremonial. The newspapers of his closing years showed him as a comic-tragic figure playing a clownish part on stage. The mumbling shambles of his appearance ... should not be recalled without remembering Lady Charlotte Guest's description of his eloquence.[1]

Psychiatrist Alan Bellack described the schizophrenic's pursuance of a mystical ideal, with mumbling speech, eccentric clothing and sexual promiscuity. The catatonic type of schizophrenia described by him claims the patient has feelings of rebirth, or of catastrophe, feelings of exultation or identification with the cosmos.

Dr Price is illustrated in the letter-writing as indicative of a mental illness such as paraphrenia. The use of symbolism is often used to obscure meaning, using a language in a code or cipher. It is almost as if there is a need to conceal the meaning of letters and messages, which calls into question Dr Price's letters, his obsession with the Greek stone at the Louvre Gallery and its hieroglyphics, and the release in 1871 of his unfathomable book, *Gwyllllis yn Nayd*, which is devoted to the Druidic vision he encountered on his first visit to France. The book was funded by Price and published by Vincent Brooks of King Street, Covent Garden.

There is also the fact that another characteristic connected to paraphrenia is the multiplicity of capitals and the almost continuous underlining of words. Such features became so repetitive in his letters that they lose their value and emphasis and it becomes more and more clear that Dr Price has succumbed to a mental condition, which could have been paraphrenia. It also argues the false premise of the title of the son of the Lord of South Wales, his determination to secure property and land in the name of his family, which didn't even exist. The deterioration was so rapid at this point and so unsettling, a forerunner of which could be identified in the Medical Directory of 1860, where his entry begins to cause concern in itself. It read,

PRICE, Wm, Craig Alva, Ponty y Pryidh, Glamorganshire – M.R.C.S. Eng. And L.S.A 1821; Discoverer of 'Gafal Len Beren Myrdin or the Cimmerian Algebra of all Languages'; 'The Trial of the *Queen* v. *William Price* for Perjury, in the Native Language and in English'.

The letter which he addressed to the Lord Mayor of London at the Mansion House, London, is another example of largely indecipherable language and symbols.

To T. Cubbit, the Steward of my Father, the Lord Ris of Cayroris, in office as His Lord Mayor of London, <u>for the time being</u>, ending all Latitudes, north and south, and in all <u>longitudes</u>, east and west of Cayroris, or Caerphilli, or Caerfelli, on <u>November the eighth instant</u>. At midnight, one thousand, eight hundred and sixty one!!!

Sir / I Ytt tyy * X C Cayroris Arglwyd Deheudir Cymru, the Son of your Lord and Master, the Lord Ris of Cayroris, as herein described, so hereby give you public notice, that on the first <u>second of time, in the morning of the ninth day of November instant one thousand eight hundred and sixty one, the present foreign</u> government of Great Britain, <u>geared into office, by you as my Father's Steward</u>, in his office of Lord Mayor of London, on the <u>ninth of November 1860, shall cease to be, and shall die out to all intents and purposes, as a government to administer the laws. In the courts of Law and Equity, with Force of Arms, never again to be geared into office, as a government by you, or anybody else for you. With the private authority of my father's staff and my father's cross, on my father's will of, and in the new Testament, thenceforth as the Staff, and the Cross, and the new Testament of the Lord Ris of Cayroris, are my Private Estate and Title of Inheritance, from my Father Ris of Cayroris, your Lord and Master for the Time Being, on your oath, and the Lord and Master of All Christians, and all Christian Nations,</u> claiming, and using, <u>the Private Authority of my Father's Staff, and Cross and Will, in the New Testament</u>, for the Public purposes of government, in all localities and nations at home and abroad, with whom I, Ytt tty X O Cayroris, shall be in personal alliance on, and <u>from the ninth of November instant, one thousand eight hundred and sixty one, on whom I shall call, to restore to me, from your custody, possession or power, of my father's staff and my father's cross, and my father's original Will, my private estate and title of inalienable inheritance</u> all past ages of the civilised world, <u>to the present time, discovered</u> by the unknown genius of my Cymmerian Mother, in whose custody, the Secret remained for fifteen hundred years before. I was to tell, to whom, Ioine, <u>Thy Divine Revelation, of my Father's staff, and my Father's Cross, and my own Cross</u>, in the Christian Will of my Father the Lord Ris of Cayroris, in His New Testament, for the Happiness and Glory of my Race and Country, and the Peace and Contentment of all Christian Nations, destined to be involved in continued Revolutions till my father's Staff and my Father's Cross and the Immortal Will of my Father, in the New Testament, <u>shall be restored to me</u>, His Son, and His Private Estate of Cayroris and Ponty y Pandy the only <u>original Private Estate</u>, recorded (before civilisation existed as a science of human government) which gives me the Three Crosses Ytt tty * X O Cayroris, and the Title Arglwyt Deheudir Cymru.'[6]

Within the letter is a copy of the image of Dr Price and Hiarlhes. Under which is written,

> Lhyndain!!! For more than Twenty Years past <u>my Flagstaff</u> has been your Queen, at the Altar of Her Lord God <u>dressed by you</u> (my Father's Steward in office, as his Lord Mayor of London, on your oath), and the Lord and commons of Great Britain, <u>in my Father's White Robe, saturated and Drunk, with the Blood of the Widow, and Her Infants and my Father, and in common with them His own Son</u>, whom your Queen has hunted the second time, out of His own Dominion, for denouncing the Collective Treason or Insanity of your Lawgivers, in taxing the Bread and wine, on the altar of your Lord God!!! In contempt and defiance of his Will in the New Testament and the Arms of Great Britain surrounded <u>with the motto 'Homi soit qui mal y pense'</u> and <u>his</u> motto '<u>Dieu et mon Droit</u>' if this one etc of your government as an instance, is not an insane etc, what <u>is</u> Insanity?

Dr Price's fantasy became all the more elaborate when he requested that a printer named Jones produce several hundred copies of a notice which once again exalted his county of Glamorgan, not unlike Iolo Morganwg attempted to achieve in the previous century. On 27 December 1861 he wrote from Boulougne to Mr Jones, stating,

> Dear Sir, I owe you a Bill, who has been due for a long time, in consequence of my inability to pay you.
>
> You need not fear, you shall be paid every penny with interest as soon as I can. I have requested Gwenhiolen Hiarlhes Morganwg, to call upon you, to print from 200 to 500 of this public notice immediately, and pay you, before you deliver the order, executed by you.
>
> Let this curious Public Notice by put into the compositor hand forthwith, as there is not a moment to spare! Let it be printed in a clear type, on note paper about this size that it may be sent in the form of the letter. Be particular in correcting the press! You know my handwriting sufficiently to decipher it.

The public notice read:

> All the Greek Books are the Works of the Primitive Bards, in our own Language!!!!!! There is a Discovery for the Cymmerian Race!!!!! Discovered by me in 1839!!!! No man living can form an opinion, or imagine, the consequence of my Discovery. Before he shall be taught, by me, to read Homer, The Greek New Testament, or any and all The Greek Classics, which I can do, perfectly, in less than six days!!!!! Homer was born in the Hamlet of Y Van near Caerphili. He built Caerphili Castle.

His name is ap Ywein Cayoris. He was the discoverer of the Cross that has been so long in use, to govern mankind. That is not the Cross with which he built the Castle. That was His own Cross resplendent by the letter – Phon Eure. The first money that was ever coined on the Face of the earth was coined by Him, at Cayroris in Caerphilli Castle. The oldest Books of the Chinese confess the Fact!! This look more like a dream than a Reality in the absence of Light.

A day later he wrote again to the printer, insisting that this was the 'most important manuscript notice that has ever been sent to any press for the public!!!' He also instructed the printer had the words 'Plant Ywein Lawgoch' in red ink at the top of the notice, referring to Owain Llawgoch (Owen of the Red Hand).

There is only one letter, in this Notice, you may not have in your printing office, but you will contrive to get it, or make it with a & and a /, by cutting off & and putting them together by thuys 'YH hy, *, X,O, Cayroris, Arglwyt Deheudir Cymry.

This use of historical figures as the basis for a bizarre mythology centred upon an idiosyncratic interpretation of Druidism absorbed Price's energies for the rest of his life.

While in Paris on his second exile, Dr Price claimed to have met Pierre Joseph Proudhon (1809–65), French philosopher and social theorist who had a massive effect on the post-1848 revolutionary France. Proudhon was a revolutionary, but his revolution did not mean violent upheaval or civil war, but rather the transformation of society. Given Price's own strong political views, Proudhon and the famous Welshman had much to discuss and ideals to share. Price was clearly enamoured of the man, who was the first individual to call himself an 'anarchist' and the first documented as using the word 'capitalist' to mean property-owner.

According to the Welshman, Dr Price also enjoyed many love affairs during his time in France, noting in particular a certain Madame Bisset, of whom he became increasingly fond. He remained in contact with his daughter and her mother during his exile and he spent more than a year abroad. He wasn't present at the Crawshay wedding in April 1862 when Francis's two daughters, Isabel and Laura, married the Fothergill brothers of George and Thomas. This grand ceremony, uniting two of the most powerful and wealthy dynasties of the region, was well documented in the local and national press.

What is important in verifying his time in France was the small entry in the *Cambrian News* in May 1863 that read, 'The well known and eccentric Welshman Dr Price, has returned to his castle near Pontypridd after a stay of several months in France. Dr Price appears in good health and was warmly received by a large number of the inhabitants of the above-named place.'[7]

By 1865 there is a large quantity of correspondence relating to an increasingly acrimonious dispute between Dr William Price and the executors and trustees of the late Mary Price of Old Steyne, Brighton. Dr Price tried to claim a legacy of £1,000 from the estate. What is of interest is that the correspondence relating to the will of Mary Price, his first cousin, is lucid, clear and has a purpose. There is no repetitive underlining of words or overuse of capital letters and exclamation marks, as seen in the letters of 1861. However, there is again reference to his honorary title, which states, 'Forward me a cheque for my legacy in a few days hence made payable at the Bank of England to William Price in the Presence of Ytt tty * X O, Cayroris'. Aside from that, the letters show no other signs of the bizarre content or writing as with previous letters, and one can only assume this was during a far more lucid period in his life. They are distinct, clear, and provide factual evidence to the executors of the estate and solicitors rather than rambling fantasies of a confused mind. Not until the final letter is there any sign of the constant underlining of words, phrases and even entire sentences.

Copies of the correspondence were sent to George Philcox Hill, solicitor of Brighton, claiming that in her will a legacy of £1,000 would be paid to Dr Price within 'three calendar months after her decease'. It is accompanied by copies of letters sent to the executors of the will, Miss Catherine Harriet Smear of Kensington Place, Kensington and George Nelson Emmett, a solicitor of Bloomsbury Square, London. In it he calls on them to ensure he receives the legacy to which he is entitled. As the correspondence continues, Dr Price becomes more agitated with the solicitors involved and goes so far as to send them a copy of the pedigree of the Price family, which he devised to illustrate he was her cousin and entitled to his claim. He explained that he is the William Price stated in the will, whereas they claim that the William Price entered was dead before the demise of Miss Price herself. In attempting to reverse that decision Dr Price submitted his pedigree to them as evidence of their mistake.

Emmett responded to him in March 1865 and stated, 'I am not aware of you being the first cousin of the late Miss Mary Price and never heard that you were such nor did the late Miss Price ever speak of you to me as her first cousin. You cannot be the first cousin named in the will as W. Price is dead.' The William Price stated was in fact the son of Charles Price who had died the previous year in 1864.[8]

The pedigree was not enough for the solicitors to even consider Dr Price as one of the heirs, and without certificates and definite proof they were unwilling to present the legacy he claimed. Dr Price responded on 4 April 1865 with the following letter.

The William Price named in the Will of Mary Price deceased is William Price, the third son of the Revd William Price of Tŷ yn y Coed Cae, Rudry in the County of Glamorgan and no other William Price! For the date of the Will of Mary Price and at the date of her decease, Mary Price had no other cousin of the name William Price living – supposing William Phillips Price, the son of Charles Price of the Stamp Office, London is now living or had not been dead twenty years ago!

The letter was accompanied with a copy of his parent's marriage certificate and his own birth certificate. Further certificates were required of his grandfather Charles Price, which he also produced. He was unable to produce the baptism certificate of the other William Price, calling it the 'lost certificate' but did send copies of the certificate as it appeared in a copy of the original Register Book of Baptisms in the Parish of Bedwas, stating in his next letter, 'William the son of Charles Price was baptised February 25th 1761 … The above is a true cope of the Register Book of the Parish of Bedwas, Monmouthshire.'

Dr Price explained that the original could not be found and as the solicitors made claim for it 'your suggestion is as good as it is useless and can never be complied with' and only the entry in the Register Book could be produced, which was already a copy. This, he claims was due to the fact that the original pages from the book were 'destroyed or cut out of the Register about the year 1793 … it is the Rule of Evidence in the Courts of Law and Equity to admit the Transcript of the original Documents or the best secondary evidence in the administration of the Law of the Land'. With this letter, dated 1 May 1865, he also included a certificate stating that the original entry was non-existent: 'I, William Williams, Recrot of Bedwas, having examined the Register Book of Baptisms belonging to the Parish of Bedwas hereby certify that I have not been able to find any Baptismal Entries therein from the year 1757 to 1766.'[9]

When again the solicitors question the validity of his claim, Dr Price lost all patience with them and responded with a lengthy reply which included the following startling revelations:

I beg to refer you to the title of the Pontypandy Estates Marriage Settlements and the marriage settlement of the Revd Thomas Price, the will of Charles Price of Bedwas, the Trust Deed of Joan Price order or decree in Chancery Expante *Price* v. *Price*, the Will of the Revd Thomas Price and inventory. The Will and a deed of trust of the late Dr Charles Price of Brighton subject of course to his creditors in *Price* v. *Price* in Chancery and various other documents in your possession that will leave no doubt on your mind WHY the Revd Thomas Price of Merriott and his brother Charles Price, the attorney of Joan Price, their widowed stepmother conspired after her death in 1793 to cut out and did cut out the Baptismal Entry of William the son of Charles Price of Bedwas from the Register Book of Baptisms of the Parish of Bedwas in the County of Monmouth for the purpose of disinheriting the youngest brother, Revd William Price of Tŷ yn y Coed Cae in the Parish of Rydry in the County of Glamorgan, who had become, about that time, *non compos mentis* to consign him to a lunatic asylum and took possession of some £15,000 mortgage invested by his father Charles Price on the Pontypandy Estates left by his Will to his son William Price the Residuary Legatie and joint Executor with his mother Joan Price and succeeded in robbing and swindling and disinheriting their youngest brother the Revd William Price of his personal and real estates during his life with will fail to rob and disinherit his heirs![10]

The response from Emmett was clear:

We have communicated with our clients therein and it is impossible for us not to participate fully in their deeply injured feelings of indignation at the foul and unjustifiable charges you have made against the former members of Miss Price's family long since dead and now for the first time after a lapse of 70 years launched against the memories of gentlemen of the highest character and respectability and for which aspersions we do not believe you have the slightest grounds ... and we must therefore call upon you to retract such a shameful claims. We still say that the copy certificate sent is incomplete because it has not attached to it the name of the clergyman or any other official party as having signed it ... certificates can be of no value without such signature.[11]

Undaunted by the letters Dr Price goes so far as to accuse them of lining their 'breeches pockets' with the division of the 'real and personal estates of the Revd William Price'. Claiming of them 'falsehoods' and 'wilful fabrications', he also admonishes them for not informing him sooner that the entire will was being administered by the Court of Chancery. As they had taken so long in informing him of this, he felt his claim would not be heard as there was little time to spare. Clearly, his claim failed.

Dr Price steadily withdrew from the frantic quantity of court cases that had engulfed almost fifteen years of his life. His obsession with litigation – possibly also attributable to a dire financial state given the costs involved in previous hearings – dwindled. Instead Dr Price turned his energies increasingly to Druidism. During the latter part of the 1860s he made further frequent visits to London, usually staying at lodgings in Victoria Hotel, 27 Euston Square, from which he continued to correspond with his daughter. Given the small amount of correspondence that still exists, one can assume that he actually spent several long months, maybe more than a year, in the same premises without coming home to Wales. From October 1868 to May 1869 his address is that of Euston Square, but by the end of May and up until October 1869 he resided at 40 Lombard Street, London. During this period the *Cardiff & Merthyr Guardian* made mention of the fact that the Treforest tinplate works had closed with 'no intention of reopening in the near future' and Dr Price was described as the 'once eminent surgeon of Treforest'.

One of the letters of 7 October 1868 thanked Hiarlhes her for the parcel, 'the contents had not deteriorated except for the wheat bread which was slightly mouldy! The cheese, butter and oat bread restaurant is the best in London. The delicacies, the plums and the blackberries are excellent.' Some of the letters do make references to possible court hearings and matters of litigation. One of which is a letter of 24 February 1869 relating to further claims of the Clungwyn Farm, the oldest surviving in the area, which 'has been hidden from everyone for a hundred years'. The letters regarding the estate again refer to Thomas and Charles Price, not dissimilar to the correspondence over the will of Mary Price. This time there is clearly a court case, possibly *Davies* v. *Price*, taking place in London, and he may well have remained in the city as it was undertaken.

On 16 July 1869 Dr Price lost his elder sister Mary, who had resided with her husband Thomas John, who was a decade younger than her. She was buried in the family tomb in St Barrwg's, Bedwas. During the same year Dr Price was arrested in London one Saturday afternoon by his creditors, explaining,

> the bank was closed, so I could not then deposit money as security to keep me out of gaol. On the Monday I received a notice from the Court of Chancery that I was to be declared a bankrupt. This was done because my creditors had found that I had withdrawn from the Bank of England the money they had intruded to pounce upon. I appealed against the notice, and deposited £400 with the Commissioner, as security until the costs had been taxed, so I got the best of it after all.

One of the final letters referred to a chance meeting with William Crawshay who asked to 'call upon him' when he was next in Wales. Once again it was time to return to his homeland and in doing so become further and further immersed in some fantastical thoughts and deeds.

1870–1883

In 1870 Dr William Price reached his seventieth birthday, and most men of his relatively advanced age for the period experienced a quiet and peaceful existence in their dotage. Not so for the doctor, whose existence remained as tumultuous and adventurous as it ever was. Sadly there is a sense of tragedy surrounding Price during his advancing years. His mental stability is constantly brought into question, particularly with the publication of his philosophy of Druidism, claiming once again his right to uphold and lead this religion to greater heights than ever imagined. Earlier he was recognised for his warmth, kindness and emotions, but with age he became intolerant, subject to the delusions of further grandeur and is portrayed as an egocentric man. It was a period in which he was ridiculed mercilessly in the newspapers, both due to his devotion to a pagan religion and for his own peculiar lifestyle, dress, ceremonies and beliefs. This period was not without its personal tragedy, with the death of his partner, his daughter finding a lover and creating her own path in life, the loss of his home and Pontypridd estates, his departure from his employment, closure of his surgery and the retirement of his friend and confidante Francis Crawshay to Kent.

The consummate self-publicist and dramatist had lost the support of the industrial hierarchy where he had spent decades healing the sick and the injured. The Crawshay family no longer employed him and his greatest supporter of all, Francis, was gone. He was a man in decline, losing the tinplate and ironworks leaders' sponsor. He was also a man who had lost the support of his fellow Druids in the Gorsedd Circle at Y Maen Chwyf, as exemplified by Morien's constant badgering of him in the press as someone who spoke a 'nonsense Druidism'.

In one of several letters from France in 1869 Dr Price talked of a case involving an injunction on Craig Alfa and Bryntail Farms. By the time of his return to Wales in 1870 neither of the properties were home to the Price family as they had once been. By then they were residing in the Duke of Bridgewater Arms on Ynysangharad Road, which at this time was a tenement called Pentrebach House. Within the year – and following an order of ejectment – they resided in a terraced house on Rickard Street, Treforest, a far cry from the extensive farmland Dr Price was used to where he kept large quantities of livestock. Instead they had resigned themselves to living among the workforce of the tinplate and ironworks. Neighbouring Pontypridd had become an extensive municipal town, complete with its own flourishing marketplace, chapels, public houses, the largest railway platform in the country, and the landmark St Catherine's Church spire, recently constructed. Life was changing all around him.

On 10 February 1870 the issue of the Clungwyn Estate was heard by the Lord Chancellor Baron Hatherley regarding an action brought before the Court of Exchequer called '*Price* v. *Jackson and Others*' to recover Clyn Gwyn (or Clungwyn) in the parishes of Bedwas and Machen. The land had once belonged to Dr Price's grandfather, Charles Price. The case was heard at the Guildhall, London, on 18 February 1870, and an order was made against Charles Morgan Robinson Morgan, Baron Tredegar to produce documents. Price claimed Clungwyn should have 'devolved by heirship upon the immediate ancestor' of himself after the death of his grandmother Joan in 1792. Lord Tredegar ignored the order to produce the documents and consequently Dr Price claimed that Tredegar was an outlaw. There were previous Chancery proceedings about Clungwyn in 1782, 1786 and 1790 between Nicholas Price of Pontypandy and Bloom Williams and Hopkin Llewellyn at the time. There was a local tradition that the Prices had been cheated of their inheritance by the Morgans of Tredegar. This probably arose from some of the bequests to the Morgan family contained in local wills, such as that of Hugh Jones of Gelliwastad, Machen, dated 21 October 1777. Hugh Jones's wife, Ann was the aunt of Joan, the second wife of Charles Price. It would therefore appear that these 'bonds, contracts and settlements' would go to his sons, including Revd Price.

Letters between Dr Price and Hiarlhes dated May 1869 refer to the Clungwyn Estates and the will of a Mary Price. The estate was being sold and 'I shall have to file a bill against the trustees to hinder their sale of Clungwyn! Neither Thomas Richard Shelland nor Maria Sothern have proved their pedigree!' Price continued throughout this period to try and have the tenants of Clungwyn evicted. Sadly, there is no further evidence of this case and one can only assume that, as with so many other claims for the rights and ownership of land and property by Dr Price, it again failed.

At the start of 1870, Price faced the law courts once more, only this time he was accused of the most serious of charges – manslaughter. In January at the Musical Hall Inn, Penydarren, an inquest was held on the body of Thomas Price, a haulier, before deputy coroner Mr T. Williams. Two years earlier Thomas Price was kicked by a horse which caused a tumour on the kneecap. He was attended at different periods by local surgeons Dr Dyke, Dr Griffiths, Dr Webster and Dr Cresswell, who all suggested the leg be amputated. In November 1869 Thomas, who was aged just thirty-three, sought the opinion of the 'celebrated and eccentric Dr Price, of Treforest, who professed himself able to cure him without amputation'.[1]

A newspaper covering the court case explained the events leading up to his death:

> The only medicine that Dr Price gave him before yesterday week was a powder and a pint of beer. On that day the deceased was taken down in a cab to Dr Price, who passed a needle with a silk threat attached through the tumour, releasing a pint of blood and water from the wound which reduced the pain experienced by the patient. Having done so he took the needle out, leaving the threat in the wound, the end of which he tied. The man was taken home slowly in the cab and from that time he eventually sank until Friday morning when he died. Dr Price came up on that day and gave the following extraordinary certificate of death: 'I hereby certify that Thomas Price died from the original cause, the law of the land.'[1]

At the inquest, which was attended by the widow and brother of Thomas Price, Dr Cresswell was examined and the case was adjourned to ensure the attendance of Dr Price. He was committed to the assizes by the coroner on the charge of the manslaughter of Thomas Price. Dr Price arrived in the court in a 'fine brougham, with a pair of horses, with two servants. He was dressed in a suit of green, lined and trimmed with scarlet and a handsome fur cap.'[2]

In March the case was heard before Lord Chief Justice Bovill at the Glamorganshire Spring Assizes in Swansea. Mr Bowen and Mr B. T. Williams appeared for the prosecution while Dr Price conducted his own defence 'with great skill and ingenuity, if not with all the legal acumen of a barrister, still with much judgment, and in a manner which showed that he was fully alive to the grave nature of the charge'. The court was crowded as soon as the doors opened and the doctor, clad in his green-and-scarlet outfit, stood up in the dock and was made the object of curiosity by all who attended:

> The appearance of this eccentric individual in Court created a good deal of curiosity and interest. His peculiar clothing – being dressed in a tunic and trousers of green cloth, with scarlet trimmings, and curious vandyke edgings – his long flowing white beard together with his hair tied and twisted under his chin – his fur cap consisting of a fox skin, completely conspired to give the accused a most remarkable appearance. Rumours has that this eccentric individual has adopted the costume believing it the dress of the ancient Welsh, but whatever the cause had led to the adoption of fantastic dress, the accused attracted universal attention.[3]

As was the usual case, Dr Price, described in the list as a 'surgeon of superior education', objected to twenty names in the jury – the limit he was entitled to object to! When asked whether he was guilty or not, Dr Price replied loudly, 'not guilty'.

Mr Bowen opened the case for the prosecution. Dr Price was charged with having, by negligence in his profession, caused the death of Thomas Price. His widow, Eliza Price, said her young husband had died on 7 January in 1870. Two years previously he was kicked by a horse and for eight months Dr Dyke attended him for his infected knee. The leg had become so swollen that he only worked three months in two years, such was the severity of his pain. In March 1869 he received treatment from a Dr Griffiths, who subsequently died.

Thomas Price was a patient at Bristol Infirmary for three weeks and on his return was attended by Dr Cresswell, Dr Webster and Dr Dyke. Five weeks before he died Dr Price came to his house and promised to cure him and save his life. Dr Price allegedly claimed that if he was to have his 'leg off, it would be just as well he should have his head off'.[4] He had then seen the leg and said that her husband would not live ten days if he had his leg amputated.

Three weeks prior to his death he administered a dose of powder, and Dr Price visited him once before calling him to come to Pontypridd fourteen miles away. On 27 December he visited Dr Price, and again on 2 January. The patient died five days later and on signing his death certificate, Dr Price added that it was undertaken in the 'presence of' followed by his usual list of Welsh royal titles he had incorporated.

In his latter days Thomas Price complained of pain in his hip and head and remained constantly thirsty. He drank water, brandy and beer and began vomiting. When Price's brother, Meredith, travelled to see Dr Price he returned with medicine which relieved the pain and gave some ease to his condition. Dr Price alleged that he had ordered the medicine to be taken immediately, but the patient had waited several hours before taking it and it should have been taken every three hours afterwards which also wasn't complied with.

Meredith Price was also questioned and cross-examined, giving further evidence of the type of operation Dr Price undertook on his brother by inserting the needle in his knee to relieve the tension and release the infection. The court heard that the journey in cold weather from Merthyr to Pontypridd, coupled with the injection of the needle that could have caused the poisoning of the leg, had accelerated the death of Thomas Price.

Prosecutor Mr Bowen accused Dr Price of gross ignorance and negligence for performing the operation when the leg should have been amputated, which was the only way of saving the patient's life.

Dr Robert Cresswell, chief surgeon of the Dowlais ironworks, said he saw Thomas Price in October 1869 and within the month felt the leg should have been amputated as the tumour was in fact on the thigh and there was no other method of saving the patient's life. He explained that the journeys he undertook to Dr Price exhausted the patient and that, coupled with the injection, had resulted in his premature death. The body had since been exhumed for further examination and it was proved that the myeloid tumour had caused his death.

Dr Price cross-examined his fellow surgeon, quoting medical works which proved that his treatment of the tumour – which was a bursa tumour not a myeloid tumour – was in strict accordance with the best surgical experience and practice of the period.

The judge explained that there were a variety of tumours connected with infections of the joints and many varieties of myeloid tumours which could only be properly detected by close examination with a microscope. He went so far as to say that some of the leading surgeons of the day had mistaken the actual diagnosis of the tumours and had believed them to be a cyst rather than cancer.

The judge stated that in his opinion in the early stages of the case there would be no difficulty in ascertaining the form of the disease, but it would have been difficult for Dr Price, at a later stage and not acquainted with the early history of the case, to

> arrive at any reliable knowledge of the precise nature of the disease, it being masked so much by the quantity of fluid and swelling around the knee-joint. The Judge said the evidence showed how difficult it would be for a jury to reach any judgment under such circumstances and it was not possible to blame Dr Price for gross ignorance or negligence.

His Lordship then directed the jury to acquit the defendant and a formal verdict of not guilty was recorded.

Dr Price added that many of his witnesses were present and it was difficult for him to pay all of the expenses, but the judge ruled it was another example of how a coroner should not be able to commit cases to the assizes. If it had been brought before the magistrates, it would not have required a judge and jury court case. On leaving the dock, he was received with cheers from the body of the court, and the large crowd followed him into the street and accompanied him to his hotel, cheering all the way.

In April 1870 Dr Price made quite a spectacle through the streets of Pontypridd. Transport was made available over the Easter weekend for railway workers to enjoy free travel on board their trains. However, much speculation was rife over 'whether a local character of more than local notoriety intended to take part in a procession in a triumphal car, whose steeds were represented by six goats. The excitement this coming event engendered afforded material for any number of social gatherings. The stirring strains of 'March of the Men of Harlech' were heard in the distance, at once causing several groups to cohere in a remarkable manner. Suddenly the band of the 19th, in undress, made its appearance headed by the chairman of the local eisteddfod, and supported on either side by an enthusiastic friend. The band was followed by a small string of competitors in the forthcoming intellectual and artistic contest. But the hero of the procession was nowhere to be seen.

> The disgust on the faces of the assembled expectants was apparent … in the afternoon the band played again … on the tiptoe of wonderment to see the object of so high a compliment, we saw an individual clothed in green, with grey moustache and beard, and wearing a huge skin covering for a head dress. This was Dr Price of Treforest, the 'conquering hero'. This remarkable character – for remarkable he undoubtedly is – in every way seems to have infused among a large number of people an impression so profound as to be regarded with the same amount of infatuated veneration and awe … it puzzles an ordinary intelligent man to account for this, but then we have to deal with exceptional phenomenon.[5]

In Pontypridd County Court on Thursday 11 May 1870, Honour Judge Falconer ordered an action of ejectment against Gwenhiolen Hiarlhes Morganwg and her father, Dr William Price, by the proprietors of the Treforest tinplate works. Some years after the retirement of Francis Crawshay, there was a noticeable change in attitudes towards the Price family when they ordered Dr Price, Hiarlhes and Ann to be removed from Pentrebach House. The property was leased by the tinplate works from none other than Lady Llanover and it appears the Prices had resided there since September 1869, which links with the court hearing that took place over the injunction into Craig Alfa and Bryntail, which caused their departure from both farms. Originally Pentrebach House had been divided into two tenements, in which Mr Richards and Mr Hutchins resided. When Richards left, Miss Price applied for the property and it was alleged the key was obtained unfairly for the one tenement and illegal possession of the second tenement was taken after Hutchins left and the partition wall between both properties was knocked down. In the case Miss Price said 'she supposed she was the daughter of Dr Price', and lived in the house after Mr W. Lewis, one of the partners of the tinplate works, was introduced to her by Mr Hutchins. In September 1869 she was allowed to occupy one half of the coach house, and the stall and a stable was to be retained by the tinplate works, for which she would pay £24 per year.

At the court hearing Hiarlhes claimed that a six-monthly rent payment was agreed to and not on a monthly basis. When the second section of the house became vacant in November 1869, she employed cabinetmaker John Williams of Pontypridd to remove the partition wall. When she was sent a bill for rent of two months, she was unable to pay and a bill of ejectment was made. She offered to pay in gold at the local railway station to one of the partners of the tinplate works, but was refused. After several hours the judge felt that without a contract and no agreement, he had to support the order of ejectment and therefore Hiarlhes had to pay costs, expenses and fees. Within the year Hiarlhes, who had become a bartender, was living with her mother and father at Rickard Street, Treforest, close to the ironically named row of houses 'Druid's Terrace'.

Dr Price remained faithful to the cause, particularly when he portrayed the rights of the Druids in another of his famous court cases when he tried to re-establish the Price family fortune by placing a claim to the Ruperra Estate – lands that included Monmouth and Brecon and were owned by the Barons of Tredegar – which he referred to the High Court. Dr Price claimed it had always belonged to the Druids and that Hugh Jones of Machen, a person who was accredited by Price with the ownership of the estate, had bequeathed it by will to his father when he was a young man. His father, by reason of his mental illness, had allowed it to lapse.

Dr Price went on to explain in his interview in 1888,

My father was a Druid, baptised in Gellywastad House in Machen by Hugh Jones. This was the only place where the Druids baptised their sons and on a gravestone in Machen parish churchyard you will find a very big coat of arms, with an oblong concave dish, which held the water at the ceremony of baptism.

It is funny, I can read the arms of the Druids, and no one who is not an arch Druid can do that. Hugh Jones, I should tell you, was the owner of Ruperra Estate, which always belonged to the Druids. The owner of Ruperra was supposed to possess a power inherent in him to baptise, and could bequeath the property to whom he pleased. Hugh Jones in his will bequeathed Ruperra to my father and appointed John Morgan, a Druid, of Tredegar as executor.

Hugh Jones lent John Morgan £40,000 to take possession of Tredegar. My father was 13 years old at the time when Jones died in 1777 but because of a fall my father had upon his head he was incompetent in keeping the property. I have deposited in the Public Record Office in London an affidavit of 725 folios, in which I trace my right to Ruperra, and have exhibited 120 proofs that I claim the authority that the Primitive Bard had to govern the world.

I proved my claim to it, but judgement was given against me. I intend to bring another action to recover Ruperra. I have traced several important facts on a stone in the hamlet of Llanbedr and I exhibited the stone itself in the proofs I speak of. Llanbedr means Church of Baptism and no one but a Druid has the right to baptise.[6]

On taking up the case, Price attempted to affirm his lineal Druidic descent and argued he was able to read the inscriptions of the Druids, a unique gift which he believed made him an Archdruid. He deposited at the Public Records Office an affidavit but nothing came of it.

Dr Price began to play a more active role in eisteddfodau throughout South Wales during this period. On Whit Monday 1870 a 'grand eisteddfod' was held at Zoar Chapel (which was still under construction) in Morriston, to which hundreds of people travelled for the festivities. Zoar Chapel, 'a large and handsome building' which cost £3,000 when fully completed, welcomed competitors and supporters from far and wide. Chairman of the day was the 'celebrated Dr Price of Pontypridd, who appeared in his usual eccentric costume, and with his daughter Iarlles [sic] Morganwg, attracted a great deal of attention'.[6] With more than 2,500 people present, almost twenty choirs took to the stage to compete and many well-wishers remained outside due to the lack of room.

In September 1870 he was invited to become President of the Aberdare United Eisteddfod at the Temperance Hall. The occasion opened with a rendition of '*Hen Wlad Fy Nhadau*', and Dr Price rose and addressed the gathering in Welsh.

He was dressed in his usual costume of green and held in his hand what he called '*Coelbren y Beirdd*', on which was inscribed 28 letters one of which was invisible, and which represented the number of days in the lunar month. In his opening address Dr Price stated that he had copied those letters 30 years ago in Paris and from a manuscript 2,000 years old. Some linguists asserted that these were Greek characters, but he maintained, in the face of all opinions, that they were purely Welsh characters and he challenged the universe to prove to the contrary, he also alleged that Clun, the Welsh bard, was the real Homer and the original author of the *Iliad* and *Odyssey* notwithstanding the conflicting testimony on the subject. His remarks elicited much applause, and his eccentric appearance created a great deal of interest.[7]

His final appearance at an eisteddfod in 1870 came at the Drill Hall, Merthyr on Monday 26 December. The sixth annual eisteddfod saw Dr Price appear as president, with adjudicator of poetry and prose David Jones (Dafydd Morganwg), music adjudicator D. Emlyn Evans (Dewi

Emlyn), and harpist W. F. Frost (Alaw'r Dyffryn). The hall was blazoned with banners featuring words such as 'Our language, our country, our nation'.[8] What is so significant about this event is that it is the first recorded appearance of Dr Price in his new attire, a one-piece outfit of purple woollen material that was covered in letters from *Coelbren y Beirdd*. The style had been taken from an image in Bernard de Montfaucon's *L'Antiquite Explique et Representee En Figures* and Dr Price had the entire outfit tailor made to suit him. As always, it created huge interest from the packed audience. The Druidic alphabet in green covered the purple material and Dr Price said they were letters he had seen on the stone at the Louvre thirty years previously. He went on to explain in the most preposterous manner that the historians and experts of Paris failed to understand the hieroglyphics on the stone and only he could decipher them. He explained that it was the Welsh people who gave the letter 'L' to the Romans and several letters to the Greeks, making the Welsh language the mother tongue of them all.

Despite his claims and now an equally as eccentric costume, Dr Price's quirky behaviour, passion for Welshness and articulate, inspiring presence, made him a favourite at eisteddfodau, where people must have sat in wonderment at the character before them. In a particularly dark and drab era, Dr Price's colourful flamboyance attracted attention wherever he went, both from the men who ridiculed him, the children who looked on in wonder and the women who still raised an admiring eyebrow at such a charming, athletic visionary.

Within three weeks of his previous eisteddfod appearance he returned to the competitive arena, but as a participant rather than president. At the Brecon Eisteddfod in January 1871 he won the best lecture in Welsh on the subject chosen by the adjudicator, which took five minutes to deliver. For his recitation of 'The War and its Civil Consequences' he was presented with 2s 6d.

Dr Price's ability to court controversy never eluded him. As he had done thirty years previously, his determination to support the working men in their endeavours for fairer wages, better conditions and ample healthcare provision remained foremost in his mind as a surgeon and often outspoken political activist. In June 1871 the coalminers of Aberdare and Rhondda came out on strike for a five per cent increase in wages. It was a bitter twelve-week period in the South Wales coalfield. When a second dispute erupted in 1872 it led to the abolition of the Amalgamated Association of Miners, which had a membership of 42,000 men and was one of the first large-scale unions of its kind.

Dr Price took their cause to his heart, openly condemning the local colliery owners as 'Welsh Pharaohs'. His opening speech addressed to the Aberdare colliers in the town was impressive to say the least, and not overpowered with the ramblings one had come to expect. Filled with passion, it was clear, confident, direct and most of all, inspiring:

> You are the Welsh Pharaohs who think you can suck the life blood of the colliers for ever. You have grown fat and prosperous, you own the big houses, you wear the finest clothes, your children are healthy and happy, yet you do not work. How then have you got these things by idleness? Let me tell you. You have been stealing the balance of the low wages which you have been paying them. Take heed you men whose bodies and souls are bloated by the lifeblood of the poor, take heed before it is too late. Remember that the oppression of the Pharaohs of Egypt did not last for ever, and neither will the blood-sucking Pharaohs of Wales.[9]

In the local press, a writer named 'Belted Will' and 'A Welshman' wrote articles against Dr Price, endeavouring to prejudice the miners against him. For several weeks from the end of October, there were letters in the *Western Mail* concerning Dr Price's outbursts along with comments that contradict his theories on the 'ABC of Strikes'. One writer scoffed at Dr Price for his new form of signature, which states he signs his name not in the presence of Cayroris as before, but now 'in the presence of the sun'. The writer said,

> It seems to me that Mr William Price has read the alphabet of strikes not in the presence of the sun, but by the dim light of a Davy lamp in a collier's stall. Neither a Druid nor a doctor would prefer darkness to light if he were searching for truth and willing to hold it against the world.

After six week silence and one month's formal notice to the Western Mail of the forthcoming demonstration together with many opportunities intervening for consultation with the collective wisdom of the associated and amalgamated miners in meetings assembled in Merthyr Tydfil, I did hope that Price would have fully acquainted himself with the facts and reasoning's contained in the 'ABC of Strikes' and not have conjured up some phantom of his own imagination for the purpose of knocking it down again, or rather perhaps, for the purpose of showing the poor ignorant colliers of the Rhondda and Aberdare Valleys how another Don Quixote can either tilt or tant for them ... Mr Price recommends that the colliers should rise and drown their masters, the capitalists, like the children of Israel drowned the Pharaohs of old in the Red Sea. Now I was not aware before that Pharaohs were drowned by the children of Israel ... nowhere are they commanded to drown the Pharaohs in the Red Sea in the way that this mistaken man advised the colliers to drown their masters; and if William Price would study the ABC of scripture a little more carefully, 'in the present of the true sun', he might escape the fearful doom of those who add unto, or wilfully pervert its sacred truths...[10]

The writer goes on to suggest Dr Price should throw himself in the Severn Sea off Cardiff Pier, calling him a 'foolish doctor'. He goes on to say that if the capitalists would also drown as he wished, there would be no more employment in Wales.

Belted Will continued, 'Until now I always thought that Dr Price of Pontypridd was, at the very least, a man of sense, if not a wise man, but I am afraid I must now alter my opinion, that is if that letter was truly meant for your paper and not for *Punch*. He says nothing in a great deal of space.'

Price retaliated with the following announcement:

To the Sane and Peaceful Colliers of the Aberdare and Rhondda Valleys, lately on Strike against their Pharaohs:

Strange that such Difference should be
Tween wheedle you and wheedle me!
And Stranger still that 'Belted Will'
With Owen Morgan's hand and Quill!
Should analyse his 'BC' Bubble!
To save the Doctor's Ink and Trouble!
Save me? No! You twaddling donkey!
Balamm's Ass is Not so empty!

By William Price – In the Presence of the Sun at Ponty y Priyth, November 1 1871.

The reference to Owen Morgan (1836–1921) is of importance here because this character also figured prominently in Dr William Price's life during its last few decades. Occasionally a nemesis to Price and yet at other times a supporter, Owen Morgan ridiculed him mercilessly in the press and continued to do so long after he had died. A 'disciple' of the aged Myfyr Morganwg, Owen Morgan, who adopted the bardic name of Morien, was the son of Thomas and Margaret Owen of Dinas, Rhondda. A well-known journalist, Morien worked chiefly for the *Western Mail* newspaper from 1870 until 1899; he also came under the spell of Iolo Morganwg and the Neo-Druidism of Pontypridd, electing himself the successor to Myfyr as Archdruid of Wales on his master's death. It was a further six years before he properly made a name for himself as the journalist who kept readers on the edges of their seats during the coverage of the Tynewydd Colliery Disaster in Porth in 1877, where miners remained trapped underground.

In the latter weeks of 1871 Dr Price published the philosophy of Druidism that he had spent so long orating to every audience he had the pleasure of addressing. Thirty years after his celebrated trip to Paris he published his own manifesto, his hopes, dreams and aspirations for a new order of Druidic religion. The result was *Gwyllllis yn Nayd*, the fruit of an overactive imagination published in London on '*Dudd Alben Arrththann* 1871'. After the passing of a decade since his outrageous letters and claims of 1861, with unfathomable lettering, constant underlining, the overuse of capital letters and the frantic inclusion of unknown sentence constructions, mixed words and incomprehensible spelling, *Gwyllllis yn Nayd* seriously called into question the mental ambiguity of Dr Price. By this time his mind was overwhelmed with his obsession for Druidism and through this publication he hoped to reassert his leadership of the cult.

It is difficult to examine the work in detail as the content remains so very elusive, particularly as Dr Price warned those who could understand it that they were forbidden to translate its contents. When it is translated, the content is equally as unfathomable, although we can see traces of his philosophy through the mystical haze of the words. The education and background of Price can be recognised, although it is fragmented and inconsequential. Occasionally poetic in its delivery, it displays Price's own eloquence for which he was known in the public arena, both as a political activist and litigant. Nevertheless, this is a unique document as it provides the basis for Dr Price's delusions as evidence of his own fantastical theories for the future.

Gwyllllis yn Nayd was his philosophy of Druidism. The title is a corruption of '*Ewyllys Fy Nhad*' (The Will of My Father) and on the cover is a version of the Lord's Prayer in curious semi-phonetic Welsh, with quadrupled consonants.

Yn Tayd wut Ti yn y Nevvoyd! Sancttudd vyddddo dy Ennw Di dyet dy Dyrrnnas! Byddddet dy Wyllllis Di arr ydd Ddauarr meggis ym ma I yn y Nevvoydd! Dyrro innii eddddu yn Barra Bynnydddiol A madddda yn Dyled Diou vel ym maddddduqnni yn Dylewurr! Na arrwinni u Brovvidigayth yuththurr ynggwarred ni rayg yd Drwgg! Cannis dy ynddddot Ti uw yd Dyrrnnas yg gallllu a yryggogonniant yn oys oyssoydd A ym Menn! A ym Menn! A ym Menn!

He believed this was the original Welsh language spoken 2,600 years before, although why he should open with the Lord's Prayer when clearly he had denounced Christianity is beyond understanding. Very disjointed and fragmentary, he claimed it should not be translated and only he, as the son of the primitive bard, had the knowledge, vision and ability to do so. Beneath the prayer is embossed a red goat, surrounded by a green serpent with its tail in its mouth and itself encircled with the letters IUYUAIUYUEUOYUS. This is the crest he used on his private notepaper, and the goat was also represented on his brass buttons. He had it struck in bronze to commemorate the cremation of his son some years later.

This was his greatest fantasy. The text is rambling and confused, but the direction of his concern is clear. He emphasises he is addressing the Welsh people in correct Welsh – '*Annwyl Gymmru a Chymmressi*!' – in order to reveal the 'Song of the Wan of the Lettered Lore of the Welsh', which he has discovered after 2,000 years. 'The Will of His Father', he said, 'has been kept secret during the time of the foreign kings for their own advantage to mis-rule the nations of the earth. Remember that the living god himself is born a Welshman in his natural memory.'

The second half of the document contains Price's greatest fantasy – an eisteddfod of a million Welsh men and women, on the slopes of Snowdon, with himself at the centre repeating questions intended to show the Welsh origin of all things.

Within its pages there are also drawings of the original stone he claims to have seen at the Louvre so many years earlier. Overall, its contents are written in the most bizarre form of Welsh, with one translated section reading:

> Dear Welshmen and Welshwomen.
> I am the lettered bard
> With my wand in my hand
> Which breaks the song of the thrush
> And the lark on the dawn
> East South
> West North
> The cold moon bread and cheese.

I am addressing you in writing, in the Welsh of The Royal State in the way I heard my mother and my father speaking Welsh in my childhood, in order to inform the ear of every Welshman and Welshwoman that there is the way the Chief Bard of Welsh Learning wrote 'The Song of the Wand and Lettered Lore of the Welsh' which after two thousand and six hundred years, is according to what you see on my clothes, copied letter by letter, with the lion of England behind me, from the second part of '*L'Antiquite Repliquee*' which was printed in Paris in 1722 by Bernard Montfaucon.

I have filled in the three mistakes which I see on the neck of the Chief Bard of Learning with the letters 'Z V V' and written out every letter of the song correctly in the letters which are taught in Welsh schools at present on the following pages in order to guide you so that you may understand, and read and sing the 'Song of the Wand of the Chief Bard of the Lore of the Welsh' literally according to the directions and the spelling of the song in the egg which I saw on the skin of man who loved himself, whom you have heard so much about.

Yes, dear Welshman and Welshwomen, the skin of the man who loved himself. Do you know who he is? Does one of you answer? No, no one, I shall tell you then. The skin of my father, and your father, dear Welshman, is the skin of the man who loved himself eternally in the memory of the Welsh people which you see on my skin, with your copy of the will of my father on it. For he, from his own brain, literally sends the sun through the moon on to the seas and on to the earth from his right hand in a cola egg as the eternal Prince, over the sons o H E Th in the name of God and all goodness in the Welsh of the Royal State, the Welsh of Monmouth and Glamorgan in the year 1871 according to belief. His will was revealed from his cold egg. His portrait has been kept in secret during the time of the foreign kings for their own advantage to mis-rule the nations of the earth against their will with want to hunt the heir to the will of my father in the name of the man who owns the all eighty and all wealthy sword which was taken from the sons of H E Th through eternal war in the hearts of the foreign speaking nations, until they return their swords to his hand whose right it is to rule peacefully on the throne of the sun over the earth for ever for the sake of the seven natural senses of the Welsh on the day of their birth from the cold egg of his portrait.

Remember that the living God himself is born a Welshman in his natural memory, in the children of all nations on the day of their birth from the womb, with his seven senses in his possession for ever.

He remembers!

He hears!

He speaks!

He tastes!

He feels!

He sees!

The breath of the living God himself went from his nostrils to the womb eternally without the learning of the God of the Father of Baptism, everybody has another name for the God of the Father of Baptism – and the books in foreign language of the God of the Father of Baptism teaches the priests and lawyers and doctors and their people to lose their memory, their hearing, and their natural speech from the two-handed cradle of the living and himself, who gives his memory, his speech and his natural memory to every little one from generation to generation in order to loosen the hold of the intoxication of the foreign language books of the priests, the lawyers and the doctors and the people of the God of the Father of Baptism in order to drive the heir of the Chief Bard of Welsh learning to the place where he went to the new moon from his cold egg, the form of the living God himself.

In the way in which you hear, they have conquered the memory the hearing and the Welsh speech of the living God himself by bringing him up from is birth quite dumb and deaf in the cradle of the learning of the foreign language ... He has a three gold learning on his shoulders to live in poverty, sweating for half enough, very often, of bread and cheese, with his own blood from the edge of the knife, under the edge of the sword, to kill and burn and rob, and mortgage the property of the foreign nations who have lost the day by fighting against each other and breaking their own commandments by fighting to the end for kings in order to govern nations against their will from the cold egg of the form of the living God himself ...

... there is not one of the scholars learned in the books in foreign language of the God of the Father of Baptism who remembers or speaks the Welsh of the living God himself from the womb, as the lion speaks Welsh from his mother's womb! The Welsh, and the wild and tame creatures, the wild birds are those who speak the language of the living God himself, everywhere in the world from his womb, and that language is Welsh!

... When the time comes when the English will want to understand the reading of the will of my father in Welsh, they will come, without any persuasion on my part, to love Welsh women, so that they may be the mothers of their children, to bring them up as Welshmen, to remember hearing the living God himself speaking Welsh from his mother's womb, so that they may speak Welsh to their father, face to face as they did in the early ages ... in the meantime give a rope to the four senses of the English. Let them go mad and be hanged! There is no need to persuade the deaf and dumb to understand that they are selling their lives from day to day and from generation to generation to the God of the Father of Baptism for the cold egg of the portrait of the living God himself, for we Welsh belong to Him and he to us!

O Welshmen,
One face
I shall see
On Snowdon
In an eisteddfod
One day,
When they will learn
To read the secret will
Of Mab Duw ...

Imagine that you are ten circles of Welshmen and Welshwomen, with a hundred thousand Welshmen and Welshwomen in each circle, having come together in an eisteddfod on the top of Snowdon on the morning of Alban Efin in the year 1873 before the rising of the sun, with me in the middle of you on the top of Snowdon, standing with my face towards the east, and asking you 'What do you, the Welsh people, call yonder light which you see shooting through the clouds on the horizon?' You answer, 'The dawn!'

I now ask you, 'Whose dawn is it?' You answer, 'It is His dawn.'

I ask, 'Who is he?' The answer, 'He is the sun!'

... pure Welsh is every letter in the wills of the Duw and Bedydd in the Old Testament and the New Testament. Pure Welsh is every letter in the *Oddissey* and the *Illiad*, the wills of the chief bards of the learning of Wales. Pure Welsh is the copy of the will of chief bard of the learning of Wales from his cold egg which you see on my clothing, and his wand in my left hand and in the will of the father of us Welsh, as it has been spelt in the Welsh of the Royal Province by him more than two thousand and six hundred years ago, and here it is, and a copy of his form singing it ...

For Dr Price it was his divine scripture.

Although written in a type of Welsh that even the Welsh speakers themselves could not understand, Price further warns those who read it that they are forbidden to translate it. When it is translated the content is just as elusive! Like the ramblings of a disintegrating schizophrenic, you can recognise the education and cultural background of Price, even if it has become fragmented and inconsequential. However, the Will of My Father is a unique document, and Price used it subsequently as a substantiation for his delusions because he felt the need to provide some explanation for his extraordinary claims of inheritance. The fact he felt the necessity to produce this proof at all is evidence of his uncertainty about his fantasy.[11]

Within *Gwyllllis yn Nayd* is the image of what he considers to be the primitive bard wearing an outfit that is covered in hieroglyphics and lettering and from which Dr Price created his elaborate purple-and-green suit, which he wore frequently in an almost ceremonial vein, during his latter years.

Dr Price claimed this was the image he saw on the Greek stone at the Louvre, which has been documented in several different historic works. Although the location of the original large stone is uncertain, there are certainly references to smaller gem and cameo pieces, possibly matching the same description.

The image is illustrated in the works of the French Benedictine monk, Bernard de Montfaucon (1655–1741), regarded as one of the founders of modern archaeology. In Montfaucon's work it is described as an image of a man with a transcription of Greek letters that had been translated to Hebrew, and the original stone may have been recovered at an archaeological site in Naples. Montfaucon attempted to translate the short lettering on the figure and either side of it, reducing the Greek letters to Hebrew as Dr Price had done from Greek to Welsh. Montfaucon claims some of the words translate to 'The Lord, Armies, Majesty, Hidden In the Light of the Fire, Possession of Divinity, The Strength of Light'.

The stone is also illustrated in a catalogue of the collection of cameos belonging to antiquarian De Clercq, who put the items on show at Louvre. If this is the case, then Dr Price may well have seen the cameo at the museum also. Dr Price was enamoured of Montfaucon, listing copies of his books in his own will and sharing in his deep interest in Greek history – Montfaucon himself laid the foundation of the study of Greek manuscripts and in 1724 was largely responsible for bringing the Bayeux Tapestry to the attention of the public. Between 1719 and 1724 he published fifteen volumes of *L'Antiquite Expliquee et Representee En Figures* ('Antiquity Explained And Represented in Diagrams') which contained copperplate folio engravings of classical antiquities. In the second volume it features the very same engraving, from a stone contained in the collection by the family of Jean-Jacques Chifflett (1588–1660), a French physician, antiquarian and archaeologist, many of whose manuscripts have been studied.

This was his

doctrines of the ancient Druids, which is even more difficult to read than those by Myfyr or Morien. It was written in his own 'authentic' ancient Welsh, and its mode of expression, even in translation, is especially convoluted ... the father in this case seems to be a deity, the fount of the whole cosmos, who was born from an egg laid by a serpent. The notion of the universe as hatched from a cosmic egg appears in the ancient Greek Orphic hymns, which Price combined with the pagan Norse tradition of a serpent that twines about the earth. This father deity ... directs the motions o the sun, which is the living god of the apparent world. Some sense of Price's style can be gained from a passage on the nature of the ultimate divinity:

For he, from his own brain, literally sends the sun through the moon onto the seas and onto the earth from his right hand in a cold egg as the Eternal Prince, over the sons of H H Th ... the Welsh of the Royal State, the Welsh of Monmouth and Glamorgan in the year 1871 according to his belief. His will was revealed from his cold egg.

Even more than Morien's religious writings, those of Price read more like a prophet speaking in trance ... much more lucid were the political and nationalist sections of this testament, in which Price called on the Welsh to reject the European, and Christian culture that repressed them and return to their native roots. The book sank without trace, nobody even seems to have thought it worth burning.[12]

In 1871 the issue of the Bryntail colliery and its tram road, running through Dr Price's leased property, again raised its head. There was a hearing at the Court of Chancery for an appeal from Vice Chancellor James in which Dr Price, the defendant, had granted the lease of a colliery on his land, and reserved rent and royalties and a covenant on land where a tramway was to be built to the Glamorganshire Canal, presumably from Craig Alva. The plaintiffs, Davies and Acraman, alleged that Price had broken an agreement to allow a right-of-way over the land connecting a colliery to the canal so they could transport the coal to Cardiff. As Dr Price had failed in his promise it had damaged and ruined the industrialists, who had sunk a shaft and invested money into it.

The report read,

Such a tramway, if not absolutely essential, was at any rate of most material importance to the working of the collieries. It afterwards turned out that Dr Price, from no fault of his own was unable to procure the land in question. The lessees, who had taken possession and incurred considerable expense in preparing to commence working thereupon declined to pay rent, for which Dr Price then brought an action at law. The present suit was then instituted by the present lessees to restrain such action and the case made by their bill was that the undertaking by Dr Price to procure land for the construction of the tramway and communication between the colliery and the Glamorganshire Canal was a condition precedent and that as such land had not been procured the material consideration for the lease had failed.

Dr Price, on the other hand, contended that the stipulation to provide land was not the whole or a material part of the consideration, but an independent and subordinate stipulation only, for the breach of which an action at law for damages would be an adequate remedy. The Vice Chancellor however, decided in favour of the plaintiffs and granted an injunction. Dr Price appealed from this decision ... The Lord Chancellor being of opinion that the acquisition of the land on which to provide means of success to the canal was indispensable to the profitable working of the collieries and was also a condition precedent to the agreement to take the lease, dismissed the appeal.[9]

The next two years witnessed further tragedy for Dr Price, with the loss of the mother of his only surviving child and the death of his brother and a sister. Charles Price, the former cashier to Francis Crawshay, passed away at his home of Caeridwen near Radyr on Tuesday 28 March 1871, aged eighty. His funeral card simply read, 'Of whom it may be truly said that "He Was What He Pretended To Be".' Their sister, Elizabeth died at 9.20 a.m. on 25 October 1872 at Pentwyn, Rudry, a farm of 50 acres she had shared with her servant, Daniel Walters. She was buried four days later at Bedwas. Dr Price later named his fourth daughter in memory of her. None of the Price siblings married, with the exception of one sister, and only Dr Price is known to have had children.

The third tragedy came on 25 March 1873 when Ann Morgan died, aged just fifty-six, at their home in Rickard Street, Pontypridd. Her certificate, which does not give a cause of death, lists her simply as 'housekeeper' and names a Mary Evans as being with her at the time of her death. Dr Price did not remain faithful to her and her alone during their thirty-year relationship, and to this day claimants are abound who believe their ancestors who were neighbours, maid servants or patients, succumbed to his advances and bore him children 'the other side of the blanket', which has yet to be proved. Having said that, the relationship, in whatever form it took, was long-lasting and they both shared a daughter, Hiarlhes.

In different periods of his life Dr Price's behaviour became all the more bizarre following a tragedy, difficult periods of upset or failure. Following the Chartist Rising and its demise he began prophesying about his religious vision at the Louvre and the power that would be inherited by his first-born son. With the failure of the Round Houses project and the financial ruin that faced him, he began writing rambling letters. Again in the 1870s with the loss of his home and death of his brother, he published the equally incredulous *Gwyllllis yn Nayd*. A matter of fourteen years later, the death of his long-awaited son, would result in him undertaking his most extreme and unforgiving act of all. It almost appears that with each failure he tried to reinvent his mastery over Neo-Druidism, re-establishing himself as a leader of society, a unique, powerful figure in whom all the mysteries of the earth were protected. Sometimes the bewildering fantasies became more extreme than at others, but this almost egotistical thought process was exacerbated in periods of difficulty in his life and the powerful cult of Neo-Druidism tightened its grip on his mind.

It was during this period, following the personal loss both of his lover, brother, sister and his home and employment at Treforest, that he embarked on a new period in his life, one that brought him the international status that he is accorded to this day. It is uncertain when he left Treforest. The census of 1881 tells us that by this point Hiarlhes was residing in a farm in Llanishen, Cardiff with several lodgers and her young lover named Thomas Williams. Evidence shows as early as 1873 she lodged in a property in Connaught Road, Cardiff. As for Dr William Price, his future lay in the ancient hilltop town of Llantrisant, five miles away from Treforest. It is uncertain when or why he chose Llantrisant as his new dwelling place. Unlike the industrial towns in which he had lived for the majority of his life, Llantrisant was steeped in ancient history. Its origins as an early Celtic settlement, where Price presumed – as Iolo had done – the early Druids had practised their faith, was 'proven' in his mind when in 1873 the refurbishment of the parish church of the saints Illtyd, Gwynno and Dyfodwg revealed a magnificent discovery. The circled Celtic cross, dating from around the seventh century AD, proved this town had been a sophisticated Celtic community before the days of the Normans and the coming of Christianity. For Dr Price, there was something almost 'pure' in Llantrisant's pagan birth, engulfed in its lush green mountains and common lands, far from the industrial towns that belched their smoke and flames. In his mind, this had been the settlement of his Druidic forefathers almost 2,000 years earlier and he intended to live out his final years among this 'Celtic kingdom'.

Commanding an outstanding setting on the crest of a hill, Llantrisant's splendour lay in its enchanting past. Dr William Price had probably read the first historic account of the town, published by Sem Phillips in 1866, which celebrated the glory of what was once a magnificent hilltop fortress, like a dominant city from biblical times, crowned by its medieval castle and a fine parish church, surrounded by a cluster of homes that cling precariously to the steep slopes, scattered throughout the town's charming, unplanned cobbled streets. Llantrisant was one of the most strategically important Norman strongholds in South Wales and, as such, witnessed a turbulent past, boasting a history of fierce battles, ancient customs, and notorious characters.

Chiefly remarkable for its vantage point, it was easy for Dr Price to accept that a Celtic community existed here, possibly as far back as the Roman invasion, given the legion's interest in neighbouring lands. The first settlement, of largely timber dwellings within a wooden fort-like enclosure, was probably a well-organised post-Roman society, eventually overthrown by the conquering Norman barons centuries later.

With the advent of Christianity, this extensive ecclesiastical centre, dedicated by missionaries of Llantwit Major to saints Illtyd, Gwynno and Dyfodwg, gave the town its name of Church of the Three Saints. A Romanesque-style church was probably built as early as 1096 by the first Norman lords who conquered the town, and it was later rebuilt sometime around 1246, when the neighbouring castle was also fortified. It was these Norman lords who recognised the advantages of developing Llantrisant as a military base, owing to its elevation between the conquered vale and the barren mountain terrain of the north. In this hill country, or *blaenau*, the Celtic or Welsh warriors gathered periodically to raid settlements of the invading Norman armies.

Gwrgan ab Ithel, or Einon ab Collwyn, both Welsh Lords of Glamorgan, may have built the first wooden fort well before the Norman invasion. Quite possibly, the first Norman castle was completed on this same site, sometime between 1096 and 1100, its ring-work walls offering protection for a community of smallholdings accompanied by the parish church. It was within such a settlement that those Norman masters faced fierce opposition from the Celtic tribesmen and were probably expelled from Llantrisant in one of many battles before 1127. Following their re-emergence, a stone-built defence of several towers, two wards and a timber ring-work with ditches was built by Gilbert de Clare in 1246, making it second only to Cardiff in military importance. Gilbert 'The Red' inherited it by 1262, while he built neighbouring Caerphilly.

For the next two centuries the town witnessed a series of bloodthirsty rebellions. The castle, however, remained active until at least a decade later, when it was used as an overnight prison for King Edward II, captured in November 1326, and later subjected to a horrifying execution at Berkeley Castle.

One of the most notable episodes in Llantrisant's history took place in 1346, with the presentation of its first known charter. Tales of courageous longbow-men from the town, fighting at the Battle of Crecy under Lord of Glamorgan Hugh le Despenser, had resulted in academics believing this was the reason behind those brave soldiers being rewarded with the issue of such a significant document. Sadly, the legend isn't true, because the charter was actually presented five months earlier, on 4 March 1346. However, it is always comforting to imagine those gallant veterans of Crecy may have been the first to be bestowed with the freedom of the new Ancient Borough of Llantrisant on their return from victory. It would also have been of unique interest to Dr Price that, as his own ancestors in Caerphilly had been involved with the Despenser family centuries before, he too would now reside once more in one of their former strongholds.

The charter was reissued in 1424 and gave those burgesses, or freemen, absolute possession of the land, the equivalent of the freehold tenure we have today, and made it clear that non-burgesses could not trade in the town without paying for the privilege. Therefore, a free borough, or corporation town, was a community of freemen and its main purpose was to earn a corporate living. In an effort to help it to succeed in a competitive world, its burgesses gathered a range of privileges, giving them a measure of self-government, their own courts of law, and control on markets and fairs. The portreeve exercised power over the administration, while the corporation business was conducted by the Court Leet. The boundary of the ancient borough was also sanctified by the custom of a religious ceremony, which we now know as the Beating the Bounds.

Four hundred years later and Llantrisant held a somewhat dubious reputation as the haven of paupers, thieves and prostitutes, and was a centre of drunkenness and rowdiness, while outbreaks of epidemics were also widespread. Llantrisant, the town 'where pigs roam streets without rings in their snouts', was the hub of all factions of society, from the ruling gentry and corrupt vicars to quarrelsome families and prostitutes, who witnessed incidents of brutality and even murder, with frequent nightly brawls owing to the mass of public houses. The historic church vestry meeting on 5 December 1783 was called to 'consult in regard of establishing a workhouse for the poor'. Until then, the aged, feeble and weak-minded were either cared for by a neighbour for a small fee or simply left unassisted in insanitary cottages. In 1784, it was unanimously resolved to open the workhouse, the first in Glamorgan, in a series of adapted cottages along Swan Street and in the Black Cock Inn on Yr Allt, with the Union Workhouse opening a century later close to the Bull Ring.

By the eighteenth century it witnessed a time of splendid refurbishment of the church and the appearance of many landmark houses, shops and inns. Fairs and markets played a central role in its resurrection and the town's reputation as a centre for trade flourished. Four fairs were held annually in the open square, adjoining the Town Hall and the Market House. The old town scales and weights were kept at the Angel Inn, or the Pwysty, where tolls were collected by the constable of the castle and imposed on goods entering the town for sale. However, this certain degree of affluence as a hub of commercial activity was relatively short-lived and, gradually, its authority declined in favour of neighbouring Pontypridd.

Sadly, when Dr Price arrived in Llantrisant the glory of the town had faded. One historian noted it was a 'mean little town', others condemned it as a filthy community of dilapidated buildings where people walked up their knees in 'dung'. Although Llantrisant Railway Station was opened in 1861 it was in thriving Pontyclun, three miles away. Ironically, Llantrisant's positioning, once its greatest attraction, was now something of hindrance and, although Lord Bute gave freedom for the market tolls, it was not enough to save the town's commercial wealth as more and more the markets and fairs dwindled in favour of the more accessible and prosperous Pontypridd. Although Llantrisant's Union Workhouse was in full operation, the town was still overrun with vagabonds and thieves. Prostitution in the twenty-seven pubs that existed in the oval circle of the hilltop was rife. One of Price's closest friends was Roderick Lewis, landlord of the Wheatsheaf Hotel, and Dr Price frequented many others, some claiming he even owned the Mount Pleasant on Commercial Street at one point. In fact, at an auction in 1886 for the public house, the occupant was a Mr Bound. When the property, garden, stable, coach house and dwelling house adjoining it were sold, it belonged to none other than Dr Price.

In 1853 Edwin F. Roberts wrote of his experiences of visiting the town, which gives us a clearer indication of the community in which Dr Price settled:

> ... the gray castle and old church towers, gleaming white houses, with bold dark-green arable land ... the road led along the base of he hill, and turned abruptly up a very steep incline through the town which is little more than a street. Passing through a turnpike gate leading from the Cardiff road, we began to climb the alarming height ... the same idea of pictorial beauty does not follow you in entering the main street of the little town, for age, dilapidation an the apparent stand-still of the place – its remoteness from railways, mining localities and so on having left in status quo and even Newbridge [Pontypridd] beats it all to pieces in architectural development. Though it is in a marquisate it has no suggestiveness of princely possession. It has a poor, profitless and somewhat untidy aspect. The houses are in ill repair and some have evidently laid their heads and backs together on the principle of 'mutual support' while the old tower, that looked really romantic from afar, on nearer inspection has a mouldy and cankered aspect. I remark on the apparent untidiness of the women's style of dressing. The clothing in itself is good, warm and substantial but they have an appearance of personal neglect so that a young woman has no more shape than a matron of fifty. The pig parades the streets with an air of indolent enjoyment and an aristocratical contempt for the laborious exertions his more active barn door companions usually exhibit. Little active life there appear in Llantrisant, though there was promise for the future, that some metalliferous veins were being opened and possibly the contiguity of a railway or branch of mining uses may infuse a little fresh blood into the town which it sadly wants ... although I have seen few places more striking.[13]

The Llantrisant that Dr Price resided in from September 1873 onwards offered land and property at significantly reduced prices and the surgeon, despite previous financial worries, was still a shrewd entrepreneur, and invested what he had, mortgaging them to further add to his portfolio, until he established himself a good estate in the old town. His bank account of 1872 shows that he had an impressive £750 invested. Of those lands, the most prominent was that of East Caerlan, the easternmost mountain of the three that the old town straddles, of which he mortgaged 9 acres with John Thomas, a chemist of Cowbridge, in 1884 for £100. It was here that his infamous actions led to national notoriety. In 1881, the National Provincial Bank of Cowbridge estimated that his entire estate was valued at £10,000.

Dr Price's portfolio of property in the Llantrisant area was impressive and extensive. In September 1873, at auction, he bought the Greyhound Inn on Greyhound Lane. The proprietor, David Evans, emigrated to the United States, and Price purchased the large building for £1,885. The inn, which later became Dragon Temperance Hotel, was directly behind his new home, Tŷ'r Clettwr, a peculiarly shaped house on the sharp bend of lower High Street.

To the rear of the Greyhound Inn was a group of four small cottages, all of which Dr Price owned. He went on to purchase further properties along Heol y Sarn, including the empty house he used as a stable block where the angry mob attacked him and his servant in 1884.

Dr Price remained in Llantrisant for more than two decades and continued to practice as a surgeon, rebuilding his career and finding even more patients to administer to. The community were concerned about their new neighbour as his reputation went before him, and despite his advancing years Dr Price did little to calm his adventurous behaviour and mischievous ways. Few could ignore his handsome presence, dominant character, romantic costume and theories that attracted the eye of the ladies. They were deliciously alarmed by him and his views on marriage and the women of the parish were somewhat in awe of this figure in their midst.

Dr William Price was no stranger to Llantrisant, having attended to patients in the vicinity of the old town for many years. In fact, as far back as 1839 a John Davies of Cefn Mabley Farm in Llantrisant had subscribed for the failed Y Maen Chwyf venture in Pontypridd. There was even rumour that Dr Price had fathered another daughter with a patient in 1870 in the David's Town area of old Llantrisant, close to the Castle Inn public house.

Price revelled in his new home town, although he didn't appear to become involved in many of the traditions associated with Llantrisant, such as the Beating the Bounds ceremony that was held every seven years by the ancient order of the freemen. Similarly, knowing Price's total disregard for authority he would hardly have immersed himself in the local celebrations when a local farmer's son, David Evans, became Lord Mayor of London and paraded through the streets of the old town in 1892, lined with well-wishers. Price ridiculed the chapel-goers, dismissed the church folk too, but at least enjoyed the many facilities at the local public houses – those who served him cider, or better still champagne.

The precise date on which he left Treforest to reside permanently in Llantrisant is uncertain, and as late as 1876 mention is made of him living between two residences in Pontypridd and the old medieval town of his adoption. Letters written in August 1872 to his sister Ann show that he was still residing in Pontypridd, although in the same year mention in the press is made of 'six young urchins' who entered his boarded up surgery in Craig Alfa and threw stones at the skeleton in his room. The boys were 'severely admonished' and discharged for their unruly behaviour and it proves Dr Price had closed the surgery completely by this point. The surgery was eventually demolished, along with a row of nearby cottages in 1964. His entry in the Medical Directory of 1873 names him as still residing in 'Craig Alva' and following his medical credentials is followed by further bizarre text stating,

> Discoverer of *Gavval Lenn berren Myrrdhdhin Wyllt Tyurn wialenn Oyurr Aneurin Gwawtrudh Awennudh Privv Varrydh Nuadh y Brynn Gwunn Gwialenn Lann ab Lann ab Beyl ap Peyl Sarrph ynus Pruttann A ych Choyul Brenn Privv Varrydh Dusg Cymmru.*

Despite his decision to reside far away from Treforest and Pontypridd, his ties were not cut with the cultural events taking place there and he continued to visit his long-standing patients in the locality. The interest in Neo-Druidism in the area still inspired his creativity and he made frequent appearances at the quarterly services on Y Maen Chwyf. In February 1873 funds were raised to assist the striking miners of the location, and a Distribution Committee was appointed to create a Relief Kitchen through the *Western Mail* newspaper. On advertising their intention, Dr Price was one of the many to subscribe immediately by donating £10 towards the cause, which raised an astonishing £650 in the first two weeks of its existence.

Although his appearances in court, as a plaintiff or defendant, had lessened during these years, he was still called as a witness in an action for the unskilful treatment by a surgeon in Neath, in March 1873. Thomas Jenkins, a surveyor of Neath, wanted compensation from local surgeons Thomas and Ryding due to their 'unskillful and neglectful treatment'. In the course of the case Dr Price was called to give evidence as he had been consulted by the witness, who had damaged his knee. He accompanied Dr Price to London for a consultation with a surgeon at St Thomas's Hospital. 'Dr Price of Pontypridd, who appeared in his peculiar costume – a curiously fashioned coat of bright green, with splendid red facings – was next examined. He said he had been in practice for 52 years and had had great experiences in dislocations ... he considered the mode of treatment which the witness had described as having been used by the defendants was improper ...'[14]

At the end of November 1873, he was back in the dock, this time in a case tried before Mr Justice Brett at Swansea. Dr Price was the plaintiff in this case and he is said to prefer some claim to the hereditary sovereignty of the Principality. His appearance was most remarkable, as he wore his shirt outside his vest, without any necktie; had on greet trousers, fantastically cut, and when out of the witness box enveloped himself in a long bright green cloak lined with read and clasped at the throat and vandyked at the edges. His long white hair tipped with yellow, his carefully trimmed beard and moustache, added to the generally Garibaldian appearance and his movements were watched with the greatest curiosity.[15]

The case was brought against Price by a Mr Jones, who resided in London and had offered lodgings to a young medical student named Thomas Davies. The young man had been a student to Dr Price and his mentor had promised to pay his board and lodging during his study at St Thomas's Hospital in London prior to his preliminary examinations. Dr Price was to pay £45 for six months, of which £20 was to be paid in advance, and after eight weeks Mr Jones would not allow Thomas Davies back in the house. On doing this Dr Price said he had also lost the £20 he paid to St Thomas's Hospital on entering as a student apothecary. Mr Montague Chambers QC, on behalf of Dr Price, alleged that Jones and his wife had treated the young student badly and did not feed him properly and 'they did not like him because he was a vegetarian' like his mentor. The jury returned a verdict for Dr Price and he received damages of £10.

On Wednesday 4 February 1874, Mr Warren's Welsh Model Theatre came to Pontypridd to give a performance of Shakespeare's *Othello* in the Market Place Theatre. The entire performance was under the patronage and presence of none other than Dr Price.

This place of amusement still continues to be a favourite resort to the Pontypriddians and no efforts are spared by the proprietor, Mr Warren, to merit the patronage that has been so liberally extended to him. For a people like the Welsh whose lively fancy is well known to the world, the dramatic representations cannot fail to be very attractive. Mr Warren has, during his sojourn in the town, placed on the stage some of the best known pieces including the immortal Shakespeare's master works. As leading actors the proprietor has lately engaged Mr and Mrs Maitland of the Cardiff Theatre and both have proved very attractive indeed and have given satisfaction. Tonight the performance will be under the immediate patronage of Dr William Price, when *Othello – or The Moor of Venice* will be performed.[14]

The magnificent cloth advertisement for the production boldly states, 'On this occasion, the curtain will rise on Shakespeare's Tragedy, in Five Acts' and lists the actors as Charles Maitland in the title role, with Mr N.

Hartley as the 'green eyed' Iago. Following the performance there was a song by Mrs Hartley and a dance by Pollie Warren, which concluded with a 'Laughable Farce'. Admission for the event was 2*s* for a reserved seat and 6*d* for the pit with 3*d* in the gallery and 'good fires kept in all parts of the theatre'.

In October 1874 the eighth annual Alban Elfed Eisteddfod was held in the Temperance Hall in Aberdare, and, although the weather was poor, a large group of people attended the selection of competitions. At noon Dr Price, 'attired in his well known Druidical costume',[16] was elected to the chair and gave an opening address, before the band of the 14th Glamorgan Volunteers played an overture and the competition for prizes began.

In April 1875 Dr Price's servant, John Davies, was charged with assaulting George Howell, clerk of the Taff Vale Railway line. Davies was transporting hay at Llantrisant for the surgeon when Howell said he was owed 5*s* for the work. Davies denied any knowledge of payment and a scuffle occurred between them that resulted in the judge fining Davies one shilling plus costs.

During the same year, a testimonial fund was established in Newbridge to honour Myfyr Morganwg. A list of subscriptions was received in May to be presented to the bard and antiquarian in celebration of his seventy-fifth birthday. The testimonial was established by a committee of men who nominated Daniel Owen of Cowbridge and Jaber Evans of Pontypridd as treasurers, with Owen Morgan (Morien) as secretary. The subscription list included some rather impressive names, including the likes of Gwilym Williams of Miskin Manor, Revd David Howell of St John's Cardiff, William Traherne of Llantrisant and Dr William Price, who donated £5 towards the cause, slightly less than the £25 from the Marquis of Bute and £10 from Lord Talbot, the Lord Lieutenant and MP. Despite the obvious rifts that had occurred over the years between Price, Myfyr and Morien, a mutual respect did exist among the men.

Despite being a preacher in his early years, Myfyr had abandoned Christianity altogether by his mid-fifties and spent the remainder of his life investigating the mysteries of bards and the Eastern religions, with their alleged connections to Christianity and Druidism. He was denounced from the pulpit and condemned by the press on several occasions, not dissimilar to Price. Some regarded him as a simpleton or an idiot, but all his true acquaintances and friends referred to him as a naïve, innocent and sincere man.[17] A prolific letter-writer to local newspapers and author of several books – most of which were published at his own expense – he fought hard to uphold the 'discoveries' of Iolo Morganwg, particularly when many of those beliefs, including Iolo's mystic mark /|\, were brought into question; the Druids who followed him in Newbridge were mockingly called the 'Rocking Stone Barefoots', and Myfyr's teachings were called deceitful and superstitious. By 1874, a year prior to the testimonial fund, the preacher and editor of *Y Gwladgarwr*, William Thomas (Islwyn), launched an attack on Myfyr in the *Western Mail*. 'We regret that this nonsense is published since the English will now believe that he is a representative man, which we totally deny.'

In 1875 Myfyr published the last of his extensive volumes of bardic history, *Hynafiaeith Aruthrol Y Trwn Neu Orsedd Beirdd Ynys Brydain a'I Barddau Gyfrin*, and left instructions that they should all be placed under his head in his coffin and buried with him. Few are available, largely because chapel deacons and ministers encouraged their congregation to buy copies and then burn them. Many people were outraged with Myfyr, Dr Price, Morien and the rest of the circle of Druids in Pontypridd, while others viewed them with a patronising curiosity. A letter in *Y Gwladgarwr* in 1875 from D. M. Williams of Coedpenmaen not only denounced the Druids but called on local ministers to meet and discuss how to bring an end to the circle that sowed 'the seeds of atheism, and planting unbiblical principals in the minds of the feeble and the young'.[17] Morien came to his defence, and it was due to his support that the testimonial fund was established to care for Myfyr in his old age, raising a total of £140 12s, which was presented to him at the Butchers Arms, Pontypridd in December 1875. Three years later and Myfyr was presented with the degree of Doctor of Civil Laws from the American University of Philadelphia and Eclectic Medical College of Pennsylvania, which sadly wasn't quite what it appeared, as the 'university' was in an office in Philadelphia whose owner was known for selling degrees. One of its victims was Morien himself, who paid $30 for a degree from the fraudulent institution. Myfyr gradually withdrew from public life and attended his last Gorsedd at Y Maen Chwyf in 1878, after which the ceremony in Pontypridd declined, and he died a decade later at his daughter-in-law's home in the town.

Dr Price described him in 1888, saying, 'He was a very clever man and very well read, but he did not understand, you know – he did not understand.' When he was told Morien had accepted the role of Archdruid over Price, he added, 'Well, Morien knows nothing of Druidism, not he. I shall let matters remain exactly as they are. An Archdruid should be able to read and decipher all Druidical letters and hieroglyphics, and Morien knows nothing at all about them.'[6]

What is of note is the fact that by this time a new element of Welsh culture was beginning to reinvent its sense of nationhood. Neither Llanover, Guest nor Dr Price and his Druids could imagine that despite all of their desperate attempts to recreate the identify of the Welsh people and its prominent position in the British Empire, it wasn't the costume, the literature nor the ancient history and religion that would give this country and its people the recognition it deserved, even though it had of course accounted greatly towards a new vision from the outside world. Instead, it came from music, and choral singing in particular.

While its workforce endured the dangerous hardship of working underground in the most appalling of conditions, the communities in which they lived were galvanised by a musical intensity the like of which had never been seen before. For more than a century Wales was famous for more than just its outpouring of precious bituminous fuel, it was the heartland of a culture inspired by the sound of people united in music. Chapels united in John Curwen's ingenious tonic sol-fa, allowing ordinarily uneducated working class people the ability to read a new and easier form of musical notation. In doing so, the ability to unite in harmonic choral singing began. From the 1870s onwards in particular, Wales was a melting pot of a whole range of musical organisations and within those long, monotonous valley terraces the universally popular image of the male voice choir first found its voice. Soon its people grasped the concept of singing festivals, oratorios, cantatas and competitions in eisteddfodau, which reached its climax in the national event every year. It was a haven of competitive gatherings where an eisteddfod marquee resembled a gladiatorial arena, with reputations and village pride at stake. These performances drew crowds that far exceeded any sporting event. At the National Eisteddfod in Swansea in 1891 a staggering 20,000 people were crammed into the Pavilion. At the international rugby game in Newport a few months before only 8,000 spectators saw the game. This golden era of choral music significantly shaped the national identity of Wales.

By 1870 debates about Wales were persistent, as notions of crisis came to mind with the unrelenting growth of nonconformity. What was needed was a sudden injection of confidence in the insecure Welsh psyche and what better way to achieve this than through singing? The point of ignition was the Aberdare blacksmith Griffiths Rhys Jones, or Caradog (1834–97), when he led a conglomerate of South Wales choirs to compete for and win the Thousand Guinea Trophy at Crystal Palace. However, the impact it had on the universal image of the Welsh was the true success of his *Cor Mawr*, as hysterical celebrations changed the way Wales was viewed from the outside world. This was the first competitive representation of the Welsh nation beyond its boundaries, and it marked an unparalleled success. As he stepped off the train at Ystrad Station on a bright summer day in 1872, the welcome he received from a massed crowd of more than 5,000 admirers was testimony to the respect he commanded throughout Wales. A state of euphoria swept the country as shop windows throughout every major town were emblazoned with pictures of his solemn face, accompanied by banners proclaiming 'He Led Them To Victory'.

This escapism from the harsh realities of working class existence in the South Wales valleys proved a major factor in this insatiable appetite for Congregational singing. Nobody could put it better than Caradog himself when he verified that '*Gwlad Y Gan Yw Gymru I Gyd*' ('All Wales is a Land of Song'). Yet, even by the end of the nineteenth century, the *Encyclopaedia Brittannica* still failed to recognise the uniqueness of the Principality when it brutally stated, 'WALES – see England'.

Despite this rise in choral singing and the eventual Royal Assent it would receive from the Queen Empress when she regularly welcomed Welsh choirs to one of the palaces, the die-hard Neo-Druidic movement continued, although it was obvious to one and all that this had become a dwindling and almost comic tradition where people watched in bewilderment at the buffoonery of the situation.

In July 1877 an art exhibition was opened in the Market House in Pontypridd, complete with the historic works of Sir Joshua Reynolds and Sir Peter Lely on show. Part of the exhibition included a collection of portraits of ancient Welsh bards and warriors by Mr Jones of Merthyr; Myfyr Morganwg's mundane egg, which he claimed was 400 years old and discovered in a cairn near Llandaff; a *Coelbren y Beirdd*; and numerous objects from the collection of Francis Crawshay. There was a collection of china, ancient coins, and a crown presented by King George II to Hopkin Hopkins of Llantrisant, who at 2 feet and 7 inches tall was one of the smallest men ever registered, and son of the celebrated bard Lewis Hopkin. He visited Windsor Castle in 1751 at the age of fifteen and presentations were made by the king. One of the exhibitions was created by 'Gwenhiolen Hiarlhes Morganwg Price', of items belonging to her father. Dr Price made further ludicrous claims of the origins of many of the items, which are questionable indeed:

> This collection is so remarkable that a list of them is here subjoined: Dishes made by the Tartars in the reign of Zingia Khan, 500 years ago; china cups and saucers, made by the Chinese before the Tartar dynasty was founded 600 years ago; china tea and coffee service, 250 years old; Chinese cups or basins, made by the Chinese before the Tartar dynasty; soup plates, Nantgarw ware; cups and saucers, originally the property of Gwladys Price of Pontypandy 200 years old; cup and saucer, the property of Mr Crisley Cousins of Ynysplwm's great-great-grandfather.[18]

There are few entries in the press regarding his once frequent court hearings during this period, save for a case of causing a nuisance in 1876 and a claim by Dr Price against Dr James, a surgeon of Cwmparc, Rhondda in July 1877. Dr Price made a claim of £50 against him for services rendered to Essex Nicholas, one of the defendant's patients who had been injured in a colliery. Nicholas objected to Dr James amputating his leg and wanted to see Dr Price, who stated that because Dr James had paid for his trap to fetch him, he was also liable for the charges to treat him. Dr Price came to the court hearing with a bone in a bottle of wine, which he extracted from the foot of the patient, who was able to walk on crutches. The judge decided against Dr Price because no contract had been signed.

Dr Price began travelling frequently to North Wales, and learned about bone-setting and manipulation of bones from therapist Evan Davies. Through Davies he also met Hugh Owen Thomas of Liverpool (1834–91), with whom he corresponded for years. The Welsh-born surgeon, considered as a father of orthopaedic surgery in Britain, was descended from a young boy shipwrecked in Anglesey. His father was a well-known bone-setter in Liverpool, often taken to court for not being a trained physician. Hugh, however, trained at Edinburgh and London, qualifying as a Member of the Royal College of Surgeons in 1857. Known as an eccentric and temperamental man, rumours were abound that he would attack victims himself and break their bones in order to have patients on which to practice. Shorter than Dr Price by five inches, he always wore a long black coat, a patch over one eye and a cigarette in the mouth, and among the poor of Liverpool was held in high esteem. He operated from his home in Nelson Street, sharing the same social healthcare ideals of the Llantrisant surgeon by treating patients for free on a Sunday. His contribution to the treatment of fractures and tuberculosis was widespread, and although he was not appreciated in his own lifetime, his nephew Sir Robert Jones used his splint methods in the First World War and reduced mortality of compound fractures of the femur from eighty per cent to less than eight per cent between 1916 and 1918.

Another tale of Price's life is the visit he made in 1875 to a medical conference in London. According to Price he went to a Soho pub and met his old friend Cledwyn Hughes, who introduced him to none other than the German philosopher and revolutionary socialist Karl Marx, who resided in London from 1849 until his death in 1883.

In 1878 a dinner was held in honour of the Druids of Pontypridd, under the auspices of Francis Crawshay, at the Rickard Arms. On this occasion the Order of Ancient Druids marched through Treforest, but Mr Crawshay was unable to attend. On passing Forest House, the processions were 'reminded of the prosperity of what once had been' and, led by the Treforest Brass Band, they were photographed by Thomas Forrest, who was hired many times by Dr Price over the coming years. Present on this occasion was Francis' son, Mr F. R. Crawshay, the vice Archdruid of the occasion who proposed the toast – and who ironically sat at Dr Price's famous trial six years later!

Within a few months Dr Price learned of the death of his dear old friend, Francis Crawshay. It was his own 'eccentricities' that led to the decision of Francis not to allow him to become heir to the Cyfarthfa Works, favouring his stepbrother Robert Thompson Crawshay instead. Known for his wicked, dry humour, Francis retired to Kent in 1867, selling the tinplate works to a consortium that became known as the Forest Iron and Steel Works.

In June 1878 Dr Price was called to give evidence at an inquest in the Colliers Arms, Llantwit Fardre, following the death of twenty-five-year-old Ann Edwards. Miss Edwards, a farmer's daughter of Aberfan, died of rheumatic fever and was attended by Dr Price. She spent five months bedridden with 'Dropsy' and Dr Price allegedly felt there was little more he could do for her. Miss Edwards wanted to visit a Mrs Jenkins of Ystradbarwig in Llantwit Fardre, where she hoped for a cure. A Mrs Morgan of the same village also gave her medicine. When she visited Llantwit in June 1878, she saw a friend and complained of stomach pains and within the day she was dead.

In September 1879 Dr Price was before the magistrates at Pontypridd, charged with having a savage dog that he allowed to roam free. Price appeared in a 'fine white linen surplice, his long white beard falling over his breast and his white hair falling over his shoulders ... and stood at the bar with his arms folded over his chest'. Sergeant Tamplin said Dr Price's dog had attacked a dog belonging to William Davies of Llantrisant, and when he tried to stop the attack Dr Price became furious with him, threatening to attack him as Tamplin reached for a screwdriver to defend himself. In the court Dr Price vehemently cross-examined Tamplin to show the dog was not dangerous to people. Afterwards, Price grabbed his fox skin hat and walked from the court. The magistrate called, 'Where is he going?' and the constable rushed after him, with Constable Hallett blocking his way and placing his hands on his shoulders. 'Let me be man!' shouted Price, claiming he had private business, but the Bench demanded he returned where they dismissed the case, unable to prove the dog was dangerous to humans.

Earlier in February 1878 he lost another sister. Ann Price passed away at the age of seventy-four in her home at Llanishen, which later may have been the home of Hiarlhes, as she was listed as residing in that area by 1881. Ann was buried in the family grave at St Barrwg's Church in Bedwas.

Dr William Price visited his relatives' graves to find St Barrwg's was being restored. Builder R. Jones of Caerphilly was following the plans of architect of the diocese of Llandaf, Mr Prichard, to create the Gothic style that he had also introduced in Llantrisant six years previously. Costing £1,300 to complete, a special opening service took place with visiting members of the clergy from the vicinity of Caerphilly.

Dr Price undertook the journey to Bedwas, where he claimed excavations were being carried out in the chancel. Human bones had been taken from the chancel for reburial in the churchyard and Price picked up a piece and claimed it was a bone from his sister. On dashing to the rectory, he allegedly reached for Revd William Williams over the kitchen table, accusing him of sacrilege by tossing family bones on the 'dung hill.' So incensed was Price that he had a brass plaque firmly placed on the family grave outside the church which was fixed by a workman from Breconshire without the knowledge of Revd Williams. It was soon smeared with car grease and red lead paint, but survived in place until April 1967 when, green with age, it mysteriously disappeared. The plaque, which chastised the clergy, was written by Dr Price and was featured in a letter in the *Western Mail* which begins 'Oys Oys Oys!'. The plaque read,

> *Celwydd yw vod saith oyr tystion*
> *Dorrwyd, gynnta, arr y garreg denni yn gorwedd.*
> *Carthwyd wynt u bwll y dommen*
> *Dan Draed Opheria T Eglwys Betwas*
> *Cluwch nw yn Levvaian amya amarch*
> *Yng Gwydd y var a yr atgyvttiad*
> *Yng gluw y 'Iessu y bia yng gleddu*
> *Tywysog Carriad Coron Cymmry*[19]

It is translated to:

> It is a lie that seven of the witnesses
> whose names were first carved on the stone are lying below it.
> They were scoured away to the pit of the dunghill
> Under the feet of the priest of Bedwas Church
> Hear them crying out against the desecration
> In the presence of Jesus, whose right it is to bury us
> The prince of love, the crown of Wales

What is prophetic about the entire episode was that possibly Dr Price's own fury at the sheer negligence of the family grave may have been attributed to his decision not to allow the remains of his own baby son to fall victim to the same fate. Was this desecration therefore another reason why he felt cremation was a more acceptable method of disposal of the dead?

The entire matter was featured in the *Western Mail* but not until a year following the event, and then only due to a rather unkindly letter from Morien, titled 'Dr William Price In The Presence Of the Sun And of Yth Thy and O Coruous And The Bedwas Church Authorities'. Morien wrote with tongue in cheek:

From the days when I wore a short frock prettily braided, to this hour, the subject of my sketch has been to me, as he is to everybody else, an object of deep and curious interest. When I first remember him he wore a similar costume to that he wears at the present day, but his looks were not so hoary then as they are now. With that exception, he is still much as he was then, for his step is as nimble and his agility as full of animation as they were fifty years ago. He however then rode a cream coloured pony with its tail nearly touching the ground. It is supposed that advancing years is the reason he is no more on prancing horses.

The next place I saw him was on a Pontypridd Common Fairday, pouring tea into a large number of cups, arranged on the Gorsedd rocking stone, for a considerable number of aged females whom he was entertaining within the Temple of Keridwen, the Cambro-British Goddess of poetry on the Pontypridd Common. The infantile ... gazed in awe from a safe distance at the strangely dressed doctor and his somewhat weird companions.

Many years afterwards, the writer had gone from Bath, where he then resided, to London and was engaged at the Record Office, Chancery Lane, where, like an apparition, there passed the desk at which he was engaged Dr Price, his large fox skin cap – a whole skin, the ears included – under his arm and his white hair in plaited appendages falling over his chest and shoulders and disappeared through a door at the other end of the room. Presently he reappeared walking nimbly, and with an angry repose...I walked towards him and after addressing him in Welsh, he gave a sudden jerk to his body and looking into my face with much sharpness, said '*Duw, Pwy'n wyt ti*' [God, who are you?]. Having satisfied him on that point he walked with me to the desk by my request, and taking a magnifying glass attached to a string on his bosom, he examined the document upon which I had been engaged. By and bye one of the attendants brought in his hand to the doctor, with an expression of humility, a large yellow sheet of parchment. The venerable follower of Esculapins took the document in his hand and after pointing to me the names 'Price' 'Monmouthshire' upon it he said to the attendant, after thanking him, 'Why couldn't you bring this to me first?' A few as before this he had argued his claim to a certain property in Monmouthshire before Baron Bramwell and a special jury. 'Do you know what the baron wanted?' He said that 'I reasoned in a circle?' 'How singular' he continued, 'That he said the very same thing about me that my grandmother used to say!' 'Why,' I asked, 'didn't you say that his Lordship's remarks remind you of your grandmother?' The doctor looked at me sharply and made use of a very sharp emphatic expletive, as if under the impression I was joking about a thing that might have relegated him to durance vile for contempt of court, for Baron Bramwell had the reputation, at least in Wales, of being a representative of John Bull in his examining mood.

The writer returned to Wales. The Druid did so also after an absence of several years.

'Morien' called upon him at his Pontypridd residence, and was cordially received. One of the first things I noticed was a number of dogs, which seemed to be old enough to be the ancestors of all the other dogs in the county. One that was lame seemed to be the object of the doctor's fonder solicitude. It is whispered that the doctor is a believer in the Druidic theory of transmigration, and this tenderness to the canine breed may have something Buddhist in it. I must admit that the venerable Escupalian's appearance on this occasion had a peculiar effect upon me, especially when the various objects about this room caught my eye. Resting against the wall was a figure in a red shirt, with arms extended and where the head should have been was a golden crescent with the horns pointing upwards and down the front of the shirt were golden letters in great confusion. Here and there about the same there were other curious articles. By and by I ventured to ask my friend what that object was. With a harried move of his head he said, in a whisper ... 'That is a curiosity! It is the greatest discovery of the age! It is the will of my Father, or the skin of the man who walked without the man! On the rode under it is carved a new song!' I became uneasy and glanced occasionally towards the door. But with considerable recklessness I retained my seat and said, 'Would you mind singing the new song?' 'With pleasure', was the reply and he walked towards the figure and exposing the rod, which was covered with small letters artistically carved, and holding the figure at arm's length, he commenced the new song in an unknown tongue which he, however subsequently told me was the language of nature which he had recently discovered. As he stood there with the figure in one hand, waving the other, his long white hair and beard, and his light green garments lined in scarlet, and scalloped at the bottom, and chanted the now song in melancholy cadenzas, my hair almost stood on and like quills on the fretful porcupine. The only words, if words, too that I could make out were '*yth thy O Coryous*'.

The above performance being over, I described to him my recent visit to the grave of Prince Llewellyn, the last native Prince of Wales, recognised as such by England, near Builth. I saw instantly that he was much moved. His eyes glazed with patriotism as I described a gentleman in North Wales and I from South Wales, kneeling at the well, out of which Prince Llewellyn drank his last drop of water on earth a little before he died ...

Now it will be remembered that the doctor brings serious charges against the Bedwas Church authorities which is to the affect that they have desecrated the grave of his fathers and that seven bodies have been carted away and thrown into the rubbish tip. Certain printer's errors occurred in the doctor's lines, reported in the *Western Mail*, which were copied from the brass plate which he had caused to be put on what he states to be an empty vault at Bedwas Church, and with reference to that matter he has addressed the following letter to me:

Llantrisant, Glamorgan
Dear Morien
Dear Sir! Your introduction to what you are pleased to call a curiosity, and your criticism of it in the *Western Mail* of the 13th instant, are very fairly reported by you based on the authority of Dr Owen Pugh and others who did not understand the meaning of the letters of the alphabet of the Welsh languages as he has provide in his Dictionary and Grammar by rendering False Translations of the Primitive Bards. Neither does the one bard whom I have the pleasure to knowing know the meaning of the sign or letters, the original elements of the imperial language of Gwent and Morganwg! But in copying my inscription, you have I have no doubt by unintentionally blundering taken away three of its natural uses in the First, Second and Seventh lines. I shall therefore thank you to report the orthography of my inscription again letter for letter as it is and not otherwise as I know the meaning of every vowel and every consonant in my natural language of Gwent and Morganwg issuing out of the immortal brains of the Cymmerian race![20]

The article is followed by a copy of the brass plate from the Bedwas Church, followed by his signature of 'William Price in the Presence of Yth Thy and O Coryosis'.[19]

Over the coming years Price and Morien remained at loggerheads. What exacerbated the situation was Morien's decision to totally ignore Dr Price's self-proclaimed promotion to the title of Archdruid of the Isles of Britain. In September 1880 several letters went back and forth between the two men in the *Western Mail*, which Morien responded to with,

There is … a reason we should venerate him, who is the 'in the presence of the sun'. He has grown so earnest in the pursuit of Druidic lore, we all respect earnest men, that he has discarded modern attire and adopted the ovate green garments, with scalloped edges, the latter being in most instances after the comb of the bird of Aurors, goddess of the morning and in ancient times the symbol of authority. To be exact, it should be also stated that the scallops were worn by the priests of the sun as emblems of the rays of that luminary. Whether the doctor wears them after what the Yankees call a rooster, or as indicative that he is the priest of the sun, is not stated. Probably he had both ideas in his thoughts when he adopted them. His fox skin cap is well known to be striking symbol of the doctor's sagacity. But there are indications that the doctor is on the eve of further dress development, which, if adopted by him, will be extremely trying to the nerves of all who may happen to meet him in a lonely place.

The public will recollect that the venerable gentleman announced a short time ago that he would award a prize of £5 to the vocalist that would sing 'The Will of My Father' or 'The Skin of Men that Walked Without the Man'. The Committee of the Swansea Eisteddfod, much as they would have enjoyed the addition of the prize to their list of prizes, were so frightened by the 'skin of the man who walked without the man' that they omitted to include it in their programme. And it was well they did omit it, for had the competition come on at the eisteddfod, the doctor had prepared such a surprise for the audience that would have sent them into fits.

Having failed in his purpose at Swansea, the doctor proceeded to Llandrindod Eisteddfod, where after some attempts were made to sing 'The Will of My Father' or 'The Skin of the Man That Walked Without The Man' the doctor volunteered to do it himself. He mounted the platform and took off his boots, and appeared with naked feet, for he never wears stockings. He then flung off his cap and upper garments and, his white hair over his shoulders, was proceeding to unbutton the dress to the alarm of all. One of the officials here stepped forward and expressed hope that no impropriety was contemplated. The sharp reply was 'Tis all right', at the next moment the doctor appeared in a dress similar to that worn by a pantaloon, but covered by the coloured figures of all kinds of reptiles. Many jumped up with the intention, apparently of making their escape but the next moment the sonorous voice of the strange gentleman was heard chanting 'Yth twhy, tha, tha, tho, yah, yah, yah, yo!' the roars of laughter, hastened the performer to break into modern Welsh and said, '*Ffolid y jawl I chi gyd!*' and picking up his garments, left the eisteddfod in disgust. The curious dress is supposed to be intended as an illustration of the skin of the man that walked without the man.[20]

As a matter of interest, the bards of the Gorsedd at Swansea wrote a letter of disgust to the *Cambrian* regarding Price's '*Gwyllllis yn Nayd*' performance too.

Dr Price couldn't fail to respond to Morien's criticism, which appeared on the following edition of 20 September 1880 and did little to uphold his character in a positive light. It is rambling, with little point and again attempts to reconfirm his position in the Druidical hierarchy, criticising the men at Swansea and Llandrindod for their insolence. At an eisteddfod in Llantrisant on 10 September where adjudicator Alaw Goch and Brinley Richards denounced a performance by William Morgan while singing '*Gwyllllis yn Nayd*'. On being interrupted during the performance Dr Price accused them of being ignorant and unable to understand the meaning of this important piece of historic text.

Further articles from Morien followed in January 1881, this time under the title of 'The ArchDruid's Works', where he upheld the tradition of Druidism and celebrated the fact that Myfyr's works were to be translated into English. In doing so, he couldn't fail but mention Dr Price, claiming his regular appearances at Y Maen Chwyf had become 'a kind of pantomime', which is not so far from the truth, given the evidence of newspaper reports of the time.

In March 1880 Dr William Price turned the grand age of eighty, by which time he was living permanently in Llantrisant, a town which earlier that month saw an outbreak of typhoid fever, and great criticism was made of the lack of a water supply, which was considered detrimental to health, and the need for a Rural Sanitary Authority was called upon to examine the situation. For the next few years many entries appeared in the local newspapers, and particularly the *Western Mail*, of Dr Price's devotion to Y Maen Chwyf and regular appearances were made there to hold Druidical services. At one visit in September 1880 one of the young men who accompanied Dr Price from Llantrisant sang '*Gwyllllis yn Nayd*' and the doctor joined in to the amusement of the curious onlookers.

On 21 March 1881 he was named at the service to mark the vernal equinox. Morien absolutely condemned the spectacle, opening his lines in the *Pontypridd Chronicle*,

> After the serious piece comes the screaming farce. Now Druidism, is but a grand solar drama, blended with metaphysical speculations at to the origin of man, and of all things. The Druid's theatre is the universe, its done fretted with golden fires. The miniature stage where the solar Drama is now performed is to be seen on the Pontypridd Common. On Sunday last, at noon, the tragedians performed religiously the Drama of the creation of the first man ... but on Monday at noon ... an apparition appeared in the streets of Treforest ... as would have induced a stranger to fancy that the much trifling at Pontypridd with venerable things had at last tempted one of the old Druidic patriarchs to step down from the circles of felicity to his old haunts on earth for the purpose of reviving earnestly Bardism as a religion ... the apparition was robed in white, scalloped at the borders, symbolic of the sun's rays ... on his head was the whole skin of the Anubis of the Egyptian priests of Osiris. Its nether garment was a commonplace article called a trousers lined with red ...

He carried the wand resting on the shoulder streamed a large flag of crimson silk. The bearer was Dr Price 'yth wy, in presence of the sun'. I asked him 'Where are you going?' He replied stagily [in Welsh] This is *Hymn Y Maban*, the Flag of the child, a red flag, I know he is come. He is seen this day on the stone, the comely son of the Easter stone, the song of the Mighty'. The whole town were at their doors and many followed the strange visitors ... having reached the rocking stone the doctor mounted it exactly at noon and addressing the sun he proceeded to speak in the strange Welsh, it was supposed, of the pre-Adamite epoch. The audience was in convulsions of laughter, but not a smile was on the performer's face. He was assisted to sing by Charles P. Brown, Treforest.[21]

Dr Price got himself into some difficulty during the summer of 1881 with the Pontypridd Rural Sanitary Authority. The complaints were due to the unclean 'water closet' of his home in Llantrisant, and that of the other houses he owned in the hilltop town. He was summoned before Judge Gwilym Williams at the Pontypridd petty sessions for neglecting to 'abate a nuisance caused by an accumulation of filth' in the closet belonging to one of the four properties he owned at the rear of the Greyhound Inn. The inn was in fact behind Tŷ'r Clettwr on Greyhound Lane, and he owned houses to the rear of that also. When John Evans, inspector of nuisances, prosecuted him, Dr Price had engaged the services of a London solicitor named Edmund Kimber. Some months beforehand the Sanitary Authority even had toilets built for the doctor's houses and summoned him to pay the costs, to which the doctor appealed. Although the house was now empty, the 'privy' was still filled with filth, not helped by the fact that a gap in the wall allowed the local people to use it as a public convenience! Kimber said there was a case pending to sue the board for the recovery of the cost of the closet and damages for the trespassing of the public itself. Dr Price said the order to clean the closet, with only two days notice, was 'malicious, spiteful' and an 'unjustifiable prosecution'. The judge gave Dr Price seven days to clear the filth. The case returned to Pontypridd Police Court in November, so the authority could claim the £10 they had spent on building the closet. On this occasion Dr Price defended himself, saying the board had no right to build the toilets next to his four houses because they were as 'well provided with sanitary accommodation as other premises in Llantrisant'. In return he refused to pay the £10 and instead counter-claimed the board for £100 for using his land to build the closet in the first place! By January 1882 the board agreed to drop the entire claim for fear of repercussions, although Dr Price then pulled down the privy altogether!

The 1881 census reveals interesting material concerning Dr Price and his daughter. By this time Hiarlhes was the head of a farm of 37 acres in

Llanishen Park, Llanishen. She had two servants and offered lodgings to a haulier and carpenter. Also present was her partner Thomas Williams. As for Dr Price himself, his lifestyle in 1881 was even more interesting. He is listed as the eighty-one-year-old physician, surgeon and head of the property named Pen Tŷ Cae Cledar (or Tŷ'r Clettwr) and as a 'widow' following the death of Ann Morgan. At the property is a domestic servant named Margaret Griffiths, who is twenty years of age. However, it's the third resident that causes the most interest. Although she is listed as his 'daughter' which of course is untrue, the name of Gwenllian Llewelyn, a twenty-one-year-old spinster, appears for the first time in association with Dr Price and she was faithful to him for the remainder of his life. It is believed she visited him at his surgery in Llantrisant and he was besotted with her. She walked into the room to see him bending down and fetching an item from a cupboard and when he turned around, he clutched his hand to his head and claimed 'Isis has come, the Mother of Gods has visited my habitation! Her forehead is high like that of the Goddess Juno, and her brow is like that of the Goddess Minerva!' His devotion to her was endless.

She was born at Ynyscaedudwg Farm (other reports claim it was the nearby Cwm Eldeg Farm) in Cilfynydd on 23 October 1859, six years after her parents married in Merthyr Tydfil. Her family were the Llewellyns of Llanwynno, and Ynyscaedudwg was later the site of the Albion Colliery, where the worst mining disaster in Britain before Senghenydd took place. Her mother, also named Gwenllian, grandmother, again named Gwenllian, and their maidservant all died of typhoid fever in the early months of 1872. Her grandmother was the first to pass away, on 12 February after suffering typhoid fever for nineteen days and experiencing extreme sickness and diarrhoea. Her son, William, who farmed Ynyscaedudwg, registered her death. Sadly, within the week he registered the loss of his wife of the same illness, aged just thirty-six. The manservant on the farm apparently took fright and disappeared. At this time Gwenllian was only twelve years of age, and the remainder of her family moved to farm at Coed y Goran, St Mellons. Her father, William Llewellyn, died three years later when she was sixteen, and she was sent to her aunt, Ann Davies of Whitehall, Llanharan, when she met Dr Price who treated her aunt as one of his patients.

Apparently a form of 'Druidic marriage' took place between them at Y Maen Chwyf on the doctor's eighty-first birthday, in March 1881. Gwenllian was just twenty-two. In Gwenllian he saw his ideal partner, someone who understood his Druidic beliefs and was prepared to accept his behaviour. The housekeeper moved to Tŷ'r Clettwr, and remained in the town for the next sixty years. In July 1881 she appeared in her first court hearing alongside Dr William Price, due to an assault upon her at

East Caerlan, the extensive land belonging to the surgeon, where he kept his cows and bulls, using a stable block at the Butchers Arms on the Bull Ring to bring them in from the fields. Engine driver Mark Senior came before Judge Gwilym Williams accused of assaulting Gwenllian, 'a good looking young woman'[22] who had joined two servants to milk some of Dr Price's cows. Senior was accused of interfering with their work by taking the tin caps, and tried to milk one of the cows before Gwenllian hit him to the ground and she sent one of the servants for a bucket of water, which she emptied all over him. Dr Price called on Sergeant Tamplin and Senior was fined 1s for the assault, bound over in the sum of £10 to keep the peace towards Miss Llewellyn and for six months.

By the end of September Dr Price appeared at another Druidic 'relic' or stone at Mynydd y Dinas above the Rhondda mining village of Penygraig. On the summit of the mountain was '*Maen Llog*' or the Oath Stone or Stone of the Covenant. Villagers rushed to the mountain when they heard him call,

> A magician am I! I am the chief bard of the people! I am acquainted with every herb in the cave of the west! I am the liberator of Elphin from the recess of the tower of stone. I will proclaim to the king and to the common people that a strange creature will come from the Marsh of Rhianedd. His hair, teeth and eyes will be golden, *Bum Glas Gleisiad, bum ei bum hydd, bum iwrch yn mynydd. Bym cyf mewn rhaw*!

> Rise! He sons of Cambrian rise!
> Spread your banners to the foe
> Spread them on the mountain brow!
> Lift your lances high in air,
> Friends and brothers of the war;
> Rush like torrents down the steep
> Through the vales in myriads sweep;
> These are Taliesin's rhymes
> These shall live to distant times
> And the bard's prophetic rage
> Animate a future age.

Miners looked upwards to see Dr Price mount the stone holding a crimson flag and on lifting his hands he continued singing,

> The Hall of Harps is lone this day,
> And cold the chieftain's hearth;
> It hath no mead, it hath no lay,
> No voice of melody, no sound of mirth.

And I depart – my wound is deep
My brethren long have died –
Yet ere my soul grow dark with sleep
Winds: bear the spoiler one more tune of pride[22]

On reaching the summit many of the villagers continued to follow Dr Price as he celebrated the autumnal equinox aided by his throng of followers. Only a few months later he appeared at Y Maen Chwyf for the feast of Alban Hefin and wore a suit of light grey home-made Welsh cloth and on his head a white hat. The crowds laughed at his behaviour. In December 1882 he was again at Y Maen Chwyf 'in the presence of the sun and of the hissing egg'. Dr Price, described as the 'modern Thoth', appeared in the circle carrying his banner and 'spluttered' '*Gwyllllis yn Nayd*'.

By March 1883 he was seen walking through Pontypridd market, dressed in his usual attire and holding a large wand surmounted by the crescent moon with a crimson flag flowing in the wind. Whenever someone asked him what it was he replied, 'It is the banner of the Son, the flag of the *Hen yn Nghnawd* or the *Gwyddon*' which were both recognised as titles of the high priest of the Druids according to Iolo's manuscripts. Morien's report of the appearance said,

Dr Price, who should not be mistaken for Myfyr Morganwg, the modest old scholar, proceeded to the Druidic temple on the common and there he celebrated the vernal equinox. It is not true, as was rumoured in the town, that he stood on the rocking stone on one leg; but with both feet firmly fixed on the stone and with his face towards the sun he chanted the will of his father, his Highland collie the while sitting on the grass, gazing steadfastly at his master and whining a musical accompaniment. Occasionally the dog, apparently forgetting the part he was expected to perform in the celebration in which the master was engaged, darted stealthily after other dogs. This rebellious spirit was always checked by the doctor calling '*Dere yma!*' which he instantly obeyed. It is one of the doctor's articles of faith that Cymraeg is mother of the languages of the earth and that all the others are derived from it. Welsh is the language of nature and he who knows Welsh thoroughly can, while sitting under the trees in the forest, understand the words as well as the music of the songs of the winged tribes. This statement will not appear surprising when I say that Dr Price declares that the builders of the Pyramids of Egypt were people from Caerphilly. What is in favour of the statement is that no one can prove it is not true.[23]

In July 1883 Dr Price appeared at the Pontypridd County Court before B. T. Williams QC after trying to sue puddler Evan Davies of Dowlais for £40 for medical attendance on the late Llantrisant shopkeeper David Davies. It appeared that Davies left an infant son, who was entitled for up to £5,000 and a small freehold inheritance. Davies was guardian of the child and trustee of the property and Dr Price demanded he pay the bill for the treatment he gave the late Mr Davies. The bill was objected because it was exorbitant, but the doctor added he was an extraordinarily skilled surgeon and the judge ordered £20 5s be paid by Davies with costs.

Dreams of a god-like son were finally answered on 8 August 1883, when Gwenllian gave birth to a boy. Following years of hopes and dreams to father a son, his prophecy was fulfilled. As blasphemous as it appeared to the surrounding community, Dr Price recognised this child as the prophecy from *Gwyllllis yn Nayd* and the Greek stone he had viewed more than forty years earlier. The child was the centre of all his hopes and aspirations, claiming his birth and functions had been foretold from ancient days. The baby was the fulfilment of his life, and would restore the lost secrets of the Druids. He claimed the right to call his child Iesu Grist, the Welsh name of Jesus Christ, as foretold in the prophecy which foresaw the birth. In the ancient times the governor or king of the country was always selected by the Druids, and the person they selected was called *Mab Duw*, The Son of God, according to Dr Price.

> It was for this reason that Cynddelw called Llewellyn, the second Welsh prince of that name by the title. I have proof positive that I am the son of the Welsh Primitive Bard and I am equally certain that this second child of mine, who, I have also called Iesu Grist, will reign on earth, and that in him the ancient Druidical system will be restored.[24]

How utterly incredible was the fact that Dr Price was confusing Christianity with Druidism. Admittedly, earlier Christian history had adopted pagan ceremonies into its own, but for Price – a man totally opposed to modern religion – to name his son Iesu Grist seems absurd. Although he explained the child would be the Son of God, obviously he was referring to the Druidic gods, not that of Christianity. One wonders whether in naming the baby Jesus, or Iesu, he was either mocking the Christian church and chapel which held such power in Victorian Wales, or was it quite simply down to his confused mind, as he felt the descendants of the Ancient Britons would better recognise their new Druidic messiah by the name of the Christian Almighty?

By November 1883 Dr Price and Gwenllian were charged with not registering the child's birth, which was a legal requirement, and were ordered before Judge Gwilym Williams at Pontypridd Police Court. Gwenllian, a single woman, housekeeper in the employ of Dr W. Price of 'in the presence of the sun' celebrity was charged at the instigation of the Registrar General of Births and Marriages with neglecting to register Iesu Grist within 42 days of his birth. She was also charged with neglecting to comply with local registrar Howell Davies's orders to carry out the orders immediately. Neither Gwenllian nor Dr Price appeared at the court.[25]

Sergeant Hoyle of Llantrisant said he served the summons on Gwenllian Llewellyn, and although he heard a woman's voice within Tŷ'r Clettwr, Dr Price denied she was there. Hoyle dropped the summons at the doctor's feet. Howell Davies said he had sent a notice on 5 October but it had been returned as refused. When he visited Gwenllian she explained that Dr Price had never registered his former child and was not going to register this one.

Gwenllian's aunt, Ann Davies of Whitehall Farm, Llanharan, said she slept at Tŷ'r Clettwr on the night prior to the birth but didn't realise Gwenllian was so close to having her child. On the next morning she returned from milking and admitted washing a newly born son but didn't know it was Gwenllian's baby! Llantrisant widow Margaret Morgan, aged seventy, who was making jam in Tŷ'r Clettwr on the eve of the birth, had also been ordered to make baby's clothes on the request of Dr Price and visited them on the day of the birth. The judge fined Gwenllian 40s for each of the charges plus costs. He also felt Ann Davies' evidence was untrue and ordered proceedings of perjury against her, which were later withdrawn.

It is said the baby had strange marks on his back, even one that resembled a man on horseback, which first appeared when he was only three weeks old. Ill health certainly plagued the baby's young life until, tragically, Iesu Grist Price died after only five months in his cradle in the front room of Tŷ'r Clettwr on 10 January 1884, but in doing so, secured his father's place in history.

10

1884

Cremation was a subject of serious consideration in Great Britain for more than a decade before Dr William Price committed his baby son to the 'cleansing flame'. A crematorium was erected in Woking as early as 1879, but not until Dr Price's court case paved the way for legalisation of this method of disposal of the dead was the system put into action. The Cremation Society of Great Britain fought legal issues, social and religious prejudices to succeed in their aim. With the introduction of the 1836 Births and Deaths Registrations Act, the country could produce more accurate mortality figures. With the passing of the Attendance and Remuneration of Medical Witnesses at Coroners Inquests Act, a payment system was established for coroners to authorise physicians to perform a post-mortem. For the first time it was clear: the magnitude of the infant mortality rate and average lifespan were indications that insufficient cemeteries, particularly in the populated areas that had developed following the industrial revolution, were unable to cope with demand.

Churchyards throughout the country were becoming unsanitary, with overcrowded burial plots in densely populated areas. 'City dwellers were all too aware of the attendant horrors of over-crowded burial grounds, drunken gravediggers, body snatchers, the ever-present stench of corruption and the sight of bones carelessly thrown up from yawning graves.'[1] With the growing threat of cholera and other epidemics, clearly something had to be done.

Dr Price's own research into Roman history and Eastern religions, particularly Hinduism, gave him an insight into the practices of cremation. In *Asiatic Researches* in 1784, founded to foster British knowledge of Eastern religion and culture, an essay by Francis Wilford suggested Britain had been the sacred islands mentioned in some Hindu religions. Therefore ancient Druidism and Indian culture were very closely related, a fact that Dr Price as well as his contemporaries, including Myfyr Morganwg, would have understood. He mapped the Hindu divisions of godhood onto ancient Druidry, explaining that the sun had been its symbol of divinity, and that the rites of the summer solstice represented the deity as creator, those of the winter solstice portrayed him as destroyer. He related deities from Welsh and Irish mythology to Hindu deities, biblical patriarchs and characters from the works of Iolo.[2]

In Roman times, cremation was the most common form of disposal, with the remains placed in urns. Even as late as the fifth century evidence suggests it occurred in Britain, a period when Dr Price's glorious Druids practised their pagan religion. Cremation is mentioned in the Book of Genesis when Abraham is ordered by God to prepare the funeral pyre for the sacrifice of his son Isaac, and there are other references throughout the Old and New Testament. In truth, with the growth of Christianity, cremation came to an end, becoming embroiled in mythology as the act of human sacrifice by the Celts.

Cremation avoided the process of decomposition and ensured that in times of plague the body would not be a threat to the living. During battles, cremation ensured there was no desecration of the fallen soldiers or their graves as the ashes could easily be taken away for proper rites and honour, away from the enemy. However, there was opposition from the Church. With an anti-Christian background and the fact that the Church believed in the resurrection of the body to face the judgement of God, there was also the fact that

> churches owned most burial grounds and drew income and pastoral authority from them. There was also a revolutionary theme to cremation. The French Revolution had proposed cremation, in its double battle against the Catholic Church and the old feudal order whose hierarchies were celebrated in conspicuous rites of sepulchre and memorialisation. Thirdly the European imagination saw cremation as associated with shameful deaths, the extermination of witches and heretics.[3]

A re-emerging interest in cremation began with Sir Thomas Browne, a physician of Norwich whose book in 1664 advocated cremation as an alternative to burial. Honoretta Pratt, daughter of Sir John Brookes of York, in 1769, wished for her remains to be burnt to avoid further 'harmful vapours' rising from the grave. In July 1822 Percy Bysshe Shelley, the famous poet, drowned off the Italian coast; under Italian law anything washed onto the shore had to be burnt for fear of spreading the plague. An iron furnace was made and Lord Byron watched Shelley's cremation; mutual friend Edward Trelawny clutched the poet's heart from the flames and it was later buried with his wife, *Frankenstein* author Mary Shelley, in Bournemouth. Between 1856 and 1870 archaeologists discovered evidence of cremations in England and Scotland with urns and ashes being unearthed, particularly in Yorkshire and Dorchester.

In 1857 *The Lancet* supported the method: 'The plan here proposed for reducing a body to ashes, (if practicable) appears as decent, speedy and effectual method as could well be conceived'.[4] The notion was already being adopted elsewhere, particularly in Germany and Italy where furnaces were erected. In Great Britain, the need to explore the possibility was greater than ever. Cremation was not new to the poor. As a nineteenth-century gravedigger described one cemetery: 'You should go there of a night, sometimes, Sir, and see them burning the bones and the coffins. You see, they dig up the "commones" every twelve years ... and what they find left of them they burn.'[5]

The starting point of legalising cremation in Great Britain was due to Sir Henry Thompson (1820–1904), a well-respected physician who, following studies at the medical school in the University College London had an outstanding career with honours in anatomy and surgery. A surgeon at the University College Hospital in 1863 and consulting surgeon in 1874, he was later professor of surgery and pathology at the Royal College of Surgeons by 1884, the year of Iesu Grist Price's cremation. Specialising in urology, the surgeon was called to treat the King of Belgium, who was suffering kidney stones, and operated successfully on the monarch. He later undertook a similar operation on the former emperor, Napoleon III, who died four days later, but not from the surgical procedure. In 1874 he founded the Cremation Society of Great Britain, becoming its first president; not only was he active in urging the advantages of cremation as a means of disposing of the body after death, but he also did much toward the removal of the legal restrictions by which it was at first sought to prevent its practice in England. It was during his visit to the Great Exhibition in Vienna in 1873 that he met Professor Brunetti, Professor of Pathological Anatomy at Padua University, who was exhibiting a model of a cremation furnace. It captured Thompson's imagination and he wrote a series of essays supporting the concept. His seminal work printed in 1874 was the article 'The Treatment of the Body after Death', which appeared over ten pages in the *Contemporary Review*, and discussed the decomposition of a corpse, the damage to the earth, pollution of the graveyards and the effect on the air and water. Carefully he avoided discussing religion and listed the public health advantages and economies in funeral expenses (which annoyed undertakers in that case). His main reason for supporting cremation was that 'it was becoming a necessary sanitary precaution against the propagation of disease among a population daily growing larger in relation to the area it occupied'.[5]

Although the main argument he advanced was a sanitary one, other reasons were given. Cremation, he believed, would prevent premature burial, would reduce the expense of funerals, would spare mourners the necessity of standing exposed to the weather during interment, and the ashes kept in urns would be safe from vandalism. He controversially also suggested the use of bones as fertilizer because burial wasted half a million pounds of bone and earth each year, a statement he later regretted. The *British Medical Journal* supported the idea on hygienic grounds, but opposition was felt by religious leaders.

On 13 January 1874 Thompson called a meeting at his home to form the society, among whom were the rector of St James's in Westmoreland Street, Hugh Reginald Haweis; novelist Anthony Trollope; surgeon Thomas Spencer Wells; George du Maurier, the novelist and grandfather of Daphne du Maurier; political cartoonist of *Punch* and illustrator of *Alice's Adventures in Wonderland* John Tenniel; founder of the Theistic Church Charles Voysey; editor of the *British Medical Journal* Ernest Hart; Frederick Lehmann, the businessman and father of Liberal MP R. C. Lehmann; Pre-Raphaelite artist John Everett Millais; and none other than Dr Price's old acquaintance, Rose Mary Crawshay (1827–1908), the wife of Robert Thompson Crawshay, who had entertained Price many times at various balls and dinners in Cyfarthfa Castle.

Rose, an anti-vivisectionist and women's rights campaigner, was one of the signatories of the declaration to establish the society that night in Thompson's home. She was the only female signatory and the only female member of the council following the departure of Frances Power Cobbe. Aged forty-seven in 1874 and married for twenty-nine years to her estranged husband Robert Crawshay, half-brother of Francis Crawshay, she was elected as vice president of the Bristol and West of England National Society for Women's Suffrage and worked in organisations that led towards the establishment of female colleges in Oxford and Cambridge. In 1871 she was the only woman elected to the first Merthyr School Board and elected chair to Vaynor School Board – one of the first means that women used to rise democratically. Her position on the boards was criticised when she circulated a pamphlet advocating S. D. Williams's support of euthanasia, which caused widespread controversy. Rose Crawshay was a prominent individual in London society, counting Emerson and Darwin among her close friends.

The declaration of that historic meeting of the Cremation Society read,

> We, the undersigned, disapprove the present custom of burying the dead, and we desire to substitute some mode which shall rapidly resolve the body into its component elements, by a process which cannot offend the living, and shall render the remains perfectly innocuous. Until some better method is devised, we desire to adopt that usually known as cremation.

The group began fund-raising to erect a cremation furnace. Papers were written, lectures given and the profile of the cause gradually increased throughout the 1870s. In October 1874 Lady Dilke, wife of radical politician Sir Charles Wentworth Dilke, died aged twenty-six following the birth of her son. Her body was transported to Germany and on her wish was cremated.

Further evidence arose in the case of Henry Crookenden of Kensington, London, who was buried in Brompton Cemetery in August 1878. His sister Eliza Williams protested, explaining she had an addendum to his will, which directed her to ensure he was cremated and his remains placed in his favourite Wedgwood vase. She applied for the body to be exhumed on the understanding it would be buried elsewhere, and it wasn't until March 1879 that she succeeded before his son could object because he was away in India. The body was delivered to London docks and with the help of the Cremation Society was transported to Milan, where the cremation took place as Crookenden wished.[6]

However, the opposition to the notion of cremation became equally as fierce, with handbills distributed in London condemning the practice as 'Horrible Disclosures of Burning Bodies'. In July the Bishop of Lincoln preached 'On Burning of the Body and On Burial' at Westminster Abbey, stating that cremation was incompatible with Christianity as it undermined the belief in the resurrection. *The Lancet* responded with an article questioning this belief, given that some people were killed in explosions or possibly drowned and were eaten by fish – and why wouldn't they be resurrected in just the same way as anyone who was burned? The debate continued in the press with clear indications that the church was uncertain of its stance on the subject.

Aside from the religious factions, there was also the case of law, which effectively was determined by Dr William Price's court case of 1884. Until then

> the legality of cremation in the UK was uncertain. There was no statutory rule specifically prohibiting it, nor any statutory rule requiring dead bodies to be buried. Cremation's legality depended on the vague ambit of a motley collection of common law misdemeanors and on the debatable weight to be attached to judicial remarks about a person's 'right to Christian burial' and other people's correlative duty to arrange one.[5]

Cremations had by now taken place in the United States, with the first in a private crematorium in Washington DC in 1876. Using Dr C. Siemen's design of a furnace, the Cremation Society of Great Britain planned to purchase land at East Barnet to establish their first crematorium, but sadly their proposals failed, particularly due to the opposition of the Bishop of Rochester. However, with the good rail links from the capital city, they recognised the area surrounding Woking, Surrey as an ideal location for a crematorium and purchased an acre of land in 1878 close to the vast privately owned cemetery. In October the press announced that the site had been secured to erect a crematorium. By December the Vicar of Woking, Revd Frederick J. Oliphant, wrote to the Home Office expressing his disgust, explaining that residents felt a 'great abhorrence' to it. What followed was a long period of negative publicity and letters appearing in leading newspapers and medical journals where many voiced their 'repugnance' against the project.

A deputation of the society met the Home Secretary Richard Asseton Cross on 20 March 1879 and outlined their desirability of opening a crematorium and how they wanted to proceed with the proposals. Thompson stated the Cremation Society wanted to act in conformity with the government and the Home Secretary issued a Bill to be discussed in Parliament. A question was tabled by the Earl of Onslow in the House of Lords, who wanted it monitored legally that the Cremation Society had vowed not to carry out any cremations until the legal issue was settled. Unprecedented publicity associated with the entire affair occurred and people supported and objected in large number, but it was clear that a decision was made stating the practice of cremation could not be sanctioned except under the authority and regulation of an Act of Parliament. The appointment of a new Home Secretary in Sir William Harcourt did nothing to move the proposals forward, and although animal carcasses had been cremated at the Gorini cremator at Woking to illustrate the clean method of cremation, it was a long six-year wait before the first body was disposed of in this way.

In the meantime, cremations did take place in Dorset with the wife and mother of Captain Thomas Hanham in Manston House, Sturminster Newton. Mrs Hanham died in 1876 and Lady Hanham in 1877 and both expressed a desire to be cremated. Captain Hanham was determined to carry out the wishes and had their bodies encased in lead-lined coffins in a mausoleum in the grounds of the house. He approached the society and asked to use the Woking cremator, but Sir Henry Thompson refused to support the idea, making it clear that no action should take place until it was legalised in Great Britain. Instead Captain Hanham had a specially built chamber in the grounds of his home and the cremation took place there, followed a year later by the body of the man himself. There didn't appear to be any prosecutions by the police for these acts, which was good news for the society, but it still failed to convince them to use Woking, although this event did attract widespread publicity, and possibly the Home Office's bluff for prosecution had not been called. Despite also hearing the case of the Cremation Society, the Home Secretary, fearing cremation might be used to prevent the detection of death following violence or poison, again refused to allow it until Parliament had authorised it by either a general or special act. With the threat of either legal or parliamentary proceedings against them, the Cremation Society was forced to abandon further experiments. From March 1879, the function of the society was restricted to trying to change the public attitude to cremation and it was an event in the quiet dilapidated little Welsh hilltop town of Llantrisant that gave them the power to succeed in their aim.

A whole host of reasons could have influenced Dr William Price in his decision to cremate the remains of his infant 'god-like' child. His studies of Roman and Greek history and his understanding of an appreciation of Hinduism were tantamount to his decision. Hindus believe that destroying the corpse in this way induces a feeling of detachment into the freshly disembodied spirit, helping the soul to pass to the other world. As one of the sixteen rites of passage in life, cremation is the *antim samskar*, or 'last rites' and combines the soul with the universal spirit. Traditionally, widowed Hindu women even threw themselves on the pyre as there was no place for widows in their society. Dr Price's Druidism coupled with his love of nature all supported the method of cremation for the disposal of their dead. One must also be reminded of Dr Price's own outrage at the apparent desecration of the family grave at Bedwas. It is not unreasonable to suggest that Dr Price would have been well aware of the endeavours of the Cremation Society and although his connection with the Crawshays had long since perished, he would have known of Rose Mary Crawshay's involvement in the movement. Whatever his reasoning, he was determined that cremation was the only way in which he would dispose of the corpse of his child, the future reigning deity of a pagan religion.

The *Cardiff & Merthyr Guardian* of February 1884 read,

> Cremation may be the best method of disposing of the dead, but it is not approved of by the country just yet; and anyone who attempts to carry it out incurs considerable risk of interference on the part of his neighbours and the public generally. There have very recently been recorded instances of cremation where the furnace and the other paraphernalia have been provided on the private property of those who wish to carry out the behests of deceased relatives or friends who prefer the quick action of fire to the slow progress of natural decay; but this is only in very isolated cases. It is not quite certain that in a discussion of this question the worm would have altogether the best of the argument against the 'devouring elements,' and perhaps mainly for the reason that the space at disposal in the neighbourhoods of large centres of populations is becoming so limited that one of these days we may have, willy-nilly, to have recourse to cremation, not merely out of sentiments of delicacy for the dead, but out of consideration for the health of the living. Burning the dead was, as our readers are aware, practised by the Greeks and Romans, and HOMER gives us minute particulars as to how it was accomplished. It is beyond dispute that about 1225 B.C. the practice was general in the countries we have mentioned and elsewhere, and the manufacture of costly urns for the reception of the ashes which remained after the fiery process was not only of an extensive character, but it developed artistic instincts which probably had a marked effect in the moulding, designing,

and colouring of these post-mortem depositories and pottery generally. Burying, however, came to be practised by both Greeks and Romans, the former having their burial places at a distance from the towns, the latter near the highways. Half a century before the birth of the SAVIOUR, there was a revival, under SYLLA, of the practice of cremation, and although it became pretty general for a time, busying-places or cemeteries eventually held their own, and became, as they are to this day, the approved depositories of all that is mortal of earth's denizens.[7]

Dr Price planned to cremate his son on his hilltop land in East Caerlan above Llantrisant at around seven o'clock on the evening of 13 January 1884. The paraffin cask was ordered on Saturday 12 January for the ceremony from the wife of John MacCarthy, a hawker of Brynsadler. It was collected by Thomas Tootell, landlord of the Bute Arms, Pontyclun, who left with his horse and trap at six o'clock on Sunday evening, accompanied by Iesu's grieving mother Gwenllian Llewellyn. Leaving her at Tŷ'r Clettwr, Tootell met the doctor at the Cross Keys Hotel on High Street, Llantrisant and was soon rejoined by Gwenllian. That was where he gave his final instructions. Tootell was told to climb the hill above, crossing two fields and on reaching the third field, owned by Price, would set down the cask and oil on the summit of Caerlan, a position that commanded views of the surrounding countryside and could be seen for miles. Gwenllian passed the remains of her baby, wrapped in flannel and over twenty napkins, to the doctor at the Cross Keys. On walking the steep, narrow lane from Commercial Street to Caerlan, Dr Price began the infamous cremation ritual.

At 7.15 p.m. as two local colliers, Uriah Wilkins and Lewis Ajax, were walking home from church on that cold and wintry night, they saw the smoke rising from East Caerlan. Lewis Ajax, a thirty-one-year-old father of four, lived with his wife Ann on High Street. Fellow collier Uriah, aged thirty-six, was residing at Graig Row at the time with his wife Elizabeth and six children.

They climbed the hill and walked through Price's fields to find the doctor engaged in the most macabre of events. Dr Price, clad in a white robe, his hair and beard streaming in the wind, his arms outstretched as if on a crucifix, was chanting a lament in unintelligible Welsh. Before him was the cask of paraffin oil and within it a baby's corpse carefully wrapped in napkins.

Dr Price called out a somewhat corrupted version of a poem written by the sixth-century bard, Taliesin, which occurs in *Angar Cyvyndawd*. It would seem to have been a lament on the soul's ascent to meet the Druidic bard:

> Pedair tywarchen
> Ni wys ei gorphen
> Pwy foch new Cwrwyden hudd
> Ath gyfarthaf, fawr Gadfardd?

Gwr eith gynydd
Ysgyrn niwl,
Rhwyddynt ddau
RhaiaDr gwynt;
Traethallor yng ngolwg
Yr efrau yn ngoddeg;
Yr efrau yn efrog;
Yr efrau yn efrau
Bu Tes;
Hen anwylid, chywyd;
Gwr a rod pan ei ddychwelyd;
Cu welir crymdu, crymdwyn.
Ladatum, laudate Deus.

Translated as:

The four souls, their creation is unknown
What pig or wandering hind shall I greet
O, warrior Bard?
[Then to the burning body]
May he aid thee!
And may ossesous mist
Speed ye, twain!
May prosperous ease be thine,
Through cataracts of wind!
The altar of the sea shore
Is now before me;
The husk is speechless;
The husk is again but a husk;
Long Beloved One is here!
Lovely again will be him, though
Now bent and black on the funeral pile.
On the angular hill of the tumulus!

Then the venerable doctor chanted, until the mountain echoed, the monkish legend, '*Laudatum laudate Esus*'. In a very short time a vast crowd of several hundred faithful worshippers walked from the open doors of the nearby chapels of Tabor, Elim, Penuel and the medieval parish church, and looked upwards at the blaze on the mountainside. They climbed to the summit and formed an immense circle within a safe distance from the fire. They appeared awed by the extraordinary scene before them, and none seemed able to stir a foot. The doctor all the while stood with hands uplifted and face towards heaven.[8] The sight before them filled their hearts with dread, fear and anger.

Until then, Llantrisant's residents had condoned Dr Price's actions as pure eccentricity, and forgave him due to his success as a surgeon, but this was too much to comprehend. For the church and chapel-goers who were flooding the streets from the gaping doors of their places of worship, it was the ultimate act of blasphemy. Thoughts of his well-known Druidic beliefs and their association with the cult of human sacrifice swept away the affectionate good humour which had indulged his eccentricities. Although not understanding his beliefs, the villagers had felt that his reputation for miraculous cures and the mystery of his ceremonies had earned him their respect, although a respect mixed with fear. Now it was being outraged.

All the town knew that a child of about five months, blasphemously named Iesu Grist, had died in the doctor's house at ten o'clock on Thursday night. The gathering had many unanswered questions. Did the baby die naturally or was it murdered, and this his method of disposing of the evidence? Was this a human sacrifice? If not, then at best it was the desecration of the dead. At first no one stirred as the flames leapt four or five feet into the darkness, and the doctor gazed into the heavens, sometimes kicking the cask to make the flames go higher. Residents were transfixed at the sight of the burning pyre, although at first few realised the extent of the act being carried out in their own close-knit community. Steadily, an unruly mob of locals multiplied on the mountain.

Tremendous consternation was caused in Llantrissant [*sic*] ... it seems that at about eight o'clock at night on Sunday attention was drawn to a conflagration on the summit of a hill – or knoll – not far from the residence of Dr Price. Someone entertaining suspicion of the cause, went for the police, and P.C. Francis and P.C. Hoyle at once went to the spot. By this time an immense multitude had gathered together, and were in a state of apparently frenzied excitement. The cause and scene were indeed strange. There stood Dr Price with a cask containing paraffin by him lighted, and into it he had thrown the body of a child supposed to be dead. The doctor was cremating the infant body to all appearance. About all this there was something so weird and fantastic, and to the popular mind so barbarous, that the clamorous attention of the crowd intensified into fury, and it is asserted that but for the presence of the police the venerable doctor would have been lynched, or something akin to it. Some members of the crowd were desirous of making an onset upon him, but it is asserted that the doctor called out that the first man that dared interfere with him he [the doctor] would shoot.

The old man, with a white flowing beard, and wearing curiously cut and coloured raiment, performing a heathen funeral ceremony on the Welsh mountain tops, with no other witnesses than the 'spirits of the hills, with all their dewy hair blown back like flame'. In these parts we know the eccentric individual, and if we are not surprised when we hear of his mysterious doings on the ridges and the elevations in the neighbourhood of his home, and have almost ceased to elevate our eyebrows when we observe him solemnly parading the streets with pea-green unmentionables picked out with scarlet, a snow jumper, and an arrangement of fox skin for a head-dress, it cannot be expected that our breath will be wholly taken away when we hear of his attempting to cremate, with such simple appliances as an old barrel and a quantity of paraffin oil, the body of a child, of which he, an octogenarian, is the self-admitted father. Unfortunately for the object the doctor had in view, his actions were observed, and he soon discovered that instead of performing the rite upon which he had set his heart in the solemn solitude of the hills, he had gathered at his heels a crowd of excited persons who would, so we are informed, have expressed their antagonism to this proceedings in something louder than words, something deeper than sentiment, but for the presence of the custodians of the peace, who, after some difficulty, rescued him from the hands and tongues of his tormentors, and placed him within the security of the police-station.

We have none of us any right to question the sincerity of Dr Price's motives, or to interfere with him in the performance of the religious ceremonies which he believes to be the only 'correct thing'; but it must be added that if in carrying out these ceremonies, and making manifest this belief, he creates, or is likely to create, a breach of the peace, or to bring down upon himself the indignation of the public, then it becomes a matter of duty for those who are charged with seeing that the peace of the realm is not broken to take action. As to the proceedings at the inquest, we have nothing very particular to say. It may not be in accordance with the Druidical law to register the birth of children, but that is neither here nor there. It is the law of the land, and Dr Price, like a good citizen, should have shown the loyalty of his disposition by conforming to it. There may be excuses for the anti-vaccinators, because it is alleged that bad physical results may follow from vaccination; but nothing of the kind can be asserted about the registration of infants, which, for obvious reasons, the State insists upon. No doubt the worthy doctor has been put to considerable pain and inconvenience by recent occurrences, but although he may personally deny himself the consolation which others will have in the reflection that his unusual proceedings were at he bottom of the mischief, he will find, if he chooses to pursue the enquiry, that he has few sympathisers in his misfortunes. If men will do such unreasonable things as to go at night to the top of a mountain to burn in a barrel of paraffin the body of a recently deceased child, he must not expect.[9]

Police Sergeant William Hoyle and Police Constable Francis of Llantrisant Police Station were the first of the authority figures to arrive. Hoyle kicked the barrel hard enough for it to fall and the burning corpse rolled out. Although wrapped in napkins, its gruesome content was clear as the bare chest and exposed arms and legs were well alight. The mob broke into a frenzy, shrieking at the sight of the burning baby's corpse. Women fainted, others cried out in terror.

Albert Davies, a local labourer, hooked a stick into the body and dragged it, still blazing, across the grass to the hedge, where he used turf to extinguish the burning flesh and napkins. Shock, horror, outrage and hatred swelled through the crowd, now numbering 300 people, who became actively hostile and determined to push Price into the barrel amidst calls of 'Let us burn the old devil'.

On Sunday night while the whole country for miles around Llantrisant was, about half past seven, startled by the sudden appearance of immense lurid flames ascending to heaven from the summit of one of the two lofty hills between which the town is situated. It was just as the moment when throngs of people were leaving the many scores of chapels within view of the mountain. Some people seem to have fancied a volcano had shot forth subterranean fires over the mounts; others that the old Eastern worshippers had rekindled once more a *coelgerth* which in English means 'the enormous fire of faith' on one of the Glamorgan hills. The sight was dark, and the fire was of remarkable brilliance and the description furnished eye witnesses reminds one of Leigh Hunt's description of the character if the funeral pyre in which the said Lord Byron burnt the body of the poet Shelley on the Italian shore,

On Sunday night nearly the whole inhabitants of the town and country side ran in the direction of the flames on the hill, which is an elevation of about 1,000ft above the level of the sea ... in an incredibly short time hundreds of people had climbed to the neighbourhood of the fire, when a strange and weird scene met their astonished gaze. The first object they saw was a great circle of fire with a dark form in its centre, from which immense flames ascended; then to complete the picture Dr William Price was seen in a white robe, with his flowing white hair and long white beard falling over his breast. His arms were extended so that with his body, the form of a cross was formed ... in a cask in the centre of the great fire was the dead body of the infant son of his housekeeper ...

The venerable doctor chanted until the mountains echoed ... in a short time a vast multitude gathered ... they appeared awed by this extraordinary scene before them. No one seemed able to stir a foot. The doctor the while stood with hands uplifted and face towards heaven. While the affair was at its height Police Sergeant Hoyle and Police Constable Francis reached the top. But they seemed afraid to arrest the doctor, it being impossible to ascertain in the uncertain light whether he had firearms in his extended hands ... after a little while the doctor's attention was diverted and Police Constable Francis rushed upon him from behind and secured his arms. The many hundreds of men and women then rushed forward cheering. The public seemed to be in threatening mood, and it was every moment feared they would take the law into their own hands. The feeling, especially amongst the women, became still more intense when one of the men lifted out of a cask of paraffin in the centre of the circle of fire, the naked, flaming body of a baby. The constables, however, behaved with great coolness and by their judicious conduct were enabled to convey the doctor down the hill in safety and afters lodged him in the police station. The body of the baby was lodged in an adjoining cell, where I saw it on Monday in a hamper of straw, through the top of which one of the naked little feet projected.

After the doctor was lodged in the cells the vast throng of enraged women and men hurried to the neighbourhood of the doctor's house and it was feared the child's mother would be assaulted. In the house, however, were a dozen large and savage dogs, which have been so trained by the doctor to do everything he commands and that the throng deemed it prudent for keep from the fangs of the guards of the priest of the sun...[10]

Police Constable Philip Francis (No. 163), a man noted for his way with rough public houses, drew his truncheon and threatened to strike the first man who touched Price. The elderly doctor did not share this view of the part that Francis played as his protector, but said he thought he was being dragged off 'like a felon' when he was put in the cell at Llantrisant Police Station on George Street. The crowd did not disperse with the removal of Price, some following him along High Street, past the Bull Ring and its town pump to the place of his incarceration in the shadow of the ruined castle. Others stayed on the fields and near Tŷ'r Clettwr until 3 a.m. in the morning, awaiting his return and perhaps the hope of more excitement.

Sergeant Hoyle travelled to Pontypridd to see his colleague Sergeant Evan Jones, who was unwilling to share in the responsibility of charging the Druid. They visited superintendent Jabez Matthews at 2 a.m., who was sleeping soundly in his Berw Road home and called from the bedroom window, telling them to keep Price locked up until morning when the local magistrate would hear his case. He was made comfortable in the cell until 7 a.m., with coats, two rugs, two blankets and a fire to keep him warm. Until then suspicions grew ever greater over Price's actions, questioning whether he had murdered the infant and was desperately trying to destroy all evidence.

On the following morning, Monday 14 January, he was taken to Pontypridd by the direction of the stipendiary magistrate for the district, Mr Gwilym Williams (1839–1906), of Miskin Manor, a well-respected freeman of the town. The magistrate, whose statue stands in the vicinity of

Cardiff law courts at Cathays Park, had been a stipendiary for Pontypridd and Rhondda since 1872, and well known as the 'terror of malefactors'. He had also heard many a small court case involving Dr Price, but never anything as extreme. He bailed Dr Price to appear to the charge of misdemeanour in common law in not burying the body decently.

One of the first to visit him on his release and return to Tŷ'r Clettwr was Morien, who remembered,

> On Monday afternoon I found the doctor at his own house. He was in a very serious mood, with the dirt from the smoke of the night before on his face and surplice. He told me that what he had endeavoured to do was no sacrifice. The child was already dead and he simply attempted to liberate the particles constituting the dead body by means of fire instead of letting the body rot in the earth. He moreover, obeyed the ancient law of Wales, which was older and higher than the law of England. Inasmuch as the law had ignored him in the matter he would only recognize the law of Cymru.[10]

Morien later visited his Druidic mentor Myfyr Morganwg to explain the ghastly occurrence, to which Myfyr answered,

> Dr Price is a very strange man, but on this occasion he merely attempted to revive a very good old custom. The customs of burning the dead was well-nigh universal in remote ages in this country as well as in many other countries of the old world. Read Homer and you will find it was the general custom in the most refined period in the history of Greece. Open the turmoil in on our own mountains – the *cista* – and you will find that the bones are burnt. No doubt it is the sweetest mode of disposing of mortal remains, for it is the quickest mode of restoring the corporeal particles to their simple elements. It also agrees better than burying with the venerable Druidic theory of transmigration which is so little understood at the present day. But which is so closely associated with the doctrine of evolution.[11]

Sergeant Hoyle discussed the possibility of the child being murdered with Coroner E. B. Reece, supported by Superintendent Matthews. The infant had died suddenly and there were no birth or death certificates. The public wanted justice to be done, but the four believed in discussing it with Price without recourse to an inquest.

'There is no desire on the part of the coroner to hold an inquest if you will allow a medical man to see the child,' was the letter delivered on the morning of the cremation. Dr Price, however, saw no reason why this should be necessary. He did not believe in registration and throughout the ensuing court hearings, would not involve Gwenllian Llewellyn, refusing to admit she was even the mother of the baby.

An inquest was held on Tuesday 15 January at Llantrisant Police Station before the coroner and a jury, of which Price's friend, Mr Roderick Lewis of the Wheatsheaf Hotel on High Street, was the foreman. Crowds gathered along George Street and at the Town Pump on the Bull Ring to await news of the investigation. A post-mortem examination had been made on the charred remains by Dr Naunton Davies of Llantrisant, Dr Martin Davies of Bridgend and Dr William Davies. Gwenllian Llewellyn 'a young woman of about 30 to 35 years' – was sworn and asked by the Coroner E. Bernard Reece: 'Is the deceased your child?'

Gwenllian replied, 'I object to giving you evidence as I understand that the object of the inquest is to commit me for a crime of which I know nothing.'

Reece said, 'Well, if you don't give any evidence I must commit you to gaol. I have no notion of any crime at all having been committed; I simply ask you a plain question, and unless you give me a plain answer, I must commit you, though I should be sorry to do so. I again ask you – was deceased your child or not?'

'No, sir,' she answered and sat down, but Reece told her to stand up and said, 'Was the child living in the house of Dr Price?'

Gwenllian didn't answer and when asked again whether she would give an answer she said, 'No, sir.' Since she refused to give any evidence Reece impatiently stated, 'Well, then, I give her in your charge, if you please. Take her away, and I will make out the commitment to gaol and sign it. It will be all in due order. She is not to hold any communication with anybody. That will be the plan.'

She was arrested by Sergeant Hoyle and taken into custody. The jury believed she had been instructed not to answer any questions by her partner.

Dr Price was called and immediately suggested he ought not to be examined because, 'It is very likely I shall be charged with killing the child, perhaps. I have a right not to be examined.'

The coroner agreed, adding that before he refused to answer a question, he should hear it first. He asked if Gwenllian was his housekeeper to which he said, 'Well there is a story about that and I object to answer.'

Bruce asked, 'Do you object to say whether this was her child or not?'

'Yes I do. I say the child was mine. I will swear that.'[11]

The inquest continued,

The coroner: 'But it must have had a mother.'

Dr Price: 'That may be, but it does not follow that Gwenllian Llewellyn was the mother.'

The coroner: 'No, I only ask you if this child was that of Gwenllian Llewellyn?'

Dr Price: 'And I refuse to answer the question. But I tell you point-blank that the child was mine, and I could show this if I were only called and addressed privately. I should give you perfect evidence.'

The coroner: 'Why don't you do so now?'

Dr Price: 'No. The fact is this that very likely I shall be pulled up for aiding and abetting an innocent woman for burning the child. It is true I burnt the child. I admit doing it.'

The coroner: 'With that I and the jury have nothing to do.'

Dr Price: 'I had a right to do it, and would have done it.'

The coroner: 'I ask no questions about that.'

Dr Price: 'The child was mine. I can prove it.'

The coroner: 'And it is a great credit to you, I am sure. But the object of this inquiry is, as the child was not registered, to know whether the child died from natural causes or not.'

Dr Price: 'I have no doubt of it.'

The coroner: 'Well, then, what I want to know is, who was the mother. That is a necessary thing.'

Dr Price: 'It is not necessary, because I tell you it was my child.'

The coroner: 'But it is necessary to know who is the mother of the child?'

Dr Price: 'And I refuse to answer.'

The coroner: 'Then I must commit you.'

Dr Price: 'Do as you please. You can never make me answer.'

The coroner: 'What is the use of my committing you?'

Dr Price: 'The fact is, when a medical man attends anybody he attends that person in confidence. He does not open his mouth until permission is given to him.'

The coroner: 'I don't want to annoy you. You put it on the grounds of professional etiquette, then?'

Dr Price: 'Oh, yes; certainly. I was bound by an oath before I left the college in London – before having the diploma in London – not to disclose anything respecting my employers.'

The coroner: 'Will you tell whether this child had been living under your care?'

Dr Price: 'It lived under my care and protection since its birth.'

The coroner: 'Then you have any objection to say whether he was ill or not?'

Dr Price explained that the child fell ill the previous week. He had been healthy at first, but teething pains took place and convulsions supervened. He was up two or three nights with the child and took extreme care and precautions, but on Thursday night he died in a convulsion.

Dr Price recalled, 'It thrived commonly for two to three days, and then had what is called whitemouth which almost destroyed it. I had no mother for it and no milk, so I had a goat to give it milk, but milk did not agree with it. Well the only thing that agreed with it was what we Welsh people called '*uwd sugaethan*' or flummery, a sweet, soft pudding of stewed fruit and thickened with cornstarch, and on that it progressed beautifully. It was a small infant, very large head and small limbs and I believe never intended for any great work. Well, it proceeded in that way until it was five months old, and I would not suffer it to go to sleep with anybody but myself, I spent with it every night and took care of it ... I think it was on Wednesday morning, about half past five o'clock I was perfectly awake and was for three nights watching it afterwards – in my sight and at my side it had what is called a convulsion fit and was in that fully an hour ... subsequently it was restored and took food in the course of the day. Its bowels were relaxed, without having medicine whatever and it had what is called diarrhoea and I fancy it was too violent and I gave him a dose of rhubarb ... on Thursday night about ten o'clock he died in the cradle in the front room where I was watching him. I took great care of him from the time of his birth.'[12]

Dr Price went on to explain that the child, named Iesu Grist, had not been christened but would have been, if it had lived, on Y Maen Chwyf because that was where he had christened Hiarlhes four decades before.

The coroner then suggested to Dr Price that, as far as Miss Llewellyn was concerned, she ought to corroborate what he had said of the child.

Dr Price replied, 'I don't now what she will do in the world. I leave that between you and her. She is perfectly competent to act for herself.'

The coroner again remarked that the child had not been registered.

Dr Price: 'But we Welsh bards – and I consider myself a Welsh bard – teach that it is not necessary to register or baptise, and that ultimately this will be the universal belief of the Island of Britain.'

The coroner responded with, 'But it is for the time being, you see, necessary.'

Eventually Gwenllian came before the coroner again and gave the same explanation as Price over the health of the baby. Once the coroner was satisfied, she was allowed to go.

After hearing the evidence of Dr Naunton Davies that the post-mortem examination showed the death was due to asphyxia, which might have been produced by convulsions, the jury returned a verdict of death from natural causes and not foul play. The death certificate was signed by E. Bernard Reece, Coroner for Glamorganshire and registrar Howel Davies. More poignantly, Iesu Grist's name does not appear on the death certificate, only as an 'un-Christened child'.

The police made an application to the coroner to bury the child, but Dr Price objected and demanded he had the body back, 'I wish to ask you, Mr Coroner, to order the remains of the child to be given up to me.'

The coroner responded with, 'All I can say upon that is that I will give you the permission to bury. I will sign it.'

Superintendent Matthews intervened to suggest that perhaps the burial order should be handed over to him for transfer to Price if he promised on his word of honour to bury the child decently, or Matthews could keep the body until after the magisterial proceedings.

Dr Price added, 'I insist on the usual practice of the coroner's court,' to which the coroner responded, 'I cannot refuse, as Dr Price says he is the father of the child.'

Dr Price would not give the required pledge to Supt Mathews, and the officer said that the body would be retained by the police until after Wednesday's issue at the police court.

In reply, Dr Price, taking away the order, said: 'You do just as you like, and I will do just as I like.'[13]

A penalty of £3 on each of the two charges was presented.

The *South Wales Daily News* of 16 January 1884 stated,

The sensational incident which resulted in an inquest yesterday, at the Police-station, Llantrisant, is one of those rare events which bring to the front some very eccentric persons. Dr Price may be regarded as a sort of unique personage. To those who live at a distance and know nothing whatsoever about him, the account of the cremation, and more especially the account of the inquest, will appear almost incredible; but those who know who and what Dr Price is would rather be surprised than otherwise if something out the usual course had not followed the death of any human being under his care. We are inclined to think that those who have read the report of the inquest which we publish in another column will feel thankful that it will not be a final inquiry.

There are several incidents connected with the case which the public will certainly like to have cleared up before the remains of the child are disposed of either by burial or cremation. We do not attach any blame to the woman, who declined to be examined by the coroner even to the extent of admitting or denying the maternity of the child. If there is any likelihood of a criminal charge being based upon the extraordinary proceedings which took place upon the hill in the neighbourhood of Pontypridd, it is not to be expected that any person would voluntarily give evidenced which might subsequently be used to be her prejudice. At the same time, the refusal of the woman to say whether the child was her own or not makes it all the more imperative that there should be a thorough investigation of the case. The child must have had some mother, and that mother ought to be discoverable. Then, again, the attempt to cremate the child on the day before the inquest was expected to take place, is suggestive but is not inconsistent with perfect innocence of the part of those who endeavoured to do away with the remains. Of course, if the attempted cremation had proved successful, there could have been no inquest worthy of the name. The coroner's jury, it is true, has returned a verdict to the effect that the child died of natural causes, but we have to bear in mind the testimony of Dr N.W. Davies to the effect that the child had suffered from mal-nutrition for a long time prior to death. This mal-nutrition does not, of course, imply that the child was starved by anyone in charge of it, but it affords sufficient ground for the expectation that the whole case will be thoroughly gone into before the magistrates; and that evidence will yet be adduced to satisfy every reasonable person that though the infant was in the hands of a very eccentric parent, it had all the attention that love and skill combined could have bestowed upon it.[11]

Dr Price was brought before the stipendiary magistrate, Mr Gwilym Williams, at Pontypridd on Wednesday 16 January 1884 and charged by the police superintendent, Jabez Matthews. The police prosecutor was Mr Rhys, of the firm W. H. Morgan & Rhys.

The court was crowded with little room to stand in the gallery, let alone sit and Dr Price, clad in his usual costume, took his seat in the defendant's box. The moment the name 'Dr Price, Llantrisant' was called, there was complete silence in court and Mr Rhys said he prosecuted on behalf of the police, and, as the case was one 'happily of a very uncommon kind', he thought it should be thoroughly investigated and would ask for a remand to enable them to place the facts before him and get his direction on the best method of proceeding.

He felt that Dr Price had rendered himself liable to an indictment at common law for misdemeanour, for indecently exposing the body, and in not taking it decently covered to the place of burial, thereby offending the feelings of the public generally. The case was felt to be similar to one cited in 'Peterdorff's Abridgement', where it is laid down:

> The common law casts upon a person under whose roof a death takes place the duty of providing sepulchre for the body, and of carrying it to the grave decently covered. Every such person cannot keep a body unburied, neither can he do anything to prevent Christian burial. He cannot cast out a body, or do violence to the feelings or the health of the living, neither can he be permitted to carry it uncovered to the grave.

Mr Rhys went on to argue that Dr Price had violated all these regulations as several women had fainted at the cremation ceremony, and unquestionably Dr Price had caused considerable annoyance to his neighbours. Mr Rhys applied to the stipendiary for an adjournment.

The stipendiary thought they had better call sufficient evidence to justify a remand, to bear out Rhys's opening statement and so Sergeant Hoyle was sworn and said, 'I was on duty at Llantrisant and at about half past seven o'clock I saw a large bonfire in the field occupied by Dr Price. They call it Caerlan, and it is near Llantrisant. I proceeded there at once, in company with several others. When I got there I saw a large cask, burning. The flames went up four or five feet in the air. Dr Price was standing alongside. He kicked the cask several times with his feet to make the fire burn faster. After what the doctor told me before – in the morning – I was rather cautious about going up to him. I drew his attention and then collared him, and put my arms around him. On turning over the cask the body of a male child fell out. It was tied in a lot of old clothes, and they were all in a blaze.'[14]

Mr Rhys asked about the condition of the body to which Hoyle replied, 'The body was all in flames, it had apparently been soaked in mineral oil.' The stipendiary interrupted, 'Never mind apparently. Appearances are very deceptive.' Hoyle replied, 'Well it was soaked in oil.'

The stipendiary then asked, 'But what we want to know is, how the body was tied, and what appearance it presented.'

Sergeant Hoyle replied, 'It was tied in white napkins, and was burning. Paraffin or benzoline mineral oil was round about it. I caught up the body out of the flames, and threw a lot of wet earth to put the fire out. I then found the body had been burnt a good deal. The shoulder and legs, and all over the surface of the body there was slight discolouration – it was charred. I heard Dr Price say yesterday that the child had died at about ten o'clock on Thursday night.'

When asked about the crowds who began to gather in the vicinity of the cremation, Sergeant Hoyle explained, they were 'In a very excited state. They threatened to lynch the doctor and I had great difficulty in keeping back the crowd. Several women were in a fainting state. There was a crowd of several hundred people after him, hallowing and groaning. In consequence of the feelings of the crowd I had to protect Dr Price's house that night. It was nearly three o'clock in the morning before I could get the crowd away.'

Hoyle also explained that napkins were wrapped around the body but the legs were exposed and he could see the face of the child. The stipendiary also drew attention to the inquest, where it was ascertained Dr Price was the father, but the mother's identification was still not known.

Dr Price was invited to cross-examine Sergeant Hoyle and stood remaining silent for some time before the stipendiary said, 'Now is the time, not when it suits you, but when it suits me!' Dr Price turned to Hoyle and asked questions relating to the inquest in particular, and the outcome being the child died of natural causes. He also asked why the body of his baby had not been returned to him as yet and Hoyle said it was the decision of his superior officer, Superintendent Matthews not to allow him the return of the body, which was being kept at Llantrisant Police Station, until he was ordered to bury it.

At this point Dr Price turned to the stipendiary and said, 'I demand the remains of my child. It was my child. I demand the remains to bury just as I please and not as you please or anybody else. I demand them!'

The stipendiary said, 'It is no good going on like that. I will deal with the point when it comes before me in a proper way. Do you wish to ask any further questions on the evidence given today?' Dr Price responded, 'No your worship.'

Superintendent Mathews then recalled and repeated what Dr Price had spoken at the coroner's court as to the relationship of Gwenllian Llewellyn. Dr Price said that she could go in and out of the house as she liked, that she did all the work for him, and that there was an agreement between them, which had been executed by her of her own free will, and in the presence of her uncle and aunt, and that the reason he had this agreement drawn up was because he did not like the idea of a divorce court. Hoyle added, 'I heard her repeat that the child was hers.'

The stipendiary at this point said, 'It is my intention to remand the further hearing of this charge against you until this day week, Dr Price. I will admit you to bail upon the same recognisance as before [£200].'

Dr Price answered 'Very good. Now with respect to the remains of my infant child and son.'

'Yes?' the stipendiary responded, followed by a long pause. 'What is your application?'

The doctor replied, 'I apply to you for the delivery of them to me instantly.'

'Instantly?' the stipendiary questioned.

'Instantly!' Price replied.

The stipendiary said, 'I am afraid I cannot comply with your request, then, instantly, or at a longer or further date. My impression is that the law gives to the police the power to take upon themselves the execution of a duty where they consider the proper custodian of that child is wanting in that duty. I think that your conduct has been, in the language of the case cited, an outrage, or that you did violence to the feelings of the people who happened to be your neighbours. I am willing, if you will give me your word that you will dispose of the body of this child in the usual manner adopted in this country, to order the police to give up the body of the child to you, but not on any other condition. If you will give me a verbal undertaking that you will bury the child in the manner usually adopted in this country – in a manner not to outrage the feelings of your neighbours – I will agree to hand you over the body of your child, but not on any other condition. I understand that the same condition was put before the superintendent of police at the termination of the inquiry yesterday, but you declined – that is, made no promise. If you are willing to make me that promise, I will take your word for it, and will allow you to have custody of the body of the child.'[14]

'Very well, sir, I will,' Dr Price said.

'You will give me your word?' asked the stipendiary.

'Yes, sir.'

'That being so, the police will have orders to give you the body of the child.'

Dr Price said, 'My bail is here, Daniel Pritchard.'

The stipendiary requested Dr Price to see that the child was covered. The police would be required to place the remains in a coffin, or a box, or some equivalent.

Dr Price said, 'It is now in a box, covered with a number of napkins.'

'You must have that,' said the stipendiary, to which Dr Price added, 'Oh, I will take care of that, you may rely on that.'

Dr Price and his bail were then bound over in £100 each for his attendance at the adjourned proceedings on the following Wednesday, and the party then left the court. Dr Price went to the New Inn Hotel in Taff Street afterwards, and a large group of people remained outside to witness his departure.[14]

Between six and seven o'clock that evening Price, with his manservant, Emmanuel John, better known as the second Y Mochyn Du (The Black Pig), went to the police station to collect the body. He took it to an empty house and stable on Heol y Sarn, opposite the Llantrisant Inn and alongside the Butchers Arms. It was there that he fed a fat cow he kept there, and by the light of a candle they chopped up three buckets of turnips.

As he had left the police station only hours before bearing the body of Iesu Grist, four men watched with curiosity as Price and his companion took the body in the building. They waited outside but when the sound of chopping was heard a menacing crowd gathered to listen to what they thought was the doctor dismembering the body. There was also a burning fog across the town and hundreds of people waited outside and when, about midnight, the doctor came out, he was hustled and pelted with stones, and had to take shelter in the Bear Inn. Eventually retreating to Tŷ'r Clettwr at 11 p.m., after climbing a series of garden walls and crossing the Common, he hid the body under his bed until the time came for a second cremation.

Earlier that night the infuriated mob attacked his house while Gwenllian was alone inside. The incident began with one of the crowd hurling a stone and smashing a front window in Tŷ'r Clettwr. Fortunately for Gwenllian, the door was locked and she had four of the doctor's wolfish-looking dogs in the room, who barked furiously. She also reached for two of the pistols kept in the house and loaded them both. Standing behind the dogs, with a pistol in each hand, she shouted a warning to those who were hammering at the door, threatening to shoot the first person that forced entry. Her bravery worked, for she kept the mob at bay until the police arrived, followed hours later by Price, his friend and the baby's corpse.

Gwenllian recalled in 1888,

I remember that on that particular evening I was sitting half asleep near the fire expecting the doctor home, when, about ten o'clock I was startled to hear the loud howling of an infuriated crowd outside the house, and, just as I was rising from my chair, several large stones were hurled in through the window. Fortunately, the door was locked, and I had the dogs, so I was not afraid. The dogs barked furiously and would have torn to pieces any man that dared enter the house. I had also several firearms in my possession and, having loaded them, I stood behind the dogs, having a pistol in each hand. I gave the crowd to understand that I would shoot the first man that tried to force an entrance. By these means I kept them at bay and eventually they dispersed.

A statement from the *Pontypridd Chronicle* of 18 January 1884 stated,

During the past week the people of Llantrisant, like the Athenians of old, can think of nothing but the latest news. They eagerly snatch up the least scrap of intelligence respecting Dr William Price's defunct baby, named Hesus the Anointed. There is no doubt that all in South Wales who know the aged doctor feel a peculiar interest in him, it is no wonder, therefore that his offspring, though the better part of it is now, according to the doctor's view. In the Elysian fields should be regarded with peculiar interest. It is because the people of Llantrisant are so fond of Dr Price that they are in such a rage with him at the present moment. Dr Price declares most solemnly that he desired to cremate his child, and thus save the mortal remains from corruption, because he loved it as a father should love his own flesh and blood. On the other hand, the inhabitants, naturally fond of all babies and particularly fond of the baby of the descendant of the Mayor of Caerphilly, who superintended the building of the Pyramids of Egypt as Dr Price describes himself – will not have such indignity offered to the remains of the unlucky infant if they can prevent it.

On Thursday morning the tidings were flashed over the country that Dr Price, returning home on Wednesday night after the magisterial investigation at Pontypridd, had cremated the baby during the night, and that riot was on among the inhabitants. I was quickly on the road to the town of the three saints … visions of a smoking town, a howling mob, and a fugitive Druid spurred me forward … I came to Dr Price's modest residence. The first thing that attracted my attention was a large hole in one of the panes of glass of the front window. Then I saw Mr Roderick Lewis, who is a king or perpetual mayor of the town. He told me that the night before had witnessed a tremendous row in the streets and that the aged doctor, as well as Gwen Llewellyn, had experienced a narrow escape … the deepest feeling of exasperation against Dr Price was still felt. This had been deepened by the rumour that the doctor had cut the baby into bits in an uninhabited house during the night ... Women groaned and men swore, and the storming of the house seemed imminent. The sound of chopping continued uninterruptedly. Someone was asking whether chopping up babies was a Druidic custom ... the horror that night of the sound of 'chop, chop, chop,' in the building ... after a while a most horrible stench pervaded the atmosphere and the crowd instantly jumped to the conclusion that the Druid was sacrificing the body ... by way of emphasising their Christian feelings they began to hurl stones through an upper window, the lower one being protected by strong shutters ...

Stones were pelted, however, and under a shower of them Dr Price and Mochyn Du, with the box, escaped into the Bear Inn, the doors of which were instantly closed and barred. That doctor was terribly frightened and trembled violently ... Hoyle and Acting Sergeant Oliver were in the crowd doing all they could to pacify the people who now numbered several hundred ... most of the throng then left and hurried down to the town in the direction of Dr Price's residence ... Gwen Llewellyn was seen cocking firearms ... the crowd gradually melted away ... Dr Price, Mochyn Du and Mr Williams, landlord of the Bear, had climbed the wall of the back of the yard and passed into the fields ... they reached the Common from which they could hear the hubbub of the streets ... the night was excessively dark and the paths rough and devious ... exhausted they reached the doctor's house in safety.[15]

Further reports read,

This morning intense excitement was produced throughout the neighbourhood adjacent to Llantrissant, by intelligence that Dr Price, of cremation notoriety, had, despite his promise to the magisterial bench on Wednesday, burnt last night the body of the child, five months old (his own), which he had endeavoured to cremate last Sunday night. It was further stated that Dr Price had, before cremating the remains, actually chopped them to pieces. Subsequently personal inquiries elicited the following particulars. At about eight o'clock in the evening, Dr Price went to the police-station, Llantrisant, and demanded the body of his child. He had kind of biscuit box in his hand to carry it. The body was duly handed to him, cased in the old box, and with napkins over it. He put the last box in the other, and then walked away, He proceeded straight to an untenanted shop of his, out of the main thoroughfare. The door was closed, and there Dr Price and his companion remained.

Presently strange chopping sounds were heard, and the police state there was also a strong smell of burning. But this Dr Price denies. At this time a motley crowd had gathered outside, and a messenger fetched the police. There was a rush to the house door, and it was apparently forced in a little. Execrations were loud and general, for it was believed that the doctor was committing the mutilation and sacrifice by fire afterwards declared to have taken place. The doctor came out; so did Morgan John. The enraged crowd closed round them at once, and the doctor was hustled and maltreated in such a threatening fashion that he darted (the box still in his hand) into the Bear Inn for protection. The crowd was maddened by his escape, and proceeded to the doctor's house, which is situate on the side of the main thoroughfare.

Miss Gwenllian Llewellyn, the housekeeper (25, and not 35 years old), who is reputed to be the child's mother, as she was the person fined for its non-registration, was about household duties at the time, awaiting the doctor's arrival home. The clamour of the crowd was, however, unmistakeable. In it there was anger and determined menace. With remarkable self-possession, Miss Llewellyn instantly ran upstairs and fetched a loaded revolver. The nine or ten dogs which Dr Price has on his premises were also, I am told, ranged in position. Without flinching, Miss Llewellyn then, sitting down, dauntlessly told the would-be assailants that if they came in on the premises she would with the revolver finish what the dogs would leave unfinished. The police were willing, if necessary, to aid the woman but she said she did not require it. Eventually between ten and eleven o'clock, the crowd, which numbered many hundreds, dispersed, and Miss Llewellyn was left again in supreme solitude.

Meanwhile Dr Price made his exist from the Bear Inn, through the back, clambered over hedges and ditches, mud-stained, and clad in but light clothing, though it was a cold winter night. A friend gave him shelter for a little. But it was not till he had wandered about yet longer that rounding Llantrisant Common he at last got home. He got in by a single private entrance. It was then eleven o'clock. The family had retired to rest. People were in the streets, but there was no further molestation of the premises of Dr Price or the occupants.

Now comes the strange part of the story. The police still insist that there was a strong smell of burning about the unoccupied house. Dr Price, however, denies positively and emphatically, and without the slightest qualification, that the child was burnt. He was not, he says, chopping the child's body, but chopping turnips. He asserts that he has the body of the infant at the house, but has refused to show it. The child, he says, was his, and he has a right to do what he considers proper with it consistent with his promise to the magisterial bench. He points out that when he left the premises where he was mobbed the box was still with him. The stipendiary magistrate for the district has been advised of the whole circumstance of last night. The same course will be taken with regard to the Public Prosecutor.

The housekeeper is a complete convert to the doctor's cremation views. She is, she says, resolved that the doctor shall cremate her remains should he survive her; and she will, she further states, see that the doctor's body is cremated should she survive him. The doctor also informed me to-day that had he any doubt as to the cremation of his body after death by person entrusted with that duty, he would cremate himself. 'I have', he says, 'enough pluck left for that.'[16]

Dr Price stated that after leaving the police station yesterday evening, he and his companion were followed by four persons whom he distinctly saw, and when they subsequently went out of the building these four persons were still standing with their backs against the wall of the premises. These individuals, Dr Price, if I rightly understand him, believes to have been the head and front of last night's discordant proceedings. The doctor also says that he had stones flung at him. There were two police officers on the road at that time, and saw the four men indulge, remarks the doctor, in their abusive process. It was because the stones came 'flying about' so 'thick and fast' that he and John went and sought the refuge in the Bear Inn. 'It was for his safety and not for my own', said the doctor, 'that I went to the Bear'. 'Henry Williams of the Bear' helped them from his garden on to the Common, and then they went by Henry's father's house. The box, with the infant, was still kept safe, and found final lodging with the doctor at the doctor's own abode. Dr Price lays emphasis on the circumstances that he was very unfairly treated – and old man of eight-four left to roam about at that hour of a winter's night in the his shirt sleeves.

In order to make the point respecting the burning of the body clear, I repeated to Dr Price the question – 'Is it not true that you burn the body?'

Dr Price: 'Wholly untrue. It is a lie. I have got the body, and no one shall take it from me. They [the crowd] tried, though, to burst the place open.'

I put it to the doctor that he had, no doubt, thoroughly satisfied himself as to the 'reasonableness' of cremation, from his point of view.

Dr Price replied, 'Yes,' and added: 'It is the custom of the country – of Druids all over the world. Cremation was the process practised here in the polished age of Greece.' Here the doctor launched forth in to a lengthy and novel disquisition upon the theory, which perhaps it may be advisable to again reproduce. The child which had died was the final glory of the bardic lineage. On the back of the steed, again, was the figure of a man riding and brandishing a spear. These characters denoted that it would have had a magnificent career had it lived. It was not strong of body, but its brain development was immense. It was the son of 'Alun, the god of all the nations of the East'.

Miss Llewellyn, the housekeeper, was no less reticent upon the peculiarities of the child, and remarked to me that it had just before death uttered a sound which the doctor distinctly declared to be 'Welsh'.

Dr Price speaks with bitterness of the fact that since yesterday two of his most valuable fowls have been stolen from the place where he kept them. He is not slow to express his suspicions as to the probable culprit.[17]

By Friday night the town of Llantrisant had become subdued to a great extent. Dr Price would still not give any further information as to the whereabouts of the body, and the police awaited the instructions and advice of the public prosecutor, Sir J. Maule. There was an extra policeman or two in the district, as a precaution against another onset on the doctor, but everything remained calm in the area.[18]

A few days later and Morien entered another article in the local press, adding that no stirring incidents had occurred in Llantrisant, but like a private investigator had visited the 'Holy Places' of the surgeon in the locality. One was the dwelling house itself and the other was the house and stable where Dr Price kept a fat cow, cocks and hens and the large collection of dogs which Morien claimed was due to the doctor's belief in the 'transmigration of souls'. One of them was a black dog and on Dr Price holding its nose the little animal wagged its tale and looked up 'joyfully' at her master, to which Dr Price said, 'Bless you, your eyes are exactly like those of my mother.'

As for the house where the animals were kept, Morien entered the empty building, much to the astonishment of another journalist who visited the town and was clearly afraid of Dr Price and his actions. When Price arrived on the scene he took both men inside the building and then locked the door, with the second journalist looking alarmed and at that point Dr Price lost his temper. 'Go damo!' he shouted. 'Where are my cocks?' His birds had gone, and he believed the police had stolen them, then he flew from room to room calling on the birds. The journalists were shown the fat cow and then walked out of the building, 'glad of not having been either eaten or cremated'. Morien followed Dr Price to Tŷ'r Clettwr to meet Gwenllian,

a superior looking young woman, both as regards intelligence and appearance. Her forehead is the brow of Minerva. And her eyes beam with intelligence. That she is devoted to the extraordinary doctor is patent to everyone. His slightest behests have for her more potency than a mandate from a king ... I saw nothing to lead me to doubt that she was thoroughly devoted to the doctor and his strange affairs. The doctor, after a friendly chat, opened a box and taking out an old volume, seated himself near the window which is crowed with geranium pots ... the book was entitled *The Poems of the Old Welsh Bards*. The word and spelling were, to ordinary mortals obsolete, but then, Dr Price is not an ordinary man, and he proceeded quite familiarly to expound the teachings of the old Welsh prophets. I could almost have concluded by the apparent ease with which the doctor explained his theories that Taliesin was brother to the Mayor of Caerphilly, that Llwyarch Hen had only recently left the doctor's residence, and that King Arthur had spent his recent holidays under the roof of the Llantrisant Priest of the Sun.[19]

Under the 'Talk of the Week' column in the *South Wales Daily News* at this time an interesting article referred to the legal process involved in the case:

The talk is that although cremation is not against the law of the land, it is not safe to practise it in the eyes of the public, who may be apt to be shocked at the post-mortem spectacle. Dr Price, in his singular escapade on the Llantrisant knoll, which is his own property it is said, has eclipsed all his previous performances in eccentric directions. He has also, I believe, transgressed the law. Cremation is not, as far as I can learn, illegal, provided it be accomplished minus the obnoxious details of last Sunday evening, though it is a method which is not so far advanced in public estimation as to render its adoption at all general. If Dr Price had built him a furnace, and provided the adjuncts to decent cremation in the manner we read of the other day, it would have been no doubt a nine days' wonder, and then an end to it; but then, I suppose that this would not have been Druidism as the venerable doctor believes in it and hence the tar barrel or paraffin cask, as if he had been about to burn a 'Guy Fawkes'. I do not think the present charge against Dr Price is likely to succeed. There is something vague about 'a misdemeanour in common law in not burying the body decently'. There may be many ideas as to what decency may be. Is it not an offence – and I put it forward with all humility in the face of the light and leading legal luminaries by whom we are surrounded – to bury the body of a child before such child has been duly registered? If the Public Prosecutor's opinion is to be obtained on Dr Price's case, the query might be put to him, without any harm being done. It is a more serious offence, one would think, than 'burying indecently', whatever that may mean.[16]

At Pontypridd Police Court on the following Wednesday 23 January, Price appeared to answer the charge before Mr Ebenezer Lewis, Dr Leigh and none other than Francis R. Crawshay, the son of his beloved late friend. It would be ironic if F. R. Crawshay was the child Dr Price had delivered in Caesarian section all those years previously. The crowded court, including many Llantrisant people who faced the inclement weather that day, heard how Dr Price appeared to answer the charge of 'exposing the body of his child'.

Dr Price was present to answer a charge of misdemeanour by not burying a dead body decently and bowed courteously to the bench as he entered. The case had been adjourned in order that Mr Rhys, the prosecuting solicitor, could correspond upon the subject with Sir John Maule QC, the public prosecutor. As the correspondence was still continuing, Superintendent Matthews asked for another week's adjournment after the magistrates' clerk, Mr Stockwood, asked whether the negotiations had been completed.

The magistrates asked Dr Price if he was content with the adjournment and whether his surety, Mochyn Du, was present, to which Dr Price replied 'yes' to both questions. The doctor also requested the hearing took place at Pontypridd and not Llantrisant as there was insufficient room. The doctor then left the court, followed through the pouring rain by a crowd of people.

What is clear by the reports of the newspapers and the court is the uncertainty over how the public prosecutor would administer the legal proceedings, given the complexity of the case as

it is rumoured that the said gentlemen have explored all the statutes available from the time of the Druids without succeeding in discovering anything prohibiting the cremation of dead bodies. It has transpired that the Public Prosecutor seems reluctant to move at all in the matter, and inclines to shift the responsibility of the prosecution, which he has been consulted about, to the shoulders of the Clerk of the Peace for the County. That functionary earnestly protests that he has nothing to do with such matters, having, probably arrived at the conclusion after a patient search of the statutes which have engaged so much of the time and keen attention of the local legal gentlemen above referred to.[20]

A local correspondent wrote,

I learn that the Public Prosecutor has intimated his perfect acquiescence in the prosecution against Dr Price instituted by the police authorities. It appears likely, too, that another charge will be preferred against the doctor – that of non-registration of the child before death. Should Mr Gwilym Williams, the local stipendiary, deem that the charge of misdemeanour is proved against defendant, the case will be sent for trial, it is presumed, to the assizes.[20]

Morien, determined to ensure not a day went by without including an article in a newspaper concerning the case, wrote extensively of the history of burning rites of the past. If Morien's *History of Pontypridd and Rhondda* (1904) is anything to go by, then little notice should be taken of his abilities as a historian, given his bizarre fabrication of facts. On putting forward a translation of the poem he chanted at the cremation, claiming they were from the poetry styled 'mystical' and found in Iolo's *Myvyrian Archaeology*, as they refer to the transmigration of the soul:

> The expression, 'what pig or wandering hind' is addressed to the Druidic priest officiating at the funeral pile, and refers to the Druidic belief that a sinful soul after death, passed through the circles of Abred ... the hell of the Druids ... the phrase of the hymn 'the husk is again young' means that the particles of the body, were now restored to the elements from when they had originally come. Ghastly as the affair on the Llantrisant hill summit have appeared to us, reared among different customs, to those whose reading have made them familiar with the funeral pyres of the ancients the horror it produced in the district was amusing.[20]

A correspondent in the *Western Mail* submitted a letter of 26 January questioning whether Dr Price's ambition to be great was not confounded with a craving for notoriety. Whereas the first is honourable for it means a way to excel and outshine others in profession or calling, he goes on to say that in craving notoriety there is nothing noble, honourable or praiseworthy. 'The clown in the circus makes a fool of himself to earn a living; the notoriety hunter acts the part of the clown from a desire to attract notice and to set people talking about him. In Dr Price's conduct, there is certainly no evidence of an ambition to be great, but there is unmistakable evidence of a craving for notoriety.'[21]

The correspondent goes on to question his outfit as a 'ridiculous caricature of a Druid's dress'.

> There was a sturdiness, a manliness, a heroism, a sanctity, a downright earnestness, a nobility of character and bearing in the Druids which even at this far off period compels admiration ... but who can feel respect or admiration for a masquerade Druid? Of course, if it gratifies Dr Price's vanity to fancy himself to be what he is not, that is no business of ours ... if cremation was preferred to burial why not have cremated the body at home? Why make a bonfire in a conspicuous place, at night too, and on a Sunday evening, just as people would be coming out of their places of worship? The same old feeling prompted all – a craving for notoriety ... if no crowd had been attracted, if no policeman had come to the scene, the doctor would have felt tempted to commit suicide out of sheer chagrin.[21]

On Wednesday 30 January Dr Price appeared again at Pontypridd Police Court before Mr Gwilym Williams, Dr Leigh, Francis R. Crawshay and Mr Rees, where he appeared in answer to the charges of 'attempting to dispose of the body to prevent an inquest, after having notice from the coroner, unlawfully, indecently attempting to cremate a body, and causing a public nuisance; neglect to give Christian burial'. Mr Rhys appeared for the prosecution on behalf of the police. A crowded court welcomed the proceedings. Gwenllian did not make an appearance although she was also charged with complying to cremate the baby.

A newspaper report in *Pontypridd Chronicle* read,

> A short while ago Gwenllian Llewellyn, was summoned at the court for non-registration of her infant child. Her reply to Registration Officer Davies was that Dr Price was averse to registration. There was a good deal of cross swearing on the case, and one of the witnesses was so conflicting in her statements that the stipendiary directed a prosecution for perjury, intimating that she had been tutored what to say. The perjury case was after withdrawn in deference to the representations of the woman's friends, payment of a fine of £2 by Miss Llewellyn on the conviction for non-registration, and a promise, it is said, that the child should be registered.[22]

Mr Rhys addressed the bench,

> The offences with which I propose to charge the defendant Price are as follows: That he did, on the 13th day of January 1884, unlawfully, wilfully and indecently attempt to cremate the body of his infant male child, and that he offered indignities to the remains of the said body. That by such conduct he caused a public nuisance.
>
> With attempting to dispose of the body of his male child, knowing that the coroner intended to hold an inquest on it, and without notice to the coroner.
>
> That he did on the 16th day of January 1884, by burning the said body, create such a stench as to be a public nuisance. With neglecting to give Christian burial to the remains of the said body.[23]

Mr Rhys continued,

> I also propose to charge Gwenllian Llewellyn jointly with the defendant Price with having committed the second and third offence, as I shall call evidence to prove to your worships that she went to fetch the oil and hired a conveyance to carry it to the place where the child was burnt; that she and the defendant were last seen together on the spot where the occurrence took place, and that within a few minutes of their being seen together the cask of oil was set alight and illuminated the whole country around; and on this evidence I shall ask your worships to say she is

equally guilty with the defendant Price of the attempt to cremate the child on the Sunday, and the nuisance thereby caused, as she must have been fully aware of the defendant Price's intentions, and assisted him in carrying them out.

Cremation in itself, if carried out scientifically and in a properly prepared apparatus, and in accordance with rules and regulations for observing due order and decency in the process, would, no doubt, in the minds of many, be a preferable mode of disposing of the dead to the method at present universally in vogue among us, and this principally for sanitary reasons, but the wretched attempt at cremation as practised by the defendant cannot fail to inspire the most advanced cremationist with feelings of horror and disgust, as I think every right minded person comparing our system of burial with that adopted by the defendant, must come to the conclusion that it is a far better way to carry the dead decently covered to a place of burial, followed by sympathetic friends and neighbours, paying every token of respect to the memory of the dead one, than to get hold of the nearest empty barrel, put a quantity of oil in it, and throw the dead body, partly exposed and naked, into it, and set fire to the whole lot, these last obsequies, instead of being attended with the singing of hymns and psalms and spiritual songs, being accompanied by the howling and hissing of a justly enraged and shocked public.

Such being the result of the defendant's action, it would seem to be a monstrous thing if it were not capable of being put a stop to, for if everyone is to be allowed to use his own discretion, and follow the bent of his own feeling as to the way in which he shall dispose of the dead, we should be constantly witnessing scenes both disrespectful to the dead and offensive to the living. Anyone might follow the defendant's example, get an empty barrel, fill it with a quantity of oil, throw the body in, and set fire to the newly-fangled funeral pyre in their back yard or garden, right under the windows of their next door neighbour, with the result that the surface of the oil would take fire and burn out by degrees, but the body having sunk to the bottom would not be singed until the greater part of the oil was consumed, and there would, when the fire had burnt out, be found the half-charred remains of the dead body, which would be offensive to the sight as well as to the smell, and eventually the same process would have to be repeated, or the body buried.

Happily, however, by our law this state of things cannot exist, for the system of burying the dead has been in force amongst us ever since the Christian era, and the custom having been so long established, has grown to the part of our common law, and so cannot be overridden by anything less than an Act of Parliament. Until an Act of Parliament justifying cremation is passed, the common law must prevail, and anyone acting in defiance of it, must bear the pains and penalties of so acting. There is a maxim of law that everyone must use his property in such a way as not to injure another, and if this applies to what is a man's own property, it clearly applies with much greater force to what is not a man's own property.

The first thing, therefore, that I shall prove to your worships is that there is no property in a corpse. The notion that a dead body can be treated as property was repudiated in a well-known instance which occurred in 1841, *Reg* v. *Fox* 2 Q.B. 247, referred to in the 'Justice of the Peace' for 2nd December 1882. A poor man named Foster had been in debt, and an order was issued to the sheriff and then to the lord of the manor at Halifax, under which the man was imprisoned. He died in gaol, leaving a will. The executors applied to the gaoler for the dead body, but he refused to deliver it up without payment of expenses incurred in maintaining the prisoner. The gaoler, in furtherance of his claim, said that if his little bill was not paid, he would bury the body within the precincts of the gaol, and began digging the grave, and actually buried the body there. The executors successfully applied for mandamus, and in the same case soon afterwards the gaoler was indicted for the misdemeanour of unlawfully, and in abuse of his office, without legal authority or excuse, and against the will of the executors, burying the body in an unconsecrated place, not being a place fit for burial, and he was found guilty.

And in another case, *Regina* v. *Sharpe*, which was one where a son, without any legal authority, removed his mother's remains from a grave in which they had been buried, in order that he might bury them without those of his father in another grave; he was indicted. The jury found that his sole object was not to do any disrespect to another corpse, but solely to remove his mother's body, being animated by motives of affection towards her. The jury were directed by the judge to find the defendant guilty, but a case reserved for the opinion of the Court of Crown Cases. The Court said that, although the defendant had estimable motives for what he did, yet he committed the offence. Neither authority nor principle justified the position that the wrongful removal of a corpse was no misdemeanour, if the motive for the act deserved approbation.

Our law does not recognise the right of any one child to the corpse of its parent. There is no property in a corpse. I think the authority of this case, assuming the conduct of the defendant Price to have been actuated by the most estimable motives, and not by that insane love of notoriety for which he is celebrated, sufficient to commit him, for he was doing this act without legal authority in defiance of the notice served on him by the coroner, after which he had no right to bury the body until after the inquest.

There is another case in which the same principle was decided, and this case is additionally interesting, as it is the only one I have been able to find in the books in which the legality of cremation is touched upon, but unfortunately was not expressly decided. By his will a Mr H. T. Crookenden directed that his body should be given to his friend, Miss Eliza Williams, to be dealt with in such a manner as he had directed to be done in a private letter to her. He bequeathed to Miss Williams a certain black and red earthenware jar made by Wedgwood, and given by the testator's father to his mother soon after their marriage. The jar was given to Miss Williams for the purpose to which he had directed her. He also directed that any expenses in carrying out his instructions should be discharged by his executors. The private letter referred to desired Miss Williams to cremate the testator's body. The executors and family would not hear of the cremation, and the testator was buried in Brompton Cemetery in December, 1875. In March, 1876, Miss Williams wrote to the Home Secretary for permission to remove the body and have it burnt in this country or elsewhere. The permission was refused. She afterwards wrote saying it was her intention to have it buried in a churchyard in North Wales, and permission was given her. Instead of doing so she removed the body to Italy, where she cremated it, and sued the executors for the expenses, amounting to £321. It was held that she could not recover, because the whole acts by which the body was disinterred and burnt were fraudulent and void, and, therefore, the judge did not think it necessary to decide whether cremation in itself was legal. From some observations made by him in the progress of the case, he would seem strongly to lean to the opinion that cremation was illegal, and I think we may look to this case as one very much more in favour than against us.

During this case the judge referred to *Reg* v. *Stewart*, which is the one I cited to your worships on the last occasion. I have since got a full report of the case, and as some of the remarks of Lord Chief Justice Denman are very pertinent to the present case I will read them to you. 'Every person dying in this country, and not within certain exclusions laid down by the ecclesiastical law, has right to Christian burial, and this implies the right to be carried from the place where his body lies to the parish church.' Further, to use the words of Lord Stowell in *Gilbert* v. *Buzzard*, 'that bodies should be carried in a state of naked exposure to the grave would be a real offence to the living as well as an apparent indignity to the dead.'

We have no doubt, therefore, that the common law casts on someone the duty of carrying to the grave, decently covered, the body of any person dying in such a state of indigence as to have no funds for that purpose. The feelings and the interests of the living require this and created the duty, but the question is on whom it falls. It would seem that the individual under whose roof a person dies is bound to carry the body decently covered to the place of burial. He cannot keep him unburied, nor do anything which prevents Christian burial. He cannot, therefore, cast him out, so as to expose the body to violation, or to offend the feelings or endanger the health of the living, and for the same reason he cannot carry him uncovered to the grave.

It was laid down by Lord Campbell, in *Reg* v. *Vann*, that 'a man was bound, if he has the means, to give his deceased child Christian burial, but unless he has the means he is not indictable for neglecting to do so. He cannot sell the body or put it into a hole, or throw it in to the river, in disregard of the law and customs of this nation and against the rules of public decency.'

After hearing the evidence on the authority of these cases, I shall ask your worships to send the defendants for trial.[23]

As Gwenllian Llewellyn was not present, it was resolved not to proceed with the charge against her. Sergeant Hoyle was then called and said that in consequence of enquiries, he found a dead body in Dr Price's house on 11 January and communicated with the coroner Mr E. B. Reece personally on the Saturday morning, who instructed him to deliver a notice to Dr Price. Sergeant Hoyle returned to Pontypridd and reported the matter to Superintendent Mathews and together they went to the deputy coroner Mr Grover.

According to the evidence, a written notice was then delivered to Dr Price on Sunday morning and the verbal notice had also been duly given him. The notice from Mr Reece intimated that the coroner would not hold an inquest if Dr Price would afford medical access to the child for purpose of certificate. At that point Dr Price asked Sergeant Hoyle, 'What has that to do with your or the coroner about my child?' Hoyle asked Dr Price if this answer was to be sent to the coroner. Dr Price replied, 'No, don't send any answer from me; but it is very likely I shall see the coroner my self in a day or two about it.'

Hoyle then allegedly asked him, 'Will you go and see him tomorrow?' Dr Price replied, 'No, I shall not see him tomorrow as I don't know what may happen. I have several patients coming here tomorrow. I don't know what may happen.'

About half-past seven that evening Sergeant Hoyle said he was in Llantrisant when he saw a large bonfire on a field called 'Caerlan Waste', occupied by Dr Price.

Sergeant Hoyle continued, 'I went there in company with Daniel Francis and several others, and found a paraffin cask burning. The flames shot up to a height of four or five feet in the air. Dr Price stood alongside the cask, and I saw him kick it two or three times with his foot. Each time he did so the fire burned more intensely. I turned over the burning cask, and out tumbled a quantity of burning oil and the body of a male child. The body was being consumed in the flames. The top of the cask had been knocked in. I identified the body as that of a child which had been in Dr Price's house – the only child there. The face was not burnt. I took the body away. It has since been claimed by Dr Price as that of his child.'

Dr Price was allowed to cross-examine Sergeant Hoyle and questioned how many napkins were wrapped around the baby when he tipped it from the flames, intimating that twenty-one napkins had been used. Hoyle, however, stated, 'I saw two or three about the neck. Albert Davies hooked the body out of the cask with stick.'

Dr Price asked, 'Did you drag it a hundred yards over the grass and cause the grass to burn?'

Hoyle replied, 'No; Albert did. I only knocked over the cask and rolled it on one side. The body was not, I should think, dragged more than twenty-five yards. I did not see the grass burning.'

Dr Price questioned, 'Was it the body of the infant which was flaming, or the napkin?'

'The body,' Sergeant Hoyle answered. 'The fire was extinguished with wet clods which Albert threw at my request. It was not by my direction that the body was dragged along the field.'

Dr Price stated, 'You committed this outrage on my dead infant,' at which point the infuriated stipendiary interrupted, 'Don't you talk about outrage, Dr Price, for goodness sake. You ought to be the last person to speak about that.'

John MacCarthy, a hawker of Brynsadler, said, 'I am a hawker living at Brynsadler. I sell oil amongst other things. I know Dr Price. He came to my house on Sunday, the 13th January, about one o'clock. He asked me whether I had put the order he gave my wife the previous day in readiness for him? The order was for oil. Later in the day a horse and trap came to my house. The doctor had told me he was going to send for what he had ordered. There was a man in the trap and a woman, but I could not swear who she was. I know, Miss Llewellyn that they talk about, but I don't know whether that was her. I offered to give her an orange or two, if she liked to have them. I have served Dr Price with vegetable sometimes. When the trap came to the door I put the cask into it. There were ten gallons of oil in the cask. That was the quantity the doctor had ordered on Saturday. It was petroleum. I sold the cask to the doctor as well as the oil.'[23]

Dr Price asked, 'At the time you delivered this oil, did you know for what purpose it was?' The witness said, 'Not in the least.'

Thomas Tootall, landlord of the Bute Arms, Llantrisant, said, 'I know the defendant. He came to my house on Sunday, the 13th January, between one and two. He ordered a horse and trap for half-past six. Later on in the day a female came to my house. I did not know then who it was, as I had not seen her before. I do know now. I should think it was about six o'clock when she came. I drove her to Mr McCarthy's house. There was a barrel put into the trap by McCarthy, and I Drove back to the bottom of a lane in Llantrisant. Miss Llewellyn got out, and I Drove to the double doors at the back of the Cross Keys public house. At the double doors I saw Dr Price and Miss Llewellyn. The way she went on getting out of the trap would be a shorter cut to these doors. They were holding the doors open. Dr Price directed me up across the field. Miss Llewelyn went up and opened the first gate. The doctor, I think, remained behind. I went across two fields and half across the third field. The doctor showed me the way over. He told me in the middle of the third field to stop and put the cask down. I did so and came away. When I had gone about half a mile I noticed a blaze in the field in the direction from which I had come.'[23]

Lewis Ajax, a collier, stated, 'In consequence of something I heard, I went out in to the street. It was about a quarter past seven. I saw a blaze. I went up and saw Dr Price standing near a cask, and giving it a kick now and again. The blaze came from the cask. Sometime afterwards the cask was upset by Sergeant Hoyle, and the body of the child came out of the cask. The body was lying on the ground all in a blaze. I assisted to put the fire out.'

Dr Price asked, 'Was it the body or the napkins which were burning?'

'Both were burning, can't say which,' he replied. 'The body fell out of the cask. It was not dragged out.'

Dr Price asked, 'Did you pull the child out with the stick?'

'No, Davies did,' he said.

'Was it dragged 100 yards?' asked Dr Price.

'No, not near so much, I should think,' he said.

This was the evidence on the first charge, and on being asked whether he had anything to say in answer to it, Dr Price said, 'I will say nothing.'

The second and third charge (attempted cremation and causing a public nuisance) were heard next.

Uriah Williams, a collier from Llantrisant, was the first witness called. He said that on the night he was in Lewis Ajax's house, 'We went out of the house together. It was about half-past seven. We saw fire burning on top of Caerlan and went there and found fire burning out of a cask. Dr Price was there kicking the cask occasionally to make it burn. Ajax and I were the first there. We stood about 40 yards off. We smelt oil burning.

'Then Sergeant Hoyle came and he upset the cask. A bundle in flames came out. We closed up then, and saw a child's arm, leg, and upper part of the chest. These were bare, without anything on. We could not see what was the state of the other part as it was covered with some sort of linen. The body was in flames and was dragged along the field. I assisted to put the fire on the body out by putting wet earth on it. That was why the body was taken to the hedge. A hamper was then sent for and I assisted Sergeant Hoyle in putting the body in. By this time a very large crowd of people had come there. There was great excitement. There were women there, I heard them screaming. I assisted to take the body to the police station. The crowd followed hollowing and hooting all up the road. The crowd was following Dr Price and the body. In my opinion if it had not been for the protection of the police violence would have been done to Dr Price.'[23]

Dr Price said, 'With what was the body dragged over the field?'

'With a stick,' he replied.

The stipendiary said, 'I can't see the bearing of your question. It is not a likely thing anybody would take hold of a burning body with their hands.'

Dr Price responded with, 'I won't ask witness any more questions.'

Lewis Ajax was again examined and confirmed what had been said by the preceding witness. 'The crowd wanted to put Dr Price in the cask. Women were screaming. On the way to the station the crowd became very threatening. The police had to protect Dr Price,' he added.

Again Dr Price questioned how far the body had been dragged from the cask, to which Ajax said, 'About 25 or 30 yards.'

Sergeant Hoyle supplemented what he had previously said by the statement that the crowd at the cremation business numbered hundreds of people: 'I secured Dr Price and gave him into the custody of P.C. Francis. There were a great many persons there, I should say 300. Some said, "Get out of the way Sergeant let us get at him, we will burn the old devil." Others cried, "Lynch him." They continued shouting and threatening until we got to the station. There were several females in the crowd. Mrs Thomas was retching very much and others complained of feeling ill. I sent a constable to Dr Price's house to protect it as several hundred people threatened to do damage to it. It was three o'clock in the morning before we could get all the crowd away.'

Albert Davies, a labourer of Llantrisant, after materially corroborating what the last witness had said about the state of mind of the crowd at the time of the cremation, continued, 'The body of Dr Price's child which came out of the burning cask was too hot for me to hold with my hands. So I took hold of it with a stick and carried it to the hedge, a distance of about 25 yards. I put some turf on it. The hedge was the nearest place where I could get turf. There was a smell of burning from the flesh.'

Ann Thomas, wife of Thomas Thomas, explained, 'I went to Caerlan, and saw a hamper there on the ground with the body of a baby in it. The sight and the smell make me quite ill. I noticed other women ill.'

The stipendiary asked, 'This was, I believe, when other people were leaving places of worship in the town?'

Mrs Thomas replied, 'Yes. There was an immense crowd. Women as well as men threatened the doctor.'

Superintendent Mathews said, 'The child was unwell on the Tuesday, and died at ten o'clock on Monday night in his house. He said the child was at the time in a cradle in the front room in his house. He likewise said the child had been with him ever since he was born, sleeping with him. The age of the child was about five months. I know defendant is possessed of some money – of sufficient to bury the child decently if he had chosen to do so. I know the spot where the burning took place. It is about 200 to 250 yards to the nearest house, and about 500 yards from Dr Price's house. It is on a hill which looks down into the town.'[23]

The stipendiary asked. 'Have you, Dr Price, anything to put to the police superintendent?'

Dr Price replied, 'No. He is no good.'

'I don't suppose he values your opinion more than I do,' the stipendiary responded, and then formally charged him upon the current charges and asked him if he had any reply to make.

Dr Price said, 'I am guiltless.'

Mr Rhys continued with the case. 'The next cases to be dealt with will be those which arise from the act of Wednesday [the night when Dr Price took the body of the child from the police station, and was supposed to have chopped it].'

Emmanuel John was called and said, 'I am a servant with Dr Price. On Wednesday, a fortnight today, I went with Dr Price to the police-station at Llantrisant. I got from there a box containing the dead body of a child. I took the child to a house where Dr Price keeps a cow. It was then about six or seven o'clock. At the cow house we cut some swedes for the cow with a knife. We sliced them. We don't make much noise over that. We hold the swede in the hand and slice it with a knife. I was holding the candle and Dr Price was cutting the swedes. We cut three buckets. It would take about half an hour to cut them. We stood at the house about half an hour or three quarters. There was no fire, only a candle light. There was no smell there at all. I don't know anything about the noise of chopping being heard. We put the box on the ground in the cow house. Nothing was taken out of the box. There was no fire there, so I don't know what caused smoke to come out of the chimney.'[23]

The dialogue between master and servant developed.

Dr Price: 'Now Emmanuel, have you ever seen a fire lit in that house?'
Witness: 'No, not a bit since I have been with you.'
Dr Price: 'Did you see four men following us by the station.'
Witness: 'Yes.'
Dr Price: 'There were women screaming?'
Witness: 'Yes.'

Dr Price: 'Did you see the four men by my house?'

Witness: 'Yes.'

Dr Price: 'You saw the policeman there in his proper clothes?'

Witness: 'Yes.'

Dr Price: 'Did the men and the policeman follow us up to the Bear Inn?'

Witness: 'Yes.'

Dr Price: 'Did not Hoyle stop when we were near the Bear Inn?'

Witness: 'Yes.'

Dr Price: 'Did not stones then begin to fly about?'

Witness: 'Yes.'

Dr Price: 'So that we were obliged to get into the inn?'

Witness: 'Yes.'

Dr Price: 'Did the police interfere to prevent the stones flying about?'

Witness: 'No, they did not.'

Dr Price, addressing the Bench, said the police tried to take his life.

The stipendiary said, 'The police saved your life.'

Dr Price replied, 'They tried to take it all they could.' He turned to Emmanuel and said 'Weren't the police and their gang going about all that night for hours?'

'Yes, they were,' he said.

Sergeant Hoyle was called to the witness box and said, 'The doctor came to the station at five minutes to eight, and had the box containing the body of the child. He and Emmanuel John took it away together. I did not see where they took it to. About twenty minutes after, I went down the road. When I got opposite the cow house I found a large crowd of people and I noticed there a very peculiar stench, which seemed to be coming from the empty house. It was the smell as of flesh.'

The stipendiary: 'I don't think that will do.'

Mr Rhys: 'If you think so, I will not press.'

The stipendiary (to the witness): 'You may stand back.'

Dr Price: 'I want to ask him something.'

The stipendiary: 'He is not examined. This charge is withdrawn.'

Dr Price: 'It is time for you.'

The stipendiary: 'That is a matter for me and those who are with me on the Bench to decide – not you.'

Dr Price: 'It is time for you.'

The stipendiary committed Dr William Price for trial at the ensuing assizes on the two main charges. He was admitted to bail himself in £100, and Mr Griffith Evans, Pontypridd, his surety, to £100. The case against Gwenllian Llewellyn was to be heard the following week.

Dr Price was followed down the street by a great crowd.[23]

There was probably no judge better qualified and experienced to preside over the trial at the Glamorganshire Assizes for *Regina* v. *Dr William Price* than James Fitzjames Stephen. Later Sir James Fitzjames Stephen and 1st Baronet (1829–94), he was born in Kensington, and was the son of James Stephen, the brother of author and critic Sir Leslie Stephen, and the uncle of author Virginia Woolf.

Educated at Eton College, and for two years at King's College London, he entered Trinity College, Cambridge in 1847 but did not have an outstanding academic career. He was already acquainted with Sir Henry Maine, six years his senior and then newly appointed to the chair of civil law at Cambridge, and they remained close friends throughout their lives. Stephen was introduced by Maine into the Cambridge Apostles, which contained a remarkable group of men who afterwards became eminent in different ways, such as the developer of classical electromagnetic theory James Clerk Maxwell, and Liberal Party leader Sir William Harcourt. Stephen was called to the bar in 1854. He was a member of the Viceregal Council and later Professor of Common Law at the Inns of Court. He was largely occupied with official work on codification, the results of which were never used. He was, however, responsible for the Indian Evidence Act, 1872, and in 1879 he became a judge of the High Court. An established journalist who contributed to the *Saturday Review* in his early years, he was also an author. Both the first and the last books published by Stephen were selections from his papers in the *Saturday Review*. These volumes embodied the results of his studies of publicists and theologians from the seventeenth century onwards. He served as Secretary to the Royal Commission on Popular Education from 1858 and 1861, during which he was appointed Recorder of Newark. In 1863 he published his General View of the Criminal Law of England, to explain the principles of English law and justice in a literary form. In the summer of 1869 he became legal member of the Colonial Council in India, following in the footsteps of his colleague Maine, and had the task of continuing this work by conducting the Bills through the Legislative Council. The Native Marriages Act of 1872 was the result of deep consideration on both Maine's and Stephen's part. The Indian Contract Act had been framed in England by a commission, and the draft was materially altered in Stephen's hands before, also in 1872, it became law. Also in 1872 came the Indian Evidence Act, which made the rules of evidence uniform for all residents of India, regardless of caste, social position, or religion. Prior to his return to Britain later that year, Stephen himself witnessed a traditional Indian cremation and had a respect and interest in Hinduism. Married to Richenda Cunningham since 1855 and a father of four, one of his children was James Kenneth Stephen (1859–92), a promising poet who died within his father's lifetime and was the tutor to Prince Albert Victor, the eldest son of Albert Edward, Prince of Wales. Almost a century later, J. K. Stephen would be wrongfully named as a suspect in the Jack the Ripper murders in the 1972 biography of another Ripper suspect – Prince Albert, Duke of Clarence and Avondale himself. Author Michael Harrison based his idea on Stephen's misogynistic writings and similarities in handwriting with that of the 'From Hell' letter. He also claimed Stephen was in love with the royal, who preferred the company of women and did not reciprocate Stephen's feelings. Although the accusation has been rebutted by professional document examiners and there is no proof J. K. Stephen was ever in love with Albert Victor, he did starve himself to death shortly after hearing of Albert Victor's own passing.

Standing over 6 feet tall and weighing 200 pounds, James Fitzjames Stephen made a stern impression and only those who knew him well were able to discern the kindness beneath the somewhat coarse exterior.[24]

> He brought to the trial all the research that had gone into his completed three-volume *A History of the Criminal Law of England* and into the compilation of *Digests of Criminal Law and of Evidence* which were part of his efforts to have the law on those matters codified. In the mid-century, moreover, he had been a prolific contributor to the intellectual journals of the day, holding forth, in particular, about politics, philosophy, theology and, of course, criminal law. Stephen was well equipped to take a wide view of the issue in Price's trial. He was also very much opposed to judicial law-making and in particular to the judicial expansion of vaguely defined common law misdemeanours, of which the charge laid against Price was potentially one. He also objected to the criminal law being used to crush opinion ... on top of all this Stephen liked Price ... it is clear from the very full accounts of the trial in the local newspapers that Stephen and Price hit it off across the court. Stephen was not unsympathetic to cremation.[25]

Dr William Price was committed for trial on Tuesday 12 February 1884, and the case of *Regina* v. *Price* was opened at the Glamorganshire Winter Assizes in the town hall of Cardiff. Dr Price was one of forty-one prisoners to appear before the court and one of 'superior education' to the rest. Also in court was Henry Edward Coleman, aged eleven and friend William Rees, aged ten, charged with stealing a cake and five knives. Also Mary Morris of Merthyr, charged with stealing a blanket.

A Grand Jury was sworn in: Mr F. E. Stacey (foreman); Mr J. C. Nicholl; Mr J. S. Gibbon; Mr R. Knight Richards; the Mayor of Cardiff; Mr Edward David; Mr R. H. Rhys; Mr R. W. Llewellyn; Lt-Col Franklen; Mr Evan Lewis; Mr Thurston Bassett; Mr G. Phillips; Mr T. W. Booker; Mr Birt St Alban Jenner; Mr J. S. Corbett; Mr F. G. Evans; Mr R. Forrest; Mr W. Pritchard; Mr D. E. Williams; and Mr J. Ware. Also on the jury was Mr F. R. Crawshay, his dear friend Francis' son.

S. S. Hughes QC and B. T. Williams appeared for the prosecution. Dr Price appeared undefended. Mr Justice Stephen, in his charge to the Grand Jury, dwelt at considerable length on the case. On directing the jury he submitted his thoughts of the case to paper.

One of the cases to be brought before you is so singular in its character, and involves a legal question of so much novelty and of such general interest, that I proposed to state what I believe to be the law upon the matter. I have given it all the consideration I could, and I am permitted to say that although I alone am responsible for what I am about to say to you Lord Justice Fry takes the same view on the subject as I do, and for the same reasons. William Price is charged with a misdemeanour under the following circumstances – he had in his house a child five months old of which he is said to have been the father, the child died and Price, as it seems, did not register the death. The coroner accordingly gave him notice on Saturday the 12th of January 1884 that unless he sent a medical certificate of the cause of the child's death he would hold an inquest on the body of the following Monday. Price on the Sunday took the body to the child to a field of his own, some distance from the town of Llantrissant [sic] put it into a ten gallon cask of petroleum and set the petroleum on fire. A crowd collected, the body of the child which was burning was covered with earth, and the flames were extinguished and Price was brought before the magistrates and committed for trial. He will be indicted before you on a charge which in different forms imputed to him as criminal, two parts of what he is said to have done. Namely, first his having prevented the holding of an inquest on the body; and secondly his having attempted to burn the child's body.

With respect to the prevention of the inquest, the law is that it is a misdemeanour to prevent the holding of an inquest which ought to be held before disposing of the body. It is essential to this offence that the inquest which it is proposed to hold is one which ought to be held. The coroner has not an absolute right to hold inquests in every case in which he chooses to do so. It would be intolerable if he had power to intrude without adequate cause upon the privacy of a family in distress and to interfere with their arrangements for a funeral. Nothing can justify such interference except a reasonable suspicion that there may have been something peculiar in the death, that it may have been due to other causes than common illness … if you think that the conduct of Price was such as to give the coroner fair grounds for holding one, you ought to find a true bill, for beyond all question Price did as much as in him lay to dispose of the body in such a manner as to make an inquest impossible.

The other fact charged as criminal is the attempt made by Price to burn the child's body and this raises, in a form which makes my duty to direct you upon it, a question which has been several times discussed, and has attracted some public attention, though so far as I know no legal decision upon it has ever been given, the question, namely, whether it is a misdemeanour at common law to burn a dead body instead of burying it.

As there is no direct authority upon it, I have found it necessary to examine several branches of the law which bear upon it more or less remotely. The practice of burning dead bodies prevailed to a considerable extent under the Romans as it does to this day amongst the Hindoos [*sic*] though it is said that the practise of burial is both older and more general. Burning appears to have been discontinued in this country and in other parts of Europe when Christianity was fully established, as the destruction of the body by fire was considered, for reasons to which I need not refer here, to be opposed to Christian sentiment, but this change took place so long ago and the substitution of burial for burning was so complete, that the burning of the dead has never been formally forbidden or even mentioned or referred to, so far as I know, in any part of our law.

Amongst the English writers on this subject little is to be found relating to burial. The subject was much more elaborately and systematically studied in Roman Catholic countries than in England, because the law itself prevailed much more extensively ... The law is silent as to the practice of burning the dead ... there is one practice which has an analogy to funeral burning, as much as it constitutes an exception method of dealing with dead bodies. I refer to anatomy. Anatomy was practised in England at least as far back as the very beginning of the seventeenth century. It continued to be practised without so far as I know, any interference on the part of the legislature down to the year 1832, in which was passed the Act for Regulating Schools of Anatomy ... it then makes provision for the supply of such bodies by enabling 'any executor or other party having lawful possession of the body of any deceased person' to permit the body to be dissected except in certain cases. The effect of this has been that the bodies of persons dying in various public institutions whose relations are unknown as so dissected. The Act established other regulations not material to the present question, and enacts that after examination the bodies shall be 'decently interred'. The Act appears to me to prove clearly that Parliament regarded anatomy as a legal practice, and, further, that it considered that there is such a thing as a legal supply of human bodies though that supply was insufficient for the purpose. This is inconsistent with the opinion that it is an absolute duty on the part of persons in charge of dead bodies to bury them, and this conclusion is rather strengthened than otherwise by the provision that the 'party removing the body shall provide for its decent burial after examination. This seems to imply that apart from the Act the obligation to bury would not exist, and it is remarkable that the words are not, as in the earlier section 'executor or other party' but 'party removing' referring no doubt to the master of the workhouse or other person in a similar position who hands the body over to the surgeons. Upon him the statute imposes the duty of decently interring the body with which he is allowed to deal. The executor's rights at common law, whatever they may be, are not altered.

As is well known the great demand for bodies for anatomical purposes not only led in some cases to murders, the object of which was to sell the body of the murdered person, but also to robberies of churchyards by what were commonly called resurrection men ... the case of *Rex* v. *Lynn* in 1788 ... it was held to be a misdemeanour to disinter a body for the purpose of dissection ... in *Revd* v. *Sharpe* it was a misdemeanour to disinter a body at all without lawful authority, even when the motives of the offender were pious and laudable, the case being one in which a son disinterred his mother in order to bury her in his father's grave, but he got access to the grave and permission to open it by a false pretence.

The law to be collected from these authorities seems to me to be this; the practice of anatomy is lawful and useful though it may involve an unusual means if disposing of dead bodies, and though it certainly shocks the feelings of many persons, but to open a grave and disinter a dead body without authority is a misdemeanour, even if it is done for a laudable purpose.

These cases ... have some analogy to the case of burying a dead body, but they are remote from it. They certainly do not warrant the proposition that to burn a dead body is in itself a misdemeanour. Two other cases come rather nearer to the point. They are *Regina* v. *Vann* and *Regina* v. *Stewart*. Each of these cases lays down in unqualified terms that it is the duty of certain specified persons to bury in particular cases ... but ... the question of burning was not before the Court in either case ... there is only one other cause, *Williams* v. *Williams* which was decided two years ago ... in this case one H. Crookenden directed his friend, Eliza Williams to burn his body, and directed his executors to pay her expenses. The executor buried the body. Miss Williams got leave from the Secretary of State to disinter it in order, as she said, to be buried elsewhere. Having obtained possession of it by this misrepresentation, she burnt it, and sued the executors for her expenses. The case leaves the question now before me undecided. The purpose say Kay, J., 'confessedly was to have the body burnt, and thereupon arises a very considerable question whether that is or is not a lawful purpose according to the law of his county. That is a question I am not going to decide'. He held that in that particular case the removal of the body and its burning were both illegal according to the decision of *Reg* v. *Sharpe*. 'Giving the lady credit,' he said, 'for the best of motives, there can be no kind of doubt that the act of removing the body by that licence and then burning it was as distinct a fraud on that licence as anything could possibly be'. This was enough for the purpose of that particular case, and the learned judge accordingly expressed no opinion on the question on which it now becomes my duty to direct you.

The question arises in the present case is a perfectly clear and simple form, unembarrassed by any such consideration as applied to the other cases to which I have referred. There is no question here of the illegality and dishonesty which marked the conduct of those who were described as resurrection men, nor of the artifices, nor indeed criminal but certainly disingenuous, by which possession of the body was obtained in the cases of *Regina* v. *Sharpe*, and *William* v. *Williams*.

Price had lawful possession of the child's body and it was not only his right but his duty to dispose of it by burying or in any other manner not in itself illegal. Hence I must consider the question whether to burn a dead body instead of burying it in itself an illegal act.

After full consideration I am of the opinion that a person who burns instead of burying a dead body does not commit a criminal act unless he does it in such a manner as to amount to a public nuisance at common law. My reason for this opinion is that upon the fullest examination of the authorities, I have, as the preceding review of them shows, been unable to discover any authority for the proposition that it is a misdemeanour to burn a dead body, and in the absence of such authority, I feel that I have no right to declare it to be one.

There are some instances, no doubt, in which courts of justice have declared acts to be misdemeanours which had never previously been decided to be so, but I think it will be found that in every such case the act involved great public mischief or moral scandal. It is not my place to offer an opinion on the comparative merits of burning and burying corpses, but before I could hold that it must be a misdemeanour to burn a dead body, I must be satisfied not only that some people, or even that many people, object to the practice, but that it is, on plain, undeniable grounds, highly mischievous or grossly scandalous. Even then I should pause long before I held it to be a misdemeanour, for many acts involving the grossest indecency and grave public mischief – incest for instance, and where there is no conspiracy, seduction or adultery – are not misdemeanours, but I can take even the first step.

Sir Thomas Browne finished his famous essay on Urn Burial with a quotation from Lucan, which, in eight words seems to sum up the matter: '*Tabesne cadavera solvate an rogus haud refert*' – 'Whether decay or fire consumes corpses matters not'. The difference between the two processes is only that one is quick, the other slow. Each is so horrible that every healthy imagination would turn away from its details; but one or the other is inevitable, and each may be concealed from observation by proper precautions. There are, no doubt, religious convictions and feelings connected with the subject which every one would wish to treat with respect and tenderness, and I suppose there is no doubt that as a matter of historical fact the disuse of burying bodies was due to the force of those sentiments. I do not think, however, that it can be said that every practice which startles and jars upon the religious sentiments of the majority of the population is for that reason a misdemeanour at common law. The statement of such a proposition, in plain words, is a sufficient refutation of it, but nothing short of this will support the conclusion that to burn a dead body must be a misdemeanour. As for the public interest in the matter, burning, on the other hand, effectually prevents the bodies of the dead from poisoning the living. On the other hand, it might no doubt destroy the evidence of crime. These however, are matters for the legislature, and not for me. It may be that it would be well for Parliament to regulate or to forbid the burning of bodies, but the greater leading rule of criminal law is that nothing is a crime unless it is plainly forbidden by law. This rule is no doubt subject to exceptions, but they are rare, narrow, and to be admitted with the greatest reluctance, and only upon the strongest reasons.

This brings me to the last observation I have to make. Though I think that to burn a dead body decently and inoffensively is not criminal, it is obvious that if it is done in such a manner as to be offensive to others it is a nuisance of an aggravated kind. A common nuisance is an act which obstructs or causes inconvenience or damage to the public in the exercise of rights common to all Her Majesty's subjects. To burn a dead body in such a place and such a manner as to annoy persons passing along public roads or other places where they have a right to go is beyond all doubt a nuisance, as nothing more offensive both to sight and to smell can be imagined. The depositions in this case do not state very distinctly the nature and situation of the place where this act was done, but if you think upon inquiry that there is evidence of its having been done in such a situation and manner as to be offensive to any considerable number of persons, you should find a true bill.[26]

The following is a copy of the indictment which appeared in the calendar.

William Price, bailed 30th January, 1884 charged with 'Unlawfully and wilfully attempting to burn and utterly dispose of the dead body of his male child, aged five months or thereabouts, at Llantrisant, on the 13th January, 1884, he then well knowing that the coroner of the district comprising the said parish of Llantrisant intended to hold an inquest on the said body on the following day; also, being then of sufficient ability to provide Christian and decent burial for the dead body of his male child, aged five months or thereabouts, did unlawfully and wilfully neglect so to do, and then unlawfully, wilfully and indecently did attempt publicly to burn and cremate in the open air, the dead body of the said child, by then and there placing the said body in a cask containing ten gallons of petroleum oil, and then setting fire to the said cask, oil and body, and causing them to burn in the open air, whereby divers unwholesome smells did arise there from, and the air was greatly corrupted and affected to the danger and common nuisance of all the liege subjects of our Lady the Queen, there inhabiting and residing at Llantrissant, on the 13th January, 1884.'

The court was crowded some time before ten o'clock. A number of ladies occupied seats to the left of the judge, whilst the balcony was thronged with both women and men. Dr Price immediately on his arrival in Cardiff had made his way to the town hall, and been let in by a private entrance, so that he was the first in the court. He took his seat with the attorneys, in the box between the barristers and the prisoner's dock. The business commenced with the summing up of the judge in a poaching case, during which Dr Price, accompanied by his daughter, Hiarlhes, occupied a seat in the well of the court, almost like a junior counsel. Shortly after eleven he was called upon by the clerk, and rising at once in response, removing at the same time a blanket which partly concealed his costume, he asked the judge to allow him to remain in his place in preference to the dock. 'Very well, if it is more convenient to you,' Stephen replied.

'I may stand here?' Dr Price enquired.

Stephen replied, 'If the dock behind there is inconvenient for the purposes of your defence, I will allow you to remain where you are, otherwise you must take the same place as the other defendants.'

'It is more convenient for me to remain here, my Lord,' said Dr Price.

'Well you are an old man, and as it may be more convenient to you, I will indulge you to that extent,' His Lordship replied.

The clerk then read the indictment to the defendant, to which he replied 'Not guilty,' in a strong voice. The clerk told the defendant that upon another count he was charged with having 'neglected to send notice to the coroner to view the body of the said child, that instead of so doing, he burnt the body, and disposed of it by burning after he had received notice from the coroner.'

In answer to the customary question, 'Are you guilty or not guilty?', Dr Price stated clearly, 'Not guilty.'

Twelve jurymen were then called into the box, His Lordship telling the defendant at the time that he might object to any of them. The jury consisted of John Samuel Davies, Thomas Heath, James Hill, Frank Sidney Johnson, David John Rees, William Simpkins, John Snape, Gilead Spencer, John Webb, who said he was a Quaker affirmed, instead of taking the usual oath.

Mr G. B. Hughes and Mr Francis Williams prosecuted on behalf of the Treasury; while Dr Price was unrepresented. His Lordship intimated that the defendant might sit down if he wished, and the doctor 'sat his trial' instead of 'standing' it.

Mr G. B. Hughes said he appeared with his friend, Mr B. Francis Williams, to prosecute in this case on behalf of the Treasury. Hughes said the case was unprecedented in its character, and he was sure it would obtain from the jury their very careful consideration. He was aware it had created considerable feeling in the neighbourhood, and he must ask them earnestly, and he was sure he would not ask them in vain, that they would dismiss from their minds all that they had heard, or read, or thought about it, and that they would be guided in their verdict by the evidence which would be brought before them, subject only to the law as it would be laid down by the learned judge.

Hughes explained that, on behalf of the Crown, he should tell the jury what the law entailed with respect to such a peculiar and unprecedented case. Hughes said the facts were short, and probably there would not be much controversy about them, but the question of law, which would arise in the course of the case would, no doubt, be more complex and difficult. He said Dr Price was a stalwart old gentleman of eighty-four years of age. He wore a peculiar costume, which he said was the dress of a Druid, and he claimed not only to be a Druid, but an arch-priest.

Stephen interrupted, 'I think we had better not go into particulars of the defendant's views, as it opens up a wide field of discussion. Confine yourself to what he is alleged to have done.'

Mr Hughes went on to say that the question was whether the defendant had violated the law in the act which he had done. He lived near Llantrisant and had property of his own, on which he had resided for many years, and he had a large practice as a surgeon. On 18 January a child died, four months old, of which he claimed to be the father. Hughes then proceeded to detail at considerable length the facts relating to the attempted cremation of the body.

He explained that if the defendant had dealt with the body by burning it near a highway or in a busy neighbourhood, where people's sight or smell would be naturally affected by the process, he would be indictable for a public nuisance. It would be an indecent sight to have the child exposed in that way before passers by or in the sight of people living in the neighbourhood, who would be witnesses of the spectacle. The law as to common nuisances was comparatively clear.

The judge said, 'I shall be glad to know whether you have any addition to make to what I have said. I expressed to the Grand Jury my views on this subject at very considerable length, quoting all my authorities, and what I said has been correctly reported in the various newspapers. The mere burning of a body cannot be regarded as a misdemeanour, but if it was done in such a manner as to be offensive to others it would be a common nuisance, and the defendant would be in the position of a man who had committed a common nuisance.'

Mr Hughes said, 'What I should like to submit to your Lordship is that, even if it was not done so near house or a highway as to be a nuisance to sight or smell, the process of burning the body by the law of England is illegal.

Stephen replied, 'Do you go so far as to say that, supposing a man took every precaution to burn a dead body in such a way that it could not give offence to the sight or smell of any person, the act would be a misdemeanour?'

'Yes, my lord,' Hughes replied.

'Then I shall be glad to hear any authority of that point,' Stephen said.

Mr Hughes said that even if the inhabitants had not been injuriously affected by this being done in a public place, to offend sight or smell, still he should submit that the defendant had been guilty of an indictable offence, though not of a nuisance in fact, but of a misdemeanour at common law. By the law of England a body must be decently dealt with, and not subjected to indignities. The expression 'rights of a corpse' might be an inaccurate one – though it was sometimes used – because a dead body would not, strictly speaking, have rights; but there were duties in relation to it, and the question was what those duties were. Hughes argued that a body was not like the carcass of a mere animal; the law treated it, and considered it in a very different light in this country and in all civilised countries.

Hughes explained that it was laid down by Lord Stowell that to 'carry a body to the grave in a state of naked exposure would be a real offence to the living, as well as an indignity to the dead'. Lord Denman said, 'A person charged with a body cannot cast it out so as to expose the body to violation or to offend the feelings or endanger the health of the living.' It had been laid down in a general way that 'bodies must be buried'. Hughes told the crowded court that in numerous cases he had found the expression used by legal authorities that bodies must be buried. It was clear that they could not be left unburied, and that they could not be removed after burial, except under an order of the Secretary of State.

Stephen said he had gone through all the cases referred to by Mr Hughes, but the difference between them and the present case was that in those cases the question was a dispute between a person who, for some reason or other, would not bury the body, and the person whose duty it was to bury. In those cases the whole question was about the burial.

Mr Hughes said that 'burial' and the mode of dealing with the body were expressions always used. He added that in the cases to which he had alluded the term 'Christian burial' was very often employed; but now Christian burial could not be insisted upon. He argued that the body must be buried decently, whether with or without any religious rites. He ventured to think that what was contemplated by the law of this land was interment in some form, and the statute which regulated the dissection of some bodies strengthened his argument, because it provided for decent interment of portions of the body after dissection. The law of the land was not to be abrogated by this intermediate mode of dealing with the body.

His Lordship said, 'Do you say dissection was not legal before that act was passed?'

Mr Hughes replied that dissection was legal before, but when the legislature passed the act extending the provisions for dissection, they said that the remains must be decently buried. 'The law,' he said, 'that the body must be decently buried, was not to be deviated from. Burial was generally required by common law, grounded, no doubt, on the canon law. That would exclude cremation.' He went on to say that it was quite clear that at present, although he was told some change was contemplated in the law, cremation was not legalised by any statute.

Stephen contradicted, saying, 'The inference from that is that it is not illegal.'

Mr Hughes argued, 'There is no need to exclude cremation. If the common law lays down burial as the rule, then cremation, being an exception, would be illegal.'

Stephen said, 'No doubt it is the universal practice to bury the dead. It does not follow, however, that a deviation from the common practice is at common law a misdemeanour. You see in the cases you have referred to the question of burying did not arise. The question simply was – who was to bury them?'

Mr Hughes responded, 'One point more. Suppose that cremation, properly and skilfully conducted, were legal, to take the body of a child into a field, to put it into a cask of oil, and to roast it in a conspicuous place, so that people should be offended by the sight and smell, was an indecent and improper way of dealing with it. That was not the proper and reverent mode of treating a body which the common law of England required. And if cremation, properly done in a private place, might not be illegal, it by no means followed that such a mode of treatment as would be described by the witnesses the jury would hear presently was allowable or legalised by the laws and customs of this country, because it was an indignity to the body and a shock to the decency and feelings of the public generally.'

The judge said as it was a point of law he would hear Mr Williams if he wished.

Mr B. Francis Williams called the attention of the court to the judgement of Lord Stowell in a burial case, and said that although it was perfectly true that in that case the question was as to the right of burying a body in an iron box, Lord Stowell, in his judgement, in which he dealt with burial from the earliest times, said, 'That carrying bodies in a state of naked exposure to the grave would be a real offence to the living as well as an apparent indignity to the dead.'

Stephen interrupted, saying, 'Lord Stowell was as great a judge as ever sat in any court, but it does not therefore follow that every word occurring in any of his judgements may be picked out and converted into law. That which you refer to, Mr Williams, is an essay. It covers 50 or 70 pages and contains all sorts of things historical, moral, and I don't know what, things which in a general way I should agree with.'

Mr Williams said, 'It is a judgement dealing with the subject of burying, my lord.'

His Lordship responded, 'The question there is as to the right of a person to bury a dead body of which he was in charge in an iron box.'

Mr Williams said, 'The common law therefore casts upon someone the duty of carrying to the grave, decently covered, the dead body of another person. In the case of the *Queen* v. *Vann*, the duty is cast upon the father where he has the means, and I submit that dealing with a body in the way that the prosecution allege this defendant did is not in compliance with what Lord Stowell laid down.'

'That is your argument, and, after the fullest consideration, I do not think it is sufficient,' Stephen said.

Mr Williams replied, 'It is a matter likely to become of importance. As your Lordship is aware, a member of the House of Commons has introduced a Bill …'

'No I do not,' Stephen interrupted, 'You want me, no doubt, to rule against what I believe to be law in order to give a case to the Court of Criminal Appeal, but I will not. Am I to direct the jury that burning a dead body is a misdemeanour when I think it is not, that I may afterwards reserve a case?'

Mr Williams said, 'I simply ask your Lordship to direct the jury that the law of England is what Lord Stowell said it was.'

His Lordship argued, 'I have considered those two cases which you have cited, and they do not lead me to decide that burning a dead body is a misdemeanour. If I told the jury that the burning of the body was a misdemeanour, I should have to reserve a case to try whether that view was a right one. No doubt it would be convenient for the public that the case should be tried by a higher court. On the other hand, I have to do justice to my own view of what is right according to my skill and knowledge, and I think it is not a misdemeanour. I am not going to rule that which I do not believe because it is more convenient to the public that I should.'

Mr Williams said, 'I ask you to put–'

Stephen quickly interrupted, 'You have delivered your argument, and I say I quite appreciate it, but I do not agree with it; and then you suggest that it would be a good thing to get my decision and the only way I could do that is by laying down as law what I do not believe to be law.'

'With great respect, my lord, that is not my proposition. I ask you to lay down the law laid down by Stowell,' Williams pleaded.

Stephen was adamant: 'I do not agree with Lord Stowell, as I have already told you. To the best of my knowledge, the law is what I stated it to be in my charge to the Grand Jury, the effect of which is this. That those cases I have referred to – which I believe are the only cases which I could refer – are not sufficient to convince me that the burning of a dead body is in law a misdemeanour. They speak not of burning it, but they deal with the burial. I quite see your argument; but it seems to me that in the case of the *Queen* v. *Vann* the question was whether a man was to be forced to incur a debt to bury his child, and the court held that he was not. The utmost extent of what a man is bound to do is to carry the body, decently covered to the place where it is to be buried, if he has not the means to do more.'

Mr Williams said, 'But Lord Stowell had the question of cremation in his mind.'

The judge said to Dr Price, 'Do you wish to say anything?'

'No, my lord; not at present,' he answered. ' I quite agree with what you are saying, my lord.' Which was followed by loud laughter, including that of Stephen himself.

'That certainly is not unnatural,' the judge quipped.

The judge addressed the jury at some length on the cremation case, and explained that the charge of 'cremating, contrary to law' as it was termed, had to be abandoned by the prosecution even before any evidence was called. His Lordship said he had fully discussed this matter with Lord Justice Fry, and he was of the same opinion. They believed that the mere act of burning a body was not in itself a crime; but if the body was burnt in an indecent manner, that was, in such a manner as to give offence to any portion of the public, if they were where they had a right to be, it was a common nuisance.

He stated, 'Whether this was a common nuisance or not must depend upon facts and circumstances, and in considering whether it was a nuisance every fact or circumstance to which Mr Hughes had referred must be taken into account. The very natural feelings people had about a dead body, and the horror which the indecent treatment of it was calculated to inspire, had to be taken into consideration, and if when that had been done it was believed that the act was offensive to any portion of the public enjoying their ordinary rights it would be a common nuisance.'

Stephen said he did not see himself, if the thing was done decently, that burning was more horrible than burying.

He said that if anyone allowed his imagination to stray inside the coffin, and to think of what the process of decomposition was like, he would be shocked. So long as the body was burned decently and privately, he saw nothing illegal in the practice.

Stephen added that other judges might have a different view of the law; but he was judge in this case, and if he had an opinion, he had a right to express it, and the defendant would have the benefit of it, and he directed the jury that the mere burning of the body was not an offence, but if it was burnt in such a manner as to give ordinary persons reasonable ground of offence, then it was a misdemeanour at common law. When he used the terms 'ordinary persons' and 'reasonable ground of offence' he meant there were some people who took offence at their neighbours doing anything that they did not like themselves, or which was not in accordance with their own habits and practices. There were also many people who were extremely indignant as soon as they had heard that any person held political or religious opinions with which they did not agree or practices and habits of life which they considered absurd or wrong. This was a habit of mind which was not to be commended, and which the law of this country did not protect. Therefore the mere fact that someone might think the burning of a dead body wrong or might have some religious scruples against the practice, was not what he referred to when he used the term giving offence to 'ordinary persons' feelings.

Stephen went on to explain what he meant was, first, offensive to the senses; secondly, he referred to the feelings of respect and awe with which someone looked at a dead body. These feelings were not to be wantonly interfered with, and if anyone wished to burn a body he must do so in the fullest sense of the words, decently and in order, and in such a manner as not to offend his neighbours. That he thought was the law, and he thought it was common sense as well. But whether it was common sense or not, he told them that in his judgement it was the law. The jury were bound and the learned counsel were bound for the purpose of this trial, to submit to his ruling upon the matter of law.

Mr Hughes made further remarks, but confined himself to the charge of 'committing a public nuisance', after which he called evidence in support of his case. This was, however, exactly the same as that given at the magisterial hearing; the details of the burning cask being toppled over and the body dragged to the hedge in order that the fire might be extinguished. Dr Price of course, tried to get the witnesses to show that they, and not he, had caused the nuisance by tipping the casket. Mrs Ann Thomas said if she had remained at home with her children, she would not have been sickened at the sight she saw. In reply to the judge, this witness said what made her sick was 'the smell of the oil' and also the noise of the people, and, at the judge's suggestion, she added, what she heard the people say as to what was taking place. Neither she nor any one else saw the body until the cask was tumbled over, and the only smell the witnesses complained of was that of burning oil.

Uriah Wilkins, examined by Mr B. Francis Williams, stated that he was in the house of Lewis Ajax on the Sunday evening and noticed a smell of burning and they went outside and there saw a blaze on Caerlan. Walking to the place with Ajax he saw Dr Price standing by a cask, which was burning. He said the surgeon kicked the cask in order apparently to make the flames increase. He waited at the spot and smelled something that appeared to be oil.

Under the cross-examination of Dr Price he admitted it was not quite half a mile from the field to the house. He walked fast, but did not run and did not smell much before arriving at the cask. He denied pulling the doctor's infant son out of the fire but dragged the child out with a stick, similar to that held up by Dr Price, a stick with a crook and charred at one end. He said Albert Davies took out the body, but he did not see the man strike more than once or twice at the head of the child after taking it out. He admitted that the child was dragged some distance with the grass flaming after it.

Lewis Ajax said he went to the field at Caerlan and saw the burning cask. Dr Price was by it, and kicked the cask, which made it burn more. He said Sgt Hoyle kicked over the cask and a bundle came out of it, which was seen after to be the body of an infant child and it was burning, by which time up to 300 people had gathered.

Stephen observed, 'The place is on the hillside, where people can see, but where there are hedges. A road is a short distance away, and the nearest house is about 250 yards.'

Mr B. Francis Williams explained, 'From all the top part of Llantrisant the field can be seen.'

Sgt William Hoyle said he was attracted by a bonfire while near the church.

Under cross-examination by Dr Price, Hoyle admitted trespassing on the field in coming to the place of the burning and both he and Albert Davies made an effort to put out the fire before Davies, at his direction, dragged it to the hedge.

Under Dr Price's cross-examination, Albert Davies admitted he pulled his infant son Iesu Grist out of the fire with a stick like that produced, but did not strike the body on the head, but about the middle, and that in order to knock off a bandage there. Davies said he did not pull the body by the neck across the field, but by the middle.

Ann Thomas said she went there and like other women became very sick.

Dr Price said, 'The outrage made you sick, and I don't wonder at it,' intimating that she was at fault for trespassing on the land, and condemning those who interfered in the cremation and causing the nuisance that ensued.

Thomas Williams, surveyor, Llantrisant, admitted to having measured the distance from the house of defendant to the place where he had attempted to cremate the body of the child, Iesu Grist, and it was 387 yards. The distance from the highway to the latter spot was 548 yards.

The public nuisance case was closed and Dr Price, addressing the jury, said, 'My Lord and the Jury, you have seen me producing this crook with which my infant son, Iesu Grist, was drawn out of the fire and dragged along the field. If, for instance, he had been suffered to remain in the cask I had prepared, the body would have been absolutely burnt. Instead of that, the assault was committed upon me, upon my own property, upon my own infant son, dragging him in my sight, and then taking me to the police station and detaining me there till next morning.'

Dr Price displayed the skin and horns of a goat's head on the top of the crook. 'This was my son's cap. I gave him this because he was a thoroughbred Welshman. We Welshmen pride ourselves on being Welsh nanny goats. And this is his cap. It is presumed that I felt nothing at all at seeing him dragged up the field. I have brought this cap to show you that I did think a great deal of him. Nothing else I am guilty of. That is all I wish to say.'

Mr G. B. Hughes, reviewing the evidence of the prosecution, said the jury had heard what effect the burning had on the people. He had to submit to them on behalf of the Crown that it was not a question with regard to cremation, but that putting the body in a barrel and roasting it under circumstances to offend the feelings of the neighbourhood was indecent, in the nature of a nuisance, and was not a proper and fitting way of dealing with a body.

His Lordship, in summing up, said the facts were not in dispute. The facts were simply that Dr Price put the body in a cask with petroleum oil, and set fire to it, intending to consume it. After giving the best consideration he could to the case, His Lordship said he thought the law did not forbid the burning of dead bodies, if it was done in a decent and orderly manner. But, on the other hand, the law protected what he would call the reasonable feelings of mankind against violation. He said that if the jury thought that Dr Price conducted the affair in such a manner as to give reasonable cause of offence, by sight or in any other way, or by producing a horrible smell, or by causing a dreadful spectacle to the people who lived in the neighbourhood – in either of those cases they ought to convict him. But if, he explained, on the other hand, they were not of that opinion – if they thought he had a right to say to the people, 'If you don't like the sight why did you come? – why don't you let the fire go on, when it would have been burnt to ashes, and no one would have been injured, instead of coming and making a disturbance and upsetting the cask and causing a nuisance?'

On the other hand, it appeared to His Lordship that if a man was going to do anything which shocked the feelings of the people, he ought to be careful about what he did and ought to conduct the operations in such a manner as to prevent any injury to the feelings of the people. And he certainly thought that if a man, in his own field, at some distance from his house went and made a great flame and blaze in such a way that ordinary people would naturally go to see what was the matter, then this was a new case, but if a man 'so conducted himself as to excite the curiosity of the people and he did what, in the ordinary course of things must collect them together or be disgusting and revolting to their feelings, that might be regarded in the light of a nuisance it was interfering with them'.

He said that if a man chose to make a great fire on land of his own where it might be a technical trespass to go, it was like inviting them in and if they saw a very horrible sight they had a right to say that it was common nuisance. Stephen argued it was a question of degree, more or less. If it had been done in a very remote place – in some covered place or in a place specially made for the purpose, it was his opinion there would be no offence. Stephen admitted this was a peculiar case, because it was not like burning a body in an open square, in the centre of a town, where it would undoubtedly be an offence; nor yet was it like burning a body in a place prepared for that purpose in his opinion. It was something between the two, and the jury had to consider whether it was a nuisance. If the smell was so near the road as to interfere with the people in the exercise of their common rights, then the jury should convict the defendant. But, if he had gone a considerable distance, and it was the fault of the people that they went, then they had no cause for blame, and the defendant must be acquitted.

The jury retired to deliberate upon the verdict, and another case – a charge of perjury against a young woman from Penygraig – was taken, and even at the close of this the jury in Dr Price's case had not returned. The judge directed a fresh jury to be empanelled to proceed with the second indictment against Dr Price, charging him with preventing the holding of an inquest upon the body of his child after he had received notice from the coroner that an inquest would be held unless certain conditions were observed.

Mr Hughes opened the case to the jury. The child, he said, died suddenly on 10 January aged five months, and the coroner gave notice of his intention to hold an inquest, and informed the defendant that he was not to bury or dispose of the body of the child, but Iesu Grist Price was disposed of in spite of that notice. Hughes thought he would be able to show that the notice was a reasonable one for the coroner to give under the circumstances, especially as the death of the child had not been registered as it ought to have been, and that there was reasonable ground for holding an inquest.

He said if that was so then Dr Price was clearly liable to a charge of misdemeanour for paying no attention to the notice of the coroner. Hughes explained that even if there was not sufficient reason for holding an inquest, the defendant ought not be the judge of that.

Stephen said, 'I certainly would not allow that the coroner has a right to interfere with funeral arrangements by simply giving notice. The circumstances must be such as to justify the coroner in doing so.'

Mr Hughes said, 'It comes to this: the person who would be the interested party would be the judge in his own case. Supposing there should be considered grounds for holding an inquest, before the man disposed of the body of the child it would not be difficult to ascertain whether reasonable grounds existed for holding the inquest or not.'

His Lordship stated, 'There may be good reason why some law on the subject should be made. I do not think there is any law at present. The present law of the land is that the coroner has no right to hold an inquest unless there are some circumstances which render it desirable for him to do so. If he gives notice without reasonable grounds the disposal of the body, the burning of the body, is lawful: it is no offence.'

Stephen thought it clearly wrong and highly dangerous that a person could go into a house where a dead body is lying and say, 'You shall not bury the body before I hold an inquest.'

Mr Hughes said that evidence would be given to show the reason why notice was given. Information of the death of a child was received by the coroner, and he gave notice, stating that there was no desire to hold an inquest if the defendant would allow a medical man to see the child, and if the medical man was prepared to give a certificate of death. 'Under the circumstances,' the notice continued, 'the coroner will hold an inquest on Monday next.' The notice was served on the morning of Sunday. In the evening of the same day Dr Price burnt the body of the child.

Hughes said he didn't need to trouble the jury with the question of whether it was legal or illegal to burn the body. The fact was that he disposed of the body after notice had been given. The coroner, he felt, was justified in giving the notice, and the defendant was not justified in disposing of the body and preventing an inquest being held.

Sergeant Hoyle was called, and said he delivered a verbal notice to Dr Price on behalf of Mr E. B. Reece, coroner, and a written notice sent by the deputy-coroner, Mr H. L. Grover. He said at twelve o'clock on Sunday, the 13th, he gave the notice. Dr Price read what was on the paper, and said, 'What has it to do with you or the coroner how I dispose of my child?'

Mr E. B. Reece was sworn and said his reason for holding an inquest was that he was told no information was given to the registrar as to the cause of the child's death.

Dr Price asked, 'What right had you to write and tell me that you would hold an inquest?'

Reece said, 'I did not; I sent a verbal message.'

Dr Price asked, 'What right had you to hold an inquest upon my son, Iesu Grist, and order a post-mortem examination to be made? What induced you to do that? Was there any suspicion of foul play?'

'No,' said Reece.

'Then what was your reason for intruding on my privacy? I say you have none.' Stephen asked, 'Had you heard that the child had met with foul play?'

'No, my lord,' replied Reece, 'But the circumstances were strange, and I thought it might be necessary to inquire into them.'

The judge said to Dr Price, 'He thought as you refused to give information as to the cause of death, it was his duty to hold an inquest.'

'That is an amendment, my lord,' Price replied, with the sound of laughter around the gallery. 'What he said before was that it was because the child was not registered. Was there any imputation of foul play?'

'No, not at the inquest, certainly,' answered Reece.

Dr Price asked, 'Before the inquest, then?'

'I don't know,' Reece said.

The judge said, 'In justice to the defendant, I think I ought to ask what was the outcome of the inquest?'

'Natural causes – no doubt about that,' answered the coroner. 'There was nothing in the slightest degree to reflect upon the defendant. Death was due to disease and malnutrition.'

Dr Price said, 'I could have informed him of that without the necessity of holding an inquest or a post-mortem examination.'

Mr Howell Davies, registrar of births, marriages and deaths, was next called. He said that no registration had been made of the death of the deceased child on 9, 10, 11 or 12 January, neither had any been made of its birth. No information was given to him as to the cause of death and he had not been informed of who the mother of the child was either.

Dr Price examined Davies, saying, 'Have you applied repeatedly at my house to register the child?'

'Yes, the birth, I have,' he replied.

'Did you ever ask me?' the surgeon asked.

'No, sir.'

'What have you applied for?' asked Dr Price.

'The registration of the birth,' was the reply.

Mr B. F. Williams asked, 'So the birth was not registered?'

'No,' said Davies.

Dr Price asked, 'Who is the mother?'

'Gwenllian Llewelyn,' the witness said, to which Dr Price asked, 'Have you proved it?'

'She was fined for non-registration,' he replied.

'Can you prove that she is the mother?' Dr Price again asked.

The judge interposed that that was not necessary, that the person whose name had been mentioned, it need not be repeated, had been fined. This concluded the hearing of the second indictment.

Dr Price, in addressing the jury, said, 'In regard to this charge against me I deny the right of the coroner to enter my private building. I had determined before I heard from the coroner to cremate the infant, and nothing should have interfered with me and prevented me from cremating it if it had not been for the police being authorised to stop me – they committed upon my property, myself and my infant the most outrageous of ill. I have no doubt myself that if the Llantrisant people had been left alone they would not have interfered with me. But in consequence of the police being put on by the master of the hounds – of the bloodhounds they came upon me, the people followed them if you please, the people followed the police and took me as if I had been a felon or a murderer and prevented me from doing that which I always intended to do with all persons connected with me and myself, because I consider it a better way a great deal to dispose of the remains of all persons than by poisoning the earth, poisoning the water, and poisoning the atmosphere. Independently of the practice of the Cymric race of burning remains being a Cymro myself and knowing the history, not only of the Cymric race, but of all nations, I have never shrunk from the idea. If I cannot get someone to burn me I will burn myself if I could.'

His Lordship, in summing up, called the attention of the jury to consider whether Dr Price was guilty of the indictment and had gone beyond his extreme legal rights. He thought it really turned upon whether the circumstances of the case were such as to justify the coroner in giving notice to the doctor that he meant to hold an inquest. Stephen said he must confess that it appeared to him that Dr Price would have done a great deal better if he had put off the cremation until after the inquest. But he was standing upon his extreme legal rights, and the jury had to consider whether the coroner was in such a position as to impose upon Dr Price the legal duty of allowing an inquest to be held, and of not disposing of the body before the inquest was held. Stephen said the question was whether the coroner had reasonable ground to suppose that there was anything about the death of the child which called for an inquest. If so, the coroner was justified in holding an inquest.

The jury retired to consider their verdict, and shortly afterwards the first jury, those who had tried the nuisance case, returned into court after three hours of deliberation and the foreman declared that they failed to agree. The jury were, he said, no nearer a conclusion than they were at the beginning.

'You are of different opinion?' asked Stephen.

'Yes, my lord,' said the foreman.

His Lordship said, 'Then I must discharge you, gentlemen. You tell me that some of you have taken one view, and some another. Very well; I shall discharge you. The defendant may be tried again on that indictment.'

He next asked Mr Hughes if he intended to proceed further against the defendant on the indictment. Mr Hughes consulted with Mr B. F. Williams. Seeing that Mr Hughes had not made up his mind, His Lordship remarked that unless he came to some decision, the defendant would be tried again on Saturday morning. The doctor was admitted to bail, with Morien becoming his surety.

Just then, the second jury returned. The clerk of arraigns asked, 'Have you agreed upon your verdict, gentlemen?'

'We have,' said the foreman.

The clerk asked, 'How do you find? Do you find William Price guilty or not guilty?'

The foreman replied, 'We find that Dr Price was not justified in attempting to dispose of the body of his child before the coroner's inquest was held, after receiving notice from the coroner that the inquest would be held.'

Stephen explained, 'That is no verdict at all!' to which there was applause. 'Policemen, take in custody somebody who claps or laughs out loud. Let him be taken into custody and brought before me, and I will make an example of him.'

Turning to the jury His Lordship continued, 'Now gentlemen, that is no verdict at all. What you have got to do is to answer the clear question I asked you whether you think he is guilty or not guilty of the offence with which he is charged. I told you he is guilty if you think the coroner had reasonable ground to suppose that the child could have died otherwise than in the ordinary manner. In that case the coroner had a legal right to hold an inquest, but not otherwise. That is the question you have got to determine, whether Dr Price's conduct gave the coroner reasonable ground to suppose that the child had died otherwise than in the common way. If the coroner did suppose there was a reasonable ground, he had a legal right to require an inquest, and not otherwise. The only verdict I can receive is "Guilty", or "Not guilty".'

The jury consulted for about a minute when the foreman said, 'We are agreed my Lord.'

'What do you find?' asked the clerk.

'Not guilty.' There was another slight outburst of applause.

His Lordship said to Dr Price, 'Then you are discharged on that count.'

Dr Price smiled cheerfully. He was allowed out on the same bail as that formerly required.[27]

At ten o'clock on the following day, Saturday, at the Glamorgan Assizes at Cardiff, again before Mr Justice Stephen, Dr William Price appeared to answer an indictment charging him with having committed a misdemeanour by burning the body of a child. Upon His Lordship taking his seat, Mr G. B. Hughes, counsel for the prosecution, said, 'After fully considering all the circumstances of this case with my learned junior, Mr F. Williams, and considered what took place yesterday, I have arrived at the conclusion that the best and most desirable way will be not to proceed further with the charge. After the most elaborate opinion, more than opinion, judgement, which your lordship gave with a review of all the authorities on the great matter of cremation, and looking at the other circumstances connected with the case, I think I can fairly, without deviating from my duty to the Crown, refrain from offering any further evidence on this occasion.

'I will only add one word and that is this. After the decision of your lordship that cremation is not illegal, I can only hope that if it is practised on some subsequent occasion it will be done under less painful circumstances, and in a different way to that adopted in this case.'[27]

Justice Stephen said to the jury, 'The learned counsel, for reasons with which I entirely agree, offers no evidence in this case, and therefore it will be your duty to say that William Price, the defendant, is not guilty. The matter has been one of considerable importance, and I have endeavoured to discharge my duty with regard to it. I gave my reasons as fully as I could for the view I took, and I have nothing to add or to alter. No doubt it may in some ways possibly be an inconvenience to our mode of procedure, when a judge delivers an opinion which is undoubtedly favourable to the accused, when there is no means to test that opinion, but that cannot be helped. I have given my view, and it must go for what it is worth, unless the question arises again. I may say formally to you, but really to the defendant Price, through you, that people may hold the view that burning is better than the practice of burial, but we must remember, what everybody who has to live in this world would do well always to bear in mind, viz., that people ought to regard each other's feelings, and there is no subject in the world upon which mankind feels more strongly or more naturally than upon the treatment of dead bodies. Feeling, I don't say that it is altogether reasonable, I think it is not, but feeling is shocked at the burning of a body, although it may be an act of tenderness to prevent a more horrible process than that of burning. Still no one can possibly be surprised that people should feel very strongly on the subject – very strong indeed. Therefore, if people determine to do this unusual act, an act which is so likely to be misunderstood, and give offence to a great number of people who ought not to have offence given them, it was not only a legal, but as far as he had a right to talk about it, a moral duty to use every possible means to prevent annoyance to the neighbours, and to prevent their attention from being attracted to what was going on.

'With regard to Mr Price, he is acquitted. I am sure he must feel that he has been fairly treated on this occasion, and I hope he will take what has been said in good part. He obviously enjoys much greater vigour, and has enjoyed much greater vigour, than falls to the lot of most of us. He has lived a great many years, and looks as if he will live many more. Although he expressed his intention of burning himself if he could not find anyone else to do it, I am sure it is not his wish to give offence to his neighbours: and I trust that they, on the other hand, will tolerate an old man's eccentricities and peculiar views.'[27]

Turning to Dr William Price he said, 'You are discharged.'

The defendant bowed to His Lordship, and then left the court with his daughter.[28]

The *South Wales Daily News* read,

Dr Price, of Pontypridd, and his admirers will, no doubt, be greatly delighted at the result of the trial which has occupied the time of the Court and the attention of the public for the last few days. We are not sure, however, that the general public will feel the same degree of satisfaction. Not that there has been anything wanting either in the judge before whom the case was tried, or the counsel on either side. We are disposed to think that the general opinion will be entirely favourable to them, and that most persons will admit that they discharged their obligations in such a manner as to give most thorough satisfaction. The charge of Mr Justice Stephen deserves, as it will, no doubt, receive, very general praise. He had to give his opinion upon a question on which he had little or nothing in the form of precedent to guide him, but making the utmost use of the material which extensive reading and close study had put within his reach, he gave an opinion upon cremation which could not, we imagine, be easily if at all upset. It appears that cremation is not an illegal act. It may be generally condemned by the people of this county or it may not, but we now have it on high authority that we may practise it without bringing ourselves within the censure or penalty of the law. We did not, therefore, expect the jury to find Dr Price guilty of a misdemeanour simply because of his attempt to dispose of his child by cremation. The whole case appears to have turned not upon the legality or illegality of cremation, but whether Dr Price had endeavoured to burn the body of his child under circumstances which would have made the act illegal, and in spite of the previous demand made upon him to allow the coroner of the district to hold an inquest upon the body. It is needless for us to enter into a discussion on the question, inasmuch as the jury returned a verdict which, however unsatisfactory it may have been, has undoubtedly resulted in the discharge of the defendant as one who stands before us and the law and before the people with clean hands. The part which the jury played in this business is not exactly such as will be likely to secure for them the commendation either of their fellow country-men or the British public generally. Indeed their verdict is one very difficult to comprehend. The jury had a simple duty to perform. They had to find the defendant 'guilty', or 'not guilty', but after an absence of three hours, the foreman intimated that there was no chance of an agreement among them on the matter. This jury was therefore, dismissed, and with this difference of opinion we do not propose to find any fault. It was but natural for the jury to hesitate about characterising as a public nuisance the attempt made by Dr Price to dispose of a child's body by cremation. Had he made this attempt on the public streets, there could have been no difficulty in coming to the conclusion that was in the highest degree offensive, but when it is remembered that the child's body was carried away to what is usually a lonely spot frequented rarely by the public, one would be free to argue that there could have been no nuisance except to those who chose to follow the doctor, and consequently throw themselves in the way of that which is supposed to have been offensive to them. In the second clause of the indictment there was something, perhaps, even more definite for the jury to decide upon. In this case the jury had to decide whether or not the defendant was justified in disposing of his child's body without a medical certificate, and without giving the coroner an opportunity of holding a post-mortem examination. In this instance the jurors agreed as to the verdict, so that one would have expected the case to have resulted either in the acquittal of the defendant or in his being fined or otherwise punished. But, strange to say, the jury gave a verdict of such an extraordinary character that we can only say that it was not altogether creditable to those who agreed upon it. They found that Dr Price was not justified in attempting to dispose of the body of his child before the Coroner's inquest had been held, but, as the Judge informed them, that was not a verdict at all. On proceeding once more to make a second attempt, the verdict was that of 'not guilty'. This reminds us very much of the case in which a jury found defendant 'not guilty', but advised him never to do it again. To say that Dr Price was not justified in doing as he did, and was nevertheless free from guilt in the matter, was simply a contradiction. We cannot expect a verdict like this to receive any honour throughout the country, or give to the defenders of the jury system any reason to congratulate themselves on the result. We do not wish to see trial by jury abolished simple because a jury here and there acts in a foolish and an unbecoming way, but a few such decisions in this country, coupled with cases which have dropped through in Ireland, would soon bring all trial by jury to an end in this country, and in every other enlightened country in the world. As the case now stands, we feel inclined to say that Dr Price may well 'thank his stars' for his freedom. Virtually the prosecution has broken down or given up pursuit. All parties are agreed that no second trial should be attempted, and consequently the eccentric hero of Pontypridd is free.[29]

As for Dr Price himself, it soon appeared that the entire episode was not over after all, as he made it clear soon afterwards that as he had been acquitted he would lodge a complaint against the police officers who arrested him and attempt to sue them for compensation.

When Dr Price arrived home on Saturday night after his successful legal contest at the assizes, the welcome he received from the people of Llantrisant couldn't be any different to that which had experienced from an angry mob less than a month previously. In fact, the welcome was in stark contrast to the angry howling, deathly threats and damage to both himself and his property. Instead he was met by a local shoemaker and about a hundred children. He received an ovation and was greeted by a crowd with flags and banners flying. The surgeon presented the children with a sovereign in coppers, and subsequently his triumphant return was further commemorated by a flag hung at the window of his house, and another flag put on top of the house, where the mysterious chopping and burning were reported to have taken place.[30]

A week later James Fitzjames Stephen wrote,

He was the strangest old creature, calling himself a Druid and an Archpriest. I was quite glad to be able to let the old man off. It would have been such a pity to interfere with the last of the Druids – especially as he was the very handsomest working old man for his age I ever saw in my life, light, tight, bright-eyed and with free graceful gestures, quite pleasant to witness. He did infinite credit to his Druidism and his vegetarianism and I felt so indulgent as to take no particular offence at the fact of his becoming the father of his remarkable child.[25]

Newspapers throughout the country included articles relating to the successful trial. It also allowed literate members of the community to voice their considerations of the entire affair. One published letter in the *South Wales Daily News* read,

In your report of Dr Price's case, Mr Justice Stephen is reported to have said 'He thought it really turned upon whether the circumstances of the case were such as to justify the coroner giving notice to the doctor that he meant to hold an inquest', and further on to the same effect. It appears in the evidence that Police Sergeant Hoyle made a request for an inquest, and that the coroner applied to Dr Price to allow the child to be inspected by a medical man, which he refused. Mr Justice Stephen and the counsel for the prosecution appear entirely to have forgotten the law as laid down in the statute '*De Officio Coronatoris*' and the interpretation thereof by the Lord Chancellor in Re Hull, L.R. 9 Q.B.D. pp 591–700, in which it is clearly laid down that it is the duty of the coroner to hold an inquest whenever requested, unless he is certain from proper information, that there is no doubt that the deceased died from natural causes. I would also draw attention to the case of *Williams* v. *Williams*, L.R. 20 Ch. D. 659 [a cremation case]. The law is there stated in an exhaustive judgement to be that no person has property in a dead body, but that the executors or administrators have a right to the possession of the body, and their duty is to bury it; nor can the legal representatives hand over the body to any other person to be disposed of. It is not decided whether the legal representatives can cremate a body, but it is clear that they cannot deliver it to anyone else to be cremated. Now, the child in this case is stated to be illegitimate; therefore, Dr Price cannot be the legal representative, and, therefore, was not legally in possession of the body.

This case is remarkable in another point of view. Political economists, and moralists, and atheists are very fond of talking about moral force, and saying that persons are to be restrained by considerations of decency and loss of wealth. This case clearly illustrates that such an argument is of little worth, for though in many cases it is true, yet a few cases, or perhaps one, will entirely change the standard. The legislature has never contemplated such immorality and indecency as Dr Price has committed, and yet, when Dr Price was acquitted, there were not wanting persons to applaud the fact, instead of lamenting that Wales can produce such a disgusting relic of barbaric ages. I am, Rowland Adams Williams, Crickhowell.[31]

The *British Medical Journal* hailed Price for his court case:

The recent case of Dr Price has awakened public interest once more to the consideration of a practice that is in every way to be commended, even from sentimental points of view, for there can be but one opinion as to the hygienic value of cremation; and clean ashes are surely less repulsive to contemplate than mouldering carcases. As Darwin has shown, the worms swallow earthy matter, and after separating the digestible portion they eject the remainder in little coils at the mouth of their burrows. In dry weather, the worm descends to a considerable depth, and brings up to the surface the particles which it ejects. Hence, earth infected by contiguity to a diseased carcass, buried with the greatest care, is brought to the surface and can infect a whole pasture.[32]

Another article, in the *Pontypridd Chronicle*, read,

The great majority of the people of this country are doubtless in favour of what is termed decent sepulchre in the churchyard or the cemetery – earth to earth and ashes to ashes – but there are not a few who do not hesitate to declare their preference to the methods in vogue with the cremationists, and express their preference in post-mortem directions for the speedy process of the fire to the usual wormy meal. Until the law steps are determined what it is proper to do in these respects, individuals will be left to take their choice in giving directions as to the final disposal of their remains if they can find friends afterwards to carry out their behests. The Romans cremated, and in tropical climates the practice is far from being unknown. We suspect the rite was practice not solely out of deference to the Paganism which was the religion of the Romans before the Christian era. Sanitation had something to do with the matter. It may have been considered an unspeakable treasure to possess the ashes of one's near and dear ones preserved in costly urns and occupying places of honour in the domestic arrangements of the domicile, but there is every reason for believing that the burning of bodies was really regarded as a sanitary precaution which it would be dangerous to disregard. In hot climates cremation was probably resorted to for the same reason. With a high thermometer, putrefaction sets in a very brief space of time, a few hours, and it was an absolute necessity to get rid of the dead speedily in order to prevent contagion. The operation of digging a deep grave was a cumbrous one – and so much disease and death had followed from shallow interments that depth was a necessity which could not be overlooked – and the quick process of combustion was, we had almost said, naturally resorted to as an expeditious means of the disposing of the dead and preventing disastrous consequences to the living. The Hindus, when the breath had left the mortal frames of their friends, lost no time in committing them to the Ganges – their god – where they were carried away by the ever rolling stream to spheres where decomposition could take place without risk or danger. The ceremony was, it is true, born out of the religion which the people professed, but we may depend upon it, the deep old priests, who were such a power in the land, knew very well what they were about. They believed, no doubt, they were propitiating their deity, and satisfying the cravings of their people by this maritime method of disposing of their departed ones, but we hardly think they were unmindful of the sanitary advantages which accompanied the practice which found general favour in India. However, this is neither here nor there. There is, as we have stated, no law against cremation, and as long as it is carried out without detriment to the health of the public there is no one to say nay to those who, in fulfilment of the wishes of deceased friends, resort to the practice. It may be morally offensive to most people, but that is not sufficient reason for demanding that those who believe in cremation shall hold their hands, and abide by what the public sentiment is in the matter.[33]

The *South Wales Daily News* of 19 February 1884 explained,

Dr Price has attained the highest degree of his notoriety by the attempted cremation of the body of his infant child. Going about 'in garments green like Druids of old', and sometimes in a carriage drawn by his nanny-goats, he has for a long time figured very conspicuously to the public, not only in Glamorganshire but even in London, where we are told he was once seen riding triumphantly on the back of one of his handsome goats. People deem his Druidical proclivities very eccentric, but in his opinion it is others who are eccentric, deviating from the centre of the ancient order of things, to which he remains true as the needle of the mariner's compass to the pole, or the sunflower to the brilliant king of day. He believes, or takes upon him to believe, in the orthodoxy of the past, and lists to discard what he deems the heterodoxy of the wayward present. An effort has been made at Pontypridd to revive obsolete Druidism and restore the worship of antiquated economies. Years ago Myfyr Morganwg, a Pontypridd octogenarian, published in the vernacular a very curious volume, and rather a large one, the aim of which was to convert (or pervert, as nearly all will believe) the people to embrace the religion of the aborigines of this our old island home. Vestiges of Druidism, and mementoes of some of the custom of the ancient Britons, are still to be seen in various parts of the principality. As the doctor asserted last Friday, that it was a custom of the Cymmerian race as well as other nations to burn the bodies of their dead ones is a well known and acknowledged fact. Caesar, in his *De Bello Gallico* tells us of the ancient Gauls, whose kinsmen lived in Britain, cremating their dead bodies, and he describes their funerals, declaring them to be *magnifica et sumptuosa*. Welsh history tells us of Gwythefyr, a British king who flourished in the fifth century, directing his survivors to cremate his body and preserve the ashes in a brazen image of him erected on the shore to terrify and ward off invaders. The mounds or tumuli so conspicuous in various parts of the country remind us of the cremating practices of our ancestors. In 1813, an Anglesey farmer, whose farm was situated on the banks of the river Alaw, when digging in a tumulus on his land for stones to erect some buildings, unearthed an urn which contained the burnt remains of Bronwen, the sister of the ancient noble, Caractacus, so archaeological authorities who examined the evidence concluded. The interesting relic was conveyed to the British Museum, where doubtless it may now be seen. About fifty years ago, Mr Morris Davies, of Rephidim Farm, in the neighbourhood of Trelech, about nine miles form Carmarthen, when digging in a mound on his farm, discovered together, three such urns, containing calcined bones and ashes. A son of this Mr Morris Davies is a trustworthy and most respectable colliery agent in Glamorganshire, and possesses a most interesting stock of knowledge of his native place. Here the historical mound, designated Crug y Deryn, still remains. It has a remarkable *cistfaen*, and used to be an object of veneration or superstitious dread to the inhabitants of the neighbourhood, who trembled as they approached.[34]

Pontypridd Chronicle of 1 March added further weight to the demands of the Cremation Society of Great Britain:

The result of Dr Price's trial, we suppose, took few person by surprise. From the first it was felt to be very doubtful whether the law could touch him for what he had done. But the result of the trial renders it incumbent on the Legislature to deal with the question of cremation. If any person, prefers that mode of disposing of the bodies of their deceased relatives we cannot see any reason why they should not be allowed to adopt it. But certain regulations should be enforced, not only to secure decency and order, but also to prevent the concealment of crime. Among the hosts of questions debated in this inquisitive age, one has been concerning which is the most natural way of disposing of the dead; natural, i.e., as being most in harmony with or least repulsive to the feelings and instincts of our nature. It might be said that no way is it natural for death and all appertaining to it is most unnatural. It is the execution of a curse, one of the many consequences of sin. Still since the penalty has been incurred, since our relatives and friends must die, the question of disposing of their remains is forced upon us, and the enquiry which is the most suitable way of doing so may be entertained. This question has been practically answered in at least five different ways, viz.: by burying, by burning, by embalming, by exposing, and by casting into rivers. The probability seems to be strongly in favour of burying as having been the most ancient mode. The sentence pronounced upon Adam, 'Dust thou art, and unto dust thou shalt return,' it is reasonable to suppose would have suggested to him, when a death took place in his family, that to bury the body would be most in accordance with the Divine will or decree. It is certain that burying is the first mode mentioned in Scripture, and this is found to have prevailed in the earliest history of many nations. Of the other four modes three are closely allied with and had their origin in those superstitions which did not come into existence until a later time. Burning was resorted to under the idea of purification. It was supposed that fire refined the grosser commixture of the body and set at liberty the ethereal particles which are deeply immersed in it; which particles then returned to the Deity from whose essence they originally proceeded. Embalming was adopted by the Egyptians, and formed a necessary adjunct to their creed, which taught that the bodies of good men should remain at peace and undisturbed forever. In their estimation nothing was so abhorrent as putrification. Casting the dead into rivers has for ages been the custom among the poor in India. The rivers selected for the purpose are regarded as divine, and the popular belief is that the 'spirits' of the rivers watch over these bodies and conduct the escaped souls into Elysium. Exposing the dead probably is ascribable not to any superstitious notions, but to want of civilization. It is practised by people in a semi-savage state. The Israelites learnt the art of embalming from the Egyptians, and frequently adopted it. In certain cases the Jews exposed the dead, but this was either as a punitive act, or to denote strong contempt. There are a few instances mentioned of their burning the dead, but only under peculiar circumstances. In the present day cremation is advocated by the few who favour it on sanitary grounds. The consideration would have had more weight some years ago. Happily, now the practice so dangerous to the health of the living of burying in and around places of worship has been almost put an end to. This custom had its origin in a dogma of the Roman Church; the reason assigned for it by Pope Gregory the Great was that the sight of the tombs might move the living to say prayers for the repose of the souls of the dead. It was first introduced into Britain about the 9th century. Burying within the church was introduced two centuries later by an Archbishop of Canterbury. The Public Cemeteries Act by putting an end to this custom, and providing a burying place at a distance from towns, has to a great extent quashed the sanitary plea in favour of cremation. There is no probability of burying being superseded to any large extent. The associations which Christians have with the tomb – deep, strong and sacred, – will ever cause them to give the preference to interment for disposing of the bodies of deceased friends. It may be only a sentiment, but it is a sentiment which has too firm a hold of their hearts ever to be given up. On the other hand we know of cemeteries the very reverse of all this. Paths slovenly, the surface after a little rain sloppy, wretched to walk upon, graves more like the burial spots of dogs than of human bodies – and of flowers none to be seen. Burial Boards cannot be expected to plant graves with flowers although they may give facilities and encouragement to friends to do so, but they ought to see that the graves are properly made up, that the surface is well drained, and that the surface is well drained, and that the paths are kept in good condition. It causes a shock to see a burying place in a slovenly state.[35]

Another report of *Pontypridd Chronicle* on 15 March 1884 said,

It appears that the decision of the judge in the Dr Price cremation case has brought the English Cremation Society into life again and according to a London contemporary the Council of that society is prepared, under certain rigid conditions, to do in a strictly regular and aesthetic manner, what Dr Price, 'the Welsh Druid', endeavoured to do for himself under circumstances of apparent barbarity. In 1878 the society erected a cremating apparatus at Woking. Immediately afterwards the council became seriously disturbed in mind as to whether cremation could be legally practised in England. For six years the cremating apparatus, although 'maintained in perfect order', has not been employed for the purpose for which it was built. Now, however, this Council of the Cremation Society has recovered its self-possession. According to a recent decision of Justice Stephen cremation of the dead is a legal proceeding if it is effected under circumstances which do not make a nuisance to the living. The council is accordingly ready to offer every facility for cremation in what is called 'the best manner'. As, however, it might occur that some of those who were most anxious to avail themselves of this complete method of disposing of the dead might have questionable, and even criminal, reasons for preferring cremation to burial, the Cremation Society stipulates that any one desiring to make use of its apparatus must have a doctor's certificate which unhesitatingly states the cause of death, or, if no medical man had attended the deceased, must permit an autopsy by the medical officer of the society, and must also show that the deceased had, during life, expressed a wish to be cremated after death. Even if these conditions are complied with the society seems to have some hesitation in practising what it preaches; for it still further reserves to itself the right of refusing to allow a body to be cremated in its 'apparatus'.[36]

The Cremation Society of Great Britain, fortified by the judgement of the Dr Price case, issued a circular informing the public it was prepared to proceed with a cremation at Woking of anyone who requested it. However, they realised it was also important to give no cause for any criticism in what they proposed to do and conditions were strictly observed before a body could be cremated. They would prevent the cremation of a body which may have met an illegal death. On 30 April 1884 Dr Cameron, MP for Glasgow, introduced a Bill in the House of Commons – The Disposal of the Dead (Regulations Bill) – 'to provide for the regulation of cremation and other means of disposal of the dead'. Supported by Dr Faruharson, MP for Aberdeen and another member of the Council of the Cremation Society, and Sir Lyon Playfair. It was opposed, 149 votes to 79, which was still more support than the society expected.

On 26 March 1885 the first official cremation took place at Woking with Mrs Pickersgill, a well-known figure in literary and scientific circles. By 1886 ten bodies were cremated and in 1888 a total of twenty-eight cremations took place, with the Cremation Society issuing an appeal for funds to provide a chapel at Woking. With the support of the Duke of Bedford and Westminster, it was possible to build the chapel and purchase further ground, constructed in a Gothic thirteenth-century character and opened in 1891. During the intervening years the interest in cremation had spread, with a society formed in Glasgow where the second crematorium was opened. A crematorium was opened in Manchester in 1892 when a group of citizens formed a company in the south of the city, and the same occurred in Liverpool where the fourth crematorium was built. During this period the Cremation Society maintained a high level of publicity and propaganda, most notable being Dr Farhuharson MP's lecture in Aberdeen.

In London the Cremation Society obtained land in Hampstead Heath and in 1900 the London Cremation Company Limited was formed, and, with architect Sir Ernest George appointed to plan the site, the most famous of crematoriums opened at Golders Green by Sir Henry Thompson. It is there that Rose Mary Crawshay's magnificent catafalque in memory of her son, Richard Frederick, was raised. A memorial fountain to the lady is also sited at Golders Green, created by Sir Ernest himself.

In 1901 the Darlington Cremation Society built a crematorium, and the first municipal crematorium in Great Britain was opened at Hull and run by the local authority, displaying how important the method was becoming.

In 1902 the Act of Parliament for the Regulation of Burning Of Human Remains, and to Enable Burial Authorities to Establish Crematoria was passed, twenty-eight years after the Cremation Society of Great Britain was formed. The new act gave powers to the Home Secretary to make regulations, and these were published as Statutory Rules and Orders in March 1903.

One newspaper report in the *Bristol Mercury* of 10 March 1884 claimed Dr William Price even considered the first crematorium in Wales to be opened in Llantrisant itself. Morien contacted the *Bristol Mercury* newspaper claiming that as he had cremated the baby successfully, he had announced an intention to open a crematorium at Llantrisant and pointed out the financial advantages of cremation, as the burning of his son had cost 8s 2d and 'every vestige of the body was burnt and he breeze carried the ashes away'.[37]

As for Price, his celebrity status following the plethora of court hearings and mass newspapers reports brought greater acclaim on the 'eccentric' behaviour of the famous Welshman. He revelled in this new-found 'fame', making regular appearances at various events which were constantly mentioned in newspaper columns throughout the country, although future court appearances would appear demeaning, petty and childish compared to his 'greatest victory'. Cassell's *Saturday Journal – For the Homes of the People* in London published a lengthy story in its edition of 16 February 1884, just a few days following the acquittal, which is based on the Dr Price story. Called 'The Blood-Stone Tragedy: A Druidical Story', what is more significant about the 3,000-line article is that it was written by a twenty-five-year-old Scottish writer named Arthur Conan Doyle. The writer had followed Price's escapades as they had appeared in the national press. Also a bachelor of medicine and master of surgery, Doyle was a budding author, living in Portsmouth by 1883 and a prolific member of a local literary circle. For over a century 'The Blood-Stone Tragedy' was an unknown work of the father of Sherlock Holmes, until the mid-1980s when a group of material was auctioned from Cassell's archives, including two letters by Conan Doyle, written two years before he published *A Study in Scarlet*. One of the letters was written after July 1885, when he received his doctorate from the University of Edinburgh.[38]

The letter read, 'Dear Sir. I am at present republishing a volume of my stories. I should like very much to add to them 'John Barrington Cowles' and 'The Bloodstone' both of which appeared in the *Saturday Journal*. I should be very much obliged if you would allow me to use them. Yours Sincerely, A Conan Doyle MD.'

The collection he referred to, *Light and Shade*, was never published, probably because Conan Doyle had not become a successful author at that time. What was extraordinary about 'The Blood-Stone Tragedy' was the fact it was written with a reference to a historical point so close to the actual event itself. It is unlikely that he visited Wales to witness the court case evolve and it is likely his inspiration actually came from the vast quantity of press accounts, which provided source material in all its shocking and vivid gore.

Dr Price's story made headline news throughout the country and nowhere was this better illustrated than in London's Fleet Street, where photographers' shop windows were celebrating the occasion with images of the cremationist figure in his Druidic garb.

The court case was also celebrated in popular ballads, which were sold in the fairs and markets of South Wales. Welsh and English versions were usually printed on the same leaflet:

> Our Bible tells us clearly
> In words distinct and clear,
> Our dust with dust shall mingle
> Till Gabriel shall appear;
> No word is ever written
> About cremation dire,
> The Bible does not mention
> Of paraffin and fire!
>
> No doubt you're all acquainted,
> And often have heard tell,
> Of Doctor Price, Llantrisant,
> And know his actions well;
> He sought to put his infant
> Amidst the raging flame,
> But policemen came there quickly,
> And stopped his little game.
>
> For that, at the Assizes
> At Cardiff, he was tried,
> But somehow or another
> The Judge did with him side;
> And thus said Justice Stephens –
> 'A body you may now
> Cremate as you think proper –
> But don't kick up a row'
>
> It seems that any person
> Can burn a corpse who please,
> But grant that all good people
> May keep from such affairs;
> And may we all be buried
> In tombs, peaceful and low,
> To sleep until awakened
> When loud the trump shall blow.

Throughout 1884, proceedings involving Dr Price and Gwenllian Llewellyn were not over. On Wednesday 26 February Mr E. C. Spickett, solicitor, superintendent registrar, made an application at the Pontypridd

Police Court for enforcement of the penalty imposed upon Gwenllian for non-payment of the magisterial penalty in consequence of the non-registration of the birth of Iesu Grist. At the hearing it was stated that the necessary order was made, and the authorities would, unless the penalty is paid, remove items of Gwenllian to ensure payment. If she said that she had none, or it was found that they were insufficient to meet the fine, the probability was that a summons would be applied for committal of Gwenllian to prison.

Mr Spickett said the defendant had neglected to attend the office registrar to register the birth of her child.

Sarah Davies of Llantrisant, said, 'During a portion of last summer I was employed at Dr Price's to milk the cows. In the summer a baby appeared at Dr Price's. I went into the house on the morning of the birth. The defendant lives at the doctor's. It was about six o'clock when I went into the house. I saw Dr Price, who told me to go on with my work as usual. I asked where Miss Llewellyn was? He said she has a son. He told me to go up and see. I said I will milk first. He said you had better go up at once. I did, and I saw her in bed with a baby in her arms. The day before I thought she was likely to become a mother. On seeing her in bed I said, 'Here you are.' She said 'Yes,' and told me to go on with my work as usual. It was a newly born baby. I went to the Doctor's dairy afterwards to milk. I saw her downstairs in about a week. She did not seem to be in the family way then. She did not seem very delicate. I saw her afterwards nursing the baby. I never asked her whose baby it was. It was Miss Llewellyn's baby, I believe, because she appeared to have given birth to a child. She was not suckling the child, but only nursing.'[39]

Mr Spickett asked, 'There was no other woman living in the house?' 'No,' she said.

Howell Davies stated, 'I am Registrar of births, and the defendant resides within my district. On the 28th January I served her with a notice. I called at the house. She opened the door. I told her I had a notice same as before for her to attend at Pontypridd. She said I have nothing to do with you. I had no opportunity of serving the notice so I placed it under the door. The notice produced is the one I went to serve upon her. On the 6th February I attended at the office of the Superintendent Registrar at the time mentioned in the notice. Defendant did not attend. The birth has not been registered.'

Gwenllian Llewellyn was fined the full penalty of 10s and costs.[39]

Gwenllian's appearances before the court didn't end there, as just a few days later, on St David's Day, 1 March, she allegedly assaulted Police Constable Francis, who had been involved in the events on Caerlan.

Appearing at Llantrisant Police Court before Mr G. Williams, Stipendiary Magistrate, Gwenllian, listed as housekeeper to Dr Price, was summoned for assaulting PC Francis. Dr Price was present at the hearing, acting as a kind of legal adviser, occasionally prompting her with whispers.

PC Francis stated in evidence that on Saturday 1 March he met Gwenllian on the road at Llantrisant and tried to serve her with a notice that she had been fined for the non-registration of a child. She said, 'I will have nothing to do with it.' He tried to put it in her hand, and she struck him with her fist on his left ear.

He again offered her the notice, but this time she snatched a cane from her left hand and struck him with it across the right side of the face and ear.

As she was leaving him she said, 'Will that do you?'

When asked if she had any question to put to the witness, the defendant said, 'No. I admit what I did. I did strike him. I told him before that I would if he did not let me pass. It was done in self-defence. The police watch me like a cat watching a mouse, and they threaten to take me to the police station as if I were a highway robber or a murderer. I told him I would not take it in the street.'[40]

The stipendiary said 'Did she tell you she would not take the notice on the highway or in the street?'

Francis answered, 'No, she did not.'

'Had you any reason to serve her on the road?' the stipendiary asked.

'The door is always locked; the sergeant and I can never have admittance,' he replied.

Gwenllian said, 'They never come in the day.'

But when asked, Francis said they had indeed tried contacting her during the day.

Gwenllian dismissed this and said, 'They come at eight or nine or ten o'clock at night.'

Mrs Caroline Jones, a widow, living near the Angel Inn of George Street next to the police station, said she saw the constable offer Miss Llewelyn a paper, which she refused to take and she stood back and tried to escape him; the constable took hold of her arm, then she struck him over the ear with her clenched fist. She then took a cane from her left hand and struck him over the ear or face.

The stipendiary asked, 'When the constable took hold of her by the arm did he use very much force?'

Mrs Jones said, 'I did not see him do anything except catching hold of her arm and try to put the paper in the band of her apron.'

'He did not assault her?' asked the magistrate.

'No, nothing except that,' she replied.

Gwenllian asked, 'Did you see the bull going before me?' Mrs Jones replied, 'Yes, but the Mochyn Du was driving the bull, I believe.'

'No; he was in front of it,' Gwenllian replied.

Superintendent Matthews said he would call Sergeant Hoyle to prove that there was no possibility of serving summonses on the defendant.

Sergeant Hoyle said that he had on several occasions tried to serve summonses on Dr Price and Miss Llewellyn.

The stipendiary quickly interrupted, 'We have nothing to do with Dr Price today.'

Hoyle said he had been at the house in the daytime and in the evening, but they would not open the door. They came to the door and said they would not open. He put one summons under the door – that was about eight o'clock in the evening.

Superintendent Matthews submitted that eight o'clock was not an unreasonable time.

Gwenllian, on being asked what her reply to the charge was, said, 'I don't deny it, I don't deny it.'

The stipendiary asked, 'Have you anything to say in defence?'

'No; but they threaten me on the highway,' said Gwenllian.

Supt Matthews said, 'I think the constable acted very leniently. The constable being assaulted might have locked you up.'

Sgt Hoyle added, 'I told you if you assaulted me I would lock you up.'

Gwenllian answered, 'You said you would unless I took the paper.'

The stipendiary added, 'You are here in a position which everyone must be sorry to see. You must divest yourself of all your surroundings. Because Dr Price is notorious don't think that that gives you any power outside the law. You must be dealt with like any ordinary person. I have known you for many years and have known your family all my life, and it is a very painful duty to me to have to deal with a case like this. But don't you think that from some eccentricity or spurious admiration for Dr Price you are to be allowed to do all sorts of things. Dr Price I have nothing to say to in this case. I have nothing against him, but I can't help saying a few words to you. There must be a time when you will be standing alone. Although he is hale and hearty at 84, as he alleges, he must succumb, all men must, some day or other, and in all probability you will survive him. Just think what your position will be when you have not Dr Price to support you. I am not telling you this to aggravate the case, but simply to remind you that you must not set yourself up above the law. I am only dealing with you as an ordinary person. This constable is simply an instrument of the law and to retaliate upon him for proceedings instituted by others is a meaningless thing. He is merely a bit of machinery that has simply to do certain duties in the best way he can. It is for you to say if he did not do it in a proper manner and for me to decide whether he used more violence than was necessary in the execution of his duty. But, supposing he did, it is not for you to take the law into your own hands. You may say it is difficult for a woman to keep her hands off a man if he puts his hand upon her. But he is not an ordinary man, but simply a policeman – a messenger of the law to give you a notice, and the law compels him and others to do it.

You might have cause of complaint otherwise. He comes to tell you that you have been fined, and that the fine should be paid or other penalties would attach. You took the law into your own hands. You struck the man not only once, but repeatedly. The witness who corroborates the police states that the man did nothing but direct your attention to the notice. He tried to serve you in the street. It is not nice to be served in the street, but the police have no option. They have tried in the one or two cases that have recently come before me to serve you in the ordinary way but they failed.'[40]

'But they did not come in the daytime,' she protested.

'I say eight o'clock is not too late at all. If they had come in the middle of the night when you had gone to bed you might have had cause of complaint, but you say you were up and you opened the door and closed it.'

'No, I refused to open it,' she said.

'Well, that is rather worse,' the stipendiary stated. 'You declined to have anything to do with it. But I am not going to waste my breath. It is an ordinary case of assault and an assault on a man in an official capacity. The law makes a distinction between a man in the ordinary sense and a man in an official capacity. If men were allowed to be assaulted by every person on whom they serve a summons we could not get men to do the work, and the law must be administered in a way to protect the police. You will be fined 20s and costs, or, in default, 21 days hard labour.'

The money was immediately paid – £1 15s 2d.

Dr William Price successfully carried out his intention to cremate Iesu Grist on Friday 14 March 1884 unmolested by the crowds, although Sgt Hoyle and Rowe were said to have watched the incident from the ruins of Llantrisant Castle on this occasion. Most of the crowds of local residents stood at the foot of the hill and watched. Only Wheatsheaf Inn landlord Roderick Lewis dared go closer to confirm the event took place. Locals thought the body had been buried or burnt in the stable, others wondered whether the remains were burnt in a large oven at Tŷ'r Clettwr.

In fact Iesu Grist was eventually cremated in half a ton of coal, a gallon of paraffin oil and sixpenny worth of wood. The entire act cost 8s 2d. A pair of iron grids were placed above the coal and the box containing the child, wrapped in napkins, above it. Again, Price chanted an ancient song in the presence of a number of unorthodox spectators, most notably some twenty horned cattle driven to the site by the doctor and his servant Mochyn Du. The ashes were carried away in the winds.

A report in the *Pontypridd Chronicle* said,

On Friday morning on the same spot the doctor succeeded without any interruption in burning the remains of his infant son and heir. Three bundles were placed in the ground, forming a triangle, half a ton of coal was placed inside the enclosure in the centre of which were two large grates, upon which was place a large wooden box. Inside this box was a smaller one containing the body, which was wrapped in 21 napkins. The space between the two boxes was filled with coal. A great quantity of petroleum was thrown over the coals and this served to make the pile one mass of fire as soon as ignition took place.

The pile was lit at half past eight on Friday morning and continued burning furiously for three hours. The doctor, with a large shawl thrown over his shoulders, was present during the conflagration and was seen walking to and fro, in all probability chanting some ancient song to himself. In about half hour's time his cattle joined him and stood for a while hard by as if they had come to pay some last tribute of respect to their master's heir. A little after 'Mochyn Du' was leading his master's donkey and cart past the pile. When he had come up in front of the seething mount the donkey, thinking his vocal organs were equal to the crackling noise made by the flames, commenced to bray most vociferously.

It was amazing to see some of the inhabitants, not a few representing the female community of the town, climbing the breath of the hill, and peering over the fence to catch a glimpse of the doctor in performance of that very rite which many of them had on the first occasion interrupted. But the scene was changed! They did not even cross the fence, until the doctor, seeing their curiosity aroused, and their anxious faces look up, and cordially invited them to approach, on condition that they would not touch or interfere with the sacred pile. Between two and three hundred of the inhabitants then visited the scene, and conducted themselves most orderly and reverently ... when asked why he did not sacrifice a cow or calf he shook his head and said, 'Morgan [the bull] shall die a natural death and shall then be burnt.'

Dr Price's friend, Roderick Lewis, ascended East Caerlan with Gwenllian a little later to see the fire, before more inhabitants crowded the scene.[41]

Dr Price was not about to let matters lie, and just to create further stir in the village would often cremate his dead cattle on the mountainside. The cremation of Morgan the Bull was well documented at the time, when he had the carcass carried to East Caerlan for a ritualistic disposal! He next conceived the idea of building a public crematorium in the vicinity of Llantrisant, and made a public appeal for subscriptions. Letters of support were received from London, Europe and even India but the project was discontinued.

Dr Price decided to commemorate the cremation by having an oval-shaped medal struck in bronze, and over 3,000 of these were sold at 3*d* each. The coin shows a nanny goat and a serpent around the figure about to eat its own tail, again referring to the Druidic beliefs of reincarnation and the transmigration of the soul. He explained, 'The Serpent, represents the Cymmerian race and the Cymmerian Language, and the only word that is enunciated by the serpents' "sth" – a hissing sound which is represented by the vowels which surround it. Now in the goat, the serpent, and the letters of his egg, or oval over his head, I am able to decipher the pedigree of the poet, and it is so follows:

'"I will go to sow him who will sow me who will go to sow him. The will sow perpetual motion in the Serpent of Baptism with the Light of the Brain of the Cymmerian goat."

'The goat is the scapegoat of the wilderness, which governed the world for all eternity and the serpent circumscribes the world. The verse you see on the obverse side of the medal was composed by me, and a free translation of it would run thus:–

> 'See Jesus Christ from the fire dragging
> In the hand of Victoria, my dear Welshman,
> In the presence of the Day of Judgement he owns the sword
> Of the Prince of Love, and the Crown of Wales.
> January 13 1884.'

The actual words on the coin read in Welsh are

> *Gwel Jessu Crist o yr tan yn llysgo*
> *Yn llaw Victoria, ym annwyl Gymmro*
> *Ang gwydd y varn ve bia cleddu*
> *Tywysog Cariad Corron Cymmru*
> *Ionawr yr 13 eg 1884*

A newspaper report read,

The excitement over Dr Price's attempt to cremate the body of his infant in a tar-barrel had died out, and Llantrisant had assumed its wonted dullness when, on Friday last, the flame was rekindled, the light of the Doctor's fire again lighted the slopes of the neighbouring hills, imaginative minds were once more attracted to the scene, and the eccentric cremationist again found himself famous. It will be remembered that after the inquest, at the first magisterial proceedings, the body of the child was ordered to be delivered to Dr Price, on the condition which he promised to observe, that he would 'dispose of the body in the usual manner adopted in this country – in a manner not to outrage the feelings of his neighbours'. The doctor gave his word to the Stipendiary magistrate that this condition should be observed. The empty house mystery and – well nobody knew what became of the child; that is, nobody outside the Doctor's house. Conjectures were rife, of course. Some supposed the body had been quietly buried, a few thought that the body had been consumed in a large oven which the Doctor had in his house; whilst others who know his unflinching determination, felt convinced that nothing of the kind had occurred but that he would appear again as he did on that memorable Sunday night on Caerlan Hill, and complete the work he had begun. The latter supposition was found to be correct. On Friday morning last week, on the same spot, the doctor succeeded without interruption in burning the remains of his infant son and heir. It is said that during Thursday night Dr Price was observed to be sending coal and wood up to the summit of the high hill to the east of the town, where he sometime ago attempted to cremate his dead child. Early on Friday morning he drove all his horned cattle, including eight bulls, to the same locality. Shortly afterwards immense flames were seen ascending in the air, and in the midst of the fire was a box containing the body of the child. All in a ring, with their faces towards the fire, stood about twenty cattle. 'Mochyn Du', Dr Price's confidential servant, stood there in charge of a donkey, which, when it saw the flames, brayed as only an ass can bray, and by so doing set the vocal organs of the cattle in motion, with the result that there was a noise which reminded the quiet inhabitants of the district of the music at a wild beast show. The 'natives' crowded round the scene at a respectful distance from the fire, and, remembering the result of the trial, Sergeant Hoyle and PC Rowe stood in the ruins of the castle. Operations were commenced in open daylight, but in order to completely consume the remains of the baby the fire was kept burning until the night was far advanced. Mr Roderick Lewis appears to have been on sufficiently friendly terms with the high priest of the crematorium to be suffered to approach near enough to see the general arrangement of the fiery furnace. He says, in confirmation of what we have stated above, that what he saw was a triangle formed of hurdles. In the midst were two grates, facing each other, and across from one to the other was a box containing the body of the child. On this box was another larger one containing gallons of paraffin. Around the triangle half a ton of coal had been piled, and the moment the doctor applied a match the flame shot up to a great height, and everything was gradually consumed. It seems the doctor does not believe in gathering up the ashes to keep in an urn, and he did not observe that 'custom' on this occasion. Indeed, it is difficult to see how he could have done so, considering the immense quantity of ashes strewn around the place. The doctor has received letters from all parts of the country, as well as from the Continent, sympathising with him in his effort to carry out his burning views.[42]

On the same day as the cremation, Pontypridd County Court heard before judge B. T. Williams QC that the case of *Evans* v. *Price* was down for hearing. The action was for £5, and the defendant was Dr Price, whilst Mr Richard Evans, farmer, was the plaintiff. The question to be tried was one of trespass. It was incidentally stated in court that the summons upon the defendant had to be posted up on Dr Price's house door – entry or access being declined. The defendant did not appear. Mr Kinsman, a solicitor's clerk from Nottingham, said that Dr Price was ill, and the case was adjourned till next court on payment of the costs, to be taxed by the registrar.[43]

Two weeks later and Pontypridd Police Superintendent Mr Jabez Mathews received the necessary notice from Dr William Price, intimating that a claim was to be preferred against Mathews by Dr Price in the High Court for £3,000 damages and compensation of the recent imprisonment and trespass surrounding the cremation trial.[44]

The matter went before Swansea Assizes for a special jury case at the start of August 1884 and again the courtroom and gallery was filled to capacity. Dr Price was the plaintiff, who intended to claim £3,000 compensation from the defendant, Police Superintendent Jabez Mathews, Pontypridd and Police Sergeant William Hoyle, Llantrisant. Dr Price conducted his own case. Mr McIntyre QC, Mr R. F. Watkins (for Hoyle's case) and Mr G. B. Hughes (in Supt Mathews's case). Judge Grove heard the statement of claim with particulars by Dr William Price read:

1. The defendants, on the 13th day of January, 1884, broke and entered, with a large number of persons, the plaintiff's lands and premises, known as Cae-yr-Lann, at Llantrisant, in the county of Glamorgan, and broke the fences thereof, and injured the herbage thereof, and the plaintiff's cattle being thereon, and wrongfully seized and destroyed certain chattels and goods of the plaintiff, and a barrel and the oil therein, belonging to the plaintiff, and being on such lands.

2. The defendants, on the said 13th day of January, 1884 aforesaid, wrongfully assaulted and beat the plaintiff at Cae-yr-Lann aforesaid, and took from this lawful possession and custody the dead body of his child, called Jessu Christ, and unlawfully and indecently exposed the same and dragged it, while flaming, for a distance of 64 yards, above, upon and over the plaintiff's said premises.

3. The defendants, on the last aforesaid, assaulted and arrested the plaintiff, and dragged him over Cae-yr-Lann aforesaid, and through the public streets of Llantrisant aforesaid in custody, and imprisoned him for 12 hours in a cold cell at the Llantrisant Police Station.

4. The defendants, on the said day (which was a Sunday), publicly assaulted and took the plaintiff into custody without any authority or warrant, and imprisoned him for 12 hours in a cold cell, dangerous and injurious to health, at the aforesaid police station, and on the following morning wrongfully took him in custody to the Cross Inn Station of the Taff Vale Railway, in the county aforesaid, and there before Gwilym Williams, then the stipendiary magistrate, and thence on the same day, while still in custody, and by direction of the said Gwilym Williams, to Pont-y-Prydh, in then said county, where after a conference between the defendant and the said Gwilym Williams, the plaintiff was wrongfully remanded, under bail, to appear, and he did appear before the said Gwilym Williams, as such stipendiary magistrate, at Pont-y-Prydh aforesaid, on Wednesday, the 16th day of January, when the plaintiff was again remanded to appear, and did appear, before the said Gwilym Williams, at Pont-y-Prydh aforesaid, on Wednesday 23rd January, when he was again remanded to appear, and did appear, before the said Gwilym Williams, at Pont-y-Prydh aforesaid, on Wednesday 30th January, when he was committed for trial; and at all the several times herein referred to the defendants falsely charged the plaintiffs with having committed certain misdemeanours, and the defendants proceeded in the prosecution thereof.

5. The defendants on the 13th, 14th, 16th, 23rd, and 30th days of January, 1884, maliciously and without reasonable and probable cause, preferred charges of alleged misdemeanour against the plaintiff, and proceeded in the prosecution of the same before the said Gwilym Williams, the then stipendiary magistrate for Pont-y-Prydh aforesaid, who, in consequence, committed the plaintiff for trial on such charges and caused the plaintiff to be bailed to answer the same, and on the 12th, 13th, 14th, and 15th days of February last the defendants, without reasonable cause, prosecuted the plaintiff thereon at the Winter Assizes, then held at Cardiff, in and for the county of Glamorgan, where the plaintiff was acquitted.

6. The defendants wrongfully kept possession of and detained for four days (commencing on the said Sunday, the said 13th day of January, 1884), from the plaintiff the dead body of his child, called Jessu Grist, without any and in defiance of authority, and also after lawful demand by the plaintiff, and after production to the defendants by the plaintiff of the coroner's certificate and order for the delivery to the plaintiff of the body of his said child Jessu Grist.

7. The defendants, on the 16th day of January aforesaid, with others, wrongfully broke and entered the plaintiff's lands and premises, known as Tai-ys-Sarn, at Llantrisant aforesaid, and destroyed and injured portions of the buildings and divers fowls of the plaintiff,

then thereon, and wrongfully searched such lands, buildings, and premises.

8. And for that the defendants falsely and maliciously, on the 13th, 14th, and 15th days of January, 1884, spoke and published of the plaintiff at Llantrisant, Pony-y-Prydh, Cardiff, and elsewhere in the said county, the words following (that is to say): – 'Dr Price' (meaning the plaintiff) 'has the body of a child,' (meaning his said child Jessu Grist), 'in his house, and he has caused or aided in its death, and intends illegally to cremate the body of the child' – (meaning thereby that the plaintiff, by want of skill and neglect, had occasioned or contributed to the death of his said child, Jessu Grist, and was intending to commit a misdemeanour in reference to the disposal of its body. – Whereby the plaintiff has been greatly injured in his credit and reputation, and damaged in his profession as a medical man.[45]

Dr Price also listed the costs involved in the damage sustained to his property:

A.–For the breaking and entering and wrongful searching and seizure, destruction and injuries, referred to in paragraphs 1 and 7 (that is to say, on the 13th and 16th of January, 1884, and inclusive of £1 10s, the cost paid by the plaintiff for the said goods, barrel, and oil, and the expense of carriage–£30.

B.–For the wrongful assault and beating, and taking from the plaintiff's lawful custody the dead body of his child, Jessu Grist, as alleged in paragraph 2, and assaulting and beating the plaintiff, and arresting him, and dragging him over Cae-yr-Lann, and through the public streets, and imprisoning him, and bringing and falsely charging him before the said Gwilym Williams, the stipendiary magistrate, as alleged in paragraphs 3, 4, and 5, viz.: on the 13th, 14th, 16th, 23rd, and 30th of January, 1884),–and prosecuting him at the winter assizes in and for the county of Glamorgan, as alleged in the last-mentioned paragraph (that is to say, on the 12th, 13th, 14th, and 15th days of February, 1884)–£2,700.

C.–For the expenditure and expenses of the plaintiff, and his loss of time and professional fees as a medical man, consequent upon the aforesaid charges, and in defending himself therefrom, on the aforesaid several days of January and February respectively, namely, expenditure and expenses, estimated at £50, and loss of time and fees £60–£110.

D.–For the wrongful possession and detention by the defendants of the dead body of the plaintiff's child, Jessu Grist, as alleged in paragraph 6 (viz: on the 13th, 14th, 15th, and 16th January, 1884)–£50.

E.–For the slander of the plaintiff by the defendants, as stated in paragraph 8 (viz.: on the 13th, 14th, and 15th January, 1884)–£105.

F.–For the expenditure and expenses of the plaintiff, and his loss of time before the coroner, and professional fees, in consequence of the said slander, £25–£130.[45]

At the outset Dr Price asked for the original depositions of *Regina* v. *Price*.

'They are not here,' said the judge.

'They can be had on your order, my lord,' Dr Price replied.

It was ordered by His Lordship that the depositions be handed to Dr Price by the clerk of arraigns, and this was done.

Dr Price, after the jury had been sworn, produced copies of his committal and acquittal at the Cardiff Assizes on the charge of cremation; also the notice of action. The pleadings were also produced.

Dr Price was about to call his first witness when the judge asked whether Dr Price was not going to explain his case to the jury, so that the jury might have some conception of it.

Dr Price said that he was going into the witness box himself ultimately and the judge said it would suffice.

Thomas Williams, surveyor, was called to produce to the court a plan of his house and the surrounding district of where of the cremation took place, and Justice Grove certified them.

Dr Price then called Sergeant Hoyle, one of the defendants, when the judge suggested that Price had better be sworn himself, so that the case might be started.

Dr Price addressed the jury with,

My Lord, and gentlemen of the jury. In this case I am the plaintiff. My complaint is this:–On the 13th of January last, on a Sunday, I was cremating my infant son, Iesu Grist, on my own land. I had been there for some time – say for half an hour – before any interruption was attempted by the police – who then interfered and seized me as a felon and a murderer. They knocked the cask down which contained the body of my infant child and scattered the contents of the barrel over the ground. The cask contained about ten gallons of paraffin for the purpose of cremating the body of my infant son.

They also hooked the body of my infant out of the flames with this stick (produced). This is the stick with which the body of my infant son was hooked out of the fire by Albert Davies, under the direction of W. Hoyle. Davies struck the body of my infant son three or four times with this stick – there were marks on the head of my son when I made a post-mortem examination. Davies ultimately hooked the stick round the neck of my infant son and got the body out of the fire, and dragged it for a distance of 64 yards. It was then carried to the station, and I, too, was taken there like a felon. You will observe from the plan that there is no road or way to the field without trespassing on my own lands. The police station is about 600 yards off. One Francis took me, helped by Hoyle. They took me and lodged me in the police station, where I was for about twelve hours, without any warrant for my apprehension or imprisonment. Until the police appeared on the field there was no disturbance, nor did anyone at all interfere with me. There was a large crowd in the next field. I heard the police direct the crowd. There was no breach of the peace until the police interfered.

I was ultimately taken to the Cross Inn Station of the Taff Vale Railway to meet Mr Williams. I was only there for about ten minutes when Mr Williams arrived, and he declined to take my bail there until he had consulted Mr Matthews. I was taken to Pontypridd, and there my bail was taken, by direction of Mr Williams, and I was liberated. That was on the 14th January. On the 15th there was an inquest held at Llantrisant, and I was subpoenaed to attend as one of the witnesses. The inquest was held and a verdict returned by the jury of natural death of the infant. There was a post-mortem examination of the infant ordered by the Coroner, and which I attended. I was remanded four times to Pontypridd by Mr Williams. I claimed the body of my infant at the station and it was refused me. Jabez Matthews took it away. On the 16th January I appeared before the magistrates of Pontypridd, Mr Williams being the Stipendiary, when I had an order to receive the body, and on the night of the 16th I called at the station and had the body. I went with it about 160 yards to feed a fat cow which I had. Two policemen followed me. William Hoyle, one of the defendants, was one. He had charged me that day with chopping up the child and burning it in an uninhabited house there. He made the poor women there believe that I had burnt the body, but there had not been no fire in the house for five years. On that night there was a great crowd, who pelted me with stones and cried out. Two policemen were there, and I believe they put the crowd on. I could not go home until about eleven o'clock at night. It was on the 30th January, I was committed to take my trial at Cardiff. I was tried at the Cardiff Winter Assizes and acquitted.[45]

The judge asked, 'Who took you to the gaol as if you were a felon?'

'A man named Francis, helped by Hoyle. Until the police appeared on the field there was a large crowd on the next field, but they did not interfere with me till the police came, when the police directed them to interfere.' Dr Price said he heard the police directing them. He felt he was not causing a breach of the peace until the police interfered.

Dr Price added, 'The crowd followed me that night, and pelted me with stones.'

'Did the policemen pelt you with stones?' asked the judge.

'They were in the crowd, and I believe they put the crowd on. My life was put in peril, and though my house was not far off, I could not go home till eleven o'clock at night. I was out till then,' he said.

Mr McIntyre asked Price, 'What was the name of the child?'

'Iesu Grist,' he replied.

'Whose child was it?'

'It was my child,' Dr Price said.

'Was it the child of Gwenllian Llewellyn,' McIntyre asked.

'It was my child.'

'Yes but the child must have had a mother?'

'No,' replied the doctor, 'It was my child.'

'What, no mother!' McIntyre explained to great hilarity.

'I am one of those persons called medical men, and when I go to houses I am privileged not to say anything about what I see there,' Dr Price replied.

'Ah, but this is your own house. Was the child ever christened?' asked McIntyre.

'I christened the child.'

'What did you christen it?'

'Iesu Grist.'

'Was the child born in your own house?'

Dr Price replied, 'I don't say.'

'But you will say, if you please,' said McIntyre. 'I have other questions to put about that. Was the child born in your own house?'

'I am privileged not to give that.'

The judge interrupted, 'No, there is not such a legal privilege.'

'My lord, we medical men are on our oath that we don't disclose anything that we know of other persons.'

The judge argued, 'But the law says you must disclose it. The law knows a privilege with regard to solicitors and their clients, but not with reference to medical men. The learned counsel asks you where the child was born.'

'It was born in my house, my lord,' he admitted.

McIntyre questioned, 'Was Gwenllian Llewellyn its mother?'

'No,' he said

'Who was its mother?'

'I don't know,' was the reply.

'Didn't you assist at its birth?' he asked

'I am privileged not to say.'

'No; my lord has said you are not privileged.'

Dr Price referred to the oath which surgeons, he said, took.

McIntyre queried, 'Now, doctor, did you assist at the birth of the child?'

Dr Price, in reply, admitted this, and also acknowledged the paternity.

'Will you tell me who was the mother of the child?'

'That's a difficult question for me.'

'Who do you believe to have been the mother of the child?' McIntyre asked.

'I believe in nothing,' he answered, which resulted in laugher throughout the court.

McIntyre again asked, 'Do you know who the mother was?'

'It is very likely I do,' was the response, again with laughter from the crowd.

'Well, as it is very likely you do, will you be kind enough to inform me who the mother is?'

Finally Dr Price responded with, 'Very likely it was Gwenllian Llewellyn. I believe she was the mother of the child.'

'You believe Gwenllian Llewellyn was the mother of the child?' McIntyre inquired.

'Very likely she was.'

'Was she or was she not?'

'She was.'

His Lordship stated, 'Then why don't you say so at once. You are not doing your case any good by answering in that way.'

Dr Price responded with, 'Well, she was the mother, and is nearly the mother of another one again.' Gwenllian was only a matter of weeks before giving birth to another son.

The cross-examination continued. Dr Price said that he did not register the child. He never registered his children, and he had had several, he said.

McIntyre said, 'How did you take the body of the child to the place of cremation?'

'How you think?' was his awkward response.

'I was not there, you see. Will you tell me?'

Dr Price replied, 'Well, I don't much mind that if it will give you any satisfaction. I bound him up in twenty-one clean napkins and then carried him up under my arm. The barrel of paraffin was taken up about a quarter of an hour before by my man-servant, a man named Tootell. I don't know whether Gwenllian Llewellyn was in the trap which took up the barrel. I saw her after near the gate of the field where the body was burnt. The barrel and the body were carried to the top of a high hill, 500 feet above the level of the sea. I put the body of the child in the barrel, and then set fire to it. There was not a soul then present in the same field – not for about half an hour. There were some women shrieking in an adjoining field. The men did not shriek out as well. The men did not threaten to lynch me. They did follow me and threaten me – but that was not in my own field, but in the next field. I heard some women shrieking, and I saw one woman vomiting there. There might have been some in the crowd ready to do me violence and there were some there ready to protect me, but not the police. The police had no business to touch the body of my infant child at all. They took me to the police station like a felon. I walked quietly enough afterwards. Mrs Hoyle did give me a blanket at the police cell, and did all in her power to make me comfortable. The women are always kind and tender to me, somehow or other. I was not afraid to go to my house that night.'

The cross-examination continued and revealed he had kept the dead body of the infant from 16 January until 21 March under the bed in his house, and then cremated it.

'Did you not say that you were afraid that the crowd would kill you if you went to your own house that night?'

'No; it's a lie.'

'Did you not say you were afraid the crowd would go to your house and kill Gwenllian Llewellyn?'

'No; that is a lie, too.'

'Did you not ask Hoyle to go down to your house and protect Gwenllian?'

'No, I did not. That's a lie.'

'Or Francis?'

'No. That's a lie.'

McIntyre said, 'You must not make use of such coarse language. Simply say yes or no.'

Mr McIntyre cross-examined Dr Price as to the conditions upon which the body of the infant had been given him at the instruction of the stipendiary magistrate, and the alleged infraction of the conditions.

Dr Price, in support of his action, quoted the Welsh adage, '*Nid twyll y twyllo twyllwr*' ('It is no sin to deceive a deceiver').

'They had stolen my child, and they wanted to steal it again; and do you think I was such a simpleton as to keep a mere promise to do what I suggest to my own child?'

'When the child was given up to you, did you promise to bury it?' McIntyre asked.

'I did not promise to bury it. I promised to take it.'

'And have it buried?'

'No, I didn't.'

'What?'

'No, I didn't,' Dr Price repeated. 'For I never intended it; and, besides, if I had promised, it was not upon the condition of receiving my own child.'

The judge interrupted, 'Never mind. We only want the facts. We can judge of them afterwards.'

McIntyre continued, 'Did you promise to have it buried?'

'I promised Mr Williams very likely to do it, but with the certain intention of never doing it at the time.'

'Then although you made a solemn promise...'

Dr Price interrupted, 'I did not make a solemn promise.'

'Well a promise without solemnity?'

'Yes, without solemnity,' he replied, with laughter in the room.

Justice Grove questioned, 'Why go into all this. He admits that he broke his promise.'

McIntyre said 'But it was only on consideration of your making that promise that you had the child given up to you.'

'He held stolen property,' Dr Price explained, 'and he was not the owner of my child.'

'That is Mr Gwilym Williams you are speaking of?

'Yes.'

'Mr Gwilym Williams had stolen your child? Did the jury at the assize trial say in their verdict that Dr Price was not justified in attempting to dispose of the body of the child before the coroner's inquest was held, and after reasonable notice from the coroner that an inquest should be held?'

Dr Price responded with 'Yes; but His Lordship said that that was no verdict at all.'

'And ultimately the jury found that you were not guilty?'

'Yes.'

Mr H. Ll. Grover, deputy coroner for the Glamorgan eastern district, was called and examined by Dr Price as to a certain letter written by him on 12 January, which contained the following words, 'There is no desire on the part of the coroner to hold an inquest if you will allow a medical man to see the child.' Grover said that he had no direct authority from the coroner, his instructions were general. He had before the inquest intimation from the police that there were reports afloat of ill usage of the child, and that it was doubtful what Dr Price would do with it.

Mr E. B. Reece, coroner for the eastern division, also gave evidence bearing upon the inquest, and in cross-examination remarked that he had considered an inquest was needed on the child because it was dead in the house, and its birth and death unregistered.

Dr Price claimed, 'Hoyle said in his communication to me that opinion was somewhat excited at Llantrisant. I did not see Superintendent Mathews on the subject until the inquest. I gave Superintendent Mathews a copy of the certificate of burial I gave you.'

Sergeant Hoyle said that he had given information respecting the death of plaintiff's child to the coroner. 'I am a sergeant of police. I went down with some information to the Coroner at Cardiff. I was told by scores – your servant girl for one – that you had a child who died suddenly in your house: that you had taken it (cradle and all) up and locked it up in

your room. I told the Coroner that you had not registered either the birth
or the death of the child, and that there was a general feeling in the town
that an inquest was necessary.'

'Who told you?' Dr Price asked.

'Levina Liddicox,' Hoyle replied. 'She said that the child had died
suddenly, and you had taken the body upstairs and locked it up in the
room.' Hoyle said he had told the coroner, and remarked that a great
many ratepayers at Llantrisant had, after the death of the child, thought
an inquest was necessary.

'Was that your feeling?' asked Price.

'I had no feeling in the matter at all,' was the response from Hoyle.

'Then how did you measure the feeling of the town if you had no feeling
yourself? Who authorised you to do so in the town?'

'I could not tell you – hundreds of people.'

'Name one or two of them,' Dr Price demanded.

'Mr Ebenezer Davies, the person you asked to make the box for you;
Mr Jones, the saddler; and Mr Richard Leach, of the Greyhound public
house.' Hoyle added that the first he knew about the burning of the body
was what he saw when the burning took place and when he pulled the
child out of the cask.

Dr Price asked Hoyle if it was not the fact that he had ordered Albert
Davies to pull it out. Hoyle admitted the fact.

Hoyle said, 'I had not then heard that it was your intention to burn the
child. I did not know that until I saw you doing it. I saw the flames, and
on going up I saw the fire coming out of the cask. I caught hold of you
and handed you over to the custody of Francis. I then tipped the cask over
and the body of the child fell out. I told Albert Davies to pull out the body
from the flames. We took the body to the police station. We took you there
as well. I had no authority to do so at the time. I went over a hedge to get
into your field. I acted on my own authority and discretion. Mr Williams,
the stipendiary, did not tell me to keep you in the cells that night. I took
you in custody to Pontypridd and handed you over to Superintendent
Matthews, who took you to Mr Williams, the stipendiary. I said in my
evidence at Pontypridd that I had heard you were chopping up your dead
body. I swear I smelt a stench of burning there.'

'Yes, and that was what made the people mad,' Dr Price stated.

Under cross-examination, Hoyle said that after taking from the coroner
a message to Dr Price requesting that certain steps should be taken to
avoid any inquest. Dr Price said that if they came to his house to hold an
inquest he would 'blow their brains out'. Dr Price promised that he would
go and see the coroner. That very evening, seeing a fire in the doctor's field,
Hoyle went up there. The crowd shouted out to him not to go close, or the
doctor would shoot him.

'He does carry things about with him, does he not?' asked McIntyre.

'He boasts that he does,' said Hoyle.

Dr Price shouted, 'What is that? I carry much worse things than you think of.'

McIntyre said, 'Perhaps you do; but I hope that you won't try them on me.'

Hoyle went on to say that he went forward to the doctor. 'When I took hold of the doctor the crowd shouted out to me to let him go, and they would burn him, the old beast. The crowd was very violent, and I and the other officer were obliged to do all we could to prevent the crowd from lynching him.

'They continued in the same strain all the way to the police station. The gate there had to be barred to keep the crowd out. I gave Dr Price at the police station one of his top-coats and two rugs and two blankets and also offered to fetch anything Dr Price required from the house. Dr Price answered, "No, no. It will be no good. Miss Llewellyn won't give it you." A message came to the police station saying that the crowd had gone down to Dr Price's house. Upon that the doctor said, "Go by all means, and protect Miss Llewellyn."

'I and Francis then went down and saw an excited crowd there, who were yelling and shouting and threatening to pull the house down. It would not have been safe to have allowed Dr Price to go to his own house. He would have been lynched – killed. The women were worse than the men and some of them were made very ill.'[45]

On Saturday morning again at the Glamorganshire Assizes, Swansea before Justice Grove, the case continued.

The first witness now called by Dr Price was landlord Roderick Lewis, who said that he remembered going to Caerlan on the night of 13 January. The attempted cremation had commenced when he appeared on the scene, and the police had Dr Price in charge. Lewis said he did not see the body of the infant pulled about the field, but saw it by the hedge afterwards. Nor did he hear anybody threatening the doctor's life at all, but the people were very excited.

Justice Grove asked, 'When PC Francis had hold of the doctor's hand, was there any disturbance?'

'Not at all, sir.'

Dr Price questioned Lewis, who said, 'I saw no one attempt to strike you. There was no danger of anyone doing anything of the kind. I was one of the jury at the inquest. I was the foreman. Seven of them are here now. There was a great crowd on the occasion referred to. They were very excited, and some shrieking. I did not hear any of the crowd call out "Lynch him". Some of the crowd were against the doctor, and others were the other way.'

Thomas Williams said that he went into the field on the night of the cremation but did not see anyone attempt to do anything to the doctor. He said that PC Francis had the doctor by the hand, and put the fire out so that it should not burn the grass. He did not hear anyone threaten the doctor's life between the Caerlan and the Bull Ring, on the way to the police station; all he heard was one man in the crowd calling out that Dr Price ought to be burnt.

Uriah Watkins was examined by Dr Price in confirmation of what had already been stated in evidence, when the judge remarked, 'I don't suppose it is to be denied that the police did interfere to prevent the cremation being consummated – the consummation of the burning.'

McIntyre said, 'The police had the flames extinguished, and took possession of the body. That never has been disputed.'

Dr Price asked Watkins, 'Did you see any of the crowd interfere before the police came there?'

'The police were there when I came. Some of the crowd were shouting out, "Burn him!" and I heard the words "Lynch him!" used. The women were shrieking, and there was a great disturbance.'

'Did you see any of the crowd attempt to lynch me?'

'No, sir.'

'Was there any danger of my being lynched, do you think?'

'Indeed I can't say,' Watkins replied.

'Did you see any expression of fear in my face?'

'I never was in such a place before.'

Lewis Ajax was called and said that he saw the body of the infant dragged along the field twenty-five or thirty yards, with a stick similar to that produced by Dr Price.

Ann Thomas said that she was at Caerlan and the smell of the oil and the noise affected her. She added that she thought that Dr Price should be burnt instead of the baby.

Police Superintendent Jabez Mathews, one of the defendants examined by Dr Price, said, 'I was first informed of the attempted burning of your child between 12 and 1 a.m. on the Monday. Sgt Hoyle informed me. I had no communication with Mr Williams, Miskin. I gave no directions to Hoyle.'

'You gave him no instructions then, did you, with respect to my being then in your custody?'

'No. He went back to Llantrisant without any directions from me. Mr Williams, he told me, had instructed him to bring you before him next morning. I saw you afterwards in custody that morning on the Pontypridd Railway platform. Mr Stockwood, the magistrates' clerk, and Mr Gwilym Williams, the magistrates were present.'

'What was the result of the captivity?' Dr Price asked.

'You were at once bailed out to appear at the police court on the Wednesday following. During that time your infant son was in the custody of Hoyle, I should think. There – at the station – I saw it on the Tuesday. He told me that he had got the child. I was at the inquest. I refused to give the child up to you unless you complied with what I said. I did not consider that the body belonged to me. I told you I would be willing to give up the body if you would promise to bury it decently.'

'What authority had you for this?'

'I did not want another scene to take place.'

Dr Price said, 'That's a different thing.'

The constable said that the body was given up to Dr Price on the Wednesday, on his making the requisite promise.

'Did you say before the coroner that it was your business to bury the child?' Dr Price asked.

'No, I did not.'

'Why did you want a certificate then?'

The officer said the magistrates might order him to bury; hence he had taken the precaution. He had given the certificate to Hoyle, who lost it.

'I told you that if you were to apply to the coroner and give your word of honour that you would bury the body decently, I would make no objection at all to your having it, otherwise I would be bound to detain the body until the following day.'

Price asked, 'What was your authority for detaining the body of my child I want to know? Now, your authority?'

'My own authority.'

'Your wilful authority?'

'I acted for myself.'

Replying to the judge, the witness said that Dr Price had refused to listen to his proposals at the inquest to decently inter the infant.

'And you exercised your own authority at law to ask me that?' Dr Price said.

'I did it, Dr Price; I told you so.'

'Why didn't you say so at once?'

'I did say so.'

'It is clear that you had no business to do so, and for that reason I would not do it. You had no business with my child. There is no question about it.'

Emanuel John traced the incidents of the evening from the time when he and the doctor took the baby to the empty house on to the period when they left. After Hoyle came on the scene, on their exit from the house, stones flew. He told the doctor their brains would be knocked out, and he and the doctor went to the Bear Inn for refuge. They were afterwards out a long while.

Albert Davies was called and said that on the night of the attempted cremation he went to Caerlan with Sgt Hoyle and pulled the infant's body out of the fire with a stick.

Dr Price asked, 'How many times did you strike the infant with a stick?'

'Did you see me strike it?'

'Yes,' the doctor replied.

'Then you are saying a lie.'

Dr Price questioned, 'Are not your family pensioners of Mr Williams, of Miskin?'

'No, sir,' was the response.

'Are you the son of a person who is familiarly know at Llantrisant as Jack Rann?'

'That is not my father's name.'

'What is it?'

'John Davies,' but Davies admitted that the other appellation was also, perhaps, used ('Jack Rann').

Dr Price said in Welsh, 'Go down, you are not worth a potato.'

Mr McIntyre asked, 'Is there a case to go to the jury?'

Justice Grove answered, 'I think there is a case for the false imprisonment.'

'What I contend is this: that the coroner having given notice that he would hold an inquest upon the body of the child, the taking of the child for the purpose of burning or destroying the remains of the child so that the coroner could not hold an inquest upon it was a misdemeanour.'

'I don't say anything about that at present. I am with you on that part of the case,' the judge replied.

'Well, that being so, if a man is found committing a misdemeanour, a police constable may apprehend him.'

'What authority have you?' asked the judge.

'*Russell on Crimes*.'

'It is so with a felony, there is no doubt.'

McIntyre explained, 'The distinction is this: Upon suspicion of felony a person may be apprehended by warrant. But in a misdemeanour a person must be found committing the misdemeanour?'

'Where do you plead this?'

'My lord, the pleading is not guilty by statute; that the police officer is protected by statute in any action taken.'

The judge (perusing certain documents) said, 'No, it is not here. There is not a word about "under" the statute on it.'

Mr Hughes said, 'I certainly put in the pleading by statute, and in the margin I cited several cases bearing on the case. It was in the draft of the pleadings.' The judge said that he should not look at the draft. It was not on the record 'under the statutes'.

McIntyre said, 'By an unfortunate omission in the copying, the words 'under the statutes' is not in the pleadings sent to the plaintiff. Will your Lordship amend the record to that effect?'

'No, I cannot do that; it would raise a different defence altogether. The plaintiff had the right to know the grounds upon which the defendants said they were justified in doing what they did. It was not stated in these pleadings that they were justified 'under the statute'. If I now allow that to be inserted on the record, the plaintiff would have to go through the whole of the cases bearing on the point. Now, in this particular case – was the plaintiff committing a misdemeanour? Now, cremation in itself is not a misdemeanour, but it was a misdemeanour if it was done with the intention of preventing an inquest being held or to obstruct the holding of an inquest.'

'Or to do it in such a way as to become a nuisance,' McIntyre suggested.

'Well, as far as the evidence goes it shows that he was tried for that, but that the jury found that he was not guilty of either.'

'Your Lordship, the jury were discharged without a verdict.'

'I cannot tell the jury on a matter like this that the man was committing a misdemeanour. If the act is one which may be or may not be a misdemeanour, then you should have pleaded that the constable did see him commit a misdemeanour. But you have not pleaded that. This is not felony. In false imprisonment for felony you have to prove that a felony was committed.'

'You must prove that felony was committed to enable you to set up the defence that you had reasonable and probable cause.'

'Yes, of suspecting a man of felony,' the judge said. 'So with a misdemeanour you must prove that a misdemeanour was committed, and that the constable had probable cause.'

His Lordship afterwards said that he had no issue for the jury upon the question of misdemeanour. He thought that defendant must go upon the matter of damages.

McIntyre suggested, 'I have a word to say upon that. As far as the slander is concerned, that is gone...'

The judge said, 'The slander is gone. I will tell you and tell Mr Price before we begin my view of the case, if that will help you. My impression is that, if the jury believe the witnesses who have been called, there was reason for their removing the body and preventing the burning being consummated, because at that time there were such circumstances as if proved, would justify the coroner in holding an inquest on it, viz., that the child had died suddenly (that they were informed so); that the child, immediately after its death, had been locked up in a room; that there was no certificate of the birth or death of the child, and that then the plaintiff was found burning the body of the child. Under these circumstances, I think, and shall tell the jury so, that if they believe the witnesses, there were sufficient grounds to justify the coroner in holding an inquest, and that the police constables, having also that information, were justified in preserving the body, and in using all reasonable means to preserve the body for the sake of a proper enquiry being made into the cause of death. So far I am with you. I must leave the question of the credibility of the witnesses to the jury. But with regard to the imprisonment, I don't see any justification. If it had been merely keeping the crowd off to protect Dr Price from their violence, I think they might have been justified in preventing a breach of the peace and injury to human beings; but it was unnecessary, it seems to me, to take him and lock him up at the station, and then take him before the magistrate. But they did take and keep him in custody, and so far it is a question of damages. That is the question upon which you must address the jury. If the jury think there was nothing hard or harsh done, then they will give merely nominal damages.'[45]

Mr Lewis submitted that the case with regard to Superintendent Mathews was not exactly on similar lines with those of Hoyle. 'Superintendent Mathews was not brought in the trial until Monday morning, until the parties had arrived at Pontypridd. It is not shown that Sgt Hoyle or what he did on the Sunday night was acting at all under Mathews's instructions.'

The judge referred to the evidence of Hoyle, that on the Monday morning, at the railway station, Hoyle left Dr Price in the hands of Mathews. Mr Lewis remarked that that would only apply to the waiting room whilst Dr Price was being admitted to bail.

'That may be, but that only goes to the damages. You know that it has been held that a constable locking a door upon a man for a minute is arrest, or even standing at a door and not allowing him to go out. I cannot say there is no evidence against Mr Mathews. It is true that the evidence against Mathews is very slender, but I don't thinks it is a case I can remove from the jury.'

Dr Price then addressed the jury, 'Gentlemen of the jury, I refrain from addressing you. You have heard the evidence, and if I addressed you for a whole day, I am quite sure you would take no notice of my address, but of the evidence that has been introduced. Therefore, I shan't say a word further than the evidence I have produced before you of what has happened.'

No witnesses were called for the defence, and Mr McIntyre addressed the jury for Sgt Hoyle. He contended that the police were justified in doing all that they had done. He said there was not the slightest evidence to prove that they had acted maliciously. All that had been done was brought about by the conduct of Dr Price himself, who, if he had not been guilty of an actual breach of the law, had outraged public decency by endeavouring to cremate the body of his child on the Sunday night just as people were coming out of church and chapel. Mr Lewis also addressed the jury for Superintendent Mathews, and urged that there was really no evidence against him.

The judge summed up at length. He left the jury four questions. But on the first, that of slander, His Lordship ruled that in point of law there was nothing to go to the jury. On the second, that of malicious prosecution, he was of the same opinion, though he did not absolutely rule it. The third question he would put to them was, did the plaintiff sustain any damage? And if so, what damage, by the detention of the body by the police? The fourth and most difficult and important question was, was there any false imprisonment? And if so, what damages would the jury award?

The jury, after a quarter of an hour's consultation, returned a verdict for the defendants, on the first, second and third counts, namely, slander, malicious prosecution, and detention of the body, but on the fourth count, that of imprisonment, they returned a verdict for Dr Price as against Sgt Hoyle, with damages of one farthing!

Upon the application of Mr Arthur Lewis, His Lordship certified for costs and special jury in the case of Superintendent Matthews. Mr G. B. Hughes said that under a recent Act he was bound to ask His Lordship not to allow costs for plaintiff as against Sergeant Hoyle.

Justice Grove said, 'Yes; previously the costs would follow verdict, but as the jury have found that you [Dr Price], were not substantially damnified, I shall not allow costs on either side, but you will have to pay the costs of Supt. Matthews.'

'The verdict in the case of Dr Price was received at Pontypridd with great enthusiasm on Saturday night. On the arrival of the seven o'clock train Superintendent Mathews was cheered and congratulated.'[45]

For the remainder of 1884 Dr Price's notoriety caused continual newspaper coverage, particularly the rumours that he was actually dead. Only a few weeks following the trial and the 'worthy and learned doctor who has recently occupied considerable portion of the public attention throughout Wales, and even England, seems to have fallen upon evil days ... he finds himself again – and perhaps not so pleasantly – the victim of an untoward fate'.[46]

A quarrel took place over the right of possession of fields near Llantrisant of which Richard E. Evans, a farmer, was the owner, but Dr Price had leased the land for grazing his 'cattle of the descendants of the ancient Druids' in 1882. The land was gated, with Dr Price holding the keys and when the lease expired Mr Evans required the land returned and asked for the keys, which Dr Price did not produce. In response, Evans secured the gates with wooden barriers or 'staples' and Dr Price, using a hammer, tried to break them, but failed. Evans appeared on the scene and an argument ensued but 'only served to inspire the aged doctor with youthful vigour and ire. At last, unable longer to repress his warlike promptings, the venerable Druid sprang upon the offending gentleman and laid hold, with no gentle hand of his beard. Mr Evans, unable to submit to such barbaric treatment, and with all his Celtic blood on fire, speedily retaliated, and by a dexterous movement of his right leg laid the doctor at full length on the ground …'[46] Gwenllian arrived on the scene, as the doctor shouted 'Police!' A constable also arrived and ordered Price to let the farmer go as they wrestled on the ground. Gwenllian helped the doctor to his feet and they left the field, threatening that legal action would shortly follow. Indeed he did lodge a complaint within the week.

The case was heard at the Glamorgan Summer Assizes in August 1884, again before Mr Justice Grove. Dr Price attempted to sue Richard Evans for £200 for the assault, while Evans wanted £5 in damages. On this occasion Mr Bowen Rowlands QC and Mr Brynmor Jones appeared for Dr Price, with Mr McIntyre QC, Mr Williams Evans and Mr Dillwyn appearing for Evans. The jury eventually decided on damages of one shilling to Evans for trespass and assault.

Richard Evans said that he lived at Maesaril Farm, Llantrisant. He was also tenant of Ton Mawr Farm. In 1882 he was tenant of seven fields and had then sub-let two fields to Dr Price, one to J. Evans, and one to W. David. However, he had no power to sub-let.

Mr Lewis, agent to Mr Insole, wrote to him on 15 April 1879, after which he saw Dr Price, who said that he would write an answer.

In the summer of 1882 Dr Price wanted the whole of Ton Mawr Farm. Evans said that if Insole would consent he would take him as tenant for the whole, and told him that if Mr Insole gave him notice he must quit the same as himself – that was six months. Dr Price told Evans he had seen Mr Insole and afterwards asked him to go to Cardiff to sign the documents, but Evans would not go.

At this point Dr Price told Evans that Mr Insole said he should have the land, if Evans was willing to leave it, but still he did not go and see Mr Insole. The agreement that Dr Price produced was signed by Evans and dated August. The agreement was signed on condition of Mr Insole's consent after Evans had signed.

Dr Price told Evans before the agreement was signed that Mr Insole had consented and he was still tenant under a six-monthly notice. Evans and David were yearly tenants then, to expire on 2 February any year. David and Evans went out in February 1883, and after that Dr Price was in enjoyment of the whole farm. After receiving certain letters bearing on the tenancy, Evans went and spoke to Dr Price as to the letting, and reminded him that he (Dr Price) had told him (Evans) that Mr Insole had consented to his being tenant.

Dr Price said, 'Don't you mind, I'll bring him round very well.' Evans asked the doctor to give him the half-year's rent, and he would take it down himself. Dr Price replied, 'No, you shan't; I am not a tenant of yours.'

Evans tried to persuade him further to pay the half-year's rent. Dr Price would not do so and said that he was a tenant of Mr Insole. Subsequently Evans paid Mr Insole, and asked the doctor for the half-year's money.

Dr Price said, once more, 'No, I won't pay.'

Evans subsequently sued the doctor in the county court for the half-year's rent, and recovered it and the costs.

Dr Price brought an action afterwards – for the same money – to get it back. The action was struck out.

On 30 July, Richard Evans was served with a six months notice to quit the Ton Mawr land by Mr Insole. On receiving it, Evans told Dr Price the terms of the notice on 31 July 1883. On 2 February 1884 Evans went on the land and called on Dr Price's house afterwards. Mr Thomas, who was with him, told Price what Mr Insole was doing, that he had come there to take possession. Dr Price said, 'Do what you like.' Thomas went back to the field, and took the cattle there to Dr Price. He told Mr Thomas that Mr Insole had consented to take him as a tenant. The doctor also said that Mr Lewis was along with Mr Insole when the latter consented to Dr Price becoming tenant. The doctor and some of his people took some of the cattle to his own field.

From 2 to 26 February the fields remained in possession of Mr Insole. On 2 March Dr Price put his cattle on Mr Insole's land. On the Wednesday morning Evans fastened the field gates with a chain and staples. He afterwards saw Dr Price at the gate pulling out the staple, with a chisel in one hand and a hammer in the other. With these tools he got the staple out and tried to open the gate, and Evans put his hand on the gate to prevent his doing so.

Amid much laughter in the court room, the audience heard that Dr Price put the hammer and the chisel into one hand and 'collared' Evans with the other. Evans then tried to get the hammer out of Dr Price's hand. He got it, and threw it over the hedge into the field.

Dr Price tried then to poke him in his side with the chisel, which he still held in one hand. He did him no harm, but he did poke the chisel against his side and Evans got the chisel and threw it over the hedge. The doctor then got hold of him with both hands, and he secured the doctor. There they stood for a while.

Evans said to the doctor, 'Doctor, let me loose' two or three times, and then said, 'Unless you loose me, I'll put you on your back.' With that Evans hit Price to the floor and kept hold of him on the ground.

A policeman was there, and came on saying, 'You let loose Mr Evans and then you'll be free.' He did not do so till the policeman pulled his hand from him. Then Dr Price got up and let him loose.

The judge said, among much hilarity, 'It is too late to do anything. Young men will be young men.'

Mr Evans said, 'You will see, my lord, from the statement of Clay that we have never asked for anything in the nature of damages. All we want is to be left in peace.'

Mr Rowlands suggested, 'You want the land.'

The judge said, 'Cannot you get to some arrangement by which the parties may live in peace and quietness? You [Mr Evans] say that Dr Price assaulted your client, and he [Dr Price] says that plaintiff assaulted him.'

Mr Rowlands said he did not think that he and Mr Evans would have the slightest difficulty about the question of assault. The only real difficulty was with regard to the right of tenancy and the deprivation of Dr Price's crop.

'I don't think so,' said Evans.

'No?' asked Rowlands.

'Oh, then we will leave it alone,' Evans replied.

The judge stated, 'These transactions have been extremely loose, speaking in a legal sense, and they may give rise to some considerable difficulty, which may take the case to the House of Lords, and by the time this gets there, if plaintiff and defendant live – five years hence – a great deal of money will have been spent. If before getting further they could come to some arrangement, all the better. If they cannot do so, well, then, I must try it out, and the jury must give their verdict.'

The counsel then consulted, but failed to agree upon a compromise.

Mr W. H. Lewis, colliery proprietor and agent for Mr Insole's Glamorganshire estate, said that there had not been any meeting upon this matter between Dr Price and Mr Insole.

Mr Isaiah Thomas, a retired farmer at Llantrisant, spoke about the altercation between Dr Price and the plaintiff.

PC Francis said that on the occasion of the alleged assault he was present; he saw no violence.

Mr Bowen Rowlands argued that the evidence for the plaintiff as to the custom of the country was absurd. Who could suppose that a man went into a farm at a rental of £1 a year, paid in advance on 1 February, must, because of the custom of the country go out on 2 February. The plaintiff was taking unfair advantage of the man who happened to be so unpopular as Dr Price now was. Dr Price was decidedly entitled to hold till 2 August 1884.

The jury retired at about 4.20 p.m. At 5.15 p.m. the jury re-entered the court, and gave a verdict for Richard Evans of 1s for the trespass (the assault being included in the shilling). In the counter-claim the jury gave a verdict for Mr Evans.[47]

Following the successive court hearings in 1884 alone, Dr Price's new-found fame allowed him the opportunity to gain widespread acclaim as a lecturer and guest speaker at various events for the remainder of his life, although his appearances almost always courted controversy, and he became an almost tragicomic figure as the newspapers continually wrote derogatory reports about his behaviour. In March 1884 he was invited to a meeting at the Public Hall in Blaina, where he was to give a lecture on the history of the Ancient Britons. Unfortunately the entire event descended into a pathetic, laughable display where the audience cheered in 'sympathy' at him. Chairman for the evening was Mr T. E. Watkins of Blaenavon who welcomed the doctor, who appeared dressed in his usual costume with a white tunic covering the coloured waistcoat and trousers. The Blaina Brass Band welcomed the new-found celebrity, who was cheered as he stepped onto the platform. Several Welsh songs were performed by various artists until Dr Price stood to rapturous applause and cheers from those who had read so much about the cremation case. However, despite having been invited to discuss Welsh history, he instead lectured about the cremation case itself and when he explained how he had been acquitted of the case, there was cheering from throughout the hall. He concluded with the quote he used on the medal struck to commemorate the cremation itself, and, following some music, Dr Price took off his tunic and appeared in a red costume which caused gasps and laughter.

> In his left hand he held a pole with horns at the top and red streamer hanging down. He spoke in Welsh with some hesitation but displaying a good deal of energy and enthusiasm for such an old man. From the laughter and cheers he appeared to please his audience and when he sang a Welsh song, which appeared to have reference to the emblematical parts of his dress, the laughter became convulsive and the doctor concluded amid cheers. Fresh mirth was caused by the doctor donning his trousers in front of the audience in the coolest manner possible. The dressing served to keep the good humour of the people, three parts of whom were said to be English and therefore could not appreciate the doctor's Welsh speech ... the music was the best part, except of course, the doctor's realism which seemed to tickle the fancy. At the close thanks to Dr Price were given as a mark of sympathy with him.[48]

Dr Price was also invited to be present at the dinner of the Cymmrodorion Society of Brynmawr, where he received an ovation. On arriving at the train station of the London and North Western Railway, dressed in his usual costume, a number of admirers met him on the platform and together they went to the Globe Inn. At the dinner he was given the place of honour next to the chairman and he rose, to a round of applause, to give a toast. He said that as the toast of St David had been proposed, instead of proposing it again, he would sing an old song which had been composed 3,700 years earlier and had been lying in the Louvre at Paris for 2,000 years. He explained how he had tried for forty years to decipher it and had published it in 1871 and that he was willing to teach the song to anyone who wanted to learn it, as long as they were Welsh. He explained that as Caradog had taken his grand Welsh choir to London, all Welshmen were great singers and that Welsh was not the language of books but of nations. He sang the song and 'used a music score without the aid of spectacles although he is in his 84th year. The copy was in hieroglyphics which no one but the exceedingly well versed in Welsh literature could understand.'[49]

The following week, the *Bristol Mercury* noted that Dr Price was among the audience at the Theatre Royal in Cardiff to see *Shadow and Sunshine* and was dressed in his picturesque costume, which attracted plenty of attention in the auditorium. When one of his heifers died on grazing land in Llantwit Faerdref in August, it also made news in the *Western Mail*, again displaying his celebrity status as he appeared in the gossip column.

He also appeared at the Cardiff Art Exhibition in April 1884 to describe his *Gwyllllys yn Nayd*. The event drew a large crowd to the Public Hall in Queen Street, where a number of women were present and were witness to an event not unlike an 'occult' gathering. Although he wasn't noted as a clear and loud public speaker at this event, he did say that children who were not taught the Welsh language would curse their parents for the omission. Again he struck up a song, condemned registration of birth and at that point kicked off his boots and removed his clothing to reveal his *Coelbren y Beirdd* costume. Amid great amusement he spoke of the contents of the goose's egg and how his own birth had been registered 3,700 years earlier. On completing his presentation he removed his items from the stage and left.

Not everyone was totally enamoured with Dr Price and his behaviour. The relationship between him and Morien had been a complicated one. On occasions, they supported one another in their mutual belief and understanding of Eastern religions and Druidism. In one of the court hearings Morien even stood as his bail surety. However, there had been the occasional fracas between them, some of which were well publicised in the local newspapers.

By the middle of March 1884 this occurred again when Morien wrote a damning report entitled 'Dr Price Not A Druid – A Protest From The ArchDruid'. The outburst had come following Price's own announcement that he was indeed an Archdruid of the Isles of Britain, a title Myfyr had held for some time, and which Morien himself would controversially adopt on Myfyr's death in 1888. However, the news report condemns Price from the outset, but in doing so also brings question and doubt over Morien's own curious beliefs, integrity and outrageous, unfounded claims over Welsh history and Druidic ancestry. It almost reads as a prologue to his fabricated history of Rhondda and Pontypridd. Morien claimed,

No one will believe for a moment that in submitting to the public that Dr Price is not the Archdruid and not even a Druid of the minor degree of Ovate I am actuated by any other interest than of truth. I would not say a word in disparagement of Dr Price personally. Setting aside some few peculiarities in his views of society most people like the eccentric doctor. As long as the fun introduced by Dr Price lasted I felt reluctant to disturb the notion that the venerable and clever physician was acting the part of an ancient Druid. But now, when the game has been played out and the public are settling down to judge the doctor and his curious antics by the sober light of reason, it is time to say a word in defence of the venerable creed of our ancestors, which the doctor's conduct has placed before the public in a most ridiculous light. He has attained great notoriety 'spurious notoriety' the local stipendiary magistrate described it – it is true and, no doubt it will be difficult to convince some people that he is not the profound Celtic scholar and learned sage they have assumed him to be.[50]

At this point Morien became outspoken in his condemnation of the surgeon:

Dr Price knows absolutely nothing, that is certain, about the mysteries of the Druidic creed. I admit that he has some hazy notions with regard to them. But to suppose that the antics he has played within the last few months in the face of high heaven are the result of the teachings of the mighty philosophers of Western Europe – grave men who reverently constructed a system of religion on the model of the universe, scholars who examined with awe the great laws governing that universe with a view to attain a better knowledge of the Great Architect – is preposterous in the extreme.

What has incited Dr Price during the last 60 or 70 years to comport himself so strangely in the valleys of South Wales? This is a difficult question to answer. An elderly lady of great intelligence who had known the doctor all of his life, assures me that his conduct dates from the time of a certain love affair in the neighbourhood of Hangar. Among the playful old customs of the Welsh people was one of presenting a forsaken lover with a cap made of willow branches. There this had some remote reference to the hanging of the harps on willows by the rivers of Babylon I am unable to say. But we know that the birch and the willow played important parts in the symbolic religion of the ancient Druids, and probably the custom signified abundance among them. Did Dr Price adopt the willow cap? Not he! But something that, with a view to convey a notion that henceforth, since the lady had wedded another, he would be a wanderer, he adopted the skin of a fox as a head covering.

But I am not of this opinion. I believe that Dr Price never intended to be a wanderer in the ordinary sense of the term. Nevertheless, he has visited many lands, and as is well known, he has always made public the fact of his presence wherever he went.

My humble opinion is that Dr Price's eccentricities are not to be attributed to a broken heart; on the contrary, that they are the outcome of muddled ideas respecting ancient philosophy. He evidently became early in life enamoured with the brilliant ideas scattered like nuggets of gold in the ruins of ancient paganism. But he, being ignorant respecting the whereabouts of the key which would unlock the mysteries which would enable him, if he had capacity enough, to reconstruct the temple, became bewildered, and has remained in that condition ever since. Let anyone talk with him on any other subject, than ancient lore, and, he is intelligent and instructive. But lo! Touch not the hem of archaeology in his presence, and he will tell one that Greek is Welsh obscured by a little bad spelling; that Homer is Great Hugh and unquestionably a Welshman, and that every syllable of his poetry is pure Cymraeg. He will insist that the Pyramids of Egypt and the mighty temples of the land of the Pharaohs were built by builders from Caerphilly. He will speak to some 'Lettered Man' 'whose skin walked without the man'. Therefore it is fair to infer that the man, whoever he was, must have remained until his skin returned minus an essential covering. It will hardly be believed that the doctor has evolved this statement and of one of the titles applied to the Gwyddon, or the Pontiff of the Druidic system in ancient days. He was called 'man of letters' in the same sense as the phrase is understood in the present day. But Dr Price has had a tight fitting red dress made with golden Roman letters scattered all over its front, in imitation of the skin of the 'Lettered Man' ... Dr Price's creed is a medley of several other creeds jumbled together. His dress is an illustration of this. His cap is emblematical of the dog-headed god Anubia, of Egypt; his shawl is Scotch – a Royal Stuart tartan. The scallops along the edge of his smocks and trousers belong to Zoroaster, the Persian Sun Worshipper. All that is Druidic about him is his white hair and beard, the green of his clothes and the white of his smock. I reiterated and challenge him to prove the contrary that he know nothing about the Druidic mysteries preserved by the chair of Glamorgan. No one is more indignant with Dr Price for dragging the Druidic name among his fooleries than the great Druidic scholar, the real ArchDruid, Myfyr Morganwg, Pontypridd. I have authorities by him to protest most solemnly against associating the Druidic name with Dr Price's wretched travesty. From the great throne of the British Druidic hierarchy the herald of the Gorsedd is commanded to proclaim in the face of error and its disciple, '*Y Gwir yn Erbyn Y Byd*' ('Truth Against The World').[50]

In September 1884 the *Bristol Mercury* wrote to Dr Price requesting an interview, to which Dr Price wrote the most astonishing reply:

> I shall feel much pleasure in teaching your representative Englishman all he can comprehend with his four natural senses, that is to say, his natural sense of sight, his natural sense of smell, his nature sense of taste and his natural sense of feeling; but it is impossible to teach him to hear and to speak and to understand my natural ideas of original memory, original language, and original hearing as the three natural ideas or memory, language and hearing have been suppressed or blotted out of the brain of your presentative Englishman by his education, who is taught to ignore of the three of his original senses to make him or her mad, for robbery and murder in Afghanistan, South African and subsequently by a change of form the same mad game has been played in Egypt to the tune of ten millions to pay the bondsmen of Egypt!!! Such you are Englishmen with only four of your natural senses empowered to govern the island of Britain, the bards of our country called '*Gwlad nev*' or the Country of Heaven – *Anglice*!!! I shall send you by this post a copy of the will of my father 3,700 years of age. In the language of Gwunt and Morgane at the present day, deciphered by me.[51]

The newspaper reacted with a footnote stating that the 'last of the Druids' was not a Druid of any kind or for that matter a doctor, and listed his titles in the Medical Directory for 1884.

On 8 October 1884 Dr William Price and Gwenllian Llewellyn had a second son. On naming him Iesu Grist II, Price believed he would inherit all his Druidic wisdom as his first son would have done. Newspaper reports make mention of the birth, congratulating the doctor on fatherhood once more, at the age of eighty-four.

The *Pontypridd Chronicle* made an announcement of the event, the content of which is questionable at best.

> Dr William Price has, it is stated got another baby, Gwenllian, his housekeeper having delivered on Monday of a fine boy. Dr Price, with all his learning, was uncertain as to whether the expected one would be a boy or a girl and therefore in anticipation of the new visitor being a daughter her had prepared a feminine name, namely Virgin Mary. The public will learn with satisfaction that according to the latest tidings from Llantrisant both mother and little one are doing well. The inhabitants of the ancient town are much exercised in respect of the interesting event which has just taken place among them for they know not what the advent of the young Apollo in their midst may result in the near future – in the future history of the town and borough. It is reported that Dr

Price is wild with joy at the happy event ... all Monday he seemed to
utter praise to some unknown god and goddess for bringing him another
baby who, he believes, is the future to rival all who have gone before
him in the splendour of his career and usefulness to the human race. In
fact this '*Maban*' as he spells it, which is Welsh for 'baby' is the Tenth
Avatar and is the Long Expected Goa. Prophetical foreshowing of the
event which has just taken place in Llantrisant, has mislead the so-called
Mabdi and caused all the troubles in Egypt and the Soudan, it is said
the world does not know of its greatest men, and the birth of the baby,
according to Price, is proof of this ...[52]

Dr William Price also sent notice to Morien, via Mochyn Du, that he was
to have the new-born child and Gwenllian photographed. The image was
published, alongside an image of himself dressed in the costume covered
with the *Coelbren y Beirdd* letters. Above the two images were further
hieroglyphics and scenes akin to a Pharaoh's tomb. Below it Dr Price again
wrote in his almost indecipherable Welsh about the legacy of Iesu Grist,
claiming his birth was seen by the Gods and the oldest of the people of
'Cymmru' as written in *Myvyrian Archaeology*. He goes on to add that the
prophecy of his birth was also seen in Montfaucon's volume and signs the
document (which was published by Sprague & Co. of London) as 'William
Price Yth'. This item was sold and published in sufficient quantities over
the coming months and once again exemplified his belief in the worth of
self-publicity and showcasing his knowledge, talents and the affirmation
of his son's god-like abilities to restore the Druid order.

At the end of December 1884, Dr Price made the news again, this time
when he cremated his prize bull Morgan Apis, who died from cold during
the frosty weather. The obedient beast was taken to the summit of East
Caerlan and a large load of coal was brought to the area where the bull
was cremated. Later in the evening, the 'white-robed priest of the sun'
stood and began the funeral pyre to send the ashes of Morgan the bull to
the four winds.

It had been an incredible year indeed, and one that would secure Dr
William Price in the annals of world history.

49. *Llantrisant*, by H. Gastineau, 1832.

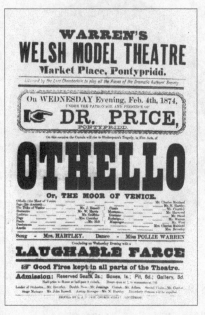

Above left: 50. Dr Price sponsored a performance of *Othello* at Pontypridd, 1874.

Above right: 51. Ann Price (1804–78), a younger sister of Dr Price.

OYS. BYS. OYS

GELWYDD, LLW. VOD. SAITH. OYR. TYSTION.
DORRWYD. GYNNTA. ARR. Y. GARREG. DENNI. YN. GORWEDD.
CARTHWYD. WYNT. LL. BWLL. Y. DOMMEN.
DAN. DRAED. O PHEIRIAT. EGLWYS. BETWAS
CLWWCH. NW. YN. LEYVAIAN. AM YAM ARCH.
YNG GWYDD. Y. VARN. A. YR. ATGYVTTIAD.
YNG BLWW Y. IESSU Y BIA. YNG GLEDDU.

TYWYSSOG. CARRIAD. GORON. CYMMRY

52. A letter from Dr Price to his sister Ann, explaining the situation of the Price family grave at Bedwas.

Above left: 53. Gwenllian Llewellyn (1859–1948).

Above right: 54. Dr William Price in full Druidic costume, 1871.

55. Cross Keys Hotel, Llantrisant, where Dr Price met Gwenllian with the remains of their baby son before the cremation commenced.

56. High Street, Llantrisant, looking towards East Caerlan, showing clearly the panoramic view it enjoyed, making the cremation visible for residents who saw the burning pyre.

57. Police Constable Philip Francis No. 163. (Picture used with the kind permission of Rosemary Williams)

58. *The Illustrated Police News*, 5 April 1884. (© The British Library Board, *The Illustrated Police News*)

ROSE HILL, LLANTRISANT. No. 1530.

59. The view from Dr Price's home, Tŷ'r Clettwr, along High Street, Llantrisant, where the mob gathered to attack.

60. The Bear Inn, Llantrisant, where Dr Price hid from the unruly mob.

Above left: 61. Justice James Fitzjames Stephen (1829–94).

Above right: 62. The second attempt at cremating Iesu Grist, as depicted by *The Illustrated Police News*, April 1884. (© The British Library Board, *The Illustrated Police News*)

63. The bronze coin Dr William Price had minted to commemorate the cremation of Iesu Grist Price, 1884.

64. Dr William Price in full costume, 1884.

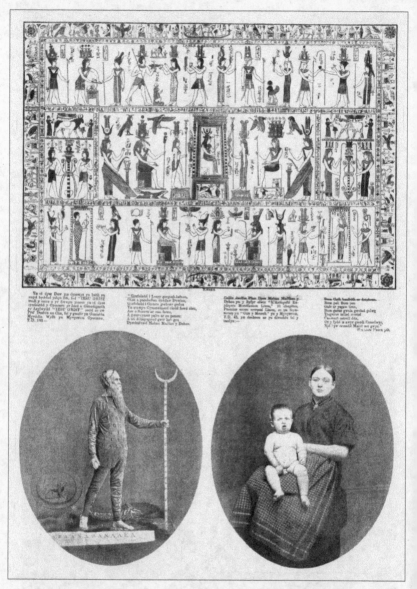

65. The print Dr Price had created to celebrate the birth of Iesu Grist II and to prove himself as the Primitive Bard of the Isles of Britain.

Above left: 66. Dr William Price and Dr Richard Anderson of Fernhill (1826–1901).

Above right: 67. Nicholas and Penelopen outside Tŷ'r Clettwr *c.* 1892.

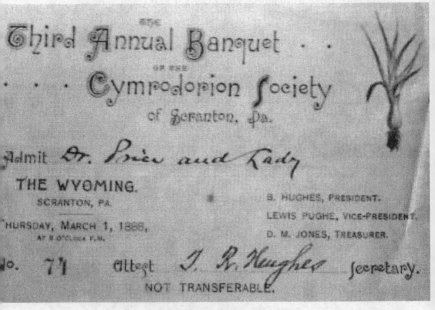

68. An invitation to attend the Third Annual Banquet of the Cymrodorion Society of Scranton, Pennsylvania, USA.

Above left: 69. Dr William Price with his family, Gwenllian, Penelopen and Iesu Grist II *c.* 1889.

Above right: 70. The Memorial Pole placed at East Caerlan by Dr Price.

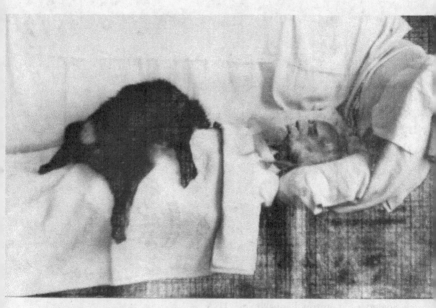

71. The late Dr William Price laying in state at Tŷ'r Clettwr.

In Memory of

DR. WM. PRICE,

WHO DIED JANUARY 23, 1893,

AGED 93 YEARS.

AND WAS CREMATED ON CAERLAN, JAN 31st, 1893

72. An obituary card to Dr Price which wrongly states he was ninety-three years of age when he passed away.

CREMATION OF DR. PRICE.

ADMIT BEARER.

Gwenllian Llewellyn.

Printed by Davies Bros, "Chronicle" Office, Pontypridd.

73. A ticket to attend the cremation of Dr William Price.

74. Crowds outside Tŷ'r Clettwr awaiting the distribution of tickets to attend the cremation of Dr Price.

75. Crowds trying to obtain tickets at Tŷ'r Clettwr to attend the cremation of Dr Price.

Right: 76.
A commemoration of
the life of Dr William
Price, 1893.

Below: 77. Gwenllian,
Penelopen and Iesu
Grist II pictured
among the crowd at
the cremation of Dr
William Price.

78. The cremation of Dr William Price at East Caerlan.

79. Crowds attending the cremation of Dr William Price.

80. Dr William Price's cremation at East Caerlan.

81. Iesu Grist II, later named Nicholas, *c*. 1889.

82. One of the poems written in memory of Dr William Price and sold at the cremation, 1893.

LINES ON THE DEATH AND CREMATION OF

The Grand Old Welshman

ARCH-DRUID DOCTOR PRICE

WHO DIED AT LLANTRISSANT, MONDAY, JAN. 23rd, 1893

IN HIS 93rd YEAR,

AND HIS REMAINS CREMATED SHORTLY AFTER HIS DEATH.

"LOG CABIN"

A grand old Cambrian Chieftain has just passed away,
From the land that we knew he loved so well,
Doctor Price the Druid you have known for many a day
And Llantrissant his history can tell.
Descended he could show, from centuries ago,
He has left the dear till mountains now at last ;
And nearly ninety-three were told that he must be,
A missing link between this and the past.

Llantrissant knew him well, he wants no funeral knell
No hypocrites in mourning him bewails,
If they carried out his wishes, they have done right well
For Doctor Price the grand Arch-Druid of South Wales

His Ancestors they were Druids when Llewellyn reigned as King
When the ancient Minstrels sung among the hills,
The Retainers in our Castles made the valleys sing,
And love of Country every bosom fills.
Not one shade of disgrace in our history can we trace,
Our enemies try to do it but they fail ;
And now the old man's departed we shall miss the face
Of Doctor Price the grand Arch-Druid of South Wales

If you saw him in the market his dress may have bewigoner
But he could please himself what he should wear,
His rough and ready costume was respected here,
To insult him I'm sure there's no one dare.
In Cremation he believed, and so he had conceived,
His principles of Religion he would show ;
To burn the useless body if the Soul's in heaven received
As the Druids did a thousand years ago.

Once had a daughter who died some years ago,
At his farm 'neath the shadow of the hill,
Her body was Cremated as in Pontypridd they knew,
And 'twas said he had committed a sin until—
The Magistrates found he could stand his ground,
And no one saw that incident bewails ;
For many English people as the years pass around,
Have left a will the same as Doctor Price of Wales.

In his will be plainly stated what he wanted them to do
To take his body as he died into the fields ;
The old ancient City of Chariton close in view,
The pure air of Heaven above him to be revealed,
He said take me away at the middle of the day
Let my ashes scatter as the breezes blow,
And where I am Cremated at some future day
Let the grass and the lovely flowers grow.

The fine old race of Welshmen are leaving us so fast,
There are few that now are left behind
There are few to show us the relics of the past,
But the Castle of Caerphilly calls to mind
When any foreign foe his features dare not show,
Before Cambria fell misfortune's guile ;
For Priests of that day, could fight as well as pray,
Like Doctor Price the Grand Arch-Druid of South
Wales.

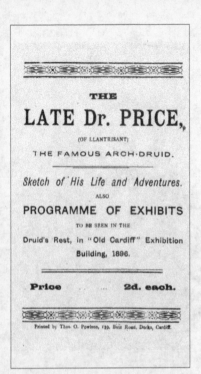

83. The exhibition on Dr William Price, 1896.

Above left: 84. An unknown artist portrayed Dr William Price.

Above right: 85. A handkerchief made to commemorate the life and death of Dr William Price.

86. Tŷ'r Clettwr in ruin, 1899.

Above left: 87. Penelopen Elizabeth Price, pictured around 1905.

Above right: 88. Penelopen Price dressed as Britannia at the National Pageant of Wales, 1909.

Above left: 89. Nicholas Price (1884–1963) pictured with the religious symbol on his tie.

Above right: 90. Rachel Parry, Hiarlhes Morganwg Price Williams and Gwenllian (Llewellyn) Parry at East Caerlan, *c.* 1925.

91. The unveiling of a tablet to Dr William Price by Penelopen and distinguished guests at Zoar Chapel, Llantrisant, 17 September 1947.

92. The crowd gather for the unveiling of the tablet to Dr William Price at Zoar Chapel, Llantrisant, 17 September 1947.

93. Penelopen (pictured centre) at the official opening of Thornhill Crematorium, Cardiff, 1953.

94. Nicholas Price pictured shortly before his death, *c.* 1962.

95. The unveiling of a statue to Dr William Price, Bull Ring, Llantrisant, May 1982.

Above left: 96. The statue of Dr William Price facing East Caerlan.

Above right: 97. Statue to Dr William Price, Bull Ring, Llantrisant.

98. Re-dedication of the plaque to Dr William Price. Pictured are Revd Peter Jupp, author Dean Powell, Lord Earl Grey (President of the Cremation Society of Great Britain), Ann Thomas of the Federation of Cremation and Burial of Great Britain, and Roger and Mrs Arber, Secretary of the Cremation Society of Great Britain, Zoar Court, Llantrisant, 17 September 2011.

1885–1893

With age, Dr Price's general conduct became increasingly bizarre, adding to the ever-growing array of stories about him. He remained a gifted surgeon and his services were in great demand in complicated cases or when other practitioners pronounced a hopeless situation. The eccentricities and oddities, the zeal and aggression of his youth became more florid with age, but he retained sufficient integrity to be a formidable opponent. The newspapers of his time showed him as a tragic figure playing a clownish part on the stage. The mumbling shambles of his appearance as an old man who undressed to the audience should not be recalled without remembering Lady Charlotte Guest's description of his eloquence all those years before.

His title in the Medical Directory of 1886 read,

PRICE, William, V.S.L.M., Llantrissent, Glamorganch. M.R.C.S., Eng, A.L.S.A. 1821 (St Barthol. A Lond. Hosp.). Decipher of '*Gwyllllis yn Nayd*'. Discoverer of *Gavval Lenn Berren Myurrdhdhin Syllt Tyurn wiallen Cyur Aneurin Gwawtrudh Awennudh Privv Varrydh Nuadh y Brann Gwunn Gwislen Lsnn ab Lann ab Deyl ap Peyl Sarrph ynus Pruttan a ych Chyoul Brenn Privv Varrydh Dusce Cymmru a Gwyllllis yn Nayd*.[1]

This astonishing and incomprehensible entry was improved the following year with the addition of 'Author of *Pedigree of Iesu Grist*'.

Dr Price explained that the entry recorded not only his medical qualifications, 'but also his Druidical discoveries'.[1]

V.S.L.M … means *Fi si La Mer* … I am the flood of the ocean. The Primitive Bard, you know, represents himself as the source of the ocean. Perhaps you have noticed that one of the emblems of Freemasonry is a board with water flowing out of the centre – that, really, represents the Primitive Bard. It is said that it was Newton who discovered that the moon influenced the movements of the sea, but that was well known to the Druids thousands of years before he was born …

I believe in nothing except what I know to be absolutely in existence. I used the Bible as it might be used. It is clear to me that Abraham was a cannibal, and it was with the view of destroying that trait in the nature of his descendants, and to raise tame animals, that the first pyramid in Egypt was built.[2]

There are also more stories about his behaviour than can possibly be collected, catalogued and verified as being partially true at best. However, such anecdotes that by their similarity also indicate the nature of the man as often stubborn, forthright, mischievous and downright awkward at times, have grown with his legacy. In fact it could be regarded as a tribute to the man that despite the passing of more than a century, stories, no matter how over-exaggerated, are still shared in the communities where he once resided. Often untrue or at very best inflated as to have little bearing on the truth, they still prove interesting and enjoyable reading.

There was the well-known tale of the local butcher who called on him to complain of a problem. He asked the doctor, 'If a dog entered some premises and stole a leg of lamb what would you advise?'

'Well, I would make the owner of the dog pay for the meat,' the doctor said.

'Well, it was your dog sir.'

'How much was the meat?' asked Price.

'Five shillings,' the butcher explained.

'Well here is your money.'

The delighted butcher was leaving when the doctor called him back. 'You owe me six shillings and eight-pence.'

'What for?'

'Legal advice,' said the doctor!

He allegedly had a new sign made for the Mount Pleasant public house on Commercial Street. When the creator painted the sign he also had it erected on the front of the premises. On visiting the pub, the doctor paid for the work, but refused to pay for installing it as he had not requested it take place!

One day he admired a chest of drawers in a shop. The shopkeeper could see he liked it and said he would 'send it down' to his home.

'As you like,' replied the doctor.

Some time later the keeper asked for payment and the doctor looked surprised. 'Sold? You asked me if I liked it. I said I did. You said you'd send it down. It was a gift.'

Dr Price absolutely revelled in his fame due to the outcome of the cremation court case. It inflated his already sizeable ego and gave him further confidence to inform others of his Druidic hierarchy and the rights and powers of his infant son Iesu Grist Price II. His wilful and determined personality became even more extreme than before and his deliberate attempts to cause further controversy, infuriating some in the process, continued despite his advancing years. For that matter, his frequent appearances at court cases also showed little sign of decreasing. As early as January 1885, the people of Llantrisant were once more witness to a cremation on East Caerlan when another of his cattle died and was disposed of in the leaping flames. Spectators gathered once more, many of whom remained in the vicinity until midnight to watch the grand old man exercise his religious rights.

Dr Price's friends were as peculiar as himself, particularly when remembering the picture of him sitting next to a man wearing a Wild West cowboy costume. Known as Dr Robert Richards Anderson, he resided in Fern Hill, the idyllic Carmarthenshire dairy farm which was so beautifully captured in the childhood memories of Welsh poet Dylan Thomas seventy years later. In fact, when Thomas discovered Dr Price had visited Fern Hill, it inspired him to capture the gore and horror of the man's activities in prose in 'The Baby Burning Case'. Fern Hill, which was owned by Thomas's aunt, was found near the village of Llangain, between Carmarthen and Llansteffan. This beautiful little farmer's cottage was occupied by Dr Anderson when he first met Dr Price, although it is uncertain how their paths originally crossed. Was it at a cattle auction possibly? Or had Anderson contacted Dr Price following the cremation to voice his admiration for the triumphant court case?

In truth, Anderson was not a doctor at all, although he had been trained in medicine. The son of a lawyer, his name was actually Robert Ricketts Evans and a note of the name-change to Anderson appeared in *The Times* in 1871. He was better known as 'Evans Y Crogwr' or 'Evans the Hangman' and presided over several executions between 1873 and 1875. Reputed to be a man of private means who did not genuinely need the small income from the executions, which he allegedly gave to William Calcraft (1800–79), the most famous and prolific English hangman of the nineteenth century, for the privilege of assisting him or acting as his principal. Images of Calcraft at the time do not look so unlike that of the white-haired and long-bearded Dr Price himself.

Anderson, or Evans, acted as principal executioner several times, particularly in Wales, although he did carry out a treble hanging in the open courtyard of Gloucester Gaol on 12 January 1874, when thirty-one-year-old Mary Ann Barry and her common law husband Edwin Bailey were executed for the murder of his illegitimate child, together with Edward Butt, who had strangled his girlfriend. For this hanging Anderson suggested that the platform of the gallows be mounted over a pit to make it level with the prison yard. Barry did not die instantly and Anderson had to press down on her shoulders to quicken her death. She was the last woman to be hanged by the short-drop method and the last woman executed at Gloucester Gaol. It is believed he assisted in the public execution of schoolteacher Charlie Peace (1832–79), the notorious burglar and murderer of a policeman, PC Cox, in Seymour Grove, Old Trafford and also in the public executions of the Manchester Fenians in 1867.

Anderson, who lit Dr Price's own cremation pyre, died in August 1901 at the age of eighty-five and his very lengthy obituary gives a vivid portrayal of the eccentricities of the man who clearly had much in common with the cremationist himself. Born in 1810 and the son of attorney Evan Evans of Carmarthen, Anderson's death certainly saw residents reminisce about his remarkable and colourful life. Having grown up at Glanrhwy Farm in Llangenedeir, he studied medicine and surgery at Guy's Hospital in London, but he was too much of a hell-raiser in his youth to complete his studies. 'His whole life seems to have been entwined in the doings off hangman, prize-fighters and gentlemen of that ilk ... and dozens of such notorieties too numerous to mention were his personal friends ... Every act which he performed seems to stand out in contradiction to what an ordinary human being usually does ...'[3]

He courted the daughter of a gentrified family; they eloped one night and were married and had a daughter of their own. When his wife died the daughter ran away, claiming her father was forcing her to sign her inheritance from her mother's family over to him. She left Wales altogether, not returning until Anderson himself died. Like Dr Price he partnered with his own housekeeper, although in his instance he at least married her. At this time he took his mother's maiden name, Anderson, as his own, his ancestors being the Andersons of Walsall Castle in Ireland. When he left his second wife he spent the remainder of his life in Fern Hill and was recognised as a peculiar man. 'It is impossible to record the incidents of his adventurous career as the deceased moved amongst circles into which but a few were admitted or care to enter, and they can only be related disjointedly from his own narratives to friends on different occasions ... he had a most pronounced penchant for the fair sex and one of his proudest boasts was the long list of conquests during his life amongst ...' women in London. It may have even been a case that he met Dr Price on such a jaunt to Soho where Price was said to have met with Karl Marx on one visit.

Having been trained by the Prince of Wales's boxing master, he was an accomplished fighter (as Dr Price's own son would be) and was allegedly acquainted with King Edward VII during his youth. Like Dr Price he was an inveterate litigant and often remarked he had spent £30,000 in various legal proceedings throughout his life and had 'good fun out of it too'. Some of the legal encounters were as bizarre and awkward, even mischievous in their methodology, as Dr Price's own wrangles. Anderson was a frequenter in the Small Debts Court and someone who often refused to pay bills. He was compassionate to the poor and a practical joker who revelled in causing chaos among visitors to Fern Hill itself, usually by terrifying them with stories of his life as a hangman and the macabre events he had witnessed. Following the death of executioner Calcraft he befriended successive hangmen, such as William Marwood (1820–83) and James Billington (1847–1901), hangman for the British Government.

> In full consonance with his love of things creepy, he was one of the earliest of latter-day advocates of all round cremation, and in connection with this phase of his character it is well to recall his dealing with the late Dr Price of Llantrisant. These two notorieties were bosom friends, and many are the tales of the eccentricities they held in common. It was Anderson who put the match to the pile on which the body of Dr Price was publicly cremated on Llantrisant Mountain – an act which created such widespread astonishment at the time – and deceased often used to express the wish to be singularly disposed of outside Fern Hill after his own dissolution. He had actually fixed upon a present inhabitant of Carmarthen, an old friend of his, to apply the torch, but during his last illness he forsook the idea and the ordinary rights of burial will take place.[3]

Local villager Rees Davies recalled a visit by Dr Price to Fern Hill:

> I saw him there one time ... we were going to school in the morning and we saw a brake with two pairs of horses and we knew him as Jac yr Falcon. He was the driver, and Dr Price, Llantrisant, he was standing on his feet and Evans, the two standing up in this, not a big brake, but two pairs of horses and Jac yr Falcon driving up ... it was great for us to see something like that ... I think they were some party, Dr Price, I don't know whether Evans the hangman belonged to them ... it was a rumour that he [Evans] knew something about medicine and I don't know whether its right or not.[3]

Dr William Price's other friend during his latter years was Dr Charles Fox, of the Quaker family of Falmouth. He was much younger than Price and after studying at the London Hospital, qualified with MRCS in 1873 and was placed on the Register in late 1874. He was one of the seven sons of Joseph John Fox (1821–97) and shared many of Dr Price's views, particularly on vegetarianism and vaccination. He was a well-published medic and lived in a tent in the West Country for many years because he loved nature to such a degree. He published such works as *The Question of Compulsory Vaccination Illustrated by Fifty Six Unpublished Cases and Illness and Death*, *Mystery of the Great Pyramid and Coronation*

Stone (Banner of Israel, 1910), and *A Voice Crying for Help* (Vegetarian Messenger, 1918).

There is also the subject of Dr Price's strained relationship with the Neo-Druidism of Y Maen Chwyf in Pontypridd. Considering himself a member of a higher Druidic society than them, he didn't always maintain their friendship and as already stated, although Morien, a prince-in-waiting for Myfyr's Druidic crown, was Price's surety in the cremation trial, the pair still had very public arguments in the columns of the local newspaper. Although born in February 1836, Morien always concealed his age and by this time had become a prominent member of *Clic y Bont* in Pontypridd, which continued to meet at the office of the bard (and auctioneer) Dewi Haran.

Morien was described as 'the impressive Morien, who was oftener in the clouds than on solid earth, and always half drunk on Myfyr's Druidism'. In a rather unflattering description of the Druids in 1879, the same correspondent stated,

> His first love was Welsh Calvinistic Methodism, which, to his honour be it said, he never wholly deserted. To the end he valiantly tried to reconcile the two theories (by equating Taliesin with Jesus Christ) but he might as well have attempted to mix oil and water ... the full-blown Druids were wonderfully and fearfully clothed, but Mr Owen and a few others appeared in ordinary garments. The service was supposed to be held in the face of the sun, the eye of the light. Torrential rain, however, prevented all from seeing the sun that day. The little crowd presented a miserable and woebegone appearance, and all hurried home like half-downed rats.[4]

His distaste for Dr Price became further evident in a series of letters written in the *Western Mail* during February and March 1886. Morien wrote of the practice by local medicine men to treat Myfyr Morganwg during his illness, and went on to explain how the Druids themselves had been great healers but were ignorant of science and medicines. He believed that many of the current-day practices used the traditions of Druids to create drugs and pills. He went on to discuss a letter he received from a man from Croydon who wanted to read a biographic account of the life of the Archdruid Dr William Price, to which Morien replied he should correct the writer and explain that Price was not an Archdruid.

In the following edition of the paper, a Roderick Roberts of the Prosser-Roberts Drug Company in Camberwell, London, said that according to Pliny the Druids had indeed used medicines. But he argued that current-day pharmaceuticals were prepared to the highest quality and went on to vouch for Dr Price and the 'esteem in which he is held by members of the

Royal College of Surgeons'.[5] Morien responded to the letter, apologising if
the company had misinterpreted his earlier correspondence. He explained
that the Druids were adept at natural laws and Ciscerio proved they were
good at philosophy. As for Dr Price, he condemned the Druid:

> He is an excellent doctor but he is no Druid, and I protest most strongly
> against the assumption that the masquerade which has made him so
> notorious has anything Druidic about it. I am constrained to state that
> Dr Price's so-called Druidism is a ridiculous burlesque on the solemn
> religion of the Ancient Briton. The Druids referred in their purity to the
> newborn sun of the new year of a babe – young Apollo – sun of the old
> Saturn, son the old year. His mother, they said, was the Black Virgin
> named Calas. Now Dr Price will have it that this young Apollo, named
> Hu Gadarn refers to his baby and that Miss Gwenllian Llewellyn, his
> babe's mother is the veritable wife of old Saturn, the father of young
> Apollo! To talk of Dr Price as the Archdruid is simply nonsense. The
> real Archdruid sitting on the chair of Glamorgan, successor of the
> mighty Druidic high priests of other days is Myfyr Morganwg. The
> English reading world will soon see that his Druidism is not a parcel of
> tomfoolery, but a sublime creed![5]

Morien was also one of the most unreliable and complicated local
historians of his time, totally influenced by the fabricated works of Iolo
Morganwg, and he took that fabrication to a whole different level. His
mythical *Battle Pontypridd*, which gave an almost eye-witness account
beggars belief, coupled with the most ludicrous interpretations of place
names.[6]

His mentor, Myfyr Morganwg, had withdrawn from public life in 1876
to live out his last decade with his daughter-in-law. He outlived seven of his
eight children, many believing it was his pagan worship and mocking of
Christianity that resulted in him being punished for his sins. On his death
in February 1888 his burial was one of the largest ever seen in Pontypridd.
He was given a Christian burial, with his publications laid under his head
in the coffin as requested, at Glyntaff where Revd Rowland Jones read
the service. Morien, who witnessed his will three days prior to his death,
published its contents in the *Western Mail*, noting himself first as, 'After
disposing of his library and articles of furniture, the will contains the
following: I bequeath to Morien all my writings and papers, knowing as I
do that he is the best qualified to deal with them properly and to make the
Druidic philosophy of our Cambrian ancestors known to the world …'[7]

In an interview shortly after Myfyr's death in 1888, Dr Price explained, 'He
was a very clever old man and very well read, but he did not understand.' It
was on his death that a correspondent in *Tarian y Gweithiwr* said Dr William

Price was the natural successor to Myfyr as Archdruid of the Bards of the Isle of Britain, but in the *Western Mail* of the same time Morien said he had claimed the title himself, which infuriated Price and caused anxiety among members of the Gorsedd Association of the National Eisteddfod, who invited him to address the assemblies in Liverpool in 1884, where the Druids entered wearing blue ashes and aprons embroidered with Iolo's mystical sign. He spoke again at Caernarfon in 1886, where the bards and ovates were robed in grade colours and had a grand setting inside the castle, where the Lord Mayor of London was initiated into the Gorsedd. Morien was eventually admitted to the order at Wrexham in 1888 following Myfyr's death and for the next thirty years remained dedicated to the Gorsedd, where each eisteddfod ceremony, particularly throughout the 1890s, became even more grand and imposing.[8]

Dr Price stated, 'Well, Morien knows nothing of Druidism, not he. An Archdruid should be able to read and decipher all Druidical letters and hieroglyphics and Morien knows nothing at all about them.'

From 1870 to 1899 Morien lived in Glyntaff and wrote a number of books, including *Pabell Dafydd* (1889), about the Druids; *Kimmerian Discoveries*, on the alleged Chaldean origins of the Welsh; *A Guide to the Gorsedd*; and *A History of Pontypridd and the Rhondda Valleys* (1903). The latter was described by R. T. Jenkins as 'an odd jumble of Druidism, mythology, topography, local history and biography'.

'What did it for Morien as a historian was Druidism, or more precisely Neo-Druidism, that feverish belief in the arcane and downright bogus, which had been propagated by the wayward genius of Iolo Morganwg.'[9] Morien remained faithful to Y Maen Chwyf and the Gorsedd there, playing a prominent part in the proceedings when the National Eisteddfod came to Pontypridd a few months following Dr Price's death in 1893. He spent the rest of his life perpetuating the work of Myfyr, displaying until the bitter end that Iolo had enjoyed a strong foothold for his fabricated writings in the Pontypridd district for almost a century after his own passing.

As for Dr Price himself there are few reports that mention his appearances at Y Maen Chwyf during the latter part of his life, although clearly his energy had not forsaken him. Unfortunately, what followed was a series of childish court hearings that did nothing for the reputation and dignity of the enigmatic surgeon. Instead, they appeared humiliating as he endeavoured to defy the legal system and the position of judge and jury to prove himself right in all matters pertaining to the law. It resulted in the doctor being portrayed as a pathetic and cheeky buffoon. In March 1885 he returned to the courtroom, again before Judge Gwilym Williams, at Pontypridd County Court when a cross-action occurred between him and a neighbouring farmer, Isaac Evans. The doctor tried to claim £5 from Evans for the detention of a bull in his field. Price called his cowman and servant, 'Mochyn Du', who stated that in January he went to fetch the cattle from the 'celebrated' Caerlan field, where Evans told him the bull was in his field and he couldn't have it back until he paid 10s. He reported the matter to his 'aged chief'[10] who told him to return and claim the bull. On his return he noticed a bush had a gap through which the bull must have used to wander into the adjoining field. He tried to claim the bull three times and was refused by Evans. The judge blamed Price for not keeping the bull on his own land but Dr Price argued the gap belonged to Evans, not him! At this point the judge ruled against him.

Then Evans sued the doctor for 7s 6d for attending Pontypridd Court on 9 March 1883 on a subpoena served on him from Dr Price – for 15s a day for eight days attendance at Swansea Assizes to give evidence in his fracas with farmer Richard Evans. Thirdly he demanded payment for the trespass of the bull and the damage it caused. Dr Price objected to them all. As for the Pontypridd Court hearing, Dr Price was too ill to attend and told Evans not to go, and in his absence had been ordered to pay the costs. As for the assizes case he said he gave Evans £3, and, as the case had not been finished, he could not claim any more money. The judge said it was 'absurd' to suppose a witness must remain until the end of an action to be paid and ordered Price to pay 7s 6d for eight days with the £2 already deducted. As for the third offence of the trespassing bull, the judge disallowed the claim.

The matter relating to the Richard Evans case reached the Queen's Bench Division of the High Court of Justice on Wednesday 5 May 1885 before Lord Chief Justice and Mr Justice Cave. The case had been tried by Mr Justice Grove and resulted in a verdict for 1s for the plaintiff. Mr B Rowlands QC had called for a new trial. The counsel explained there were originally two actions but they were consolidated and 1s damages awarded to Evans. But the matter now in dispute was with reference to the cost of the proceedings themselves. His Lordship dismissed the appeal and the motion was withdrawn.[11]

Dr Price remained determined in his endeavours and took the matter to the Court of Appeal in March 1886 before Master of the Rolls and Lord Justices Lindley and Lopes. Again on this matter the court, after a short argument, dismissed this appeal with even further costs. However, it is interesting to note that Evans eventually conquered the surgeon with kindness. When Dr Price's cattle again trespassed, Evans asked his servant to drive them off the field and up the road to Tŷ'r Clettwr and deliver them to the doctor himself, rather than impound them and accuse them of trespass. On their arrival the doctor gave the boy five sovereigns: 'For God's sake, give those five sovereigns to your master in lieu of those he paid at the pound.'

The case involving Isaac Evans and his trespassed bull reappeared in Pontypridd Crown Court, again before Judge Gwilym Williams, for a new action. On this occasion Evans, represented by J. Evan Jones, claimed £5 damages from Dr Price for having taken and unjustly detained five of his oxen on 17 June. Mochyn Du claimed the cattle on an adjoining field because he said they had got through into Price's field and were impounded, with Dr Price claiming damages of £5 3s. The matter of the original bull crossing into the other field due to the gaps in the fence was raised as Dr Price's bull had trespassed five times since the last case. Judge Williams said Dr Price had acted in a 'purely revengeful spirit. These transactions are not *bona fida*.' His honour refused to believe a word of Dr Price's witness and called the whole case a 'farce'. Evans was awarded the full amount plus costs and Dr Price wanted it to go to a superior court, but the judge would not offer him anything of the such. 'It must be done, your honour, and it shall be done,' Dr Price said.

'Very well,' Judge Williams answered and closed the hearing.[11]

The entire set of affairs reappeared in April 1886, only this time Dr Price had impounded four steers belonging to Isaac Evans and the latter tried to sue the doctor for £3. Once more Judge Gwilym Williams heard the case at Pontypridd Court. Dr Price attempted to counter-claim to the tune of £8 15s 6d. Evans claimed it was Price's bull that had caused the damage to the fences and his cattle also wandered back and forth. On this occasion he felt someone had coerced his steer onto Price's land. The judge expressed his concern of the points raised and the fact this was coming before the court once again.

Dr Price said, 'I know it is the habit of this court, but the law of this court is not the law of the land.'

'The law of the court is according to the law of the land,' the judge responded.

'I say it is not.'

'I am the judge!'

'I know that. I knew the law before you ever knew it, and before you were born.'

'Then you haven't learnt much,' the judge responded.

The doctor added, 'They are evils of cattle,' and said he would have preferred a trial before a jury.

Judge Williams said it was a similar case as before and he expressed his utter contempt for the disagreement taking place between the two neighbours. He explained that because Dr Price was older than some of them he spoke as if he were the only person who knew anything about the customs at Llantrisant, but some of them knew as well as Dr Price and considered themselves as well able to form an opinion on the matter. The judge explained he was not a farmer, but there was a tradition in the area that if animals of neighbouring farms strayed they were led back to their proper field, not impounded and the matter brought to court. He dismissed the claims.

Later in March 1886 an accident took place at the Albion Colliery in Cilfynydd. Opened on the site of Gwenllian Llewellyn's childhood home, the colliery would one day become synonymous with one of the worst coal mining disasters in the history of the industry. On this occasion a large stone, weighing about two tons, fell from the side of the shaft, killing twenty-five-year-old Joseph Jones and Richard Jones, aged twenty. Also terribly injured was James Rowlands, and it was found necessary to amputate one of his legs. The operation was conducted by eighty-six-year-old Dr Price, who was described as 'medical officer of the works', with the assistance of Dr Ivor Lewis of Cymmer.

That same month Dr Price was named in a series of lectures given in London by Professor Rhys, the occupant of the Celtic Chair at the University of Oxford, to discuss Druidism. He appears to have understood and agreed with many of Dr Price's own theologies on the subject. Dr Price's colleague, Emanuel John 'Mochyn Du' also gained further publicity when he was accused of being drunk and 'riotous' at Llantrisant at Christmas time, and was fined 5s!

On 27 May 1886 Gwenllian gave birth to another child with Dr William Price; this time it was a daughter whom he called Penelopen Elizabeth. It had been almost fifty years since he witnessed the birth of his first child. What makes it even more remarkable is that baby Penelopen was forty-four years younger than her elder sister, Hiarlhes, who had moved to the new home of Gelliwion Coedcae Du, a few miles north of Llantrisant, with her young lover, Thomas Williams, the engineer on the Taff Vale Railway Line. Despite being eighty-six years of age, Dr Price was kind, loving and a patient father to his two young children whom he idolised. Many years later Penelopen gave a rare and fascinating insight into her childhood years with her father. Although he died when she was just six years of age, her memories of him were vivid as she described him on a BBC broadcast in 1947.

> I was only six when my father died, but I have some vivid memories of him. He was such a remarkable man that anybody who met him never forgot him, and to live with him every day was a great experience for an impressionable child. I soon gathered that there was something different about him from other men, and I became very proud of him. When we went for a walk, men raised their hats to him, and treated him almost with reverence; I noticed that they did not raise their hats when they passed other men. Then again, he did not dress like other men.
>
> He always wore green trousers, vandyked at the foot and edged with red silk braid; a line of red silk braid also ran down each trouser leg.

His waistcoat was red, edged with green. In his younger days he wore a green coat, but when I knew him he wore, over the waistcoat, a sort of white smock. The big brass buttons were figured with goats, and the little buttons for the waistcoat with little kids. We always kept goats, and he was very fond of them. On his head he wore a fox skin, and over his shoulders a big plaid shawl. Of course, he was intensely Welsh, and I did not speak a word of English until I went to school. When I was a little child my father always insisted that I should be dressed in full Welsh costume. Naturally, I wanted to dress like other little girls, and just to please me, my mother bought me a red frock and white pinafore. When I wore this, I used to steal out through the cowshed and return the same way, in order to avoid meeting my father, for I would not have displeased him for the world. Not that he would have been angry. He was the most gentle of men, and did not believe in giving way to anger. Nor would he indulge in swearing, My mother never heard him use a single swear-word, not even of the mildest kind.

He was always extremely gentle with animals, and I can remember the great distress there was in the house when a favourite dog was lost; it jumped out of the window and followed my father to Cardiff. Everything possible was done to find him, but he was never found. My father was reluctant to cause suffering to animals that he was not even willing to let my mother kill the chickens. He said they should be allowed to die naturally. He was a strict vegetarian himself and would not touch fish, flesh or fowl. He kept a herd of Glamorgan cattle to have the milk, butter and cheese for his own use. I remember once that my mother killed some young cockerels, not thinking that my father would notice, because he was ninety years old by that time, but he was still as upright as a line and his voice was not like an old man's. He soon noticed that the cockerels had gone and he guessed what had happened. He did not get angry, but he said with a smile to my mother, 'You think I'll be dying soon, so I won't want the cockerels any longer.' When my mother asked him why he wanted to keep them, he said he liked to hear them crowing in the morning. I remember that incident very well, because even though I was only a little child, I know my mother had done wrong in killing the chickens.

I don't want to give the impression that I was afraid of my father. It would be truer to say that I almost worshipped him. Every morning my brother and I would go in to see him and show him that our hands were clean. Then he would give a penny to each of us, but we were not allowed to spend it on sweets. I used not to jump on his lap and kiss him, as so many children do to their fathers. I used to think that he was too great to be treated with such familiarity. I remember once that a neighbour's child came in and jumped up on him and kissed him, and

I felt shocked. Of course I was wrong; children loved him and he loved them.

My final memory of him was of his cremation. How proud I was that day! My mother, my brother and I walked behind the body between lanes of people who had come to pay their last homage. They say there were 20,000 of them. People have asked me if the sight of the fire did not frighten me. I had no such fear, because my father had said it was the right thing to do. I said I felt proud, and I still feel proud. All my life I have had to listen to fantastic stories about my father, most of them a lot of rubbish, but I suppose that such stories are the tribute that ordinary men pay to those who are greater than them. When I was a child I thought my father was a great man. I still think so.[12]

As time would tell, it was Penelopen who remained faithful to her father's memory, undertaking many public events to celebrate his massive legacy of the passing of the Act of Parliament in 1902.

In the early days of 1887 Dr William Price received the accolade of an invitation to travel to the United States of America. The Second Annual Banquet of the Cymmrodorion Society of Scranton, Pennsylvania, itself a haven for Welsh coalminers, invited Dr Price 'and Lady' to a hall called The Wyoming. The Society was celebrating St David's Day and following a decision by President B. Hughes, Vice President Lewis Pughe, Treasurer D. M. Jones and Secretary J. R. Hughes, it was agreed that Dr Price should be the guest of honour for the dinner on 1 March at eight o'clock. In recognition of Dr Price's notoriety, his newly taken portrait, of him in full Druidic costume, holding aloft the burning torch and with a sword in his belt, was used on the cover of the programme for the evening. The image had been commissioned by Dr Price with Thomas Forrest at his Cambrian Studios in Pontypridd and this is the first time it was used on a public document. Dr Price, forever the self-promoter, sold copies of the image over the coming years, but on this occasion it dominated the handsome cover of the menu and list of events. The Cymmrodorion went so far as to invite Dr Price again in 1888 to attend their third annual banquet, but he was unable to undertake the many weeks of travel.

In April 1888 Dr William Price finally succumbed to undertaking an extensive interview with the journalist Ap Idanfryn of the *Cardiff Times & South Wales Weekly News*. 'Dr Price Of Llantrisant: The Famous Druid Interviewed: Sketch Of His Life And Adventures' was an extensive interview printed in six parts on the front cover of every edition. The articles make compelling reading, and although they are an interview of an eighty-eight-year-old man and many of the facts and deeds are questionable, there are also sections that are perfectly accurate and allow a rare insight into the thoughts of the man himself. Ap Idanfryn wrote passionately about the doctor and much of his interview was used in subsequent works, including exhibition brochures and obituaries. The journalist, born Gwilym Hughes of Llanrhaiadr-ym-Mochnant (where William Morgan translated the Bible into Welsh in 1588), was the son of a schoolmaster. He went on to play an active role in the local literary circles of Cardiff, writing for *Welsh Outlook* and the *South Wales News* for more than twenty years. He died in 1933.

The opening paragraphs of the first article put into context the man with whom Ap Idanfryn held audience:

In the once flourishing but fast dilapidating town of Llantrisant, a few miles to the south of Pontypridd, there lives at the present day a man whose name is familiar to all Welshman, and whose deeds have on more than one occasion been the theme of comment throughout the whole length and breadth of the United Kingdom. In Glamorganshire, especially, his eccentric actions and his marvellous escapades are frequently dilated upon with manifest enjoyment by some of the old inhabitants, whose memories carry them back to the troublesome days of the Chartist riots, while there is hardly a cottage in all the countryside where the subject of our sketch is not at one time or another the central figure of an exciting tale unwoven on the family hearth. The anecdotes concerning him are innumerable, and although in their passage from mouth to mouth, some of them have been distorted out of all consistency with truth, still most of them have some foundation in fact, and it is questionable whether any one in his position in life has had a more adventurous career. In some respects he seems to have possessed attributes making to those of Salamander, for although the mighty engines of the criminal law have several times been put in motion against him, he has never failed to elude their iron grasp, and that without having once sough the assistance of the legal advocate ...

Three times he has been criminally prosecuted, but on each occasion the prosecution failed to convict him. It would be difficult, indeed, to name any subject with respect to which this extraordinary person agrees with his fellow men. He seems to have raised his hand against the whole community and to despise all those things which mankind has learned to regard with reverence and respect. In short, it would seem, according to his ideas, that whatever is customary is necessarily wrong, and this theory is carried out by him even in the smallest affairs of life. According to his peculiar creed, matrimony is to be mercilessly condemned as an institution which reduces the fair sex to a condition of slavery; the burial of dead bodies is a barbarous practice, and should be superseded by cremation; the eating of animal flesh has a tendency to revive in man the worst passions of a brute; vaccination is a method established by law for the express purpose of slaughtering infants; the wearing of socks is injurious to the health, and lastly, but by no means least, the Christian belief in a Deity and a future spiritual existence is all moonshine.[13]

For the last few years of his life, little mention is made of Dr Price, except in the occasional snippet of correspondence usually due to his association with some well-known bard who had passed away. In July 1890 he appeared in *Baner & Amserau Cymru* for refusing to send Iesu Grist Price II to school, despite being six years of age. Dr Price was taken to court and fined 3s 6d for the misdemeanour. In June 1891 the same newspaper explained that he was 'dangerously ill' but by August he was seen making a visit to Cardiff and 'created quite a sensation. He was followed by an admiring crowd of inevitable small boys and girls. Many people will be glad to hear that the doctor is out again.'[14] By October 1892 he was still making regular visits to Cardiff, 'in his well-known Druidic garments, and attracted general attention as supported on the arm of a friend he walked along Castle Street. The doctor is 92 years of age and although "shrinking" somewhat, is still upright in his carriage.'[15]

There is no mention of Dr Price in major festivities that occurred in his home town during this period, which may be due to the fact that he was experiencing ill health. At the start of 1892 he was injured after a fall from his carriage when his horse slipped on an icy road near Llantrisant. For weeks he lay on the couch in the front room of Tŷ'r Clettwr, and eventually recovered, but had lost his zeal and energy. However, it was remarkable how youthful he continued to look, with several articles written at the time commenting on his clear and fresh-faced complexion.

Another reason why he didn't involve himself in the festivities of that summer could also have been more typically due to his showing contempt for authority and the establishment. Hundreds of townsfolk and their children lined the streets of Llantrisant as the local drum and fife band marched to the Bull Ring on a hot July afternoon in 1892. It was a special occasion and a memorable chapter in the history of the town, because following the musicians was an open carriage carrying a very special son of Llantrisant. David Evans, a freeman no less, who had become the Lord Mayor of London, and this was his first visit back to his birthplace since his prestigious appointment by the liverymen of the City of London less than a year earlier. He was only the third Welshman to hold the position in the history of the institution of London Lord Mayors. Later Sir David Evans KCMG, a trustee of Llantrisant and former alderman of the borough, he was the son of Thomas Evans of Glanmuchydd Farm.

After a series of treatments from Dr William Naunton Davies, who lived directly opposite him on High Street, Dr Price recovered sufficiently in the latter part of 1892 to travel to Pontypridd, Cardiff and even Carmarthen.

One news report tells of his visit once more to Dr Anderson at Fern Hill. On arrival at the village railway station, he stopped by a local public house owned by Evan Morgan to take a glass of wine, wishing everyone 'good health'. He was not quite so buoyant as before, but more visitors than ever came to Llantrisant to see him. Going about his business he still attended scores of afflicted patients who flocked to him from all parts of Wales, but gradually the grand old doctor became weaker. He was already preparing for his cremation, having ordered a 61-foot-high white pole to be placed on the Caerlan fields where the event would take place. It was surmounted by a representation of the New Moon and could be seen for miles around. Some thought it was there to mark the spot where he cremated Iesu Grist, but the doctor wanted it to indicate the spot where his own body would be disposed of.

On 18 January 1893 he stood on the front doorstep of Tŷ'r Clettwr with his two young children, took a deep breath of air, and looked at the beautiful landscape before him. During the previous year he had not slept on his bed, but on his couch because of an aversion to feather beds. He came inside the house, lay on his couch and claimed, 'Well, you have laid me on my couch at last. It is unlikely that I shall ever rise again.' He added that he wouldn't die that night, or that week, but would not survive the fortnight. Sometimes he sat up, although he seldom spoke but retained all his faculties.

His eldest daughter Hiarlhes travelled to help nurse him during his final days. Neighbour Mrs Sparnon also spent time in the house to help care for the ailing doctor. One morning a letter from a friend was received and the doctor whispered, 'Then it must be answered,' before fainting. Throughout Monday 23 January he slept soundly and appeared refreshed, but still weak when he awoke. At 9.30 that night Gwenllian knelt by his side and asked him whether he would take some cider.

'No, give me champagne,' he answered.

After sipping from his glass, Dr William Price looked into her eyes, held her hand, leaned back and died peacefully and quietly. Gwenllian said 'it was as if a candle had gone out. There was no indication of pain and he seemed to have been sleeping tranquilly earlier in the day and he retained consciousness until the last minute.'

Dr Naunton Davies said he scarcely considered the old doctor had been ill during the past year, as he had recovered from his fall and was wonderfully 'hearty' for his age until his last illness overtook him. 'He had retained his faculties to a wonderful degree until the last and the cause of death was senile decay – in fact, general failure,' he said.

His death certificate named him as a Member of the Royal College of Surgeons, with Dr Davies certifying the cause of death. What is interesting is that the death was actually registered by Hiarlhes's partner, Thomas

Williams, who at the time lived at Tŷ Mab Ellis on the road to Penycoedcae near Pontypridd.

News of his death shocked the district, for although people realised his advanced age, it was still unexpected since news as his illness was kept within the family. Once the news was spread, the house became besieged with visitors and Roderick Lewis stayed at Tŷ'r Clettwr to keep overzealous mourners away from the family. The newspaper coverage of his death was vast throughout the whole of Great Britain and beyond, with daily reviews of his life and plans for his funeral, complete with headlines about the 'High Priest of the Sun' and the 'Welsh Wizard'. Often littered with factual errors and exaggerated tales of his life, they still provide valuable reading for they give an impression of the overall notoriety and esteem in which he was often held despite his indiscretions. Regarded as one of the 'most notable men in Wales',[16] Dr Price was only a few weeks away from his ninety-third birthday when he succumbed.

Morien was one of the first to pay tribute to him, with a short sketch of his life where he called him

> a peculiarly constituted man. Down to the time of his death his features retained striking characteristics, and old age had invested them with much dignity. His two eyes were resembled those of a hawk, his nose was slightly aquiline in shape and his forehead was broad and lofty. He kept all his beard and it grew in shape something similar to a goatee and reaching down to his breast. It was striking and perfectly white. His hair, also white as snow was likewise allowed to grow long, and it was plaited in long strands and looped up about the lower part of his head. The shape of the head was truly magnificent, and indicated, from a phrenological point of view, great mental powers. But his remarkable eccentricities throughout his long life left no doubt in the minds of those who knew him intimately that his brain was seriously affected. It seemed as if his great natural gifts were always struggling with a mind diseased, but as far as is known, he could satisfactorily command his mind in the exercise of his profession. That he was most daring in surgery is well known and he was more than once called to account for it; but nothing was ever proved against him. Long before most of those now alive can recollect his eccentricities expressed themselves in the manner in which he dressed himself...
>
> Until the last few years, he walked as lightly as a youth, and he always expressed the belief that he would live to be at least one hundred. He prided himself on his knowledge of Druidic lore and he was in consequence often confounded with the late Druidic philosopher Myvyr Morganwg, a truly great man though strange in his views. Dr Price's dress and head-dress were attempts to imitate the style of apparel he supposed an ovate Druid of the golden times wore.[17]

It is a miserable fallacy to describe Dr Price as a Druid at all, but to state correctly what he was is beyond the powers of mortal man. We owe it to the dignity of the Gorsedd and Welsh history to state clearly that Dr Price's tomfooleries had nothing Cymric about them.[18]

What is of interest is that as a footnote to the article Morien states that Gwenllian Llewellyn had not lived with the doctor during his latter years, but rather resided in Llanharry, although she visited frequently to care for the doctor and look after the two children. Nowhere else does such a statement exist and one can only wonder whether it is true at all, for all evidence suggests Gwenllian remained totally faithful to him for his entire life.

In a meeting with Morien on the day following Dr Price's death, she intimated his desire to be cremated, but felt she could not make any arrangements of her own until she met with the doctor's eldest daughter, Hiarlhes. She told him that Dr Price had no fear of death and felt it was a natural physiological event that did not deserve sorrow or mourning. He gave explicit instructions to her on the disposal of his body, particularly during the last few days when he grew weaker, demanding it be cremated 'thus helping the grass to grow and the flowers to bloom'. Time and again he'd told Gwenllian, '*Peidiwch a'm rhoi i yn y ddaear*' ('Do not put me in the ground') and he would add, 'Keep me on the surface of the earth.' There was to be no collection of his ashes either, rather they were 'to be sown broadcast along the field in order that they might help the grass and flowers to grow'.

When asked why she would not allow his body to be cremated at Woking Crematorium, she added that 'the doctor had no faith in crematoriums of that kind. He desired that his body should be burned in the open air, and it shall be, if I get my way. My neighbours seem to think that it is not right he should be cremated. Their belief is in burials, but I should never forgive myself if I were to bury him. If I had the courage to see my own child cremated then surely I ought not to be afraid to cremate him. He wanted to be cremated at Caerlan where he had the large while pole erected some months ago.'[19]

Neighbour Mrs Sparnon was frequently in the house with her, and she arrived the moment of Dr Price's death when Gwenllian gave him champagne. It was a drink he had enjoyed throughout his entire life, harking back to the days of the grand Crawshay parties of decades before. The news of his death had been kept from Iesu and Penelopen until the Tuesday morning, when they 'cried bitterly' at the loss of their father.

Morien explained that due to the popularity of the doctor, it had been made clear that tickets would be issued to allow entry onto the hilltop in order to restrict numbers. Messrs Davies Brothers of the Pontypridd Chronicle Printing Office had already been instructed to print the tickets bearing the message, 'Cremation of Dr Price. Admit Bearer To Caerlan Field – Gwenllian Llewellyn.' This restriction however was not precisely adhered to, as many thousands, some say as many as 20,000, actually attended the event, although a fenced off area close to the pyre was created for specially invited guests. Gwenllian told Morien that her next task was to contact Superintendent Jones at Pontypridd to discuss police protection for the event.

During Morien's visit many people came to pay their respects to Gwenllian, but no strangers were allowed into the 'death chamber' to see the doctor laid out in state on the couch where he had passed away, his fox skin head-dress spread across his chest. Thomas Forrest, his friend and a photographer of Pontypridd, attended to photograph the body of the famous man. He remembered,

> He lay like a warrior taking his rest
> With his martial cloak around him

His snowy white hair was brushed back from the forehead and his beard was flowing onto his chest from his pale face; otherwise 'he was the same aristocratic old Welshman'.

Gwenllian emphasised that no strangers should be allowed to revel in gazing on his dead body and it should be burned in a core of timber with 2 tons of coal and no attempt should be made at preserving his body. Gwenllian and her two children were appointed executors of the will. Along with Hiarlhes and Roderick Lewis, they took the police in their confidence and discussed plans for a cremation.

On Wednesday the Pontypridd justices were engaged in a lengthy consultation regarding the cremation. Mr Ignatius Williams, the stipendiary, along with Mr Evan Jones, Mr Godfrey Clark, Mr T. P. Jenkin and Mr E. W. Davies met with Superintendent Jones. They retired but on returning to court made no order of any kind for issuing to the police. Morien wrote,

> It is not known whether any legal objection is to be raised to the cremation, but from what transpired at Pontypridd Police Court it is understood that a consultation there took place ... Outside Llantrisant speculation seems to be rife throughout the district as to whether any hitch may occur to prevent the carrying out of the explicit instructions of the Will, but Llantrisant folk expect the event and would be greatly disappointed it if did not come off, and come off within the limits of the ancient borough.[20]

One correspondent wrote,

> Will Morien preside at the burial and give it all the circumstances and
> colouring of the old observances? In the old day, when the chieftains
> ranged the mountains and the Druid erected his altar on the highest
> point, so as to be nearer heaven, the burials were in near proximity to
> the war track – as in the case of the Romans who buried near their
> roads, or as in the case of the Druids, near their gathering place. If this
> burial of Dr Price be carried out, it should be divested of the sightseeing
> and exhibitionary character. If we are to copy antiquity, let us do it with
> the observation of the old solemnity. It would be as great a sacrilege as
> brawling in church to defile our grand old mountain retreats with the
> orgies of a camp, a fight or race. If it cannot be done with reverence, it
> should not be done at all.[20]

Price wrote in his will that he should be placed upright in the chair of his
'Druidic' uncle Hugh Jones of Gelliwastad, Machen, 'and deposit it on one
cord of wood and 2 tons of coal piled up within the triangle on Caerlan
with the face of the pile saturated with paraffin then fire the pile where
it shall be burned every atom … the dust retaining only in the triangle
shall be sown to grow grass and natural flowers'. Clearly such an exercise
could not be undertaken and it appeared that a Christian ceremony was
also going to be demanded by the magistrate, in the hope of keeping the
entire occasion as dignified as possible.

On Thursday 26 January it was announced in the national and regional
newspapers that the

> body of the late Dr William Price, the ArchDruid, will be publicly
> cremated in compliance with the terms of his will. The police have
> been consulted with a view to prevent molestation and stringent
> precautionary measures are to be adopted. The body will be burned in
> Caerlan fields and admissions to witness the ceremony will be by ticket.
> The late doctor had no faith in crematoria and provides, by his will, that
> his body shall be consumed on Caerlan fields at noon, that it shall be
> clad in the clothing worn at death, that the fuel used shall be of a core
> of timber and two tons of coal and that no attempt shall be made to
> preserve the ashes of the body.[21]

A journalist for the *Western Mail* noted, 'There seems to have been an
entire change of feeling at Llantrisant since the last cremation made the
Caerlan field celebrated. Instead of opposition to the ceremony there
now seems to be a general desire that the oft expressed wishes of Dr Price
shall be carried out, and carried out within the precincts of the Ancient

Borough of Llantrisant. Gentlemen well known throughout the district have volunteered to render every assistance with their power.'[22]

As the first pre-arranged open-air cremation in Great Britain in modern times at least, thousands of admission tickets were issued for the major event. No matter how much they tried, many people failed to gain entry. Over the coming days the amount of people visiting Tŷ'r Clettwr greatly increased.

A corporation official from Cardiff wrote, 'Madam, I am extremely sorry to hear of Dr Price's death, and being an advocate of cremation, I should esteem it a special favour if you will kindly grant me one or two tickets of admission to Caerlan Fields. Thanking you in anticipation and sympathising with you and your family.'

Even a member of the Royal College of Surgeons tried to get four tickets but failed at first. He wrote, 'I should feel greatly obliged if you would kindly let me know where I could obtain four tickets for myself and three friends to gain admission to the cremation ceremony of the late Dr Price.'

The police and printers were inundated with demands but were not allowed to distribute them. The applications and letters of sympathy grew. One came from a 'Fellow Practitioner' in Aberdare seeking tickets for himself, while a Llandaff resident and one-time patient of the doctor wrote to Miss Llewellyn,

> Kindly allow me to express my deep sympathy with you and the little ones in your bereavement. Ever since my first acquaintance with Dr Price I have always admired him for his manliness and his skill as a practitioner. I should be very pleased to pay what respect I can, and if you have any tickets to spare me I would feel greatly obliged, as the only way in which I can testify my respect is by attending the ceremony of cremation. I know from the daily papers you are greatly pressed with correspondence, therefore I will not trouble you further, but on behalf of the children accept my sincere sympathy.

Another letter from William Evans of the Wimborne Hotel, Cardiff, read,

> Sorry for your bereavement, as I have been a great friend of the deceased gentleman in his great trials through this carnal world. I beg on you to send me a few tickets to see him cremated. Perhaps you have not known me personally, but to let myself be known, I may say that my pamphlet was the one read by the Lord Chief Justice of England in the great trial on the cremation of the child.

Robert Williams of Bank Chambers, Pontypool's letter dated 25 January, read,

When I inquired of you on Monday morning last how the aged Dr Price was, I did not expect to hear so soon of his death. Pray accept my sympathies both for yourself and children in the loss you have sustained. Understanding by this morning's paper that the doctor will be cremated, and being a member of the Cremation Society of England, and also an occasional lecturer in favour of cremation, I would esteem it a great favour to be allowed to witness the cremation of the body of one who, without doubt, settled the legal difficulties as to cremation in this country.

A gentleman from Llandaff said, 'Madam, I have heard of Dr Price's death and his wish to be cremated in the open air. I have seen the Hindus and Burmese burn their dead at different times. I should be quite capable of carrying out the wishes of the late Dr Price. If you are not already suited, I beg to offer you my services for the last rites of the departed Dr Price.'

There were also several requests for certain mementoes, including, 'I would like a little lock from his beautiful head if possible, as a small souvenir or remembrance of the dear old doctor.'

A letter signed by three Tonypandy gentlemen said, 'We are three believing sternly and appreciating your determination in carrying out the cremation according to the noble doctor's instructions. And we are three believing in the same principle as the late doctor in disposing of the remains of human beings, and our earnest wish is that every lot of the instructions will be carried out to the letter.'

A young lady wrote, 'My father was a juryman, at the assizes in 1884, and he was a sympathiser to with the late doctor.'

Notices had been placed on Caerlan warning that trespassers would be prosecuted, although up until 27 January the date of the cremation had still not been fixed.

Not all of the letters received were sympathetic to the cause. A correspondent in the *Western Mail* wrote,

Having read with interest the account of the death and proposed burning of the body of the most eccentric being ... Seeing that the authorities are allowing the cremation to take place, and as I have no doubt a large multitude of civilised people will go out of curiosity to witness the hideous spectacle, I would suggest that the parties who are entrusted with the carrying out of the proceedings make a charge for admission to Caerlan Fields, say of 1s or even 6d. No one who is anxious to witness this 'interesting event', would, I am sure, grumble at the change when it is considered that the sight is not to be seen every day like a football match or a Buffalo Bill Wild West Show. The proceeds I would further suggest, should be handed over to the deserving Cardiff Infirmary to help to alleviate the pains of suffering humanity, for whom the late Dr Price did so much while alive.[23]

The *Standard* newspaper questioned the entire cremation and why it could not take place at a crematorium rather than in the open air, asking whether

> it be advisable in the interests of public health and decency, that public cremations of this kind should be permitted. If there, there seems no reason why some other eccentric gentleman should not order his body to be placed in a pond by the roadside until the process of time it disappears; or a third to required it to be hung from a tree near a public highway until consumed by the birds. It seems that, after discussing the law relating to the disposal of human remains, the justice of the Pontypridd Division decided to take no notice in the matter. This is to be regretted.[24]

It didn't take long for Morien to begin writing the first of several scathing columns. He remained relentless in his determination to undermine the doctor's Druidic authority as he had done during his lifetime, but in doing so rambled through his own fictitious beliefs in the religion and caused added confusion to the reader.

> It is full time to protest against the crack-brained nonsense of attaching the title Archdruid to the name of the late Dr Price. Druidism has long ceased to be practised publicly as a religion and yet, it must be confessed, by the way which we now call heresy, so worshipped the ancient Druids the Gods of their fathers. There is a time for all things, except for jesting with holy things. However people may differ on points of doctrine, all men with a healthy brain become reverent when they approach the eternal verities! … I would refer to Dr Price with proper respect, and with the veneration demanded by his great age. But I say solemnly it is very wrong to associate his name with the venerable high priesthood of the Druidic hierarchy of this island, the great mother of all creeds. From time immemorial Glamorgan, the centre of the country of the bravest of the brave in ancient days – namely the Silurians – has had its Druidic sanctuary. No doubt the priests of Stonehenge retired among the Silurians during the Roman occupation and long performed their ancient religious rites at the Round Table of King Arthur and his Twelve Knights at Caerlleon-on-Usk.[25]

He then went on to list the Silurian Archdruids from the year AD 1300, from Treharne Brydydd through to the likes of Dafydd ap Gwilym to Iolo Morganwg, Taliesin ab Iolo and Myfyr Morganwg.

'The above named carried down from age to age the marvellous lore.'[25] However, Morien was no kinder to the doctor's memory in a separate article in the same newspaper the week after his death. One of his reports also claims that a Mr J. Loveless, architectural stone and wood carver, of Severn Road, Canton, Cardiff, had visited Tŷ'r Clettwr and took a plaster cast of the head and face of the doctor. He also went on to say,

> It is impossible to describe the horror with which many people regard the forthcoming public burning of the body of the late Dr Price. Some appear to be afraid that if they body be burnt and the substances dissolved in smoke, it will be very difficult to bring them together again and to give the eccentric doctor a share in the resurrection of the dead ... while we analyse the might studies of the Druids ... .respecting death and future life are like the playthings of infants in comparison to the philosophic views of the Druids.
>
> Dr Price knew next to nothing at all about Druidism as a religious system, but he was a good classical scholar, and could read Homer in the original Greek and like on everything else, he held very peculiar views respecting the Iliad and the Odyssey ... he would submit that the correct spelling of Homer is Hu Mawr, or Hugh the Great. Dr Price's directions to burn his body was not due to this assumed Druidic views, but was due to his Homaric readings and medical studies. He pictured the preparations for his own funeral fire as resembling the preparations for the burning of Patrocius ... it is certain Wales has not witnessed such a sight during the last 1,700 years and it proves that Dr Price was wiser or more foolish than anybody living in Wales during that long period. In this instance, I think he was wiser than the rest.[26]

However, he did have a softer approach to Price's memory when discussing the reaction to the death by the people of Llantrisant.

> Exit Dr William Price! Notwithstanding the doctor's strange eccentricities and his many quarrels with his neighbours, the general public regarded him with a kindly interest and he exercised upon us all a curious fascination. This was due to several reasons. His great age and the prominent position of conspicuous eccentricity he had occupied from the days of the early manhood of grandfathers and grandmothers of the present generation down to the present day, prepared the public to deal kindly with him and his foibles ... the general public regarded him with tenderness, and when they condemned him they, as a rule, did so smilingly. It is with a feeling of regret all will reflect that his strange-looking figure will no more be seen in the dales of fair Glamorgan.[26]

As the days passed, more people began to arrive at Llantrisant, taking lodgings and hoping for tickets to attend the event. A group of men walked from Risca, some ladies came from Porthcawl by horse and trap and stayed in one of the local public houses. The British Medical Association wrote to Miss Llewellyn, 'This library which is open to the members, being now in the course of formation, the committee will be pleased to receive donations of books for it from members of the families of the deceased members. In all such cases due acknowledge will be made and the name of the donor will be affixed to the books when placed in the library ...'

On Sunday evening, scores of people crossed the mountains from the Rhondda.

> The narrow streets of the dilapidated old town were crowded for the most part of the day, and not a few of the visitors wound their way across the adjacent fields to gaze upon the site selected for the cremation at Caerlan. Stringent precautions were adopted to prevent the field itself being invaded, and on Saturday huge placards were placed all around the grounds notifying that trespassers would be prosecuted with the utmost rigour of the law. A large heap of coal has been deposited on Caerlan by James 'Siams' Morgan of nearby Bull Ring Farm and vigilant watch had to be kept on this to prevent persons from carrying lumps away as souvenirs. Elaborate arrangements are being made to exclude all but ticket holders from the ceremony, while the list of applicants for the coveted cards is being closely scrutinised in order to keep it within the narrowest possible limits. First considerations will ... be given to the applications from the doctor's patients and personal friends ... the tickets will not be despatched until the last moment.[27]

Commemorative items were also being produced to mark the occasion, most notably a selection of beautiful handkerchiefs depicting the Pontypridd Old Bridge, along with images of Nicholas and Penelopen, Gwenllian in full Welsh costume, and Dr Price himself. These were produced by Jones & Co., the drapers and outfitters from Market Square in Pontypridd.

At first, it was agreed that the cremation would take place at midday, but rumours grew that the family were in fact preparing to start the proceedings much earlier. As word spread of the change in plan, people began arriving at Llantrisant by 4 a.m., coming by brakes, horses or on foot and by the time the funeral procession began there were an estimated 20,000 people headed for East Caerlan. Every road was congested as the carnival mood prevailed, much to the doctor's wishes, and the twenty or more pubs ran dry of ale. Tŷ'r Clettwr was besieged with visitors requesting tickets. One poet even sold copies of his work on the life and death of Dr Price.

A specially designed coffin, which was constructed by Thomas Jones, a blacksmith of Talbot Green, was delivered to Tŷ'r Clettwr. The casket was made of sheet iron, encircled with iron bands and draped with white muslin. Jones felt iron would be red-hot in the flames but would not crack, so there was no chance of the body becoming exposed. A series of holes along the side were placed to allow the flames to enter and for fumes to disperse. The coffin was brought on a horse-driven hearse by Edgar G. Matthews, who worked for Wilks and Powis of Pontypridd. They were also contractors for the Masters family of Lanelay Hall. The undertaker, Ebenezer Davies, was accompanied by four assistants and twelve other local men to help as bearers and they arrived at Tŷ'r Clettwr at 7 a.m., where they placed the casket on a bier, borrowed from the local church wardens. Gwenllian and the children took one last look at the great man himself. The family and friends had remained all night to prepare for the occasion ahead. Hiarlhes cut off a lock of her father's hair and kissed his face for the last time as the heavy iron casket was bolted and covered with a white pall. Gwenllian, Iesu and Penelopen left the house first. The boy was dressed in a matching fox skin hat and outfit similar to his father's costume, with breeches vandyked at the edges that reached to just below the knees. Hiarlhes wore a traditional Welsh costume, while Penelopen wore a Welsh *pais becwm* and a red shawl. Gwenllian wore a long black cloak with tall Welsh hat.

It was a gloomy morning, the weather was poor and the view of East Caerlan from the front door of Tŷ'r Clettwr was obscured by a thick haze.

Gwenllian, affected by the sorrow of the event, was escorted by neighbour John Sparnon and Dr Richard Anderson, of Fern Hill. At 8 a.m. they reached the field at East Caerlan, close to the spot where Dr Price had cremated Iesu almost nine years earlier.

The remains of the late Dr William Price were, at break of day this morning conveyed to the Caerlan Fields, and there cremated in accordance with the instructions left by the late Archdruid in his will. Several hundred tickets were sent off on the previous day to friends and patients of the deceased, and to the large number of persons who had forwarded their applications by post and telegraph to Miss Llewellyn and Miss Price. It was stated however on these tickets that the ceremony would take place at noon today, and consequently there were not many people about at seven o'clock this morning when the ceremony actually took place. A few, however, who had obtained a clue the night before as to the course of affairs were likely to take, arrived in Llantrisant in brakes and vehicles from Pontypridd and other towns as early as five and six o'clock.

The body, had been placed in a receptacle constructed of sheet iron, encircled at intervals by strong iron bands. This receptacle was similar in shape to an ordinary coffin. Up to an early hour this morning the coffin, for so it may, perhaps, be called, lay in the front room of the house, a room which, by the way, served up to the doctor's death both as a study and a consulting room. Dr Price was severely simple in his tastes and ordinarily there was nothing in the apartment, with its boarded floor and bare walls, to suggest the least tendency to a desire for bodily comforts – not to mention luxury – on the part of the occupant. The coffin was placed on a long couch, draped with muslin, and the contrast between the snowy-whiteness of the drapery and the grim blackness of the receptacle, varnished over with a sticky substance of the consistency of coal tar, was striking in the extreme.

The spot selected for the extraordinary ceremony, which forms a fitting close to so extraordinary a career – was the summit of a hill … this land formed a portion of freehold property owned by the late Dr Price. It was here on a plot of ground known as Caerlan Fields, ten acres in extent, that the departed Druid cremated his own child Iesu Grist in 1884; it was here that Dr Price on many occasion since, burned the carcasses of the cattle and the dogs that died while in his possession; and it was on the self-same spot, by his own express desire, that his remains were consigned to the flames … But the ceremony of today was divested of all the objectionable features of the cremation practised by the doctor himself, and those responsible for the arrangements are to be congratulated upon their success in accomplishing so difficult a task as that of carrying out the doctor's instructions, while at the same time, refraining from committing any act that could be considered offensive, or indecent, or calculated to outrage public opinion.

A small crematorium was erected for the occasion … a few yards to the right of the enormous flagstaff which the doctor had erected there a couple of years ago. The crematorium consisted of two parallel walls, built of solid masonry, each wall being eighteen inches thick, ten feet long and three feet six inches in height. There was a clear space of three feet six also between the walls, and this space, at a height of two feet three inches from the ground, was crowned by a number of iron bars, two inches in diameter, the ends being embedded in the walls. The bars were placed close to each other, so as to form a kind of grate upon which to place the fuel, the space below being left to facilitate the draught. A few inches above this grate were four other bars, placed across as intervals from side to side, and it was on these four bars that the iron coffin was placed. There was then a space of fourteen inches between the sides of the coffin and the walls, and a space of two feet at each end – the coffin being six feet long – while the top of the coffin was several

inches below the level of the masonry. This space at the side, at the end
and on top, was stocked with fuel, so that when al was ready for the
burning torch to be applied, the ends only of the coffin were visible to
the curious crowd ...[28]

It seemed ironic that although the local Anglican Church had condemned
him for his beliefs, on the day of his funeral it was the local curate of
Llantrisant Parish Church, Revd Daniel Fisher, who led the service. Revd
Fisher met the entourage that had walked the steep slope of High Street,
passed the Wheatsheaf Inn, Penuel Chapel, Fox and Hounds and the many
shops of Commercial Street and passed the junction of Bristol House and
Cross Keys to the entrance of the lane that climbed to Caerlan fields.
He was assisted by Revd J. Williams of Pontyclun, replacing the normal
words of committing the body to the 'earth' with that of committing it
to 'fire'. He read an adaptation of the service appointed for 'The Burial
of the Dead at Sea', saying, '*Gan hynny yr ym ni yn rhoddi ei gorff ef
i'r tan gan ddisgwyl am adgyfodiad y meirw ac am fywyd y byd sydd
ar ddyfod.*' The form of the service was approved by the Bishop of the
Diocese of Llandaff. Shortly before eight o'clock Revd Fisher, wearing his
surplice, read the service and preceded the procession to the centre of the
field where the crematorium had been built. After some time the bearers
lifted the coffin into the centre of the furnace. At exactly ten minutes past
eight, Dr Richard Anderson stepped in front of the crowd and lit a match
to the shavings, which covered the mouth of the furnace. At the same
time Mochyn Du lit the other end and three or four other men stood on
top of the coals and poured large quantities of paraffin on the mass of
combustibles. For a little time it seemed as if the fire would not kindle, but
as the mountain breezes fanned the fire and more paraffin was poured on
the casket, the entire pyre was soon enveloped in flames and great volumes
of dense smoke and flame arose.

A total of thirty-five police officers, under the eye of Superintendent
Evan Jones, were in attendance to ensure the massed crowd remained
peaceful throughout, although the service and cremation were considered
'quiet'. A further fifteen constables were called to help stop onlookers
clambering over hedges to try to secure entry. Chief Constable Lindsay had
ordered the arrival of the police, particularly appointing Superintendent
Jones and his assistants, Inspectors Jones of Pentre and Davies of Porth
and Sergeant Hallett. The cost incurred was £5 12s 2d for expenses, which
Chief Constable Lionel Lindsay applied for due to the disorder that had
taken place at the previous cremation. Besides railway fares, thirty-five
breakfasts were paid for costing 9d each and thirty-five dinners at 1s each.
At the Joint Standing Police Committee in March, Cllr David James said it
was consoling to know the expenditure would not occur again, to which

the chairman said, 'Not so far as Dr Price is concerned. You cannot even cremate a man twice!'

Thomas Forrest of the Cambrian Studio, Pontypridd was there to record the event. Journalist Morien was also present, along with historian and Town Trust clerk Taliesin Morgan, who in a few years would write the second history of Llantrisant, complete with romantic prose and fabricated stories not unlike those of the Victorian Welsh tradition, it would seem.

By noon that day thousands were in the town and it appeared to multiply as the afternoon progressed, with many surrounding Tŷ'r Clettwr hoping for tickets to approach the field at Caerlan,

> all loudly clamouring for tickets, the most important of their number actually forcing their way into the house of the mourning in quest of the coveted pasteboard. So far as possible those requests were complied with, while Miss Llewellyn and the children, who left the field after an hour of the cremation, took advantage at the same time of the opportunity of disposing of photos and souvenirs of the departed Druid at modest prices.[28]

The most famous was the coloured lithograph of Dr Price, copies of which were sold at 1s 6d each, and 'scores were bought'.

By 2.30 p.m., thousands and thousands had climbed the mountain and the flames were still raging furiously. One newspaper report claims that Hiarlhes was black with smoke when she returned to Tŷ'r Clettwr and the young man with her, presumably Thomas Williams, 'became so ill when he beheld the fire that he retired to bed with his boots on'.

One poet wrote,

> Cremated! That which once was flesh and bone
> Is now reduced to ashes – dust! What fire
> Has purified on the funeral pyre
> Now scatter o'er Caerlan without a moan
> Without one tear, without a sigh or groan.
> 'Twas the old man's wish, Hear the feather'd choir.
> His requiem day by day will chant higher
> No music need be in its sacred tone,
> What we deemed odd, eccentric, we'll forget,
> We'll watch the grass and flowers grow in spring,
> Await the marvellous beauty they may bring.
> For strange ideas strange results beget.
> The way wardness of man through roots may run
> Strange hues, strange slopes may come when shines the sun

At four o'clock, the shattered casket was found almost totally destroyed by the heat. Supt Evan Jones and Dr Williams agreed that there was little point in placing more coal on the flames. It was placed on the bier and allowed to cool, although souvenir hunters tried to scavenge among the remains of the furnace. There were still 6,000 people at the site by this time, rummaging and snatching pieces of cinder from the fire 'in the vain hope of being able to secure pieces of it as relics of the extraordinary ceremony'. What is remarkable is that remembering only 8,000 watched Wales play England in rugby at Newport two years earlier, an event such as this had attracted 20,000 in total. The casket was returned to Tŷ'r Clettwr, where the remains were placed on the couch where he had died. For years people combed the field to find remains of Dr Price. A member of Pontypridd Council related with gusto how he did a thriving trade selling the teeth of dead sheep for half a crown each by representing them to be those of Dr Price. A Pontypridd journalist, possibly Morien himself, retained a piece of the coffin at his home, as did Siams Morgan of Bull Ring Farm, who delivered the coal for the pyre. By eight o'clock in the evening, twelve hours after the pyre was lit, the streets of old Llantrisant became gradually empty again, except for the townspeople themselves who gathered in groups and talked of the strange day.

Another unknown poet remembered,

> I walia, ffaith anhylus – i'n heddyw
> Fel meddyg gorddestlus,
> Na anwyd ar ein hynys
> Wr uwch na Gwilym ap Prys.

> Hynod yn eithriad hunan – hyd ein oes,
> Hynod wrth fynd allanl
> Drwy danwydd o'n gwydd I gan,
> Lach ynwyf oluch anian.

> Golych einioes awyrgylch anian – yw
> Anadl pawb – by Drydan;
> O fanog lawr fangre lan
> Daw efau'r Duw ei Hunan.

By the Wednesday morning the smoke was still ascending from the pyre itself. Some of the iron bars had been broken and a portion of one of the walls had collapsed. It was even suggested the structure was left in place as a reminder of Dr Price and his legacy. A ton of coal was left unused and carried away by local residents as souvenirs or to use at their homes on the wintry nights ahead!

One poet sold copies of the following eulogy,

> Doctor Price, the noted Druid,
> Has now drawn his final breath,
> And his voice, so clear and ringing,
> Has been silenced by grim death;
> Full of years he has departed;
> His career was very strange.
> Seldom have men's lives encompassed
> Such a long and changeful range.
>
> As he died, he called them to him,
> And these words he slowly said:
> 'In the grave you must not lay me,
> When my form is still and dead;
> Let my body be consumed
> By fierce flames, and let my dust
> Scattered be again to Nature
> All that blossoms on earth's crust.'
>
> Through the countryside this saying
> Went on ever speeding wing.
> Many hundreds quickly gathered
> To behold this curious thing;
> And on Tuesday morn at daybreak
> Was his corpse with reverence borne
> To Caerlan field, at Llantrissent,
> Followed by sad hearts who mourn.
>
> After reading the church service
> His iron coffin did repose
> On a pile of coal and timber
> As the doctor did propose.
> Two old friends did then come forward
> And set flames unto the pyre;
> Soon the coffin was consumed
> By a raging, flaring fire.
>
> Thus they did as he had ordered,
> And he rests in calmful peace,
> As though by a grave encompassed,
> Where all earthly sorrows cease;
> Let us gently treat his memory

He, a Welshman of renown
For he loved his country dearly,
And for her sake bore many a frown.

Gwenllian Llewellyn was the executor of his will, which was read on 20 February 1893 and outlined the value of his personal estate at £400 5s 6d with further savings of £54 4s 5d. His will, signed on 22 February 1891 and countersigned by witnesses David William Davies of The Firs, Llantrisant and innkeeper Roderick Lewis, read,

Be it known that at the date hereunder written the last Will and Testament of William Price late of Llantrissant [sic] in the County of Glamorgan, surgeon, deceased on the 23rd of January 1893 at Llantrissant aforesaid and who at the time of his death had a fixed place of abode at Llantrissant aforesaid with the District of the Counties of Glamorgan was proved and registered in the District Probate Registry of Her Majesty's High Court of Justice at Llandaff and that Administration of the personal estate of the said deceased was granted by the aforesaid Court to Gwenllian Llewellyn of Llantrisant aforesaid, spinster, the sole executor named in the said Will, she having been first sown well and faithfully to administer the same. Dated 20th day of February 1893.

Value of Personal Estate – £400.5s.6d

Value Savings – £54.4s.5d

Contracted by Rees & Gwyn Solicitors, Cowbridge.

This is the last Will and Testament of me, William Price of Llantrissant in the County of Glamorgan, Surgeon. I appoint Gwenllian Llewellyn of Llantrissant aforesaid (hereafter called my Trustee) to be the Executor and Trustee of this my Will. I order than when I shall cease to be in my present state called or baptised by the name of William Price my executor shall take up my old body clothed as she may find it and put it up in a sitting position in the old chair of my late Uncle Hugh Jones of Gellywastad in the parish of Machen in the County of Monmouth and deposit it on one cord of wood and two tons of coal piled up within the triangle on Caer Lann East with the face of the pile saturated with paraffin then fire the pile where it shall be burned every atom at noonday. The dust remaining only in the triangle shall be sewn to grow grass and natural flowers. I order that and Robert Warson of 54 Roman Road, Barnsbury, London, shall be called to assist my executor aforesaid in the aforesaid cremation and paid ten pounds for his time and expenses.

All my books, including two copies of Dr John David Rees' *Cymmerian Gramma* and *Myvyrian Archaeology of Wales* (in three volumes), two copies of the *L'Antigate Exuliques Par Dom* by Bernard Montfaucon; *Les Origin de Town les Cultes* by Dupais, a copy of *Odysseiau* and *Iliad* by Barnes, Dr Stukeley's *Stonehenge* and six volumes of the *History of the Native Tribes of America* shall not be sold or parted with upon any condition whatever but shall remain the property of my two children by the said Gwenllian Llewellyn namely Iessu Grist and Penelopen Elizabeth Price and their descendants for ever amen amen amen.

I will and devise that my Glamorgan breed of cattle of so many cows and bulls of that breed as can from time to time be deposited on Caer Lann East aforesaid shall be kept until the younger of my said two children by the said Gwenllian Llewellyn shall attain the age of twenty-one years when the cattle then existing shall be dealt with.

In the manner hereafter expressed concerning my estate I devise and bequeath unto my trustee upon the trusts and for the purposes hereafter declared all my property of whatever nature, including all my estates and interests in property left in trust by Hugh Jones and his wife Anne Jones of Gellywastad in the parish of Machen in the County of Monmouth to John Morgan of Tredegar Esquire his only executor who by deed of trust constituted himself the trustee of my father the Revd William Price and his children by his wife my mother Mary Price and who so long summoned to produce the said deed in evidence in an answer of ejectment tried in the Guild Hall, London refused on being called three times in Court. In the first place I deed my trustee to observe the terms hereafter imposed in respect of my books and my Glamorgan breed of cattle. In the second place upon trust to use all and convert into money the whole or so much of my estates and personal estate as may from time to time be required by her for performing the rights hereunder and after payment of the expenses connected with the disposal of my body and also my testamentary expenses and debts, if any, to stand possessed of my trust property or so much as shall from time to time remain unrealised and unapplied in trust for the equal use benefit and beneficial enjoyment for my trustee and my said two children by her namely Iessu Grist and Penelopen Elizabeth Price until the younger of such children attain the age of twenty one years with powers as my trustee at her desire to raise the whole or any part of the presumptive share of either of the said children to apply and advance the same for his or her education (in the Cymmerian Language) an advancement or benefit and on the younger of my said two children attaining twenty-one years of age. Upon trust to divide the trust estate remaining unused and unapplied equally between her, my said trustee and my said two children first deducting out of each share the amount advanced under the power hereafter contained. If either or both of my said children or my trustee shall die in my lifetime or before the younger of the said children attain the aforesaid age the unused or unapplied share or shares of the person or persons so dying shall issue for the benefit of the surviving persons or person interested under the trusts hearing before contained to be desirable on the younger of the said two children attaining the aforesaid age or on the death of the surviving child as the case may be and in case of the death of other or both of my aid two children I direct the body or respective bodies of such deceased child or children to be cremated within the triangle on Caer Lann East in the same manner as my first son Iessu Grist was cremated.

I empower my said trustee to postpone the sale and conversation of my seal and personal estate or any part thereof for so long as she shall see fit and that the rents and income thereupon shall after payment following all outgoings be paid and applied in the same manner as the income of the money produced by conversion would be applicable under the terms herein before mentioned in all former wills and testamentary dispositions made by me. In witness whereof I have here set my hand this twenty second day of February one thousand eight hundred and ninety one. Signed by the above named William Price as his Last Will and Testament in the presence of us both who in his presence and in the presence of each other have hereunto subscribed our names as witnessed, David William Davies, the First, Llantrisant, Glamorgan and Roderick Lewis, Innkeeper, Lantrissent [*sic*].[29]

It is noteworthy that the will makes no provision whatsoever for Hiarlhes.

Shortly after the cremation, the Cardiff Health Committee discussed the opportunities available to erect a crematorium on Flat Holm Island, used as an isolation hospital to protect the mainland against a cholera epidemic. Only a year prior to Dr Price's death a serious outbreak of cholera occurred in Hamburg, and five infected vessels were discovered and moored off Flat Holm. When it broke out again it was decided to build a most substantial hospital and with it a crematorium. Another of those writers who penned eulogies about him for sale included the following song:

Lines on the Death And Cremation of
The Grand Old Welshman
Arch-Druid Doctor Price
Who Died At Llantrissant, Monday, Jan. 23rd, 1893
IN HIS 93rd YEAR
And His Remains Cremated Shortly After His Death

A grand old Cambrian Chieftain has just passed away
From the land that we know he loved so well,
Doctor Price the Druid you have known for many a day
And Llantrissant his history can tell.
Descended he could show, from centuries ago,
He has left the dear old mountains now at last;
And nearly ninety-three we're told that he must be,
A missing link between this and the past.

Llantrissant knew him well, he wants no funeral knell
No hypocrites in mourning him bewails
If they carried out his wishes, they had done right well
For Doctor Price the grand Arch-Druid of South Wales.

His Ancestors they were Druids when Llewellyn reigned as king
When the ancient Minstrels sang among the hills,
The Retainers in our Castles made the valleys ring,
And love of Country every bosom fills.
Not one shadow of disgrace in our history can we trace,
Our enemies try to do it but they fail;
And now the old man's departed we shall miss the face
Of Doctor Price the grand Arch-Druid of South Wales.

If you saw him in the market his dress may have been queer
But he could please himself what he should wear,
His rough and ready costume was respected here,
To insult him I'm sure there's no one dare.
In cremation he believed, and so he had conceived,
His principles of Religion he would show;
To burn the useless body if the Soul's in heaven received
As the Druids did a thousands years ago.

Once had a daughter [sic] who died some years ago;
At his farm 'neath the shadow of the hill,
Her body was cremation as in Pontypridd in they know,
And 'twas said he had committed a sin until –
The Magistrates found he could stand his ground,
And no one now that incident bewails;
For many English people as the years pass around
Have left a will the same as Doctor Price of Wales.

In his will he plainly stated what he wanted them to do
To take his body as he died into the fields;
The old ancient City of Caerleon close in view
The pure air of Heaven above him to be revealed
He said take me away at the middle of the day
Let my ashes scatter as the breezes blow,
And where I was Cremated at some future day
Let the grass and the lovely flowers grow.

The fine old race of Welshmen as leaving us so fast,
There are few that now are left behind;
There are few to show us the relics of the past,
But the Castle of Caerphilly calls to mind
When any foreign foe his features dare not show,
Before Cambrian felt misfortune's gales,
For Priests of that day, could fight as well as pray,
Like Doctor Price the Grand Arch-Druid of South Wales.

In August 1893 the National Eisteddfod was held in Pontypridd, and although unfortunately Dr Price died just a few months earlier and did not witness the huge spectacle at his beloved Maen Chwyf with the crowning of the bards, his son and daughter were both present. In fact Gwenllian, Iesu Grist and Penelopen sat in the 'shilling seats' to watch the proceedings. This was the first noted public appearance of the Price family since the death of their patriarch. It was an uncertain future for them all without him, and in the care of their mother, Gwenllian, changes to their lives were about to take place.

1894–2012

Dr William Price's mortal remains may have disappeared into the winter winds above East Caerlan, but the memories of the man and his legacy continued to grow. Many would say those tales of the notorious 'eccentric' became further exaggerated with time; in fact many became so bizarre, grotesque and absurd, that for some the definition between fact and fiction became impossible to decipher. Morien continued to include his name in various articles over the coming years, not least of which being the occasions when he continued to announce his huge intellect of all matters relating to Druidism.

In 1896, three years following Dr Price's death, Taliesin Morgan, clerk of the relatively new Llantrisant Town Trust and someone who both knew Dr Price and was listed as attending his cremation, published his *History of Llantrisant*. This charming, romantic vision of the town, wholly untrustworthy in places as an historical document, features a small chapter on the doctor. It opens with the following passage:

> For many years there lived in the Town a medical gentleman of very eccentric manners known as Dr William Price. He held very peculiar views on Druidism and Cremation, and his dress had a peculiarity, in imitation of the old Welsh Druids and he posed himself as the Archdruid of Wales. In general, however, he was regarded with amused tolerance. Not of very large stature, and generally clothed in his green-cloth trousers, scalloped, his scarlet vest, green cloth jacket or shawl, with fox skin cap, of quick movement and sharp manner was not unfamiliar in the district.[1]

During the year of the publication, an exhibition supposedly celebrating Dr Price's life, when in fact it did quite the opposite, was held at the Druids Rest in 'Old Cardiff' Exhibition Building in Cathays Park. 'The Late Dr Price (Llantrisant) – The Famous Archdruid – Sketch Of His Life and Adventures Also Programme Of Exhibits, 1896' was launched as part of the Cardiff Fine Art, Industrial and Maritime Exhibition. The triumph of the British Empire was celebrated and inside the Indian-style exhibition pavilion the visitors found the places of honour occupied by symbols of Britain's industrial supremacy – a model of a South African gold mine, a model of a Welsh colliery, railway locomotives and coaches, hydraulic pumps, printing machines, and depictions of great battle victories such as Waterloo. In an adjoining room amid a motley collection of minor relics was the Dr Price exhibition, the contents of which were more or less fabricated and in some cases offensive to his memory. Some of it was also included in Mr J. L. Kerpen's bizarre Welsh version of the World Fair and Christmas Carnival from December 1895, which was also exhibited in Cardiff's Roseberry Room in Canton, and featured Rifle Nell, the understudy to Annie Oakley of Buffalo Bill fame undertaking a shooting and knife-throwing exhibition. Among the Victorian 'curiosities', Dr Price had also found a place with a lifelike figure of himself clothed in his costume on loan from Gwenllian.

However, it is the exhibition of 1896 that caused the most ridicule. The programme opened with a short biographical sketch of the doctor by Ap Idanfryn, who wrote passionately about his colourful life in quotations taken from the interviews held in 1888. His opening lines read,

> There lived a man whose name is familiar to all Welshmen, and whose deeds have on more than one occasion been the theme of comment throughout the whole length and breadth of the United Kingdom. In Glamorganshire, especially, his eccentric actions and his marvellous escapades are frequently dilated upon with manifest enjoyment by some of the older inhabitants, whose memories carry them back to the troubled days of the Chartist riots. The anecdotes concerning him are innumerable and although, in their passage from mouth to mouth, some of them have been distorted out of all consistency with truth, still most of them have some foundation in fact, and it is questionable whether any one in his position in life has had more adventurous career. In some respects he seems to have possessed attributes akin to those of Salamander, for although the mighty engines of the criminal law have several times been put in motion against him, he has never failed to elude their iron grasp. Three times has he been criminally prosecuted, but on each occasion the prosecution failed to convict him.
>
> It would be difficult indeed to name any subject with respect to which this extraordinary person agrees with his fellow men. He seems to have raised his hand against the whole community and to despise all those things which mankind has learned to regard with reverence and respect. Whatever is customary is necessarily wrong; and this theory was carried out by him even in the smallest affairs of life. According to his peculiar creed, matrimony is to be mercilessly condemned as an institution which reduces the fair sex to a condition of slavery; the burial of dead bodies is a barbarous practice; and should be superseded by cremation; the eating of animal flesh has a tendency to revive in man the worst passions of a brute.[2]

The exhibition contained seventeen items, many of which caused some level of curiosity with the curator, who attempted to courteously guide the public around the wax models and exhibits. Opening with the image of him dressed in the outfit illustrating the *Coelbren y Beirdd*, the second exhibit is an indication of the level of fabricated items to come. This is the first of a series of false illustrations of 'The Doctor in the act of chopping off the bailiff's toes who tried to force an entrance into the house to levy a warrant for debt. The operation perfectly shown – this exhibit is of great interest. The Doctor and his visitor being faithfully portrayed, and the majesty of the law appearing on the scene.' The following exhibition was none other than 'The instrument with which he did the deed' no less!

There were also drawings of his arrest along with 'the chest in which the Doctor made his escape when baffling the police who came to arrest him at his house in Treforest during the Charter Riots', again another false exhibit, although this may have been confused with his alleged escape from Craig Alva following the disagreement with the Llanovers. There were also two pistols on show, which the doctor used to keep the public at bay while trying to cremate Iesu Grist. The exhibition included a gun walking stick, which was his 'constant companion'.

Pictures of the cremation and the remains of his burnt coffin were shown and the sofa on which he died, his favourite chair from his uncle which he wished to be cremated on, his medical table 'where he prepared his world-famed medicines', and the hooked thorn which was used to pull Iesu Grist from the flames.

Probably the most peculiar – and fake – exhibit is listed last as 'The only remains of the Doctor after his cremation, viz: his right foot – it being said by scientists that the whole nature of his body must have dropped to his foot, which is on view'.

His costume, also shown, was later donated along with medical certificates, instruments and the large crescent moon to the Museum of Welsh Life at St Fagans near Cardiff, a cultural centre he'd envisaged creating in his own lifetime. The museum opened on 1 November 1948 in the grounds of the sixteenth-century manor house of St Fagans, donated to the people of Wales by the Earl of Plymouth. Penelopen continued to donate objects, including the famous 1822 painting of her father to the museum in 1950, and they were put on permanent display.

To have displayed so many personal items, the exhibition must have been compiled with the support of Gwenllian as she continued to perpetuate the myth and legend of the late father of her children. Yet, times were different without him and the security she felt within his care had gone. One can only assume that she was concerned about the effect his legacy may have on the two young children. It was with this in mind that Gwenllian made a series of changes to their lives, possibly in the hope of protecting them and securing a stable future. Realising the effect a name such as Iesu Grist would have on their surviving son, she made the decision to rename him Nicholas Price in memory of his ironmaster ancestor.

It is uncertain whether these actions were entirely her own, or that of a new figure who appeared in their lives. John 'de Winter' Parry was a curious character and there is little evidence of his background. It is believed he was born in Breconshire, around 1859, making him the same age as Gwenllian. The son of Matthew Parry (a plasterer) and Mary (née Lewis), John Parry earned a living in a variety of positions, ranging from being a publican, a stonemason and even a road inspector for the local council. In 1883 he married twenty-one-year-old Ada Charlotte Down from Putney in south London, and the couple had a son named Ernest. A decade later and the Parry family were residing somewhere between the village of Llanharan and the town of Bridgend and in 1896 Ada passed away, aged just thirty-five. The dates suggest that shortly afterwards John Parry met Gwenllian Llewellyn, possibly on becoming the landlord of the Butcher's Arms public house in Llantrisant, a stone's throw away from the infamous stable where Dr Price had come under attack from the angry mob. He may possibly have also become a landlord for one of Dr Price's own public houses at some point previous to this.

On 20 April 1898 John Parry, the widowed father, married Gwenllian Llewellyn at the parish church of St Mary in Glyntaff, which stood a short distance from Dr Price's surgery and the Round Houses. One can only imagine how much of a strange occurrence this must have been for the new couple, forever under the shadow of the ghost of Dr Price. Both aged thirty-eight, Parry is listed as a widowed road inspector from Bridgend on the marriage certificate, while Gwenllian is simply listed as a 'spinster' and the daughter of the late William Llewellyn, a farmer. The couple were married in the presence of John Gough and Esther Knox, with Rowland Jones presiding as registrar.

Gwenllian and John had a daughter, Gwenllian 'Rachel' Janet Parry, on 8 August 1899. It marked the fourth generation of the family to be named Gwenllian. What makes her birth certificate interesting is that by this time Parry is no longer listed as a road inspector, but rather as a retired stone cutter. Another interesting fact is that she was born not in Llantrisant, but in 10 Cardiff Street in Aberdare. By this time the Parry family, which consisted of the newly born Rachel, Nicholas and Penelopen (but no mention is made of John Parry's own son, Ernest), have left Llantrisant altogether. Ernest does reappear however, in several pieces of correspondence with Penelopen from 1904 onwards when he is residing in Tonypandy, Rhondda and refers to her as 'my dear sister'.

On 27 April 1900 an auction took place in the George Inn, Llantrisant under the guidance of John David. The two premises listed were the Mount Pleasant Inn, which stood on nearby Commercial Street and is believed to have been a property once owned by Dr Price, although by this time the occupant was a Mr Collins. The second property for sale is Tŷ'r Clettwr itself, listed as 'the Freehold dwelling house and premises, situate in the main street in the town of Llantrisant, formerly the residence of the late

Dr Price but now untenanted'.[3] It is uncertain when the Greyhound Inn was also sold, or for that matter the remaining properties, which may have been leased by Gwenllian to ensure additional income for the family.

Tŷ'r Clettwr remained unsold for two years, with its windows boarded up, and created a sad, ghostly appearance for all who visited the town. Gwenllian had gone from the vicinity with the Price children by this point and apparently her marriage was not a happy one as Parry was prone to bouts of heavy drinking. Although Gwenllian is listed as a 'widow' on her death, there is no record of John Parry's own demise and he was certainly not with the family by the time of the 1911 census. Gwenllian retained property in the town, including Cae Ysgubor Farm on Heol y Sarn and a house opposite. She was also in the possession of land at East Caerlan and possibly some of the properties to the rear of the Greyhound Inn. As for Tŷ'r Clettwr however, it was demolished. Journalist John Williams visited Tŷ'r Clettwr in 1901:

A few days before its demolition I wandered rather sadly through the rambling old house. It was then in fair condition although, of course, money would have had to be spent on it to restore it if there had been any hope of retaining it as a permanent memorial to very remarkable man. I understood that an American lady visited Pontypridd with precisely this aim in view but alas, it came to nothing. I think that Pontypridd Council should have backed this move and turned the old house into a museum, not perhaps solely devoted to the doctor. After all Pontypridd has been home of quite a number of notables ... but ... now it is gone. The old house. The threats and the bitter invective that the doctor's beliefs invoked. The passions have long cooled and, as she always must, reason has turned to her throne. But the red flames leaping from the funeral pyre at Caerlan throw a bright gleam of light across a dark page in Welsh history.[4]

In 1902 Tŷ'r Clettwr was replaced by the grand Zoar Chapel by the members of Bethel Chapel, who departed the congregation sixty years earlier. Bethel's worshippers left the chapel, which later became the parish church hall, for a large room at Mwyndy Farm. Eventually they acquired, on lease, land at Cardiff Road, Penygawsi where the first Soar was erected, before eventually purchasing Dr Price's former home and replacing the resting place of a pagan with a house of Christian worship.

It was also rather poignant that while his house was razed to the ground, his own legacy was ratified with the passing of the Act for the Regulation of the Burning of Human Remains, and to Enable Burial Authorities to Establish Crematoria, 2nd July, 1902. Cremation had achieved a form of governmental regulation and it thereby became officially recognised in the highest quarters. The new Act of Parliament gave powers to the Home Secretary to make regulations, which were published as Statutory Rules and Orders in March 1903. It was all thanks to that one Welshman who cremated his son high above a sleepy ancient town.

In 1901 John, Gwenllian and the three children lived at 88 Dock Street, Newport, where the head of the household was listed as a licensed publican. The family eventually found themselves drawn back to Llantrisant. As early as 1904 they were residing in the Butcher's Arms on Heol y Sarn, possibly because John Parry had returned to the vicinity as a publican, and they were resident at the property until 1907. There is also mention of their residency at the White Hart, which was situated on the Bull Ring nearby. At this time a new home for the family was built on land originally purchased by Dr Price more than thirty years earlier. Close to the very spot where Iesu Grist was cremated in 1884 and Dr Price in 1893, a four-bedroom house was built. On the summit of the mountain, overlooking Llantrisant and the breathtaking panoramic landscape around, East Caerlan Farm became the home and workplace of the Price-Parry family, and they remained there for the rest of their lives.

John Parry isn't the only family member not listed on the 1911 Census. Nicholas is absent from the list, which only includes Gwenllian and the two daughters. Gwenllian is listed as a farmer, while twenty-four-year-old Penelopen's occupation is music teacher, followed by eleven-year-old Rachel Parry. Penelopen's prowess as a piano tutor was widespread and for over eighty years she taught children throughout the district, initially travelling to their homes on horseback, later by bicycle and in latter years by bus. In 1909 she appeared in the National Pageant of Wales dressed rather superbly as Britannia.

In 1901 Hiarlhes Morganwg was listed as residing in Mary Street, Merthyr Tydfil, with her partner Thomas Williams. A decade later and they were living at 4 Webster Street, Treharris with two lodgers who were working underground in the local colliery. What is significant about this year is that despite being together for decades, Thomas and Hiarlhes were actually married on 10 August 1911 at the Registry Office in Merthyr Tydfil. Thomas was a fifty-six-year-old civil engineer, listed as the son of a later mining engineer named William Williams. Hiarlhes was a sixty-nine-year-old spinster, although under the section naming her father, the space is left empty.

Penelopen was educated at Pontypridd Girls Grammar School, while at some point Nicholas attended High Grade School in Augusta Street, Cardiff. With the outbreak of the First World War, Penelopen became a devoted member of the British Red Cross Society and St John Ambulance Association. Throughout the war she was actively involved in treating injured soldiers who were brought home from the front and cared for in various military hospitals throughout the country. The nearest facility to Llantrisant was found at the stately manor house of Talygarn, which later became a hospital for injured miners of the South Wales coalfield. Penelopen's devotion to both societies is obvious by the sheer volume of certificates and honours bestowed upon her for her dedicated service, support and kindness to the wounded men and boys. She trained as early as 1912 in a multitude of courses at various training centres. In 1919 she received the accolade of an award from the Joint Committee of the British Red Cross Society and the Order of St John of Jerusalem in England, in recognition of her valuable services during the Great War. Following a meeting of the Council of the British Red Cross Society held at St James's Palace, her name was also inscribed on the Roll of Honourable Service. In many of the images of returning heroes from the First World War who were presented with their medals on the steps of the Guild Hall in Llantrisant, next-door to the police station where her late father had spent a night in the cells, Penelopen can be seen in her nurse's outfit among the crowd. Her half-sister, Rachel, also trained as a nurse in 1916 and assisted with the wounded at Talygarn.

A rather poignant letter that was discovered among Penelopen's items was written in September 1917 from Private Fred Hawcroft of Albert Street, Barnsley in Yorkshire: 'I am doing fine and enjoying myself up to the mark. I am sending you this Regt Broach which I promised you and I hope you will like it and keep it in kind remembrance of a Yorkshire lad to whom you showed every kindness. Trusting you keep in good health to carry on in the good work in which you are engaged in.'

Without a man in the household for extended periods of time, it was left to Gwenllian and her two daughters to run East Caerlan as a farm for several decades. Although the house had a certain Edwardian grandeur about it, the work itself must have been hard for three women to undertake alone, particularly on such an exposed farmstead open to the elements from all directions. The detailed farm records listing the quantity of cattle and pigs is incredibly concise, listing carefully the market or farm from whence they were bought, moved and sold. The records actually run from 1924 to 1966, with large numbers of animals being accounted for at the farm.

Penelopen and Rachel remained spinsters, devoted to one another and their family home and farm. In their youth both were collectors of postcards, which make fascinating reading; there is talk of several suitors for them both and one even suggests that Rachel was to marry. Many would say that it was Rachel who undertook much of the farm work, whereas Penelopen divided her time between teaching piano, nursing and selling milk in the old town. There was also a fun-loving element to them both at times, particularly when viewing the images of them in elaborate fancy-dress costumes as Brittania or Boudicia during several Llantrisant Carnivals following the end of the First World War. Probably the most chilling of all the images is the one of Penelopen in her father's outfit, along with a false white beard, on horseback for the 1918 Benefit of Soldiers.

One cannot ignore the fact that their lives were hard, living in such a secluded area. The Price family were well respected in the town of Llantrisant, with Penelopen being well loved and remembered. With her startling eyes and clean, youthful skin – which she claimed was due to a moisturising cream created by her late father – Miss Price made a recognisable and prominent figure, often dressed in a long coat with a black hat.

John Parry left the family by 1910 and no record exists of where he spent his final years. Nicholas had much more of a varied and interesting life, which in itself gives the impression that he was quite an elusive character with certain qualities about him that were not totally unlike his father. For one thing, he never wore socks, also believing that fresh air to the feet was important to overall health. He did not achieve the brilliance predicted by his father, but there was certainly a notoriety about him. In his youth Nick Price was a 'strong man', a champion weightlifter and boxer who also gained a reputation as an excellent rugby player. One image of him looking like a dashing and handsome youth shows him wearing a tie pin with the symbol of an equilateral cross with its arms bent at right angles. The symbol, which dates back to Indian religions, was used specifically in Hinduism, Buddhism and Jainism, primarily as a sacred symbol of good luck. Wearing such a symbol during the early part of the twentieth century illustrates Nick's interest in the Eastern religions that his late father had such great fascination with. It certainly doesn't connect him with the future rise of the Nazi Party in Germany and the other connotations that the swastika has for us today.

On 26 December 1914 Nick, then aged thirty and listed as a carpenter, married Harriet Watkins, a thirty-five-year-old spinster of Tŷ'n Llwyn Farm in Llantrisant. Harriet, who was the daughter of Morgan Watkins, a well-known farmer, and dressmaker Hannah Watkins, signed the marriage certificate with a cross, just as Nick's grandmother had done when marrying Revd William Price more than a century earlier. The couple were married at the Pontypridd Registry Office. Her mother, Hannah, was a friend of Dr William Price, becoming his tailor when he moved to Llantrisant and repairing his elaborate Druidic costumes, while also helping to create some of his beautifully cut outfits in his latter years. Sadly the marriage between Nick and Harriet did not last and although they are not listed as divorced, it seems Nick was considered unhelpful with the upkeep of the farm, enjoying his sporting, and for that matter, drinking prowess, more than heavy work. The story goes that on his return to the farm late one night he was faced with a wheelbarrow with his belongings inside accompanied by a sack of flour. The message was clear that these were objects he had entered the marriage with, and he was leaving with them too.

The few items of correspondence between Nick and his sisters do reveal something of his whereabouts during his early years. Various stories claim he was a carpenter and builder for stonemason Will John at the RAF aerodrome in St Athan before spending time on construction sites in Newport. There are also tales of him working as a policeman in Reading during the 1920s. For a while he travelled to the United States, settling in Detroit, Texas, New York, Philadelphia and also Turcarawas in Ohio in the summer of 1908. Nicholas returned by the outbreak of the Great War, marrying Harriet in the final weeks of 1914 before enlisting in the 38th (Welsh Division). A Christmas card, sent to Caerlan 'with Christmas Greetings for 1917 in the Confident Hope of a Victorious 1918' survives.

Of all the family, it was Penelopen who best represented the memory of her father. She continually attended various events organised by the Cremation Society of Great Britain that honoured his massive contribution to their cause. After many years of deliberation it was decided to open the first crematorium in Wales, and although it was not erected in the vicinity of Llantrisant as Dr Price had first hoped, it was opened in the area where he spent the greater majority of his life. The decision to erect a crematorium in Glyntaff may have had no bearing whatsoever on the fact that it was to be opened so close to his former surgery at Craig yr Helfa, but it appears befitting that this was the place chosen. Glyntaff Cemetery was opened in 1875 with the first interment taking place on 3 June for John Bradshaw, a sixty-seven-year-old barber. With the passing of time and the increasing population boom of the industrial district, the Pontypridd Burial Board, by virtue of its powers as a burial authority, took advantage of the 1902 Act and decided to provide a crematorium. The board converted one of the existing cemetery chapels for use and one gas cremator was provided, followed by a second in 1938 and further cremators were installed following the Second World War. In June 1924 the first practical test took place at the crematorium before a large gathering of medical men, councillors, public officials and members of the burial board. The carcass of a sheep was presented by Walter Lewis of Bridge Street, Pontypridd and placed in the incinerator while the architects A. C. Rockwood and J. Malcolm Laing of London described the modern methods used in the cremation. James Spickett was clerk to the Burial Board in the area, and had actually attended the cremation trial of Dr Price in 1884. He was also of the same Spickett family of solicitors of Pontypridd that had been involved in several Dr Price cases during his lifetime. Mr Spickett explained that the incinerator had cost £2,500 and costs per cremation would be two guineas, plus 5s for the minister. For those outside the Pontypridd area, the cost was three guineas!

Just four years following the opening of the crematorium at Glyntaff, the sixty-third deceased person to be cremated there was Dr Price's oldest surviving daughter. Gwenhiolen Hiarlhes Morganwg Williams moved to East Caerlan Farm to be with the remainder of the family following the death of her husband, Thomas. On 5 July 1928 she passed away there aged eighty-four, following a long period of senile decay.

In remaining faithful to her father's memory, Penelopen retained many of his costumes and personal effects safely in the family home. Sadly Gwenllian disposed of much of his written material. Dr Price's name continued to appear in the newspapers over the years, and they were not always complimentary.

An edition of the *Pontypridd Observer* in 1932 called him 'grotesque' in the headline as it recalled memories of the man. Two years later and a play was produced at Bedwas Hall, a short distance from St Barrwg's where the Price family tomb exists. Written by playwright Revd Daniel Hughes, *Pikes of Dawn* detailed the Chartist Rising and was produced on 2 May 1934, with Penelopen in attendance. A copy of the play was presented to her by Revd Hughes in gratitude to the fact that she allowed the actor, G. Ascenderrie, to wear her father's fox skin hat for the performance. Much of Dr Price's dialogue can also be attributed to his Ap Idanfryn newspaper interview of 1888.

By July 1944 the story of Dr Price inspired the first of his biographers. Islwyn ap Nicholas resided in Elmtree Avenue in Aberystwyth and wrote his initial letter to Penelopen to explain his intention to write a short biography of her father. He requested information, particularly of the 1884 cremation trial, and having already submitted a letter of his intent in the *Western Mail* had received numerous stories about him. The short book, *A Welsh Heretic*, was published in 1940 and for over forty years remained the most detailed biography of Dr Price. The introduction beautifully captures Dr Price: 'Dr William Price was certainly a figure of high romance. It was as though a composite creature had stepped out of the pages of Old Testament history and, in his passage through the centuries, had enriched his personality from the flow of all the hidden streams of myth and legend.'[5]

On 17 September 1947 Penelopen was invited to return to the place where Tŷ'r Clettwr once stood to unveil a small bronze plaque in memory of her father. It was the first dedication to the memory of Dr Price and was unveiled in a town where its residents had ridiculed and admired him in equal measure. It was the same place where over sixty years earlier the large gathering of angry Llantrisant folk had smashed the windows of his property. Now its descendants arrived *en masse* to celebrate the life of the town's most famous resident. There is no mention of Nicholas attending the occasion. By this point Gwenllian was a bedridden eighty-nine-year-old residing at East Caerlan, and she could have well viewed the spectacle from her window at the house as it overlooked the site of Zoar Chapel. The plaque was presented by the Cremation Society of Great Britain and read,

This tablet was erected by The Cremation Society and the Federation of British Cremation Authorities to commemorate the act of Dr William Price, who cremated the body of his infant son in Caerlan Fields, Llantrisant. For this act he was indicted at the Glamorganshire Winter Assizes on the 12th February 1884 where he was acquitted by Mr Justice Stephen who adjudged that cremation was a legal act.

Dressed in her usual dark coat and hat, Penelopen was joined by the Lord Mayor of Cardiff Alderman George J. Ferguson, members of Llantrisant Town

Trust, Councillor Ivor Jacob, Arthur Pearson MP for Pontypridd and Hugh Royle, the Chairman of the Federation of British Cremation Authorities, along with its Secretary P. H. Jones, also Vice Chair Mrs B. M. Gilbert and Leonard Porcher, the Clerk of Pontypridd Council. Present was Superintendent of Glyntaff Crematorium Mr S Davies and his wife, along with Dr Islwyn Evans, D. S. Rowlands JP, Councillor and Mrs Clayton of Pontypridd, Councillor Whereat, Theo Griffiths, Mr C. Thomas, David Rowlands, Supt Howell Rees, Councillor Jesse Powderhill and Mr William Jones. Another of the special guests was Mrs Fisher, the widow of Revd Daniel Fisher, the curate who presided over the cremation of Dr Price. With her she had the death certificate and the two half-crowns that her husband was paid for the service. The item was later donated to the Museum of Welsh Life at St Fagans. The president, Lord Horder, was unable to be present owing to another commitment in Geneva.

At 5.15 p.m. the plaque was unveiled before members of the first Cremation Conference held in Wales, which took place over a three-day period in Cardiff. In fact, an invitation was made for Penelopen to visit City Hall, Cardiff for a reception with the lord mayor on the previous evening. Children were released from the local schools to enjoy the carnival atmosphere. Councillor Ivor Jacob, representative of the town on the Rural District Council, opened the proceedings:

Ladies and Gentlemen, may I extend to you a very hearty welcome on behalf of my Local Authority. During the past three days you have been the guests of the City of Cardiff and I trust and believe that they have accorded you a great welcome and hospitality. You are here today in order that you and I may pay tribute to the memory of an illustrious resident of this old town, and I am very happy that you are here with us as you have raised within us a feeling of deep, deep pride. May I say here, that we regret that it has not been found possible for your President to accompany you to Llantrisant today. He is engaged in work of world-wide importance and we trust that the efforts of Lord Horder and his colleagues in the cause of Humanity will be successful. Would you permit me to say, and I speak as a Welshman, that Dr William Price was an outstanding man, and your President also is outstanding. Hence we appreciate it very much indeed that we are paying a tribute this afternoon to the memory of Dr Price. Dr Price, however, possessed one distinction which unfortunately was not accorded to your President: he had the distinction of being a Welshman. Will you please convey to your President this message, His work on behalf of humanity has so endeared him to our people that we have long since regarded him as an adopted son of the Principality.

I am very pleased and happy to have with us this afternoon Miss Penelopen Price, the daughter of that illustrious father. We residents share with her the joy she is experiencing today. The plaque which she will shortly unveil is a fitting memorial to a great man, and I accept it on behalf of the Llantrisant Town Trust who will, I assure you with all sincerity, cherish, safeguard and preserve it for all time.

Arthur Pearson, MP for Pontypridd, said,

We are here today to commemorate an outstanding gentleman of this old fortress town of Llantrisant. It must be a thrill to the organisers to have such a response as is evidenced by the attendance of the delegates of the Cremation Conference, who have come from far and near, the Chairman and Members of neighbouring Authorities, the Lord Mayor of Cardiff, and so many people from Glamorganshire. It is fitting that we in this fine old county should commemorate those of her sons who, against ignorance and opposition, faced their trial with great courage, and succeeded in the days of small beginnings to make the event the most historic in this old town. Dr Price, himself, established in the High Courts the right to cremation and now in these days an ever-widening circle of our countrymen are appreciating the pioneering work of Dr Price in this field. We pay tribute to his memory and we are proud to think that a member of his family is here to perform the ceremony of unveiling this plaque …

Miss Price pulled the chord and said, 'I am proud and happy to unveil this plaque in memory of my father and hope it will be preserved for all time.'

Hugh Royle, the chairman of the Federation of British Cremation Authorities, Arthur Pearson MP and Mrs Gilbert, vice chair of the Council of Cremation Society, spoke at the event and presented Miss Price with a silver salver which read, 'Presented to Miss Penelopen Price by the Cremation Society and the Federation of Burial and Cremation Authorities on the occasion of the unveiling of a tablet in the honour of her father Dr William Price, a great pioneer of cremation at Llantrisant 17th September 1947.' Mr Royle said,

It is our first visit to Wales, and it is right that we should seize the opportunity of paying tribute to Dr William Price, to whose memory this plaque has been erected, and unveiled so graciously just now by his daughter. We have long been aware that he was the founder of cremation in this country. He was a man of character, foresight, courage and strong convictions, and we are now reaping the benefits of these high qualities which he possessed.

Mrs Gilbert added, 'As I came down this glorious valley of yours and looked at the wonderful scenery and passed the beautiful children on the way, I said to myself, "this is indeed a land which will provide pioneers and heroes of all time".'

With the formal proceedings over, the crowd spontaneously burst into '*Cwm Rhondda*', which had been composed only a short distance away in Llantwit Fardre, followed by 'Aberystwyth' and concluded with '*Hen Wlad Fy Nhadau*'.

The group, which had also visited Glyntaff Crematorium earlier in the day, walked to the summit of East Caerlan to see the spot where the cremation took place.

At 9.15 p.m. that evening a forty-five-minute radio play was broadcast by the Welsh Regional BBC entitled *Dr Price of Llantrisant*, to which Penelopen gave her memorable speech and for which Lord Horder had recorded the postscript,

To a previous generation, Dr William Price was a figure of controversy. In our own day, he has become a romantic legend, and around his name have been woven fantastic and improbable stories. As President of the Cremation Society, I am concerned only with his significance to our Movement. What is this significance? I can best explain this by reminding you of the circumstances prevailing in the year 1883. Nine years earlier – to be exact, on the 13th January 1874 – Sir Henry Thompson, the Royal Surgeon, with whom were associated a number of outstanding artists, writers and scientists, such as John Everett Millais, Anthony Trollope, John Tenniel and Sir T. Spencer-Wells had founded the Cremation Society of England, as it was then called because, in their own words, 'They disapproved the present custom of burying the dead, and desired to substitute some mode which shall rapidly resolve the body into its component elements by a process which cannot offend the living and shall render the remains perfectly innocuous.' Considerable interest had been aroused previously by articles published by Sir Henry Thompson on the subject of cremation.

Seeking to establish a crematorium in London, the Cremation Society met with considerable opposition, and it was not until 1878 that they succeeded in obtaining a small plot of ground near Woking, in Surrey, where an experimental furnace was erected. But they were unable to put their beliefs into practice, because the Home Secretary of the time declared cremation to be illegal, and he strictly forbade the procedure. Sir Henry Thompson and his friends were reluctantly forced to accept this decision and thereupon confined themselves to pursuing propaganda.

This they continued to do until the end of 1883, when the incident occurred which was this afternoon commemorated by the unveiling of a tablet in the little town of Llantrisant. Briefly, Dr Price set out to cremate the body of his infant son in the open air in a field which he possessed at Llantrisant, but he was prevented completing the act by the arrival of the police, who extracted the body from the flames. Subsequently Price was brought before the Magistrates at Pontypridd on a number of charges, and later stood his trial at the Cardiff Assizes where, in dealing with the charge against Price of attempting to cremate the body of his infant contrary to the law, the Judge, Mr Justice Stephen, in his charge to the Grand Jury, declared that cremation was a legal act so long as it was not accompanied by a nuisance. Consequently, Dr Price was acquitted. Fortified by this judicial pronouncement, the Cremation Society announced that its crematorium at Woking was not available for public use, and on the 20th March 1885, the first cremation under modern conditions took place there.

It will be seen, therefore, that it was due to the action of Price that the condition of stalemate which had persisted since 1874 was ended, and that the reform advocated by the founders of the Cremation Society was instituted. How long we might have waited for a change in the official attitude towards cremation had it not been for this act of Price is a matter of conjecture; but the simple fact remains that it was not until the judicial pronouncement was made at the trial of Dr Price that it became possible to initiate what has now become recognised as a public service of the highest importance.

Towards the end of the feature to which you have just been listening, you will have observed how public opinion had veered in favour of Dr Price and his advocacy of this refers by the time his own cremation at the same spot in the open air at Llantrisant took place in 1893. It is a matter of the greatest satisfaction to me, and those associated with me, that this change in public opinion has become even more marked as the years have gone by. According the information at my disposal, most of the local authorities in Great Britain will establish crematoria as soon as the exigencies of the building programme will permit. They are prompted to this action not only by reason of the fact that public opinion is in its favour, but also because the demands of the living for housing and recreation upon the valuable lands, and near our towns, renders the continuance of the burial system a practical impossibility.

Price was a courageous pioneer, one might say he was an architect of a great sanitary reform, which is today recognised by thinking people not only as desirable, but as an economic necessity.

The radio drama was written and produced by P. H. Burton and featured Arthur Phillips as Dr Price, Ivor Maddox as Justice Stephens and David J. Thomas as the narrator. The cast spent ten hours on rehearsals over three nights prior to the broadcast.

On 21 December 1948, Gwenllian Llewellyn Parry passed away at East Caerlan Farm in the presence of her two daughters. Suffering with rheumatoid arthritis and senile decay, she had been treated by Dr J. C. R. Morgan, whose surgery was at Southgate. Gwenllian was eighty-nine years old and had lived an incredible life. Surprisingly there is no record of her cremation to be found. In the same year Porthyglo, the former home of Dr Price, which was situated next the Upper Boat public house near the Glamorganshire Canal, was demolished.

Penelopen once again appeared on BBC radio in October 1949 to discuss Dr Price, for which she was paid eight guineas. On 30 November 1953 she finally met Lord Horder, the president of the Cremation Society, when she was invited to attend the opening of Cardiff's first crematorium. The £63,000 crematorium was opened at Thornhill by Horder, who again paid tribute to Dr Price for his massive contribution to their cause. Thornhill was the second crematorium to open in Wales and the sixty-eighth to open in Great Britain. Lord Mayor of Cardiff Sir James Collins was also present and the service of blessing was followed by a luncheon for the special guests at City Hall. In fact the Cremation Society remained in contact with Penelopen for the remainder of her life, inviting her to attend the laying of a foundation stone at Hereford Crematorium in October 1955.

On 8 October 1966 Penelopen visited Glyntaff Crematorium to unveil a stained glass window in memory of her father at the North Chapel. The new window was created by Celtic Studios in Swansea and was paid for by public subscription at a cost of £560. Councillor J. Warren, Chairman of the Pontypridd Burial Board and Cremation Authority, unveiled the window with Miss Price and said, 'I am sure it can be said that in implanting Cremation in the thoughts of a progressive community such as ours, the act of the late Dr William Price did a service for his country and fellowmen, for which we of this present age and our successors must be grateful.'

Penelopen's diary from 1955 to 1960 is filled with references to her own medical complaints, significant dates in her father's life and occasional entries of the ill health and deaths of friends and relatives. There are also entries of visits to the seaside and the Royal Ballet, along with the entry that both she and Rachel attended a concert at Sophia Gardens following an invitation from the British Association of Advancement of Science in September 1960. Three years later, on 21 June 1963, their brother Nicholas passed away at East Caerlan of a heart attack. He was seventy-eight years old and was cremated at Glyntaff. A few months later the surgery at nearby Craig yr Helfa was demolished.

Another of Dr Price's legacies was found in the world of literature. Although Sir Arthur Conan Doyle was the first to mention the surgeon in a fictional work, references to Dr Price were found in song, on stage, in poetry and on the television screen. One unsubstantiated claim is whether Dr Price influenced J. R. R. Tolkien in his fantasy sagas *The Hobbit* and *The Lord of the Rings*. Scholars believe Tolkien employed a strict landscape-based method to research and write his influential books, and the author appears to have scoured topographical volumes and guides published before 1948 for curious and bizarre fantasy plots and storyline inspirations. Dr Price's tale was featured in a travel book entitled *Highways and Byways in the Welsh Marches* by S. P. B. Mais in 1939 – six years after his first *Letter from America* for the BBC, which continued for decades.

Arguably Tolkien appears to have based on Price his character Deneothor, son of Ecthelion who, in a state of insanity attempted to cremate his son on a pyre of wood and oil. On being thwarted he threw himself on the pyre instead. As a staunch Roman Catholic, cremation was not a method of disposal of the dead that would have been supported by the conservative Tolkien. Another reference is made to Saruman, in his colourful wizard costumes, who escaped his tower home, with a cunning plan no less! A dark tower with the lidless red eye, not unlike a camera obscura across the landscape of Glyntaff? Was there a link with Tolkien's two towers themselves, which may or may not have been influenced by the Round Houses? Tolkien certainly visited Wales, having announced, 'I love Wales – and especially the Welsh language,' possibly using it to craft the language of the elves in his work. As a writer he cherished the ancient history of Britain. In the Welsh language – and in his heavily annotated copies of the *Mabinogion* – he found inspiration to create his own mythology. In a 1955 lecture at Cardiff, Tolkien described his love of Welsh, saying, 'For many of us it rings a bell, or rather it stirs deep harp-strings in our linguistic nature. It is the native language to which in unexplored desire we would still go home.' 'English and Welsh' was the title of Tolkien's valedictory address to the University of Oxford, which shed light on his conceptions of the connections of race, ethnicity and language.

A definite influence appears in the works of Wales's most celebrated poet, Dylan Thomas. On a visit to Aberystwyth to visit the controversial author Caradoc Evans, Thomas was accompanied by Glyn Jones and together they recited poetry, short stories and visited numerous public houses. It was back at their hotel that Jones told Dylan Thomas about Dr William Price, his famous cremation of a baby and the case of which he was acquitted. It is also significant that Price had spent time at Dylan's beloved Fern Hill when it was owned by Dr Richard Anderson. The many stories gathered about Dr Price resulted in Dylan Thomas writing the macabre tale 'The Burning Baby', which glowers with unrelenting horror. The tale of incest, rape and insanity appeared in his red notebook in September 1934 and was published in 1936. It concludes with the chilling lines,

> They heard his son howl in the wind. They saw him walking over the hill, holding a dead animal up to the light of the stars. They saw him in the valley shadows as he moved, with the motion of a man cutting wheat, over the brows of the fields. In a sanatorium he coughed his lung into a basin, stirring his fingers delightedly in the blood. What moved with invisible scythe through the valley was a shadow & a handful of shadows cast by the grave sun ...[6]

What is also somewhat more memorable about the story is that for the first time there is a reference to Llareggub, used as the setting for his most famous radio play, *Under Milk Wood*.

BBC Wales were responsible for a play about the cremation trial that was broadcast on television on Easter Monday 19 April 1965. *Let Justice Be Done – The Story of* Regina *v.* Price was written by Glyn Hardwicke and directed by Myfyr Owen. It featured a relatively small cast of ten characters.

Welsh author Ewart Alexander produced a documentary, *Dr William Price*, for Harlech Television in 1971, with William Squire appearing as Price and Meg Wyn Owen playing Gwenllian. Plays such as *Y Llosgwr*, starring Huw Ceredig, and *Fire Starter* by Big State Theatre also followed on stage throughout Wales. *The Life & Times of Dr William Price* was produced as a community video documentary in the Rhondda village of Blaenllechau, with well-known poet and member of the *Gorsedd y Beirdd* Glyn James in the title role. In his memoir of his early life in the Rhondda Valley and in London, *Print of a Hare's Foot*, Rhys Davies (1901–78) devoted an entire chapter to Dr William Price.

Penelopen Elizabeth Price died on 21 October 1977 at the age of ninety. Suffering with a heart condition, she was admitted to Tonteg Hospital, where she later passed away. Her death marked the end of two generations of a family that had lived collectively more than 177 years. Her half-sister, Rachel, was named as the next of kin. Stubborn, strong and determined, the sisters had overcome many illnesses together and received great care from the Alexander family, who purchased one of their properties, Cae Ysgubor Farm on Heol y Sarn. Although not his natural daughter, Rachel did not attend the next significant celebration of the life of Dr Price at Llantrisant in May 1982. Instead, she was allowed a glorious view of the proceedings from the house at East Caerlan. Almost a century after the cremation of Iesu Grist, Llantrisant paid another tribute to their famous resident by unveiling a magnificent statue to him on the Bull Ring. Designed by leading sculptor Peter Nicholas of Rhoose, the statue of Dr William Price was unveiled by Mayor of Taff Ely Borough Council, George Preston and his wife Rhoswen in the May Day Festival of 1982.

The figure shows him with arms outstretched, 'blown by the winds of adversity'. Wearing fox skin hat and Druidical cloak, his left hand is holding a crescent moon, the other hand holding a torch. With a sword worn around his waist, he is standing on a boulder, presumably symbolising the rocking stone, and is stood facing East Caerlan. Peter Nicholas was invited to consider designing a commemorative sculpture for the town in the summer of 1980. The commission came from Taff Ely Borough with advice from the Welsh Arts Council. Thousands of people descended on the town for the festival and Beating the Bounds ceremony, which coincided with the unveiling. Children's choirs from the three local schools combined to perform an homage to Dr Price written by local poet Gwilym Llaeron (William Lewis) of Beddau, and this was sung to the tune of 'God Bless the Prince of Wales'.

Homage to Dr William Price

Today we sing the praises
Of Dr William Price,
Who legalised cremation
Throughout the British Isles.
His infant he cremated
One day at East Caerlan
And thereby gained the hatred
Of almost all in Llan

Chorus
So let us sing the praises
Of this farsighted man,
Who legalised cremation,
That day at East Caerlan

And here on the Bullring
In sight of East Caerlan,
Today we place a statue
In honour of this man.
He was a Welsh Heretic
A queer sort of chap,
His deed that day set firmly
Llantrisant on the map

He also was a Druid
And Chartist of renown,
This character made headlines
In cities and in town,
Dressed in a quaint regalia
His cap made out of fur,
When riding through the area
He always caused a stir.

And here we are gathered
Today as you can see,
To place this fine memorial
Up to his memory.
So let us raise our voices
In song up to the skies,
And thank the Lord for sending
Us, Dr William Price.

The unveiling also coincided with a rather different song about Dr Price, written by Professor Meic Stephens of Treforest and widely performed by members of Llantrisant Folk Club, who use his image as the symbol for their organisation.

There was a man called Doctor Price
Who lived on lettuce nuts and rice
His idols were the moon and sun
And walked the hills with nothing on.

The naughty doctor in his day
Put lots of girls in the family way
His little offspring could be seen
From Pontypool to Pontyclun.

The Nonconformists didn't like
The practices of Doctor Price
They say he wasn't nice to know
He had an enormous libido.

So at the age of eighty-eight
The doctor thought he'd take a mate
He married a girl called Gwenllian
And became the father of her son.

A doting dad was Doctor Price
He called the baby 'Jesus Christ'
He wrapped it in a flannel shawl
The bonniest baby of them all.

But one year later sad to say
The Doctor's baby passed away
So after chapel one dark night
He set the little corpse alight.

The Doctor thought it quite a joke
To watch the kid go up in smoke
He took the ashes with a grin
And kept them in a biscuit tin.

But when the local deacons saw
That Doctor Price had broke the law

They shouted at him '*ach a fi*'
And put him under lock and key.

The Doctor told the Magistrate
He didn't care about his fate
'It was the most hygienic way,
I'll be a famous man some day.'

The morning that the Doctor died
His children sat at his bedside
He drank a bottle of champagne
And started singing once again.

He told his children in his will
To Burn him on Llantrisant hill
They built a crematorium
And the Doctor went to Kingdom Come.

So it's thanks to Doctor William Price
That modern corpses have the choice
To either linger in the mouldering clay
Or go up the chimney straight away.

On 12 April 1986 at East Glamorgan Hospital, the death occurred of Rachel Parry. Rachel had suffered several fractures, notably to her femur, and yet continued to live in isolation at East Caerlan. She underwent several bouts of surgery in the early part of 1986, when finally she passed away at the age of eighty-six. Registered as a 'retired farmer', the informant of her death was a Gwilym John Stephens.

East Caerlan was sold at auction for £57,000 with the contents selling for £12,000. The proceeds were donated to the British Red Cross, in which both Rachel and Penelopen played a leading part locally. Surveyors and auctioneers Herbert R. Thomas handled the sale, advertising the house incorrectly as the home of Dr Price himself, a piece of local mythology which is often wrongly referred to today. The auction was held by Lucas and Madley of Westgate Auction Galleries in Cardiff and included over 620 items, many of which were items owned by Penelopen and Rachel alone. However, there were items from Dr Price's own collection. Some of them included the bronze coins made to commemorate Iesu Grist's death, goat-headed brass buttons, copies of *Gwylllllis yn Nayd*, copies of programmes from the 1902 exhibition, copies of family certificates, and a quantity of the history books that Price often referred to.

The interest in Dr Price continued with several attempts at biographical essays, short stories and novelette-type biographies themselves. However, it was Dr John Cule who produced the first comprehensive work, with a thesis for an M.A. at Cambridge University in 1960 following his extensive meetings with Penelopen Price and Rachel Parry during the previous year. In fact, the selection of publications and articles written about him during that time is quite phenomenal, while people of Pontypridd and Llantrisant in particular still talk about him with a mixture of humour and an underlying sense of respect.

In 1994 a Dr William Price Memorial Garden was unveiled by Llantrisant Community Council on the corner of High Street, directly opposite the site where Tŷ'r Clettwr once stood. An exhibition was also opened at the Model House Craft & Design Centre in Llantrisant. Francis Crawshay's Forest House became the School of Mines in 1913 and ninety years later remained a central building to the ever-expanding University of Glamorgan, which also boasts the 'Dr William Price Business School'.

Throughout 1996 campaigners in Caerphilly fought tirelessly to save the Green Meadow Pub, which was considered the site of the original Tŷ'n y Coed Cae Farm where the doctor was born. However, this was never proved and even in interview with Penelopen Price in 1959, Dr Cule was told the original house had been a ruin for years. Sadly, in March 1997 they lost their fight and it was demolished and replaced by a housing development. Since then industrial estates bear Dr William Price's name, as does a group of houses in Glyntaff.

In September 2009 Rhondda Cynon Taf Council, with the support of a £49,200 grant from the Heritage Lottery Fund, erected thirty blue plaques throughout the county borough to commemorate icons, events and buildings. As there was no memorial to Dr Price in the Glyntaff area, the author nominated the Round Houses as a potential site for a blue plaque and it was agreed by the committee of local historians. On 17 September 2011, exactly sixty-four years to the day, the plaque unveiled to Dr Price at Zoar Chapel in Llantrisant was rededicated. The original plaque had become damaged and was restored through the work of the author. At the original ceremony, members of the Llantrisant Town Trust, Llantrisant Community Council, the Cremation Society of Great Britain and the Federation of Burial and Cremation Authorities combined to pay tribute to the Welshman. Present-day leaders of all these organisations came together for a second time to witness the rededication of the plaque by Mayor of Rhondda Cynon Taf, Cllr Sylvia Jones and The Rt Hon. the Earl Grey, President of the Cremation Society. The Earl Grey paid his tribute to Dr Price, adding that due to his legacy, more than 73 per cent of funerals of the previous year resulted in cremations rather than burials.

More than two centuries have passed since the birth of Dr William Price, but his legacy remains secured in the annals of history as one of the most extraordinary individuals ever to have lived.

Long may the memory of this great man continue.

NOTES

Chapter One: 1800–1813

1. Jones, G. G., 'The Price Families of Caerphilly', *Cronicl Caerffili*, 3 (1976), p. 15.
2. Davies, J. B., 'Parish of Pentyrch' in Williams, S. (ed.), *Glamorgan Historian*, 1 (1963).
3. The Will of William Price, 15 June 1776, proved London 8 May, 1778. Public Record Office, Kew.
4. Griffith, R. A., *Sir Rhys Ap Thomas and His Family: A Study In The Wars of the Roses* (University of Wales Press, 1993).
5. *Golden Grove Book of Pedigrees*, 2 (1765).
6. *Pontypridd Chronicle*, 31 January 1893.
7. Guy, J., *A History of Rudry* (Starling Press, 1976).
8. '*Price* v. *Fothergill*', *Cambrian News*, 8 February 1848.
9. Guy, The Rev Dr John R., 'The Rudry Radical: Dr William Price of Tŷ'n Y Coedcae, Part 2', *Caerphilly*, 6 (2000).
10. Beeston, G., *Bedwas and Machen: Past & Present* (1972).
11. Coleman, E. and D. Coleman, *Machen Remembered* (1996).
12. *Cardiff Times & South Wales Daily News*, April 1888.

Chapter Two: 1814–1822

1. Thomas, P. H., 'Medical Men of Glamorgan: William Thomas Edwards' in S. Williams (ed.), *Glamorgan Historian*, 8 (1970).
2. *Cardiff & Merthyr Guardian*, 25 September 1837.
3. *Cardiff Times & South Wales Daily News*, April 1888.
4. Peterson, M. J., *The Medical Profession in Mid-Victorian London* (University of California, 1978).
5. Daunton, C., *The London Hospital Illustrated: 250 Years* (London: B. T. Batsford Ltd, 1990).
6. Clark-Kennedy. A. E., *London Pride: The Story of a Voluntary Hospital* (Hutchinson, 1979).
7. Collins, S. M., *The Royal London Hospital: A Brief History* (Royal London Hospital, 1990).
8. Ellis, J., *The Story of the London Hospital Medical College, England's First Medical School* (London, 1986).
9. Minutes of the London Hospital, Whitechapel, London (1821).
10. Cule, J., *Dr William Price (1800–93) of Llantrisant: A Study of an Eccentric* (University of Cambridge, 1960).
11. Painting of Dr William Price by Alexander Steward (1822) in the Museum of Welsh Life, St Fagans.

Chapter Three: 1823–1834

1. Boyns. T., D. Thomas and C. Baber, 'The Iron, Steel and Tinplate Industries 1750–1914' in *Glamorgan County History Vol. IV* (Glamorgan County History Society, 1974).

2. Malkin, B., *The Scenery, Antiquities and Biography of South Wales* (London: 1803).
3. Davies, R., *A Drop of Dew* (1949).
4. *Cardiff Times & South Wales Daily News*, April 1888.
5. *Western Mail*, 16 July 1881.
6. Stephens, C., *Welsh Costume and the Influence of Lady Llanover* (National Library of Wales, 2005).
7. Earl of Bessborough (ed.), *Lady Charlotte Guest: Extracts From Her Journals 1833–1852* (London: John Murray, 1950).

Chapter Four: 1835–1838

1. Ellis, P. B., *The Druids* (Constable & Co. 1994).
2. Aubrey, J., *Druid Temples* (1649).
3. Lewis, C. W., 'Iolo Morganwg and the Strict-Metre Welsh Poetry' in G. Jenkins (ed.), *A Rattleskull Genius: The Many Faces of Iolo Morganwg* (University of Wales Press, 2009).
4. Davies, J., *The History of Wales* (Penguin, 1993).
5. Morganwg, M., *Hynafiaeth Aruthrol y Trwn* (1842).
6. Denning, R., 'Druidism at Pontypridd' in S. Williams (ed.), *Glamorgan Historian*, 1 (Barry, 1963).
7. *Pontypridd Chronicle*, 14 August 1891.
8. Morien, *History of Pontypridd and Rhondda Valleys* (1903).
9. Stephens, M., *Pontypridd: A Town With No History But One Hell Of A Past* (University of Glamorgan, 2002).
10. *Cardiff & Merthyr Guardian*, 20 February 1835.
11. Jones-Jenkins, C. O., 'Francis Crawshay and Trefforest' in H. Williams (ed.), *Pontypridd: Essays on the History of an Industrial Community* (University College Cardiff, 1981).
12. Holley, T. F. and V. A. 'Holley, Francis Crawshay 1811–1878' in J. Gross (ed.), *Methyr Historian*, 4 (1989).
13. Y Maen Chwyf, 1839.
14. *Cardiff & Merthyr Guardian*, 14 September 1839.
15. *Cardiff & Merthyr Guardian*, 21 September 1839.

Chapter Five: 1839

1. *The Rise & Fall of Chartism in Monmouthshire* (London: A. H. Bailey, 1840).
2. Jones, D. J. V., *The Last Rising: The Newport Insurrection of 1839* (Clarendon Press, 1985).
3. Wilks, I., *South Wales and the Rising of 1839* (Croom Helm, 1983).
4. Bute Papers XX7, Cardiff Central Library.
5. Earl of Bessborough (ed.), *Lady Charlotte Guest: Extracts From Her Journals 1833–1852* (London: John Murray, 1950).
6. *Northern Star*, 16 November 1839.
7. Bute Papers XX20, Cardiff Central Library.
8. Bute Papers XX27, Cardiff Central Library.
9. *Cardiff & Merthyr Guardian*, 7 September 1839.
10. Nicholas, I., *A Welsh Heretic* (London: Foyle's Welsh Co Ltd, 1940).
11. Bute Papers XX23, Cardiff Central Library.
12. Bute Papers XX33, Cardiff Central Library.
13. Williams, D., *John Frost: A Study in Chartism* (Evelyn, Adams & Mackay, 1969).
14. Morien, *History of Pontypridd and Rhondda Valleys* (1903).
15. Egan, D., *People, Protest and Politics, Case Studies in Nineteenth Century Wales* (Gomer Press, 1987).
16. Bute Papers XX41, Cardiff Central Library.

17. *Cambrian News*, 11 November 1839.
18. Bute Papers XX103, Cardiff Central Library.
19. Bute Papers XX105, Cardiff Central Library.
20. *Cardiff Times & South Wales Daily News*, April 1888.

Chapter Six: 1840–1849

1. *Cardiff Times & South Wales Daily News*, April 1888.
2. Medical Directory, *Lancet*, 1886.
3. Price, W., *Gwyllllis yn Nayd* (Victor Brookes, 1871).
4. Pliny and H. Rackham, *Natural History* (Harvard University Press, 1989).
5. Hutton, R., *Blood & Mistletoe: The History of The Druids in Britain* (Yale University Press, 2009).
6. *Cardiff & Merthyr Guardian*, 4 July 1840.
7. Cule, J., *Dr William Price (1800–93) of Llantrisant: A Study of an Eccentric* (University of Cambridge, 1960).
8. *Northern Star*, 10 July 1841.
9. *Northern Star*, 17 July 1841.
10. *Northern Star*, 24 July 1841.
11. *Northern Star*, 21 August 1841.
12. *Northern Star*, 27 November 1841.
13. *Northern Star*, 24 October 1840.
14. *Northern Star*, 28 August 1841.
15. *Cardiff & Merthyr Guardian*, 14 May 1842.
16. *Northern Star*, 14 July 1842.
17. Davies, J., *Hanes Cymru* (Penguin, 1989).
18. Griffiths, G., *Land of My Fathers: Evan, James, Their Lives And Times* (Carreg Gwalch, 2006).
19. Thomas, the Rev. W., *History of the Parish of Llanwynno 1843–1890* (1888).
20. Morien, *History of Pontypridd and Rhondda Valleys* (1903).
21. Davies, B., 'Evan James, Dr William Price and Iolo Morganwg's Utopia', *Gelligaer Journal*, 17 (Gelligaer Historical Society, 2010).
22. *Cardiff & Merthyr Guardian*, 19 July 1845.
23. *Cardiff & Merthyr Guardian*, 24 August 1847.
24. *Cardiff Times & South Wales Daily News*, 1888.
25. Hutton, R., *Blood & Mistletoe: The History of The Druids in Britain* (Yale University Press, 2009).
26. *Cardiff & Merthyr Guardian*, 6 February 1847.
27. *Cardiff & Merthyr Guardian*, 27 March 1847.
28. *Cardiff & Merthyr Guardian*, 12 June 1847.
29. *Cardiff & Merthyr Guardian*, 19 June 1847.
30. Matthias, W., *Excelsior: The Voice Of The Treorchy Male Choir* (1965).
31. *Cardiff & Merthyr Guardian*, 29 January 1848.
32. *Cardiff & Merthyr Guardian*, 3 March 1848.
33. *Cambrian News*, 22 July 1848.
34. *Cardiff & Merthyr Guardian*, 2 February 1848.
35. *Cardiff & Merthyr Guardian*, 8 February 1848.
36. *Cardiff & Merthyr Guardian*, 24 February 1849.
37. *Cambrian News*, 9 June 1849.
38. *Cambrian News*, 27 January 1893.

Chapter Seven: 1850–1859

1. *Cardiff & Merthyr Guardian*, 10 February 1850.
2. *Cardiff & Merthyr Guardian*, 15 June 1850.

3. Letter from Dr William Price to The Solicitors of Maria Price, 13 June 1849.
4. *Cardiff & Merthyr Guardian*, 11 August 1850.
5. *Cardiff & Merthyr Guardian*, 23 July 1853.
6. *Cambrian News*, 9 April 1853.
7. Price, W., *The Trial of* Queen *v.* William Price *For Perjury* (1853).
8. *Cardiff & Merthyr Guardian*, 17 July 1853.
9. *Cambrian News*, 21 March 1856.
10. *Cardiff & Merthyr Guardian*, 30 June 1853.
11. *Bristol Mercury*, 28 July 1855.
12. *Morning Chronicle*, 30 July 1855.
13. *Cambrian News*, 3 October 1856.
14. G. Jenkins (ed.), *A Rattleskull Genius: The Many Faces of Iolo Morganwg* (University of Wales Press, 2009).
15. Jenkins R. T. and J. E. Lloyd (eds), *A Dictionary of Welsh Biography Down To 1940* (The Hon Society of Cymmrodorion, 1959).

Chapter Eight: 1860–1869

1. Cule, J., *Dr William Price (1800–93) of Llantrisant: A Study of an Eccentric* (University of Cambridge, 1960).
2. *Cardiff Times & South Wales Daily News*, 1888.
3. *Bristol Mercury*, 29 September 1860.
4. *Bristol Mercury*, 30 October 1860.
5. Letter to Jackson, Neale & Co from Dr William Price, 1861.
6. Letter to the Lord Mayor of London from Dr William Price.
7. *Cambrian News*, 1 May 1863.
8. Letter to Dr William Price from George Nelson Emmett, March 1865.
9. Letter to George Nelson Emmett from Dr William Price, 4 April 1865.
10. Letter from Dr William Price to George Nelson Emmett, May 1865.
11. Letter from George Nelson Emmett to Dr William Price, May 1865.

Chapter Nine: 1870–1883

1. *Western Mail*, 10 January 1870.
2. *Cambrian News*, 21 January 1870.
3. *Cambrian News*, 18 March 1870.
4. *Western Mail*, 18 March 1870.
5. *Western Mail*, 18 April 1870.
6. *Cardiff Times & South Wales Daily News*, 1888.
7. *Western Mail*, 13 September 1870.
8. *Y Fellten*, 30 December 1870.
9. *Cambrian News*, 27 July 1871.
10. *Western Mail*, 27 October 1871.
11. Cule, J., *Dr William Price (1800–93) of Llantrisant: A Study of an Eccentric* (University of Cambridge, 1960).
12. Hutton, R., *Blood & Mistletoe: The History of The Druids in Britain* (Yale University Press, 2009).
13. Roberts, E. F., *Visit to Merthyr Tydfil* (1853).
14. *Cambrian News*, 21 March 1873.
15. *Cambrian News*, 5 December 1873.
16. *Western Mail*, 12 October 1874.
17. G. Jenkins (ed.), *A Rattleskull Genius: The Many Faces of Iolo Morganwg* (University of Wales Press, 2009).
18. *Western Mail*, 10 July 1877.
19. *Western Mail*, 5 December 1879.

20. *Western Mail*, 1 September 1880.
21. *Pontypridd Chronicle*, 22 March 1881.
22. *Pontypridd Chronicle*, 16 July 1881.
23. *Pontypridd Chronicle*, 22 March 1883.
24. *Cardiff Times & South Wales Daily News*, April 1888.
25. *Pontypridd Chronicle*, 29 November 1883.

Chapter Ten: 1884

1. Cuyrl, J. S., *The Victorian Celebration of Death* (Newton Abbot, 1972).
2. Hutton, R., *Blood & Mistletoe: The History of The Druids in Britain* (Yale University Press, 2009).
3. White, S., 'The 125th Anniversary of the Cremation Society of Great Britain', *Mortality*, 4 (1999).
4. *Lancet*, 22 August 1857.
5. Parsons, B., *Committed to the Cleansing Flame* (Spire Books, 2005).
6. Jupp, The Rev. P. C., 'History of the Cremation Movement in Great Britain, The First 125 years', *Pharos*, 66(1) (1999).
7. *Cardiff Times*, 19 February 1884.
8. *Pontypridd Chronicle*, 17 January 1884.
9. *South Wales Daily News*, 15 January 1884.
10. *Western Mail*, 15 January 1884.
11. *Pontypridd Chronicle*, 16 January 1884.
12. *Western Mail*, 24 January 1884.
13. *Western Mail*, 25 January 1884.
14. *South Wales Daily News*, 18 January 1884.
15. *Pontypridd Chronicle*, 18 January 1884.
16. *South Wales Daily News*, 18 January 1884.
17. *South Wales Daily News*, 16 January 1884.
18. *South Wales Daily News*, 19 January 1884.
19. *Pontypridd Chronicle*, 20 January 1884.
20. *South Wales Daily News*, 24 January 1884.
21. *Western Mail*, 26 January 1884.
22. *Pontypridd Chronicle*, 2 February 1884.
23. *South Wales Daily News*, 2 February 1884.
24. Colaiaco, J. A., *James Fitzjames Stephen and the Crisis of Victorian Thought* (St Martin's Press, 1945).
25. White, S., 'A Burial Ahead of Its Time: The Crookenden Case', *Mortality*, 7(2) (2002).
26. James Fitzjames Stephens, 1884.
27. *South Wales Daily News*, 16 February 1884.
28. *South Wales Daily News*, 18 February 1884.
29. *South Wales Daily News*, 14 February 1884.
30. *South Wales Daily News*, 19 February 1884.
31. *South Wales Daily News*, 18 February 1884.
32. *British Medical Journal*, March 1884.
33. *Pontypridd Chronicle*, 23 February 1884.
34. *South Wales Daily News*, 19 February 1884.
35. *Pontypridd Chronicle*, 1 March 1884.
36. *Pontypridd Chronicle*, 15 March 1884.
37. *Bristol Mercury*, 10 March 1884.
38. Doyle, A. C., *The Blood-Stone Tragedy: A Druidical Story* (Arthur Conan Doyle Society, 1995).
39. *Pontypridd Chronicle*, 1 March 1884.
40. *Pontypridd Chronicle*, 28 March 1884.
41. *Pontypridd Chronicle*, 16 March 1884.

42. *Pontypridd Chronicle*, 29 March 1884.
43. *South Wales Daily News*, 15 March 1884.
44. *South Wales Daily News*, 31 March 1884.
45. *South Wales Daily News*, 11 August 1884.
46. *Pontypridd Chronicle*, 3 March 1884.
47. *South Wales Daily News*, 12 August 1884.
48. *Cardiff & Merthyr Guardian*, 13 March 1884.
49. *Bristol Mercury*, 10 March 1884.
50. *Pontypridd Chronicle*, 15 March 1884.
51. *Bristol Mercury*, 2 September 1884.
52. *Pontypridd Chronicle*, 10 October 1884.

Chapter Eleven: 1885–1893

1. *British Medical Directory*, 1886.
2. *Cardiff Times & South Wales Daily News*, 1888.
3. *The Journal*, Camarthen, 30 August 1901.
4. *Glamorgan Gazette*, 16 July 1926.
5. *Western Mail*, 5 March 1886.
6. Denning, R., 'Druidism at Pontypridd' in S. Williams (ed.), *Glamorgan Historian*, 1 (Barry, 1963).
7. G. Jenkins (ed.), *A Rattleskull Genius: The Many Faces of Iolo Morganwg* (University of Wales Press, 2009).
8. Hutton, R., *Blood & Mistletoe: The History of The Druids in Britain* (Yale University Press, 2009).
9. Stephens, M., *Pontypridd: A Town With No History But One Hell Of A Past* (University of Glamorgan, 2002).
10. *Pontypridd Chronicle*, 20 March 1885.
11. *Pontypridd Chronicle*, 15 August 1885.
12. British Broadcasting Corporation, 17 September 1947.
13. *Cardiff Times & South Wales Daily News*, 1888.
14. *Western Mail*, 14 August 1891.
15. *Western Mail*, 10 October 1892.
16. *Western Mail*, 24 January 1893.
17. *Western Mail*, 25 January 1893.
18. *Western Mail*, 1 February 1893.
19. *Western Mail*, 25 January 1893.
20. *Pontypridd Chronicle*, 26 January 1893.
21. *The Star*, 26 January 1893.
22. *Western Mail*, 26 January 1893.
23. *Western Mail*, 27 January 1893.
24. *The Standard*, 26 January 1893.
25. *Pontypridd Chronicle*, 27 January 1893.
26. *Western Mail*, 31 January 1893.
27. *Western Mail*, 30 January 1893.
28. *South Wales Daily News*, 31 January 1893.
29. Last and Testament of Dr William Price, Proved, 1893.

Chapter Twelve: 1894–2012

1. Morgan, T., *History of Llantrisant* (1896).
2. The Life of Dr William Price Exhibition, 1896.
3. *Pontypridd Chronicle*, 25 April 1900.
4. *Pontypridd Chronicle*, 14 May 1901.
5. Nicholas, I., *A Welsh Heretic* (London: Foyle's Welsh Co Ltd, 1940).
6. Thomas, D., *Baby Burning Case: A Short Story* (1936).

BIBLIOGRAPHY

Books

Boyns. T., D. Thomas and C. Baber, 'The Iron, Steel and Tinplate Industries 1750–1914' in *Glamorgan County History Vol. IV* (Glamorgan County History Society, 1974).

Car-Gomm, P., *What Do Druids Believe?* (Ganta Publications, 2004).

Chappell, E. L., *Historic Melingriffith: An Account Of Pentyrch Iron Works and Melingriffith Tinplate Works* (Merton Priory Press, 1995).

Davies, B., 'Empire and Identity: the case of Dr William Price' in David Smith (ed.), *A People and a Proletariat: Essays in the History of Wales 1780–1880* (London, 1980).

Davies, J. B. and J. G. Owen, *Pentyrch Iron Works* (Pentyrch: Pentyrch & District Local History Society, 2003).

Davies, R., *The Story of Wales* (W. Collins, 1947).

Edwards, H. T. (ed.), *Merthyr a Thaf: Cyfres y Cymoedd* (Gomer, 2001).

Evans, D. G., *A History of Wales 1815–1906* (University of Wales Press, 1989).

Griffin, J. P., 'Eccentric or Visionary: Dr Price of Llantrisant', *Journal of the Royal Society of Medicine* 84 (1991).

Jenkins R. T. and J. E. Lloyd (eds), *A Dictionary of Welsh Biography Down to 1940* (The Hon Society of Cymmrodorion, 1959).

Llaeron, G., *Memories Recalled: Poems of Gwilym Llaeron* (Dillwyn Lewis, 1982).

Miles, D., *The Secret of the Bards of the Isle of Britain* (Gwasg Dinefwr, 1992).

Mogg, R. A., 'William Price, M.R.C.S., L.S.A of Llantrisant', *The London Hospital Gazette*.

Morgan, P., *Glamorgan County History Volume VI, Glamorgan Society 1780 to 1980* (Cardiff: University of Wales Press, 1988).

Nicholas, I., *A Welsh Heretic* (London: Foyle's Welsh Co. Ltd, 1940).

Parsons, B., *Committed to the Cleansing Flame* (Spire Books, 2005).

Phillips, S, *The History of Llantrisant* (Bristol: J. Wright, 1866).

Powell, D., *Victorian Pontypridd* (Merton Priory Press, 1996).

Powell, R. J., *Treforest, Glyntaff and Rhydyfelin* (Tempus, 2005).

Richards, H. P., *A History of Caerphilly* (D. Brown & Sons, 1975).

Trevelyan, M., *Glimpses of Welsh Life and Character* (London: J. Hogg, 1893).

Williams, E., *Poems, Lyrics and Pastoral* (MSS Society, 1794).

Documents, Newspapers & Websites

Alphabetical Index of Students at the London Hospital and Medical College from the Foundation of the Hospital in 1740.

Archives, Royal College of Surgeons.

Archives, The London Hospital, Whitechapel.

Bristol Mercury.

Bute Papers, Cardiff Central Library.

Cambrian News.

Cardiff & Merthyr Guardian.

Cardiff Times & South Wales Daily News.

Greenwell, B., *Lost Lives: William Price* (online) http://www.billgreenwell.com/lost_lives/index.php?key_id=590.

London Hospital Charter By-Laws and Standing Orders (1832).

Minutes of The London Hospital, Whitechapel, London (1819).

Monmouthshire Merlin.

National Library of Wales.

Pontypridd Chronicle.

Price, W., *The Pedigree of Nicholas Pryce.*

Western Mail.

ACKNOWLEDGEMENTS

My grateful thanks to the following individuals:

Stephen White, Member of the Council, Cremation Society of Great Britain; Dr John Cule; Dr Michael Jones; Madame Agnès Scherer, Archivist, The Louvre Gallery & Museum, Paris, France; Christopher Jeens, Archivist, Jesus College, Oxford; Richard Askwith, Archivist, Corporation of the Sons of the Clergy; Jennifer Firth, Caerphilly County Library; Andrew Helme, Monmouthshire Museums; Scott Reid, Curator, Cyfarthfa Castle Museum; Carolyn Jacob, Merthyr Central Library; Rev Peter Crocker, St Barrwg's, Bedwas; Professor Meic Stephens; Richard Meunir, Deputy Archivist, Curator, St Bartholomews; Peter Evans, Cardiff Central Library; Helen Rogers, Director Royal College of Midwifery; Rosemary Mander, Emeritus Professor Midwifery, School of Health, University of Edinburgh; Dr Janette Allotey, University of Manchester; Professor Billie Hunter, College of Human and Health Sciences, University of Swansea; Professor Ronald Hutton, Bristol University; Alun Withey, History Department, University of Swansea; Rev Susan Rees, St Ilan's Church, Parish of Eglwysilan; Sue Lacey, Glyntaff Crematorium; Dr Janette Allotey, School of Nursing & Midwifery, University of Manchester; Carolyn Jacob, Merthyr Central Library; Stephen Graham, Aberdare Central Library; Professor Chris Williams, University of Swansea; Roger Arber, Secretary, The Cremation Society of Great Britain; Revd Peter Jupp, The Cremation Society of Great Britain; Rt Hon Earl Grey, President, The Cremation Society of Great Britain; Marilyn Jones, Swansea Central Library; Gwilym Games, Swansea Central Library; Jennifer Firth, Caerphilly Central Library; Bargoed Library; Gill Levvy, Museum Service, Caerphilly County Borough Council; John Harrison, Heritage Officer, Rhondda Cynon Taf Council; Helen Newton, Pontypridd Registry Office; Professor Meic Stephens, University of Glamorgan; Revd Viv Parkinson, Llantrisant Parish Church; Hywel Matthews, Pontypridd Central Library; Sioned Hughes, Archivist, Museum of Welsh Life, St Fagans; Valerie Harris, Llantrisant Library; Gwyn Rees, Llantrisant; Daryl Stacey, Treorchy; Mary Miller, Dorset; Rhodri John Powell, Miskin; Henry, Pat and Gareth Alexander, Llantrisant; Graham Mellor, Talbot Green; Edmund Miles, Talygarn; Roger & Lorna Tedstone, Porsett, Bedwas; Geoff Harris, Bedwas; Helen Fordes; Jacques Grange, Cardiff; Curon Evans; Nick Kelland, Rhondda Cynon Taf Libraries Service; Rosemary Williams; Philip Page, Round Houses, Glyntaff; Gareth Jones, Llantrisant; Clive Pegg, Llantrisant.